and

the

Blues Began

▲▲▲

Alan Lomax in 1941

The Land Where the Blues Began

▲▲▲▲▲▲▲▲▲▲▲▲▲▲▲▲▲▲▲▲▲▲▲▲▲▲▲▲▲▲

Alan Lomax

THE NEW PRESS
NEW YORK

Grateful acknowledgment is made to the following for permission to reprint previously published material:

Alfred A. Knopf, Inc.: Excerpts from *All God's Dangers: The Life of Nate Shaw* by Theodore Rosengarten. Copyright © 1974 by Theodore Rosengarten. Reprinted by permission of Alfred A. Knopf, Inc.

Bantam, Doubleday, Dell Publishing Group, Inc.: Excerpts from *"You Live and Learn, Then You Die and Forget It All"* by William Ferris. Copyright © 1992 by William Ferris. Reprinted by permission.

Crisis/NAACP, Crisis Publishing: Excerpts from "Mississippi Slavery in 1933" by Roy Wilkins from *Crisis: A Record of the Darker Races*, April 1933.

Louisiana State University Press: Excerpts from *Blow My Blues Away* by George Mitchell. Copyright © 1971 by Louisiana State University Press. Reprinted by permission.

Macmillan Publishing Company: Excerpt from *Big Bill Blues: William Broonzy's Story* as told to Yannick Bruyoghe, originally published by Cassell & Company (London). Copyright © 1955 by Yannick Bruyoghe. Reprinted by permission of Macmillan Publishing Company.

Mississippi Folklore Register: Excerpts from "Black Fife and Drum Music in Mississippi" from the Fall 1972 issue of *Mississippi Folklore Register*, the journal of the Mississippi Folklore Society, Center for the Study of Southern Culture, University of Mississippi.

Scientific American: Excerpt from "The Mule" by Theodore Savory from *Scientific American*, December 1970.

First published in hardcover by Pantheon Books, a division of Random House, Inc., New York, 1993
This paperback edition published in the United States by The New Press, New York, 2002
Distributed by W. W. Norton & Company, Inc., New York

LIBRARY OF CONGRESS CATALOGING-IN-PUBLICATION DATA

Lomax, Alan, 1915–2002.

    The land where the blues began/Alan Lomax.

    p. cm.

    Includes bibliographical references and index.

    ISBN 1-56584-739-3 (pbk.)

    1. Blues (Music)—Mississippi—Delta (Region)—History and criticism. 2. African-Americans—Mississippi—Delta (Region)—Music—History and criticism. 3. African-Americans—Mississippi—Delta (Region)—Social life and customs. I. Title.

ML3521.L64   1993

781.643'09762'4—dc20   91-52627

The New Press was established in 1990 as a not-for-profit alternative to the large, commercial publishing houses currently dominating the book publishing industry. The New Press operates in the public interest rather than for private gain, and is committed to publishing, in innovative ways, works of educational, cultural, and community value that are often deemed insufficiently profitable.

The New Press, 450 West 41st Street, 6th floor, New York, NY 10036

www.thenewpress.com

Book design by Laura Hough

Printed in the United States of America

10 9 8 7 6 5 4 3 2 1

To the black people of the Delta,
who created a Mississippi of song
that now flows through the music
of the whole world

Contents

▲▲▲▲▲▲▲▲▲

Preface

▲▲▲▲▲▲▲▲

Although this has been called the age of anxiety, it might better be termed the century of the blues, after the moody song style that was born sometime around 1900 in the Mississippi Delta. The blues has always been a state of being as well as a way of singing. Leadbelly once told me, "When you lie down at night, turning from side to side, and you can't be satisfied no way you do, Old Man Blues got you." A hundred years ago only blacks in the Deep South were seized by the blues. Now the whole world begins to know them.

In order to hear the blues, when I was very young, my girlfriend and I slipped into the black ghetto of my Southern hometown under the cover of darkness. If we'd been caught there, we would probably have been expelled from the university. Nowadays everyone sings and dances to bluesy music, and the mighty river of the blues uncoils in the ear of the planet. Indeed, the blues may have become the best-known tune humans have ever sung. At the same time, all of us are beginning to experience the melancholy dissatisfaction that weighed upon the hearts of the black people of the Mississippi Delta, the land where the blues began. Feelings of anomie and alienation, of orphaning and rootlessness—the sense of being a commodity rather than a person; the loss of love and of family and of place—this modern syndrome was the norm for the cotton farmers and the transient laborers of the Deep South a hundred years ago.

I'm a poor boy and a long old ways from home . . .

This song arose in a period much like our own. Our species has never been more powerful and wealthy, nor more ill at ease. Homeless and desperate people in America and all over the world live in the shadow of undreamed-of productivity and luxury. So it was in the Mississippi Delta in the early years of this century. Boom times in cotton gave a handful of planters easy riches, while the black majority who produced the cotton lived in sordid shanties or roamed from job to job. Some blacks attempted to become free enterprisers, but were so hemmed in by caste barriers that very few succeeded in rising in the world. The rebellious were kept in their place by gun and lynch laws, ruthlessly administered by the propertied.

Our times today are similarly out of joint, similarly terrorized. Technology has made the species rich and resourceful as never before, but the wealth and the resources rest with a few individuals, corporations, and favored nations. Most earthlings, most nations, are distanced from technological luxury, and that imbalance is presided over by armed forces capable of destroying the planet itself. Rage and anxiety pervade the emotions and the actions of both the haves and the have-nots. And the sound of the the worried blues of the old Delta is heard in back alleys and palaces, alike.

In such threatening situations most people grow careful about speaking out. The fate of whistle blowers and nonconformists is well known. Those most favored by fortune become the most reticent about the inequities that profit them. The poor eat humble pie and only smile—when their masters are present. Everyone learns to remain silent in the face of monstrous ironies. In the South I grew up in, for example, almost everyone had convinced themselves that blacks were happy. In fact, they were excluded from public facilities, were poorly paid, badly housed, constantly insulted and bullied, and were without equal rights before the law. Nevertheless, everybody, especially the oppressed and disenfranchised, kept quiet. Working-class blacks who talked ran the risk of losing their jobs, if not their lives. Blacks who hobnobbed with strangers might also land in serious trouble. Whites who protested were stigmatized as "nigger lovers" and faced social exclusion or worse.

This was the way things were when my father, John A. Lomax, and I began recording Southern black folk songs in the field in the 1930s. I realize now that during a summer I spent in the field in 1935 with the brilliant black folklorist Zora Neale Hurston, she never elicited any accounts of oppression from anyone, nor did she discuss such matters. I presume that she considered this too risky, and I am sure she was right. This book is a long-delayed account of my personal attempts to penetrate this zone of silence, and how I managed, finally, to record the way the black laborers of the Delta saw their situation.

The portable recording machine, which my father and I were the first to use, provided the first breakthrough. It was heavy (five hundred pounds) and it engraved a rather noisy sound groove on aluminum discs. Even so, by making it possible to record and play back music in remote areas, away from electrical sources, it gave a voice to the voiceless. It documented music, such as the complex polyphony of the blacks, which notation could not represent. Thus the portable recorder put neglected cultures and silenced people into the communication chain. The performers were heartened when they heard their own music and often spoke into the microphone as if the machine were a telephone, connected directly to the centers of power. One black sharecropper began, "Now listen here, Mr. President, I want you to know they're not treatin us right down here . . ." The poignant songs he and others recorded for us stirred New Deal Washington and won support for our activity. In a few short years the image of a remarkable African-American indigenous culture had been put on permanent record—a black Texas, a black Alabama, a black Virginia . . .

Bit by bit, I learned to use these early machines to probe into the singers' feelings. You had to be quick because the first discs held only three or four minutes per side. It was important to keep the machine out of the picture, so I generally sat between it and the singer and flipped the discs with my back to the turntable. Soon conversations about songs lengthened into life histories. By the time of the Delta trips I was using big acetate discs. Acetate was harder to engineer than aluminum, because you had not only to keep the mike focused and monitor the volume, but also to prevent the acetate chip from piling up under the recording needle. However, the tracks were much quieter, and best of all, every side could hold fifteen minutes of sound. This meant long events—church services, games, storytelling, work scenes, extended reminiscences—could be documented.

Every time I took one of those big, black, glass-based platters out of its box, I felt that a magical moment was opening up in time. Never before had the black people, kept almost incommunicado in the Deep South, had a chance to tell their story in their own way. For me the black discs spinning in the Mississippi night, spitting the chip centripetally toward the center of the table, also heralded a new age of writing human history—and so it proved. The recorded prose, when transcribed, curled and capered beautifully in print. It was as good as the best of Shakespeare's "vulgar" scenes, or Dickens's—writers who I suspect had recording machines in their heads. So in the 1930s and 40s, I set down the first oral histories—singing biographies of Leadbelly, of Jelly Roll Morton, of Big Bill, of Vera Hall, and many more.

However, I still remained unsatisfied about the candor of my Southern interviews. It was clear that Southern blacks would not readily confide in a white folklorist. Therefore, I approached Fisk University, the Princeton of black colleges, with the idea of doing a joint field study with my department at the Library of Congress. The aim was to establish a center for black folklore studies at Fisk. If prestigious Fisk became involved in folklore work, I reasoned, black intellectuals might overcome their prejudices against the oral traditions of the rural and unlettered blacks, prejudices expressed in searing language by Richard Wright in *Black Boy*. Moreover, I felt that I would learn much on a biracial trip into the Deep South.

Charles Johnson, head of sociology at Fisk, liked my notion of doing a study of an urbanizing cotton county as a way of accessing the continuing importance of traditions. For this reason we picked Coahoma County, the cotton capital of the Delta, as the site. The composer John Work agreed to do the musical analyses. Lewis Jones, Johnson's highly skilled field assistant, headed a team to carry out a systematic social survey of folklore over four generations. My work, to record the field interviews, was made easy because Lewis and other black members of the team vouched for me. The story of my experiences in Coahoma County fill the first four chapters of this book.

World War II permanently interrupted Lewis Jones's write-up of the Delta data. For my part, I came away from the study unsatisfied. I felt that although the Fisk survey placed the lore in its temporal social context, it had missed the creative and cultural forces bubbling in the cauldron of the Delta. The penetrating studies of Delta life done in the same period by John Dollard and Hortense Powdermaker depicted the Delta black majority as passive victims of a complex and cruel system. But these characterizations gave no sense of the creative forces at work in the lower depths of the Delta society.

The Fisk study came closer to the people of the Delta but failed to show that the Mississippi working class whom Richard Wright so despised had a dynamic culture that constantly enriched their surroundings. Clearly, these underprivileged blacks had transformed every situation, every aspect of their environment—dance, orchestration, religion, work, speech—making them over in their own image. But the Fisk study had failed to locate the cultural wellsprings of this underprivileged majority and to describe the dynamics of their constant creativity.

During the forties and later, I continued to interview Delta musicians and returned to Mississippi several times to make tape, stereo, then video recordings. Year by year I learned how to ask better questions. The further the recording session was from the Delta, the more openly the blacks spoke about their lives. I took my Delta material overseas with me and puzzled over it as I worked on a world anthropology of folk and primitive music. Gradually, I began to see Delta culture as the product of the reaction of a powerful African tradition to a new and often harsher social environment. On my return to America I carried this insight further. Together with a team of specialists I spent a number of years on a global study of the relation of performance style to culture in twin surveys of the treasures of ethnographic recordings and film. This work put the African-American drama in perspective, as one of many encounters between African and Eurasian performance styles. Out of this study came ideas that illumined the Delta research.

It became clear that black Africa had distinctive performance styles, quite as formal as those of Western Europe. Moreover, these expressive patterns clearly represented and reinforced the fundamental structures of African society. Their broad provenance throughout Africa south of the Sahara indicated that, even though they had been transmitted orally and nonverbally, these cultural traditions were both powerful and stable. Careful comparison showed that black African nonverbal performance traditions had survived virtually intact in African America, and had shaped all its distinctive rhythmic arts, during both the colonial and the postcolonial periods. It was this unwritten but rich African tradition that empowered the creativity we had encountered in the lower depths of the Mississippi Delta. The error in African-American studies had been to look to print and to language for evidence of African survivals. For instance, musicologists discovered that American blacks performed many European-like melodies, but failed to notice that the whole performance context—voicing, rhythmic organization, orchestration—remained essentially African.[1] Such scholarship turned university-trained black intellectuals and writers away from the heritage of their parents, who had a nonprint, nonverbal heritage that the educated falsely labeled "ignorant." Nonetheless, it was because of this culturally biased "ignorance" that African culture had been largely passed on in America—that is, through nonverbal and oral channels, out of the reach of censorship.

Every one of the the world-renowned black American genres from ragtime to rap bears the mark of this "folk" heritage. Clearly also it provided the resources employed by the Delta blacks in manifold adaptations to their harsh destiny as an uprooted and exploited people. Gradually, I saw how, through every trial, Delta blacks had been buoyed up and propelled forward by the nourishing river of black cultural practice, maintained in the isolation of the Southern ghetto. Like cunning Br'er Rabbit, the African-American creative tradition was "bred and born in the briar patch" created by Jim Crow.

A flood tide of supportive African sociability, eroticism, and life-giving laughter, welling up in black family and community life, endowed black life with a certain invulnerability in the face of sharp adversity. Our studies established solid connections between the modes of every day and the characteristics of song and dance styles. For example, these wider investigations showed that the ability to sing in good concert, and to dramatize strong feelings in dance, were present wherever cultural conditions constantly brought black people together for sociable activities. The large extended families, the neighborhood self-help groups, and the community-led religious services of the blacks provided such sociable occasions and fostered ease in morale-building group performances.

Therefore, it could be argued that the new song styles of the Delta symbolized the dynamic continuance of African social and creative process as a technique of adaptation. Moreover, the birth of the blues and the struggles of its progenitors could be seen as a creative deployment of African style in an American setting, the operation of African temperament in new surroundings. In a sense, African-American singers and dancers made an aesthetic conquest of their environment in the New World. Their productions transfixed audiences, and white performers rushed to imitate and parody them in the minstrel show, buck dancing, ragtime, jazz, as nowadays in rock, rap, and the blues.

It is the gradual discovery of this river of black African tradition flowing through Delta life that gives form to the experiences chronicled in these pages. The field recordings, the life histories, the yellow pages of my field notebooks, the encounters and conversations often dimly recollected after fifty years—all revealed some bend of the big river where the blues were born. As the work went on, the eloquent people of the Delta spoke more openly, and it was a source of deep satisfaction to me that at last I, a white Southerner, could penetrate the Southern façade and learn something about what life was like on the other side of the Jim Crow line. The tales and songs return again and again to a few themes—to the grievous and laughable ironies in the lives of an outcaste people, who were unfairly denied the rewards of an economy they had helped to build. One black response to this ironic fact was to create the blues—the first satirical song form in the English language—mounted on cadences that have now seduced the world. It is heartening to realize that both the style and the inner content of this new genre are bold symbols of an independent and irrepressible culture.

The experience of Southern working-class blacks, who created the blues in the postslavery period, was in some ways more bitter than slavery itself. Promised equal rights and opportunities, blacks were, by and large, denied both. They put their hand to the plow, to the railroad hammer, to the lines of the mule team and, in effect, built the South—for subsistence wages. Faulkner's decadent planter class knew how to exploit them and, when they felt it necessary, resorted to the most savage exemplary violence to keep these vigorous and ambitious people in line. As always, such cynical violence imposed from the top led to violence within the exploited group—a very ugly emotional safety valve.

These conditions—described in the following pages—continued, especially in the Deep South, with little change until World War II, and, even after the Johnson political reforms and the inspiring successes of the integration movement, have not entirely disappeared. Thus they form the immediate background for our present. The Delta scene was, perhaps, more savage than that in some other parts of the South because it was a sort of industrial frontier. Yet it is fair to say that the grandparents, even the parents, of the majority of American blacks were painfully acquainted with the lifestyle described in these pages. Now that people everywhere begin to taste the bitterness of the postindustrial period, the Delta blues have found a world audience.

A.L.
New York City
June 1992

The Land
Where the
Blues Began

▲▲▲▲▲▲▲▲▲▲

Chapter 1

▲▲▲▲▲▲▲▲▲▲

My Heart
Struck Sorrow

MEMPHIS

There is an impulsive and romantic streak in my nature that I find difficult to control when I go song hunting. I know that I should first put on my best suit and pay formal calls on the mayor, the local professor of music, etc., ask their advice, win their support, and then gradually slide from the front gate around to the back pasture where the songs live. However, music professors are uncomfortable with me and I am downright unhappy in anything but sport shirt and blue jeans; so, even after being snubbed, lectured, arrested, and once or twice shot at, I still persist in plunging straight for the bottom where the songs live, and I am always surprised when the big bullfrogs of the pond start croaking and the ripples keep spreading and causing me trouble later on. When I returned to the South in 1942,[1] after a long absence, I made the same mistake and ran straight into trouble.

The weather was partly responsible. Texas born and bred, a hot day puts me into a euphoric frame of mind. That August afternoon the thermometer registered 101 in the shade and the hot wind roaring off the melting tarvia through the windows of my flivver had me singing all the way to Memphis. I fancied I could smell the Mississippi, which for me is southern America in a liquid form, signifying fried catfish, roasting ears dipped in butter, and watermelon in the cool of the evening, washed down with corn liquor and accompanied by the blues. I knew this was to be my last song-collecting jaunt before the army got me, maybe the last time I would ever hear the alley blues and the hallelujah spirituals that I believe are the best art our country has produced. Memphis and Beale Street, the home of the blues, lay just ahead, and I had a terrible thirst.

I didn't stop to reflect that Memphis and the South might have changed since my last visit, especially under the tensions of the war. After years of living in the North, my speech and my manners were no longer straight Southern, and I was unaware that my protective camouflage had faded somewhat. Memphis was the front gate to home for me, and I walked as if I owned the place. I drove straight to Beale Street and strode into the Monarch saloon where Handy and Jelly Roll had played, slipped a quarter in the jukebox, put my foot on the brass rail, and called for beer. But the bartender did not sail into action with a schooner and a spigot and a dish of free lunch as he had done on my last visit. As the jukebox cleared its throat with a frozen smile and began to boom out the blues, the black barman glanced at the owner, the owner shook his head slightly, and the bartender jerked his thumb at a card tacked to the wall. It read:

THIS IS A COLORED PLACE.
NO WHITES SERVED.
SORRY.

He didn't look sorry. He just grinned a little as he said, "You must not be from around here, mister, or you'd know that things have changed on Beale Street. Mister Crump say, 'If we gonna segredate one way, we gonna segredate the other.' Yessir, that old gun got two wrong ends now, and you looking straight down the other one!"

This was justice. This was logic. But it was crazy logic and double injustice. I left my quarter to amuse the nearly empty Monarch and went away. But nowhere in Beale Street's mile of cheap stores, eating joints, and juke joints could I find a barman who agreed with me that this new regulation merely multiplied the insanity of the old barrier between whites and blacks. Beale Street had changed from a sort of blue branch of the Mississippi to a dry gulch, and as I shuffled along it, aimlessly, glancing into the dance halls and bars where the fun was going on, I learned what it was like to be a black man in the wrong part of town.

A very thirsty hour later, I heard two guitars in quiet conversation behind the screen door of a tailor shop. I didn't dare open the door or say a word. I just leaned against the wall to listen as a whiny, rather humorous tenor voiced my own sentiments:

I walked all
The way from East St. Louis,
From East St. Louis here,
And I got nobody,
No one to feel my care.

Willie B. stuck his head out of the door. Willie wore a big black Stetson on his ruff of kinky hair and his black face wore a smile. "Whyn't you come in where you can hear better, mister?"

"There's a law that says I can't."

"That's right, Willie," said someone inside the shop. "Them new laws."

"Besides, they don't sell beer in tailor shops."

"Yeah," said Willie B., "but they a man crost the street sells it in bottles."

"I always thought that blues and beer went pretty good together."

"I believes in the three B's myself," said Willie. "Beer, blues, and Willie B., which is me."

"I'm goin down to the river, sit down and begin to cry," sang the voice inside the tailor shop. *"If the blues overtake me, I'll drink that old river dry."*

"I've got a dollar for the man crost the street," I said.

"Take it, Willie B., take it and fly," said the voice behind the screen door. "We'll meet you in the outside garden."

Willie B. had already recorded for a commercial label, and later he asked that his full name not be used in connection with the recordings he made for me. He took the dollar and was halfway across the street when his friend appeared. The man had a guitar in his powerful brown hand. He was tall, lanky, silky-muscled, with a long oval Sudanese face. He introduced himself as William Brown.[2] It was dark, so we shook hands. Most people have forgotten that it was dangerous back then for a black and a white person to shake hands where someone could see them. Texas-born, I had acquired the habit only recently.

"I likes a man from off," said Brown. "Come on, let's us go out to the garden. And Willie B.," he hollered, "tell the man to send along three po-boys. I pay him tomorrow."

The garden was a vacant lot with a huge billboard where a girl with a very rosy face was drinking a Coca-Cola twelve feet high. Our table was a stone. Our seats were bricks piled three high. But the beer was stinging cold and the stars seemed to draw closer as Brown began:

Now I'm broke and I'm hungry, ragged and dirty, too.
What I want to know, sweet mama, kin I go home with you?
I'm broke and I'm hungry—

A powerful flashlight shot its beam in my eyes and then played over the faces of my friends.

"What the hell is goin on over there?" said a cracker voice.

"The blues," I yelled.

"Easy, mister," Willie B. whispered. "That police is pointin his gun over here."

There were two rather decrepit Memphis policemen on the sidewalk.

"Where you from? What's your name, buddy? What are you doing on Beale Street?" All this with two flashlights in my face.

As I was explaining that I was on a mission from Washington to record the blues and had found two good singers . . .

"Washin'ton. Jis what I thought," said A.

" 'Sociatin with niggers," said B.

"Whyn't you take all this nigger crap back where you came from?" said A.

"We don't like it here in the South," said B.

"Where's yuh draft card?" said A.

I felt for my papers. They were all in my car at the other end of Beale Street.

"Jis what I tole you," said B. "Jis a white tramp with a coupla goddam nigger vagrants."

"Otter run um in," said A.

"Git movin, you damn niggers," punching my friends with his nightstick.

"And you, you nigger lover," said B., not touching me, "you walk ahead and mind you walk straight."

The Library of Congress cultural mission to record Delta folk songs made a rather sorry spectacle as it straggled down Beale Street, past doorways filled with brown faces, past the Monarch, toward my car. I turned once and said to Brown, "I'll meet you here in a half hour." Brown nodded and A. hit him in the shoulder with his club and he stumbled and fell in the gutter. "Thought I tole you to move along," said B., and laid his hand on his gun.

At the car I showed the cops who I was and demanded their numbers.

"That ain't no Memphis permit," said A., "that's a damn Washin'ton permit. Been too damn many folks from Washin'ton stirrin up trouble round here."

"And you don't need our numbers," said B. "Just tell um up at city hall ol Mack sent you."

"Yeah, and don't let us ketch you on Beale Street without no permit again," said A., "or we'll run you in. Now git."

At the Memphis city hall they were a good deal more suave. "As a Southerner, you ought to understand," a pleasant young man explained. "Our labor is being corrupted. Agitators putting wrong ideas in their heads. Trucks coming over the river from Arkansas recruiting our labor at fancy prices. And trainloads of um leaving everyday for jobs up No'th. They're gettin so uppity, it's dangerous for a white man to go to Beale Street after dark. Some boys down there would kill you for five dollars . . . Now tomorrow evenin I'll talk to the chief and he'll arrange for you to go round with a plainclothes escort. They can take you to some mighty hot places where folks do everything but—" he laughed a little. "Hope you'll forget about old Mack," he added. "He's a little old-fashioned in his way, but he's a good man. 'Bout that permit, I reckon the mayor would give you a license to make your records, if he sees things like I do. But, of course, I can't speak for him . . ."

I picked up Brown and Willie B. round the corner from the tailor shop.

"Let's lam outa this town," said Brown.

We crossed the long river bridge. Down below us the Mississippi poured on south, talking to itself in its big quiet voice.

"What did them cops at city hall tell you, Jack?" asked Willie B.

I said nothing.

"Leave the man alone, Willie," said Brown. "Can't you see his feelings are hurt? Let's us fergit about damn Memphis laws and git out to the bottom somewheres where nobody gonna bother us. Let's us go to Hamp's Place and git this man something to drink."

Hamp's Place was a shack in the middle of an enormous Arkansas cotton field. A country store in the daytime, night transformed it into a dance hall and gambling joint. The light blue walls were plastered with brilliant snuff, baking powder, and roll-your-own advertisements. But the main business of the store was selling country moonshine, as clear as springwater and as fiery as the 4th of July in West Hell. The price was reasonable, so we bought a jug and passed it round, and the crap game in the corner broke up and the Arkansas folk gathered round quietly to hear Willie and Brown perform.

Willie B. had made commercial recordings. In the hard white light of the juke, you could see that, although he was in his twenties, his eyes were streaked with brown and his face had that muddy, blurred look typical of alcoholic blacks.

"First song I gonna sing for you, mister, is a little number already out on records. It went good—good from what they tell me."

"Did you get your royalty?"

"My what?"

"You heard the man," Brown said. "Your so much for every record."

"Yeah, that white man gimme ten dollars for every song put on his machine," said Willie B., turning his vague, blurred gaze in my direction. "Three records. Sixty dollars. And this hat besides," flinging his Stetson down to the floor. "That's how they treat a man up in Chicago. They recognizes musicians up there. Not like down here. Down here . . ."

"We know bout down here," said the bartender. "We wants to see how that microphone work."

"Well," said Willie B., "the circumstances of making this song is a girl I had—she fell. She went down like the moon before day, otherwise, but I loved her. That's why I say . . ." And he began to sing in his whiskey-harsh voice:

Four-o'clock flowers bloom in the mornin and close in the afternoon.
Well, well, they are only so much beauty and they fades so soon.

I'm a hard-workin man and I never gets my lovin soon,
When I think about it in the mornin, it aches my heart in the afternoon.

I'm not jealous but I'm superstitious, most workin men is that way,
If I catch you playin hooky, Lordy, what a day, what a day . . .

"She was only beauty, you understand," Willie B. added tenderly, speaking half to himself. "But she went down. She was my first love, but then she gone with the wind. She never did get to hear that number I made for her. Maybe on some jukebox or on the radio. They'd announce it—'This next blues by Willie B.,' and she hear it and she know exactly who the record was singing about . . ."

Willie smiled, but the smile did not untie the puzzled frown that knotted his brow. He waved his hand grandly toward the recording machine, and ordered, "Now show these folks what I'm talking about, while I gets me another little drink."

I played the record back.

"That's a ghost," said a wizened little old farmer in the corner. "It purely a ghost."

"Don't talk old-fashioned, man," said Willie B. "It ain't nothin to do with ghosts. I tell you exactly how it work. You know what a cotton gin is?"

"Sho," said the old fellow.

"Well, this the same idea. Just like a cotton gin take two, three wagonloads of cotton and squeeze it down to just one bale so you can ship it where you want to go, this microphone squeezes me and my song down into that little wavery line and they can ship me out to wheresonever they want me to sing. See the mystery?"

The old man took his pipe out of his mouth again, spat. "I still say hit's a ghost," he said.

Willie B. stalked off to the bar, muttering about how some people won't ever be educated, while I turned to William Brown, the man I'd had my eye on from the beginning.

"Give us the blues, Brown."

"I'm not a composer, I just know old, scatterin verses."

"The older the better, Brown."

"Well, I ain't got no voice, but I'll give you the words of an old Memphis song." William Brown began to sing in his sweet, true country voice, poking in delicate guitar passages at every pause, like the guitar was a second voice commenting with feeling on the ironic words of his blues. The noise in the room died away. The little old man took the pipe out of his mouth and forgot to put it back in again, leaning forward so as not to miss a note. This was the real blues, America's *cante jondo*, not a whit inferior to that great Spanish art in vocal and instrumental skill, and fresher in sentiment and broader in its range. The blues in print give you the skeleton only. If you've never heard the blues, get yourself a record and listen and then come back and join us at Hamp's Place. William Brown's song can last until the morning:

Now I'm broke and I'm hungry, ragged and dirty, too.
What I want to know, baby, kin I stay all night with you?

Well, I peeped in my window, but I couldn't see through my blinds,
Heard the bedsprings poppin and heard my baby cryin.

If I can't come in, baby, I won't be back no mo.
When I leave this time, you can hang your crepe on your door.

I say your hair ain't curly and your doggone eyes ain't blue,
I say your hair ain't curly and your doggone eyes ain't blue,
And if you don't want me, what in the world I want with you?

"That's the blues, that's the Delta blues," said the old man, putting his pipe back in his mouth, when Brown had finished. "Boy, what you want to drink?" He fumbled in the pocket of his ragged overalls, fished out an old handkerchief, untied a knot in one corner, and took out a quarter, "Here, Hamp, give this boy a drink. He bound to be dry. He been *singing*."

Brown looked pleased for the first time since we had left Memphis and downed the half water glass of fiery stuff. "Makes a man think, don't it?" he said, patting the old man on the shoulder.

"I mind a girl called Ca'line," said the old man. "She wasn't so big now, nor so bright, but she was supple. I mind me . . ."

Willie B. came blundering from the bar. "Nuff of them old wore-down songs," he muttered. "We gotta put this in high. Give it a modern kick. Now listen," he said, turning his drunken gaze on me. "You pretty nice white man. Least I believe you are. And I'm gonna give you my latest composin for your record. But don't you put it on no radio. Do, and I'll be on you like that Memphis cop was on Brown here." Willie laughed and the others looked embarrassed. " 'Member how that was? Well, this is a record of my knowledge of the Japs. The title is *A Jap Girl for Next Christmas from Santy Claus*." He began in his broken voice:

Goodbye, goodbye, I got to leave, girl, Uncle Sam done call,
I got to fight for you, America and God,
I got to fight for you, America and God.

"This is one of my recordings because I'm an American citizen . . . I am an American citizen," he muttered, glaring around. "These Memphis cops call me vagrant, but I'm a musician. I'm a recording artist for the Vict'ry company. Known all over the world. But these Southern laws don't recognize a man by his talents. They just think a . . ." He paused and brought his face close to, mine. "You ain't from round here. You don't play no part in all this mess goin round here. You don't know nothing about it, and I, Willie B., better known as 61, because I rambles 61 Highway from Chicago clean down to New Orleans with my guitar for my buddy, I am going to tell you . . ."

Then Willie B., for a few minutes conquering his drunkenness, reproduced with irony, with perfect mimicry, an encounter he had recently had with a Memphis policeman, a conversation in which his story was so long and convoluted that the policeman finally walked off and left Willie B. holding the street-corner stage:

"So old Mack he come up to me one day—see, they needin labor bad on all these plantations south of here, but now us boys going North and findin out we don't have to take this old Southern stuff no more—"

"That's right, boy," said the old man. "Preach."

"So old Mack come up to me and he say, 'Nigger, what you do for a living?' And I said, 'Mister Mack,' I said, 'I'm not doing anything but playing music, and if I said I wudn't, I'd lie to you.' " (Here Willie B. fell into the whine, half fawning and half insolence, which poor whites love as much for its comedy and its falseness as they do for its surface of currying favor.) " 'Mister Mack, I been disabled for work ever since I got ganged up on at roadhouse playin piano. Any job that I could get that maybe I could make, I just can't carry on by not havin full control of my left arm. I have a good vim when I come on in the morning, Mister Mack. Sometimes I last for three hours, sometimes four. Sometimes that left arm go down on me about twelve. Now you know me, Mister Mack, you know I used to be one of the best cotton pickers in the Delta, fore my arm went down. Nowadays I can pick till eleven, maybe twelve, if the cotton ain't too tight, I'll make till round eleven, then I begin to lose speed. And you know a man can't pick no cotton with one hand. And that the reason, Mister Mack, I tried to take up this guitar playin of mine, trying to scramble up some way to make a livin, just being a little jackleg musician." Here Willie B. began to mumble. The alcohol was taking over again. "Just some sort of an old blues singer," he muttered, and his head flopped on his breast and he began to snore.

Brown looked at him sadly. "Tha' boy used to be good once," he said. "But whiskey gittin him. He worry too much. He always mad."

"Oughta leave him alone. Oughta leave that boy just to play," said the old man. "We others pick the cotton. Oughta leave him to play."

"But I heard it was getting better down here," I said.

"That's what you heard," said the old man.

"But some folks have changed, haven't they?" I said.

"Well, that's true," said the old man. "Some few have changed. But it all minds me of a tale my grandaddy used to tell. One time the dogs and the rabbits had a convention and the dogs 'greed not to run the rabbits no more. So two rabbits were standin up by the road one day—they was talkin over the business they'd probably been doin—so one rabbit looked way down the road and he seen an old lean hound dog comin. He say, 'Looky yonder now, I better be goin. Ain't that a dog comin yonder?'

"Other rabbit say, 'Well, now, don't you remember how the dogs voted in that convention not to run the rabbits no more? He not gonna bother us.'

" 'Yeah,' he say, 'but, brother, that son-of-a-bitch yappin over there in the bushes liable not to been in that convention.'

"And that's exactly the way I am bout white men down here in the Delta. Some of them might of done changed their ways, but how a man gonna tell by lookin at um?''

Brown took a long drag at his cigarette. "That's just the way I feel, daddy." He walked to the door and looked out at the big, fertile Delta, her green belly turned up to the moonlight, and stood there quietly, rubbing his shoulder where old Mack had struck him down. "I'm gonna miss all this when I'm gone. I was raised around here. And I know I'm gonna miss it."

"Where you goin?" asked Hamp.

"Somewhere I'll be treated like a man," said Brown.

"Taking Willie B.?" I said.

"Naw," said Brown, looking down with compassion at Willie B. snoring over his guitar. "That poor boy never goin nowhere. I'm leavin before I get to be like him."

LITTLE ROBERT

It was already dawn when I dropped Brown and Willie B. off in Memphis and found a bed somewhere. The blazing noon sun woke and revitalized me as I drove south. Willie B.'s Highway 61 ran straight through mile after mile of flat, treeless Delta plantations, where the houses of black sharecroppers rose like grey stones in the green sea of cotton.

The Beale Street episode had been fortunate, not so much for the songs I had recorded as for what I had learned about the singers. The Memphis police had, in a few brutal words, swept aside the barriers of shyness and superiority that, as a Southerner, had cut me off from black singers. I saw that, if I could be normally civil out of sight of the "law," I could learn from them much that I wished to know.

I was only a few miles from a goal I had long looked forward to, the home of "Little Robert." In folk as well as in fine art, there are especially gifted individuals who make great advances that preoccupy the less talented for generations afterward. Robert Johnson of Tunica County, Mississippi, was one of these exceptional men.

A commercial recording team had found him on one of their annual Southern tours, had waxed a dozen songs and published the records, but he hadn't been specially noticed among the scores of other blues singers who were recorded in the twenties and thirties—the roaring days of the "race" record business, when millions of blues records were sold, almost all to working-class blacks. A few whites became aficionados—for years Blind Willie Johnson's *I Just Can't Keep from Cryin* and Memphis Minnie's *Bumblebee Blues* were the companions of my often lonely nights in the field.

John Hammond, the patron of black jazz, put me on to Robert Johnson. He had discovered the unpublished masters of Johnson when he went to work for Columbia Records. Later on, one memorable evening in 1939, as I played through Columbia's stock of "race records," I found this same batch of recordings. All alone that weekend in that New York office building, I played and replayed these masterworks. Recently, all of Johnson has been reissued on CD and he has won international recognition. But in 1939 only a handful of us appreciated him. At that time I was surveying all of the so-called race catalogues of the major record companies,[3] and it was clear that Johnson's recordings stood out as the finest examples of the blues along with those of the great Blind Lemon Jefferson in the twenties.[4] Blind Lemon's blues sold so well on black-oriented Paramount Records that he had his own lemon-colored label. At the peak of his success, a jealous woman put poison in his coffee. His voice still rings out of the scratchy records of the twenties like a rooster crowing before day, and his guitar, tuned in the neo-African scales of his tunes, is as subtle as moonlight on the Mississippi. And these recordings inspired rural blacks to sing the blues all over the South. My guess at the time was that Robert Johnson probably had been one of Lemon's brilliant disciples, since Johnson's style seemed to resemble Blind Lemon's—the high-pitched delivery, the brilliant countermelodies between phrases, for example. At any rate, it was clear to me then that Johnson was one of the two or three great originals of the blues—as remarkable a singer as he was a lyricist and arranger. Hammond wanted him for his epochal Carnegie Hall Spirituals-to-Swing Concert in 1938, but the South had swallowed him up. No one I knew had a clue as to his whereabouts, until William Brown had said, "Now Robert Johnson's a boy you ought to hear, too. Come from Tunica County. His mama live down there, seem to me . . ."

Mrs. Johnson's dwelling was a painted wooden shack, wobbling uncertainly on its cedar-post supports just higher than the sea of ripening cotton that rolled up to the gate. In the narrow dooryard a withered rosebush was dying among the weeds and a slick brown chinaberry tree held out clusters of decaying yellow berries to the sun. A skinny little black woman sat on the gallery watching us. She wore a black sack of a cotton dress, dusty from the fields, her feet were bare, and her face looked out from under a fantastic cap of little grey pigtails like a brown acorn in its cup. She said nothing as I opened the gate, regarding me with a calm gaze that seemed to come from far off.

"Yessuh, I's Mary Johnson. And Robert, he my baby son. But Little Robert, he dead."

She said no more than this; she did not sob or cry out. Her eyes glistened with the dull light of someone whose eye sockets are drained; but slowly she bent forward, her grey head bowing toward her knees, as if grief was weighing her to the earth. Nothing in this place moved. No breath of wind shook the yellow berries of the chinaberry tree or the dead green of the cotton. In the west a mirage lake shimmered in the cotton field like a pool of silver tears.

Country people are not afraid to look Death in the face. He is a familiar in their lives, especially in the violent jungle of the Delta. They have seen him in the houses drowned by the great river and in the towns splintered by tornadoes; they have seen him in the faces of the young men shot down in a gambling hall or in the guise of an old fellow who came home to die after a hard day's plowing, his body on the cooling board still bent from years stooping over the cotton rows.

Mrs. Johnson raised her head, looked into my face shyly, and then said, "I'm mighty happy that someone came to ask about Little Robert. He was a puny baby, but after he could set up, I never had no trouble with him. Always used to be listenin, listenin to the wind or the chickens cluckin in the backyard or me, when I be singin round the house. And he just love church, just love it. Don't care how long the meetin last, long as they sing every once in a while, Little Robert set on my lap and try to keep time, look like, or hold on to my skirt and sort of jig up and down and laugh and laugh.

"I never did have no trouble with him until he got big enough to be round with bigger boys and off from home. Then he used to follow all these harp blowers, mandoleen and guitar pickers. Sometime he wouldn come home all night, and whippin never did him no good. First time there'd be somebody pickin another guitar, Little Robert follow um off. Look like he was just bent that way, and couldn help hisself. And they tell me he played the first guitar he pick up; never did have to study it, just knew it.

"I used to cry over him, cause I knowed he was playin the devil's instruments, but Little Robert, he'd show me where I was wrong cause he'd sit home and take his little twenty-five cents harp and blow all these old-fashioned church songs of mine till it was better than a meetin and I'd get happy and shout. He was knowed to be the best musicianer in Tunica County, but the more his name got about, the worse I felt, cause I knowed he was gonna git in trouble.

"Pretty soon he begun to leave home for a week at a time, but he always brought me some present back. Then he took to goin off for a month at a time. Then he just stayed gone. I knowed something gonna happen to him. I felt it. And sure enough the word come for me to go to him. First time I ever been off from home, and the last time I'll go till the Lord call me. And, Lord have mercy, I found my little boy dyin. Some wicked girl or her boyfriend had give him poison and wasn no doctor in the world could save him, so they say.

"When I went in where he at, he layin up in bed with his guitar crost his breast. Soon's he saw me, he say, 'Mama, you all I been waitin for. Here,' he say, and he give me his guitar, 'take and hang this thing on the wall, cause I done pass all that by. That what got me messed up, Mama. It's the devil's instrument, just like you said. And I don't want it no more.' And he died while I was hangin his guitar on the wall."

Mrs. Johnson's skinny little body began to tremble and she rose to her feet, clasping and unclasping her hands. Her gaze was no longer directed at my face, but over my head. She came down the steps into the yard and began walking up and down as she finished her story, speaking in short hysterical ejaculations, clapping and almost dancing.

" 'I don't want it no more now, Mama, I done put all that by. I yo child now, Mama, and the Lord's. Yes—the Lord's child and don't belong to the devil no more.' And he pass that way, with his mind on the angels. I know I'm gonna meet him over yonder, clothed in glory. My little Robert, the Lord's child."

Her slim brown feet, the last vestige of her beauty, raised little puffs of dust as she danced about the yard calling on the Lord and Little Robert. She had forgotten me. She was happy. She was shouting, possessed and in ecstasy. And so I left her.

TUNICA BLUES

Son House, Robert Johnson's teacher and mentor in the blues, lived on another plantation a few miles away. He was a handsome, intelligent, sensitive man, by profession a tractor driver for a huge cotton estate, by preference a musician, very modest about his own accomplishments and fulsome in praise of his pupil. "Little Robert learnt to play quicker than anybody we ever saw round this section. He used to hang round us other fellows at the barrelhouse when we play a dance and when we take a break he pick up our instruments and try to play. We'd laugh and hurraw him about it, and he'd sull up and go off in a corner and pout. Just as proud as a peafowl and terrible nervy. So then he went off one day, say he goin to Arkansas and, when he come back, he was struttin. Guitar slung round his shoulders and four or five harmonicas stuck in a great big broad belt round his waist. And play, that boy could play more blues than air one of us. Folks would say he couldn't, but we know, us musicians, that he was the man. What little I know, I taught him, but he put his own soundin in it, and sing with it, sing all night."

In fact, Little Robert added Lonnie Johnson's tricky orchestral style to the licks of Charley Patton and Blind Lemon that Son House passed on to him. Like other much-recorded New Orleans musicians, Lonnie Johnson had Creolized the blues, reorganized their lyrics so that each one told a story, and set them to book-learned harmonies. Little Robert played some of Lonnie's sophisticated progressions, but he set his highly ornamented, almost Oriental vocal style over them. Son House went on:

"Bogalusa was his hangout, where one of his girlfriends lived. Bob was a terrible man with the women, like all us guitar players." Son looked at his sweet-faced wife and they both laughed. "And I reckon he got him one too many down there in Lou'sana. So this last one, she gi'n him poison in his coffee. And he died. Wasn't but twenty-one; even the church folks felt bad about it. I always did think that was funny how him and Blind Lemon died the same way, cause he played Blind Lemon's style, but more so, and I reckon if he lived, he would have been a better man, cause he wasn't blind.[5]

"How it come about that he played Lemon's style is this—Little Robert learnt from me, and I learnt from an old fellow they call Lemon down in Clarksdale, and he was called Lemon because he had learnt all Blind Lemon's pieces off the phonograph."

Now *I* felt like shouting. Son House had laid out one of the main lines in the royal lineage of America's great guitar players—Blind Lemon of Dallas to his double in Clarksdale to Son House to Robert Johnson.

"But isn't there anybody alive who plays this style?" I asked.

"An old boy called Muddy Waters round Clarksdale, he learnt from me and Little Robert, and they say he gettin to be a pretty fair player—that's one," replied Son House. "And they's me, but I about done quit. I'm gettin to be an old man."

"How old are you?"

"Thirty-nine, and I can't run round all weekend and work all week like I used to. Got something else on my mind now but the blues." He laughed and glanced affectionately at his pretty brown-skinned wife, sitting opposite. "Now, if you don't mind, I'd like to ask you one question—why is it that a white man like you would get in his car and come all the way down here to Mississippi to talk to a fellow like me about the blues? You understand why I'm asking you this? It's not because I want to say something wrong or to hurt your feelings . . ."

"I realize that . . ."

"But it's a puzzle to me . . . I'm used to plowin so many acres a week and sayin Yessuh and Nossuh to the boss on the plantation, but for sittin down and talkin about my music with some man from college like you, I just never thought about it happenin to me. So I want to understand it better."

Mister House really meant it, so I said, "History wasn't just made by kings and presidents and people like that; we've found out that the people who plow the corn and pick the cotton have had a lot to do with it. My job is to help you get down the history of your own people."

"That's good," said Son, "that's mighty good-soundin to me. How it sound to you, hon?" His wife gave us both a smile. Son went and looked out over the cotton fields a long while without saying anything. Then he turned to me, "Come on," he said, "I want you to meet my boys and we'll try to make some of our music."

I don't know where Son took me. Down dusty roads, along a railroad track, into the back of an aging country grocery store that smelt of licorice and dill pickles and snuff. There was a jug there that gurgled, and it was so hot that Son House and his buddies stripped to the waist as they played. Of all of my times with the blues this was the best one, better than Leadbelly, better than Josh White, Son Terry, and all the rest of them.[6] There was a harmonica player who howled and whined through his instrument like a hound dog on a hot trail. There was a mandolin player who did not pick his instrument delicately, but trailed cascades of blue-silver chords that lit up the harmonica's chase like the hot moonlight of Southern midsummer nights. A second guitarist picked bass-string obbligato to the big country feet that whomped out the rhythm and turned the whole frame building into a huge African drum. At the center of all this was Son House, a man transformed, no longer the quiet, affable person I had met, but possessed by the song, as Gypsies in Spain are possessed, gone blind with music and poetry.

"*Hitch up my black pony, saddle up my bay mare,*" he sang, his words conjuring up nights of coupling in the tropical heat of Mississippi. His voice, guttural and hoarse with passion, ripping apart the surface of the music like his tractor-driven deep plow ripped apart the wet black earth in the springtime, making the sap of the earth song run, while his powerful, work-hard hands snatched strange chords out of the steel strings the way they had snatched so many tons of cotton out of brown thorny cotton bolls in the fall. And with him the sorrow of the blues was not tentative, or retiring, or ironic. Son's whole body wept, as with eyes closed, the tendons in his powerful neck standing out with the violence of his feeling and his brown face flushing, he sang in an awesome voice the *Death Letter Blues:*[7]

Well, I got a letter this morning,
How do you reckon it read?
Well, I got a letter this morning,
How do you reckon it read?
"Hurry, hurry,
Cause the gal you love is dead."

You know I got my suitcase
And I took out down the road,
You know I got my suitcase
And I took out down the road.
Boys, when I got there
She was layin on the coolin boa'd

I walked up close
And I peeped down in her face,
I walked up close
And I peeped down in her face.
"You's a good old gal,
But you got to lay there till judgment day."

I fold my arms
And I slowly walked away,
I fold my arms
And I slowly walked away.
Says, "You's a good old gal,
But I just can't take you place."

"And now," said Son, after the bottle had gone round the band, "let me sing you about the old-time walkin blues—that's when you bound to leave somebody—you don't much want to, but you gonna go ahead on anyhow."

He began to sing with the harmonica puffing like a wild and sorrowful wind, and the guitar beating out a heart-stopping rhythm, like trees being torn up by their roots.

I got up this mornin,
Feelin round for my shoes,
Know by that I got the
Walkin blues.
Say, I got up this mornin,
I was feelin round for my shoes.
I say, you know by that now I
Got the walkin blues.

Oh, the blues ain't nothin but a
Low-down shakin chill.
If you ain't had um
I hope you never will.
Oh the blues
Is a low-down old shakin chill.
Well now, if you ain't had um, boys,
I hope you never will.

The music stopped and Son House opened his eyes and lit a cigarette, but somewhere a deep note was sounding, on and on without stopping. We looked at each other in astonishment. I thought that my machine was responsible and I switched it off. The sound continued. Son came out of his trance. "That's somebody honking outside," he said. "I better go see what the matter."

In a minute the horn stopped and Son was back, looking smaller, the flush of the music gone, his cheek ashen. "It's my bossman. You better go talk to him."

A white man in khaki work clothes was sitting at the wheel of a pickup truck, his face pale with fear and anger. He looked so small, so shrunken after what I had just seen and heard that I almost burst out laughing. He wanted to know what this sweating, ill-kept white stranger was doing in the local barrelhouse with his best tractor driver. I explained as best I could, but the glory was still on me and I am afraid I made a mess of my story. He didn't look at me as I spoke, nor, I believe, hear anything I said. He appeared to be looking at a pinpoint somewhere far down the graveled road ahead.

"Well," he said, "when you've got your full of nigger music, come by the house."

I held out my hand in a feeble gesture of friendliness, but he ignored it and drove off. Back in the barrelhouse we tried another record, but the spirit had gone out of the musicians and they broke off in the middle of the song. I told Son goodbye and drove by the plantation manager's house. "Follow me," he ordered, starting up his truck. "We're going to talk to the sheriff. We've all been told to keep on the lookout for foreign agents."

Every county in the South is a small empire, with its own autonomous power. This county system of government has the virtue of allowing a small area, a small parcel of votes, the opportunity to shape a local lifestyle, independent of the state and national pattern, so often controlled by party politics. A county can vote to be dry when all the surrounding counties are wet, and this means you have to drive over the county line to buy bonded liquor or come to an understanding with the bootleggers, who have, in turn, their own understanding with the local peace officers. In the old days a county could refuse to participate in the state road-building program, and, when you hit the county line, you might drive for a tormented hour along a washboard gravel road before your tires began to whisper on the concrete again. At some few county lines in the South, there were signs that read NEGRO, DON'T LET THE NIGHT CATCH YOU IN THIS COUNTY. KEEP MOVING. These signs might not be the work of the county officials, but, since they were stained by time, it was obvious that they had seen them and either approved or feared to take them down. In the South, every county has its own peace officers and its own penal system—the county farm and the chain gang—and some of these have been celebrated in song. One from roundabout Tunica County runs:

In the South, when you do anything that's wrong,
In the South, when you do anything that's wrong,
They'll sho put you down on the county farm.

They'll put you under a man called Captain Jack,
They'll put you under a man called Captain Jack,
Who'll write his name up and down your back.

Since it was obvious that Captain Jack didn't write his autographs with a pen and since it was also clear from the silent fury in the face of my companion that I had somehow offended the autonomous forces of Tunica County, I felt a bit nervous as the plantation manager and I walked up the steps of the pinnacled and turreted American Gothic county courthouse. We passed under the brownstone portico and into the cool interior, with its familiar odor of brass spittoons, wood oil, disinfectant, stale tobacco, and the county lockup. The components of this latter smell are too unpleasant to enumerate; we leave them aside and speak of the chill they produced at the pit of the stomach. As a collector of American folk songs, I knew something of county jails, certain of which have been celebrated from coast to coast:

The lice and the bedbugs are as long as a rail,
They'll heist their bristles and shake their tails.
  And it's hard times in the Durant jail,
  It's hard times, poor boy.

I had bailed fiddlers and ballad singers out of such places and, if my nose informed me correctly, I was now headed toward one. It all depended on the sheriff. The familiar lines kept running in my mind:

And here's to the sheriff I like to forgot,
He's the worst damn rascal in the whole blame lot.
Your pockets he'll pick and your clothes he will sell,
And you're bound to get lousy in the Durant jail.
  It's hard times in the Durant jail,
  It's hard times, poor boy.

My impression of the Tunica County sheriff is blurred by time and nervousness. He was large, red-faced, with stern baronial manners. He wore his white

Stetson like a crown, and I believe there was a six-shooter on his comfortable hip. He did not appear to have heard of the Library of Congress, nor of my employer, Archibald MacLeish, so I explained I came from Texas and was descended from a long line of Southerners, with two grandfathers who fought on the right side in the Rebellion. He unbent a little.

"Well, sir, if you were raised in Texas, you're bound to know that you can't go around on people's plantations associating with their nigras. That's what the trouble is, ain't it, Bill?" glancing at the plantation manager.

"That's it, sheriff. I wouldn't have minded if he had asked my permission and then got these nigger musicians together down at my shed or something. I just didn't like the way he seemed to be sneaking in. You know how we've all been warned to look out . . ."

"You were just doing your patriotic duty," said the sheriff. "See, we've had too much of these Northern agitators, running around and stirring up trouble. And now our country is at war, we've been told to be on the lookout for Jap agents . . ."

I wondered what Jap agents would blow up in Tunica County, but I kept my skepticism to myself. "Yessir, sheriff, I understand now. I was just so anxious to get my work done and record this music that I am afraid I sort of forgot my Texas raising," I said.

"You shore did. You've just been up there in Washington too long. Now, I understand that you went up on the gallery of that Johnson woman's house. Down here, when we go to see a nigger, we never go up on the gallery, we stand in the yard and maybe put one foot up on the step, see. We don't want to get too intimate with um."

"Yessir, I see."

A shiver went up my spine. Who had reported me? There had been no one on the road to Mrs. Johnson's house. It stood by itself in the middle of a cotton field. Yet this sheriff knew exactly what I had done there. Someone had gone to him. Mrs. Johnson? Son House? Clearly, I had encountered an intelligence system at work here in the black South. It was like being in a spy movie.

"And then I hear you also went in one of them barrelhouses with four or five of the roughest niggers in this county. What if one of them had cracked you over the head with a bottle or cut you up with a razor? These Delta niggers'll do anything when they get a little white lightnin in them. Where would I have been then? In trouble with the whole state of Mississippi. They'd blame me . . ."

"But I had to go in there to make my records."

"Well, next time see to it you have some police protection when you have to go. Now, we come to something I can't really believe, now that you tell me that you were raised in the South. I heard you shook hands with a nigger! Is that so or not?"

"Oh, no sir, you know I'd never do a thing like that," I assured him. "Why, if my family were to hear of my doing that, I reckon they'd disown me."

"And they'd be right, wouldn't they, son?" beaming at me with the smile of a good Christian who had established a point in the Gospels. "Well, I'm mighty relieved to hear that wasn't so. For I reckon I'd have to hold you for a while, just to check up.[8] But I'll take your word for it. Understand, I sympathize with what you're trying to do. There's nobody likes to hear nigger singin as much as I do. You say we've got some talented niggers here in Tunica?"

"You've got the finest blues combination I've heard."

"That so. Well, we'll have to get um on the radio down in Clarksdale. What're their names?"

"Well, Mister Son House is the—" I knew I'd made a mistake before the words were out of my mouth. The sheriff's red face turned beet color. His eyes narrowed to pinpoints.

"You call a nigger Mister," he snapped. "I don't believe you're from Texas at all. I don't believe you're from Washington either. You're a fake. You're probably an agitator. Maybe even a spy. And I'm gonna hold you till we can check with the FBI."

A big steel jail door opened right off the sheriff's office. Cold, dank air crept in my shirt collar. I don't know what I said then. Memory is kind, sometimes. It couldn't have been pretty, because when I had finished, the sheriff turned to the plantation manager. "What do you think I ought to do, Bill?"

"Aw, let him go, sheriff. He says he's not gonna stay in Tunica anyhow."

"Okay, Bill, since it's your charge, it's really your say-so. Where are you going next, feller?"

"The next county down—Coahoma."

"Well, I'll just telephone um that you're comin. Sheriff Greek Rice will know how to take care of you." He gave me a thin smile and picked up the telephone. Neither of the men looked around as I left the office.

WE'RE ONE NATION HERE

The hot flush of shame and rage lasted all the fifty miles into Clarksdale, the county seat of Coahoma County. I had a taste of the humiliation every Southern black experienced every day of his life, and it was hard to swallow. I felt I had been bluffed into an apology, but as a member of the first interracial team to work in the Delta, I felt I had to be careful. We planned to spend several weeks on a survey of the music of one of the capitals of the blues, Coahoma County, and so I drove straight to the county courthouse square. As I parked, another car drew up beside me. A husky young fellow dressed in an expensive gabardine suit leaned into the car window and pulled out his badge.

"I'm from the FBI. You Lomax?"

"Yes, I am."

"Where you stopping?"

"I haven't stopped anywhere yet. I'm just going in to see the sheriff."

"That's a fine idea," he said. "He's a nice fellow. Tell him a straight story and you won't have any trouble. I'll see you later, maybe."

He got in his car and I walked up the shady path into the capitol of Coahoma County.

Sheriff Greek Rice was cut from different and more modern stuff than the Tunica sheriff. A handsome, youngish man, sober in dress and manner, he said nothing to intimate that he had heard of me, and listened attentively, regarding me with cold grey eyes, while I explained that I had come with a number of trained sociologists from Fisk University to make a scientific survey of the function of folk music in Delta country.

"You won't find much here," he said quietly. "All these vagrant musicians have moved out of the county. You and your boys can make all the records you want, so long as you get permission to go on the plantations from their owners. But we don't have time for any more problems than we've got. There's a war on, you know." There was a pause during which he pulled a big leather-bound book out of his desk. "Well," he said briskly, "give me the names of your people."

"Señor Eduardo _____, student of sociology from Argentina; Miss _____, English student from Columbia University."

"She colored?" I nodded, while we looked at each other, poker-faced Texan at poker-faced Mississippian. "Then there's Mister Lewis Jones."

"Another nigra?"

"Yes."

The pale eyes lit up with controlled but baleful light. "We don't call niggers Mister in Coahoma County."

"I know," I said, returning his stare. "I was indicating the fact that Jones is male."

Greek Rice scratched out "Mister" in his ledger and wrote "male" and in a moment completed the list. Then he said quietly, "You have my permission to go ahead, but let me warn you, don't make any trouble. If you start something, we'll finish it." His eyes indicated the armed deputies who lounged at the end of the office. Then he swung his chair round and sat looking out the window as I left with the stare of the deputies on me.

When I came out of the county building, I saw that a crowd had gathered round a platform on the cool green courthouse lawn. The two or three hundred black people who composed the audience were listening in apathy while a handsome brown-skinned woman in an elegant tea dress addressed them in the ringing tones of the schoolmarm.

". . . and this afternoon we are here to pay honor to our selectees, who will soon be crossing the seas to fight for our democratic way of life. Members of our group have always taken their part in fighting for the liberty of our beloved land . . ."

The look of the hundred young men drawn up in rough military formation in front of the speaker's platform ran the gamut from boredom to sullen despair.

". . . and we, who stay behind to back our boys up with food for victory and purchases of defense bonds, should not be found weeping and wailing, we should send them off with a spirited song in their ears . . ."

The bosomy lady turned to a prosperous-looking black seated at the piano, who began in a meaty baritone:

My country, 'tis of thee,
Sweet land of liberty,
Of thee I sing . . .

I looked around. Almost no one had joined in. The inducted soldiers were staring straight before them, their lips closed. I wondered if they knew the words, or whether they simply refused to repeat them at this moment.

Land where my fathers died,
Land of the pilgrims' pride,
From every mountainside
 Let freedom ring.

The song ended, by mutual consent between the soloist and the bosomy lady, after two stanzas. Then two ministers were introduced to pray over the young men. Only a line or two of the first prayer remain in my memory: "O Lord, help these boys to do their duty, and if they do it with thy help, we know you will make peace reign."

Somewhere in the midst of this I must have dozed off, for when I woke with a start, a much larger and more powerful black minister was well into the middle of his address: ". . . and we has more privileges and resources of liberty than any other people who tramp on God's green earth. We have all heard that there have been some trouble in Negro camps. And we are ashamed of that. As Negro soldiers, we must remember we are citizens, for our uniform is a badge of our citizenship."

One of the inductees looked up at the orator with an expression of such scorn on his face that the bosomy lady, who saw it, hastily swung round and began arranging music on the piano. Meanwhile, the words of the speaker became more enigmatic: "Who gonna win this war? The answer is God. No one will win a battle unless God fights on his side. So fear God. Sinners, don't go away to the front without God. Bring God into your program. Some think that they are wise because they are privileged, but unless God gets in charge of this country and this world, there's gonna be wife against husband, nation against nation, starvation, pestilence, and earthquakes!"

In the shocked pause that followed this prophecy of doom, the only sound that could be heard was the heavy breathing of the orator and the drone of the flies. The lady schoolteacher buried her face in her handkerchief to hide her embarrassment, and the only white man on the platform looked around nervously as if hunting for an exit.

"You can't get off from God. You cannot get out of reach of God's power and love, war or no war. You must fear God," the minister finished rather lamely. An old sister of the church said in a faint voice from the depths of the crowd, "Amen, brother."

"And now," said the minister, completely unruffled by the effect he had made, "let us all sing with uplifted voice," and he led off with a great bellow, and the ladies in the crowd chimed in:

Lord, I want to be Christian in my heart,
In my heart, in my heart . . .

The chairlady, who had doubtless arranged the program, looked almost ready to cry as she introduced the last speaker, the secretary of the chamber of commerce, a dapper, middle-aged white businessman. He had evidently decided to indulge his feeling of good fellowship to the full and sprang athletically to the rostrum.

"Now the first thing I want to say to you folks is I think we ought to thank Lillian"—the black schoolmarm old enough to be his mother was evidently "Lillian"—"and the other members of the committee for the way they've organized this grand ceremony for our boys. Two weeks ago we had a send-off for our white boys, but it wasn't a bit better run or more full of community spirit than this occasion. And we want you boys to know that we who stay at home will be right behind you with our food-for-victory program and our purchases of war bonds. Your sacrifice is just as great as the white boys' and we of the white community feel we must render respect to you in your fight for the ancient liberties of our country. We American Legionnaires realize the sacrifice you boys are making. For we're all one nation here, aren't we? So in a spirit of fellowship, I wish you godspeed and a safe return."

Then this remarkable man, the light of the community spirit fairly shining in his little belly, struck a soldierly attitude, snapped a salute, and began:

"I pledge allegiance to the Flag of the United States of America, and to the Republic for which it stands, one Nation, indivisible, with liberty and justice for all."

His voice barked on to the end, but only the schoolmarm joined him. The minister did not know the words and gave up after a few ineffective mumbles. The inductees stared stubbornly at the ground. There was not a handclap or a movement in the crowd as he finished. He flushed to the eyes and stiffly walked off the platform and disappeared. "Lillian" looked ready to cry. Only the minister was master of the situation. He turned to the pianist, whispered something, and began singing, waving his black-coated arms.

I'm going to lay down my sword and shield,
Down by the riverside, down by the riverside . . .

The whole crowd swung in behind him. Even the inductees, to a man, opened up and sang as they marched off to the station, until the words could be heard a mile away:

Ain't gonna study war no more,
Ain't gonna study war no more,
Ain't gonna study war no more . . .

THE NEW WORLD

As the crowd on the courthouse lawn dwindled away, I looked round for my friends from Fisk who were to have met me, but as they were nowhere to be seen, I walked on downtown to have a look at Clarksdale.

Clarksdale was founded on a burial mound up along the banks of the brown Sunflower River, which meanders sleepily twenty miles across the county before it debouches into the Mississippi. In the days when the river was the main highway, Clarksdale was an obscure settlement, much less important than a number of river landings, but, because of its position on the eastern edge of the county away from the danger of the periodic floods, it got the station when the railroad was built through from Memphis to New Orleans. Another railroad came and, finally, the big north–south highway, and Clarksdale became the capital of the rich cotton country. While the river landings turned into sleepy villages, Clarksdale thrived, its stores in 1937 doing a total business of $13,000,000.

Clarksdale is a pleasant shady place. White houses, set far back on cool green lawns, betokened a pleasant and easy way of life. Tennessee Williams's grandfather owned one of these houses, and the future playwright spent some years here. The business district might have been that of any prosperous Midwestern American city. I had to remind myself that it was the cotton capital of the nation, locus of the biggest cotton plantations in the South. It was here that Tennessee Williams did the research for *Cat on a Hot Tin Roof*. Williams was a Southern realist, and I have no doubt that at the time of my visit his fabled "Big Daddy" was an important figure at the meetings of the local bank, meetings that determined the policy of the cotton lobby in Washington. These quiet streets of uptown Clarksdale in no way prepared me for what I encountered when I crossed the railroad tracks and walked into Clarksdale's black business district, the social and amusement center for all the plantation workers for thirty miles around and called by them, with ironic humor, the "New World."

In this other world the streets were crowded and animated. Businessmen in fine suits shouldered their way through crowds of plantation workers, some in their town best, others in patched overalls. Slick young sheiks in Harlem drape-shape coats, watch chains hanging below the knees of their peg-top trousers, watched the chicks go by, some in poor cotton dresses, some in the latest fashions. We all sighed as a magnificent half-Chinese, half-black girl, her skin a tawny gold, her mouth curled with the challenging smile of youth, her long slim legs winking through the slit of her tight Chinese skirt, floated past us like a pale-gold goddess. Knots of older men, with sweat-scarred faces and black hands knobbed and calloused from the plow, discussed the weather and cotton prospects. Gales of laughter occasionally arose, the men bending over with it, flailing their arms against it, staggering away under the load of it, but soon drawn back into the jokester's circle.

Flivvers of every make and vintage lined the curbs—Fords, Chevys, Overlands, great black veteran Buicks, ancient touring cars out of the twenties, pickups, trucks, only here and there a wagon. The crowd poured in and out of the vehicles, stopping for long chats on the sidewalk, disappearing into the stores for purchases and into the bars for drinks—a fairly prosperous crowd with plenty of time to waste and anxious for amusement. This was lay-by season. The cotton had been planted, plowed, thinned, and hoed clean of weeds. For the next two months the sun would do the work, swelling the green bolls, cooking them until in September and October the snowy cotton would burst out, and everyone in the county would be busy from dawn till dark getting the crop picked. Then the streets would be almost empty and silent.

Now, however, the county was resting between labors and had come to town, looking for fun. And the New World was doing its best. Peanut vendors and Mexican hot-tamale salesmen peddled their wares. Fried catfish was proclaimed available in every restaurant window. Wagons bulging with huge green watermelons stood at every corner. Inside the bars—the Dipsie Doodle, the Red Wagon, the Chicken Roost, and Catfish Bill's—jukeboxes moaned and blasted. Blues, hot spirituals, jazz sweet and jivey—everything that Chicago had recorded to please Mississippi—washed across this pleasant, country crowd while they milled and gossiped on the sidewalk in the evening light.

I was a white stranger, but my experiences with Willie B. and Son House made me feel somewhat at home here. I was filled with deep excitement that at last I had slipped under the barbed wire that had always separated me from blacks, and could now begin to see something of the lives that lay back of the music that I was devoted to. I knew I was cut off from these people by a chasm that I could not bridge alone, but now I had black comrades who would vouch for me. Where were my friends from Nashville? As I hurried through the laughing, chattering multitude, no one looked at me, but everyone was aware of me, for they stepped aside as I approached, especially the older people, and so I moved through a path of empty air that enclosed me and isolated me as effectively as if I had been in a glass bubble.

The human traffic swirled heaviest at the corner of Issaquena and Fourth. As I turned down Fourth, into the heart of the New World, I heard a high voice singing:

Uncle Sam ain't nary woman, but he sho can take your man . . .

I edged into the knot of listeners at the doorway of the Dipsie Doodle as the guitar voiced its silver-stringed comments on the line:

Uncle Sam ain't no woman, but he sho can take your man . . .

Here a harmonica joined the guitar and howled out its response to the blue melody. This must be the latest jukebox record, I thought as I moved closer.

He will take and he will carry him to some far old distant land.

Later, when I played that song for a young officer from the Central Naval Recruiting Service, he was shocked and concerned. He demanded to know my source, so he could try to suppress this subversive song.

The singer concluded. He was one of the young inductees whom I had seen listening sullenly to the windy speeches of official Clarksdale, but now transformed into a laughing minstrel. A black felt hat cocked on the back of his head, his powerful hands dancing along the neck of the guitar, he sucked and puffed with furious energy at the harmonica held up to his mouth on a steel frame, the instrument gleaming against his skin like a wide silver smile. Two or three pretty women in high-heeled shoes and cheap cotton dresses stood close to him, while in the little clear space that the crowd left, a blowsy woman in Mother Hubbard and felt house slippers, half drunk, hands twined in the air above her head, her eyes closed, was doing grinds in time to the music.

Lord, lemme tell you, lemme tell you,

sang the young draftee.

Tell us, baby doll, tell mama,

the girls shrilled.

What Uncle Sam will do.
He will take you out of jitterbuggin,
Put you right in a khaki suit.

The blowsy dancer opened her eyes, flung her arms round the singer's neck, and sobbed wetly. "Ain't gonna let um do that to my little Dave, my blues-playin daddy."

Young Dave⁹ pushed her off with a shrug of his powerful shoulders. His fingers ran down to the bottom of the keyboard and the notes spurted up like a crystal fountain. Pressing his powerful body close to one of the young women, he hollered:

Stop me from all my lovin, put me in a khaki suit . . .

The girl gave a squeal of pleasure; Dave made his harmonica whinny like a stud stallion. Then he saw me for the first time and, the smile fading from his face, he sang as if to cover himself:

Oh, man, I would rather be an ar-my man,
Baby, baby, but I would rather be an army man,
Gittin tired of these crowded old buses, gonna ride on a special train.

Dave played chorus after chorus of his incredible runs at the bottom of the fingerboard, as if he couldn't bear to let the tune go.

"Don't matter whether you like it or not, man, you booked and you bound to go, Dave boy," said an old fellow.

"What's it got to do with you, old man?" said the young woman, slipping an arm round Dave's neck.

The old man grinned. "When Uncle Sam git all these young gamecocks, you'll be cluckin for us old roosters."

"Fore I call for you, old veteran, the worms be eatin you for chicken fricassee," shrilled the girl. The crowd rocked with laughter. Dave flung the final crystal shower of notes out of his guitar. "Come on, baby, let's git a drink. They don't serve nothin but water where I'm goin."

"Honey, I ain't gonna buy you no drink, I'm buyin you a bottle." And with her slim honey-colored arm round his strong brown neck they went laughing into the bar, with the crowd after them. I wanted to talk to this young genius of the guitar, but I felt too timid to follow him into the noisy bar; besides, I suspected Dave had something better to do just then than talk about the blues.

BLIND MAN BY THE WAY

While the people of the county found a new evening of pleasure in their New World, I strolled along, wrapped in my envelope of Anglo-Saxon shyness and superiority. We had grabbed off everything, I thought, we owned it all—money, land, factories, shiny cars, nice houses—yet these people, confined to their shacks and their slums, really possessed America; they alone, of the pioneers who cleared the land, had learned how to enjoy themselves in this big, lonesome continent; they were the only full-blown Americans.

Somewhere ahead someone was playing the maracas. I hurried on, looking for an African with a shiny gourd in his hand, and so I first passed him without seeing him. Then I realized the rhythm was behind me and I turned back and saw him standing at the corner of a narrow alley, a slight brown-skinned old man, his face in shadow. A shapeless felt hat was pulled low over his dark glasses and below his wispy mustache. A thin hand held a harmonica, through which he was sadly puffing a melancholy tune. In his right hand he clutched a cane and a tin cup with a few coins, and his cane beat out the slow rhythm of his blues, the coins in the cup jingling and swishing in syncopation.

"All I've got is a wearied mind," he sang, and the song described him well. His shapeless black suit was in tatters. His cast-off shoes, several sizes too small for him, were split to ribbons along the sides so that his toes dragged the sidewalk. Over his greasy shirt dangled an ancient string tie, as decorative as a dried navel cord. From his uncertain, wandering movements one could see he was blind, and to judge from the slightly putrid odor that hung around him, sick as well.

"Yes, all I've got is a wearied mind," he rumbled in his street singer's voice, the lusty bass that can conquer traffic noise and go on day after windy rainy day, through town after town—the voice that is so hoarse from exhaustion that it seems about to die away, but that sings on forever, growling for food and shelter and a few pennies. I dropped a half dollar in his cup, and he

broke off his song at once. A clawlike hand grabbed the coin and secreted it somewhere in the rags. The dark glasses turned to me.

"Bless God, must be some big preacher or somebody," the blind man whispered to himself. "Somepin told me I must come to Clarksdale today. And look how lucky I is. Got a half dollar already. Thank you, Rev'run, thank you, suh!" He spoke in a sort of ghostly whisper. "You mus'n think hard of me for singin one of these little no-harm blues. I don't mean um. But this is the only way I gets my sumpin to eat. I get out here on the street and sing good *Christian* songs and the folks'll pass me on by. But if I get out here and holler—'Things about comin my way'—they give me a few pennies."

"But you know you're doin wrong," I said in the most ministerial tones I could assume.

"Yessuh, but I keeps my mind off of blues when I sings um," sighed the blind man. "I don't ever sing um less they makes me. I tells um sometimes, 'Listen,' I say, 'you can't find it in the Bible where there is blues in heaven.' And none of um can answer my point. I can't study the Bible so good, but that's right, ain't it, Rev'run?"

"That's right, son," I said, choking.

"Every day gonna be Sunday over there, won't it, suh?" he said, clutching hold of my arm with a terrifying blind man's grip. "The Lord gonna give us honey and wine. Won't have to be hongry and thirsty. When we leave this old mortality, we'll see with a spiritual eye and sing with a new voice. Be just like my old granmama used to sing for me." His blindness was an advantage in one respect—he never knew whether he had an audience or not. He turned from me and addressed his empty circle on the thronging sidewalk:

All right, friends, come on now,
It takes some wind to pull this thing,
But if you hep me out,
I'll blow it for you a few minutes.
Just one piece before I go.

The stick began its drumbeat on the sidewalk. The tin cup with the pennies swished a spicy counterrhythm—like a maraca in a Cuban rumba. His feet, spread wide apart, took two different parts in this one-man rhythm band, rocking heel-to-toe, with the accents coming on the toe of the left foot. Out of the battered little harmonica the notes of the song poured dark and rich with vibrato. The blind man could make his poor, cheap instrument speak the words of his song and, whenever his faint, deep voice fell away in weariness, the harmonica sang for him, thus:

I'll see Jesus, hallelujah,
When I lay my burden down,
I'll see Jesus, hallelujah,
When I (harmonica sings) *lay my burden down.*

I'm goin home to live in glory,
When I (harmonica sings) *lay my burden down.*

I'm goin home, way over in heaven,
When I lay (harmonica sings) *lay my burden down.*

"You have lots of burdens," I said, taking him by the arm, leading him away from the noise of the street, down the alley.

"Yet unstill I'll make it through somehow or nuther. After I'll lay my burden down over yonder in the restin place, there'll be no more trials," he said. "Anyhow I know I'm all right with you. If you travel with the Lord of Jesus, you all right. But if you don't, sumpin gonna slip up on you.

"Don't think I don't know where I'm at. This here's Hen Alley. I stay right down yonder." He pointed with his cane at a grey, rotting shack, leaning for support against its next-door neighbor. "This is the po part of town, but the folks mighty good and kind."

At the bottom of Hen Alley we came out into a vacant lot, in the center of which stood Clarksdale's Holy Roller church, a white frame building with a huge white sign that proclaimed, THE CHURCH OF GOD AND CHRIST AND THE SAINTS IN HOLINESS—COME AND BE SAVED. There was nobody about, so we sat down on the steps.

"I wasn't born down here in this devilish Delta country," he, the blind harper, said proudly. "I come from up in the Hills round Como, Mississippi."

Memories of the great river in flood dominate the folk geography. For them the Delta is the great crescent of land south of Memphis that was once covered by the river in its flood and is now protected by the levee. The higher country to the north and east, never inundated by the river at its flood peak, is called the Hills.[10] The Hill people, living on poorer land and more old-fashioned in their ways, look with a combination of envy and fear on the restless, pioneering

Delta. As they move into the Delta, the Hill folk fertilize it with their richer, more traditional culture.

The old blind man went on: "My daddy left out when I was just small and never did come back. So I couldn't play with the other children. Had to chop wood, feed hogs, pick up chips, chop cotton. I suffered from a swimmin in the head, and one time I fell off a wagon and both wheels runned over my head. I lost my sight from that fall when I was a big boy, bout sixteen. They sent me up to Nashville to the blind school and I stayed there a year and a half. Talkin bout *cold*—the wind just sifted right through you up there.

"But they learnt me music. I got to know A,B, C, and all the notes, and then when I got that down pat, I could play anything by ear. Come back home and live with my stepfather. He play banjo, guitar, fiddle, the quills, anything with a string on it or a hole in it. He taught me lots and from then on I been on the streets, playin everywhere."

Absentmindedly, like an old dog howling at the moon, the blind man raised his harmonica and began to play. Spiritual after spiritual. The modern *Precious Lord, Take My Hand*, old songs he'd learned in the Hills, like *Let Your Heart Catch on Fire* and *Lamb of God*. The Nashville ABC's contributed little to these songs. The accompaniment was led by the harmonica, overblown till the reeds vibrated like the human voice, tonguing out slides and quarter tones, making the little instrument moan like a singing deacon on the mourner's bench. I asked him if he had ever made up any songs of his own.

"Just one time," he replied. "When the great storm come to Tupelo, Mississippi. You must remember that. I heard about it over the radio. Said the folks was dancin and raisin sand in some great big tavern. Had three or four Seabirds playin. Didn't hear that God was workin, raisin up a storm. Then that tornado hit the juke and I was layin in my room that night and listenin to the rain and wind on the glass and this song come to my mind:

> *It was late one Friday evenin*
> *In wicked Tupelo,*
> *The storm begin to risin*
> *And the wind begin to blow.*
> > *Wasn't that a storm at Tupelo?*
> > *Wasn't that a storm, wasn't that a storm?*

"But, Rev'run"—the blind man's tone became confidential—"you must know the real reason for all that. Tupelo was a town where they had done some mighty mobbin. They took and hung three or four hundred colored folks, hung um unmerciful. And one of them colored boys they hung spoke to um—up there where they gonna hang him—and said Tupelo wouldn never do no good no more. And that's what happened. Four or five years later come this big tornado, like a big ball of fire turnin over and over till you couldn't hear nothin but it lumberin and roarin, and it tore Tupelo all to pieces. Only eight folks were saved in the whole town. Because those people had forgot there was a God. Is that right or not, Rev'run?"

I mumbled something, but the blind man paid no attention, caught and carried by his own thoughts. "Now I don't know what them colored boys had been doin. Maybe had touched something they should have left alone. Maybe they should have been punished. Maybe it was somebody else and the wrong ones was caught. Maybe so and maybe not. But we don't know. They didn't wait for no trial. They took God's justice in they own hands, what they say," said the blind man as he put his harmonica in his breast pocket. "These Tupelo folks didn't wait on the mercy of the Lord. And look what happen to um . . .

> A mother and a father
> Standin lookin and cryin.
> The storm had dashed their house down
> And all their children lay dyin.
>> Wasn't that a storm at Tupelo?
>> Wasn't that a storm?

At that very hour, unbeknownst to Turner Johnson or myself, another high wind was rising in Tupelo, a wind that would eventually shake the foundations of racial prejudice and would blow like a Southern storm through the whole country. For Tupelo was Elvis Presley's hometown, the place where he learned from the blacks how to perform in black style, his pelvis twisting, his left thigh swinging, his voice swooping into blue notes. This handsome young cracker from Tupelo put black and white singing styles together in a way that won young white lovers and singers in the English-speaking world over to the black side. Elvis Presley sold more records than any other singer in history and ushered in the age of rock. And the haunting quality in Elvis's voice, the note that captures and holds you, echoes the dark and tragic history of Tupelo that sounded in every note Turner Junior Johnson sang.

"It mind me of a little tale the old folks tell up in the Hills," he said, "Once there was a buzzard and a hawk, sittin up in a tree. The hawk looked down in the fence and seen a rabbit. He say, 'Brother Buzzard, yonder go a rabbit. How we gonna git him?' "

"The Buzzard look round at the hawk and say, 'Why, we just wait on the salvation of the Lord.'

"Hawk say, 'Yeah, well, that salvation liable to be too long about comin.' And he took him a dive after that rabbit and broke his own neck in the crack of the fence.

"Buzzard say, 'I *told* you to wait on the salvation of the Lord. Now, I got you to eat.' "

The blind man laughed a long, ghostly laugh, bending over his cane and rocking back and forth, filled with glee by this favorite theme of black folktales—the sudden reversal of fate in favor of the patient against the aggressive, the cunning against the strong, the humble against the powerful, Br'er Rabbit against Br'er Fox, John against his old master, Jack against the devil. When he had recovered his breath, he excused himself and asked me to lead him back to work.

"I mightily do enjoy talkin to you, Rev'run," he said as we walked back up Hen Alley, "but weekends is my best go for a little change. Rest of the time I washes rugs. Fifteen cents a rug. You know a man can't live on that. So you find me again, playin the blues. Say, you want to know my best musician in the world? Well, I'll tell you what, he don't live down here in this hot Delta. He's a Hill man. Now you go up roun Como and you ask for a man they call Hemphill. Sid Hemphill, he the old boar-hog musician taught my stepdaddy— play anything. You go and try him and you'll remember *me*, you sholy will. Pray for me now."[1]

I slipped another half dollar in Turner Junior Johnson's hand and left him snuffing out a little no-harm blues through his old harmonica. I will always be grateful to him. I did follow his lead, did meet his "old boar-hog music man," and *he* introduced me to the main find of my whole career—the African fife-and-drum dance bands of the Mississippi Hills. But that came later in this long hot summer. (The impatient reader can turn to p. 314.)

THE DIPSIE DOODLE

A cool evening breeze was blowing the sweat away. The tamale man sold me two dozen slivers of red-hot delight wrapped in steaming corn shucks for twenty-five cents. Just as good as home in Austin. A half a watermelon in a green snakeskin jacket, its meat redder than roses and sweeter than love, cost another quarter. That was supper. The Dipsie Doodle sign advertised beer, so, conquering the scruples suitable to my newly acquired title, "Rev'run," I went in.

The first impression was of lots of life but little traditional folklore. The jukebox was giving us Ellington's *In the Mood,* and the dancers, who might have been from Harlem or South Side Chicago, thankfully didn't appear to notice me. The big electric music maker in the corner again blinked its neon eye and the room was suddenly transformed. Robert Johnson, the Little Robert of Tunica, Blind Lemon's foster child, began to sing out of the nickel-plated mouth of the machine, and the couples who had been dancing Harlem became Mississippians again, slow-dragging round the floor to the weary rhythm of the blues, the pull of rough boards on flat-footed shoe soles making their bodies vibrate against one another erotically.

I got to keep movin, I got to keep movin,
There's a hellhound on my trail.

I couldn't watch that dance for long with any calm, so presently I took out my notebook and approached the jukebox, research-bound, for we planned not only to record more than fragments of folk song that still remained in this urbanized county, but also to study the musical shrine of that generation, the mechanical phonograph. I am not exaggerating when I say that this neon-lit, chrome-plated musical monster was for the people of the Delta not only their chief source of new songs but also an important symbol of democracy, one way for them to assert their racial solidarity. They put their money on the records they liked, and the rest went unplayed. Next week the owner of the joint told the owner of the mechanical phonograph to send him more records of the type preferred. In those days the neighborhood jukebox always had a sprinkling of records to suit all the musical preferences of the folks who lived nearby and patronized it. Thus a good way to size up the ethnic composition of an area was to look at the selections on neighborhood machines. Where Poles lived, you'd find polkas and mazurkas; where the Irish lived, Irish tenors and Irish reels. All this, of course, has changed since big distributors—controlled, it is said, by the mob—have taken control of the boxes and the racks.

In the Dipsie Doodle I found that all the records were by black artists and nearly all were blues whose roots lay in the Delta. Most of the singers no longer lived down home. But they knew how to contrive a song that appealed to the home folks, and a great number of record companies, and hundreds of jukebox operators with their machines in thousands of beer parlors, were living off this fact, and living well. The name of the principal manufacturer of these tireless music makers was Seeburg, but who wants a man whose name sounds like "Iceberg" to have a part in the game when you're out with your ladyfriend? So everybody in the Delta called the machine the *Seabird* or rather, with their soft accent, the *Seabuhd,* a name full of the tenderest, the most romantic associations.

"What'll we do tonight, baby?"

"Let's go down to the Doodle and play the Seabuhd."

What feminine heart, already anxious for diversion, could resist the temptation to play a Seabuhd, what could sound more innocent, what could be a more ingenuous pastime for country couples, but what, I thought as I jotted down the titles this Seabuhd would sing for a nickel apiece, could so soon and so subtly put ideas into a young girl's head as the offerings of this hypnotic machine?

Biscuit Baking Woman
Don't You Lie to Me
Shot Gun Blues
When I Been Drinking
Country Boy Blues
Coal and Ice Man Blues
Terra Plane Blues

I had got this far with my list when someone pushed at my arm. The army-bound guitar player was regarding me with a drunken stare.

"What do you want?"

"Me? Nothin. A man over here say he want to see you."

"Tell him to wait."

"I don't think *you* gonna want to wait when you see who it is." He smiled enigmatically.

More of the Memphis trouble, I sighed, as I followed Dave, threading his way through the dancers. He led the way to a booth in a relatively quiet corner.

"Here your man," said Dave, jerking his thumb at me. Then he slid into the booth, with his arm round his girl's waist. I must have looked surprised, for there was my research party, the team of my friends from Fisk University: Allen, the slim, lazy, brilliant young music professor, who hid his intensity behind a big loose grin; Eduardo, the keen, dapper Argentine sociology student. I thought both looked at me with a little hostility as I shook hands with the young English major from Columbia, an extremely handsome octoroon who had come along as an observer on the trip. And finally, regarding me from the corner of the booth with his sardonic but kindly gaze, was Lewis Jones, the man upon whom the success of this trip depended. Jones had a powerful build and the face of an Algerian corsair; but when he came South with his sociologist's notebook in his pocket, he was careful to move along as lazily as any plantation-conditioned black and his face, when interviewing a white overseer, wore an expression of rapt and humble concentration. No plantation boss could resist the sincere but respectful Professor Jones ("Call me Looey and I'd feel more at home") when he knocked at the back door and, hat in hand, asked them to help him in his study of the "colored" problem. The toughest cracker overseers have confided their troubles and their secrets to Jones. The Baptist minister felt honored after a confidential chat with the distinguished young Fisk professor. And the working men in the cotton patches never forgot the warm, friendly young feller who leaned over the fence to talk about the weather and the crops. And so Lewis Jones came to be one of the best-informed men about social conditions in the Deep South, holding what he knew in deep reserve, betraying his inner tension and his driving creative energy only in an occasional slight stutter.

This man, my much-admired friend, was looking at me sleepily, smiling his little sardonic smile. No one seemed especially surprised or pleased to see me. The fact that they were a day late was not mentioned, nor did anyone inquire what had happened on my journey. I felt more like a stranger with them than with the crowd dancing to the jukebox.

"Sit down and have a beer," said Lewis. "I was just explaining something to Dave here."

"This the one?" said Dave. "He don't look like he could do all that much."

"It's not just him. It's what's backing him up. He represents his whole group. They're solid behind him, and he knows it, whether he thinks about it or not. But me now, or Allen there—"

"But you big professors or something, ain't you?" Dave protested. "You come from a big rich college up North."

"That's right. But down here in Mississippi we're just *niggers* to every white man that looks at us, it don't matter whether we got a million dollars in our pockets and a hundred titles to our names. That right, Allen?"

Allen grinned and nodded cheerfully. Eduardo was following the conversation with a bright objective interest. I was too embarrassed to speak, but the slim young woman from Columbia blushed with shame and anger.

"Mister Jones, this isn't slavery or Reconstruction. This isn't Nazi Germany. This is America in the nineteen forties. You're talking about an attitude that's going out. And you're using a term that's insulting to your whole race, yourself included. I have to stand for it in public, perhaps, but not among friends—I—"

"Listen, darling," drawled Jones, smiling at her affectionately, but with more than a touch of malice, "this is your first trip to the South. The rest of us have lived here a long time. Me and Dave, especially, have been prowling up and down these old alleys and back roads at all hours of the day and night and we know what the *backside* of the South is like—not just the part of it they show to photographers, but that juicy old, funky old *backside*."

"I even *like* some parts of it." Dave gave his girl a big hug and she giggled.

"And Dave and I know that every Negro got to have his white man, his boss, to look after him when he get in trouble with the white world. Now I don't know about the rest of you, but this is *my* white man on this trip," concluded Jones, clapping me on the shoulder and laughing as I winced.

Allen and Eduardo joined in Jones's laugh. The beauty glared at Jones and me, while I wished I might disappear altogether from the Dipsie Doodle and the state of Mississippi.

"And," said Jones, grinning at the girl, "you are his nigger, too. What do you think he was doing at the sheriff's office this afternoon? Tell them, Alan."

"Well, I had had so much trouble on the way down, I thought it might be better if I went in and gave the names of the party."

"There, you see what I told you. We are registered in the minds of the authorities who control the destinies of everyone in Coahoma as Lomax's colored folks." Jones was still laughing.

"But how did you know I went there?" I asked.

"The grapevine, Alan. Over here in the New World we don't have the police or the power, but we have the fastest and most efficient sort of intelligence system. Doesn't anything happen on the other side of the tracks we don't know about right away, if it concerns us."

"That's right," said Dave, turning proudly to his girl. "I knew my draft number fell three days before the letter got to me."

"It's all too disgusting," said the girl from Columbia bitterly.

"It's real, honey, it's real, and not always disgusting," said Jones. "But you'd have to be born in Texas where me and my white man come from to understand it. My father had one of the best pieces of land down near Hearne, Texas. He taught the three months' school they had for the Negroes, and he was the first registered member of the Republican party in that county. And he voted. Voted on election day. Used to walk across the courthouse square, all by himself every election day. Every white cracker in town watching him. Walk into the courthouse, ask for his ballot, and vote."

"That man was crazy," said Dave.

"No, he wasn't, Dave. He had principles and he had a white man behind him. The local boys finally decided to stop my father from voting. Sent around a message they were going to burn our house down election morning. My father was sitting on the front porch cleaning his rifle after supper that evening, Mama was in the kitchen washing dishes, crying, when Old Man Bates came through the gate. He was the roughest man in the county. Owned a sawmill where he worked peon labor. Led every lynch mob that ever came up. He had his gun on his hip as usual that evening. He walked up and howdied my father. Then he said, 'Put your rifle up, Sam, and you and your family go to bed. And I'll just hang around here on the porch. Nobody in Hearne's gonna burn this house down. Do, they're burning me with it.'

"We all went to bed. And next morning there was Mister Bates on the front gallery. Everything just as quiet as always. He asked my mother for a cup of coffee, thanked her, and said, 'I'll see you down at the courthouse, Sam.' And went off. And my father voted as usual that day."

"He'd been there all night?" asked Eduardo.

"All night long. The word got around and the mob hadn't even formed. You see, he liked my father. My grandmother had belonged to the Bateses. And you can tell by looking at me that she had been more than just a slave to him. So Old Man Bates was our white folks. Just like Alan is my white folks now."

Lewis embraced me rather drunkenly, looking into my face with his tormenting smile. The girl from Columbia rose swiftly. "I can't stand any more of this," she said. "I'm going to bed." Eduardo and Allen rose and followed her.

"Better not reject him," Lewis called after her. "You may need him later on."

The girl walked angrily out of the door. "Too bad," said Dave. "Look like it's always the best-lookin chicks got the hottest tempers. Well, if this is your white boss, maybe he be mine, too. Maybe he git me outta this army mess. Think you can do that, mister?"

"I'd try almost anything to hear you play that guitar one more time." We both laughed.

"Well, I'm booked and bound to go day after tomorrow. So you-all come out to the house sometime tomorrow evening and I'll play for your machine. That be okay?"

"We'll bring a bottle," said Lewis.

"Pat, man," said Dave, grinning back. "Now me and this chick gonna snatch us some air."

When they had gone, Lewis said, "Sorry I had to do that to you, Alan, but I knew you'd want to record him. I think my little parable helped. Have another beer and look at this."

He spread out a crumpled copy of the *Clarksdale Times* on the table.

"Here's something we can record tonight, if you're interested." He pointed to a news item on the back page. "If you noticed that the streets were crowded tonight, this is the reason."

MORE THAN THREE THOUSAND NEGROES
ATTEND STATE BAPTIST CONVENTION HERE

MAYOR DYER TO MAKE WELCOMING ADDRESS

FATHER, HAVE MERCY

At least five hundred black Baptists were packed into the auditorium of the big, wooden First African Baptist Church when we set up the recording gear and lowered the microphone from the balcony, over the pulpit. The crowd below had the animation of a first-night audience. Well-dressed ministers walked up and down the aisles gossiping with their friends. Bosomy matrons chatted and laughed across the back of the benches. Hundreds of fans bearing the ad PATRONIZE THE MOSS FUNERAL HOME—WE GIVE FAMILY SERVICE stirred the muggy August atmosphere.

After an interminable hot wait, the organ began to play and a robed choir rose and sang a conventional hymn. I looked at Jones reproachfully and soon switched off the machine. "Wait awhile," he whispered. "All the Baptist leaders of Mississippi might be worth listening to."

As the singing went on, a group of well-dressed ministers gathered on the rostrum. Then a door opened at the back and the mayor of Clarksdale came in, followed by the bishop of the church. After the opening prayer the bishop rose to introduce the mayor, one of Clarksdale's leading physicians, who seemed quite cool under the gaze of the crowd.

The bishop had the golden voice and the silver tongue of the old-style country orator. His introduction of the rather ordinary-looking little white mayor would have made the angel Gabriel retire behind his wings.

"Fellow Baptists, fellow Mississippians, ladies and gentlemen," he rumbled, "I now have the honor to introduce to you one who needs no introduction. Therefore, I shall instead offer my little tribute to the man." He paused and swung his gaze round the room. When he began again, he was not quite singing, but there was that in his voice which suggested song.

Back yonder, before the world in which we now live
Was shaped and fashioned in accordance with
The plans and specifications of the supreme architect
Of the *Universe*!

"*Well!*" responded some ladies in the crowd, not severally, but all together and in precise rhythm as if the rising inflection on "Universe" had touched them somewhere deep under their silk skirts and tickled them into delighted exclamation.

It was way back yonder (*the bishop closed his eyes and spread wide his arms*)
Before the morning stars clapped their hands
    and sang *together*!

"Ye—ess!" intoned this time a whole company of the ladies, making a chord that any heavenly choir would have been proud of.

It was before the beasts roamed the dense forests,
Before the fowls tried their wings at beating the air,
Before the little fish swam the mighty deep.

"Yes, yes," exclaimed half the congregation as one voice.

The character I am about to introduce and present to you
Was still hidden away in the confines of God's eternal wisdom!

"Glory, hallelujah!" shouted one old lady, rising to her feet.

About sixty years ago in the little city of Cockrum, Mississippi,
Was born a little boy of Christian parents I am sure who taught him
The spirit early in life of dealing justly with all mankind
    regardless of race or *color*!

"That's true—preach, preach!" shouted a hundred voices.

I'm talking about a man who is not only mayor of Clarksdale,
A city of twelve thousand one hundred and sixty people,
But a Christian gentleman of the very highest type.

Apparently, Mister Mayor was accustomed to all this. He delivered a brief but cordial speech of welcome, and then scurried away. The time had come for a song, a spiritual, and I couldn't wait for it to begin. In the past I had tried to capture the lambent sound of black congregational singing and had always failed. The earlier portable equipment simply could not cope with a church full of black Baptists singing their hearts out, improvising harmonies and swinging round a perfect beat better than the best New Orleans marching band. Anybody present might "heist" the tune and lead; everybody present joined in, each person at his own pitch with his own ideas, but magically joined together in harmonies to make Dvořák and Stravinsky hunt for cover. Only Russians could match the black Baptists. You couldn't get the sound or the fervor into a studio or onto an aluminum disc. Now I was ready with good microphones, good acetate, and a professional recorder. I switched on the amplifier and lowered the needle onto the spinning acetate blank.

My astonishment and chagrin grew by the moment. First came a lady in a long dress, clutching her handkerchief beneath her ample bosom, leaning against the piano and emitting pear-shaped tones like a concert soprano. Then, after an opening vamp, a berobed choir arose and performed with a vigorous young maestro directing them. It was hard to tell which was more out of tune, the pianist or the choir. Where, I wondered, was the fluid and spontaneous harmonizing of the past? These ladies were clearly having trouble with this music, especially with the harmony imposed by the piano. They limped and croaked uncomfortably along, and I sweated in agonizing sympathy. Instead of the sound rolling like sweet thunder through the church, the congregation tried and mostly failed to join the refrains. I just couldn't believe I was in a

Southern black Baptist church. Their second song was worse, if possible. "What is this?" I whispered. "It's the latest thing. They call it gospel," Lewis told me, grinning at my discomfiture.

On the last quavering chord I switched off the recorder and we went outside for a breath of fresh air. At a little street fair in front of the church, Lewis introduced me to a Reverend Martin in the booth offering gospel songbooks and sheet music for sale. Martin was eager to explain.

"You see, in the modern Baptist church we are trying to move on past the wonderful old cornbread spirituals and sermons, as they say, with gravy on them. We want to bring our people forward with a new and more progressive type of music, created especially for modern worship by our leading composers. The old sister leading songs from the back row is being replaced by an educated musical director. His job is to spread our new, more intelligently composed songs."

"But what is more progressive about a musical director, when your old sisters could already harmonize beautifully without any direction?" I asked.

"That's not the modern, educated way. They need direction to learn the more modern songs we want them to have. This is a new day, and we must adapt to it. Take your own case. You're not here taking notes with a paper and pencil—you have the latest thing in recording equipment. The old must give way to the new."

Reverend Martin was a most persuasive fellow. But I blundered on.

"But what about *Go Down, Moses* and *Steal Away* and all the wonderful spirituals—you know that they are considered great music by everyone in the world. Are you just going to throw all that away?"

"Absolutely not," said the Reverend, offering me a songbook. "A lot of them are right here in this gospel songbook, in spanking-new arrangements by our best gospel writers. And they have their place in the reformed Baptist order of worship."

I looked at the book as we wandered on through the fair. There were some of the great old songs, all right, but they were set like conventional nineteenth-century hymns, with no intimation of the fabulous head arrangements that their "unprogressive" country congregations always gave them. I thought of the hours I had spent with musicians trying to puzzle out the amazing intricacy of those "old-fashioned" renditions. In the end, we realized that we were looking at an original African-American way of handling harmony. So far as I know, this is an unresolved and neglected mystery. The new gospel songs were handled well, with rather jazzy arrangements, but still essentially within the frame of conventional European tradition. There were some appealing tunes that might have been written by Stephen Foster, sentimental, rather than noble and epic like the spirituals. The impersonal, heroic vein of *Joshua Fit the Battle of Jericho* had vanished. The new songs were all ego—pleading with the Lord for personal dispensations—"When I'm on my dangerous journey, stand by me—precious lord, take my hand, lead me on, let me stand, I am tired," etc., etc. Clearly the ideal gospel worshiper was to feel defeated, helpless, alienated, and totally dependent.

I expressed my dismay to Lewis. "What is going on, Alan," he explained, "is a big power struggle in the church. The preachers are taking charge. It used to be that the sisters and the old deacons ran the service. They raised the songs, they kept them going, and those songs brought the mourners through. But they've lost most of that power now. The preacher controls the choir and the pianist and the music director. And so now he runs the service. His bunch holds the floor with the new gospel songs that the old sisters and deacons don't like and can't sing. The church is pushing those songs right across the country. My guess is that there's a tie-up between the big preachers and the publishers somehow. One thing for sure, there's a lot of money being made out of the whole thing."

Later on I got to know the principal gospel composer, Thomas Dorsey, a remarkable talent, who had arranged for the Louis Armstrong Hot Five sessions and a raft of jazz and blues recordings. With the decline of jazz, Dorsey explained to me, "I turned my collar around and originated gospel harmony. I've done well."

Gospel likewise has done well, producing big stars like zingy Rosetta Tharpe and glorious Mahalia Jackson, becoming re-Africanized as the black quartets and then congregations took it over, wove in the old spiritual patterns, heated up its rhythms, and sang its respectable pants off. Perhaps human song reached its peak in the performances of gospel quartets like the Soul Stirrers and the Blind Boys of Atlanta.[12]

Next, gospel, as its jazzy origins well prepared it to do, crossed over and became "soul," a new, black genre of pop ballad. Love's longing was expressed with the fervor of the worshiper at the peak of the service, and in matching musical terms. Soul singers like Aretha Franklin and Patti LaBelle, who crisscrossed—that is, moved from gospel to soul and back again and then back over—infused soul with gospel, gospel with soul, doubling and redoubling their emotional intensity until *Georgia on My Mind* sounded like *Salvation's in My Soul*.

In the process gospel has become a world-reknowned idiom, so far eclipsing the folk spirituals and shouts from which it sprang that the older forms have been virtually forgotten. Even scholarship now passes over these older idioms. I, for one, bitterly regret this tendency, since it threatens the continuance of the finest song genre of this and perhaps any continent, namely the black spiritual. I feel this all the more strongly since I witnessed the forced replacement of the spirituals by gospel in the Delta.

What I witnessed that night in Clarksdale was the first step in the process I have just described—the singing sisterhood of the folk research being silenced and brought into line by a male religious coterie, masking their drive for power and profit with platitudes about progress and education. Lewis and I stood outside the church in the dark, listening to all this unhappiness. The folk of the Delta were being required to sing in tune with the piano and in a harmonic style that was foreign to them, and the sound was agonizing. "I am tired, I am weak, I am worn," shrieked the choir. The age-old female religious collective was being replaced by a male-dominated hierarchy.

Lewis shook his head. "That choir can't yet do what it's supposed to. I mean, the educated ministers want choirs that they can *program*, so *they*, the ministers, can build services to suit themselves. That means the congregation will be following the choir and the piano or just listening. The old sisters and brothers used to raise the songs and lead the service. Now they're not even supposed to say 'amen.' "

I thought of the very West African *vaudou* rituals I'd seen in Haiti. There most of the ritual consisted of holy dancing and singing by the largely feminine congregation, with brief inputs by the cult leader, dealing with the spirits. This African pattern, which had permeated the American folk church, was now being eliminated.

We moved on through the Baptist street fair, munching away at the kind of watermelon that never travels north of the Mason-Dixon line. Presently, we came to a booth with a sign, CHARLES HAFFER, JR.—NOTED GOSPEL SONG WRITER AND BIBLE LECTURER. A huge black live oak of a man stood behind the counter, his deep voice rumbling out of a General Sherman mustache:

These days got everybody troubled, not only I and you.
It's got the rich and the poor, and every nationality,
So they don't know what to do.

Clearly, he was blind, another blind singer, but a man bold and sure of himself, his face strong and calm, closed eyelids adding to the commanding repose of his face.

When he came to an end, we asked him about his songs. Haffer opened the briefcase in which he carried his ballad sheets. What a package of death and disaster he handed us! *The Sinking of the Titanic, The Natchez Fire, The Storm at Tupelo, A Song of a Great Disaster, Time Changes Everything, These Days Got Everybody Troubled.* The subtitle of the last one caught me—*A Patriotic Song of the European Conflict,* taken from the following scriptures: Josh. 10:10–11; Dan. 12:1–2; Matt. 12:1–8; Matt. 24:21–22; Rev. 16:12–14. Eleven stanzas advocated the aid-short-of-war program that had been the subject of hot debate during 1941. "Let's record," I said. Haffer looked worried. "It might not be understood in Washington," he said, "since our country is now at war."

I assured him that no one would criticize him since we had all been confused about the issue at the time. "Besides," I added, "maybe I'll get a chance to play it for the folks in Washington."

The Noted Gospel Song Writer took this calmly. "Well, you can do that, if *you* want to," he said very gravely. "I've just been trying to do my duty by informing people about what is developing. Although I am blind, the Lord has blessed me with good understanding and a wife who will read me all the papers."

I switched on the turntable. "How does it go?" I asked. Haffer cleared his throat and began with the chorus:

These days got everybody troubled, not only I and you.
It's got the rich and the poor, and every nationality,
So they don't know what to do.

This was not quite singing, at least in our prettified, provincial view of singing. More like a midnight mountain in the Cameroons humming to itself, a musical lion at his evening devotions, or the old man of the tribe judicially measuring out his advice and prophecies, mixing them with groans—this was the voice of the street evangelist, a husky rumble, with such vibrato that you might imagine the vocal chords were not flesh but hemp. Yet every syllable of each five-dollar word came out clear as a tabloid headline; and somehow, the long and heavily weighted verse rippled cleanly over the slow, driving beat of the blind man's foot as it marked the rhythm. I looked at his broadsheet as he sang.

"These Days Got Every Body Troubled"

A Patriotic Song Of The European Conflict (Part One)

Taken From The Following Scriptures: Josh. 10:10-11; Dan. 12;1-2; Matt. 12:1-8; Matt. 24:21-22; Rev. 16:12-14

Composed And Published By

CHARLES HAFFER, Jr.

Noted Gospel Song Writer, Arthor, and Bible Lecturer

1503 O'Hea Street   Phone 990-J   Greenville, Miss.

1 If you stop and listen, I'll sing to you a song.
  About the appoiling disaster, while the war is going on.
  I'll tell you how it started, and when it all began,
  I'll tell you about the suffering; but I can't tell when it will end.

C H O R U S

These days got everybody troubled, not only I and you
It's got the rich and the poor, and every nationality,
So they don't know what to do.

2 It was in the month of September 1939, war broke out in Europe,
  And made everybody troubled in mind.
  Germany invaded Poland, and whipped them in eighteen days
  Drove their leaders in exile, and reduced their people to slaves.

3 Now England and France were allied and came to Poland's relief,
  And fought together side by side till France was finally beat,
  After they signed the armistice and France's soldiers went home.
  England was left with the bag to hold and had to fight alone.

4 Germany and Italy, together with Japan, made and signed a 3 power pact,
  In an effort to rule the land
  Denmark, Norway, Holland, Belgium, and Jugoslavia too
  Were all invaded by Hitler, and placed under German rule.

5 We here in America, a land which God has blessed.
  Live in peace and contentment from east unto the west:
  Realize the danger which we are up against,
  That's why we are spending billions for National Defense.

6 Hitler is mean and hateful, violates international law,
  That's why we are giving to England everything short of war.
  He is a ruthless cold blooded murderer, and that in first degree.
  He has conqured most of European land, and now he wants to rule the sea.

7 Like Satan he walketh about seeking whom he he can devour,
  Having the mouth of the lion, and the dragon gave him his power.
  He's a military strategist, full of hellish tricks,
  And the number of his names is six hundred and sixty six.

8 Our ships that sail the ocean, bringing goods to you and me,
  Were all forbidden by Hitler to sail the seven seas.
  He told us in substance, "you keep your ships at home."
  For they'll certainly be destroyed if they enter the war zone.

9 Our governme nt was patient, and tried to be good,
  Tolerated that foolishness as long as it possibly could.
  But one day Congress reclaimed that freedom of the seas
  And now our ships are permitted to go wherever they please.

10 Thousands are taken prisoners, hundreds of thousands killed
   Thousands are left wounded, to die on the battle field
   Still others to face starvation, and die from hunger and cold
   All we can do is ask the Lord to have mercy on their souls.

11 These must be the days that Daniel spoke about,
   At that time Michael shall stand up, and the dragon be cast out.
   May-be, these are the unclean spirits that John the apostle saw,
   Going forth unto the kings of the earth, causing them to make war.

Prices: 10c   2 for 15c   3 for 20c   4 for 25c

The sheet he handed me linked him to the British street singers of the sixteenth and seventeenth centuries who kept the public informed of the latest news by composing, singing, and publishing ballads. Their "broadsides" were, in fact, the earliest newspapers and, like the tabloids of our time, dwelt on scandals, murders, and disasters, the more lurid and dreadful the better.

Haffer's market was the Baptist Church, which, as the ministers at the convention had made clear, considered its missions in Liberia as important as the war effort, if not more so. Yet Haffer certainly was trying in his way to win his own crowd over to the war party. I changed the subject.

"This song about the Natchez Fire," I asked, "was it popular?"

"Oh, popular, popular, that song was popular! I don't have no direct record, but I must have sold two thousand copies of it."

"Have you heard other people round the country singing it since?" I asked.

"Sho, lots of people sing it. They buys my songs and sings um, and changes um. Sometimes they take um and reprint um and put their name on my songs. I've run across a lot of that." Haffer chuckled, and I guessed that this remark was aimed at me. "I just give you an idea of how it goes," he said. "It's that's what we call a *warning* song. When we write about disasters, our object is to warn the unconverted or the careless or unconcerned Christians."

"Do you think that if a man dies in sin, he goes right to hell?" I asked.

"Well," Haffer looked grave, "that brings in a lot. I don't know about that, but I *think* the man goes to the grave. There's nothing in the song that consigns anyone to no eternal torture. It just shows that the wicked are to be destroyed. It *warns*, like this one about the great storm of March 16, 19 and 42. Here's how it goes."

On a Monday evening in March, between four and five o'clock,
Great buildings like play-toys began to leave their blocks.
A fierce storm was raging, which passed through six states,
Leaving a trail of death and destruction in its wake.
     What a storm that evening,
          In different parts of the land.
     What a storm that evening,
          Men died on every hand.

Two clouds commenced rising, in the east and in the west,
They rose higher and higher until they finally met.

They clashed against each other, as it were a ball of fire,
There came a terrible roaring, like a hundred Fourth of Julys.

A man and his wife were frightened, and gave themselves up to die,
Put their arms around each other, together they wanted to die.
Their house was blown to pieces, goods scattered everywhere,
But when it was all over, they were left standing there.

There was a woman with a baby, she was carrying it in her arms,
The storm destroyed the woman, but the babe was left unharmed.
God works in a mysterious way, his wonders to perform,
He hears his children when they pray and makes the storm be calm.

"Now, the people seemed to appreciate that song *mighty* well. Just like they enjoyed my song of the storm that happened at Tupelo on the first Saturday night in April 1936. I used practically the same tune."

What a storm in Tupelo
Heard for miles around,
What a storm in Tupelo,
While so many people went down.

Another blind street singer and another song about Tupelo, Senator Bilbo's town, cursed by the battered black man before they swung him up. Ballad making is not just rhyming the news; it fixes an important event in the memory of the people and shapes it to conform to their moral dilemmas and emotional needs. "The wicked shall be destroyed," these black poets shout, and the people, listening, are comforted; God will avenge their wrongs.

"I began my work in 19 and 09," said Haffer, "writing different compositions in the way of song ballets, and the first song I ever wrote about a disaster was in 19 and 12 about the sinking of the *Titanic*. There was big talk about this ship that was thought to be unsinkable. It claimed a lot of attention, how the women refused to leave their husbands, how the lifeboats was let down wrong, how many were saved and so forth. At that *time* it was an interesting song.

If you'll stop and listen,
I'll sing to you a song,
About the time on the ocean
When the Titanic *vessel went down.*

I'll tell you about John Jacob Astor
With his handsome bride,
Refused to get in the lifeboat
And remained on the vessel and died.
> *Wasn't that a mighty time,*
> *Wasn't that a mighty time,*
> *Wasn't that a mighty time,*
> *When the* Titanic *vessel went down.*

The bias of poor blacks comes pretty clear in this ballad. The unsinkable
Titanic is just another white folks' brag. The rich folks who could afford
the luxurious passage pay for their past sins of greed and pride. Meanwhile,
Po Shine wags his head sagely and "ain't sheddin no salty tears" when they
all drown, as a bawdy rhyme, very popular in Coahoma County, makes
clear:

It was on the fifth of May
When the great Titanic *went down.*
Po Shine was on the bottom of the deck.
The captain and his mate was havin a little chat.
Po Shine ran up to the top of the deck,
Say, "Captain, captain, the water is now
Coming in the boiler room door."
He say, "Go back, Po Shine, and pump the water back;
We got one hundred and fifty-two pumps to keep the water back."
Po Shine dashed his black ass overboard and began to swim.
The captain say, "Come back, Po Shine, and save po me.
I'll make you just as rich as any son-of-a-bitch can be."
Po Shine looked back over his shoulder and said,
"What good is money to me, in the middle of the sea?"
Went right ahead.
Just then a millionaire girl walked from the bottom of the deck.
She say, "Come back, Po Shine, and save po me.
I might turn your wife, it's true."
He looked back over his shoulder and said,
"Honey, you're purty-lookin jelly roll, it's true,"
He said, "There are a thousand
In New York as good as you."

He swim right ahead.
Just then a whale, he jumped up and grinned.
Po Shine looked back
Over his shoulder again at him—
Jumped up and walked the water
Like Christ did in Galilee.

When the Titanic *went down,*
Po Shine was down in Harlem,
Almost damn drunk.
The Devil was laying across his bed.
He got up and walked to the door
And looked out and he said,
"They been a long time comin,
But they welcome to Hell."

It had been a long time since Charles Haffer, the blind gospel songwriter, had drunk his red-eye to toast the *Titanic,* yet his religious ballad thinly veiled a very similar sentiment: *They* been a long time comin, but they welcome to Hell!

I was anxious to learn, if I could, whether Haffer's was the original of the many *Titanic* songs. "Did you hear any other *Titanic* songs before you wrote yours?" I asked.

"Nossuh, but after I *wrote* that one, other people began to write, and I heard one or two more on the same things. But they wrote different. I reckon I sold two or three thousand of mine round over Mississippi, Arkansas, and Tennessee. Ten cents each, two for fifteen, three for twenty, and four for twenty-five. That's how I supports myself and my wife, and I'm with a kind of colored newspaper."

"You write for it?"

"Well, no, I just carry a bunch of papers and sell um, write subscriptions and so forth. I don't *beg* anybody for anything. I don't *ask* anybody for anything. I just sell my literature. Lots of people gives me money and don't take the *song.*"

"Make a pretty good living?"

"Well, it's hard to tell. See, I don't work every day unless it's a convention or association. Generally, on a Saturday and over the weekend, sometimes when there's no depression and everybody's all right, I do right well, right well. Maybe better than ten dollars over a weekend."

I asked him how he began making ballads.

"Well, I'll tell you. My father was a minister. I was born in Desha County, Arkansas, and my blindness come to me when I was just a boy, about the time my father moved down to Miss'ippi."

The giant blind man fell silent for a moment. I saw the hurt in his face, which looked as if the Lord had passed a hand somewhat too roughly across his forehead. He went on: "I reckon I might say I always was talented for singing. Before I was converted, I used to sing all the old jump-up songs— blues weren't in style then—we called them reels. The biggest music I know was the fiddle and the harp. They danced by fiddles those days and they had fellows they paid to come and call figures for um—I don't hear talk of that now. "Swing your partner, swing your corner." The old fiddlers played *Old Hen Cackle; Shortnin Bread; Mississippi Sawyer; Bill Bailey, Why Don't You Come Home; It Ain't Gonna Rain No Mo,* and all that stuff.

"Well, in those days, when they used to have parties, they would send around for me to sing for um. See, they had candy knockings in lay-by season, and cotton pickings—they don't have um now—when they'd clear out the cotton and plenty of something to eat and drink for people.[13]

"Back around that time the guitar came into style, and the first blues I remember originated from a sheriff named Joe Turner. He was a kinda bad man and if he'd go after you, why, he'd bring you. His blues was very famous and so was *Make Me a Pallet on Your Floor . . .*

"Yessir, we were entering into a jazz age and the old world was being transformed. Time changes everything and time changed me, too. I gave up all those worldy reels when I was converted. The first song I ever wrote was called *Stand by Me.*

"It made such a big hit that people advised me to print it and I began from that, writing different compositions. Since the year 19 and 09, I take for granted, I think I've wrote, oh, over a hundred. The way songs come to me, practically all of them that I write, I imagine I hear some voice singing and the verses come to me. The tune, even, comes to me that way. The tune that I hear it sung in, I just start singing it, myself, in that tune.

"Now they all don't come to me at once. I might get two or three verses wrote today. That song will stay off my mind and maybe in a few days it's come right back again. Sometimes it takes maybe a week or a month to get one song composed. If your mind is clouded with other things, if your situation is not so very pleasant, if you in a jam and trying to make ends meet, it takes you longer than it would if you didn't have nothing to do but write. Of course, unless it comes on me, unless I'm moved by the Spirit, I can't write a song. In fact, to be fair with you, I think all of my songs are written under inspiration, because I try not to write—I don't know—I try not to write any foolishness."

Which says it all, so far as any serious artist is concerned—try not to write any foolishness. This bard, blind and black, hedging along the pavements of the Mississippi cotton capital, pitting his great voice against the thunder of the jukeboxes, standing up to the cracker law—"Some of um talk abrup', come up cursing, 'Get out of here or we'll put you in jail'; some of um is nicer and say, 'What you doin is all right, but under the law we can't let you sing on the street,' and some of um talk fair, 'Get over on the other side of the street where you won't block the sidewalk and have all the fun you want' "—singing for his living in the open until his voice goes as rough as a currycomb, encountering the shame of his own people—"About three-fourths of the ministers likes my work and a part of the other fourth"—this latter-day people's poet of the streets yet maintains his artist's seriousness, yet says against all the world—"I try not to write any foolishness." Haffer intoned his ballad of the Second World War, a ballad that describes war as man-made pestilence, but which asserts on the streets of Mississippi towns, darkened by prejudice, that the American black is, in spite of everything, a shining and courageous patriot.

> *There is strange things happening in the land,*
> *Strange things happening in the land,*
> *War's going on, caused our hearts to mourn,*
> *Strange things happening in the land.*

1.
Oh you read the Holy Bible,
Matthew does record,
Pestilence and earthquake
And also rumors of war.
You see it's God's own will
The Bible should be fulfilled,
Strange things happening in the
*   land.*

2.
Nations against nations,
Rising up in this land,
Kingdoms against kingdoms,
You better understand.
No need to be surprised,
The end is drawing nigh,
Strange things happening in this
*   land.*

3.
Daniel spoke about it,
John the Revelator, too,
Jesus substantuwated it,
And the prophecy must come true.
God can't lie,
He declared man must die,
Strange things happening in this
* land.*

4.
Now Wilson said to the Kaiser,
"Please let my vessels be."
Kaiser said to Wilson,
"Keep your vessels off of the sea.
If you put um on the streams,
They'll meet my submarines."
Strange things happening in the
* land.*

5.
He tried to fool the Negro,
By saying, "They oughtn't to fight.
They have no home or country,
No flag or civil right."
But the Negro knew the best,
And their deeds proved the rest,
Strange things happening in the land.

Strange things happening in the land,
Strange things happening in the land,
I say war's goin on, caused our hearts to mourn,
Strange things happening in the land.

The blind black prophets bawling their wares outside the Baptist convention pictured a world constantly punished by God with storms, wars, and disasters because of mankind's wickedness. Clearly, these folk poets and their audience believed that this punishment was deserved, and here they voiced age-old beliefs. The balladmongers of old England hawked song sheets like those of Blind Man Haffer, telling of monsters swallowing whole fleets at sea, of plagues sweeping through cities, of maidens carried off by dragons, an endless recital of disasters—vengeance falling upon a wicked world. The fairy tales of peasant Europe are peopled with ogres, cruel tyrants, witches, fire-eating dragons, vicious stepmothers—all finally brought to account through their own wickedness. These fictitious monsters mirror the very real tyrants who, for eons, have subjected slaves, serfs, peons, women, children, and, recently, blacks to deprivation and humiliation, and to savage violence if they resisted. For millennia all of us have been comforted by bedtime stories in which these villains had their bloody comeuppance, preparing us for the even more savage adventures of our compensatory dreams. All these violent fictions channel the rage that fills all our hearts when we are unjustly and cruelly treated and cannot fight back.

Haffer's ballads of disaster, however, did not prepare me for what I was to encounter when Lewis and I reentered the church where the Baptist convention was proceeding. By then every seat was filled. The worshipers had dressed up to the nines, many of the ladies wearing bonnets decorated with plumes and birds. You could see these were folks who counted for something in their Delta communities. The time had arrived for the ministers, seated in a row on the dais, to show their leadership. One after another they stepped forward and led the congregation in prayers—long, beautifully intoned utterances—to which the congregation responded in melodic phrases. Together they created a sort of free-form song, in which the parts continuously overlapped in the African style. One minister succeeded another in displays of keening and oratory.

I confess that I blacked out at times and did not attend to all that happened. Even playing back later to hear what had been recorded, I found I could not focus for long on this scene. It was too intense, too pain-filled. It had the emotional level and the sheer force of operatic recitative, yet there was no make-believe. The agony was real. The impassioned coloratura of the ministers, the musical cries of the congregants, plainly came from the throats of tormented people. Perhaps some of these black Baptists had property and money, but they had no rights before the law, and their very existence depended on their acceptance of a lower caste position. The grave minister was chanting, pouring out their troubles in his prayer, and the congregation was responding to every turn of his warm baritone.

Oh, Jesus (Oh, Jesus), my rock
In a weary land (Yes),
Our shelter
In a time of storm.
Please have mercy tonight. (Yes)
Oh, Lord *(more high-pitched agony, shriller)*, Lord (Lord),
Lord (Lord), Lord Jesus *(scream)* (Howdy) *(woman shouts)*
I know you heard me one Sunday morning
When I was in sin.
(Palms smacked together for emphasis, with agony. First strong responses
from women, as shouting fervor begins.)

You got on my side.
You cut a-loose my stammering tongue,
Set my heart on fire.
(Long pause, filled by the clear-voiced "oo-oo" of women.)
Lord (Lord) Ooo *(scream of* All right!)
Ooo—when I can't even make it no more,
(Pause—someone begins to hum a tune)
When we can't get together no mo',
Oh, you promised You'd lead me. (Yeah!)
Oo *(high-pitched cry)*, go over here.
Oo (Lord), you push back the dark clouds
Over yonder
Where there no more crying (Yeah!), no more heartaches (Yeah!),
No more sorrow. Oo, get me home.
Let me sit down, rest for myself

Certainly the agony of this service in part reflected the agonizing scenes at railway depots all over the Deep South, where mothers and sweethearts were bidding hysterical farewells to sons and lovers going overseas. Many of these people were virtually illiterate. Many had no developed conviction about the war and few had any clear ideas about where their sons and husbands were being sent. The next minister expressed these confused and painful feelings.

Oh, Lord,
Oh, Lord,
My Father,
We need You this evening . . .

*(He's putting an "aah" on the end of every phrase. The congregation
   is beginning to sway in the storm of feeling. The minister begins
   to inhale noisily, like an exhausted swimmer.)*

. . . that are causing men to die.
Mussolini needs You this evening,
He's causing men to die.
Oh, Lord,
Have mercy on us.
Oh, Lord,

Oh, Lord,
We know no sinners here this evening,
But let every one of us
Tell Him to get Him to get behind us.
Have mercy, my Father.
Now bless the convention workers,
Bless the ministers.
You know the world, the world, the world—aah. *(A tremulous cry)*
Come over here and baptize us.
They makin war on every hand,
The world, the world, the world.
There is no shame there.
The world, the world, the world. *(Again, a long wailing tremolo)*
It's got us wringing our hands and cryin,
Shedding burning tears,
And when the war is over,
Oh, Lord,
When I can't pray no more,
Oh, Lord,
When I can't go no more,
When I got to lay down and die.
Oh, Lord,
Oh, Lord.

*(He starts crying, and one of the men of the congregation says, "That's
all right, buddy." These next lines were performed in a staccato and
high-pitched voice, full of anger and fear.)*

You know I can't help from loving You.
Because You loved me myself,
Long before I knew what love is.
And when my time have come
I've got the king's crown in coming glory.
And when I come down to the river,
Help me to pull off my war coat and enter.
I'll enter in the name of the Lord,
Make my enemies out a liar,
Make us able to bear our burdens.

A handsome young minister with a voice like a silver trumpet began to pray, and suddenly I tuned in. Like every Southerner, I had been raised to believe that blacks were contented with their lot. We had been taught not to think about the bad housing, the poor schools, the exclusion from restaurants, the Jim Crow rules about bathrooms and drinking fountains, the beatings, the police brutality, even the lynchings. A prosperous and expanding America had taken almost all this for granted. We had all got used to the convenience of a black undercaste that would do all the hot, dirty jobs for whatever we paid them and thank us for giving them a chance. We were used to the smiling and subservient black, because the Southern police customarily arrested any black who even wore a sullen look.

In those days there was silence across America about these things, a silence that deepened in the South, except, my ears were telling me, in church meetings like this. The prayer meeting, which had literally turned me off, was, I realized, a theater where these sorrows could be voiced and shared. The grievances might be veiled, I thought as I looked round at the sorrowing faces, but the grief was unrestrained. Meantime, the voice of the young minister rose higher and higher.

Please, sir, have mercy.
Oh, Lord.
Oh, Lord.
Oh, we want to thank You.
Please, Sir, have mercy.
You kept back the hands of Death.
You beat our enemies and made them behaaave.
You made um let us alone in Clarksdale.
Please, Sir, have mercy.
Oh, Lord,
Oh, Lord.

They all knew there was little mercy in their surroundings. They had heard about what had happened to Bessie Smith in 1937 in their hometown. Wounded in a local car wreck, the great blues singer was refused admission to three Clarksdale hospitals because she was black. In the end she bled to death without medical attention, while her friends pled with the hospital authorities to admit her. And this incident was typical of the Deep South.

The placatory outcries of this fine young man, filled with pleas to an all-powerful but kindly master "to please, please have mercy, sir" were an unpleasant reminder of the subservience that was life insurance to every Delta black.

Oh, Lord, please, Sir, have mercy.
Oh, Lord,
Our Lord,
We been travelin a long time.
Ohh-ho-ohh— *(howling melody, like a rising wind)*
Mmmmoooh—we've been bothering You tonight, Lord,
But You know we need You, Jesus.
Can't git along without You.
Bless our 'sociation,
We humbly beg Thee.
Bless our convention,
We humbly beg Thee.
Stand by Reverend Cozey when he's fallin.
Oh, prop . . .
Oh, catch him when he about to fall.
Oh, Lord. When the battle is over with,
Oh, we got to come off the battlefield.
(The congregation goes into a frenzied response, many people shouting.)
And we can't meet in Clarksdale,
We can't meet at another convention.
You that promised me a long time ago.
Oh, You'd make up my dying bed.
Mmmmmm. Mmmmmmm.
Oh, come on.
Oh, come on.
Ooooh, rock me, Lord *(woman shrieking)*
Mmmmmmm. Mmmmmmm.
Oh (Look out, Reverend), till I stop crying (Yas!)
Oh, sweetest manna. Mmmmmm. Mmmmmm.
Oh—my head.
Oh, You promised,
Oh, that You'd meet me.

Oh, Lawd *(rising cry)*
Ay-hey-hey,
Come on and meet me.
Oh, don't let me
Come into Your Kingdom crying,
Mmmmmm.
ROCK! OH—ROCK IN THIS WEARY LAND!

The voices of the preacher and the convention blended in a sound that shook the building. Tears streamed down many faces. And yet this was the normal end of a very conventional Delta church service. I felt witness to things I knew little about, feelings that were beyond my comprehension. My heart had struck a depth of sorrow and hurt such as I had never imagined. I began to see what a painful road I was to travel in the land where the blues began.

Chapter 2

▲▲▲▲▲▲▲▲▲▲

There Is a Hell

GOOD LAND

The good Baptists the previous evening had wailed as if they were living hellish lives in a part of the infernal regions. Some of the women especially seemed almost crazed with grief recalled and had to be restrained and comforted by their sisters. The next morning, however, as Lewis Jones and I drove out to our first recording date along Route 61, the highway of the blues, the Delta wore an almost heavenly look. Green fields of waist-high cotton spread away to the horizon under a gleaming blue sky. Little white cabins dotted the green like sailboats on a fertile sea, and every few miles we passed fine plantation establishments, tucked under shady live oaks.[1]

We were in the heart of the Delta, the vast floodplain of the Mississippi stretching south from Memphis along both sides of the great river, and endowed by its yearly overflow through the ages with the deepest topsoil on earth. This treasure made its white owners not only rich but arrogant,[2] although their main achievement had been to enslave and exploit the black laborers who actually cleared and tilled the land. The blacks had not only applied their inherited African agricultural skills to the development of the Delta, but had transformed remembered West African music into a new style, called the blues, which was now uncoiling in the ear of the whole world. In the creation of this Mississippi of song, the principal contribution of Delta whites was the melancholy despair with which their sin-haunted religion and their inflexible racism filled the hearts of their black neighbors.

Lewis Jones, who had for years been the eyes and ears of the Fisk University Department of Sociology in the rural South, was acting as guide and mentor on my return to the Southern netherworld. He and his team of young black sociologists had made a survey of the social background of black music making in Coahoma County. My task was to record and expand their findings. Without the sponsorship of this unflappable bronzed Dante, its denizens would never have talked so confidingly to my microphone.

The startling cruelty and violence of their stories is due in part to the fact that the Delta had been frontier until very recently. At the end of the Civil War only a few ruined plantations perched precariously on bluffs and Indian mounds along the river, transformed into islands by the spring floods. In those days most of the land was a subtropical jungle of forests, swamps, and snake-infested bayous, home to brown bears, seven-foot water moccasins, and hundred-pound catfish, and its human inhabitants were as much at home in canoes and skiffs as on land.

Reclamation of this virgin wilderness land began in the 1870s and continued up until the 1930s, and its way of life dates back to those pioneering years rather than to the period of slavery. As we meandered across the shining plain of cotton, Lewis told me about what he and his team had discovered. The Delta had just been "territory" in Civil War times, but as levees began to hold off the floods, settlers poured in from the farmed-over uplands to the east, the so-called Hills. They prospered, and stories drifted back to home folks that, in the Delta, greenbacks grew on trees and the ponds were filled with molasses. There was plenty of work for axmen to clear forests and plenty of land for good farmers to raise cotton. The plantation owners needed hands and did everything they could to attract labor.

"If land was renting for ten dollars an acre, they'd give it to you for nine, and you could sell your own cotton. We made a bale to the acre. In '86 I made eighty-four bales. Those days deer and bear tracks were more common in your cornfield than pig tracks today. You could might near feed your family with your gun and your fishing pole"—this from Phineas Maclean, in his eighties, a survivor from this early river period. Like others of the pioneer generation, Maclean thought that life had gone downhill in modern times. But he was still making a crop every year when we found him on Sherrod's Plantation, cultivating land he'd been working for sixty years.

"I come in here in '79, young fellow," he growled. "And life now ain't like no life at all compared to back yonder. Why, I have caught fish right where you are standing. Them times we didn't have no levees holdin back the waters. The river could come in and replenish the land every year. Didn have to put on no fertilizer. We made a bale to the acre. In '90 I had sixteen bales of cotton out of doors to be disposed at my say-so.

"All this here was in woods. And every year, when the crops were laid by, July and August, you'd hear the axes ringin and the folks singin:

July and Augus', tu-lum,
July and Augus', tu-lum,
July and Augus', tu-lum,
Two hottest months in the year, tu-lum.

"Near bout every farmer have him a log-rollin, with the neighbors comin in, plenty to eat, plenty whiskey, and playin them ol ring games in the evenin.

Call for your whiskey,
Pay before you go.
Bound to marry that pretty little gal
Let the wind blow high or low.

"No times like that today. Why, now a man can't even make his own cotton crop—they sends in a machine to break your land, plant it, plow it—you settin there with nothin to do. In my time we worked! We worked! Sometimes one ax gang gainst another one to see which the best.

"I remember Old Man Wooten say his niggers could outwork O'Neill's niggers. When O'Neill heard that, he went out in the night and cut his trees half through, and next day O'Neill's folks got through fore Wooten's niggers was good started. Old Wooten got hot over that, and he whip his niggers nearly to death. He was known to be mean, old Wooten was.

"Oh, it took a heap of work to clean the boogers, bears, and mosquitoes off this Delta. Most people nowadays don't know that we had to move all those logs by hand. Way we did it was to roll our log onto four sticks. That made handholds for eight men, four to a side. Then they would call out, 'Hands on your pole! Now bow and come! Bow and come!' An that log would move. Put that one on the pile and go again. But some them logs so heavy, you'd lose your grip on the lifters. Then you'd have to go to cuffs—see the cuff round yo wrist and it tied to a loop round yo stick. Then you double yo fist and lift on the words *'bow and come.'*

"An if that didn move it, we bring up the bull band, where the men have a harness over they shoulders and the lifting pole fitted to that. Sometimes, just for fun, team would let go all holts and leave one man 'tach to his bull band. That band gonna pin that man flat on the ground, and hold him there till they lift the log. They'd cut all such fool as that, most half drunk sometime.

"Evenin, much to eat. Fife-and-drum music or fiddle fuh dance. Old ladies be quiltin, watchin folks in the ring play, where the girl have a chance to choose partner and gi' um a kiss. Carryins on!" said old Phineas, chuckling. "We had us a time back yonder."

Into the twentieth century, when prisoners or forced-labor gangs were at work clearing the Delta swamplands, they continued to handle the logs the way old Phineas described. Walter Brown, the scarred poet of the Greenville riverfront, remembered how that work was done.

WALTER BROWN: No, I never will forget that. They was clearin new ground. And they had those four-foot, six-foot, ten-foot logs.

ALAN LOMAX: Is that in the swamp?

W.B.: In the swamp. Bringing the logs out through mud and water. They had hand sticks. They didn't use no pavement or nothing like that. They just used they hands. And eight mens would hep pick it up and get it to the water, and four mens would tow the log.

A.L.: How heavy was it?

W.B.: Heavy! They'd be eighteen inches and twenty-four inches thick, from six to twelve feet long. A driver would be over every group of men. The next place, you got another driver. Next place you got another driver. No driver wants the other one to send out more wood than you sent. So that's why they drive their mens hard—they want to do as well as the next man do. They wouldn have no mens my age on those sticks, just them youngsters, eighteen, nineteen, twenty years old, up to thirty, able-bodied men, you know. Man like that could pick um up and they'd move on. And then they'd holler:

Looked at the sun and the sun was red,
I looked at my partner, he was falling dead,
*But we just kept on **moving.***
It was tough.

We just kept on moving,
*We **had** to move.*
>   *Look out, Shot,*
>   *Here I come,*
>   *And you standin up there,*
>   *With your big shotgun.*
But we gotta keep moving.
>   *We got a man,*
>   *He done fell dead,*
>   *But alls I heard*
>   *Was what he said,*
Keep on moving.
He goin to heaven,
He goin to hell,
But wherever he is,
I wish him well.
>   *Keep moving,*
>   *Gimme another partner,*
>   *Give him to me quick,*
>   *I need another hand*
>   *On the end of this stick.*
>   *Keep moving.*
>   *Boom-a boom-a boom-a boom-a boom*
Come on boss,
'F you hear me cry,
I can't tote this stick
On both sides.
>   *Keep moving,*
>   *Send me a man—*
>   *Keep moving,*
>   *Double hands.*
>   *Where I can make it*
>   *Like a man.*
A-boom-a boom-a boom-a boom-a boom
KEEP IT MOVING!

Our gnarled Delta veteran's boom-booming like Vachel Lindsay's *Congo* all but labels his log-rolling chant as a continuation of the joyful, drum-accompanied songs his ancestors had sung as they cleared their jungle continent. It also reflects the mood of the pioneer-era Delta, which was often sanguine in spite of hardships and a badly skewed social system. Blacks were acquiring land, establishing their own communities, and rising in the world. Even though most worked as tenants and common laborers, they had moved past slavery and Reconstruction and were part of an expanding economy. Many of the positive characteristics of African culture still infused daily life. In the first place, they were continuing their African vocations. Black Africa has long been the most intensively agricultural of continents, and it was the heritage of black skills in raising crops and herds in the tropics that opened the hot lands of the Americas for settlement.

These African-American farmers, whose ancestors had been yam and millet gardeners and men of the hoe, had, in the USA, acquired the ripened skills of European husbandry and become proud-standing plowmen. In this cotton county, as Lewis Jones put it to me, "the men did the plowing; the women and children chopped cotton in the spring, and the whole family picked it in the fall. During most weeks of the year, most Coahoma folks were busy traveling between cotton rows with a sack, a hoe, a plow, or a tractor." Still, much Delta work was done with the dash and rhythm of the age-old communal style of black Africa, which turned the heavy, hot work of the tropics into community jollifications. In all these activities black women and children played a prominent part, both in Africa and in the New World.

Also, one now realizes, the new neighborhoods forming in the Delta, at the crossroads and on the big plantations, remained quite African in their processes. The shopping and meeting points at places like Jonestown, Lula, Friars Point, Bobo, and Stovall usually comprised several large (extended) families that worked and played and got religion together, as had the lineages in African villages. Although there was some movement of tenants between plantations, most folks stayed in or near the place they were born and raised, so that there were friends or relatives on hand when things went wrong. Their inherited sense of solidarity grew with segregation.

Since their black inhabitants belonged to a caste not permitted to marry or socialize across the color line, even as children in school, they retained an African way of doing things that shows up in every department of life. Their nonverbal African cultural heritage remained vividly alive, and all through African-American history it has fortified black morale as the group confronted an often hostile white culture. Recently, as the study of films and recordings has supplemented written documentation, we have become aware of how pervasive and powerful this continuance of African behavioral style has been, notably in the performance arts.

OLD-TIME RELIGION

All agree that the main institution of black Delta life was the church. There was usually at least one church, often paid for by the plantation owner, in every neighborhood center. The church, in political fact, was the only place where blacks were permitted to assemble and carry out organized activities in large numbers. Thus worship became the main venue in which these transported Africans could continue to be as sociable as they liked to be. There were meetings all week long and on Sundays, which might last all day and into the evening. These meetings were well attended, especially by women, for they were not only the center for respectable society, but community theaters in which the women, most notably, could act out their troubles in a supportive setting. They called it getting happy, shouting.

"Shouting" is the Southern evangelical term for "jubilating"—often dancing—before the Lord. "It's what you do when you get happy, that is, enter or enact a religious trance. You can shout all by yourself at home or in the fields, and people have and do, but shouting is usually a social affair," as Miss Fannie Cotrell, eighty-nine, of Lula, Mississippi, explained to us.

Miss Fannie was a little more prosperous than some folks we met because she'd spent her life as a domestic servant. She told us, "The body can be used as a trumpet by the spirit." But, she went on, "A meek and mild spirit is better than a rowdy mind. I saw one good old man so taken by the spirit that it took four deacons to sit him down. Some folks just pats they hands. Some just lightly jump up and down. An they's some that walks the aisles."

Miss Fannie began to gather steam. "I have known women walk the benches—yes sir! They just step from bench to bench, right across the church, and not get hurt! Other folks is more quiet. I have seen them fall from the mercy seat and remain there on the floor from ten at night until the next morning—with some folks staying there to pray for them."

We began to feel that Old Lady Cotrell might get happy herself, as her voice rose. "And this one girl—her name was Mamie—she fell out in church one evening at three P.M.—after that she never spoke or ate or moved till Wednesday morning. She was just like a doll, laying there—never opened her eyes. Her parents thought she was dead, but the doctor come and took her pulse and said she wasn't sick or nothing. Then on Wednesday morning she rose—she *rose*—triumphing, shouting, and praising the Lord. *She was under conviction.* She had always been very haughty, but she became one of the humblest Christians."

Chair-bound scholars often write as if such holy dancing were something out of the ordinary. In fact, most dance in early society was religious in character. As for African ritual, it principally consists of symbolic dances that bring the Gods to the service and honor them there. This tradition took many forms in the New World, including that of the present-day Holy Rollers. I have seen *vaudou* dancers in Haiti become snakes and coil round the rafters, men become women and in giggling sopranos demand comfits and perfume, and women take masculine personae and call for black cheroots and rum laced with bull's blood.

Damballa, we do-ey.
Kissou mande salado,
Domitans silibo, Ayee, bobo.

I've joined in the *rushing* dance of the Bahamas, where a file of flirting couples prance and slide round and round the outside aisle of the church, feeling so light they sing:

If I had the wings, like a dove I would fly . . .

The Georgia Sea Islanders shout to bring in the New Year, shuffling and singing round the church. Their rhythmic antiphonies call up biblical heroes, as did the Haitian and African chants that summoned the spirits to the dancing floor.

Moses, Moses, don't get lost,
In that Red Sea . . .

"O Eve, where is Adam?"
"Adam in the garden,
Picking up leaves."
(miming leaf picking)

Read um, John, read um.
Oh read um, le' we go . . .
(miming the perusal of a book)

The oldest Delta generation affectionately remembered such danced spirituals, especially *Rock, Daniel,* which was sung in church to make folks shout,
and at watch meeting to help bring in the New Year.

LEADER: *Put on your warfare shoes,*
    OVERLAPPED CHORUS: *Rock, Daniel.*

Put on your warfare shoes,
Rock, Daniel.

When you rocked, they explained, it wasn't dancing, because you kept your
feet far apart, never crossing them (that would be dancing),[3] but dragging
them flat to the floor, so that your hips rocked. African hoe agriculture
requires a wide ground-hugging stance. In dance, this foot sliding generates
multipart complex rhythms in the relaxed and loosely hung torso. In sum,
Rock, Daniel kept a full-fledged African slavery-time dance style alive in the
Delta Baptist church. One oldster said that sometimes a man and a woman
rocked face-to-face, holding on to each other's shoulders. On Saturday nights
they used it as a "ring play," the term for social dancing in the slave South
and the nearby Bahamas.

Everyone had sternly told me that the spirituals, locally called "hallies"
(short for hallelujah)—those most beautiful of religious songs—had died out in
Coahoma, replaced by Dr. Watts's hymns, by gospel, and by Holy Roller shouts.
But I set myself against this and arranged to hear some of the older members of
the Mt. Ararat Baptist Church recall what they could of the beloved old genre.
The church stood near the crossroads on the King and Anderson Plantation—a
plain white one-story building with steepled bell tower.

We arrived after the service had begun. A woman, just received into membership, had got so happy that the white-robed sisters of the church had to
hold her down. "I know I got religion," she whooped. "I've had it for sixteen
years, unless God is deef!"

She had reached a secure haven, Reverend Savage assured her. "Church is
as safe on water as it is in fire. In fact, the church is the safest place I know.
I've read a lot of insurance policies, but I've never read one that'll guarantee
you resurrection."

Then, in a deep voice that required no microphone, he began to sing:

Oh let me ride,
Let me ride.

The whole house answered, and in a moment the church was overflowing with the rich harmonies of old-fashioned congregational singing.

Low down, chariot,
And let me ride.

I was almost as happy as the lady convert, feeling that here at Mt. Ararat I'd probably record the great old hallelujah spirituals, and so I leaned back and enjoyed the preacher, Reverend Savage. Every turn of his sermon, it struck me, dealt with a major problem of these sharecroppers, who never could be sure of when or what their white landlords would pay them.

His title was "Payday in Heaven," where there was no Jim Crow and no postponement of payday. His opening paragraph addressed the two main problems of his congregants—the color caste line and poverty, rooted in segregation and a dishonest economic system.

"Since Satan's been defeated and driven from the territo'," Savage began, "God don't allow no different ways and no different kingdoms. Jesus can see man from his mountain height. Jesus can see what he doin in the field, and He says, 'Get to work in my vineyard there, and whatsoever is right, I'll pay you.'"

Even the laggards would get their due, the minister assured them. "Now, some folks gonna wait until the last hour to join the church—so feeble they can hardly make it to the do'—but Jesus will pay them anyhow."

His voice now rang against the church walls; "If Jesus cried with a loud voice, it's all right for me to cry out in a loud voice."

Reverend Savage began to inhale gutturally and to roar magnificently on his exhaled lines. He was dealing with the most painful part of his congregants' lives—those thin paydays when husbands brought home only a few dollars to compensate a whole family for a year of slaving in the cotton patch.

I see the angel coming with the payroll on his shoulder,
"Servant, come on home anyhow,
I know you been mocked down there,
I know you been cryin on the way."
But here come Gabriel
With one foot on the sea, and one on dry land.
He's got your pardon in his right hand,

Sayin "I'm coming quickly and reward every man.
If you've been lonesome down here,
Jesus gonna take you by the hand up in glory!"
Small payday here, large payday in the mornin.
They don't lynch over there,
They don't talk about you over there,
No hearse's rollin over there.
Every day will be Sunday,
Every month will be Jubilee.
In a few more rising suns
Payday gonna come, chillun,
Payday gonna come.

He'd spoken to all the miseries of these downtrodden folks and given them something to hope for. By the time he'd done, women were shouting all over Mt. Ararat Church. I wondered what the plantation manager would think of all this; probably Big Daddy was all tied up in family problems. The church gradually emptied, leaving only a small group who had come to sing the old-time songs for Lewis and myself. It's not easy to describe what ensued. These were older people—stooped, quiet, gentle. When they began to sing, they took us into another realm, filled with true holiness, in which we relived the trials of the biblical prophets and the sufferings of Jesus, just as their slave ancestors had. First old Brother Joiner rose and addressed our little group in his deep, grave voice:

"Christian friends, we're gonna sing one of the old slavery-time spirituals that my old grandmother taught me a long time ago. It takes Daniel for a reference. Daniel went through the same troubles that we are going through down here. (*One of the ladies:* Amen.) Daniel was persecuted, put in the lion's den for the word of God. Now my granma told me that they wouldn't allow them free access to worship like we have today.

"They would get off in some secret place in the woods and would put their heads around a big old iron washpot to keep Old Marse from hearing their voices. (*Voice off:* That's right.) And they'd sing about '*I'm gonna tell my Lord how you do me here*' and begin to shout around the old pot. (Amen.) So now I would like everybody to sing with an uplifted voice."

Brushing back his big mustache, old Brother Joiner began to sing in a deep groaning voice, the little group following right along:

I'm gonna tell my Lord,
  Daniel,
I'm gonna tell my Lord,
  Daniel.

(Here at last was the old Delta
shout, with a double clap
giving a dance beat, and
the overlap between lead and
chorus on its short phrases
happening every couple of
seconds. True African turn
taking!)

How you done me here,
  Daniel,
How you done me here,
  Daniel.

(They remember what happened
to their ancestors—whippin a
slave, strip him to the waist,
take a cat-o-nine tails and bring
blisters and then bust the
blisters with a wide leather
strap—blood runnin down to
his waist.)[4]

This ain't none of my home,
  Daniel,
This ain't none of my home,
  Daniel.

(Old Marse would sell babes from
the breast, mothers from babes,
husbands from wives. He wouldn't
let them holler and cry, say,
"I'll have you whupped if you
don't hush.")

Slip and slide the street,
  Daniel,
Slip and slide the street,
  Daniel.

(They singing off they trouble.
Slippin and slidin mean,
when we get to heaven, we gonna
have a *good* time. And we
forget all about our troubles here
below.)

The group of oldsters had sung in now.[5] Their sound was mellow, mellow as a June cantaloupe, mellow as cornbread and butter, as they filled in the needed harmonies with humming, sometimes with moans and little wailing cries. They clapped, they patted their feet, they rocked. Their eyes shone with pleasure as they swayed into verses that Old Man Joiner improvised—

Puttin on my warfare shoes,
Livin on borried land,
Gittin in a hurry now.

—his leader's part lasting only a second or two, with each line leaving the group to fill out the stanza. Here was turn taking—sharing—the basic African aesthetic at work. Then, out of a momentary pause, one of the old ladies took over the lead, shrilling David's warlike song.

O David,
Play like you played for Saul.
O David,
I ain't afeered to die.
O David.
Let me tell you what David done,
Killed Goliath, that mighty one.

Oh, it was rolling now! That church house was running over with the big sweet sound these few old folks created. Casey, the oldest man present there, rose. His voice shook a bit, but he proudly told how Samson sabotaged his persecutors.

Well, Samson burnt down a field of corn,
Well, they looked for Samson and he was gone,
Well, found old Samson in three or four days,
They bound his hands and they carried him away.
While walking along, he didn't see no one,
But looked on the ground and saw an old jawbone,
Just moved his hands, rope popped like thread,
When he got through slaying, four thousand was dead.
Crying, rock me, Lawdy,
Shake me, Lawdy,
Don't let me sleep-a too late.
Gabriel gonna sound his trumpet in the morning,
Gonna swing on the Golden Gate.

Then Brother Joiner rumbled out a spiritual about the greatest of the Bible heroes.

Makes me sorry to think about
   Jesus,
   Sholy he died on Calvary,
   Calvaryyyy——
   Calvaryyyy——
   Sholy he died on Calvary.
Don't you hear the hammer ringin?
Don't you hear Savior groanin?
   Sholy he died on Calvary.

(They had this way of singing
praises to God, who had poured
out His heart's blood that they
might have the right to the
tree of life. And when they
sing the song, it reminds them
of what Jesus said, "It is through
my death and suffering that I
may come again.")

With his deep voice trembling in sorrow, Elder Charley Drake sang of Jesus' trials. The sound of the chorus swept through the nearly empty church.

They took my blessed Lord,
They bound him with a purple
   cord,
They carried him fore Pilate's bar,
They splunged him in the side,
And he never said a mumbalin
   word,
   Oh, not a word,
   Oh, not a word,
   Oh, not a word,

(My papa never had a lickin in his
life. One day the master says,
"Son, you've got to have
a whopping," and my papa
says, "I never had a
whippin and you can't whop
me now." And master
says, "But I can kill you."
And he shot my papa down.
Ma took him in the cabin, put
him on his pallet, and he died.)[6]

Hester Jones, a gnarled old lady with a voice like a man, launched a slave's conversion spiritual.

Went out one day and I prayed to
   the sun,
   Hallelu, hallelu,
That the Holy Ghost tell me my
   work was done,
   Hallelu, hallelu.

(The old folks had a way
of asking for a sign that
the prayer would be
heard—let the sun bow,
let the star move.)

I went out one time and prayed to
   the star,
   Hallelu, hallelu,

That the Holy Ghost tell me my
work was done,
Hallelu, hallelu.

As I listened to these touching songs, I was overcome with wonder. How could these worn farm laborers and their slave ancestors, driven, demeaned, and cruelly exploited, have created songs so full of nobility and love? As if to answer my unspoken question, Brother Joiner told the story of his conversion, with an eloquence transcending the rules of diction.

"Sisters and brothers and all that go to make up this congregation . . . *I know* for my*self* that I been born again. How I know I been borned again? Because I *prayed*, I mean I *prayed*. I'm just gonna tell you a little of it. I converted in 1900 in *Tinn*essee—twenty miles the other side of Memphis. That's forty-one years ago. And, er-uh, in them days and times, when a revival would start, we'd run prayer meeting a week. You know, you know, when I get to talking about it, you know, it just stirs me all up, it just gets all *over* me. (Yes, Lawd!)

"I'd go to sleep at a certain time, I'd tell the Lord to *shake* me, he'd shake me at prayer time—and I'd git up and steal on out to my praying ground, and—you talkin about the head getting wet in the midnight dew—mine got wet. Mine got *wet*! And, when I got sho-nuff to praying, I didn't want to see nobody. I didn't want to *meet* nobody. It was just like he told you about stars and the sun. Now they say, 'Oh, that's all foolishness.' Of course, it may be all foolishness to *you*, but t'ain foolishness to me.

"*I* couldn't drink water. I couldn't *eat*. I couldn't rest nowhere I *went*. And, er-uh, the last prayer I prayed was one Saturday mornin and they say, 'We're gonna have a mourners' meeting. We want the mourners to be here at sundown.' Well, I didn't have but more'n two miles to go, and it didn't look like to me I'd ever git there—looks like the weight of the *world* was on me. And I met one of my playmates comin on a mule—he was riding—and he looked at me he say, 'You prayin, ain't you?' Say, 'Yes.' And he just *moved* on. When I got to the church, there was just two or three brothers there. And they said, 'Here's one mourner—we're gonna start.' And they started. And I got to saying, 'Lord, have mercy,' and when I found myself, I's sayin, 'Thank God. Thank *God*.' "

He spoke with mounting fervor—liquid tones of love in the voice—his old eyes flashing soft fire—his mustaches quivering with emotion—the sweet voice of a boy breaking through the harsh tones of the old man's voice.

"And I want to tell you all I didn't stop—everywhere I went, I wanted everybody to know it. I went to town and everywhere, and that was the gladdest and the *happ*iest time *ever* I felt in *all* my life. My hands looked new to me. My *feet* felt new. The *light* shined brighter. The *people* looked better. And it just felt like to me then if I could throw my *arms* around the world and carry *all* to *Heaven*."

Old Lady Fannie Jackson, another oldster, began to sing.

Free at last, free at last,
Thank Godamighty, I'm free at last.
Free at last, free at last,
Thank Godamighty, I'm free at last.

I went down in the valley to pray,
    Thank Godamighty, I'm free at last.
My soul got happy and I stayed all day,
    Thank Godamighty, I'm free at last. . . .

When I asked Charles Drake what kind of freedom the song meant, he replied that the sinner was praying to be freed from sin. But because I felt sure *Free at Last* was actually an Emancipation anthem, I pressed on.

"Don't you think the folks sang that when freedom came?"

"No, no," he said flatly. "That song is just for conversion."

When I glanced at Lewis, he winked. Obviously, Drake didn't know us well enough to admit to singing an Emancipation hymn.

"There's some pertaining to that," he said, "but *I* don't know um . . ."

In a way, he was right, of course. The song has a double significance, and one of them concerns the convert's victory over his hellish thoughts.

I remember the time and I 'member it well,
When my Lord freed my soul from hell.

In the background, an old woman began humming,

O Freedom, freedom over me . . .

Nowadays we begin to find out from the slave narratives and elsewhere how deep the anger has been, how almost ungovernable the rage. The great Bessie

Jones told me, after we'd been recording for several months, "You know someday all you white folks will woke up dead. See, we has people work in many kitchens all over the country, and on that certain day, we can send out the word—'Poison today.' Then most of you-all be dead at the same time." She laughed. Yet Bessie was the most loving friend a person could have. She was a mother of the church; she had been born again; she'd been washed in the blood of the Lamb, and she loved everybody.

Seek and ye shall find,
Knock and the door shall be opened,
Ask and it shall be given
When the love come tumbalin down.

Thus runs the old song. In those early times in the South, blacks were admitted to church membership only if their conversion vision proved to the congregation they had been born again, cleansed of hate, and were ready for heaven.

Two angels came from heaven
    And rolled the stone away,
Two angels came from heaven
    And rolled the stone away,
And the Lord will bear my spirit home.

In the silence someone said, "We done forgot most of that old stuff nowadays."

"What do you mean, old stuff?" I asked.

"Why, them old slavery-time songs—we don't sing that no more. Now I'm some old, but when I was young, we had passed all that by for Dr. Watts."

Reverend Savage had returned. "I don't know if you and Lewis ever saw a Dr. Watts hymn book. Maybe it was left out of your education. But not in Mississippi. It helped us get rid of the hallies and all that old stuff and go back to the classics."

He handed me a much-worn little grey book that could fit in the palm of one hand: *Hymns and Spiritual Songs*, 1st edition, 1707. In fine print it held the texts to a couple of hundred hymns, with authors like Wesley, Calvin, etc.—the classic hymns of the Protestant church, such as *Amazing Grace, On*

Jordan's Stormy Banks, A Charge to Keep I Have, written in the high-flown style of the seventeenth and eighteenth centuries.

And am I born to die
And lay this body down,
Or must this trembling spirit fly
Unto a world unknown?

Here were the solemn psalms of the Puritans and the Calvinists, so beloved on the American frontier. I had heard them among the Amish in Indiana, who dragged out the tunes with so many flourishes that a single phrase might last almost a minute. Deep in the Kentucky mountains I had recorded the white Primitive Baptists performing them, trailing each other in high-pitched heterophony at a graveyard pace that made me weep. The seriousness of their singing had touched the converted slaves during the Great Revival. As blacks turned to literacy, their leaders put these old psalms at the core of their service. It seemed to be a step away from African folkiness.

"You see," said Savage, "when our deacons give out these songs, line by line, and our congregations repeat them, they are acquiring culture. My old daddy always said Dr. Watts dignifies the service."

In fact, however, blacks had Africanized the psalms to such an extent that many observers described black lining hymns as a mysterious African music. In the first place, they so prolonged and quavered the texts of the hymns that only a recording angel could make out what was being sung. Instead of performing in an individualized sort of unison or heterophony, however, they blended their voices in great unified streams of tone. There emerged a remarkable kind of harmony, in which every singer was performing variations on the melody at his or her pitch, yet all these ornaments contributed to a harmony of many ever-changing strands—the voices surging together like seaweed swinging with the waves or a leafy tree responding to a strong wind. Experts have tried and failed to transcribe this riverlike style of collective improvisation. It rises from a group in which all singers can improvise together, each one contributing something personal to an ongoing group effect, yet all sensitive to all the parts—a style common in African and African-American tradition. The outcome is music as powerful and original as jazz, but profoundly melancholy, for it was sung into being by hard-pressed people.

Reverend Savage lined out in a deep groaning voice:

Ah know my Lawd—He heah mah cry—
And pities every groan—

The little band of hallie singers took up the psalm and simply sailed with it. Their dozen voices filled the church. Lewis's eyes glistened. "Listen to those old ladies go," he whispered. The little chorus was about two-thirds feminine. Thinking back, I realized that women had outnumbered men two to one in most black services I had attended in the United States and the West Indies. In Trinidad the shouting Baptists were predominately women. In Haiti, I remembered, the *hounsi,* the servitors who danced and sang the gods on and off the dance floor, were all women.

When I looked at the world data, I found that large feminine choruses were notably frequent in Africa. In fact, the size of the feminine choruses seems to match the importance of women in the work force. Big female choruses occur in the tropics, where women do most of the work in the fields. Their gardens are usually close to the village, so that they can safely take their small children with them to work. This practice continued in America, under slavery and after. A Delta veteran shares an early recollection of his mother:

When I was three I used to go out in the field and tell my mother—I didn't call her mother then, I called her Lily—I'd say, "Lily, if you give me some titty, I'll help you pick some cotton." And she sat down on a sack and she let me suck some titty. And then I'd tell her, "You better go and pick, cause I ain't gonna pick no cotton, cause I'm goin back up to the house."

A handsome, upstanding farm wife, mother of six, proudly told us how she had worked in the field as hard as a man since she was a child:

I started in the field when I was eight years old. I used to cry to go to make a day. And my mother she didn't want me to go. So there was an old white man not staying too far from us—all of them be in the field but me—he asked what I was crying for. I told him I was crying because I wanted to go and make a day just like the rest of them. They started me off at a dollar a day. I was getting just what they was getting. From then on I come all the way through. I cleaned up new ground, I cut down trees, I cut wood. I can cultivate. I can plow, I can even sweep. And then I can plant. I done did all of that all the way through in my life and days. I worked twelve years, just me and my girls. Farming twelve years—didn't have no men's help at all—and I made it.

One of my friends remembered what a worker his great-grandmother had been—a sort of female John Henry of the cotton patch:

She was named Morelia Davis and she loved fat meat and she was fat. She had one tooth in the front and she cleaned a bone cleaner than I can with my twenty. I believe she was born in Transylvania, Louisiana, and she lived on to 121 years. When she was 101, she could pick more cotton than a gin could gin. When she'd start in to pick, she'd break off a cotton stalk and take it and whup one hand and then she'd take it and whup the other hand.

She'd whup it hard and she'd say, "You-all go to work. You-all ain't *doin'* it."

Then she'd set up and laugh—"haw, haw, haw." And she'd sing a song about Sister Kate.

Come on there, chillun,
Sister Katie, we got to go,
Sister Katie, we got to go,
Sister done gone,
We gotta go,
We gotta go.

And she'd whup her hands again, says, "You-all doin pretty good, but you better go to work. Go to work now."

It was tough and valiant women like these who led the song services in church and whose personalities and experiences shaped the spirituals. Often their troubles were bitter, as Morelia told her great-grandson:

Just like if you got a field of young heifers, time come for to breed them, and you got four or five stalls of breeding bulls, like tangerinas and black heifers, and red freeze heifers. You want this one to have a white face, you put her there. That's what they did to the women in their time. When they get to be fourteen, fifteen years old, they breed them with whatever man they had in their stalls.

A little man like you gonna be didn't know what a woman was in slavery day. They took any man that weigh from 195 up and they put them in stables, like they do stud horses, and jacks and bulls. "They didn't have to work. They keep them for breeding and stuff."

If they didn't make babies, they put them on the plow.

That's right! If the man was great big, they put a harness on him and make him pull the plow. The little man walk behind him and shake the lines.

I said, "Sho enough!"

"They didn't have no choice," my granmama tole me.

LITTLE SALLY WATER

Like the slavers, the Bantu clan lineages, spilling into the empty lands of Africa, valued women for their capacity to bear and rear children. They were needed to help their families survive. Premarital sex was allowed, and a baby born out of wedlock was proof of a girl's fertility and made her more desirable as a wife. On pioneer Mississippi plantations both sexes were crowded together in communal dwellings, and slave women were rewarded for bearing children, without concern for their paternity. These attitudes carried over among the black sharecroppers in the Delta, where a young woman's pregnancy was seen as proof that she really loved her man. Since children all did chores and helped to weed and pick the cotton, the more children the better. One guitar-playing friend supported a wife and twenty-one offspring by driving a tractor and making music on Saturday nights. Such a houseful of children could prove a blessing, even if a no-account father ran off and left them.[7]

We's a big family—eight head of chillun an me, the oldest girl. My old man went away and left my mama when we all small—twelve years ago, the twenty-third of June. My mama raised us all by herself—she run the farm and raised us with nobody to help. When my old man come back two years ago, she chase him off the place—say she didn't want none of him. She didn't never want no more husband. She do better by herself. Cose all the children helped.[8]

Those little shacks in the cotton fields seemed to have elastic walls when it came to kids who needed a home. If a woman couldn't provide for her children or wished to be free of them, some member of her extended family, some neighbor, some old person needing company and someone to wait on them would take them in. True to the spirit of the African extended family, one old fellow, living on a pittance, shared what he had with the little orphans of his kinfolks.

I ain't got but three kids of my own, and they grown and off up North. But I got four children living with me now. Two of them my dead sister's children, and them two little boys in there my niece's children. Bill, he's my baby sister's kid. He was nine days old when his mother died. We raised him. He thirteen.[9]

A neighbor down the road became a foster mother for a little stream of bastard babies.

Now these two boys live here. They ain't mine, they just given to me. My sister's girl . . . give him to me two months fore he was born. And then after he was born, that Thursday, she called me and told me, "Say, Annie," say, "here your boy." She was young and wild. Wanted to go. Didn't have time to fool with no children. And this other one here, this little one, I'll tell you how we got him. He was four months old and he was sick. And my niece, she was wild, loose in the world, and didn't want to fool with the child. And when she brought me the child, child wasn't much bigger than that little stool over there. Well, just as usual, I'm a good old neighbor. I'll take anybody in my house.[10]

Good mornin, little schoolgirl,
Good mornin, little schoolgirl,
Can I go home with you?
Can I go home with you?
You can tell your mama and your papa
I'm just a little schoolboy, too,

sang Sonny Boy Williamson, piercing small feminine hearts.

I'm goin to Memphis
To git my hambone boiled.
These little women roun Clarksdale
Gonna let my little hambone spoil,

warned handsome young Muddy Waters, causing young ladies to tremble. These blues couplets belong to the powerful undercurrent of African-American eroticism that has come to influence Western culture. Carried on the tide of black popular music, it broke past Western prudishness and has drastically liberalized sexual attitudes in the United States. In the Delta caste ghetto, where the blues were born, this African permissive pattern was simply taken for granted. Little boys and girls began their sexual lives early, and by ten, it is reported, were inured to intercourse with their playfellows. The rhyme goes;

> *"Mama, Mama, look at Sis,*
> *She's out on the levee, doin the double twis."*
> *"Run in here, you dirty little sow,*
> *You tryin to be a bad girl and you don't know how."*

By twelve or thirteen many girls had left home and married—none too soon in poor families, unable to hold together in the plantation system. These girls had been mother's little helpers all their lives, always responsible for looking after their numerous siblings. Thus they had a repertory of games, singing and otherwise, to keep their little charges out of mischief. The importance of hide and seek in the Deep South setting is signaled by the elaborate and plaintively beautiful song that "It" must sing before he (or she) rushes off to hunt the hidden. Apparently, a good deal went on in those hiding places.

> *All hid— Alll hid—* (a high, ineffably sweet call)
>   (The lead hits a hot lick)
>   *Way down yonder by Abbie's quarters,*
>   *Some old lady bout to lose her daughter.*
> *Who all hid—Who all hid?*
>   *Last night and the night before,*
>   *Twenty-four robbers at my door.*
>   *I got up, let one in,*
>   *Hit him in the head with a rollin pin.*
> *Alllllll hid . . . All who not hid, holler "Aye."*
>   *Way down yonder in daybreak town,*
>   *Billy goat buttin the levee down.*
> *Here I come. Here I come.*

The best afternoons Lewis and I had in Coahoma County were spent in schoolyards and dusty back lanes, recording these children's sports. Willowy girls, just moving into womanhood and as graceful as gazelles, usually led the games. The younger ones from ten down through six followed them with adoring looks and in swinging synchrony. Littler ones, down to three, stumbled along, doing the best they could—everybody helped, nobody tried to exclude the small fry. These kids knew ancient ones like *London Bridge*, or *Needle's Eye*, which they had edited as follows:

THE OLDER WHITE VERSION	THE SEXY MISSISSIPPI VERSION
The needle's eye that doth supply	*Oh, you're lookin so sweet,*
The thread that runs so true,	*And you kisses so sweet.*
There's many a beau that I've let	*The needle's eye,*
* go*	*Seconds fly,*
Because I wanted you.	*Threads that needle right*
With a bow so neat, and a kiss	*Through the eye.*
* so sweet,*	
To have this couple meet.	

They sang a chasing game made up of onomotopoeia about the needle of a sewing machine:

EVERYBODY: O Bob-a-needle,	(The children have formed
LEAD: Bob-a-needle is a-runnin.	a ring. Bob-a-needle
	trots round the ring and
Gonna catch Bob-a-needle,	drops the handkerchief
Bob-a-needle is a-runnin,	back of one child, who
	tries to catch him before
Better run, Bob-a-needle,	he finds a place in the ring.
Bob-a-needle is a-runnin.	Meantime, everybody
	is dying laughing.)

The littlest ones liked the one where you squat down close to the ground and imitate a rabbit—doing a kind of a Mississippi *kazatsky*. The dancer slaps out notes on his mouth and cheeks on cue, then gets up and shakes that thing, always skipping away out of trouble, like a mischievous child. This goes with a hot, off-beat clap. Very old, very African—I've seen films of Pygmies doing things like this. Rabbit is, of course, a lineal descendant of Hare, the trickster hero of many African tales, a sly individual who uses his wits and his speed to get him out of the trouble his nature gets him into.

I met Mister Rabbit in the peavine,
I ax him where was he gwine.

He quirled his tail up on his back—
"I'm huntin for the muscadine." (a wild wine-making grape)

Sally Walker, do your bes,
Pop your mouth, shake your dress.

Keep a-kickin, Br'er Rabbit,
I'll see you later.

The smallest ones would try to kick out from their squatting position and fall over, while the older girls did it and failed to keep their skirts down, and everybody giggled and laughed. Many of the games trained for physical competence, but their principal focus was practice in social skills, with courtship the main concern. The games allowed the girls to be very bold, and to try out all sorts of ploys in the safety of the dancing ring. In this kissing game, a girl sat in a chair in the middle of the ring, announcing:

I'm in the well.
  How deep?
Fifty feet. (This measures how deep a kiss she wanted—
            one player said 500 feet to much giggling.)
  What it take to get you out?
Sweet kiss.
  Who from?

The girl, if not too timid, can now name the one she wants to kiss her and then receives her reward, perhaps even deeper than she fancied. Then the chosen one replaces her in the chair and the game goes on. The perennial favorite, *Sally Water*, has the girl kneeling in the middle of the ring. As her friends sing, she mimes their words, then shakes her little backside round the ring till she gets to the one "she loves the best." There she must be kissed.

Little Sally Water, settin in a saucer,
Rise, Sally, rise, wipe your weepin eyes,
Shake it to the east, Sally, shake it to the west, Sally,
Shake it to the very one that you love the best, Sally.

Not long ago these games were played by mixed groups and the erotic feelings were strong. I asked a seventy-year-old lady who it was she'd kissed in the girlhood game *Sally Water*. She began giggling and hid her face in her hands. Her old cronies chimed in laughing—"It were Jimmy, Jimmy, you remember." "Cose I remember," the old lady shrieked, as she ran off into the dark to recover her composure.

In these black ring games everyone got a turn to show off their best step. Everyone learned about choosing and being chosen. That was the theme of game after game—the rapid choice of lovers. Turn taking, sharing, but above all choosing, swiftly and boldly, then pleasuring the one chosen, and on to the next—they called this "stealing partners." Sexually active at ten or eleven, with marriage maybe only a couple of years off, a Delta country girl needed to know how to sort through the males, and how to move between marriage partners. Indeed, the most popular of the stealing-partner games was one with the refrain "satisfied."

> *It takes a rockin chair to rock.*
> *SATISFIED!*
> *It takes a soft ball to roll.*
> *SATISFIED!*
> *It takes a song like this*
> *SATISFIED!*
> *To satisfy my soul.*
> *SATISFIED!*
> **I ain't never been**
> **SATISFIED!**
> **I ain't never been**
> **SATISFIED!**

Those young black girls sang "satisfied" in perfect and saucy unison, with tremendous swing and an offbeat clap that sent chills up my spine. Here was black Africa again, just as in the hallies—a two-phrase tune to a steady beat, a leader improvising against an overlapping chorus, a syncopated offbeat rhythm that made both the words and the youngsters dance. I can never forget those slim black girls, seeming almost to take wing as they skimmed the red dust on those golden summer afternoons, the verses exploding like firecrackers on the 4th.

> *Milk in the pitcher,*
> *Butter in the bowl,*   SATISFIED!

Can't get a sweetheart
To save my soul.

I got a man
And a sweetheart, too.
My man don't love me,
But my sweetheart do.

If I live,
Get to be twenty-one,
Going to marry me
Some woman's son.

When I marry,
Gonna marry me a king.
First thing he buy me
A diamond ring.

I got a letter
In the bottom of my trunk.
I ain't gonna read it
Till I get drunk.

Went down there
To the new ground field.
Rattlesnake bit me
Right on my heel.

> **That didn't make me**
> **SATISFIED.**
> **That didn't make me**
> **SATISFIED.**

For those who may be shocked, think back about what really went on in your own childhood—playing house or doctor, probably much more. In the Delta things were more open. Black children were usually not reprimanded for playing at being little adults. In the West Indies, in fact, some parents, supervising the singing games in the backyard, might smack their own kids if they were not "winding" properly:

"Wind there, child, rock that little bottom! Do like your mama!"

The Coahoma game song that sticks most in my memory was played with switches. The children ringed up an inward-facing circle, laced arms, and held on tight to each other. Meanwhile, *It* walked slowly round the ring, looking for a way out. Right behind her came Red Wasp, giving *It's* legs an occasional cut with her little switch. *It* shrilled out:

> IT: *Red wasp is stang-ing me!*
> RING: *Can't get out—of here.*
> IT: *RED WASP IS STANG-ING ME!*
> RING: *I CAN'T GET OUT—OF HERE!*

The switching grew harder. The walk changed to a trot, then to a run, as the switch stung bare legs. *It* tried to push past arms and then legs, then flung herself against the human barrier as the cuts came faster and the chant grew shrill.

> *RED WASP IS STANG-ING ME*
> *I CAN'T GET OUT—OF HERE!*

Finally, face streaming with sweat, *It* burst free and ran, the Red Wasp hotly pursuing.

> *RED WASP WAS STANG-ING ME,*
> *I done got out—of there!*

Those wild cries still ring in my ears. I once was mortally afraid of disturbing a red wasp's nest in the woods, for their sting is horribly painful to a child. The image of a cloud of red wasps pursuing and stinging is nightmarish to a Southerner. Yet I sensed another level of anguish in this game with the red wasp—a Delta child's view of what my red-faced kind were doing to her parents and kinfolk, intimidating, maybe even lynching them, certainly locking them into a cruelly exploitative system that they couldn't escape. In that tightly closed room of caste and class, the children were the ones most victimized. They had no way of escaping the bitter punishment their angry parents inflicted on them. A brief chronicle of their torments reads like Dickens's Dotheboys Hall, yet in those days this malignant severity was considered necessary and healthy. One woman remembers:

When I was young every woman in the place was my mother. If I did wrong and one of them saw me, she'd whip me, and then she'd tell my mother and I'd get another whipping.[11]

An older man recalls his boyhood:

My father whipped me so much I was afraid of it. He would make me take my clothes off to whip me. In January—snow and ice—I ran out without my clothes and stayed two or three hours. He didn't catch me. Then my step-mother grabbed me. She was very fat—very fat, and she put my head between her thighs and whipped my rump. I bit a plug out of her and ran off. She called my father. He broke off a broomstick and began to hit me. I said if he hit me again, both of us was going to die.[12]

A levee-camp veteran remembers his mother's savage chastisements, yet speaks of her affectionately:

My mama thought I had stole a pistol from somebody—I hadn't but she believed I had. Well, she put me in a sack, tied the sack up, and hung me up and whupped me. That was the worst whippin she ever gave me. She whipped me with a strap and a stick. She really beat me.

How did she get you in a sack?

I never resisted my mother. I never even scuffled with her. If she called me, I just stood there while she did whatever she gonna do.[13]

The great Nate Shaw remembered his childhood torments at the plow:

The weather was warm and the gnats was awful bad. And, doggone it, it looked like they would eat me up. I was just nine years old. So I would fight gnats and my daddy got mad with me for that and he come to me and picked me up by the arm and he held me up and he wore a switch nearly out on me then dropped me back down. . . . He put me to plowin a regular shift at twelve, thirteen years old. . . . It didn't suit my daddy to have his mule actin up like that and his boy can't control him. He'd say, "Nate?"
    "Yes, sir."
    "What sort of plowin is you doin there? What sort of plowin is you doin?"

He was like to blow me down. I'd tell him, "I's doin the best I can, Papa, I's doin the best I can."

Next word was, "Drop them britches. Drop them britches."

He run around to the old horse mule and begin to untie the line from one of the bits. He'd get the line loose and go to doublin it, double it once or twice so it wouldn worry him to beat me with. Then he'd walk up to me and if I weren't gettin out of my britches fast enough to suit him he'd grab me and snap my little old galluses down and drop my britches, stick my head between his legs—and when he got done with me that line was hot. But I say after all that: a child ain't got no business buckin his parents; parents ain't got no business beatin a child.[14]

"I got to keep movin, I got to keep movin," sang little Robert, the bard of the Delta.

Blues comin down like hail, blues comin down like hail,
And if they keep on worr'in me,
It's a hellhound on my trail.

Or perhaps a red wasp. No child, certainly not a bluesman, coming through a rural Delta childhood missed the hot sting of the switch, the hard palm, the lash. All had run away from it as if the devil himself was behind them. All, in the end, had capitulated, and had been cruelly punished many times, saving up their wrath, but still saying "Yes, ma'am" to mama and "Yessuh, Mister Charley" to the white bosses. All were buried too deep in the great green and white valley of the cotton system to fight back or to leave or even to know where to hide. Their families, their mules, their crossroads, their fields, and maybe one town comprised what they knew for sure, and most of them could barely read or understand the signs or the maps that could lead them away.

"Besides," Lewis Jones remarked, "why should they leave? This is their country. Look at it, it's a really pretty place. Looks like a formal garden."

SHARECROPPING

Lewis and I were ruminating over this as we drove to our next appointments through the orderly green cottonfields of the King and Anderson Plantation. At a memorable meeting with young Anderson and his overseers, they had at first flatly refused to allow us on their plantation. "President Roosevelt himself couldn't come on our place," they assured us. Then, perhaps recalling Fort Sumter and its unhappy consequences, and thinking they had gone a little too far, they decided to give us a temporary visiting permit.

KING AND ANDERSON PLANTATION
Alan Lomax and members of his party can
visit tenants on this place, providing this
does not interfere with work.

GOOD FOR 2 WEEKS.

Signed by the plantation manager.

Lewis Jones and I had this *laissez-passer* stuck to the windshield as we drove down County Road Number Whatever-it-was.

"This a public, a county road we're on?"

"Right."

"It runs *through* King and Anderson, but they don't own it?"

"Right," said Lewis.

"Yet we can't be on it without this pass."

"Right," said Lewis wryly. "But you lack understanding. That big white house over there is really a castle, you see, and we are riding through a fief, right out of olden times. We can't do that without permission from the lord of the manor."

"In other words, the Bill of Rights ends back there a couple of miles."

"Land. Land is power and money. The white folks own most of the good land, and it's just about impossible for blacks or other poor folks to get hold of any of it. Some of these plantations are enormous—three, four thousand acres. The biggest is fifteen thousand acres—takes eight hundred families to farm it."

"And I guess those black tenants would like to have some and be on their own."

"A lot, a lot of them. They try, and a few make it. It's a very, very hard road. You start by saving up to buy a mule and some plows. That may take a few years. Also, Negroes have a real hard time getting bank loans. So only five or six percent of the colored farmers in this county are owners. The majority are sharecroppers. That means the landlord supplies the land and a house and maybe the tools, the tenant and his family supply the labor. In the fall the two parties share the crop, half and half. Usually, the landlord sells the cotton and then pays the cropper what he wants to pay him."

"About what does a sharecropper make a year?"[15]

"Here on King and Anderson they do pretty well. We've studied a hundred of the three hundred tenant families on the place. On the average a family of four, farming about eighteen acres, earns $324 cash, *after* they pay off what they owe the commissary."

"I don't believe you."

"I knew you'd say that. That's why I've brought you out to meet Jim Cephas, that fellow yonder. I've persuaded him to show you his records."

We had come to a stop in front of one of the green-painted, cream-trimmed King and Anderson tenant houses. A lean black man was walking down the path toward us. Lewis kept on as the man neared our car.

"I told you the tenant gets half—but only after the landlord deducts what we call the 'furnishing.' You see these families, when they move in, don't have much cash and supplies, so the landlord furnishes them food and maybe some clothes from the plantation commissary. The trouble is that the tenant never gets to look at the books. So he doesn't know what he's been charged for and how much"

"Nawsuh, he sho don't," said Jim Cephas as he got into the backseat. He was a quiet man, preternaturally gaunt, burnt black with the sun, bib-overalled and broganed.

We shook hands. There were no other preliminaries. Lewis had prepared the situation. All of us were a little nervous. In nearby Arkansas, farm union organizers had recently been beaten up and killed.

"Show him what you have, Jim," Lewis said.

Jim Cephas dug into the pocket of his bib overalls and pulled out the much-thumbed account sheet, reproduced below.

"This is what the manager give me last settlement time, to show me how much I was due," he said somewhat tremulously. "See, I thought we had done pretty well, me and my family. I'm lucky enough to have two chillun size enough to help me out, *and* my wife, she outdo mos men. An we promised my girls a new dress apiece . . ."

He went on as I looked over the typed, legally valid record of what two adults and three youngsters had made for a year's labor in the cotton field.

TO: James Cephas

Bale no. 3077	570 lbs.	10 cents/lb.	$226.00
Bale no 5309	238	9 cents/lb.	214.20
Bale no 3800	234.5	8 cents/lb.	187.60
		TOTAL COTTON	**$627.80**

Cotton seed at $14.00/ton—13,970 lbs.................... 97.19

$724.99

Less levee tax.. $13.97
Less gin charges   75.64 .... 90.81
Net.. 634.18
To company.. $317.09
To tenant.... $317.09

TENANT'S CREDIT **317.09**
ADVANCED TO TENANT **222.25**
CASH DUE TENANT AFTER ADVANCE IS PAID... **$84.84**

"What did you say when you got this?" I asked.

"Nothin. Nothin. What for me to say? He not gonna show me the books. He egvance me food and some clothes, but I don know how much he charge for um. I gotta take his word that I owe what he say. If I don't, then I get on his bad side and I got to move."[16] He fell silent for a moment. "But the wuss part is I got to take this little weasly money home to my wife. An I know I can't pay for what she done promise the chillun. That's the wuss part."

A Texas sharecropper's song ran through my mind:

His clothes is full of patches,
His hat is full of holes,
Stoopin down picking cotton
From off the bottom boll.
　Po farmer, po farmer,
　Po farmer,
They get all the farmer make.

Lewis asked, "What was the furnishing, Jim?" We talked as we drove along the red gravel road at King and Anderson's.

Jim said, "I reckon it was for sending in the tractor to plow that time. I didn't ask for it. In fact, I didn't need that tractorin, but *he* decide to send it. We raise most of what we eat, so the only things I gets from the commissary are flour and lard and sugar, such stuff as that, and a few clothes. But I don't know what they charge me."

Lewis added, "If a cropper raises a question, they act insulted, call him a bad Negro and get him off the place before, as they put it, he spoils the others. We have heard of farmers with squads that go around at night and beat up on the ones they call 'impudent.' "

"That's right," said Jim. "They sho do, sho do."

One report on the Delta noted:

The function of shootings such as these is to intimidate all colored farm workers in the area to the point that they will not object, either as individuals or as a group, to the economic and caste domination of the white landlords.[17]

"Or a white man," Lewis went on, "will ride over to the cropper's place with his Winchester across his saddle. If the cropper cracks a word with him, he may blow him down, and then swear the cropper was going for his gun. Nothing will come of it, because their word goes in the courts. None of that happens often, just often enough to keep the folks quiet."[18]

Jim Cephas nodded. "Um-hmmm. It don't always go just that way. One year there I done pretty good with my crops, so I bought me a little old ramshackle car. One afternoon I was driving across the lot. The plantation manager came over and accused me of trying to run over him. He shoved at me through my window, talking about how a little nigger was gittin uppity buying a car.

"I didn't say a word. I just eased down and took hold of the old .32-20 on my car seat. That white man got so scairt he run, and the news that a nigger had run a white man spread all round. I began packing to leave. That night the plantation owner come over and what he said was, 'No nigger had better think he could do that and get away.' Told me to stop telling other folks I had pulled a gun on a white man. Told me to say if any Negroes asked me about it, that it was a lie. So it look like I'm here, don't it?"

Lewis laughed. "Cephas, I'm your witness that you are very much here!"

Jim Cephas went on: "But all that hooraw makes you want to leave. My own daddy, look like all he did was move us around—over into Arkansas, then back over this side. He never did good, no matter how hard we all worked—"[19]

Lewis broke in: "But sometimes they wouldn't let you move."

"That's another point," said Jim. "One time old boss told Daddy we couldn't move till we paid him them fifty dollars he claim we owed him. So

Daddy tried to slip off. We had our stuff bout loaded in the wagon—had an old wagon an a pair of mules—and he come in with guns and he tuck all our little furniture, our beds, our dishes and pots and frying pan and coffee pot, Mama's picture of Grandma, tuck the mules, tuck the wagon, tuck everything. Well, Papa had to agree to stay and work it out. And we did—in two years."

Lewis added, "Plenty of men would go off looking for work—and maybe not come back."

Jim Cephas chuckled, "I tried, but I couldn't. Leave that woman with all them chillun? Plenty did, plenty did."

He turned to the window of the car. "Hey. You-all want see a woman all that happen to? Just pull in at this house here. This where Ola Perkins live. I know her good."

SHOTGUN HOUSES

It was a two-room windowless shanty with a little gallery shading the front door, a house of the shotgun type, meaning that when both front and back doors are open, you can shoot right through the house without hitting an obstacle. Actually the shotgun design, known to be African in origin, acts as a breezeway, the air moving from the shady front gallery, cooling the two rooms, and out the back.[20] Both doors of Ola's "shotgun" were open when we drove up, and you could see the cotton patch out back of the house.

Ola Perkins was cooling herself on the front porch. A younger woman rocked a baby in the porch swing. At thirty-five, Ola was a fantastic and pathetic figure—more than six feet tall, rake-thin, blind in one eye, and dressed outlandishly in purple stockings, a black skirt, a torn tan jacket, and a yellow, green, and blue cap. She spat streams of snuff into the yard as she told her story.

"I's the head of this here family. I have my second man living here with me and my daughter, but the crop is in *my* name and the settlement comes to *me*. See, when I married this here man, he had just run off from a plantation over yonder where they had him charged with a big crop bill he couldn't pay. So to keep from being charged with that big bill, I made myself the head of the family, and that way I'm not 'sponsible for his debt."

Her daughter, who was nursing a little bit of a baby, looked mighty young to be a mother. In fact, she was twelve years old. We asked Ola why she let her marry so young.

"All of my girls got married by thirteen. Some of them just wanted to, and this here one, she bear her first baby before she were twelve. See, I had a gang of children by my first husband, who died. That was good back yonder, when we need children to help with the cotton. Now, with these tractors and things, nobody don't need no big head of children. I reckon that's why my girls has been gittin about so soon. But whatever happen, they can always come back around to me."

Ola, the head of this cropper family, sent a plowman's squirt of tobacco into the yard. Her daughter kept the swing moving, and the baby slept peacefully on while two flies drank at a little dribble of milk at the corner of its mouth. Just so long as there are babies, I thought to myself, these women can stand almost anything. In the end, they're the ones who suffer the most, as this feminine life story shows.

He farmed, my father. After him and my mother separated, my mother she farmed one or two years, and then she started cooking for white peoples all the time. She didn't get paid much for cooking. You know they'd give her a little something, and the rest of it would be clothes for me, you know. She didn't get no money. All they give her just something they didn't need, a frigidaire or stove or something, and then a little money.

Now my mother got married twice after her and my father separated. And she left both of them. And she died ten years ago after she had an operation, but my second stepfather, he was the real cause of it. Of her dying. Fighting her and everything. They was fussing the way a man and a woman will do when a man go out and stay all night long.

And so this is the way they separated. She went over to this house and he was over there with this lady and they were sitting there playing cards and the lady was sitting on his lap. And so mother had me by the hand and it was dribbling rain and we was standing out there, and when the curtain would blow up we could see my stepdaddy sitting playing cards with the lady in his lap. She ask me who was that, and I'd say "That's Daddy." And I was four years old.

So when the game broke up, Mama went round there. And when they opened the door, she walked in there and they ran out in the field across from that house and he hit her with a piece of four-cornered stove-wood and broke her arm in two places. I just went to hollering and saying, "C'mon, Mama. C'mon, Mama!"

Mama was wearing a raincoat and her arm had done swole up so big that when the doctor got there, he had to cut that raincoat off her arm. He put a brace on it. And so she told my Daddy, "When the doctor takes this brace off me, you better be gone because I'm going to kill you." And so my Daddy knew she meant that, and he went to the fields and he come back. He said. "How you feel?" She said, "Feel fine, but I'll feel better once the doctor gets this brace off." He says, "Well, I'm gone." And she said, "You better be gone." And so he walked on out and went up the road. I went to the door and I told him, I said, "When I get grown, I'm going to kill you myself, wherever I see you at."[21]

Such tragic histories indicate the heavy burdens borne by Delta women. I remembered watching a woman in rural Mississippi coping with a brood of eight or ten children all one long summer afternoon. She lived in a rather miserable three-room shack with a small backyard, fenced off from hogpen and cow lot. It was one of those days when the thermometer walks off into the woods to cool off. Eight or ten black kids, between four and ten years old, were swarming round the yard, up the back steps, into the kitchen, and then, after a noisy visit there, boiling back down the steps, out into the backyard, and back again. They teased, played, fought, cried, laughed, hollered, above all never stopped moving and making a racket.

I was leaning against the back doorsill, talking to their mother. She was washing up and starting supper. The stream of kids would swarm in on her like a cloud of gnats, snatch food, knock things off the table, turn over chairs, fool around—nothing mean, just playful. She would bat at them, talk to them, pick up the ones who were hurt and comfort them, but all the while go on with the heavy work she had to do. In a few minutes here they would come again. Yet I never saw her really lose her composure. This was her destiny. She obviously had been well prepared for it, growing up as assistant mama; yet I could see in her weary face and her sagging shoulders that these children boiling around her legs were tearing her to pieces. One of her favorite hymns was "I'll take my burden to my Lord and leave it there."

However, the alternative—not marrying, not raising a family—might be even more unhappy, as another Delta woman tells us:

It's miserable to live alone by yourself. You think of so many things just laying woke at night. You just thinking you could marry, or I would get somebody but he might be this or he might be that. You would leave and go to another place, you might not do so good there. Most of the time you already have enough problems. And me, I have nobody here to talk to, nobody to say nothing to since Aunt Rosa died, and when the wrong somebody come, I don't say nothing. Sometime you want to go somewhere. Sometime you would say, "I would get up so-and-so," some food, but there's nobody there to eat with you.[22]

For the great majority of Delta women, battered or lonely, religion was the remedy, just as it had been for African women. They could "get happy at home," as this lady says:

I was shouting awhile today. Wasn't nobody here but me. Whenever I feel like praising God I just go to praying and read my Bible and I'm just as happy as I can be. I enjoy myself.[23]

THE HOLINESS PEOPLE

In church, Delta women could show their community that, in spite of living on the lip of hell, so to speak, tempted to give way to promiscuity, drunkenness, child neglect, and rage, they had maintained their feminine integrity. In church they testified before everyone that they were still pure of heart, emotionally resilient, and women to be depended on.

Both male and female ministers preached in the Church of God service I recorded, but even more important was the testimony of the largely female membership.

No one can spoil my life, because I haven't spoiled it myself.
Oooooo-yeah Glory, I'm living a spotless life, Amen.
The Lord brought me here, Amen.
The Lord gonna carry me away, Amen.
I ain't gonna move till he say move, Amen.
My soul is glad for Jesus.
He keeps me free from sin every day of my life.
And I have no mind, Amen,
To do the things that's wrong, Amen.
I thank God for putting me on the highway of Holiness.

You can't help but sin, Amen,
But I can report victory over sin and shame, Amen.
Because He baptized my soul with the Holy Ghost, Amen.

An immensely fat woman in a red turban and striped dress sang high and shrill, with a steady hot clap, guitars and tambourine back, and the whole church was heavy on the overlapped chorus.

It's stop, oh now,
    Your condemnation.

The song defies the gossip that poisons these little groups.

It's stop, oh now,
    Your condemnation,
It's stop, oh now,
    Your condemnation,
No condemnation in my life.

Here again, just as in the hallies and children's games, the black choral style was the mode of these strongly feminine cults. However, the singing lacked the tonal unity of the hallies; it was far more individualized and diffuse, reflecting the breakup of the black community and the individualistic striving that had become part of black lifestyle. Yet in one respect the jazzy Holiness hymn performances were even more African than the hallies. A stomp-down orchestra of guitars, tambourines, and piano, very much like an African drum set, accompanied the singing as the whole church clapped and danced to their syncopated beat. This clearly African mode of worship, totally unacceptable to conventional denominations, was spreading all over the world through evangelical churches such as this one. The tempo and the volume mounted:

Why, I rose this morning,
    No condemnation,
I can tell the world,
    No condemnation,
I feel all right,
    No condemnation,
No condemnation in my life.

The whole church was singing, clapping, and dancing the holy dance. One woman was jigging up and down the rostrum with her guitar. The song changed to the battle cry of the Church of God that has spread to thousands of Holiness churches all over the planet:

> *I'm a soldier*
> > *In the army of my Lord,*
> *I'm a soldier*
> > *In the army.*
> *I been wounded*
> > *In the army of my Lord,*
> *I b'lieve I'll die*
> > *In the army.*

Women were going into trance all over the little church. Talking in tongues:

> *Haw-haw—haw-haw-haw,*
> *Ta-tel iddle-iddle uh,*
> *Ta-tel iddle-iddle uh.*

Rolling on the floor. Acting out their tensions. I believe, along with others, that the high frequency of feminine possession in African ritual is due to overload. Bantu women not only have normal domestic duties, they also do more than half the agricultural work and often are in charge of marketing activities. African-American women have not only borne a similar burden of work and responsibility, they have also suffered the twin Delta torments of poverty and lower-class status. No wonder these women banded together to express their inborn holiness and to share their troubles in a ritual setting.

There they found champions to take up their cause. The talented men of the black community, using the relative immunity of the pulpit and employing biblical language to veil their meaning, denounced the wickedness of the Jim Crow system. During the last two hundred years, these black ministers created a highly dramatic order of service and a style of oratory of unmatched eloquence. Its beauty sheltered and consoled its hearers. Their orally composed folk sermons, which far outdo those of Reverend King, likened their oppressed congregations to the children of Israel and to the heroes of the Old Testament, thus thrilling and heartening their listeners, particularly the women. The art of the black sermon flourished especially during revival services, and it was at one of these that Lewis Jones and I recorded a sermon that epitomized the woes of the Southern sharecroppers.

HELL IS A PLACE

It was the lay-by season, when the cotton had been thinned and chopped for the third time and man could do no more for the crop. Now it was in the hands of the Lord and at the mercy of the rains, and the people had a season of relative leisure in the dog days of July and August. This was the time for barbecues, for fish fries and ice-cream sociables, the time when watermelons hung ripe on the vine and the frying chickens ran their last races from the pea patch to the chopping block. Some folks went off to the bayou with a fishing pole and a bottle of moonshine. Others went visiting their relatives. The young devils slipped off to the country jukes and danced to the blues. But for the staid and respectable majority, the great event of summer was the week- or two-week-long revival meeting at the neighborhood church.

A new minister had been called in. He had driven down from Memphis in a big, expensive car. A thick golden watch chain hung across his well-cared-for belly. He wore fine clothes, and there was a hint of condescension in his jovial manner. Church attendance had been falling off, but he had remedied that. The first night everyone, including the most hardened sinners, had packed the church, curious to see how the stranger could "go," and whether he lived up to his reputation. He proved to be a powerful speaker and really "tore up the pulpit." The folk came out subsequent nights to see "could he hold up?" Before the week was over, he had caught many of them in the net of his great voice and had them weeping and confessing their sins on the mourners' bench.

The service began late, for it was undignified and unpleasant to hurry a good thing. Respectable ladies in their best dresses dominated the crowd. The young women wanted to follow in their mothers' footsteps and also to walk home through the dark, after church, with their beaus, who were hanging around outside, skylarking and cutting the fool. Here and there a husband hunched up beside his wife, looking a little embarrassed, since the men had grown to wonder over the years whether the world ran according to God's plan and the preacher's promises. A knot of soberly dressed deacons sat near the pulpit. These were the good old religious men of the community, who took up collections and helped the minister. They were in his confidence, and their grave demeanor showed that they were persons of importance.

It was one of these men, the "singing deacon," who began the service. He heisted one of the old Dr. Watts hymns, the favorite music of the old folks present. The whole church swept through the song, dragging out the strange, wailing tune, swelling the chorus till the windows rattled from the great tones of this human organ. Then slowly they let the sound die as one of the old sisters in the "amen corner" filled the silence with a quick two-beat rhythm, tapped out on the floor with the toe of her shoe like a tiny African drum, heard in the distance or remembered. Which of the old ladies' feet was moving beneath a voluminous skirt? It was impossible to tell. The effect, however, was electrifying. It exposed the excitement, the tension sealed up in this audience. It was a presage of the final moment in the sermon, when the preacher would be shouting at exactly this swift tempo, and half the congregation would be dancing and leaping in ecstasy.

The old women "moaned" the hymn into silence. The mysterious foot tapping gradually disappeared. There was a great coughing and shuffling of feet. The singing deacon began in a heavy voice that flung a tune into the air. The congregation swung in behind him, hands and feet whomping out the beat.

DEACON: *One glad mornin*
              When this life is o-ver,
CONGREGATION: *I'll fly away.*
DEACON: *To the sky,*
              Hallelujah, by and by,
CONGREGATION: *I'll fly away.*
              I'll fly away, oh glory,
              I'll fly away.
              To the sky,
              Hallelujah, by and by,
              I'll fly away.

The song went on and on, the pace gradually growing swifter, the fervor rising. When foot and hand and voice had roused the people sufficiently, the deacon dropped his voice and wound up the singing. Heads came together on the pulpit, where the preacher conferred with his deacons for a moment. Then he rose. It was like the curtain going up in a theater. A hush fell over the church. With the easy, graceful stride of a trained actor—he was more than that—the minister walked up to the pulpit, leaned on the great Bible, and looked all around calmly. Slowly, he picked up and laid aside the purple ribbon that marked his place in the Bible, and running his finger down the page, read the text in a dry, grating voice:

"And he cried and said, 'Father Abraham, have mercy on me and send Lazarus, that he may dip his finger in the water and cool my tongue, for I am tormented in the flame.' "

From somewhere in the church, the rapid, electric current of foot tapping began again quietly. It was to continue, taken up by one woman after another, until the end of the sermon. The minister launched into the first part of the sermon, addressed to the younger and better-educated members of the congregation. He spoke slowly, with more than a hint of sarcasm in his voice, drawling out his words, pausing long between lines, but even so, back of the words, a slow but insistent rhythm was established, as if somewhere, far in the distance, too far to be heard but not too far to be felt, a drum was resounding in time to the minister's measured phrases and faintly stirring the blood.

You know, since we've had a little learnin . . .
Since we've had a little polish and a little culture . . .
Hell's gone out of business!
Fact, it's almost out of existence,
According to the notion and theory of some . . .
But as far as the Scripture is concerned,
And as far as I am concerned,
There's still a Hell . . .

Now all the ministers that are up here on the dais—
This fine array of young men you see here, along with myself—
They used to preach about Hell so . . .
That even in the wintertime folks would say,
"Raise the window, it's gettin warm in here!"

(He chuckled and a ripple of laughter stirred his audience. Then he grew serious.)

But we have left it *off* so long until—
Folks don't believe there's any use in tryin to shun Hell!
But, folks, there's a Hell . . .
Some of us call it Hades and others Purgatory . . .
But that's just a full-dress suit on the word—Hell . . .

In fact, that's the modernest style of givin you the slant on the place you
    wouldn't want to live eternally . . .
But it's just as impossible to do away with Hell . . .
As it is to do away with Heaven.

The first fact I wish to call your attention to—is—
There is a Hell. There is a **Hell!**
      Sinners,   without a change of mind,
                  without a change of purpose,
                  without a change of motive,
                  when this life of yours is ended,
                  whether now or sometime later to come . . .
    Eternally your life hereafter will be spent in Hell!
Now I may add that there are a lot of people who have their
    names on the church rolls,
There are a lot of people who frequent the church building,
Who, in Judgment, shall find themselves sent to Hell.
In fact, the church is a nice place to go **to Hell from!**

(He chuckled, enjoyed the laughing response, and almost sang the
following verse.)

A man gets shot down in a dive.
Oo—his people come to the eulogy at the funeral,
And they stand around and they lament,
They're sorrowful, they're broken, because
Their relative, their loved one met death in a dive!
But we who only have our names on the church rolls,
We who pretend to be that we really know we're **not!**
We who really have not been regenerated or **born again!** . . .
Are good for Hell **out of the church!**

(The last line cracked out like a pistol shot. Then he paused and adopted
a tone of sweet reminiscence, his voice, here and there, sounding like a
jazz horn blown tenderly.)

If you think with me for a moment, you'll recall that David
With a—all of his experience with God,
With it even havin been said of him by God
That he was a man after His own heart!

David got on easy on a certain occasion
About who was goin to Heaven and who was goin to Hell.
And he said, "Lord, who shall stand on Thy Holy Hill?
And who shall dwell in Thy Holy Place?"

"He that hath clean hands and a pure heart
And has not lifted up his soul unto vanity,
Has not sworn deceitfully and has not put his money out to usury
Or taken up reproach against his neighbor, but sware to his own hurt!"
Say—**He** shall dwell!
But the other fellow's goin to Hell!
    And unless there's some changes made
    Some of these folks right out of the church—

(He broke off with a threatening grin, as laughter again stirred the congregation and some of the old sisters slapped their hands and said, "Amen, amen, Lord.")

Christ said on one occasion,
"They're gonna come from all directions
And they're gonna knock and say—'Lord, Lord, open to us.' "
And He said, "I'm gonna say to you, 'I don't know you.' "

Say, "Lord, we know you . . .
You remember when you were in the world—
We fed you when you were hungry,
We came to the jail to see you,
When you were incarcerated in prison,
We visited the sickroom, when you were shut in and ill."
    And he'll say, "I don't know anything about you.
    Depart from me, ye workers of iniquity!"

(He began to speak now in God's voice, doom-filled, angry.)

You know the Church is not to be **toyed with!**
And the everlastin state of man's soul is not a thing to trifle with!
Eternity is too long a time to be mistaken about
Whether you're goin to live in Heaven or in Hell—too long!
    Job said that there's a Hell . . .
    Certainly, if the righteous can see a thing
    That's so far away from what he really is,
    The man that's right at it ought to see it!

(The mellow singing quality lulled you in the early lines of the next stanzas, the rhythm grew more rapid, until the last verses fell upon the heart like a black-snake whip.)

God said of his servant Job that he's perfec' and upright . . .
Not that he had attained perfection in the flesh, while he dwelt here,
But his **mind**, his **mo**tive, his **heart**, his **pur**pose,
Was **fit** and **set** on doin the **will** of **God.**
(You pretty perfec' when you can keep your mind thinkin about God!)
    But Job said, when his friends came around to kind a cheer him—
    During that time when the Lord allowed Satan **his** time—
    He said, "There's no **use** for you folks to argue with me!
    Hell itself is naked and open before the eyes of the Lord!"

David speaks out again and says that "the powers of Hell encompass me
    about."
And he says, "Where can I **creep** that I can be away from Thy presence?
If I take the wings of the mornin and fly away to the remotest place,
Thou art there. If I make my bed **in Hell, Thou** art there!"
Folks, there **is** a Hell!

There **is** a Hell!
And another thing about it, you don't believe there is a Hell,
You just watch some of these Hellish folks!!

(The tempo was now twice that of the beginning of the sermon. The minister's voice, now fuller and harsher, began to shout out his anger in certain lines. He lashed his people, and they responded with sharp ejaculations that punctuated and reinforced the rough music of his verse. He began in a quizzical tone.)

Why do I **believe in snails?**
    I'm not a biologist.
    I don't know all about the animal life
    And—and the various trends of their na**ture!**
Well, why do I believe in **snails?**
    Oo—oo, when I go out in the woods
    And when I begin to look around on all the sights about,
    And I see that slimy trail there, circlin about—
I know a snail's been along there.

The reason that I know there's a **Hell;**
Some of the **Hellish notions people have**
Tells me **the Devil's still in existence!!**

Of course, as some would have it,
His agents been put outa business.
Well, he'd like to have me for an agent—
In fact he'd rather have a preacher for an agent than he would anybody
    else!
        It's his business to try to get **me** to **quit!**
        It's his business to **bend** my **life so** that's its power **will** be lost!
        That's the work of the Devil!
        That's the results of Hell!

There **is a Hell!** Not only **is** there a Hell, but
Hell is a **place** and not a **state!**
(Do you hear me, Brother Lomax?)
Hell is a **place** and not a **state!**

*(With his swift thrust at me, where I knelt over the recording machine, he
had now vanquished the white man with his microphone. But more
important, he had made an agile transition into the second part of his
sermon, the section of folktale, of humorous anecdote, and of many sung
lines, designed to divert and then capture the large middle-aged group in
his congregation. Here were his solid citizens, the heads of families and
their wives. Here were the workers, independent of mind, cynical, worldly,
and eager to be amused. And they enjoyed every touch of folk humor. Now
his voice began to crackle and break with half-concealed laughter, but at
the end of every peroration the anger rasped out, the thunder of doom
rumbled.)*

Oh, you know here lately, you know, we've got it so, you know,
That you all can just hardly get about, you know.
And you know you're in a Hell of a condition.
Circumstances at home—and you ain't got no money in the bank,
And can't wear a full-dress suit and can't put on an evening gown
And fishnet stockins with your toe out!
You're livin in a Hell of a condition!
Your circumstance is bad—but **that's not Hell!**

Conditions and circumstances are exponents of Hell, but **it's not Hell!**

Hell's a **long** way down the road from the stop of conditions and
    circumstances,

Conditions and circumstances are **just stops where**

The Hellish people get on board the Hell-bound train!

You know some would believe that Hell is just an external state—

    It's without—somewhere out yonder—

    When you get tired of it, you can pick it up and move it;

    When you get tired of it again, you can pick it up and move it again.

But Hell is a place!

    Just like Heaven is a **place: He—llll is a place!**

    Just like Heaven is **up—Hell's down!**

    Just like God reigns above—**the Devil reigns beneath!**

*(Now on a wave of wordless humming from the old, experienced women of
the congregation, he half sang the next two stanzas, berating the men who
neglect their families, leave their wives, orphan their children.)*

When I think of a man—regardless of what he suppose to be,

That would send men out with all their cruelties

And drop bombs and fire and incendiaries upon defenseless people!—

Then, brethren, let me come home!

That's over in Hitler's territory—

Let—me—come—home!

Or when I see a man that will do more for—(you'll pardon me!)—

For some other woman than he'll do for his wife and his children—

I say the Old Man's loose again:

I say Hell's walkin around on earth!

(singing now)

    He's makin forty-five dollars a month—five children and a wife—

    He's gotta have an automobile to drive the other woman around—

    And his wife's gotta make a crop with them little chillun.

You mean to tell me there's not a Hell?

You mean to tell me that the agents of Hell are not operatin in the man?

    (As soon as we are born, we go about speakin lies!)

(intoning the words of a hymn)

    All we, like sheep, have gone astray,

    Each wanderin in a different way . . .

Folks, there's a Hell! . . . Not only is Hell a place,
But Hell wasn't made for folks that'll believe . . .
If you believe, you don't have to go to Hell.
But if you don't believe, that's what's gonna send you to Hell.
(groaning)
Aw—ww, God'll **forgive you.**
God'll forgive you for anything you do,
He'll forgive you for sayin anything
But that His Son did not come in the likeness of human flesh!
To take away and forgive the sins of the flesh!
If you say that, you got to go to Hell.
But if you believe and be baptized, you shall be saved.
Don't believe 'cause I say "Believe," but cause the
    record says "Believe."

(Now with trombone tones, with lovely snatches of melody, with accents thwacked out by the flat of his palm on the Bible, the minister returned briefly to the text and the theme of his sermon—the parable of Dives and Lazarus—but only briefly, for he at once introduced a subtheme, more appropriate to this, the second part of his sermon—the phrase "faring sumptuously." As he played variations on this succulent line, he attacked the community for their concern for worldly things instead of for the church; he upheld the good old ways and the good old days, when the community and the family took care of its own, and charity was more important than fine looks.)

If you please, here's a man . . .
    You know some people believe that what you wear will keep you from
        goin to Hell?
    If they can just make a little money, and get off with the upper ten,
        you know—
    "I'm not goin to Hell because I'm in society . . ."
    But your clothes don't keep you from goin **to** Hell!
Here's a man, here's a man that wore fine linen.—
    Aw—ww, this little tapestry that you spread on your table,
    And these little fifteen-dollar suits that you buy and call linen,
    Isn't to be compared with what Dives wore. Dives had pure linen.
    The catacombs **out yonder** and all the silkworms afforded him the best
        of linen.

Says this man wore fine linen—

> Not only fine linen, but he had purple, too.
> And you know anybody that could wear fine linen
> And purple, too, was somebody.

Not only did this man wear fine linen and purple, too,

> But he **fared sumptuously!**

Listen, everybody—you know, here lately, you know . . .

> The women don't have to bake biscuits anymore—
> Got a toaster right on the table—
> Call the bakery and he'll send the bread down—
> And she slips it in there and slips out!
> **Farin sumptuously!**

I think about these young people here tonight,

Most of them sleepin on Fairy Felt mattresses,

And can't get up to come to prayer meet on Sunday
> mornin!
> **Farin sumptuously!**

Their fathers back there slept on hay and slats all night,

Got up early next mornin and got to church on time!

> **Farin sumptuously!**

Back yonder we had to go fifteen and twenty miles to get
> to school,

And we didn't have but two months . . . Now we got a
> school on every turn row!
> **Farin sumptuously!**

Nowadays we got somebody to advise mothers

During the very early days of prenatural birth—

Somebody to tell her what she should do and what she
> shouldn't do,

What she should eat and what she shouldn't eat!

> **Farin sumptuously!**

And you know we're farin so sumptuously,

Ain't no more ugly folks now!

You know you can go down to the beauty shop

And get just as pretty as you please for two and a half!

> **Farin sumptuously!**

Even the men don't have to look bad anymore;

Let your hair grow out and they'll slick it back!
    Farin sumptuously!

(The church rocked to the rhythm of these short stanzas, giving the Lord's view of modern times. A crescendo of responses had risen higher and higher. Now, on the pulse of this patterned shout from his listeners, the preacher put his hands on his hips, leaned back, and his voice rang out like a great, wild trumpet shouting in the dawn, as God became a presence in the church.)

Aa—o—oh! God is tired of it, just like he was tired of Dives!
When you're farin so sumptuously, there's always someone in your way—
That God wants you to pay some attention to.
While you're gettin along so well, there's somebody at your door.

You know you get to talkin to us about mission work—
And we'll work our heads off and do foreign mission work—
But com**munity** missions and **home** missions!

(He pretended to be too disgusted to go on, but the beat carried him on and he began to sing again.)

Somebody here tonight got a husband who's a sinner in the house!
    O—oh glory! You better not say anything to him!
Somebody here tonight who got a son in the house who's a sinner!
    And you better not say anything to him!
Somebody here has a daughter tonight who's a sinner in the house!
    And she better not say anything to her!
But they talk about doin mission work!
God bless your soul!
You want to do some mission work!
Go—on—back—home!
Get—down—on—your—knees!
Tell God what's goin on at home
While you're farin so sumptuously!

(The voice at first trembled with irony, then moved quickly into music.)

You know, it just makes me feel sick, you know,
Seein big folks ridin round in their long automobiles

(Singing now, he appealed to the old African strain of sharing, of communal concern for the helpless.)

And there's a woman lives **right next door,**
She has to get up every mornin and get her little **knapsack,**
And there she **go** through the **rain, sleet,** and **snow,**
Down to the surplus-commodity **house,**
And she have to get down **there** and stand in line for **two,** three **hours,**
Shiverin in the **cold** and **rain . . .**
And get the little sack and put it on her **back,**
And here she go, wobblin **on back home—**
And that man, ridin in that fine car, **won't even pick her up!**
Farin sumptuously! **God Almighty!**
(tremendous shout from audience)

God wants you to look **around** and **see what's goin on!**

(He paused. An old woman, as bent and withered as a dried tree root, was weeping. The church was full of voices, responding to the naked suffering he had exposed and to the rhythm he had established, for the tempo had again doubled. Now he would double it again, for he was moving swiftly into the third and last part of his sermon. He had become the epic poet, speaking in the language of the Bible, denouncing the greedy rich from Dives to Big Daddy, sorrowing for the poor and oppressed from Lazarus to the landless, homeless black laborer. He addressed the old heads in the congregation, whose situation was the most precarious. They expected soon to see the Lord, to look him in the face, and to be possessed of the Holy Spirit, as were their slave ancestors, as were their African ancestors. He was preparing them for the touch of holy fire that would knock some writhing to the floor, send others shouting and weeping through the aisles, and set others dancing the holy dance. From now on he would be singing most of the way. From now on the elders would respond in precise rhythm to every line he spoke. And the tempo of the hidden drumbeat would rise and rise and rise.)

This man was farin sumptuously!
God says, "I'll tell you what I'll do—
I've got a child down in the world named Lazarus.
He's a poor man . . ."

(And thank God you don't have to be rich to get into Heaven!
Thank God you don't have to have a lotta money to be a child of God!
Eevv—ry**body, oh glory!** that **bow down on their knees**
And give God their hearts can journey into glory . . .)

    I heard him as he **said to Isaiah** back yon**der**—
    "Oh **e**veryone that **thirs**teth **come** to my **fount**ain
    And buy **milk** without **money** or **price!**"
    I heard him again as he **spoke** through **Matt**hew.
    Said, **"Come** to me all ye that **labor** and are **heavy-la**den
    And **I** will **give** you **rest.**"
    You don't **need money,** but **just come on!**

    I see Him as he gets to Laz'us yon**der**—
    And carry him and lay him down at the **gate**—
    Didn't take him inside—just **take** him up to the **gate** there.
    And in my **mind I** can see that **old sick** man,
    Sittin down at the palace **gate there,**
    Kneebones smotin tog**ether,**
    Skin is all **sores**
    From the **crown of** his head
    Down to the **sole of** his **feet**—
    And they tell me that the **dogs**—
    Brought over the **dogs**—
    Come **by** and **licked his sores!**

You know, when I think about this passage of the Scrip**tures,**
I think about back yonder in my boyhood **days,**
Out **yon**der in the **count**ry, you know,
When **I** cut my foot on a tin **can**—
Those **old** folks just believed in **Doctor God!**
They didn't call nob**ody.**
They go out **yon**der and c**alled** old **Rover,**
And take my **leg** and **hold** it **tight**
And let that **dog** lick my **sores.**
Oooo—ou—ou—**yes!**

    If you're not farin so **sump**tuously and **believe**
    God will make everything **all right!**
"And moreover the dog came and licked his sores."

(The preacher was in his full stride, his voice a low growl, then playing through three octaves. The lines grew shorter and shorter, the rhythm quicker, the beat stronger. The technique of the African epic storyteller was in full swing, and the congregation shouted together to punctuate the end of each line. As God's surrogate, the preacher spelled out the redemption of the poor outcaste and the doom of the selfish, the uncharitable, the nonsharer—both black and white.)

And God got **tired,** where he was standin **in Glory.**
And he **walked** to the banister one **day**
And he **looked** down **yonder and saw Laz'us layin** there,
Says, "I'm **tired** of my **servant layin** there.
I bel**ie**ve I'll **call** him **home,**
But bef**ore** I'll **call** him **home,**
I believe I'll call the **rich** man
And **kill** him **yonder!"**   **THAT'S RIGHT!**

Old Man **Dives died.**
He **couldn't** even **have** a **fun**eral.
Didn' **an**ybody **cry** about him.
And he **went** on **down** in **Hell,**
And I can **hear** him **now** declarin—
    "Fa—ther **Abraham!"**
I **hear** him **call**in—
    "Oo—oh, Abraham!
    I **want** you to have **mer**cy on **me!**
    Oo—oh—oh—oh-**oh!**
    I want you to **send Laz'us down here,**
    And **dip** his **finger** in the water **here,**
    Cause **I'm** tormented in the **valley."**
And I can hear Abraham say—
    "Things are too wide **open** down **there.**
    I **can't send** him."
He said, **"I'll** tell you **what I** wish **you'd do—**
    I **wish** you'd send him **back** to **my** father's **house—**
    I've **got** five brethren down **there.**
    Tell them to **listen** to Moses and the **prophets."**   **AMEN!**

You must **hear** what I **say!**
How can you **hear** without a **preacher?**

How can **you** preach the **text** as **he** says?
Aa—ah, **yes!** I'll preach **one more time!**
And go **ho**—ome to **Glory!**
And everything will be all right.
I can understand **Abraham . . .**   **PREACH!**
    You know there's **a great gulf!**
        Great gulf!
  Great gulf!
        Great gulf!   **PREACH THE**
                                            WORD

    And it's **fixed!**
    And when Jesus say a thing is **fixed!**
    Brethren, it's **sho**—**nuff fixed!**
        Aw—**ou**—**ou, fixed!**
        And you can't **come over there!**
You **got** to **hear** the **preacher!**
    And they **got** to **sing** and **pray** over you!
And you **got** to **come** by the Bible **band!**
    And they got to **sing** and **pray over** you!
And you **got** to **read** my magazine!
    And you **got** to **take** religious worship!
Aw—ou—ou, **fixed!**

(The phrases were rifle shots. Foam flecked the orator's lips. His voice rasped the nerves like a file. Gasping intake of breath after each line. People were shouting, women screaming, dancing. Pandemonium, as the roll of God's chosen ones, the blessed ancestors, the Christian pantheon, was called.)

Oo—**ou**—**oh!** yes!
Soon in the **mornin, Christians,**
When this **warrior** will have es**caped Hell,**
Where **Dives** will rem**ain** for a **thousand years . . .**   **YES!**
And **one** thing I **want** to do when I **get there**—
    I wanna see **Abraham,**
    Isaac, and **Jacob.**
        I wanna see **Nehemiah**
        And his Gospel **hammer.**   **PREACH!**
    I wanna see Jere**miah,**

I wanna see **Job,**
Hosses pawin in the **valley!**
    I wanna see **him**
    That's been **sleepin** down **yonder,**
    With the **dry** bones in the **valley.**
I wanna see **Amos, Hosea,** and **Joel**
    I wanta to see **Hezekiah,**
      Zephaniah, and **Zacharias!**
Amos, Moses, and **Joseph.**
Matthew, Mark, Luke, and **John!**
Ou—ou—ooh! **yes!**
I want to get over there.
I want to see Jesus.

(Now the minister's voice suddenly dropped away almost to a whisper. The storm had suddenly passed.)

The man who died for me . . .
The man who saved me from Hell . . .

The people stomped the aisles, flailing the air with their arms, leaping and shrieking in an abandon of rage and sorrow that blotted out memory and time, leaving only a hot, searing track across the darkness of the spirit, like the trail a rocket leaves in the eye of the mind, a fiery trail throbbing with anguish and danger.

The crying and singing drove me out of doors. I found my Fisk friend, Lewis Jones, nursing a cigarette on the back steps of the church.

"You can see they know who's responsible for the way things are," he said. "They talk about Dives because they're afraid to name the right names."

"What would happen if they did?"

"You're kin to Big Daddy, not me—you know what would happen—what did happen."

"You mean the Ku Klux—"

"And putting you out your house, and fixing it so you can't get a place to farm."

"But the ministers—hasn't anybody tried them?"

"The preachers run right to the man with everything they hear. That's why they have those fine cars they ride around in. By the way, I haven't told you they shot through the top of our car this afternoon."

"Who did?"

"We didn't stop to ask. They didn't hit anybody. They just wanted to let us know that we weren't welcome."

Lewis flipped away his cigarette, the coal still live. It spun like a little red rocket into the dark and then hissed out in the wet Johnson grass. Lewis chuckled. "I'm beginning to understand that old song they sing down here—

I'm a poor boy and a long old ways from home . . .

Chapter 3

▲▲▲▲▲▲▲▲▲▲

The Ugliest and
the Fastest Man

PREACHERS

Old John's Barbershop in Clarksdale was a place where all of us—white, black, college and folk—could meet unobtrusively. Or so we thought. Lewis Jones had invited some of the county's best "liars" (tale-tellers) to come and swap stories. I believe there was a nominal prize involved. Thus, one evening after the day when hell had been located in Coahoma County, a few of us—including Lewis Jones and his nondescript recruits—were sitting around Old John's. Barbering was going on as usual, except the radio was off and my recorder was on.

Lewis Jones had a way of stuttering over his opening gambits that made them seem indirect. "Would you-all say that we caught some pretty good preaching the other night—I mean, what did you all think of the Reverend?"

"Well, I'll say one thing for him—he went down with the crowd, it look like, but to my knowins, he stretched it out mighty much, till it got so thin you could see right through it." This in a laconic drawl from Will Stark, a lean, lantern-jawed individual who might have passed for white.

"He done all right for one of them high-toned educated ones—he built up a head of steam, I'll admit." The speaker, a stocky, barrel-shaped fellow named Asa Ware, always talked in a rush. "But for me, give me the old-time religion, give me a man from way out in the country that stop his mules in the middle of the cotton field and calls on God right across the handles of his plow. That's the man can put the gravy on his text on Sunday—"

A younger man broke in. "Don't want to cut you off, Mr. Ware," he said, "but you forget that all preachers are really alike." This was M. C. Orr, reputedly the readiest wit in town, as Asa was in his end of the county. "Yep, where it really counts, you can't tell the diffunce."

"What do you mean by preachers all the same?" Lewis grinned, guessing what was to come.

"Because they all thinkin about one thing, and that ain't the Bible," said M.C. "I'll tell you how that go. There was an old preacher in the pulpit, see, and his old deacons had faith in this preacher—anything he said, why they all tried to do it. So he was up in the pulpit preaching and he says:

Aa-ah, ladies and gentlemen-ah,
Now they's nothin in this world
Nothin that I've run up on yit,
That's better to me-ah
Than a good old-time religion.
I-I've had money-ah,
And I own a car-ah,
And I've got my own buildin-ah
And I got everything I need-ah,
But I never found nothin yit on earth, to me,
As good as a good old-time religion-ah.

Now if anybody here
In the church,
Anywhere around-ah,
Can get up now
And tell me *any*thing
Is better to them
Than a good old-time religion,
Git up now and speak.

"So they had an old brother, you know, was settin way back there in the back of the church and *he* went to git up, see. So, when he got to his feet, this preacher looked down there and seed him, he says, 'Listen, John, I'll kill you if you get up here in this church tonight and name what I *know* you thinkin about!' "

The barbershop rocked with laughter. Will Stark spoke up.

"I say it's *two* things on a preacher's mind—that and something to eat. When I was livin down in the south end of the county, I had a wife name Molly, see. So I came home one day and Molly was out there, runnin round and round in the yard, tryin to catch a chicken. I said, 'Molly, what you doin, tryin to catch that chicken?'

"She say, 'I want him for the preacher.'

"I say, '_____ the preacher!'

"She say, 'I did, but he still want chicken.' "

"Now wait a minute"—M.C. broke through the chuckles—"you boys ain't gettin down to the nitty-gritty. What I say is these preachers *always* tendin their flocks. Night *and* day. See, this preacher, when he come to this certain community, he always put up with one certain deacon. That deacon had a right young wife. She was a nice young thing and the preacher, you know, was crazy for her. Every time the boy would go out to cut wood or something and this gal would pass by the preacher's door, he'd be beggin her, 'Come in, honey, come in.'

" 'Aw, go on, Reverend, you better go on now. I'm gonna tell my husband on you.'

" 'Oh no, don't do that, don't do that. Be ashamed of yourself.'

"So the preacher kept a-worryin her, a-worryin, a-worryin, so she *did* tell her husband. He say, 'Aw, don't pay any 'tention to the Reverend. That's all right.'

" 'Well, you got to do something about it. I get tired of the Reverend pesterin me all the time. I ain't studyin him.'

" 'All right,' the boy say, 'I'll break him up.' So this boy sent her off to her mother's without the preacher knowing and then told the preacher, 'Reverend,' say, 'I'm got to go off tonight and I can't be at service. Will you omit your service tonight and come stay with my wife till I get back? She scared to stay alone.'

" 'Why, sholy, young man, I'd be glad to,' say, 'you know I would. Colored brethering like you, don't you know I couldn't afford to turn you down?' say, 'If you got to go off on business or something like that, I'll be glad to omit service and stay with your wife.'

"So the preacher hurried up and went to church and got up before his people and says, 'Now I got something to tell you I had happen to me today,' say, 'I din't know I stood so high in this community, I didn't know I was trusted that well, I didn't know I was thought that much of a gentleman.' Say,

'One of our young brethering here says he's got to go off tonight on special business and his wife at home by herself and he asked me to come stay with her till he come back. So if you-all will excuse me, I would like to go back and keep this girl company. I know she's afraid there now by herself.'

" 'All right,' they say, 'go right ahead, Reverend.' He grabbed his grip and back to this boy's house he went—and the old boy up in the bed, had put on his wife's gown and nightcap, and he spoke real fine and mincy-voiced like he was a woman. 'Do you want me to light the lamp, Reverend?'

" 'No, no, no, no, needn't light the lamp.' Pulled off his clothes and crawled up in bed, took the boy up in his arms and begin to talk, 'My little honey.'

"But pretty soon the preacher began to think something was wrong and in just a minute he was sure of it. He didn't say nothing, just turned over and got right out on the side he got in on. Got into his pants and walked right out the door. Boy say, 'Come back, Reverend.'

"Reverend say, 'No. Uh-uh . . . Oh, I knowed it wasn't nothing but a trap.' Say, 'I felt it was a trap, but anytime you set a trap like that and bait it, yourself,' say, 'you'll catch *me*.' "

"You haven't even got close to the point, yet, Brother Orr, and you know it," said Asa. "These preachers so bad they even fool round with they own deacon's wife. This preacher I'm talkin about stayed on one night in the deacon's house, you know, and this deacon had a good-lookin wife, and this preacher liked her. So the deacon told the preacher, said, 'Brother, now you can lay down there until you git ready to go up. I'm goin up here to plow some.' He told him, 'All right.'

"So he was laying in the bed, and his wife just kept passing back and forth through the room. And the preacher had done got up, you know. And every time she'd pass through the house, you know, by him, he'd smack her in the behind, you know. He says, 'Sister, I want to ask you something.' She say, 'Well, ask me anything you want to ask me, if you wanta,' say. He say, 'Well, how about us doin something?' She say, 'Well, it's all right, but those people live right out in front of us—if we shet the door, they'll know us doing something. Git over, shet the back door, the old man will see me doing something. How we're gonna do?' So he says, 'Well, let's us stand up right here side of the house.' She says, 'All right.'

"So he backed up, stand by the side of the house. They commence doin what they want to do, you know. And just about the time he commence doing what he want *good*, you see, another deacon passed on by the window. And just as he passed on by the window, he looked up and see, the preacher looked back and seen it. He said, 'Well, Reverend, what are you doing?' 'Why, I'm just telling the sister to come to the prayer meeting early tonight.' "

The man being shaved was so tickled by this story that he got up out of the barber's chair with lather on his face and walked around the room until he got his laugh out. In the hubbub someone chortled, "Man, and they puttin this on record, *on record. Everybody* gonna hear about our Mississippi preachers." Here Mississippi laps over into the world of Chaucer's Wife of Bath and Balzac's well-hung amorous monk Amador, and the legion of lecherous priests and concupiscent bishops in Catholic Mediterranean folklore. Yet for sheer brevity and punch there's nothing that quite matches the following Delta yarn.

The listener is reminded that the most lavishly hung of all animals is the male donkey, or jack. One day the peer of all such sexually prodigious animals strayed across a railroad line and was sliced up by a train. A devout old widow woman happened by and saw the magnificent member lying there. "Lawd have mercy," she shrieked, "they've kilt the parson."[1]

Lewis later explained some of the rancor in these tales. The church was the stay and prop of the women in this turbulent land, and they constantly sought consolation and comfort from their religious leader. Frequently, and often with the tacit approval of the community, their minister gave them everything they wanted and sometimes more. He also wielded great power, as head of the main black community organization and its principal spokesman to the white establishment. Lewis shook his head over the way ministers "kept the lid on things" and how many "ran to the bossman with stories" about the daring few who tried to rally their people. This is a far cry from the heroic image of Reverend King and his valiant company of the freedom marches in the sixties. Apparently, by that time the black church had developed a new leadership. But in the Delta folklore of the forties, the preacher was still a venal trickster. This, at least, is how Will Stark depicts him:

Now this preacher, he live right in the community where he's pastoring. He was a man raise a lot of hogs. One of his deacons, his main deacon, would slip over there every once in a while at night and steal one of the preacher's hogs.

And this deacon had a little boy. He never carry that boy at church. Make him stay at home on Sunday. Didn't buy him no clothes to go to church in. So the little boy found out his daddy was stealin the preacher's hogs, and one Sunday, when the preacher was taking dinner with the deacon, the little boy sat down in the yard, playing, looked up and seen the preacher coming. He started to sing:

Papa stole the preacher's hogs,
We got plenty, plenty pork now.

So the preacher stopped, you know, and listened. He thought he caught it at first, but he wanted to make sure. So he walked a little closer and the little boy was watching him under his eyelids and kept on singing:

Papa stole the preacher's hogs,
We got a plenty-a pork now.

The preacher walked up. "Howdy, son."
"All right. How're you, Rev'run?"
"What's that song you singin?"
"Oh, it ain't nothin—just a little song I sing."
"Well, would you promise to come to church tonight and sing that song?"
"Yessir, I could come out there and sing it, but I ain't got no shoes to wear."
Say, "I'll buy you some shoes."
Say, "I ain't got no suit."
Say, "I'll git you a suit."
Say, "I ain't got no hat."
Say, "I'll git you a little hat."
Say, "I ain't got no money to put in my pocket."
Say, "I'll give you some money to put in your pocket."
So the preacher turned around right then and went back to town and got the little boy a suit, shoes, hat, and come back and give him fifty cents to put in his pocket. The little boy come on to church that night. Old Reverend got up and say, "Come on up, son, come right on up to the front." His daddy, sitting back there, didn't know what was coming off. The little boy stepped up there on the pulpit where the preacher was and old Reverend say, "Now, I have a little boy here, just a lad of a boy, who is going to sing a song, and I want you all to pay strict attention. Every word of this song is just as true as you see me standing here."

Everybody was looking at the boy and wondering what he was gonna sing. They didn't even know he knowed no song—knowed he'd never been to church. So old Reverend told him, said, "Now, son, don't be afraid. Raise yourself up and be strong and I want you to sing with uplifted voice."

The boy pulled his little coat up on him, you know, cut his eye over at his daddy, started off singin:

Passed by the preacher's gate one day
He was playing a game of cards.

Old preacher begin to bug his eyes and look.

He gave me this little hat that fits so well,
And this half a dollar not to tell.

So old Reverend, he jumped out the back window of that church and they didn't see *him* around there no more.

Few English-American folktales use songs as part of the narrative. They occur occasionally in Grimm or other European tales, but are given just as verse to be read. In the black West Indies and Africa, however, the majority of stories are graced with one or several little songs, in which the audience usually joins, often dancing as well as singing. Our barbershop crowd didn't sing, but they noisily approved the discomfiture of the rascally pastor. Then M. C. Orr, the young master of words, voiced the scorn that many males felt for their religious leaders by telling this Southern favorite—"The Preacher and the Bear":

My paw is a preacher, one of the biggest preachers in the state. I remember the day behind yesterday, my paw was sitting on the porch, reading the Bible, he say, "Son, go out in the backyard and get the dog and gun and let's go hunting."
I said, "Paw, today's Sunday. You ought to be somewhere preaching."
He said, "Go on and do what I told you."
I went on out in the backyard and shouldered the dog and whistled for the gun and we go on down in the woods. Get down there and the dog get in behind sumpin. Run the sumpin way off cross the woods and run it up a tree. Me and Paw got over there and so many leaves up the tree, we couldn't see up there and so Paw told me, "Go up there and see what it is." I say, "Paw, bein you just a little older than I am, you go up there."
Paw climbs up the tree and gets on a rotten limb. Down come Paw and down come the limb and down come sumpin else. It wasn't no coon and it wasn't no possum, it was a great big grizzly bear. Me and Paw didn't have to shift nary a gear—we's already in high. By Paw having a little more speed than me, Paw gets in front of me. I told him, "Paw, let's have a prayer meetin.

You's a preacher." He says, "Son, prayer's all right in prayer meetin, but it ain't worth a damn in bear meetin."

UGLY FOLKS

The bunch at Old John's laughed as if this were a new story, although they'd all heard it many times before. But the chortling died down almost as soon as it had begun. Old John's Barbershop got so quiet you could hear the overhead fan. I looked up from the recording deck. There, looming over me, was a "police." I stood up.

"You mind tellin me what's goin on in here?" said the cop. He was sallow-skinned, squint-eyed, and with that mean I-know-about-handling-niggers expression all over his face.

"Now, Mister Cholly," Old John began.

"Don't you butt in. I'm talkin to this white man here."

I said, "We're recording a lying contest—you know, old-time Mississippi lies, recording them for the government library."

"Sounds like a goldurn lie to me," he says. "Don't you know you're in the wrong part of town? Got any identification?"

I fumbled for my driver's license. I was respectful. None of the blacks had so much as moved. Here in the wrong part of town we were outside the law. This man was the law. The choices were all his. He could do whatever he liked to any of us without recourse. So we took it easy while he studied my driver's license.

"Just like I thought, down here from Washington, stirring up trouble." He moved his weary, ugly old face closer,

"How old are you, boy?"

"Twenty-six"

"And why aren't you in the army. Probably a draft dodger." I knew he was running out of ammunition now. "Lemme see your draft card."

"Gee, I hope I have it with me."

"Don't and I'll sholy have to run you in."

The tension built while I spread the contents of my wallet on the turntable. The last crumpled bit in the most remote corner was the card with my draft status. I gritted my teeth and handed it over. He ruminated. He fumed. Then he handed it back.

"Well, it looks all right, I reckon. But listen what I'm tellin you. Don't stay over here in Niggertown too late or we can't be responsible. Understand?"

"Yessir."

He slammed the door and left. We watched in silence as he shambled off past the spinning red, white, and blue barber pole. Then M.C. broke the silence. "You know what, I don't believe that man is as mean as he is ugly."

"He so ugly people shame to be around him," said someone else.

The whole barbershop exploded, everybody topping everybody with lies about ugly people, laughing, pouring out their annoyance at the mean cop.

"Now see, some people ugly because they can't help it. Some because they've got hurt or something. But some just contrary ugly, ugly cause they want to be. We just seen one of *them*."

"He look like Uncle Joe—every time *he* look in the mirror, he faint."

"I know a man so ugly you have to turn a pot down over his head to let it break day. That's an ugly man!"

"Well, I seed a man once—honest to God it's true—I seed a man so ugly he had to back up to get a drink of water."

"He the one with eyes so near the top of his head, that when he get ready to see, he have to pull his hat off."

"You know they say God don't like ugly. So he can't expect to get in heaven. He not ever gonna die. He just gonna ugly away."

M.C. capped them all. "I may not be so ugly," he chuckled, "but I beats ugly. I'm black!" He took up a sort of chanting rhythm. "Now, you people will have to excuse me for being so black. It was eleventeen of us brothers in our family, and the older we got, the blacker we got. The youngest brother was named Invisible—he's never been seen. Maw had to sprinkle talcum powder on that boy to tell where to spank him at. It was so many of us black children in the family till one morning Paw just got tired of it and told Maw, 'You better pick out the best-looking, because I'm gonna drown the rest of um.'

"I reckon that must have been me, because I'm still oozing around here.

"Now there's a lot of people don't know when they was born, but I know the day I was born, right up to the minute. The day I was born there wasn't nobody home but me and my paw. My maw was uptown, shopping. Maw come home and looked at me, say, 'He ain't like me.' Paw say, 'He ain't like me.' You know, it made me mad. You know, it made me so devilish mad I started to pack up and go back."

M.C. went on with everybody grinning: "Just to look at me, you wouldn't think I'm a married man, but I'm married. I got a wife so big and fat and greasy I have to put ashes in the bed at night to keep her from slipping out. We got one of the cutest, one of the slickest, one of the blackest little coal-oil stoves you ever seen.

"You know, peoples, times is hard. The harder times gets, the higher sumpin to eat gets. Take a little common thing as pork chops, cost four dollars a ounce. You know that's too much to pay for pork chops. Pinto beans, three dollars an ounce. You know, that's too much to pay for beans. Chitlins—four dollars a yard. That's too much to pay for hog bowels.

"Times is so hard, the ladies can't buy powder to powder their face, have to powder with flour. I was out this morning, taking my morning stroll, met two nice-looking ladies, all powdered up in flour; and the sun had begin shining hot and, begod, if they didn't have biscuits hanging under their chins."

M.C. had drawn a lot of laughs during the first sallies in this old-fashioned minstrel sketch. Like many blackface routines, it has the rush of language and images and the change of pace typical of black witticism, but it is, basically, a painful racist caricature devised for white consumption. The minstrel show dominated the American consciousness for almost a century, and the curious and ironic result was that many blacks came to accept its racist distortions as their own, and often trotted out such moldy but mellow things as M.C.'s skit when asked for black folklore.

Ugliness has been an ever-recurrent theme in black humorous banter, and there are literally scores of "lies" on ugly people, like those they told at Old John's. Dark skin color has been a part of this "ugliness" syndrome since the time of slavery, when blacks were pressured to accept white European prejudices. Being light-skinned was often socially advantageous, so that some mothers hoped their children would "marry light" and thus move up the color-caste ladder, while dark skin often brought social difficulties. Even the marvelous and successful "Black Is Beautiful" campaign has not altogether eliminated color prejudice in the black community.

The overall preoccupation with ugliness, so prominent in black lore, is, I believe, rooted elsewhere in the American black experience. One of the most troubling aspects of being a slave was being forced into intimate association with strangers of different background, language, and appearance. Such intergroup differences rouse the most violent emotions; witness, for example, the antagonism between the English and the Scotch and the Welsh, between northern and southern Italians, between Japanese and Ainu—the list is endless. Striking differences of stature, physiognomy, and temperament separate the peoples of the Congo and the Guinea Coast, the desert and forest folk, the tall Nilotes and the Pygmies. Yet slavers and plantation managers threw people from scores of these radically different African nations together in close quarters and forced them to live and work together as well as marry each other, in spite of age-old fears and antipathies—all this while requiring that the slave pretend to admire and respect his often abhorred white masters.

The shock effects of these experiences still endure. In Latin America black national differences have resurfaced in religious and magical practices, as well as in color-caste systems of nauseating complexity. In 1935, my Bahamian street friends told me there were seven different color-castes in Nassau, seven shades from dark to light that determined admission to social clubs. In the United States such repressed intergroup antagonisms have continued to fuel aggressive interaction and to manifest themselves in rituals of insult, like "the dozens" (see below) and "sounding," where extravagant references to appearance become a game: "Man, you so ragged, ugly, and dirty, they take you for a stack of garbage and haul you off!" "Man, *you* so ugly, they throw you in the Mississippi and skim ugly for six months!"

During M.C.'s comedy sketch about blackness, laughter had grown more faint and chilly at Old John's. Will Stark's next tale shifted the focus to other concerns—the need to be on guard in dealing with whites. Here Rabbit stands, as usual, for the black man and Dog for the white man.

Asa Ware chuckled and said, "That minds me of the convention when the animals all got together.

"One time all the animals held a meeting to find out how they could get 'long with each other better. All were present and accounted for when the Rabbit come in. He was late as usual, and the hall was crowded and there wasn't no seat in there but next to the hound. The flies was bad and bothered the hound and, you know, the hound would snap at um. The Rabbit would jump down off his seat every time the hound would snap. So the chairman called Rabbit to order. 'Mister Rabbit,' he say, 'keep your seat. You's late already and you gonna get fined directly.'

"He says, 'All right. But I motion you put a muzzle on this gate-mouth son-of-a-bitch next to me fore he makes somebody hurt theirselves.' "

OLD JOHN

I felt that it might be time for me to put in my two cents, since we had survived an unhappy experience together. "Excuse me," I said, "but was Old John's Barbershop named after the man that always fooled Old Massa?"

"Us *two*," the barber grinned. "After old slave John and after *me*. When they ask me, 'Who was John?' I tell them he was an old man back in slavery time, a sensible old man, like me, who tried to git out of as much work as he could, and, when they didn't ration out enough meat, he would get his anyhow."

"Old Massa told him, 'John, I been missing hogs every night, and the last one I seen in the pen was you. I believe you stealing my hogs.'

" 'Oh no,' says John. 'I ain't been stealing your hogs. Not Old John.'

"Well, that Saturday night John decided to slip off and take him a little shoat. The first shoat he grabbed, Old Massa caught him at the gate, say, 'John, I'm gonna make you eat up every damn bit of this hog yourself. You been stealin, now I'm gonna see you do some eatin.'

"He had the cook stew that old shoat down in one of these old washpots and cook up a big pan of cornbread. The first thing Old John grabbed was the head, shock it by the ears, and et the head up. Took the middlins, fold um up just like you do a flapjack, and et *them*. Took them there hams, knocked the gristles off them, et them, and then he turned and say, 'Captain, if you'd give me any more'n this to eat, you'd-a killed me sho!' "

This John was the slave trickster hero I had hoped to hear about—the lineal descendant of Little John in Robin Hood, Ti Jean in French and West Indian tales, Jack or Jacques in countless wonder stories, John the Revelator in the Bible, and John Henry, the steel-driving man. The viewpoint implicit in the trickster's exploits helped Old John to survive and to get the better of his all-powerful master. In that code, stealing from a fellow slave was viewed as criminal, while depredations against the master were counted as acts of virtue since masters were viewed as the true thieves. An old Gullah proverb put the matter thus: "Ef bukra [white man] neber tief, how come neggar here?"[2]

Old John, the barber, went on shaving his customer as he talked about his slavery-time namesake. "Now Old John had the reputation that he could guess anything. Way he did it was to creep and hide and find how they was gonna test him, and then he'd know the answer in advance. His old marse kept bettin and winnin money on him till at last he bet five hundred dollars that they could put anything under a washpot and John could tell them exactly what was there. You know, one of them big old fifty-gallon washpots they boil dirty clothes in.

"So they did that. They send Old John to the spring so he couldn see what they doin, and while he was gone, they put a big old coon under the pot. All the folks gathered round and Old Marse call John, 'I've got five hundred dollars betted that you can tell us exactly what's under this here washpot.'

"Old John start to reach down and touch the pot, but they holler an tell him, 'No, no, John, don't touch it. You just *look* at it and tell us.'

"So Old John stand there and scratch his head and act like he studyin deep. He took his time because he knowed they didn't know they had done caught on to him. Fact of the business, they hadn't. He studied and studied and then he said, 'Well, Old Massa, look like you done caught the old coon at last!'

"His massa bust out hollerin, 'I told you Old John could do it, I told you he could!' "

THE FASTEST MAN

The barber hollered like Old Massa. That woke the customer who was being shaved. He started straight up in his chair and narrowly missed having his throat cut. While the room settled down, I glanced hopefully at Asa Ware, the chunky cotton farmer. Somehow his stories got close to the gristle, where it hurt. Sure enough, Asa responded with the old lie about the mule who got tired of doing what he was supposed to do. He told it in his rapid-fire style:

John was driving an old mule named Jack, and Jack got tired on the road. John said, "Come up, Jack." Jack just looked around at John. So John report back to him, say, "Come up, Jack." Jack looked around and say, "I been comin up for thirty years, I ain't comin no more."

John broke for the house and told Massa, "Jack talkin."

Old Massa say, "You lyin, John. I believe you lying again." So, well, John carried him down to where old mule was standin in the road. Old Massa hadn't so much as walked in seven years—had John carry him wherever he had to go. Then Old John tell that mule, "Come up, Jack."

Old mule looked around and say, "I been comin up for thirty years, I ain't comin up no more." Scared Old Massa and he went to runnin. Run till he come to a big oak tree. Couldn't run no more. Set down to rest. And his little feist dog set down right beside him. Both of um just pantin. Old Massa say, "Lord, I ain't run so much in seven years."

Little feist say, "I ain't neither."

Then Old Massa really run sho-nuff.

This story, which has been found all over the black South, evoked wicked glee in John's barbershop. It sees Old Massa as far more cowardly than his black servant. Again and again, in these tales, John performs feats his master is afraid to attempt, and, when something frightening happens, the master always outruns his slaves. Will Stark told this one:

Back in slavery time one old white man had something wrong wid his legs, couldn't walk, had two slaves carry him every step he go. One night these two boys ask him could they go to see they girls that night and he told um go on.

Well, they was some free people went fish whacking the same night and they kilt plenty of fish. On they way back home they come to the graveyard, laid their biggest catfish down at the gate, went on in and start dividing up the fish. So when those two boys come home from courting, they heard them free people dividing up their fish, "Dis one yourn; dat un mine. Dis yourn; dat un mine . . ."

They run and tell their boss, "Massa, the Lord and the devil out there in the graveyard, dividing up the souls."

"I believe you're lyin, boys, but take me down so I can see for myself. You better not be foolin me!" So they tote him down there and he listen at the cemetery gate and hear them free people say, "Dis un yourn, dat un mine. Dis un yourn, dat un mine . . ."

So when they finish counting, one fellow say, "Well, let's us get ready to go, and don't forget the big old catfish at the gate there."

Great God, Old Massa got over his sickness right there. He was home and in bed by the time his boys got there.

The laughter at the expense of skittish Old Massa was not totally unkind. Fleetness of foot was important to black survival in the Deep South. In a very real sense all blacks were potential fugitives who had to be ready to move like lightning, even run for their lives, at any moment. Flight was an essential act for the slave avoiding the lash, the peon escaping the forced labor camp, the sharecropper running away from debt, the prisoner with the bloodhounds on his trail. Gun law ruled the Delta economy; physical discipline of the severest kind ruled the household. The best thing was to get out of the way when the white man got mad, when an angry father came home, when you disobeyed Mama, or when a disgruntled gambler decided to shoot his way out of a crap game. M.C.'s next story took us into this risk-filled world.

"I was out to a dance one night," he chuckled. "And whilst I was out there to this dance, a big racket come up. Guy come up wid a gun, say, 'I'll kill you, I'll kill you!' Backed off, you know, and commenced shooting—Bung! Bung!

"I commenced running and I were running so fast until I outrun the sound of the first shot two miles and a half, so when I stopped, I heard that first shot again and I thought that man was still shooting. I lit in to runnin again, got to my house. Quick as I hit the steps, I said, 'Annie, open the door.' Look like it took three weeks for her to open it, I sit down to rest my feet, but they were so hot I called for a bowl of ice water to wash um in. Had icicles on my mustache two feet long. I went to bed, take six hours rest, got up and walked to the door, and along came the sound of that gun shooting its first shot."

In the active sensual life of the Delta, a quick retreat out the bedroom window and down the road was a useful social skill. A philanderer had to be able to move in and then move out smartly, because jealous husbands or boyfriends were often armed.

"I knowed a fellow once, he was bad about lyin on people," said Will with a sly grin. "In other words, a lot of people try to make peace and a lot of people try to break peace. Well, Sam was peace-breakin, just lyin, you understand. This time he told the neighbors a lie on John's wife.

"So John called him one mornin—they had always been friends—John called Sam, 'Sam, come here.' Sam goes up there. 'What you want, John?'

"John say, 'Now I told you to quit lyin on me, didn't I?'

" 'Yes, you did tell me, but I ain't lied.'

" 'Yes, you did,' says John. 'You lied on me and you lied on my people, now you done lied to my wife. I'm gonna kill you.' John had a Winchester with him. Sam didn't have nothin. So John put out with that Winchester, shot at Sam. Doggone, Sam taken off right down the side the ditch and through the bushes and John took that .30-30 Winchester and cut a limb right above Sam's head. Then Sam taken off running sure enough.

"As Sam moved across the field there, he jumped a deer. Him and that deer—you know a deer can naturally run—him and the deer was running side and side and Sam ask the deer, say, 'You been meddlin in John's business, too?' The deer was runnin so fast, he was gruntin: 'Unh-unh-unh-unh.'

"Sam say, 'I says, is you been messin in John's business?' You know, when the deer couldn't get away from Sam, he got more scared than ever, so he went, 'Baaa!'

"Sam say, 'Baaa, hell. If you been messin in John's business, you better take that damned chair off your head and get moving!' "

Everybody in Old John's knew about being shot at. They all were used to the risks that faced a young man courting a girl in a strange community. He might have to run for it if he wanted to avoid "having his ass kicked." A fast mover was in every way a better lover, as M.C. made clear in this subtropical slice of science fiction.

"There's a girl had company once and there were three boys courting her," he said. "And this time she was cooking breakfast and she wanted some steak for dinner. And this boy, he went ten miles to the butcher's shop and back before the stove got hot.

"The other boy come in and she wanted roas'n'ears. She went up to him and said, 'Boy, I was just fixing to serve dinner and I would like to have some roas'n'ears with dinner.' So he jumped out there and cleaned out ten acres of land and harvested before the stove got hot. And just before she got the dinner on the table, you know, the other boy walked in. Says, 'Honey, I'm just fixing to fix dinner.' Says, 'Come in and eat dinner with us.' Says, 'But I'd like to have some cool water.' And *he* went two miles down in a cedar grove and gets two buckets of water and gets halfway home and the bottoms of the buckets fall out. He runs to the blacksmith shop and gets him some tools, come back and cuts down two trees and hew him out two buckets and caught that water before it hit the ground. Fast, man!"

As I laughed with my friends over these fantastic tales, I began to realize that speediness and flight were basics in the folklore of the Deep South. The favorite ballad hero of the Mississippi penal system was a racehorse.

Stewball, he start off
Like a passenger express train,
And old Molly, she rambled
Like a midnight shower of rain.

There was Long John, who outran all the bloodhounds.

Had a heel in front
And a heel behind

Till you couldn tell where
That boy was gwine.

Old Riley, escaping prison across the Brazos River, walked the water like Christ. When the *Titanic* was sinking, Poor Shine came up out of the hold where they had him shoveling coal, took a look at all the big whales and fishes in the Atlantic, and next thing you know, he was shooting craps in Liverpool. His adventure is told in full on earlier pages.

Quickness of wit in conversation was as much admired as fleetness of foot. In his insightful studies of African-American lore, Roger Abrahams[3] developed the image of "the man of words" as a core concept of the black tradition. This "man of words," be he preacher, raconteur, lover, boaster, riddler, songster, or street-corner jokesmith, had, above all, to be speedy and changeful in his improvised use of language. Like the "big liars" gathered in the barbershop, he poured out a torrent of wisecracks, tall tales, and extravagances of all sorts over his dazzled hearers. In the Bronx today they call this "snapping." A "snapper" must never be at a loss for repartee to throw his rivals off balance. Essentially, Abrahams's man of words is a master at lightning changes of subject and viewpoint. The feats of the Jamaican reggae rhymester, the Trinidadian calypsonian, the American rapper, and for that matter the jazz musician, all depend upon instant improvisation.

These observations seem to be part of a much larger framework. In recent years, partly to find answers to the many questions the Delta research raised for me, I mounted a comparative, cross-cultural survey of performance style. One of the clearest findings has been that black African performance scores on velocity and changefulness were the world's highest—making the most use of marked shifts of level, direction, limb use, pacing, and energy in dance and of changes in voice quality, tempo, register, ensemble, mood, meter, harmony, and melody in music—along with the greatest facility in shifting style collectively in close coordination. Black style is outstandingly accelerative, collectively accelerative. Indeed, it is plain that this focus on coacceleration is one of its most distinctive features, both in Africa and in the Americas.

In graffiti sprayed on the run in the subways, in acrobatic feats matching antic postures in break dancing and basketball, in the rimshots and quick breaks of jazz, in the sizzling tempi of hard rock, in the rapid-fire philosophizing in reggae and rap, ghetto blacks have used their high-velocity African heritage to create art forms suitable to a jet-propelled age. Most recent and speed-possessed is rap. Do-wopped rap magically transforms the orchestras recorded on two turntables into a rhythm section that accompanies the high-speed danced performances of the most dense, most rapid and extravagant torrent of rhymes and text of any known song form. For sheer speed, rap rivals Rumanian panpipe playing, Caucasian dancing, and the footwork of James Brown and Michael Jackson, the fastest steppers we noted in our world survey. For high-energy coacceleration, a rap group is like a black basketball team moving down the court to score a basket.

Among its best-known manifestations is the swift flow of snapping, where several voices overlap so quickly that everyone seems to be talking at once. One of these conversational games, and sometimes a dangerous one, is called "the dozens," in which a pair of youngsters aim salacious rhymed insults at each other's mother. Sometimes the language grows so painfully insulting that a fight will break out. People have been killed over the dozens. Ordinarily, the dozens are laughed off, as these sexually loaded barbs fly back and forth at a furious pace.

VOICE 1:   *I saw your mama floatin down the stream,*
           Eatin cow chips and cold ice cream.

VOICE 2:   *Stood by your house and pulled up a nail.*
           Sign on the door say "Pussy for Sale."

VOICE 1:   *I _____ your mama on a coal-oil can.*
           You jumped out sayin, "Coal-oil man."

VOICE 2:   *I _____ your mama wid a walkin stick.*
           She swore, by God, it was an elephant's dick.

The pell-mell hurling of such childish garbage often caused fights, especially, one imagines, when one participant was the man of the house that a father had deserted. The dozens served as a channel for forbidden emotions, angry as well as incestuous. Bad-mouthing somebody *else's* mother or having yours bad-mouthed by somebody else was an approved avenue of emotional release for a kid whose heart was burning with filial rage or lust. It was the Delta custom to wean late, often as late as four or five years, but, after this initial permissive period, to institute severe childhood discipline. Child labor in the kitchen, the cow lot, and the field was essential to the poor black family's survival, and uncooperative or rebellious children were instantly and painfully brought into line. Mothers hit out with rope ends, harness, stovewood, whatever came to hand. Above all, the work-toughened palm of the parent fell hard and frequently. The best solution for the child was to take to its heels, and to joke and fantasize endlessly.

"I used to go rabbit hunting a lot." Old Will Stark smiled. "And I never did have but two shells. I *got* to get me a rabbit because I was hungry and ain't got but two shells now. If I shot at the rabbit and miss it, I'd lay my gun down and run up side of him and feel his hips, see if he fat. If he wasn't fat, I'd let him go and catch me a fat one."

This jape evoked mild chuckles and then, amazingly, out of the blue smoke of Old John's Barbershop leapt a mythic tale as old as mankind—the story of the young hero setting out to seek his fortune. I had not understood just how young this lad was in the perspective of those present. As in Dickens's novels, he was usually no more than nine or ten years old. At that age a boy from a Delta broken home was considered quite able to take care of himself, and many of the life stories in the pages that follow begin with a boy leaving home that early.

The young Delta hero, like the hero of so many wonder tales, usually encounters a demonic master, a Mister Greensnake. The "Mister" suggests that he is a white man and a demon figure as well—"the fastest man in the world." It follows that Mister Greensnake is a boss no tenant or peon or prisoner could ever elude. When the boy tries to get away, Mister Greensnake brings him back to peonage, but by then the boy has learnt Greensnake's secrets. There ensues the ageless magical flight with rapid-fire protean transformations. The story has no end. The boy is in flight with Mister Greensnake relentlessly pursuing—a true picture of black destiny in the Delta as the blues began.

Asa Ware built up tension by telling the story as rapidly as he could speak, like a man talking for his life:

Mister Greensnake was one of the fastest mans in the world. Been everywhere and knowed everything and do everything.

It was a little boy come long, walking down the road one day, you know, hongry. He didn't see nobody to ask for nothing to eat, so he goes in this man's house and set down to the table and go to eatin. Greensnake's wife hears him in there and asks him, "Son, what are you doin here?"

"Well, I'm only eatin."

He said, "Lady, hide me somewhere, please." She put him in the closet.

By the time she got him in the closet, this man hit the house, say, "Old lady, where is that boy was here?"

"I got him in the closet."

She bring him out and let the man look at him, and he liked him pretty well. He take him back to the table and let him finish. So after dinner he took him down to the new ground and learn him how to work.

The boy worked, I think, about six or seven months. Greensnake begin to like this kid and learned him some of his pranks what he could do. The boy got smart and decided to slip off from Greensnake. He went home.

Where he lived, way out in Texas, there was a man coming along one day, says to the boy's daddy, "Sam, bring your chicken down to town tomorrow; we're gonna have a chicken fight."

"I ain't got no chicken."

The boy said, "Papa, tell him you'll be down there in the morning with your game rooster, spurs on his feet five inches long—comb, three."

Boy gets up, walks to the end of the gallery, turns a somersault, turns to a game rooster, crowed three times. Daddy picked him up, carried him on downtown. Whip out everything down there.

The next week or two, there's gonna be a hoss race down there. This boy began to feel superstitious, says, "Papa, there's gonna be a hoss race down there tomorrow." He says, "Hit's gonna be a man down there, name of Greensnake, he's gonna want to buy me." Says, "I'm gonna turn into a black stallion, silver saddle on, silver bridle on, brass studs." Say, "If he wants to buy me and if you sell me, take the halter off."

Papa say, "Okay."

So by two o'clock the brass band commenced playing and the boy gets out there and commenced running. He won everything in the yard, and when this boy's daddy got ready to ride off, Greensnake walked up and say to him, say, "I want to buy that hoss."

He say, "I wouldn't take fifty thousand dollars for him."

Greensnake say, "I'll give you seventy-five thousand dollars."

He say, "Take him."

When Greensnake riding off, the old man hollered, "Aw," say, "I didn't sell that halter."

Greensnake say, "When I bought the hoss, I bought the halter."

Told him, "Naw, naw, I wouldn't take fifty thousand dollars for that halter."

Greensnake say, "I give you seventy-five thousand dollars."

This man said to his son, he said, *"Son, let your papa go rich once in life."*

Boy say, "All right."

Greensnake had a yard boy working for him. He told that boy, he say, "Listen, now, whatever you ever do, don't you ever pull this halter off this hoss. Let it stay on him."

The boy carried the hoss down to the stream to drink some water and he act like the halter is choking him. But the boy is scared to pull the halter off.

A man up in the road had a load of wood in his wagon and he saw that halter was choking that hoss and he hollered to the yard boy, say, "Pull that halter off that hoss so he can drink some water." Yard boy said, "Mister Greensnake told me, whatever I ever do, don't never do that."

Old man jumped off his wagon, run down there, snatched this halter off. The stallion cut a somersault, turned into a catfish, jumped into the sea.

This yard boy ran back up the hill, told Mister Greensnake about it. Mister Greensnake come running down, say, "Whar did he git in at?"

"Right here," he say. And Mister Greensnake cut a somersault, turned into an alligator eighteen feet long, got in after the catfish, and run him all over the sea.

The boy seed Greensnake was gonna catch him. He run out on the bank and turned into a humming bird in the air. Greensnake turned into a bald eagle and git after him and run him all over the world. The boy seed this guy was gonna catch him.

There's a good-looking girl at home, sitting under a tree, you know, waiting on her company. The boy flew there, cut a somersault, turned into a ring and got on her finger. Greensnake flew down there, cut a somersault and turned into a man, dressed to kill, plenty clothes, big stripes in his pants, diamond stickpin, courtin that girl. All his talk, "Baby, give me that ring."

Just about the time he over'suaded her to give him that ring, boy jumped off her finger, cut somersault, turned into a box of mustard seeds, flew up in the air, and busted. Greensnake cut somersaults, turned into an old hen with a hundred chickens picking up them mustard seeds. Just about that time I left.

And so did the bunch at Old John's—chuckling together at the triumph of black wit. I was thinking of the last stanza of the Texas ballad about the grey goose. The death-defying goose, after being shot, boiled, carved, sent to the sawmill, and thrown in the hogpen, flies off, honking defiance, and trailed by a newborn string of goslings. Perhaps here is the moral of the Delta myth— even with a hundred chicks to help him, Greensnake could never pick up all those nearly invisible mustard seeds. The many that were missed would take root and sprout everywhere, as the black folk of the Delta were about to do.

Chapter 4

▲▲▲▲▲▲▲▲▲▲

Lonesome Whistles

Lord, I hate to hear that lonesome whistle blow,
It say, "Trouble here and trouble down the road."

The sound of the steamboat and railroad whistles, drifting across the green fields of the Delta, wrought transformations as swift and magical as the charms of Mister Greensnake. Farm boys and plowmen left home to become professional boatmen, muleskinners, and railroaders, learning the pains and pleasures of the lonesome road. Their herculean labors brought daylight into the swamps, tamed the big muddy rivers, and built the roads along which wealth and change came to the Delta. Meanwhile, every day on the job, every night in the lawless jukes and barrelhouses, they proved their manhood and reestablished their protean black heritage.

Some of these black workers lived as free laborers, growing accustomed for the first time to regular paydays. Others were held and worked by force as peons in camps deep in the wilderness. Yet others landed in prison and were used as forced labor by the county or state. All were segregated, as well as exploited, living and toiling as all-black teams under white bosses. In consequence, because they were "unschooled" and thus ignorant of official culture, they were free to continue and develop their own fabulously rich cultural heritage. Old African habits survived, endowing every situation in a web of sociability, where banter, laughter, song, and often synchronized movement involved everyone present. This rich outcaste culture continued to expand invisibly, passed on orally and along nonverbal channels, as pervasive as blood and air. The steamboats, the railroad lines, and the green shoulders of the levees became theaters in which the African-American drama was acted out, with a sound, savor, and vitality all its own.

In the work teams and construction camps, in the cruel chain gangs and fetid prison dormitories, in the gambling houses, dance halls, and gin mills, every occasion when these men came together by day or by night was shot through with the lightning of black wit and black tunefulness. The give-and-take of black comradeship never ceased. My good friend and colleague Zora Hurston captured the brilliance of these scenes in her great *Mules and Men*. But she did not report the downside—the peonage, the pitiful wages, the long hours, the brutal, often murderous bosses, the monstrous absurdities of Jim Crow. Her turpentiners and railroaders were probably afraid to venture onto this risky terrain. Perhaps she, out of concern for them, did not ask them to, or, if they did, dared not publish what they confided to her. We shall never know. At any rate, in the twenties and thirties it was too dangerous to talk or even sing about these matters. The South was virtually sealed up.

Even after months of living with and being interviewed by me, Leadbelly never spoke of these things to me. Try as I might, I was unable to move into this forbidden territory until I came into the Delta with a partly black crew and worked with Lewis Jones, the best of Southern fieldworkers. Even then, black self-censorship held firm. And it wasn't till I talked to blacks who had moved North and then returned South after the Supreme Court had ruled against segregation that I was able to record truly candid accounts from black workers of the Deep South. These make up the substance of the chapters that follow. The experiences they recount provide both the background and the loam of song out of which the blues grew.

At the conclusion of our work in Coahoma County, Lewis Jones felt that our folk history could best be seen in terms of the three main modes of transport and communication that progressively linked the Delta to the outside world and brought change into an old rural culture. In a measure, this is true. The steamboat flourished in the early plantation era. The railroad brought in land speculation, profiteering, and in its train, sharecropping, which broke up the local communities and sent many men looking for outside jobs. With the highway came the era of rural displacement, of constant out-migration, of the jukebox and the church choir. Coahoma County musical history had three periods, each signaled by a typical sound—a steamboat blowing for a landing, a locomotive whistling on a three-mile grade, and a Greyhound bus blaring

down Highway 61. The first of these sounds was the calliope whistle of the
Mississippi steamboat, just as the first blues was the one the deckhands sang:

Po roustabout ain't got no home,
Here today and tomorrow gone.

In their day, the Mississippi River steamboats were the wonders of Western
America. Beating the brown belly of the mighty river to froth with their great
paddles, filling the sky with black clouds from cathedral-like smokestacks, at
night their furnaces breathing dragonlike flames across midnight waters, gliding through the semiwilderness of the Southwest like swift heavenly chariots,
loaded down with well-dressed dudes, fancy women, double-jinted roustabouts, and new cotton millionaires—these floating palaces roused the awe of
the Delta songsters.

The big Kate Adams *headin down the stream,*
With her sidewheel knockin—"Good God, I been redeemed."

Every oldtime riverman we met claimed to have worked on the famed *Kate
Adams*. They talked of how she lived up to her reputation as the fastest boat
on the river by beating the *Jim Lee* in a race from Hell's Point, Mississippi,
to Helena, Arkansas, in 1883. To the folk along the river, these beautiful
steamers were living beings.

Kate Adams *and* Jim Lee *had a race,*
The Kate *throwed water in* Jim Lee's *face.*

The *Jon W.*, most magnificent of the passenger boats, was 750 feet long, 91
feet wide, paneled in carved mahogany, and seated five hundred in a dining
room lined with mirrors and carpeted from wall to wall. Its elaborate steam
whistles, which could produce many chords, constantly caused horses to run
away with their buggies and on one occasion brought on a rainstorm. The
greatest ambition of every boy up and down the river was to be able to
recognize and imitate the *Jon W.*'s whistles and those of every boat on the
river. Their secret dream, of course, was to roam the river on a stern-wheeler.

Far more black than white youngsters realized these ambitions, for the riverboat crews were largely black.

Samuel Clemens was an exception to this rule, but even the nickname he won as aspiring riverboat pilot was a black-folk creation. On the day of his final test for a river pilot's license, his cronies played a practical joke on the young greenhorn. In those pre-sonar days a black leadsman was posted in the bow of the boat to sound the water periodically with a weighted line, and then call out the depths to the pilot in the wheelhouse. Clemens's cronies bribed the leadsman to fake his calls during Sam's test. Thus, when Sam took the wheel and was barreling along in what he thought was deep water in midstream, the leadsman abruptly changed his call from "no bottom" to "mark twain," which meant that the water had grown shallow. Sam quickly steered in another direction, but to no avail—again came the warning "mark twain." Soon the boat was skittering all over the river like a water-bug, and the call came "quarter less twain." Then "half twain," which meant the steamer was about to run aground. Poor Sam fainted dead away. He woke to hoots of laughter, a reviving glass of bourbon, and a nickname that became world famous—Mark Twain, the signal to the river pilot "You're headed into low water" or "Look out!"

The leadsman's line was a thirty-three-foot rope with a lead-filled pipe at its end. It was marked at four feet from the lead by a piece of white flannel, at six feet by a piece of leather, at nine feet by a piece of cotton, and at twelve feet by a piece of leather split into two thongs. This last was "mark twain," the split-leather thong set at two fathoms, or twelve feet, signaled by the cry that warned the river pilot of trouble at hand. "Mark three" was a piece of leather split into three thongs. The leadsman could estimate pretty closely where he was between these twains and qualify them with calls like "quarter less twain" or "half twain." At "mark four" there was a single strip of leather with a round hole in it, and beyond that the next call would be *"Nooooooo bottom!"*

On the blackest night, in the thickest fog, while the big boat slid over the dark water, the leadsman could judge the depth of the river by the feel of these marks between his fingers, while his periodic calls kept the pilot in the wheelhouse informed. The sequence that made Mark Twain forever famous might have run as follows:

No bottom,
Mark fo',

Quarter less fo',
Quarter less th-ree,
Half twain,
Quarter twain,
Quarter less fo',
Half twain,
Quarter less twain,
Mark twain!

There was more than romance to these Mississippi packets; they were superbly designed river carriers. One boat took 7,000 bales of cotton in one load, looking like a floating cotton bale with smokestacks poking out. The record for one season's transport was 77,000 bales, but many boats averaged nearly that. At a dollar a bale, the year's profit, in real dollar value, was hefty, and thus these flat-bottomed, wood-burning paddleboats ruled the river for a good century. The last of these floating money factories was the *Tennessee Belle,* which was built in 1927 and worked the river profitably until 1942 when she burned at Natchez, forever remembered by the old rousters.

All the loading and unloading, the lifting and toting, was done by a throng of black roustabouts, who napped on deck between jobs. A Mississippi packet, drawing only a few inches of water, could slip up a shallow bayou, broach its prow right on a plantation levee, and shoot out its gangplank near the load. Immediately, the roustabouts began trotting back and forth, unloading the supplies brought from town and loading local produce for market. The quicker their turnaround, the higher the profit. Thus the roustabouts were the heart and muscle of the big stern-wheeler. This steaming enterprise depended on their "shoulder bones" and they knew it. They daily performed lifts and carries that are far beyond what today's trained lifters could do, and they weren't working with carefully balanced barbells on padded floors. They were handling boxes, barrels, bales, and often live, struggling animals, moving up- or downhill on bobbing gangplanks or slippery mud. Two of the rousters could carry a mule, kicking and bucking, right up the gangplank.

Ray Lum, the fabulous animal auctioneer, recalled the feats of these rivermen: "I had this bull that was blind, weighed fifteen hundred pounds. When the boat come in, they lowered the gangplank. I says, 'Captain, load that bull there first.'

"He says to his rousters, 'Pick up that bull.'

"They picked him up, a fifteen-hundred-pound bull. They picked him up plumb off the ground, held him in the air, and carried him on the boat. That was the way they loaded him.

"Old John Rouser was in on that deal. Old John Louser-Rouser, they call him. He was there that day. He was a rouster that was noted to everybody that knew about boats. When he'd go up the gangplank, he'd rock. [Just as W. Brown tells us later on p. 154.] He could throw a bale of cotton on his shoulder and trot right up the gangplank with it. John Rouser lived to be a ripe old age. I knew him all down through the years."[1]

There is no intimation in the rivermen stories that follow that the rousters felt their lot was a miserable one. Indeed, they clearly preferred the wild freedom of the river to the plantation life they had escaped. Small as their pay was, it was better than the farmer's pittance. Moreover, they took pride in their feats of manly strength and their independence. The air turned blue with their powerful and erotic lingo, and the sun flashed no brighter than their laughter, as they transformed their toil into an African-American *bamboche*. Thus these rugged black men made the riverside scene their own, they humanized it, by "rocking," or dancing, their loads along, and by improvising tunes that whooped and moaned like the whistles of their beloved steamboats.

Many country boys ran away from home to seek their fortunes on the river. One of these was Henry Truvillion, who ended his days as a Baptist preacher and track caller in the East Texas pinewoods. His wailing roustabout holler may be ancestral to the levee-camp and prison hollers from which the blues arose. One verse indicates that the song goes back to 1884. Sung with falsetto leaps in a changeful vocal style, like the levee hollers, it also has an ornamented melody, with blue notes and a descending three-phrase form.

Truvillion began with an epic description of the riverside scene.

Now boys, we're on the steamer Natchez,
And we got to load this here cotton and cottonseed here
Before anybody can shut his eyes like he's asleep;
So we might just as well tear around,
Get us a gobo apiece.
Let's go on and load this stuff, what do you say?
We're up here and got it to do.
Where you at there, you old nub-fingered nappy?
Let's hear from you, blow your horn, let's load some cotton.

1.
Oh-h-h-h,
Po roustabout don't have no
*   home,*
Makes his livin on his shoulder
*   bone.*

2.
Oh-h-h-h,
Wake up, sleepy, and tell your
*   dream,*
I want to make you acquainted
*   with the two blue seams*
*   (cotton sacks with blue seams).*

3.
Oh-h-h-h,
If yo shoulder bone gets so' this
*   time,*
Git you a little sody an
*   turpentine.*

4.
Oh-h-h-h,
I left my home in '84
And I ain't never been there no
*   more.*

5.
Oh-h-h-h,
I know my sweetie goin open the
*   do'*
As soon as she hear the Natchez
*   blow.*

6.
Oh-h-h-h,
The Natchez up the bayou an she
*   done broke down,*
She got her head toward
*   Memphis, but she's New*
*   Orleans boun.*

7.
Oh-h-h-h,
Did you hear Daniel in the lion
*   den?*
Lord, have mercy, hear me now.

8.
Oh-h-h-h,
Po roustabout don't have no
*   home,*
Here today and tomorrow gone.

9.
Oh-h-h-h,
Fo' day was my cry, midnight
*   was my creep,*
I got a sweet little gal in big
*   New Orleans I does all I can*
*   to please.*

10.
Oh-h-h-h,
Catch this here sack, boys, and
*   leave it go.*
Take her down the river further
*   cause they ain't no mo.*[2]

Most of the movers and shakers of that era had gone where the last whistle echoes before Lewis Jones and I began our Delta research. However, I managed to find three men who had worked on the steamboats. The first was a grizzled river veteran named John Williams, who smoked the stub of a pipe like an Irishman and talked in the abrupt and ironic style common among Delta seniors.

JOHN WILLIAMS: My father died when I was twelve years old and I had two younger brothers and a mother and I was a grown man, well's to say, I tuck charge of seventeen acres of land, worked it just well's any man. Me'n my mother made a crop and raised them boys *up*. My mother died in 1919—she was a hundred and nine years old.

ALAN LOMAX: That made her born in—1810.

J.W.: Yessir. She went through slavery time. Through slavery *time*. And when she was my age she could pick six, seven hundred pound of cotton. I don't *reck*on so—I *know* it. Take an ax, cut just as much wood as any man. Don't care where he's from.

She had a little rock that she tote in her pocket, and when she get ready to light her pipe, she put some cotton on top of it, and on that put the little rock, and strike it with steel to make her own fire to light her pipe. Throw the cotton off and let the baccer go to burnin.

Now you know that's *wise*. We look at it wrong. That was wise in those days. You wouldn't find a man in this town, in these days, would know how to take steel and a rock and start fire. He may be graduated and he ain't got that much sense. *(laughs)* That's right. Yeah. God *reveal* things unto you when you give the case up to Him and you say you don't know how. God'll hep you. God can't hep a man that is wise *and* strong. He's a God to strengthen the weak.

A.L.: I guess your mother told you lots about slavery.

J.W.: Yessir. I hope that time never come now. If it ever come, I won't serve it—because the Lord said we *won't be slaves no more. (He states this with great formality.)*

But I tell you—they's just as much folks die now as they did in slavery time—*more* dies now in this free time because men these days they weaker and wiser, and they got different things to ride in—automobiles—airplanes. In slavery time they walked and rode on wagons. And then again, wages— wages killin men now. Men'll go out on the job tomorrow, work for five, six dollar a day and work out there in *all that weather* all day long, and believe he doing right. Slavery time, why they'd run um in the home. Course they picked cotton on ice, my mother said.

A.L.: Well, when did you first start in a steamboat?

J.W.: I start to steamboatin in 'ninety-three. I was a grown man, all right, and I fit it eight year. I went down to the *Tennessee Belle*. She had five thousand bale o' cotton. A young man meet me on Washington Street, says, "Deacon," says, "don't you wanna labor some?"

I said, "I'd like to labor some."

Said, "*Belle*'s over there—five thousand bale."

I went on over there and I ask the mate for a ticket and he looked at me. My hair was real white. Say, "Git back, old man, you can't cut it."

I don't care how good a man—you can be the size of Jack Johnson—if you never rolled cotton before, the third bale of cotton, you burn out. You'll be sweatin just like somebody throw water on you. Now if you ain't got sense enough to stay there till you burn back *een*, why, you quit.

So, I walked up to a fellow, I says, "Say, pardner, let me roll a few for you." He gi'n me the hook and went on up on the levy, and I tuck it and went to rollin cotton bales. The mate thought I was rollin for another man, but I was rollin for myself to let him see how I *could* roll. So when I rolled down on the boat the first bale of cotton, I saw a fella—me and him use to steamboat together—his name was Dick—he carried one eye. He was captain of the watch.

Dick said to me, "John Skipper," says, "I'm glad to see you laborin," says, "I want you een-side here to help me stack this cotton."

"I ain't laborin," I says. "This old man said that I can't cut it."

Says, "Oh, he don't know better."

Well, the mate was as close to me as from here to that table, and he heard what I said to Dick.

So Dick said, "Go on over on the labbord side." I went on across. Then he saw I knowed the labbord from the stabbord.

I come on back, got another bale, me and my pardner. Then I looked back over my shoulder. The mate was comin. I told my pardner, "Shove off heavy and peekay the hook." And he just squat and shove off and wave the hook around—what you call peekay the hook.

Old mate walk up to me and say, "You can get a ticket."

I say, "I know I can. Tain't black hair you want on the boat—you want cotton!"

All mens—the majority—when you head git grey, don't reckonize you are a man. Say, "You are goin back to child." It's ignorance for a person to think that. If a man is a hundred years old—*if he can't walk*—he yet a man. He ain't no child. You say anything to that old man on the street, and he'll hurt you to your heart. That ain't no child! A man is *always* a man, until he fall down here on a bed of affliction where he can't handle hisself and you got to *work* on him, *he* gone to a *child*. I'm able to go to restroom and come out, and you tell bout I'm a *child*? No, I'm not no child.

I reckonize all mens as—a man. *Some* kind of man. If he ain't a good man, he's a triflin man. That's all. *(laughs)*

A.L.: What kind of wages did a roustabout make, in the time when you were working?

J.W.: Well, in the summertime, when water's high, when all the green mens come out the country and run after the man for ticket, I have steamboat' for a dollar a day.

A.L.: I don't understand why water high and water low would make a difference.

J.W.: Well, you must see that when the water high you got a level bridge. When the water low the bridge is slanted. And you got the bare hill to walk, after you step off the bridge.

A.L.: They have to pay you a lot to walk that slope.

J.W.: Yessir. When the water is low they pay you a lot, and when it's high they don't pay you much. Then, I've got high as a hundred and twenty a month.

Yes, I'll tell you. I've worked harder than any man een this town, I must say. Ain't a man in this town has worked hard's I worked. But work don't kill *nobody*. Misunderstandin. Don't care how hard you work, it don't hurt you. Cause God tell man to work. Don't hurt you to work.

A.L.: How did the mates treat the roustabouts on the job?

J.W.: *(hesitates before replying):* If a man was stubborn and didn't want to work, the mate would take his whip, pop him—bow! bow! They had their sacks on their shoulders, one right behind the other, running down the hill, on the stageplank, on the boat, run on back just the same. But them old mates would really give it to us on the head or back, any old place, if he got in a hurry. We'd be singin:

I went to the landing,
I folded up my arms.
I never missed my dog (woman)
Till the boat was gone.
Oh-h-h, ee-e-e-e.

Roustabout, you got no home,
You makes yo living
On the shoulder bone.
    Lord, we work hard, babe,
    And they know we work hard, babe,
    And they know they work hard, babe,
    And you know you work hard.

A.L.: What would they sing when they got to the top of the bank?
J.W.: *I wished I were Captain Ringo's son*
      This morning.
  I wished I were Captain Ringo's son
      This morning.
  I wished I were Captain Ringo's son,
  Stand on the head and see her run
      This morning.

In 1947 I played old John Williams's story, along with some other bits of my Mississippi recordings, to Hodding Carter, the longtime liberal editor of the *Greenville Citizen*, the man who'd knocked Bilbo out of his Senate seat. Carter sat listening in astonishment. In all his career as a Southern journalist and a friend of the black Mississippi community, he said he'd never heard such frank talk from the black "lower depths." "I've tried and failed to cross that line," he told me. "As a Southerner, I congratulate you. But I don't think you realize what a dangerous position you're in." He paused, then went on. "Alan," he said, "promise me one thing. Take those tapes you've played me, lock them in the trunk of your car, and start driving. Don't stop till you cross the Mississippi line, because if they catch you with those tapes in this state, I won't be able to help you. You'll be a goner."

All this seems very melodramatic as I write it nearly fifty years later. However, I kept my tapes locked in the trunk while I did continue recording, and was not unhappy when my first-of-all-portable recorders gave up the ghost and I had to take it home for repairs. I drove north, looking nervously at state police cars and humming a parody on the old Parchman couplet:

Maybe I've done sumthin a little bit wrong,
Stayed in Miss'ippi just a day too long.

ROCKING

The Deep South had changed a good deal by the time I met Walter Brown, king of the Greenville riverfront, in 1978. This old-time rouster felt he could spill the beans to me. Brown had been cut up in so many fights that he had to wear a plastic badge specifying his blood type. He was a practicing poet, and his passion for history had him knocking at my motel door one morning at 6 A.M.

"You've slept long enough, Lomax," he shouted through the door. "We're gonna make history today."

I opened the door. There was skinny old Walter and a bulging hunk of a man, whom he introduced as his old river buddy.

"Me and Arthur roustabouted together. Now we gonna show you how the work was done and the songs was sung. That right, Arthur?" Arthur grunted. Walter went on, "Arthur and me have fixed up our totin machine and it's waitin down on the levee. For when you get up and get your crew ready."

I knew why they were in a hurry, so I took care of that. When we all had had a snootful, we went down to look at the "totin machine." It was a rope sling with two loops hung between two heavy bars. While Arthur arranged a big gasoline drum in the sling, Walter talked for the camera.

"When I was young," he said, "I worked on the *Tennessee Belle* and the *Kate Adams.* You know what a cotton hook is? Those days I have taken two cotton hooks and throwed um back over a five-hundred-pound bale of cotton. And laid it over on my back and toted it. And stacked it. Such as tractor tracks and whole cows for food and different things. Me an one man—me and just one man could load um.

"Show us how you did it," I asked.

"That's what this totin machine is for."

He joined Arthur and they shouldered the parallel bars of the sling, one at each end. As they lifted a big drum, Walter explained: "Me an one man! He had it on one end and I had it on the other and we used to do like that." They rocked back and forth, shifting weight from side to side, the drum swaying between the bars as they shuffled ahead, keeping their feet flat on the ground. "The steward used to call us his bulls. We used to carry the load like this goin down the gangplank, goin over the water. And we'd get out there and we'd stagger like that, you know, like we gonna fall with it?" (He chuckled as he staggered.) "And just keep on rockin, man!"

Come here, dog, and get your bone.
Tell me what shoulder you want it on.

Arthur and Walter shuffled and rocked past the camera and then put their burden down.

ALAN LOMAX: What did you rock for?
WALTER BROWN: It make it light.
ARTHUR: It seem like your rhythm make it more light on ya.
W.B.: That'd be the sleight of it, you know. When you do that rock to this side, that'd lighten this side and when you go back, that'd lighten this side. And you just stand there and rock with it. Goin down the plank, you know—staggering, playin with it and goin on.

As Walter Brown sang on, I realized this was the old roustabout holler Henry Truvillion and John Williams had sung, but set to a sort of dance beat.

Whoa, look at my men,
How they movin on.
Keep a-rockin, boys,
And bring that cotton on.

Walter went on: "We would be rockin! I was young—it was fun to me. I weighed a hundred eighty, eighty-two pounds and three fifty, four hundred was nothin for me to pick up, because I rocked the load."

Old Walter and Arthur were revealing to us, I guessed, the ultimate significance of the terms "rock" and "rocking." They belonged to the ancient and honorable order of black burden bearers, of lifters and toters, roustabouts and longshoremen, who had loaded and unloaded the cargo of canoes, caravels, and clipper ships, and who had carried the loads to the riverbanks and the seaports or moved the bales and bundles across country when mankind was on the move. In black Africa there never had been either wheeled vehicles or animal transport. Thus from the glory days of Timbuktu to the time of Stanley and Livingstone, long lines of black porters had conquered the vast savannahs and breached the jungles of Africa on foot with burdens on their backs.

In our world study of movement style we found that black Africans tend to approach reality bilaterally, that is with equal activity on both sides of the body. That is why, I believe, the musical instruments that Africans invented or favored were harps, drums, xylophones, "thumb pianos," and the like—all requiring parallel movement by both hands. The familiar West and Central African dance pose is an equilateral wide stance, with the arms cocked at the sides, both moving as the trunk swings laterally. Its basis is a relaxed middle body, where shoulders and hips can swivel and rotate independently, so that the whole body frame leaps and dances as the dancer shuffles or slides forward, feet flat to the earth for maximum traction.

What I have described, what Walter Brown demonstrated for us that day on the Mississippi levee, is that selfsame body style—the way that Mississippi roustabouts and perhaps their African porter forebears handled heavy loads. By rocking from side to side, the pressure was shifted from leg to leg and, at the same time, the body rocked forward with a surge of energy, which propelled the mover ahead.

Rocking, then, seems to be, first and foremost, the way to move heavy loads in the heat, when all you have is manpower. That this movement also mimes sexual intercourse endows rocking with pleasurable associations. In a word, it is at the very core of African cultural survival. This is where I found it on my journey into the Delta—first in *Rock, Daniel*, the holy dance of the slavery-time black Baptists, linking it to African ritual; second, on the bank of the levee, where it enabled the Mississippi roustabouts to perform herculean tasks. Now the whole world is trying to learn how to rock, and I sometimes wish they had Walter Brown to show them how to do it and explain why it is important to do it the right way.

WALTER BROWN: Now when our boat would get close to a landing, women would be all along the bank like that, you know, standing up on the levee, holl'in, "Hey! Hey! Hey!" *(in falsetto)*

When the *Katie* used to git just yonder, she would make that blow. And that levee there would be lined with women, meeting us.

She'd blow—whooooaa.

ARTHUR: Three longs and one short.

W.B.: Whooooaa—whooooaa—whooooaa—whuh. You would see women comin from everywhere. Meeting they men!

ARTHUR: Meeting payday!

W.B.: Payday. Folks come to meet all the roustabouts, the cooks, the chambermaids, and everybody.

ARTHUR: When that *Kate Adams* blow like that, she's tellin the roustabouts sumpin.

W.B.: When she make them three longs an one short, it'd be sayin, "What you brought us, *Kate*? What you brought us, *Kate*?" Ho-ho! Captain Mike Moore was the pilot, and he'd reach up there and grab the whistle rope and he blow like this *(makes motion like pulling the whistle rope)*: "Womens, womens, womens—your man's in town!" Yeah! He sure could blow it, boy, he could *blow it*! *(Walter and his friends laughed, remembering how those whistles, as if they were African talking drums, signaled the women on shore.)*

ARTHUR: And them women knowed every boat's whistle that come in here! If the *Tennessee Belle* come in, they knowed it, or the *Issaquena*—they knowed every boat.

W.B.: And captain on that *Arthur Harder*, he *knowed* how to blow that whistle. He was kinda deformed. One of his legs trembled, so he put him a strap on his whistle.

ARTHUR: Fixed it with a foot control.

W.B.: Then he would stick his foot, the one that trembled, in that stirrup, and that old whistle would sort of sob-like till every woman in town would come runnin.

ARTHUR: That was the *control* boat. That meant payday. They had an old song:

> *When the* control *boat blow,*
> *You know I got to go—*

W.B.: See, the men had been gone a whole month, and they ain't gon be in town but two or three days. So nachully the women gonna put that temporary man out the door. He must leave so the woman can take care of the man who was workin, the one comin in on that boat.

A.L.: I don't understand.

W.B.: See, the woman be takin care of her *kid man* with the money that she made offa the one workin on the boats. When that boat blowed, she'd put the *kid man* out. And he'd have to stay gone till the boat go back out.

ARTHUR: He was a playboy.

W.B.: Playboy!

A.L.: Did the guys on the boats know about those men?

W.B.: No.

ARTHUR: No, they didn't know about it.

W.B.: I caught one at my house one time.

A.L.: What happened?

W.B.: I left him right there, him an her. I just got my clothes and left um there.

Somebody snickered, then there was a considerable pause. Brown had not made it clear whether he had shot the couple before he "left them there" or simply decamped. As he veered off onto other topics, I was remembering the blues verse about

Why does the rooster crow so long fore day?
Say, why do that rooster crow so long fore day?
To tell the kid man that the real man is on his way.

Walter Brown went right on: "I been all up an down this river. I been from here to Cairo, Illinois, and back to New Orleans."

A.L.: Arthur, was it a good life on those boats? Did you enjoy the work?

ARTHUR: I was eatin and sleepin, didn't have to pay no rent *(laughs)*, no board bill or nothin.

W.B.: And go in the kitchen and get anything you want.

ARTHUR: Anything you want to eat.

A.L.: How much of the time did you have to work?

ARTHUR: Oh, off an then on. Wasn't all day. You sleep half the time, till they get ready for us. When they'd get ready for us, they'd call us and we'd go on out and unload an do everything, then we'd come right back an lay down.

W.B.: He used to ask me, he said, "Partner," he said, "do you think it's too heavy? If you do, we gonna put it down." I said, *"No, we not gonna put it down, we got to rock it round and round."* And we'd carry it on down, we didn't care what it weighed.

ARTHUR: We did more downhill tote than we did up. When we unload from the truck, we had to go down on the walk.

W.B.: And, ah, we didn't never lay nothin down. Me an this man here *(thumbs toward Arthur)* ain't never laid no load down. If it was so heavy that eight people had put it down, me an him would tote it.

ARTHUR: That's all we'd do—get it up. When we'd get it up, we gone.

W.B.: We would get it up! And we'd be rockin.

Then he and Arthur rocked up on the levee, like old John Rouser, improvising new words to the oldest song of the Mississippi Delta, reliving their African version of life on the big river.

Come here, dog, an let's git your bone.
Tell me what shoulder that you want it on.
Everybody talkin about I and I.
Nobody know nothin bout that Roustabout.
Roustabout, baby, Roustabout,
Nobody know about that Roustabout.

Tell me, gal, what you been waitin on?
I been away from her home too long.
Home too long, gal,
Home too long.

Everyday is-a payday here,
But I ain't had nothin in-a forty years.
Forty years, gal, forty years,
I ain't had nothin in-a forty years.

Tell them people they can look for me,
Few more days and-a I'll be free.
I'll be free,
Few more days and I'll be free.

Tell Roberta to unlock that door,
I been where I ain't-a been before.
Tell her to look at her keys,
Then remember to think of me.
Oh, poor me, baby,
Oh, poor me.

FIDDLING FOR THE DEVIL

One of the musical survivors of the river period was eighty-six-year-old Alec Robertson. When we met him in 1942, he was the *chef d'orchestre* to the one-legged black giant who preached and prayed and beat the bass drum in the Holiness chapel. Alec was as yellow and crumbly-looking as a December willow leaf and his hands were two little claws, but he still played a whole lot of guitar. Any evening at all between eight and twelve you could find him up there on the pulpit framming those stomp rhythms while everybody got happy, for the Holiness people were in their protracted meeting and you'd find them in church every night of the week and all day Sundays right on till nearly Christmas.

Once Alec Robertson had been Satan's chief ambassador in Coahoma County. He had "fiddled for the devil for fifty-seven years" at Hillhouse, Rena Laura, Sherrod's, and up and down the river, but just at the penultimate moment in his seventy-fifth year had turned his back on all that. His Holiness ladyfriend, "Missy," paid rent for a little room behind a garage in an alley, gave him a few dollars for eats, and in order to keep him straight, the chapel folk had put an even more senile and sinful oldster in his charge with instructions to keep him away from the bottle. Alec had gone a bit spotty under the strain of so much renunciation, but he was sure of one thing:

My mind, my mind,
My mind done changed.
That old hateful mind I had,
My mind done changed.

"What I mean by mind changing, I used to be rough, but, since I got religion, it changed all them old habits, like you used to be a gambler or something like that, you know. And I don't think a man ought to sing that song unless his mind *is* changed. I have given up sin; I don't do nothing wrong that I know of—coveting my neighbor's wife, telling lies, all such things as that . . .

The band in Gideon, the band in Gideon,
The band in Gideon, over in Jordan,
The band in Gideon, the band in Gideon,
Oh how I long to be there, too.
The saints all singin, the saints all singin,
How I long to be there, too.

"That's old-timey. A shout. That's when you jump up, shouting your joy. That's in your Bible. The old folks happy. They go round shaking hands, fellowshippin. Years and years back in '79 and '80, they didn't know nothin about these new songs; they used to make up their own and just rock.

Move, member, move, Daniel,
Rock till I get home . . .
O sister you'll be called on
For to march in the field of battle
When the warfare shall be ended.
Hallelu!

"That time I was out in the world and I knew more coon songs than anybody in this part the country, I reckon. I can sit here all day and sing them fast coon songs, but I wouldn't do that now for your microphone because they would hear it coming through the radio and that would make a knock on me."

Alec looked wise, and his ancient companion giggled and nodded furiously at this evidence of his friend's sagacity.

"But these records aren't going on the radio," I said. "They're just going down as history. What you ought to do is just sing little snatches of the songs you used to sing."

"Well now, I don't believe I want to. It's against my profession—all these square dances, composing um like that would be bad for me. Wouldn't they be broadcast?"

"No, just put away as history."

"Oh, I see."

"If these were records for broadcasters, there'd have to be a band to play with you," I temporized.

"Oh, well then, that's a different thing. Then I could give the musics. I was thinking they'd be broadcasted over the air. Well, then, how do you like this one?

Mama, make Cindy behave herself,
You better behave yourself!
Mama, Mama, make Cindy behave herself,
You better behave yourself!
Keep on fooling round,
Take a stick and knock her down.
Mama, make Cindy behave herself.

Now it might seem peculiar, in view of old Alec's reluctance, and his broken voice, that so much trouble should have been taken to induce him to mumble over his tattered songs. However, we had found no other secular musician of the Coahoma river era, the days of logrollings and rough-and-tumble square dances at Hillhouse. His repertoire was our most accurate index to the ditties of Coahoma's pioneer days, and it dovetails into the music of the Hills (see chapter 7).

"Now a square dance," said Alec, "is something like *The Old Hen Cackle* and *Fisher's Hornpipe, Billy in the Lowground* and *Leather Britches.* There's no words to them, you know. *The Arkansas Traveler, Mississippi Sawyer, Chicken's a-Crowin in Sourwood Mountain*—you make them cackle when you play—*Old Joe Clark,* and *Lynchburg Town*—*they* all works in the violeen.

"We'd have a caller," Alec went on, "might say most anything. Get an old fellow bout half drunk, he wouldn't care what he was saying them times: 'All to your places like hosses to your traces. Honor your partner, salute your partner, swing your partner, promenade! Then swing corners; right hand to your partner and left hand to your corner. March around. All salute partners again. Then first couple pass to the right. You dance with my partner and I'll dance with yours. Then next couple round. Then swing corners and all promenade and start again.'

"Dance! You ought to seen me buck dance!"

Where you goin, buzzard?
Where you goin, crow?
Goin down the hillside,
Knock Jim Crow.
> *First to the heel*
> *And then to the toe,*
> *Every time you turn around*
> *You knock Jim Crow.*

"That was my buck-and-wing I used to dance on the stage."

Alec clearly stated the general Delta belief that secular amusements put their practitioners into Satan's camp. "Thank God I didn't die then. The devil had his hands on me principally. That's because I used to drink so much. I drink so much, if I'd-a kept it all, I spec I'd have a river by now. I'd do anything a person could do—dip snuff, chew tobacco, drink whiskey, cuss, and run around. Gamble—why I'd wake up in the night wanting a game. Meet you in the road there and sit down right in the road or behind a big tree and shoot dice; look and see if I can see an officer. I do all them kind of mischief, but I never bootlegged. I couldn't never keep enough whiskey to bootleg."

Alec made with thumb and little finger the eloquent gesture of a bottle tipped up high, then licked his lips and rolled his eyes with such a wet grin and such a plaintive expression that it made my throat dusty. The old days were coming back to Alec, the days when he made more money than he could handle, fiddling, picking guitar, and leading his own little square-dance band—the days around 1910 when there were fifteen string bands in the county and all busy, playing serenades to young white ladies, playing excursions on the river, or ripping off the two-steps, polkas, waltzes, or schottisches. Hillhouse had been Alec's principal hangout in the eighties and nineties.

"You asking me have I seen anybody shot down there at Hillhouse. No— but I have walked over dead men. I would hear a gun shoot, but I couldn't tell you nothing that happened, you understand. Course, Saturday night, that was a picnic night for people to get killed, but I was playing there, with my four-piece band, and I never fit. We was down there to play. See, they'd have a picnic and a dance at Hillhouse and pay me twenty-five dollars for two days' singing and *all* the whiskey my people could drink and everything else out there, especially womens.

"I wasn't a man, you know, would just go and bully a person. And I didn't believe in just shooting sharp amongst the women, you know. I always studied myself. If she would chance it, I would chance it, but I wouldn't chance my life. I never was thataway.

"Now I had boys in my band—sometimes they'd have to run through the woods gittin away into town. Sometime I'd pay a violeen player to go with me and two hours later they'd be after him with a shotgun or a pistol or something. Violin players are terrible. I used to tell him, 'You gonna get killed.' And one of them did get killed—Charley Lee shot him right here in Clarksdale, shot one another down right in the street over a woman.

"Both their white boss gonna give um assistance—like my boss gonna give me 'sistance and your boss gonna give you 'sistance—and so they went out like two bulls and shot one another down. I went there and looked over it, stepped right in between um and give one an apple and the other an orange. I saw Charley hand George a cigarette and ask him how he feelin. 'How you feelin, George?' 'I'm feelin all right, Charley. How you feelin?'

"It seems strange to me. People shoot one another down and then ask how they feelin.

"The white folks was just as rough as the colored. They'd get fightin in there and shooting and have us all breaking out the house. They'd be drunk or fightin over women or over gamblin. I used to roll money in wheelbarrows for them gamblers—Virginia Kid, Nate the Kid, Jimmy the Kid, Sam Ivory—they lived right down at Hillhouse. You'd have to pay five dollars at the door to git in where they gamblin; they just dump in; then win seven, eight hundred, thousand dollars. So you can see us dollar gamblers wasn't no good there. But it was us got killed—mighty seldom those big gamblers."

Alec's weary old eyes glittered. He'd saved a surprise for the end.

"Those were the days," said Alec, "when we made music for the white folks in the week and for our own color Saturday nights—the days, back around 1903. Back then I used to play in the rhythm section of Professor W. C. Handy's band. You know, he come in here to lead our Clarksdale band, don't you? W. C. Handy, he was a gentleman. But I reckon he could afford to be . . ."

BRASS BANDS

W. C. Handy, composer of *The St. Louis Blues*, came to Clarksdale in the river period, to lead its brass band. Post–Civil War America had a regular mania for English- and German-rooted brass-band music. Indeed, right up through World War I the brass-band concert was the *ne plus ultra* of American small-town entertainment. The prosperous Delta was not behindhand in this respect. The Delta's best-known plantation owner supported a brass band among his slaves, as a former band member told us.

"Jefferson Davis organized a band for his Negroes, and he hired a man in Vicksburg named Charles Morgan to teach them boys music. After they got so they could play, he bought um a uniform, and he name that band the Davis Bend Band. Escort him everywhere he went. Fourteen men in the band. Played *Grand National, Fool's Watch, Mount Rose, Dream On, Flee as the Bird to His Mountain, Not Guilty, I'm a Soldier, Farm Quick Step*, all that kind of stuff. I played myself. Yeah, I played *Dixie*."

All through our Delta research we met blacks who had benefited from their association with the white planter aristocracy. Some children of mixed-blood or faithful slaves or houseservants had been endowed with land, were sent away to school, helped in business, given white-collar jobs. Others managed to acquire property and to prosper as farmers. Jefferson Davis helped one devoted retainer to found the independent black community of Mound Bayou, which before the days of night-riding reaction regularly sent a black man to Congress.

The social studies of the Delta discovered a black upper class, composed of the wealthier lighter-skinned families, who held themselves aloof, as an upper caste, from the black sharecroppers and day laborers. It is their attitude that underlies the color prejudice that sullies black folklore. But the success story of this upper-class group, their social climbing and their decadence, hardly concerns us, since few of this group had much to do with the growth of the indigenous black music of the Delta.

The exception was a retired bank clerk named Stack Mangham, whom Lewis Jones found living in Friars Point. Stack told us about his close friend, W. C. Handy:

Music has always been my hobby. When Handy was here, I'd go out and play, make four or five dollars. I'd always give it to him to help him stay here. Me, I had a good job, made good money.

You see, I worked in the Planters Bank as a clerk for thirty-two years. There was a man here named Sam Hurst, a wealthy man and a big politician and one of the stockholders in the bank. They wanted a porter at the bank and the cashier asked him to find one that would be reliable. He proposed me. The first day I was there one of the bookkeepers got sick and the cashier asked me to do a little writing. After he found out I could do it, in six months I was promoted to a clerkship. I made what was a big salary here—fifteen hundred dollars a year and a bonus for thirty-two years.

Fact is, I made more than some of the white men who worked there, and I think some of the new men complained about that. One day Mr. Holland, president of the bank, called everybody in his office and made a little talk to us. He said, "We pay everybody here according to what they are worth to the bank. If you don't get paid as much as somebody else, it's because you aren't worth as much as that man is." Nothing else was ever said.

Old Man Millsaps who founded the bank was the richest man in the state. One day he came in the bank and saw me working and said to Mr. Holland, "If you whitewash this fellow he'd be all right." Mr. Holland said, "Stack can do as much work as any five men in this bank. He can go out and play music all night and come in here and turn out more work than five of them."

I can't remember when I first became interested in music. My father was an old-time singer. When I was a boy, he had a choir and trained them to sing by notes. He had learned back in slavery. His old master had taught him shape notes. The first instrument I played was cornet. I just picked it up and learned it myself. Then I learned clarinet. When Handy came here, I was playing the clarinet. They had a white band here and a man had bought him a clarinet, but he couldn't learn to play it. He sold it to me for fifteen dollars. I sent to Philadelphia and bought myself an instructor for seventy-five cents.

There was a band in Arkansas, at Helena, that used to come here and play. Charlie Banks and I decided we would organize one of our own. This was the first band in Clarksdale. The band Handy came to teach was the second band. Where we had twelve pieces, the band Handy directed had twenty. The white people of the town gave us our first uniforms—cost ten dollars a suit. The music played was nearly all marches and waltzes. After Handy came here, he began to teach us overtures and classical music. We would play for the societies like the Masons and the Sir Knights and Daughters, and for political campaigns, march around and go up there in town and play on some main corner for about a half hour.

Our ten-piece orchestra played for dances, for both white and colored, but mostly for white. The white dances would pay you five dollars a man and expenses. Colored dances were given as what we called "script" dances—so much at the door.

We were playing practically the same music they play now, only we called it slow drag and barrelhouse, and now they call it jazz and swing. I hear pieces I used to play thirty years ago that are popular. A few years ago *Harvest Moon* was popular, and *Playmates.* We played it as *Iola, Maple Leaf Rag,* composed by a Negro—Scott Joplin.

Those days, there were different attitudes toward secular music. I had a little trouble in my church once. They brought up my playing in the orchestra as an excuse. Traveling musicians and musicians in shows were supposed to be bad. An incident I remember was funny was when Eugene Booze married at Mound Bayou and we carried our band down there. The people cut up about us playing in the church. I remember one old lady saw the trombone and she hollered, "Look, there's the devil's pitchfork." That was about 1901.

I didn't pay much attention to the blues and that music until Handy came here. He didn't either at first. I remember when we first became conscious of it. We were playing down at Cleveland for a dance and the people had been dancing, but they had gotten tired and sleepy and nobody was dancing much except a few couples on the floor. We took intermission and three fellows came in there with a guitar, a mandolin, and a bass violin, and started to play and the people began to get wild. Everybody woke up and got interested and began to dance. Handy got the idea. He went back in the corner and took his pencil and a piece of paper and copied a part of what they were playing. When Handy went from here to Memphis, he finished the piece after working on it for a couple of years and called it *Mr. Crump,* and later the *Memphis Blues.* It's the same thing we heard that night at Cleveland.

When Handy came here, his ambition was to write marches. He brought a march with him that he had written that was published as *Hail to the Spirit of Freedom.* He said then that he was going to be the March King—another John Philip Sousa. I think that was the only march he wrote. After he got interested in the blues, he never wrote another one.

Handy found at least one more blues while he lived in the Delta. One night he was waiting for a train in a deserted station at Tutwiler, a small town a few miles north of Clarksdale. His train was hours late; time dragged interminably until a poorly dressed man slumped down on the hard bench next to the composer. He was carrying a battered guitar, and soon he began to play what Handy now knew was a blues, but in a novel way. By sliding his knife along the guitar strings (like a bottleneck), he produced a silvery, crying tone that followed the gliding notes of his song:

I'm goin where the Southern cross the Dog . . .

He sang on and on, with variations. Handy was scribbling away. It was just a one-phrase melody, but hard to put down in notes. It had intervals that did not match the piano scale, little quavers that changed with each repetition, and often the voice stopped and the guitar filled the space with strange sounds that no guitar Handy knew had made before. All of us could tell him now that this was slide guitar with a country blues played by an ancestor of Muddy Waters and Robert Johnson. But this was 1903, the first time anyone had heard a blues holler set to guitar.

I'm goin where the Southern cross the Dog . . .

W. C. Handy, although he was a little nervous in that dark station at three o'clock in the morning, was beginning to feel a composer's happiness. This tune was as strange and as spicy as East St. Louis and Memphis blues. One thing puzzled him.

"What's the Dog?" he asked.

"That's the ol Yellow Dog line,"[3] said the singer, "better known as the Yazoo and Mississippi Valley. It cross the Southern down here round Moorhead. And I've made me a song about that—an old railroad song."

A new era had just begun, and Handy had it in his notebook, the era of the railroad blues.

I hate to hear that lonesome whistle blow . . .

As the railroads pushed into the Delta and ran their spurs out into the cotton lands, the cotton business boomed. In the river period only those plantations near a waterway had easy access to the market. Now the cotton moved along shining rails rather than narrow muddy roads. The organizers of railroad development suddenly became the real powers in the state, for the planter government in Jackson was willing to do anything to persuade them to work their magic. The man who actually organized the Illinois Central, which eventually became the dominant north–south line in the state, was, in origin, an obscure con man named Collis P. Huntington. By the end of his life of dealing in Mississippi land grants, manipulating the legislature, and swindling the U.S. government, he had become one of the most powerful men in America. Meantime, Big Daddy and all his friends were pushed to the wall by his oversweetened financing and by his exorbitant demands for profit.

Far below this cloudland of money and corruption, the right-of-ways were filled in through the swamps and the cool steel rails pushed out into the green tangle of Delta woodlands. Black railroad gangs laid the track and kept the lines in repair. It is their story that concerns us, because it is their spirit that infuses the Delta railroad songs. One afternoon long ago I watched one of these black railroad-building gangs at work.

DRIVING STEEL

The track ran up over the sandy hill, cutting a blazing yellow track into the piney woods. At the crest of the hill two hammermen were driving spikes, black torsos gleaming in the sunlight, their mauls swinging fast and wide, the spikes spurting into the oak ties. Behind them, rising through and clouding the green tops of the pines, rose a curtain of smoke from the waiting construction locomotive.

Old Blue, the grey mare I was riding, was a railroad horse and she could walk the ties like a person. She carried me past the spikers, through the veil of smoke, and we came to the locomotive, sighing in the forest. Down past it Old Blue and I came upon a steel gang laying down a new line on the roadbed. A long flatcar with a moving belt along its top poured out a stream of railroad ties, and as these heavy six-foot timbers rolled off the end of the car, they were caught one after another by the tie toters, who shouldered them like so many matchsticks and skipped off with them down the right-of-way. As each man reached the end of the growing file of ties, he tossed his down in order and came running back along the wobbling timbers, as surefooted as a squirrel. Five of these tie toters formed a human beltline, swiftly and skillfully laying down the line of ties for the steel rails that were soon to follow. One of them, a tall yellow-skinned man in a ragged coat, would now and again throw back his head and cry out a long series of wailing notes, each held out and ornamented with many quavers, the words something like

> *Ooo, baby, doncha go-oo, while the blood's runnin warm,*
> *While the blood runnin warm in your veins,*
> *Oo-oo, Lord Godamighty.*

There was now a row of about a hundred ties along the roadbed. The human beltline paused, and the engineer in the control cab leaned back to light his pipe, but in moments the steel gang sprang back into action. Two men began levering a long rail of steel toward the edge of the flatcar. They heaved together till the breath burst out of their mouths and a twelve-foot steel rail rolled over the side of the car and fell into three steel arms below, then was shunted downward to the track. As it came scooting out along the ties, the yellow man and his ebony partner grabbed it with huge iron pinchers and yanked it along until their buddies could catch it and lay it on the ties.

Swinging from the hips, they rammed the end of that rail into the buckle. Clang! It was joined. The steel man who squatted down to screw the buckle tight had to leap out from beneath the wheel of the already moving train. As he jumped to safety, grinning and swearing, his buddies bent over with laughter, the smoke puffed out of the locomotive stack, and the flatcar rumbled to the end of the newly buckled rails and stopped, and again the stream of ties began to flow down the roadbed.

As I sat on Old Blue, smoking and watching these men sweating, laughing, singing, and urging each other to "come on while the blood's running warm," the little spur line grew on down through the wooded valley. Each task had a special song. Sometimes a steel caller employed wild sweet cries to keep the lifters together as they handled the rails. At times, several work songs were being sung simultaneously—chants for tie toting, for dealing steel, for buckling, for spiking down—and mingled in wild and spontaneous heterophony. This rich and powerful river of song carried the gleaming rail line into the hot green woods. Meanwhile, the men of the steel gang, who handled the rails and ties like straws and their heavy mauls and wrenches like toothpicks, never slackened or stumbled, never got in each other's way. The foreman, a quiet Mexican with a white smile, told me that his gang laid an average of a quarter mile of track every day.

Track work goes by stages. When Old Hannah stood in the middle of the sky, the steel gang laid the last rail of the day and turned back down the spur to the spot where I had first come upon a pair of hammermen at work. After they drank deep from the water bucket, they all picked up mauls and began spiking down the rails they had laid and buckled together. They worked in pairs, each man with a six-pound hammer, their blows alternating regularly on the head of a spike until it seemed to flow into the tie and catch the edge of the rail like a live thing. For half an hour the eight men dogged down the rails with their mauls, and the spur was done.

All this time their foreman had not said a word to them. They had carried out this complex operation entirely on their own, efficiently and speedily, not in silence in white style, but noisily, with joking, singing, laboring like demons in the thick heat of the pinewoods, where I could hardly venture on horseback. I realized that this was how the heavy work of the Deep South had all been done—by black labor, not by brute force in any sense, but by skilled craftsmen, thriving in the semitropical heat.

As they drove the bright steel rails into this Southern forest, they put together multiple strands of melody and movement in conformity with the highest canons of black style, creating an African-American ballet on the spot. Thus they and other black railroad men transformed railroad building into a rhythmic creation, that belonged to them and that sang of progress, in African style.

Later in the afternoon I walked to the bunk car, where the crew was waiting to be carried into town. The car was like a furnace, the air solid tobacco smoke and profanity. Some of the steel men were lying asleep, their sweat forming little pools on the bare benches where they lay. Others were roistering like kids after school, playing tricks on one another, mock-fighting, bantering. Roars of laughter burst out. But underneath the hubbub ran a steady current of proud talk about their work. They were reliving this day and other adventurous days on the job, and they spoke with pleasure and excitement. The talk was frothy with profanity. Two men were trying to shout each other down and this woke one of the sleepers. He glared around him: "For Christ's sake, when will you bastards stop talking about the goddam railroad. Don't we get enough of that on the job? Change the conversation."

SHAKE, SHAKE, MATTIE

Shake, shake, Mattie, shake, rattle an roll,
Shake, shake, Mattie, Mattie, wanna win my gold.

It was sometimes hard to get a real railroad man to talk about anything else. Railroading was the best job available to blacks in the Deep South. A railroad man got some respect from his bosses, who needed skilled men and a happy gang to get the work done so the trains could run on time. The money was steady and better than on any other job, and a woman considered herself lucky if her man worked on the railroad. As the song said,

Mattie, when you marry, get a railroad man,
Every day'll be Sunday and a dollar be in your hand.

The railroad spurs that linked the Delta plantations to market towns and brought the logs to the sawmills had fanciful local names like the Yellow Dog and the Peavine. Their engines, equipped with musical whistles, sang of escape routes to a wonderful free world somewhere else. Anonymous black musicians, longing to grab a train and ride away from their troubles, incorporated the rhythms of the steam locomotive and the moan of their whistles into the new dance music they were playing in jukes and dance halls. Boogie-woogie forever changed piano playing, as ham-handed black piano players transformed the instrument into a polyrhythmic railroad train. Boogie was just one of the sanguine, we're-going-someplace styles that black folk musicians, unique among world composers of that time, created to express feelings of liberation the railroad introduced into life. The honking, gasping, chugging railroad music that Southern blacks discovered in the harmonica now speaks to everyone, across all borderlines. For the blues poets of the Delta, the railroad ranked next to women as a subject.

When the blues overtake me, gonna grab that train and ride.

When a woman blue, she hang her little head and cry,
When a man get blue, he grab that train and ride.

Yonder come that train, red-blue lights behind,
Red for trouble, blues for a worried mind.

If you've ever been down, you know just how I feel,
I feel like an engine ain't got no drivin wheel.

There were great black railroad ballads, too, like *Casey Jones* and *Railroad Bill,* but the finest black railroad songs were those that lubricated the work of railroad construction and repair. These songs are conspicuous in the African-American repertoire for the sweetness of their melodies, the gracefulness of their rhythms, and the lightheartedness of their lyrics. Almost every couplet brings a smile, for most of them carry a double meaning that is a great comfort to a man swinging a ten-pound hammer all day long in the broiling sun. Indeed, the tools used by railroad trackmen are extremely heavy, but since the jobs are steady and the pay regular and give a man a sense that he is doing something worthwhile, the fantasies that throng the songs are usually pleasant ones. More likely than not, Julie or Rosie or Mary was happy to see her railroad man home for supper and bed, because his work truly provided for his family.

"It's a good job, I mean, you can raise a family with the job," a section-gang man, Wilbert Puckett, told us. "Back then you didn't make too much money, but it was enough, you know, to have a job, to support your family off of."

"It was good enough for me to put five kids through high school and college, too," added his partner. "Course it was tough, but I made it."

Another man joined in: "A lot of mens have got hurt handling steel. Steel is very dangerous. It's heavy and if they hadn't devised some method of handling that steel with a big bunch of men, they'd always be putting out money on hospital bills and injuries, see. And they had to have some system to protect that, you know, to prevent that from happening all the time. And at its best, we have accidents with it."

"When you come to work on Monday morning at seven o'clock," said another. "You get out there on the job working, singing comes according to what job you doing. Now you take lining track, that singing was just a rhythm that the labor used in keeping the time and getting the track lined like the bossman wanted. But wasn't no joy in singing whatsoever. I mean, that it was just a part of the way we men set up to work, to get the job done."

His friend disagreed: "Singing on the railroad is just like a band on a football field. That band gives the team spirit to play and that singing gives you pep to work."

> *All right, now,*
> *Up under the rail*
>   *up on the tie,*
> *Up under the rail*
>   *where the tie lie.*
> *Up under the rail*
>   *up under the tie,*
> *Up under the rail*
>   *where the tie lie.*
> *What'd the old lady say*
>   *when she came to die?*
> *Hand on her pussy and*
>   *the other on her thigh—*
> *Oh, Lord, have mercy,*
> *Oh, Lord, have mercy!*

TRACK CALLER

The railroad man whom Lewis Jones located met us at the motel where I was staying. His name was Houston Bacon. Bacon looked about forty, a lithe, loose-jointed, light-brown-skinned man, red at the cheekbones, with a quiet voice and a quizzical smile. He'd been a track caller on a section gang for more than a decade. He'd brought a six-inch section of rail and a knife so that he could rap out the rhythms of the varied jobs.

It takes constant maintenance work by the section gangs stationed all along a railroad to keep the rails in line and the roadbed solid. The track caller is often paid a bit more than regular gang members, because his sung recitative starts, stops, and coordinates their efforts as well as sets the pace of all the tasks the gang carries out. He acts, in effect, like a musical assistant foreman, who, while he coordinates the work with his chants, keeps everybody in a good humor with his banter.

Houston Bacon, like so many other Delta blacks, was orphaned at an early age and began to support himself by the time he was eight years old. But he appears to have been as lucky in life as he was at cards, as he told us:

I'm right knowledgeable about this railroad business now, but it didn't come down to me from my father. I just happened on it. See, I left home young. My father died when I was eight years old and, after he died, I didn't want nary another man over me and I walked off. I had a brother stayed in Memphis and I called myself going down to stay with him. So as I was going down the road a man named W. M. Donald picked me up in his car and say, "Boy, don't you want to go with me?"

I say, "I don't know where you're going, sir."

"You ever hear of the Wolf River bottom?" I tell him, "Yes, sir."

"Well, we running a levee camp down there and I could let you drive the water wagon and pay you four or five dollars a week—I do better than that, I'll give you a dollar and a half a day if you come on and go with me." So I went along with him to the levee camp in the Wolf River bottom out from Memphis.

Well, I was young and I didn't know no one out there on the job. The man would give me five dollars sometimes, the next Saturday give me four; give me my clothes, my something to eat, my candy and my cigarettes. One little gal on the job there—he'd let me give her candy and cigarettes if I wanted to; but I couldn't give nobody else candy and cigarettes. If I did, next payday I didn't git none.

Mostly, I didn't know what to do with my money. I'd just keep it. I was just a little bit of an old boy, you know, and the womens would pat me on my jaws and they'd say, "Hey, give me a dollar." So I'd hand um a dollar and I thought I was doing a big thing, but I didn't know nothing about nothing.

So I had money, you know, and a fellow named Joe Davis and another, named Buddy Davis—one of them picked a guitar and the other one picked a mandolin—commenced to like me. They called me "they son." After they called me "they son," I'd go around with um and play a git-fiddle and that way I went with um and followed um and, when they'd git broke, I'd break back to Mr. Donald's and he'd hire me every time I'd come—call me his "little boy." Then I'd make some more money.

At last, one time out rambling around, we got broke and Buddy, he start to work for Mister House cutting right-of-way on the railroad. Mister House ask me if I could cut and I told him "Yessir." Buddy told him, "Yessir, that's my son, you can put him to work," and so I started to work and worked there a little better'n a month out in the bushes, cut a few ties, toted water, and then "the ax fell." See, a man like Mr. House gets an allowance every month. One month the allowance will let him work ten men, and maybe the next month eight, and that throw two mens off. Well, he cut off the youngest men and, as I was a young man, the ax fell on me and I got cut off, me being nine years old at the time.

Myself and Buddy, we went back to town and they played around in one or two little nightclubs and things. Then I got a chance to be a little sheik on gambling, you know. I stuck with my buddies and gambled while they played music. They carried me to the harvests and I found out that I could pick berries and things like that. I just run from berry harvest to sugarbeet harvest to grain harvest, back on the river around, and on the railroads backwards and forwards. We never stayed no place long, and all the time I was learning to be a real good gambler. I got me a toby [a charm] and I'd just set him in the house where I was gambling and most generally I'd win.

I remember a little song I used to sing when I was dealing cooncan:

I'm a ten-card dealer and a 'leven-card layer,
A dice shooter and a poker player.

O shush, grouchy Stella, don't say a word,
I'll get you that dress if it's in Vicksburg.

Boys, she want a dress cost a dollar a yard.
I'm gonna git that dress if it busts my heart.

O fair baby, don't you weep and moan,
You got a job long as I got a home.

I'd not be singin to no rhythm of the cards. Maybe I'd be shufflin and dealin, maybe I'd just be drawing and singing.

Quite natural, when you playing cooncan, your hands is always faster than your eye. Everybody say "I'm gambling fair," but don't no man gamble fair. He gonna cheat you if he can and tell you it's a fair game. Hand's always faster than the eye, but you have to know what you doing because when they see you lucky, they gonna try to find out how you is winning. But me, I used to play "green and lucky," and they'd say, "He's a hardworking boy and he's just got lucky." That way I could break everybody who came along, because the whole world will play a working man as a fool.

And I found out that a working man has a better show for gambling and hustling than anybody else. Why? Because he'll get out and work hard and so nobody think to watch him, but the hand is always quicker than the eye and I used to tote a pat hand all the time and nobody could see I had more than two cards. And when my card come along, I'd just fall out. Then you'd hear that other song I remember a little bit of:

Jack of diamonds once in time,
It did run my buddy blind.
>   *Jack of diamonds's a hard card to play.*

That old Jack (the one-eyed jack card) *can't see so good,*
He will fall and make you lose.
>   *Jack of diamonds's a hard card to play.*

You take a man, the biggest portion of the time when he be singin, that's a broke man. When a man git broke, he git hongry. Every woman he see, pretty near, look good to him. He just sits around thinking of what he could have done with the money when he did have some. As long as he got money, he's thinkin bout nothin but bettin.

See a man bettin a quarter or fifty cents, ain't much to him. You can't do much with him. But a man that's gamblin a right smart amount of money, like they's as much as three or four hundred dollars in the game, he could win good. But if he happen to git busted, why, then he'll start to singin. You can practically always tell a broke man. He gonna want *every*thing he see in the house. If somebody come by selling pies, he wants that. He wants to drink. He wants to talk with women. Everything going wrong with him and he'll go to singing and hollering.

Take that ace, deuce, and queen,
It gonna turn my money green.
>   *Jack o' diamonds's a hard card to play.*

Now that broke man liable to git lucky, too. He may take a nickel or dime and clean out the whole house.

I remember all them little funny things from the days I used to be a rambler. See, I'd never work long at a time anyplace—maybe two or three months or something like that. Yet, after while, I gradually settled down. First

I worked in one railroad gang from '29 up until '36. That was when I was with my first wife. Me and her, we have separated. I quit that wife and the job, too, and come here to Clarksdale, and I been working at the same job and settled married ever since.

I reckon I just got tired of loafing and running around through the world. I just got tired of living that kind of life. I'd been practically all over the U-nited States and I'd been lucky enough to be out of the U-nited States twice, so I said, "Well, I'll settle down. Be a man!" So now I'm regular track caller on the section of the I.C. line. You gonna hear me out there every good day singing and hollering on that railroad.

What do I sing? All sorts of foolishness to make the work go easy. Like we be unloading steel from the car as it move along—one piece about every fifteen feet. Every time I say "Chunk i'on," a steel rail go off the car and hit the ground—Ding! You may think that's fast, but we work fast at everything we do. Six, eight, ten, or twelve men in the gang. One man deals—shove his wrench up under one end of the rail, sort of cock it up a little bit. That give other men chance to shove their lining bars up under the edge, and when I say "Chunk i'on," that rail gone.

Get you bars and let's move on down a little bit.
We gonna drop off a few for the man,
Ain't got but nine more.
All right, bars under him.
Ready?
Chunk i'on!　Ding!
Chunk i'on!　Ding!
Chunk i'on so—　Ding!

Wope! We gonna move on down a little further.
Ain't got but nine more.
Gonna pinch on down a little bit, Shorty.
You know what Eadie gonna tell you tonight—
"You want a pair of bloomers, you better come on!"
That man gonna tell you toreckly he don't want you.
All right, Shorty.
Chunk i'on!　Ding!
Chunk i'on!　Ding!
Chunk i'on again—　Ding!

Move on, Shorty,
You see that crossing down there,
So creep on, terrapin.
Chunk i'on, chunk i'on so—   Ding!

Shorty is just the name I give my partner. Every man out on the job gonna be called some alias name to make for more sport and fun at the work. And then we always be bringing some girl into the thing just to keep the spirit more brighter.

You done unload your rails on the ties now. Now you got to go back and set your rails in the buckles so they hold together. You got four men on one end of the rail and four men on the other, handling that steel with dogs, meaning great big pinchers.

I holler "Get your dogs on it" and the men catch hold the rail. Then I holler "Raise up" and the whole gang snatches the rail up off the ties. "Jump i'on"—we jumps it four to six feet until the steel is right on the end of the tie plate.[4] Then you "jinte i'on"—it fits right on in a slot between the buckles. And when it jintes, it rings.

Dogs on it!
Loaded so.
Raise up all along.
Jump i'on!   Blang!

Raise up all along.
Jump i'on!   Blang!
Nod his head, Shorty.
Way up yonder.
Why don't you straighten that rail there?
Straighten it up, Shorty, like you done last night.
You know how you done it last night.
You gonna fumble at the hole thataway?
I know good and well you didn't do that last night.
Jinte it on back there, Shorty.
Jine hard!   Blang!

Four men on each end. And when I say "Jump i'on," they snatch it up and jump it along about six feet. They's one man back there guides it when its head is cocked up in the air. When I tell him "Nod its head, Shorty," he moves the head of the rail down so we can fit it right in the hole. Then you say "Jinte i'on" and we slam them rails together and moves right on down and git the next one.

Jinte on back there.
Jinte hard, Shorty.
Nod his head one time
Way up yonder.
Jinte on light!
You gonna see Eadie when you get home this evening?
Jinte on light!
Jinte hard now!   Blang!
Move on down now,
Creep on so.

Yessir, we works just as fast as I be singin. We don't take but two or three minutes to a rail, and I have laid as high as a rail a minute. That means take a rail out of a curve—take the nuts out of it, uncouple it, put in a new rail, take bars and couple it back together and complete it. One rail, one minute. Twenty rails, twenty minutes. We got to do that when a train due.

That's workin mighty fast, naturally. Some men can't stand the gait. They'll break down. That will happen to any man when he workin too hot. That's something everybody got to watch down here in this part of the world—gettin too hot. You take the average man nowadays, he work too free. He don't know he's too hot until he's done collapsed. When I get too hot, you know what I do? I quit and walk off. Set down. And *rest*. If I don't feel I can make it, I go on home. I ain't gonna get too hot and fall out like some do.

That some of the responsibility of the track caller—he must call the work up to what his men can do . . . So I was tellin you about couplin up and spiking down and now we get ready to line the track up straight. I do the callin and my gang do just what I tell um. They pull to my singin.

O Lu-lu-lu
I'm gonna tell you all about it now.

My wife
Louisa

In bed
With a fever
So bad
Hate to leave *her.*

(The track-lining gang is ready with their heavy iron-lining bars, jammed under the section of rail that is out of line. The foreman, twenty yards ahead, sights down the track. The track caller, paid to amuse the gang and provide the beat for them to heave together, begins to improvise couplets in a sweet, fluty voice. He paces the work, pushing it, but not letting them overdo, employing the subtleties of African rhythmics so that men heave as one.

(The gang heaves and sings together on the accented beats, until the foreman sees the track has come into line, yells "Whoa-up!" and tells them how far up to move their bars for the next efforts, and this goes back and forth till the gang is at the right point; then the caller begins to rhyme again.)

FOREMAN: *Whoa-up! Half ahead there.*

CALLER: *How you like that?*
   F: *Come up a quarter.*
    C: *How's that?*
   F: *All right.*

Well, if you can't rap with them linin bars,
Well, don't stop inside them shanty cars.
 Ho, *boys, way* over,
 Ho, *boys, way* over.
  Whoa-up, move up in center now.
   How's that?
  Back up two irons. That's right.
  Hit it hard.
Take a mule
And a track *jack*
For to line
This track *back.*
  Hey, get up in the quarter there.
  Ain't got a quarter, give you fifty cents.

Lawd, Lawd, Lawd, Lawd.
What the old lady say when the meat give out?
Settin in the corner with her mouth poked out.

> *Here,* Ring,
> *Catch a* rab*bit,*
> *Here,* Ring,
> *Catch a* rab*bit,*
>> *Whoa-up. Now go up in the quarter and hit it.*
>> *Just one more pull now.*

(And then to divert his weary gang, the caller playfully brings in images of their favorite subject—the reward awaiting the men home at the end of their hard, hot day.)

Lawd, Lawd, Lawd, Lawd.
Uncle Bud got geese, Uncle Bud got ducks,
Uncle Bud got gals that really can fuck.

    Light
    Tech *it*
    Bare*ly*
    Stretch *it*
    Light
    Tech *it*
    Bare*ly*
    Stretch *it*

Houston continued:

Now you might think it's funny that a track caller like me should carry on so much foolishness on the job—joreeing, we call it. Well, I always like to have somebody like Shorty in my gang because I always can tease him about first one little thing and then another. That way we all have a little fun, make him *hot*, you know. You work along there, never say anything, and everything will be going *dead*, see; but if you have a little spirit, your work goes along easy. A day's work would be hard and worrisome to you if you thinkin bout nothin but your work. So I tells a little funny tale, just anything to keep everybody jolly and happy.

Like sometimes I might tell um about the little boy that went off to carry dinner to his papa at the gin and on the way watched um switching cars down on the railroad. He come running back home and got after his mama to play a new game with him. "What's that, son?" "We gonna play train, Mama. I show you how." "All right, son, I'm ready." So the little boy give her the signal. "What's that mean, son?" "That means to back up." Then he give her the next signal. "What's that mean, son?" "That means to couple up good." She went ahead to see if she coupled up good, then he hollered, "Too-toot." "What that mean, son?" "That's the high ball, Mama, means get your black ass out of town!"

Course, we don't joree like that *all day long*. If the men are working real hot, you don't hear nothing but the caller. But, if it ain't real hot, they'll be laughing and jollying each other. That's just *they way*. Practically everybody say something and be talking and lively.

Houston's account reminded me of the *coumbites,* the name for neighborhood work parties that I had seen in Haiti, where the folks gathered to cultivate a neighbor's field. They drank rum all day as they worked. They sang. They joked and engaged in male horseplay that brought the collective sod-busting to a halt, when someone was upended on the ground. Roars of laughter broke out and robust insults were exchanged. Then, after the bottle went round in a storm of noisy remarks, someone began to tap out a sexy rhythm on a hoe blade and a lewd song was raised, with mentions of feminine sexual parts in every line. Like a giant earth mover, the hoe blades flashing in the sun, together they chewed away at the earth like a huge steam plow. The terrible tropical sun beat down. Rivers of sweat poured off gleaming black bodies and, with shouts and singing, the work was quickly and merrily done, in sociable African style.

Houston went on:

A good boss don't mind, because he know that if nobody don't say nothing, it would be a dull gang, a gang that wouldn't have no spirit for working. A boss that ain't going to allow nobody to talk, why, mighty little work he get done, mighty little. Take a man that will tell you to "go head on and put in twenty ties to the man or fifteen ties to a man and then we'll go home," well, now, he'll most'n happen to git that work done that *day*.

Every foreman got a different way. Don't no two of um work alike. Some of um love to tell you everything you got to do, That's miserable to you. You've got to do it *his* way. If you don't, the first word he'll say, "Why you trying to run my job, ain't you?! I'm boss, understand, *me*, I'm boss."

Don't never try to explain. Don't never tell him what your old boss, Mister So-and-so, done. First thing he'll say is, "That's the way Mister So-and-so learnt you how to rat on the job."

Whatsonever new foreman tell you to do, go on and do it. Regardless if it's wrong—if he say do it, do it—if it's right, do it. Always let him know that he's the boss and you ain't *never* the boss, and you'll get along. But otherwise he'll go out to break you and by the time he broke you, you done broke in a way you ain't good to yourself and nobody else, because every time you kinda lighten up to catch your breath, first thing he say is, "You rat, you don't want to work nohow."

Everything you got to do, he'll get back at you, and you'll have to walk out on him. They'll make a man fire himself. Yeah! They'll tell you, "That's all right, I can get rid of you." That "That's-all-right" is a big word. He means he is gonna get even with you, but you don't know how it's gonna be done. So when you hear "That's all right," you better walk off and leave and find you another job.

"So I hates to go from one foreman to another. I like a man don't mind a little fun. If he let you alone to be jolly and pleasant, you'll git three times more work done than you would if he dogging you. If we go along out there, jolly and laughing all day long, we git plenty of work done. Just like we're tamping ties, I'll keep singing foolishness until the job git done.

Now we got to get the tracks settin level on the roadbed. There'll be a gang of men with the tampers. Tampers are tools for packing the gravel tight in under the ties to keep the track level. When the jack crew lifts the rail up, I'm hollering at the jack man. He's hollering back. Then I'm callin up, the gang is singin with me and droppin their tampers in time to the song.

> *Get up behind me.*
>   *All right.*
> *How you like that?*
>   *All right.*
> *Gittin away.* (clicking of jack)
> *How you like that?*
>   *All right. Shake it a little bit.*
> *Talk back me now. I'm gonna catch um.*

That old black gal keeps on a-grumblin,
Bout a new pair of shoes, buddy, bout a new pair of shoes.

Pull off them shoes I bought you,
Put your feet on the ground, buddy, put your feet on the ground.

Got that un caught up. What you lookin at now?
Center ahead.
How you like that for center?
One eye.
How you like that?
All right.
Gittin away. (clicking of jack)
All right.
Gone again.

Where you goin when you leave here, Shorty?
Goin to the jinte ahead.
You like that, Shorty?
That's all right.
Gone again. (clicking of jack)
All right. Git back.
Wasn't that enough, boys,
Run a monkey-man blind?
See a heavy-hipted woman
Just reel and
Rock er behind.
Oh, look how she walk, boys,
So big and fine.
Oh, look how she walk, boys,
Way she reel and
Rock 'er behind.

(The work pace begins to slow.)

Well, every Monday mornin,
Buddy, when I rise
Got a pick and a shovel,
Big buddy, hangin by my side.

What you lookin at, Shorty?
Give me a quarter down there, Houston?
   How you like that? Goin home to dinner after while.
   Got to eat sometime, you know.
All right. Git up on it.
   Gone again. (clicking of jack)
Whoa. Shake it heavy.
   How's that?
All right, got one more pull.
   I'm gonna eat then.
Go ahead.

(The men are tiring and the caller is letting the foreman know.)

We can't tamp no nine-mile section
All in one day, buddy,
All in one day, boy.

(For the last hard moments of the job, the caller sings about women and sex.)

Oh, shake, shake, Mattie gal,
Shake-a, rattle and roll,
Well, you never know the diffunce,
Oh honey, till your belly swole.
   Oh, shake, shake, Mattie,
   Shake it up well,
   Well, you never know the diffunce,
   Oh honey, till you belly swell.
Julie Montgomery
Is a girl I trust,
Way she always a-hollerin,
Big buddy, git your money's worth.
   Oh jimp-jamp, Julie,
   Jump-a, rattle and roll,
   If God don't bless you
   The Devil gonna damn your soul.

You know what you mean when you say "jimp-jamp Julie"? Well, she shakes it up to you like she done last night. You git anything last night? No. Then you don't know nothing about "jimp-jamp Julie." When it git like that with me it's a poor go, a poor go. You don't have spirit to do nothin when you miss it. You do that, you be mad all the next day. Can't nobody get along with you. *I* gets hot with the world. I don't care what happens. I want to see Jimp-Jamp Julie. When she jump mighty well, then I'm pleased and happy the next day.

Yes, thank you, I'll take a dram of whiskey. I takes one whenever I can get it and don't care who know it. I don't mean I go out and do like some folks—go out and get sloppy drunk. You can't take care of your job if you do things like that. You have to have a guide to everything. You can overdo any*thing*. A man can set in the house and overdrink water, you know.

You catch a man what don't never drink no whiskey and be out in the exposure, well, he always be hurtin or achin and he can't halfway pick up all the time. But if he drink a little whiskey along, that help him. That gives him pep to keep his nerve up. When they fixed it so's working man couldn't get whiskey, that was the worst thing they could do. That's the life out of a man.

I used to keep me a half pint of whiskey all the time with a rock candy in it, and I never would have as much as a bad cold. Didn't care how much it rained that day, I'd go home and stay by the fire, drink my whiskey, and let my clothes dry on me. Never would pull my clothes off. You come home wet and pull on fresh clothes, you doin yourself a lot of harm. Just dry um right on you and drink that whiskey and that run all the cold from the inside out on the outside and the clothes'll lift right off you. Folks call that foolishness, but you take a man been through it, he know how to take egvantage of it. That whiskey will help you . . .

Houston paused as the door opened suddenly. The owner of the tourist camp didn't bother to knock. She just stuck her head in the door. She saw Houston sitting on the edge of my bed with his glass in his hand. "I expect you better not let the boys sit on that bed," she said to me. "Yes, ma'am," said Houston, and got up off the hard cot. Nobody said anything more, and the woman left. I switched off the recording machine and we sipped our whiskey for a minute.

Finally, Houston said, "That's a yahoo. A yahoo come to town. Otherwise known as a peckerwood. Did you get her down on your record?"

"Yes," I said. "What you were telling me about whiskey right before the woman said 'I expect you better not let the boys sit on that bed.' "

I mimicked her voice, and Shorty and Houston laughed. But we couldn't get the ball rolling again. Everything had gone flat. Later I drove Houston home, and on the way he confided in me that he had once invented a machine that would generate 250 volts of current without using fuel. "They" tried to steal the idea, so he had destroyed the only model. He asked me what the address of the patent office was.

"I'll make me another one now I know how to write the government," he said. "The yahoos down here . . . I'll sing you one of their songs."

He and Shorty grinned at each other. Then Bacon pulled a long face, threw back his head, and began caricaturing the hard, nasal style of rural white Mississippi. After every verse he gave a throaty falsetto whoop that reminded me of the way my father used to holler to amuse the family on our camping trips. My father's people were "peckerwoods" from Meridian, Mississippi, "from the upper crust of the poor white trash," he used to say.

The yahoo whoops tickled Houston and Shorty so much that the song would come to a stop after every stanza. "What's so funny?" I asked Houston.

"These yahoos—it's just a certain class of folks. If you sing this song around them, you better run. You can't fool with songs like this if you want to stay in this part of the country."

Nothing I could say would persuade Bacon to record the "yahoo" song, but he sat in the car and hummed through the following verses, shaking with laughter over each one.

Whoa, back, Buck, git over, Paul,
You steppin on my cotton, say, one and all.
Whoa, back, Buck, git over, Lamb,
You steppin on my cotton like you don't give a damn.
 I'm a rowdy soul, I'm a rowdy soul,
 Don't see a nigger in a mile or mo.

Took my gal to the party-o,
She sat on the steeple,
She let a fart and broke my heart
And _____ all over the people.
 Tell my wife when you go to the hills,
 I'm here workin at the sorghum mill.

Last year was a good crop year
And everybody knowed it.
Paw didn't raise but a bushel of corn

And some damn rascal stole it.
    I'm a rowdy soul, I'm a rowdy soul.
    I'm rowdy all around my red asshole.

"That's the yahoo," Houston said. "Down here you might could go in a rich man's front door, but if you go in a yahoo's front door, he's liable to kill you."

Delta blacks saw this apparently innocuous ditty as a highly charged satire on poor-white behavior, too offensive, indeed, too dangerous to render in their presence. One singer refused to sing it until we were safely in the car and moving down the highway. Another man, who was a convict, performed it as a gesture of impudence to a prison guard, who was present at the session. The fact that the guard only registered amusement suggests that this song is an in-joke, which only blacks know is aimed at the crackers.

Such timidity was certainly warranted by the violent reaction of Delta whites to the slightest gesture of defiance on the part of blacks; offenders might be cursed, clubbed, perhaps even killed. But intimidation only partially explains the Southwide popularity of this rustic black canard on their cracker neighbors. Blacks were the preferred plantation labor, for the ironic reason that they could be more easily cheated. Even so, the big owners, the "best" people in their community, preferred them. Thus, as a number of researchers have shown, the Southern class-caste system allowed blacks to view many poor whites as their social inferiors.[5]

Although no black could safely violate the caste rules of association and sexual contact, a sector of the black community belonged to a higher class than the poorest whites, earned more, and knew that the white upper crust preferred them as labor. Moreover, in spite of their hostile societal environment, blacks felt that they were moving up—tenancy, even peonage, was better than slavery. A man, or a whole family, could even emigrate to a Northern city. In both situations there was money to be made—better than the no-wages of slavery. So hope, fueled by the success of some prosperous blacks in their community, was a legitimate feeling, especially since there was someone to look down upon.

My name is Sam, I was raised in the sand,
I'd druther be a nigger than a poor white man.

WILL STARK, THE SAWMILL BALLADEER

Will Stark was a gaunt man, sad-faced, soft-voiced, with the angular grace of the poor white. The sun had touched his cheekbones with red. He looked like a poor white turned a couple of shades too dark by the sun. Poor-white was in his voice, too; the mellow music of black Delta speech was missing. Even his laughter was a shy, secretive chuckle.

Stark was hill-born, near Sardis, Mississippi. He didn't belong in the Delta and he felt this every day he lived.

When Will was still a youngster, he "flopped his wings and flied" off the plantation like many other Southern blacks of that time, looking for more money and more independence on day-labor jobs. He became a sawmill worker, drifting from camp to camp, as one tract of land was cleared of timber and operations shifted to another part of the river bottom.

I got on the train, I didn't have no fare,
This mornin
I got on the train, I didn't have no fare,
This mornin
I got on the train, I didn't have no fare,
You should have heard the conductor rare,
This mornin.

He took me by the hand and led me to the door,
This mornin
He took me by the hand and led me to the door,
This mornin
He took me by the hand and led me to the door,
"Don't let me catch you on the train no more,
This mornin."

In the long hot summer days, he listened to the piercing cry of the mule-skinner's holler, rising above the whine of the saws:

Oooh, hame string's breaking
And the collar cryin, and the collar cryin,
The women on the levee holl'in,
"That man is mine, O Lord, that man is mine."

I heard a mighty racket,
But didn't see no trains, didn't see no trains.
It must have been my bossman,
Gittin his money changed, gittin his money changed.

Will Stark felt in his heart he was a Southern white man, even though he always had to live and act like a black. That fate saddened him but, even as he became resigned, he kept intact, almost with pride, every sign and scar of this conflict. He had an insinuating voice and a way with language that marks the real ballad singer. Indeed, he knew more true ballads than anybody else in Coahoma County, and his repertory, being the choice of his audience, sets forth the strongest feelings and interests of that group. But the first song he offered us ran,

Coon, coon, coon, I wish my color would fade . . .

especially calculated to please me, as it had pleased his other white listeners. Like the earlier spiel on blackness I had heard at the barbershop,[6] this coon song belonged to the "comic" minstrel tradition that had become part of black protective adaptation. The minstrel show was once the only way into the theater for blacks, and they perforce took it over, with all the cruel stereotypes, as a main outlet for their talents as professional entertainers. Through them the racist minstrel songs filtered down into the whole of the black underclass. Thus Southern black country singers, when asked by a white for a song, would often launch into some demeaning blackface number, as Will did now. We tried to chuckle over these agonizing lines as he expected us to.

I had my face anointed,
I had my hair made straight,
Dressed up like a white man,
Certainly did look great.
Started out to see my girl
Just shortly after dark.
On my way to meet her
I had to cross a park.
    Just as I was thinkin
    I had things fixed up all right,
    Passed a tree where two doves

Were making love at night.
Stopped and they looked me over
And they saw my finished plumes.
Both these birds said good and loud,
"Co-oo-oooon."
    Coon, coon, coon,
    I wish my color would fade.
    Coon, coon, coon,
    I would like a different shade.
    Coon, coon, coon,
    From mornin, night, and noon,
    I wish I was a white man
    Instead of a coon.

Will grinned as he sang, the way a man with a twisted limb might grin who has learned to enjoy his buddies teasing him about it. To be black has meant to be exploited and disenfranchised, denied opportunity and education, conditioned to passive acceptance of humiliation and physical mistreatment, confined to the slums and condemned for life to these and other disadvantages of a lower caste. Will Stark had no trouble telling the truth, but I suspected he had forgotten how much it hurt him.

Black has only recently become "beautiful," even in the American black community. As remarked earlier, mixed bloods, with light skins and straight hair, had notable advantages.

"My father's father was a white man," Will Stark said, "and his mother was a full-blooded Indian. All the Negro that's within me is on my mother's side. She was a nigger."

Will Stark could draw a bead and hit you dead in the heart with a sentence, spoken so quietly you wondered if you had heard him. His black identity and his outcaste life were his mother's gifts to him. In the Delta one way for a woman to rise in the world was to become the temporary, but preferably lifetime, mistress of a white man. Often her paramour partially supported her—paid her rent and helped their half-caste offspring to own land and get an education. One of Will Stark's favorite toasts, a bawdy rhyme about a young lady who gives her seducer her "doodle-di-doo," ends thus:

Her mother say, "You goddam bitch,
I wish to God I had a switch,

I'd cut your ass both black and blue
And sew up your granny-dodgin doodle-di-doo."

Will's next song is a sentimental fantasy about this painful issue—a ballad of the Spanish-American War, when black troops served overseas for the first time. In it a black man dies a hero in saving the flag and is then recognized by his long-lost father, who turns out to be the commanding general. Here, indeed, is a wish fulfillment for a declassé mulatto like Will Stark! I noticed that he sang this one with a quaver in his voice.

While shot and shell were screamin
Upon the battlefield,
The boys in blue was fightin
The noble flag to shield.
 Came a cry from our brave captain—
 "Look, boys, our flag is down.
 Move on this field and save it from disgrace."
"I will," a loud voice said.
"I'll bring it back or die
And place it in the thickes' of the fray."
 Saved the flag, but he give his young life
 All for his country's sake.
 They brought him back and softly heard him say—
  "Just bring the news to mother,
  She knows how much I love her,
  And tell her not to wait for me
  For I'm not coming home.
   She knows there is no other
   Can take the place of mother,
   So kiss her on the sweet lips for me
   And bring the news to her."

From afar a noted general
Had witnessed this brave deed—
"Who saved our flag? Speak up, lads,
'Twas noble, brave, indeed."
 "There he lies," says the captain,
 "He's sinkin very fas—"
 And he turned away to hide a tear.

The general in that moment
Knelt down by his side,
Then gave a cry that teched all hearts that day—
   "My son, my brave young hero,
   I thought him safe at home."
   "Forgive me, father, for I ran away.
      Just break the news to mother."

"The reason I like that song so much," said Will Stark, "it tells of a soldier, his father was a general and thought his boy was home, but he slipped off and was the bravest one in there. I don't know if he was a Negro or a white, but I do know this was the Spanish-American War. And we had another about the same war I learnt from a colored boy in 19 and 18."

1.
Reason McKinley was so slow
About sendin men to war,
He was an old soldier,
Had been to war before.
   Befo the war, the late war.

2.
I went over to Cuby,
I went against my will,
I thought over one thing a
   thousand times.
"Supposin I would get killed?"
   In the war, the late war.

3.
McKinley asked me why did I
   run?
"You ain't afraid to die."
I told him no, that wasn't why I
   run,
But because I couldn't fly.
   In the war, the late war.

4.
The soldiers, they went a-runnin,
I went runnin too,
Give my feet a little exercise,
I had nothin else to do.
   In the war, the late war.

"Do you think that song was composed by a colored or a white man?" I asked.

"Colored. I know it was."

"Why?"

"Well," Will drawled, "I don't know for certain. I just picked it out because it was kinda like they thought a colored man would have done anyway."

"You mean you think a colored man would act that way in a war?"

Son House (Photo by Jeff Todd Titon)

Blind Lemon Jefferson (Courtesy Frank Driggs Collection)

A sharecropper's house on the King and Anderson plantation

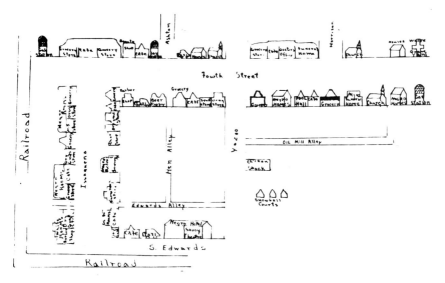

Clarksdale's Beale Streets, 1941

The Dipsie Doodle

Levee worker, 1927 (Courtesy Smithsonian Institution)

Former slave quarters, 1934 (Courtesy Schomburg Center for Research in Black Culture)

Woman with grandchild, 1942 (Photo by Alan Lomax)

Two women at Baptist prayer meeting, 1942 (Photo by Alan Lomax)

Young girls playing ring games, 1942 (Photos by Alan Lomax)

Preacher, 1942

Woman "getting happy" at church meeting, 1959 (Photos by Alan Lomax)

The *Quincy* at the landing, ca. 1900 (Courtesy Murphy Library, University of Wisconsin–La Crosse)

Loading cotton bales, the *Kate Adams* in the background (Courtesy Murphy Library, University of Wisconsin–La Crosse)

Roustabouts on the docks, ca. 1895 (Photo by G. F. Mugnier. From the collections of the Louisiana State Museum)

Chesapeake & Ohio trackmen spiking down a new rail, 1944 (Courtesy Chesapeake & Ohio Railway)

A railroad gang kicks out a length of rail near Thayer, West Virginia, 1944 (Courtesy Chesapeake & Ohio Railway)

Convicts building a levee (Drawn by J. O. Davidson for *Harper's Weekly,* March 15, 1884)

Trusty with shotgun, sandbags, 1912 (Courtesy Myrtle Bank Galleries, Natchez, Mississippi)

Wheelers, Placquemine Parish, Louisiana, 1935 (Photo by Ben Shahn. Courtesy FSA/Library of Congress)

Muleskinner with team, Mississippi River, Warren County (U.S. Corps of Engineers, Vicksburg. Courtesy Mississippi Department of Archives and History)

Levee bosses, ca. 1915 (Courtesy Mississippi Department of Archives and History)

"Well, I don't know whether he would have did that or not, but that was what they would *think* about him anyway."

Now it was quite clear whom Will meant when he spoke of "they." He went on with quiet and with urgency. "That song, it's ignorance, you know. Most of our people is ignorant. And, er-uh, they think anything that old boss like, they ought to do it. They think, er-uh, we can't live without getting help from him. As a general thing, *they* don't like a smart nigger, that is, one that knows too much for his own interests or his own race."

He was old, Will Stark, old in the ways of this place, and it had beaten him. How readily he condemned himself to "acting the fool"!

"The Southern white people, as a general thing, rather have ignorant niggers, that don't know more'n they tell um. '*You* not supposed to know . . . Do what *I* tell you to do . . .'

"They's such a few colored people in this country that can help one another. They go to get help from the white people."

He twanged his guitar and hummed the favorite song of Southern chicken thieves, black and white. For poor folks, the rich farmer's henhouse was often the only meat market open at night. Pretty Boy Floyd, the Texas Robin Hood and bank buster, went to the pen the first time for stealing chickens.

The hounds on my track,
And the chickens on my back,
I'm gonna make it to my shanty, if I can.
If I can, I don't care when,
I'm gonna keep my skillet greasy, if I can.

The times are gettin hard.
I'm gonna buy me a bucket of lard,
I'm gonna keep my skillet greasy, if I can.
If I can, I don't care when,
I'm gonna keep my skillet greasy, if I can.

"I remember here in '31, the government sent a carload of meat to give to the people that didn't have no work to do and didn't have nothing to go on." Will spoke with a sort of still horror in his voice. "They kept the meat loaded up until it spoiled and they had to burn it up, before they would give it to them." He was keeping himself separate from either of the parties involved. He could have nothing to do with either group. "And the government furnished flour and things and they even written on the sack, NOT TO BE SOLD, TO BE GIVEN OUT. But even after that, they wouldn't give it out to the colored; they burnt it instead!"

Incidents like this, frustrating the New Deal attempt to send relief to hungry Mississippi blacks during the Depression, brought federal investigations, a first and important step in opening up the solid Jim Crow Delta. Will Stark read over again in his mind's eye the official lettering on those sacks and boxes of food—NOT TO BE SOLD, TO BE GIVEN OUT. He said this in a whisper, and then he stopped and spat. For him, it was a final thing, so revolting that he could scarcely talk about it out loud. He looked up at me. I was a foreigner and a white man. How could I understand?

"Our people, *us* colored people, we try to do what, er-uh, in the *sight* of um—we try to do what satisfy um, and we get along better if we're in a tight. Some fellows say, 'I wouldn't either—if I didn't have a family.' 'I wouldn't work for what you work for—a man like you.' I say, 'I wouldn't either, but if I can do without something, them little childrens can't. It wouldn't show manhood in me to walk off and leave um.' " Then Will brushed the guitar strings and sang a dream, another chapter in the myth of the super-accelerator whom not even a bullet could catch.

> *We'll tell you folks bout a travelin man*
> *Was born in Tennessee.*
> *Made his livin stealin chickens*
> *And everything else he see.*
> > *If the police got after him,*
> > *He certainly got over the road.*
> > *Don't care how the freight train ran,*
> > *That nigger would get on board.*
> > > *Travelin man,*
> > > *He certainly was a travelin man,*
> > > *Travelin man,*
> > > *That was ever in the land.*
> > > > *Travelin man,*
> > > > *He was known for miles around.*
> > > *He didn't get enough,*
> > > *He didn't get enough,*
> > > *Till the police shot him down,*
> > > *Until the police shot him down.*

Sent this travelin man to the spring
To bring a pail of water.
The distance he had to go
Was two miles and a quarter.
>   *He went and got the water all right,*
>   *But he stumbled and fell down.*
>   *He went back to the house and got another pail,*
>   *Caught the water before it hit the ground.*
>   *Travelin man . . .*

J. D. Elder, that Tobagonian wiseman, was raised on stories of how some of his ancestors, grown weary of their hard plantation existence, put corncobs in their armpits and, as they uttered words of magic, rose in the tropic sky and sped off east toward home. The oldest slaves on the Georgia Sea Islands reportedly witnessed such an incident among recently arrived Africans. The foreman cruelly whipped them, and they "stick duh hoe in duh fiel, riz up in the sky, and tun hesef intuh buzzuds an fly right back tuh Africa." Another witness remembers that they downed their hoes, danced their way into the air, moving in a circle, faster and faster, till "dey riz up and fly lak a bud back to Africa."[7]

They caught this travelin man down in Savannah, Georgia,
Sentenced him to be hung.
The people all in this town
Thought the nigger's time had come.
>   *Allowed him three minutes to say a speech,*
>   *They was carried away in tears.*
>   *He crossed his legs and walled his eyes*
>   *And sailed up through the air.*
>   *Travelin man . . .*

Like their ancestors, who had herded cattle and hunted game on foot, blacks in the Old South depended on fleetness of foot to get them out of trouble, away from the walking boss, the patrollers, the high sheriff, and the lynch mob. Br'er Rabbit was their first hero, the Travelin Man their next.

The police took a Winchester rifle
And shot the nigger right through the head.

The nigger come tumblin down to the ground,
Everybody thought he was dead.
    They sent down South where his mother had gone,
    She was carried away in tears.
    They opened up the coffin for to see her son
    And the fool had disappeared.
        Travelin man . . .

"See, my father was a travelin man," Will Stark went on. "He traveled about and made music. He could play most any kind of music, by ear and by note. Sometimes he played cornet in a band—but he also played violin and piano. We boys took after him and all three of us were pretty tolerable at music. I learnt the banjo from my daddy, then later on I took up the Autoharp, next the accordion, and afterwhile I got to be right smart of a guitar picker. But here, late years, I've laid that all by.

"When I was a boy, where I had my chance to learn what songs I know was at dances my daddy used to give at home. And after I learnt enough on the banjo, he'd take me with him to play for the different little balls they'd have around on the plantations. My daddy would fiddle *Billy in the Low Ground, Arkansas Traveler,*[8] and he'd sing at times, too . . .

My old missus don't like me
Because I wouldn't eat black-eyed peas.
Rain come wet me, sun come dry me,
Stand back, nigger man, don't come nigh me.
Rain come wet me, sun come dry me,
Stand back, nigger man, don't come nigh me.

My old missus promised me
When she died, she would set me free.
She lived so long till her head got bald,
I don't believe she'll die at all.
Live so long you get bald,
Give out the notion dying at all.

. . . such stuff as that, and the dances would last all night, and sometimes, at Christmas, they'd last two days. Dance all night till they just give out and quit, but soon's they'd catch some sleep and get rested, they'd dance again.

"The fellow that give the ball, he had things to sell. When the folks danced a set, he'd holler, 'Promenade your partner to the bar,' and every fellow would have to take his partner to the bar and treat her. That was when you'd make your toasts . . .

May your fortune be as deep as the ocean
And your misfortune as light as its foam.

. . . and more I better not put down on record. That was before Prohibition, when people could get plenty whiskey and they didn't care for it so much. If a man got drunk, they'd just take and lay him off aside and keep on dancing. They didn't get fighting like they do now. The dances weren't rough like they are today, and the girls was a lot more particular. Naturally, there was lots of courtin. Everybody just had their fun and I remember my daddy used to sing:

I had a piece of pie,
I had a piece of puddin,
I give it all away
To see Sally Goodin.
  Hey, hi-diddle-dee,
  And a diddle-daddle-diddle.

Old man James Stark, half Indian and half white, "didn't have any money much," but he gave his son what he had—a legacy of songs. In those days, whites and blacks worked, hunted, and lived more close together than they do today, and folklore passed freely between the two groups. Its syncopation marking it as probably black in origin, *Sally Goodin* is beloved by white fiddlers from Georgia to Texas. So Will Stark's song inheritance from his "white" father stands for one side of the musical marriage that has produced present-day Southern folk music. Early on, blacks sang a few of the Anglo-American ballads that pleased them, and as they did, they absorbed this style, reworked the old ballads, and began to create their own.

In this series of black ballads, we come close to the main concerns of Delta folk at the turn of the century, just before the blues began. The story of a magical Irish horse, the "Noble Skew Skuball," was a favorite. In its American remake the race was run in Kentucky by the great mare Molly and the champion, whose name had been Americanized as Stewball. Out of that ballad came one of Bill Monroe's hits, a universal favorite of Southern bluegrass bands. With a banjo score like the last lap of the Kentucky Derby, it bears many marks of black style. Meantime, black prison gangs, with quick getaways always on their minds, filled the hot Southern bottomlands with roaring choruses about ol Stewball, coming into the home stretch "lak a midnight shower of rain."[9]

Will Stark's daddy's solo variant of the piece was sung in the flat, rather nasal, uninflected style of the Southern cracker, and to that universal favorite tune of the frontier, *The Waggoner's Lad*, or *Rye Whiskey*.

Old Stewball, Old Stewball,[10]
I know him of old,
You run in London
Twelve long years ago.

When the word was given
For the hosses to go,
Stewball, he started
Like an arrow from a bow.

Old man James Stark used to saw this out on his beloved fiddle. Then he'd light into another frontier favorite about the huge fertility symbol, *The Ram of the Derby*, the English ballad that soldiers from George Washington on have loved and that became the culminating song of the jazz funerals of black New Orleans.

1.
Man had a little ram,
His name was idle Joe.
Every wrinkle round his horn,
Measured forty miles or mo.
    Didn't he ramble,
    Didn't he ramble,
    Didn't he ramble,
    Till the man cut him down?

2.
The hair on the ram's back
Growed and touched the sky.
The eagles built a nest
For to hear the young ones cry.
    Didn't he ramble? . . .

3.

The man that butchered that ram,
He waded deep in his blood.
The little boy that held the feet
Got drownded in the flood.
      Didn't he ramble? . . .

4.

His head lay in the markethouse,
His feet out in the street.
Three girls came walking by,
Said, "Don't them nuts look
      sweet?"
      Didn't he ramble? . . .

5.

He rambled on the waterside,
He rambled on the land,
But when he went to the butcher
      pen,
There he met his man.
      Didn't he ramble? . . .

6.

This ram went up to his mother,
His tail all in a quirl.
She said, "Bear on away from
      me, you son-of-a-bitch,
I brought you into this world."
      Didn't he ramble? . . .

Will Stark's next was a version of one of the few comic ballads Dr. Francis Child thought worthy of inclusion in his canonical volume *English and Scottish Popular Ballads*. This randy tale of the blind cuckold is sung in many European tongues, but Dr. Child put *Our Goodman* at the bottom of his list—No. 273—thus indicating that it was hardly worthy of its noble companions *Sir Patrick Spens, The Douglas Tragedy*, and the rest. Among American ballad singers, however, it ranks among the top ten of their favorite English ballads, and is widely popular today among folk who wouldn't know a ballad from a battledore. More pertinently, it is one of the half dozen British ballads that black folksingers have bothered to learn and pass along. Its plot makes sense in a world of serial polygamy and rambling husbands. Also sympathetic to blacks is the saucy wife who tells her old cuckold that he doesn't know what he's looking at.

You old fool, you blind fool,
You're blind and never could see . . .

Will or his daddy or somebody added a new twist to the story. Will chuckled, as he explained. "Now, this is a story I learnt back when I was just a kid, a story about a blind man that married a lady that promised to always be kind and true to him. And he heard of a place where he could gain his sight back and he went off. When he got back home, his wife *didn't know* he'd gained his sight. She thought she could still pull the wool over his eyes. So he got his old banjo and he played to her:

1.
Lovin wife, kind,
Kind and always be,
Whose horse is that in the stable
Where my horse used to be?

2.
Say, you fool, you blind,
You blind, you never could see,
It's nothin but a milk cow
Your mammy sent to me.

3.
He say, I've traveled ten
    thousand miles,
And travel ten thousand more,
I never before seen a milk cow
With a saddle on before.

4.
Loving wife, kind,
Kind and always be,
Whose boots is them in the corner
Where my boots ought to be?

5.
You fool, you blind,
Blind and never could see,
There's nothing 'tall but a
    stovepipe
Your mammy sent to me.

6.
I traveled ten thousand miles,
Travel ten thousand more,
And I never before seen a
    stovepipe
With spurs on before.

7.
Loving wife, kind,
Kind, and always be,
Whose hat is that on the table
Where my hat ought to be?

8.
You fool, you blind,
Blind and never could see,
It nothing at all but a washpan
Your mammy sent to me.

9.
I traveled ten thousand miles,
Travel ten thousand more,
I never before seen a washpan
With a hatband on before.

10.
Loving wife, kind,
Kind, and always be,
What man is that in the bed
    there
Where I used to be?

11.
You fool, you's a blind,
Blind and never could see,
It's nothin at all but a doll baby
Your mammy sent to me.

12.
I traveled ten thousand miles,
Travel ten thousand more,
I never seen a doll baby
With whiskers on before.

This old rhyming quatrain form, ABCB, which had provided the cool channel for centuries of storytelling, was, in the Deep South, suddenly filled with the burning, bitter experience of black labor:

1.
If the sun shine hot
And the day stay long,
I'm gonna take two shady bushes
To be my home,
O Lord, to be my home.

2.
I asked that woman how about it.
She said, "All right."
I pulled off my clothes
And I stayed all night.

3.
I whipped my woman
With a singletree,
You oughta hear her hollerin
"Don't you murder me."

4.
You bring me some water
And a hammer to knock out my
*   brains.*
That rotgut whiskey
Bout to drive me insane.

Will sardonically explained how such feelings came to be: "I remember we was sawing lumber for P. F. Stone of Cincinnati and they had a lumber inspector there—he was a white man—and he'd come around and tell me sometime, say, 'Will, that lumber is a little too thin. Move your pin a hole further back.'

"I tell the block setter and he move the hole back further. Then Mister Bob, he's the superintendent of the mill, he say, 'Why the hell did you move that pin, Will? The lumber's too thick.'

"I say, 'Well, Mister Lee told me to move it.'

"He say, 'You put it back where it belong.'

" 'Put it back where *he* say, Paul,' I tell the block setter, say, 'Mister Lee say it too thin, just a leetle *bit* too thin.'

"He say, 'Well, goddam it, you tell him I say leave it in the hole where I set it. It ain't too thin. It's no such goddam thing. You tell him he's a goddam liar.'

"Then I say, 'No sir, Mister Bob, Mister Lee is a white man. If you want him told that, you tell him.' I say, 'I wasn't taught to talk to white folks thataway. I wasn't raised thataway. My grandmother partly raised me and she taught me to be obedient to white folks.' And Mister Bob just had to laugh. It tickled him."

At night in the work camps, far from the jovial solidarity of the plantation quarters, this continual humiliation turned into rage. The men needed ballad heroes too brave to "run from the gun," that is, to be intimidated by a gun-packing foreman. At night in the shanties, when the fiddles and the guitars began to whine, they sang about bad ol Stagolee, about Frankie with a pistol under her red petticoat, about Duncan, the black bartender who had the nerve to blow policeman Brady away!

> *Brady, Brady, why didn't you run?*
> *Brady, Brady, why didn't you run?*
> *Brady, Brady, why didn't you run?*
> *"I'm too brave a man to run from a gun."*

Brady's wife heard that he was dead,
She come runnin and shakin her head,
"Oh, old man, how can it be?
You killed my husband in the first degree."
> *Brady, Brady, why didn't you run? . . .*

The Memphis bully of the river, Stackolee, was the very opposite of Br'er Rabbit. He was pure anger and he killed out of irritability to relieve his pent-up rage.

1.
Say, boys,
What do you think of that?
Stackolee killed his best friend
Bout a five-dollar Stetson hat.
> *Oh bad man, Stackolee.*

2.
Bill Lyons ask, "Stackolee,
Is you gonna take my life?
I got two little children
And a lovin innocent wife."
> *Oh that bad man, Stackolee.*

3.
"*I care nothin about your children,*
Care nothin about your wife,
You done stole my Stetson hat
And I'm gonna take your life."
    Oh that bad Stackolee.

4.
Stackolee asked his woman,
Say, "*What have you got?*"
She run down in her stockin-leg
And pulled out a thousand spot.
    Oh that bad Stackolee.

5.
Stackolee was on the gallows,
He got mad and cussed.
The judge said, "*Maybe we*
    better hang him
Fo he kills one of us."
    Oh that bad Stackolee.

Then Will Stark took into the ballad of little Frankie, one of America's first liberated women. Back yonder in the mauve decade, Frankie lived and loved as she pleased, and thus became a heroine in an age when most American women were the housebound victims of stuffy nineteenth-century prudery. The song doesn't say whether Frankie made her money in the white folks' kitchen or in the barroom, but she was her own woman and could afford to buy her man a suit worth eighty-one dollars—about five hundred dollars today. When he done her wrong, she felt justified in gunning him down—cheery news to all wronged women and other humiliated persons in that turbulent age.

Frankie was a good woman,
Everybody knowed,
Paid eighty-one dollars
For Albert's suit of clothes.
    He's her man,
    But he done her wrong.[11]

Frankie belongs with the best of ballads; and the ballad was the literary wonder of the nineteenth century, inspiring Keats and Tennyson with its fleet narrative techniques, its incisive lyricism, and its quicksilver strophic melodies. Yet American blacks mastered this as well as other British song styles. Three centuries of African-American experimentation gave rise to the hoedown, the spiritual, the minstrel tunes, ragtime, jazz, the blues, rock, and gospel—each genre with a galaxy of strophic melodies that first fascinated

America and then the world. Not least among these innovations was the black ballad genre that blossomed, particularly in the Mississippi valley, round the turn of the century.

Though frontier America produced a wealth of narrative songs, the black ballads have been the most widely popular and the most telling American contributions to the British vein of *Barbara Allen* and *Edward* and *Fair Eleanor and the Brown Girl*. To prove this point one has only to draw up a list of the best-known black ballads of the United States—*Frankie, John Henry, The Boll Weevil, Casey Jones*; then, less familiar but just as fine—*Brady, Railroad Bill, Stackerlee, Poor Laz'us, Delia*. In them, just as in the British classics, an individual stands up for what he or she feels or believes and then faces the tragic consequences of this act.

For the main actors in the black ballads, however, there is no time for love or romance; retribution for their defiant acts is swift and inevitable. Their heroes are lower class, but no more or less pigheaded and violent than their British counterparts, like Fair Eleanor, who cuts off her rival's head and kicks it against the wall. Even so, in their ballad making, Southern blacks had moved past the biblical heroes of the slave songs and were celebrating blacks who were not passive, nor anonymous, but persons to be reckoned with.

Frankie was a woman, everybody knowed . . .

John Henry was a steel-driving man . . .

Po' Laz'us had never been arrested, by no one man . . .

Ollie Jackson, the gunslinging hero of the next song Will Stark sang to us, was nothing but a Kansas City coon, but you didn't fool round with Ollie.[12]

Hush, girls and boys,
Don't you-all say a word.
I'm gonna sing you a new song now
That you haven't ever heard.
*   When you lose your money, learn to lose.*

On Saturday night
Tween eight and nine o'clock,
Ollie Jackson, the gambler,
Made two fatal shots.
*   When you lose your money, learn to lose.*

"The next one is what the cokeheads used to sing," Will said. "You see, this used to be a kind of outlaw country. When they had saloons in Lambert and these little country places, they'd sell cocaine and everything and you could buy all you wanted. I ask a feller once, I say, 'Eph, who use coke on this job?' He say, 'All the people on this yard, excusing you-all three or four fellows that just come here lately.' I say, 'How does it take effect on you? Does it take you like whiskey?' He say, 'Why, you can get drunk with it and you can't smell whiskey. It make you feel better than whiskey.'

"Yessir, it was all over this country one time. I heard the people learned to use it first from jockeys. *They* used to give it to their hosses, then they got so they tried it on themselves and they liked it and they give it to the women and the women started and used it and it got among some of the men. They say you couldn't quit it after you started. You'd go crazy if you couldn't get it, after you got a fiend to it. So some of them went crazy and went to the crazy house in Jackson. Some of them got killed. And some of them walked along the street and just fell out. That stuff would eat the brains up or something. But it's played out in this part of the country and they don't nobody use it now that I knows of."[13]

Look, old girl,
If you go my way,
If you go git in jail,
I won't let you stay.
  Hey, honey, take a whiff on me.

Coke I love,
Coke I crave.
I speck it's gonna carry me
To my grave.
  Hey, hey, honey, take a whiff on me.

By the 1920s, lumbering had about played out in the Yazoo Delta, and Will went back to sharecropping. Coahoma County was no longer a relaxed frontier community, where a man could work or not as he pleased. It had become one of the capitals of the cotton industry, headquarters for the richest and most efficiently operated plantations in the South. A black man had to fit into the pattern if he wanted to stay around Clarksdale; he had to accommodate, hat in hand. The Constitution and the Bill of Rights did not apply to him. As long as he remained in the Delta, he had no civil rights. Will Stark was intimately acquainted with this system of peonage and forced labor.

"They had to work—or fight!" Will said, thus separating himself from the blacks he was discussing. "When they come after a man to work, he had to *go*. For instance, Mister Hobson or Mister Clark or Mister King or Anderson or any of these people out of town wanted some hands to chop the cotton or plow, it make no difference who he was, he *must* go. They would go into colored people's houses and git the children out who had never been worked none—schoolgirls—and make *them* go out and pick cotton. Whether they wanted to go or not, they had to go. Of course, the boss didn't do all this; the officers here in town would take um and when they got out on the plantation, they had to work—or fight."

"Did you ever hear of a case of anybody fighting?" I asked.

"Yessir, I know a lot of them, they said—fought um."

"What happened to them?"

"They just *whipped um up*. Some of um I heard they whipped to *death*. Then again some of um fought back and lived. The place where I am *now* I hear um tell a tale about the man want a boy to work and this boy didn't have nothin to eat. So the boy come to the commissary after some meal and the man told him, 'Hell, this ain't no ration day. You gonna work today.'

" 'I ain't gonna work, until I git me some meal.'

"They say Mister Barksdale called one of his agents, say, 'Clyde, come here and help me whip this nigger.'

"So the nigger whipped Mister Barksdale *and* Mister Clyde, both. Then they call Mister Murphy. 'Come here, Murphy, and help us whip this nigger.'

"Mister Clyde say, 'Mister Barksdale, let me kill him.'

" 'No, no, don't shoot him. Let's whip him.'

"And finally all three of them whipped him. But he didn't work. No sir, he didn't work. His father lives there on the place now."

"I guess the boy had to move," I said.

"Well," Will replied, "he left, but he didn't have to. Mister Barksdale's the kind of fellow, when he have a fuss with a nigger, it's all over with after the fuss is over. They ain't many like him.

"Some of them do things you might not imagine. At times, of course, they get in trouble about it. One bossman out here about Tutwiler, they fined him a thousand dollars and give him ten years in the penitentiary. I don't know whether he paid it or not," Will added skeptically, "but they *say* they fined him. He made a man work in the daytime and chained his wife in bed at night to make sure they wouldn't run away. Somebody reported it to the government one way or other, I heard.

"Some of these plantations, if you move there and start a crop with them, you have to slip off or they'll git you and bring you back and put you in jail. And of course the bossman, he rules the court and the law has to do like he say. Don't, them folks that's runnin the court can't hold their jobs.

"But not all plantations is the same. Mister Hobson's, where I used to live, a man can leave there, if he ain't satisfied, anytime he wants to. His crop is responsible for his debt. He can leave, but he must *do* like they want him to do while he's there.

"Lately, things has changed for the better around here. I don't know for sure what was the cause of it, but during this last administration [the Roosevelt New Deal], it seemed that there were some people from Washington or somewhere visiting through these counties and they found out something and so many of these rich peoples lost their plantations—I don't know exactly what was the cause, but I notice they quit a lot of that stuff. It'd be better if it wasn't for the yahoos.

Doggone my luck, doggone my luck,
I don't know my ought from my figgers.
But I got too much good blood in me
To 'sociate with the niggers.
    I'm a rowdy soul, a rowdy soul,
    Don't make no diffunce whether I work or no.

Will chuckled over the yahoo song. "That's what the white folks sing, the poor folks, up in the hills. We learnt it from them."

"Would you sing it around a poor white man?"

"No sir, no *sir*," said Will, a trifle severely. "I wouldn't on account I wouldn't want to hurt his feelings."

Will Stark skirts around a convoluted corner of Delta life, explored in John Dollard's *Caste and Class in a Southern Town*. On the whole, the big planters found black tenants less demanding and easier to handle than whites. The enforced servility of blacks gave them an economic edge over the poorest white labor, who were shunted onto the worst land. Moreover, the black families who managed to acquire land or start a business and prosper also looked down on the poor yahoos, even though they remained subject to Jim Crow and, ultimately, dependent on the favor of the ruling white elite. In other words, the caste and class lines did not coincide, so that there was a sizeable slice of the black population who could say with some justice,

I'd ruther be a nigger than a po white man . . .

Every situation arranges its own strange, but real, perspective. Will Stark, whose personality was erected around the hurts he had sustained from white rejection, really did not want to hurt white folks in return. They could call him "nigger"—that was, maybe, his mama's fault—but he didn't want to hurt them by singing the yahoo song where they could hear it. And his attitude toward Mister Bud Doggett, the local white "bad man," a ripstaver out of the frontier period of Coahoma, reflected a similar ambivalence.

"I reckon the baddest man in this county," ruminated Will, "was *supposed* to be Mister Bud Doggett, but, er-uh, Mister Doggett wasn't mean to *his* people [his black labor]. He'd take up for his people anywhere. If his people was in town, he wouldn't stand nobody running them over—the laws or nobody."

"But I heard Mister Doggett led lynch mobs," I said.

"That's right, yessir. He led all the mobs."

"Well, I can't figure that one out, Will. Some people say he was the best man for the colored people and then they turn around and say he leads the mobs."

"Here is what they claim," said Will in his weary and judicial way, quoting without comment the official opinion. "Miss'ippi was the best place on earth for a good nigger and 'twas the worst place for a bad nigger. *He* didn't have no show. When he get to play bad, he didn't have no help because all the rest of the Negroes was taught to obey the white folks."

Mister Bud Doggett, lynch-mob leader, then, was better than no friend at all. I could detect a note of sympathy in Will's account of how this bad man met his comeuppance. Ray Lum, the great animal auctioneer, was also very fond of Bud Doggett and counted him among his best friends. He remembered how he was killed:

My cousin Clint come by and said, "Ray, you tell Doggett don't cross Ellie Chapman's path. He'll kill him. Reason I'm telling you I thought you could talk to him."

"Cousin Clint, Mr. Doggett's a man you don't tell nothing to. Nobody can't talk to Mr. Bud."

It wasn't five days after that, Mr. Doggett started over to get his mail. Ellie

Chapman had told him, "If you ever cross my path, I'm gonna kill you."

I was standing at the barn door and saw Chapman step up there. They both had one foot up from the ground, and Bud Doggett throwed his gun over and shot off Ellie Chapman's tie. He had one of those little bow ties. Doggett just throwed that gun. Bam! Off went that tie. The next shot was Mr. Chapman's. I didn't see it. I'm glad I didn't. When he shot, he shot Bud right through the heart. It was just too quick. That was the last of my friend, Doggett. I cried like a baby. My best friend was gone. I haven't had a better one."[14]

"Mister Bud Doggett," Will Stark said, in continuing his memorial to the bad man, "always say a white man could whip a nigger anyhow you take it. Mister Hobson told him a white man couldn't whip a nigger if the nigger had equal terms. Put um on equal terms, Mister Hobson told Mister Bud, and the nigger would win. So when Johnson and Jeffries had their fight, you remember, Hobson bet on Jack Johnson and a whole lot of white folks bet against him. They all lost their bets to him and Mister Bud Doggett got to disputing about it and Mister Hobson jumped on him and whipped *him*. Mister Bud Doggett took it, but he told him, 'It ain't you whippin me, Hobson, it's your money. I'd kill you right here, but you got too much money and they'd hang me for it.'

"Yessir, Mister Bud Doggett was quite a man. If you'd get in jail for making a little whiskey, he'd go on your bond. He believed in whiskey and in folks having a good time and he was opposed to this new dry law. The boys in the jailhouse made up a toast to him. I'll say it for you now, but for God's sake don't let on who told it to you."

The jailhouse crowd always mixed poetry in with their whiskey drinking. Good manners and fellowship demanded a rhymed verse with every drink— the bawdier the better. There are toastmasters who can recite scores of toasts running to hundreds of lines. This genre, long popular with the street crowd in every black ghetto, is the direct antecedent of rap.

THE TOAST TO BUD DOGGETT

1.
Come all you sorry bootleggers
And listen to me,
I have a little example
I want you to see.

2.
It's better to hit your maw
Or hit your paw
Than to use liquor
Under the new Jones law.

3.
Mister Ferd, Mister Chapman,
Carries too big a gun,
And he'll shoot any bootleggers
That breaks and run.

5.
Mister Rivers take a pint,
Mister Ferd took a pint,
Mister Chapman has to have
The whole damn jinte.

4.
Mister Chapman is chief,
Brave a man as ever lived,
Never ran and never will.
His main occupation is taking
   copper stills.

6.
They'll arrest you and put you
In the Coahoma County jail,
Then you'll want bad Mister
   Doggett
To go your bail.

7.
But since he's dead
And can't bail you out,
These cold iron bunks
Will wear your black ass out.

"Yes, the boys miss Mister Bud Doggett. See, this new high sheriff, Mister Greek Rice, he's broke up whiskey and crap games, and he's barred sitting around and playing the Seabirds on Sunday. One time back he put all guitar players in jail in cotton-picking time so the folks wouldn't be too tired to go to work on Monday morning. He say, they voted the law to put the lid on, so 'Let's put it on good and tight.'

"See, Mister Greek Rice don't have to collect from these people running these dives. He's a rich man with lots of money and two or three big plantations and so he's not particular about the money. He ran for Congress once and I reckon that's what he wants—to get to Washington. So he stopped us from dancing and broke up the barrelhouses. Last year we had lots of music round here. You could have found all the guitar pickers you could want. We had lots of music. People enjoyed themselves. But Mister Greek Rice stopped us from that. Wants to make a religious town out of it. Everything must close down twelve o'clock Sunday, so everybody can git to Sunday school. I think he's doing right."

Will Stark, the fiddler's son, the sawmill rounder, tried to sound enthusiastic, but he couldn't make it. His wife, a staunch member of the Holiness Church, was always at him to join, but Will used to say, with a faint smile, "I'd have to give up too many things I enjoy." For Will Stark the closing of the jukes and barrelhouses meant the passing of the last vestige of the frontier life he had known. No more Stackerlees and Ollie Jacksons, playing the man for their own crowd. No more lowdown blues and whiskey. Will Stark was finally hemmed in between the high sheriff and the Holiness Church. Looking out over the dead green of the cotton fields that lapped up to his narrow front yard, he felt like Br'er Rabbit with the buzzard after him . . .

Once there was a rabbit and a buzzard. The rabbit hid in the holler of a tree and the buzzard stopped him up in there. He's gonna eat him. And the buzzard went off and stayed three or four days and he come back and he had a little song, said:

> *Ting-a-ling, ting-a-ling,*
> *Hootch him up again,*
> *I been flying three, four days.*

Rabbit say, "I been here three, four days."
He say, "Mister Rabbit, I'll pick your bones tomorrow."
"No, you won't."
He went off and stayed three or four more days and says:

> *Ting-a-ling, ting-a-ling,*
> *Hootch him up again,*
> *I been flying three, four days.*

Rabbit say (very faintly), "I been here three or four days."
The rabbit began to get weak. He say, "Mister Rabbit, I'll pick your bones tomorrow."
He say, "No, you won't."
He went and stayed three, four more days and he said:

> *Ting-a-ling, ting-a-ling,*
> *Hootch him up again,*
> *I been flying three, four days.*

Well, of course, the rabbit didn't answer. He's dead. The buzzard pulled the chink out. Then he pulled Mister Rabbit out and et him.

Chapter 5

▲▲▲▲▲▲▲▲▲▲

The Levee

I wouldn't tell a mule to get up,
If it was to set down in my lap.

Driving through the Delta, you hardly ever see the river, but the levee is always close by, a great green serpent running through woods, swamps, and farms, with towns nestling close to its slopes. The levee is unobtrusive, since its slope is green and gradual, but in fact it is immense—higher and longer than the Great Wall of China, very likely the biggest thing that man has ever made. It flanks and confines the giant river all the way from Cairo, Illinois, down past New Orleans, more than a thousand miles as the crow flies, but immeasurably longer as its thirty-to-forty-foot-high embankments, one on each side, follow the endless winding of the stream. Over the years this great wall of earth has loomed ever larger in my imagination, until I now see the levee as the most distinctive spiritual and cultural feature of the Delta landscape. It was the principal human response to the titanic power of the great river. The century of labor it cost, the shelter it provided, and the rich and cruel system it fostered shaped the history of the region.

It's impossible to imagine anything as big as the Mississippi levee, and, even more soul-endangering, to realize these huge dykes were erected by manpower, in major part by black muleskinners urging on their teams with wild work calls that are the only clearly African melodies we have found in the United States. These songs, which appear to be the direct ancestors of the blues, wrought an ancient black magic on the mules, stimulating them on occasion to literally work themselves to death. Perhaps this magic still pulsates and vibrates in the blues. At any rate, the levee workers, whose songs built the levees, and the white "Mister Chollys," whose money inspired them, were as tough a set of men as ever walked the American land. They tamed a semitropical wilderness—choked with vegetation, beset by noxious insects, venomous reptiles, and gargantuan spring floods—and turned it into a billion dollars' worth of cotton land.

In 1541, De Soto, seeking to cross what he called the Rio Grande (the great river), was delayed by a spring flood that rose in March and did not recede until May. "It took forty days to reach its peak and it was a beautiful thing to look upon a sea, where there had been fields. On each side of the river, the water extended across twenty leagues of land, and nothing was to be seen except the tops of the tallest trees."

Before the levees were built, the ancestors of the Choctaws raised mounds along the river where they retreated in times of high water. Big Bill Broonzy, one of the most prolific bluesmen, was born on one of those Indian mounds during the flood of 1893. The cabin was surrounded by water when his mother went into labor. There was no food in the house, and Bill's father had to set out in his skiff to get supplies. As Bill wrote the story:

> . . . he left on the 23rd of june and did not get back until the 28th with food enuff for my mother an their 12 children. . . . the old lady midwife met him, say, frank you done a good job that time. my daddy say, what you mean? she tell him, you shot both barel that time. you have got twins, a boy an a girl. . . .

Levee building began early in the nineteenth century when individual planters piled up small embankments against the floods, but the construction of opposing levees by neighbors and plantations across the river raised the floodplain and rendered these pitiful little dykes useless. The problem required more concerted effort. In 1833, levee commissions, organizing the efforts of several counties, produced a levee system that controlled all but the greatest floods. The Civil War, then, played havoc with the system, and only in the 1870s and 80s did the newly empowered levee boards erect the levees that permitted the settlement of the fertile river-bottom lands.

It is almost inconceivable, but nonetheless true, that at one stage these huge earthworks were piled up a barrowload at a time by men pushing wheelbarrows. Often the work was done by gangs of convicts, leased from the state and most cruelly exploited, driven by whips and clubs often with a reckless waste of life. If a man happened to stumble and fall into the pit with his load, "why, they just dump the next dirt on him and leave him there—cover him on up and forget him—I've seen that happen," one old-timer told me.

Many of the barrow men, or hoppers, were Irishmen, fresh out of a very hungry Old Country and ready to take on any kind of a job. These Irish dirtmen dug the Erie and other canals of the East and laid the right-of-ways for the first railroads. Levee building came natural to them. My father and I had recorded their songs all the way from

The Ee-ri-ee is a-risin
And the gin is gettin low . . .

to the state of Arkansas:

I've met with ups and downs of life and better days I've saw,
But I never knew what mis'ry was till I came to Arkansaw.

Then, magically, I met one of these itinerant Irish song makers, hitchhiking on Highway 61. Mirage lakes shimmered over the cotton fields. The concrete highway was a silver river that flowed round the crutch of the hitchhiker. One leg was off above the knee. His clothes were shabby, but he wore a brand-new black Stetson as if it were a crown.

THE BLACK-HAT MAN

"The name's McCoy. F. M. McCoy, better known as Black Hat." He grinned as he tenderly wiped off the sweatband of his faded black Stetson. The car began to move again and the breeze poured in straight from West Hell. "Sometimes they call me 'Yellow,' too, because I never got over the yaller jandice I got in Guatemala. I lost this gam helping to take this country away from the frogs and alligators. Nigger shot me, splintered the bone, and the company doctor was drunker than usual that day. Since they got my leg for nothing, I figgered they owed me a livin, so I make my residence in Greenville and push my pencils on the construction-gang circuit. A construction-gang worker is always good for a buck on payday, when an old-time barrow hopper like me is in question."

McCoy, the Black Hat Man, was the last of the Irish hoppers who had raised levees along the river. They worked with wheelbarrows and piled up the banks a few feet high along the river for a few dollars and so many jiggers of whiskey a day. When the Civil War came, they fought their Northern Irish cousins like demons to protect the slave system. The river had silted up some more during the war, and they had to go at the levees again and raise them a bit higher. They had their songs, as Black Hat recalled:

There was Ed Slocum, a man without skill,
He had to leave Denver, for a cabbage he did steal.
The stealing of cabbage wouldn't keep him alive,
And he started dead broke for the Hell's Creek Drive.

There's Elmer McGann, the worst of them all,
He's so damn lazy, he scarcely can crawl.
He'll set on his sleigh, his whip he will fling,
Crying, "Go on, you old fellers, you'll die before spring."

In the eighties, black muleskinners, working slips, and wheelers put the Irish hoppers out of work. The blacks could handle mules and the Irish couldn't. Black Hat McCoy turned foreman.

"You had to be able to whip any nigger that came along," he explained. "I never seen but two or three niggers whip a white man in all my time here. *They* didn't live long. Somebody else took it up and killed the nigger . . . If you had the guts for the jobs, you could get plenty of work.

"I remember a man offered me a hundred seventy-five dollars a month to come on as foreman. I figgered something must be the matter, must be a bad nigger around that needed working over. First day nothing happened. But about ten o'clock the second day all the women came running out on the job, said, 'Old Cokehead Hannah is whippin all the niggers in camp.'

"Those days we sold cocaine in the commissary. A nigger could get a dollar box and git on more of a drunk than he could with the same amount of whiskey.

"When Hannah got high, she'd get mean. When I went in the tent where she was working over these niggers with her singletree, I bust her side the head with the pistol butt. It took me three blows to knock her down; that's how stout she was. Then, when I got her down, I gave her a going over with my pistol and told her, 'Listen, old bitch, if there's any fighting done around here, I'm gonna do it. Come and see me when you want to fight.' I never had any more trouble out of Hannah.

"The boss and his foremen were law in those camps. These little tinhorn deputies just didn't dare come around looking for nobody. If they did, we'd run them off. Now maybe you heard that old nigger levee-camp song where they're always singing 'Mister Cholly, Mister Cholly.' Well, I happen to know that got started from Charley Silas—the big contractor who made a million and, when he went broke, walked off in the river. All the niggers heard about him when he shot the 'Mercy Man,' which was the humane officer out of Memphis. This fellow came out to Silas's camp and protested against him working mules with sore necks and shoulders. Silas told him he had a contract to fill and couldn't stop to nurse his mules. An argument came up over this and Silas shot the Mercy Man dead. It cost him fifty thousand dollars to get out of the mess.

"But those days are gone now. Every construction worker in the country is dead beat and dead broke just like myself. So here I am with my pencils, hitching around among these goddam boll weevils, and I've known the time when this whole continent was my stomping grounds—levee camps, railroad fills, canals, dams—I been a dirtman all my life and I guess it's too late for me to learn any new tricks."

I let him out where the road toward Lula crossed the road from Clarksdale, and he went off on his one leg and his crutch, his black hat bobbing in the heat waves like the head of a black, stinging thousand-legger when you throw him back in the fire.

KNEE-DEEP IN SIX-SHOOTERS

The Delta levee world was the last American frontier, even more lawless than the Far West in its palmiest days, partly because there was, so to speak, open season on blacks, considered less valuable than the mules they drove: "Kill a nigger, hire another; kill a mule, you got to buy another one." This aphorism, which would have made sense to the slave drivers of Egypt, to the masters of the galley slaves, to the brutal first and second mates of the Queen's navy, was wisdom to the greedy and often desperate men who contracted to build a section of Mississippi levee at so much per cubic yard. They corvéed their labor, they overworked and underpaid them, ruling them with pistol-whippings and the ever-present threat of lynching, against which the blacks had no recourse, since they had no legal status in Jim Crow Mississippi.

One major means of control was the rage that filled the hearts of the blacks—the helpless rage of a lower caste that dared not fight back or even speak up and that had nowhere to run to—rage that was dammed up in the black community and was taken out against their fellows. Among black levee men the saying was, "You can kill anybody you like, so long as you can work better than him. But, for God's sake, don't kill anybody can work better than you, or they'll put you under the jail."

In the levee camps everybody carried arms. One of the engineering veterans of the old-time levee board recalled that he regularly disarmed all the mule-skinners in his camp and threw the pistols in a nearby pond. "When that pond was drained, it was knee-deep in rusty six-shooters. Didn't matter how often I took away their pistols, they'd get more the next payday."

A young New Englander who came to work in a Mississippi camp as an engineer wrote home a candid and chilling account of what he saw.

Dear Folks,

There is hardly anything else in this place but negroes—about six or eight to every white man, and as a consequence every white man here virtually carries his life in his hands, for it is a place where the long arm of the law does not reach. If a white man gets in trouble with a negroe, he has to shoot and shoot quick or else get shot. Everybody carries a gun . . . and is always in a state of preparedness.

The contractor's camp, which is a short distance above here, consists of about forty tents, one white man, and about seventy-five or a hundred negroes with their "women" and over a hundred head of big strong mules. The way these levee niggers shoot one another is something fearful. One got shot in a crap game in camp above here. It didn't even stop the game. . . .

If one of the white foremen shoots a couple of niggers on the works, and it by no means is an unheard of or infrequent thing, the work is not stopped. They are buried at night and that's all there is to it. Just look a moment at the conditions and you will understand. A negro can kill a man and double quick for a short distance toward the river can get into a veritable jungle which borders all along the Mississippi and there it would be a hard matter for even the devil himself to find him. Think of one white foreman, miles from anywhere, working a hundred and fifty of the most reckless niggers in the world. It's a plain case of which you'd rather do, shoot or get shot. . . .[1]

The white levee contractors hired poor white "nigger drivers" to manage their black labor. These foremen often had a black man to back them up, a professional killer who would as soon shoot you as look at you. Such a man we heard George Adams had been, cutting the widest swath in those wild frontier times of any man in the Delta. Remember, as you read his story, that he's talking about the teens, the twenties, the thirties. By then the levee had got to be forty feet high and four hundred feet wide, but the river kept gnawing at it, sometimes breaching it, and there were camps of muleskinners every few miles to keep it in repair. These camps were out of bounds to officers of the law and thus became hideouts for escaped prisoners and for all sorts of other bad actors, female as well as male.

Right here let me mention a little incident showing the feeling of these negro women who go around with these contractor camps. A negro man had gotten himself killed and his woman came out on the levee to view his "remains." Gazing at him solemnly for awhile, she remarked, "Poor Jim, done dead," and then looking up with a broad grin on her face, said, "Guess I have to git me another man tonight" and straightaway went in search of one.[2]

The levee bosses told their men, "If you keep yourself out of the ground, I'll keep you out of jail." Clubs, backed up by six-shooters, wrote the rules and for a while George Adams wore the rule book strapped to his hip.

The weeds were waist-high on the road to George Adams's place. The house was falling down, and rot had curled the shingles on the roof till they looked like the feathers on a frizzly chicken. You could see blue sky through the chinks. It had rained in the night. The soaked bedding—a pile of ragged quilts—lay across the foot of the big mahogany bed.

George's wife was busy with breakfast. The floor sagged and stretched as she waddled around the kitchen. Probably George had married her because he liked big-legged women.

A big-legged woman with the meat shaking on her bone,
Every time she wibbles, Lord, a poor man's dollar gone.

Now her calves were like thighs and she was so big-butted she had to stoop way over to keep from falling backward. George's wife was sick and she was as filthy as her flyblown kitchen. It was hard to look at her. But she was a nice woman.

"Breakfast ready, Mister Adams. Come on and eat something." George's wife had a sweet voice.

George was out on the back gallery, waking up. Windy George, the old-time gunman of the levee camps, was making his daily escape from sleep and decay. He was eighty-nine, lean and bright-colored, with a hawk's eyes glittering over a bitter smile.

"Bring my coffee out to me," he gasped, and then coughing cut his wind off. The cough rose in waves and shook his gaunt old body like a high wind shakes an old barn.

It shook him till he had to hold on to a gallery post to keep from falling out of his chair. Then, just as it seemed to grow easier, the cough began again and mounted and went on until it seemed certain that this time George would die. When the cough left him, he sat hunkered over his knees, his face pointed toward the earth, and hawked and spat strips of yellow phlegm, and below, the hens fought to peck it up.

Windy George still could not speak. He jerked his head to his wife and she handed him coffee. George spent a long time over it. He sucked it in, then rested his bony shoulders hunched in over his chest, and warmed his old bones inside and out with hot coffee and the July sunshine. He was in his sockfeet, and his britches were unbuttoned and his galluses hung loosely over his grey winter underwear. He looked like a lean old eagle—half its feathers gone, unable to fly, starving, sick with decay, but with a predatory stare still glittering in his bold eyes. These eyes indicated the filthy yard and the dreadful shack.

"I ain't got nothing today, not atmosphere," he said, but he didn't grin in that independent and shamefaced way of the Southerner, especially the black Southerner. George Adams said everything with the least possible breath and the smallest possible degree of expression on his masklike face. His fanatic reminiscences came whispering like the wind between the teeth of a well-cured human skull:

This man you looking at is somebody has done more for the white folks than he has for the niggers. I've worked for all of um, knowed um all, drunk with some of um, all the big levee men—Charley Idaho, Charley Lowrance and

Isum McBain, Jeffry Diamond. They thought there wasn't nobody like Windy George, wouldn't take anything for me. I knowed most of this country when it was a canebrake. I've killed a many a man, but never in anger. All I shot um for, I knowed their time had come to die. If I had to do anything, I teched the trigger and told the hammer to hurry. And I never pulled a pistol unless I shot a man.

One Sunday I had to do something I hated—shoot a woman. She was pulling another woman around by the hair and slapping her on the head with a knife, down in the commissary.

"Quit hittin that gal," I said.

"Yeah! Who's tellin me?!"

"I mean it. Quit hittin her."

"I'm gonna show the world you ain't a damn thing but talk." And she come round the table at me with her knife.

I touched the trigger and knocked her double somersault. She hollered when she fell. She said, "Ladies and gentlemen, they'll sho shoot you!" Well, they took her to Memphis and in a couple of months she was right back down in camp.

It was tough peoples up and down these levees in my time. Charley Moody was the bully of the stream. Jim Smith from Robertsville. Abe Cole, the baddest of um all; he carried his cap and ball all the time, run the river, drinkin and gamblin; he went over to Clarksdale and shot at the agents, made um git down off their horses. Both white and colored was tough. I saw Charley Lowrance strip a bad nigger and carry him in his tent buck-naked and whip him cause the nigger take his grub and refuse to work. Whipped him with a buggy strap and the nigger kicked as high as a mule. Those days you couldn't walk the levee when they was short of hands. They gonna make you work.

I remember a time when the river was on the rise, I was filling sacks on the levee, heard a nigger say, "Damn levee ought to break." Old Man Dabney, levee engineer, heard the words, and wanted to kill the man—say, "Old George, who said that?"

I knowed who it was and I knowed Dabney *would* kill him if I told. He was standing there with that old carbine of his. I told him, "Just somebody in that gang over there." Well, he went off, but later he come to my house and put me to nightwatching. We was watching out for people from the Arkansas side, try to put a hole in *our* side of the levee, to take the pressure off theirs. Old Jurdon Dunn, the colored constable, told me, "If you catch a skiff comin in, don't ask no questions—just shoot."

The river was so high that it was bound to bust somewhere, here or on the Arkansas side. So we lay in behind the levee and watched.

Way later on, two white men and two niggers came rowing up in a skiff and begin to bore a hole in the levee. We layed low there till after while they said, "Mine's down," and here they come with the dynamite. I throwed my guns on um. The niggers held up their hands and said, "Don't kill us. They'd-a killed us in Arkansas if we hadna come."

The white men started to move back down the levee to their boat; I told um, "I'll kill your souls if these bullets will kill you." And we held them till Old Man Eph Larrabie, he was a regular old wildcat, come riding along.

"What's this?" he asked.

"You'll find out if you step on that dynamite," I told him.

He lit out on his horse, and in an hour and a half there was more white folks and niggers on the levee than a towboat could pull. "We knowed old Windy George was in it," they all said. I told um, "If you hurt them colored people, I ain't gonna watch for you no more. They was forced to do it." Old Man Eph, he was one of the blue hen's chickens [in other words, he was a rare bird], he killed three men at Sunflower Landing and shot at the fourth, he said, "I reckon we'll leave um alone, if Windy George says so."

They taken those two white men from Arkansas and tied plows around their necks and Old Man Dabney said, "You trying to bore the levee and drown somebody; you're gonna feel what it's like to drown." And he made their niggers row them out in midstream in their skiff and heave them in the river just like a chunk of wood. You better not be caught on the levee at night in highwater.

Me and Jurdon Dunn always nightwatched after that and Jurdon, he was a hard man; he done the thing he always said he wanted to do. Jurdon killed the man that got *him*. Those times, wasn't a Satdy passed down along the river, at Hillhouse or Sunflower landin or one of them, without a killin happened.

This nigger was playing hard at a picnic, throwin ice cream over the peoples and then askin them to do something. When he knew anything, Jurdon had a .44 in his face and told him, "I don't want to hurt you, but give me that gun."

Nigger said, "I'll give it to you, but it ain't because I want to."

Jurdon told him, "I'm just trying to keep you out of trouble." And the nigger went off.

About dark the nigger come back to the dance with a father Barlow knife about eight inches long, grabbed Jurdon's forehead from behind and popped him in the jugular. Jurdon drew his .44 and shot him in the ass as he ran, broke that nigger in two. Then Jurdon says, "Go get a doctor, boys, I'm bleedin to death." He died in a few minutes. I went down there next morning and there was blood all over the floor.

That time when Eph Larrabie killed his three men down at Sunflower's, I was working for him. Now old Eph was a man uglier than a homemade doll, and he loved to drink. When he'd get in his whiskey, he'd stay for a week, but he'd pay you, he'd pay you a dime if he owed you. He was a man that would come to the relief of his hands; he'd defend you. Ask him for money, he'd run his hand down in his pocket and say "How much?"

I did all the brickwork down at his place one time. It got cold that year and I couldn't get no whiskey nowhere. I knew old Eph had some. I knocked on his door.

"What do you want?"

"Whiskey."

"I ain't got a damn bit. I done told you, you goddam nigger, I ain't got none."

I wasn't afraid of him and I said, "I know you too well; you won't get out of no whiskey." Well, he went right by me like I was a statue, come back, says, "Here," and handed me a pint. That was old Eph—one of the blue hen's chickens.

So that time he killed his three men, he blowed his conch and we all come running to the big house. "Well, boys," he told us, "I've raised hell. Will you stand by me?"

We all hollered, "Yes, we'll stand by you." So he passed out the whiskey and gave us all guns and we all set around the gallery and the yard there drinkin and havin a time. Late in the afternoon three or four men came ridin by the house with their guns, but they didn't stop when they saw us. Anybody that would have stopped would have had trouble. I never did hear how they buried those men. Rolled um in the river, I reckon.

Now how old Eph and the other white folks come to think so much of me was the time those three bullies of the river robbed the mail boat and killed the cap'n and threw the mate overboard and set fire to the boat and run on down the river in their skiff. So we all took in after them and chased and sighted um. We knowed they was too good shots to come right up to. So Old Man Dabney ask me to see if I could wing one. I leveled down on um and winged one and they all told me to try again. So I got all three of them and the white folks got their money back. They all said, "Old George is worth a million."

"Hell, he's worth the whole state of Mississippi."

They all knew me. When I was baptized, there was white and black on the levee, thick as 'lection. I went down in the water and I said, "Goodbye, boys, I'm gone," you oughta heered those niggers holler—"Old George has sho gone under the water."

Once I caught some niggers had run off from the county farm and I carried them on in. They told me that Old Man Tom Hardy had been whippin niggers. He wanted to have the name of whippin a nigger and he had beat sixteen to death. I didn't believe um and I carried them on in. I slept at the farm in the cage with the convicts, and the guard asked me for my pistol. I told him, "You gonna sleep with your wife, ain't you?"

"Yes."

"Well, I'm gonna sleep with my pistol, then."

That night they staked out a Negro and beat him to death for something he said. Staked him out—arms, legs, and head—and next morning he was dead. That made seventeen Tom Hardy had in the graveyard.

(The summer of 1942, forty-odd years after George Adams's tale, the Clarksdale paper described the fatal beatings of two Negroes on the county road gang. The whole matter had come into the open, the story admitted, because one of the men belonged to a national burial society that had sent an investigator to examine the claim of the dead convict's relatives. The guards involved, the story added, had been punished by transfer to other jobs in the county.)

So old John Eldridge didn't like all this and he had me up before the Board of Supervisors. The grand jury heard me and they asked for the three convicts to testify, said, "Old George, you go and get um," and they give me the paper.

Now I knew I was all right because I had Old Man John Eldridge behind me. He was a tall, long, pleasant-looking man, had a plantation and a store, and if you made a ruction in the store, he'd fool you out in the yard and beat you to death. Then when he'd get drunk, he'd ride his horse right in his own store and drink out the barrel of whiskey he kept in there. He give his niggers plenty of whiskey and a little money to gamble with, but everything they made, he taken. This man was back of me.

I rode out to the farm and Tom Hardy, the whippin man, come up with them three niggers. Had um chained.

"Take off the chains," I said.

Old Tom Hardy said, "Why, that feller there will outrun a wolf."

"He's in my possession," I said. "Take off them chains. You got these *folks* tied up like they was *varmints.*"

So I took um downtown, took um to a saloon, give um a bottle of beer apiece, and then we went over in the New World[3] awhile. Old Tom Hardy stood on the railroad track watching us.

Well, them niggers went in before the grand jury, and the grand jury found two bills against that white man for killing them niggers. Tried to get to arrest him but I told them, leave that to the sheriff. They went down and dug up all seventeen of them men and old Tom Hardy got eleven years in the pen. John Eldridge said he ought to been killed, said, "I just didn't think old Tom was that kind of man."

Why, the county gang in Coahoma is so rough's that just four months ago an escaped state prisoner got put out on our gang unbeknownst and he couldn't stand it and confessed so they would carry him back to Parchman State Pen. A man's got to know how to handle hisself in this country. And *then* his luck might be against him.

I remember a case. There was this colored woman. Old Man Jones was liking her. And a nigger was liking her, too. So Old Man Jones caught the nigger and whipped him. Well, that nigger laid for him. He caught him in one of them little country stores where they didn't have nothing to sell but kidney-cure wine and canned cherries. Nigger pulled his pistol and he had them white folks falling around under counters like blackbirds in a cornfield. Nigger shot and killed Old Man Jones and he ran off. He dogleg back and forth through the county and lost the dogs and got as far as Clarksdale fore they caught him. Chartered a train and brought him back down here and hung him to a big cottonwood tree and then shot him a hundred thirty-five shots after they hung him. They shot him so in the back you couldn't lay a quarter on him anywhere on his back. They put their cigarettes out on him and left him.

Well, I was working for old Eph Larrabie at the time, and he come over and we got to talking and old Eph said, "Only thing wrong, Mister Jones ought to killed the nigger right off." And I said I didn't think so.

I said, "Do you know the reason us niggers kill you white folks off?"

"No," he said, "I don't."

"Well," I told him, "you sits up on that horse. You know you can't whip me. You know it well. I know if you get down off that horse and come at me and if I hit you, they gonna lynch me. Just as much as if I'd kill you. So, we've decided, if we got to get into it with you, we gonna kill one of you."

That's what I told Old Man Larrabie and I used to hear him tell it often. And he'd say, "Don't tell me a nigger won't shoot you. Just look at this finger I'm missing. Know how that happened? I run my finger in a nigger's bosom to get his gun and he shot my finger off, that's how I know."

Then Old Man Larrabie would laugh. If he was alive, he'd be here today to pay off. Or if he wouldn't get here today, he'd make it tonight. Ride across the county to get to me. He's done it many a time and this used to be terrible country to get about on horseback. He was my friend.

Reason he got to like me, I was a prompter at square dances. Prompter, just like the preacher in church, directs everybody. When the folks come down from Memphis, they'd all ask for old Windy George to call the Virginia Reel and all such stuff as that. So that night Eph Larrabie come up to me and give me a dollar bill to call an extry-long dance because his best girl was there and he was dancing with her. When the dance was over, I asked him how he liked it and he laughed, "You danced me down tonight, Windy, you danced me down."

That's how we come to be friends. Back in the days when I used to do all the calling for the ristocrats.

Old George Adams looked bitterly around his ruined yard, hitched his galluses up over his bent shoulders, and said in his whisper, "See, I'm somebody has always done more for the white folks than my own color. And what have I got?—not atmosphere." He spat. And below in the dust, the chickens squawked and fought over bits of his dying flesh.

I recalled the cruel verses of the levee-camp song, where the bone-tired muleskinner appeals to the bossman:

I ax Mister Cholly what time of day,
What time of day.
And he looked at me, good pardner,
Throwed his watch away,
Oh-oh-oh-oh, throwed his watch away.

"Mister Cholly, Mister Cholly,
Did the money come?"
He say, "The river too foggy,
And the boat don't run,
Oh-oh-oh-oh, the boat don't run."

I ax Mister Cholly just to gimme one dime,
Just gimme one dime.
He say, "Go long, nigger,
You a dime behin,
Oh-oh-oh-oh, you a dime behind."

"Mister Cholly, Mister Cholly,
Just gimme my time."
He say, "Go on, ol nigger,
You time behin,
Oh-oh-oh-oh, you time behind."

MISTER CHOLLY

Always, everywhere the muleskinners addressed their songs to "Mister Cholly." Nobody knows for certain who Mister Cholly was. Charles (Charley for short) was a fashionable given name in high-toned Southern families, a name with a distinct touch of "class" in that epoch. So, until you knew your boss's name, best call him "Boss," or better "Mister Boss" or "Mister Cholly," to be on the safe side. When no boss was present, you might quote him— "Mister Cholly told me . . . ," "Mister Cholly say . . . ." Perhaps this usage was a product of the levee camps, since a number of actual Mister Chollys figure in their legends. Black Hat McCoy opined that Mister Cholly was the big-time operator Charley Silas, who shot down the Mercy Man, an officer of the SPCA out of Memphis. Silas's victim was also named Charley.

Both men became legends. Some singers addressed their plaints to Mister Cholly the Mercy Man, who cared about the mules, most others to his ruthless killer.

Other old-timers told me that the original Mister Charley was Charles Lowrance, an even meaner man, they said, than Charley Silas—meanness ran his family, the Arkansas Lowrances, headed by another tush-hog levee contractor, Old Man Isum Lowrance. Big Bill Broonzy spoke of another compassionate Mister Cholly, a Charles Houlin, who gunned down the redoubtable Charley Silas in a street battle because Silas had been mistreating some of Houlin's black tenants. Later, in 1959, I met this Mister Cholly, the proprietor of a huge wide-open gambling hall for blacks in the Arkansas Delta.

So who is the Mister Cholly of the levee-camp holler? Folk memory may cast him as any one or perhaps all of these figures. Hero or villain, brutal or merciful, it didn't matter in the bad old days. Every black laborer looked to his boss for money, for help, and, at times, for protection, and thus the bolder and more powerful he was in those lawless times, the better. Often, there was no one else to appeal to or to depend on. One sultry August afternoon I went calling on one of these Mister Chollys of the levee-building period.

A few miles along the low green hill of the levee stood the fine house of "Mister Cholly" Idaho, one of the white folks old Windy George had done so much for. "In fact," George said, "I was the cause of Mister Cholly getting that place. He had a levee contract at the time and I was with him. I had heard that this plantation was to be sold and I told him, 'If you git it, you'll be gittin a good place—fifteen hundred acres and every foot of it in cultivation.'

"Well, you know what that feller done—he was settin at the dinner table in the bosses' tent and I was sittin off from him, watching—he studied a minute, then went out, got on his horse, and rode off a-flyin.

"When he come back, he say, 'George.'

"I say, 'Suh.' "

" 'George, you shore as hell put me up to something.' "

The stars shone through the fizzled roof of George Adams's shack and George dreamed up his "windies" of his life with the white folks, of his adventures as a gunman delegated by the white folks, of his partial acceptance by the white folks. Mister Cholly Idaho, sitting in the cool parlor of his fine white plantation house, did not recall George Adams.

"In my days on the levee, I worked so many of them," he said quietly, "I just couldn't say how many. But I'm proud of this—I never crippled a nigger in my life." Black eyes stared coldly out of a stern face. This was a puritan, telling himself a story of iron self-discipline and self-sacrifice.

"Yes, I've handled labor in here for forty-six years and I've never crippled one. And that's a good record. Some of these foremen would beat um up just to act smart, but I didn't whip a nigger until it was necessary and then I'd make a good job of it. I'd take him out behind the house and wear him out with the belly band off the harness. I'd make him like it. He'd know he was in the wrong and he'd take it. They had a song about me . . .

If you be a skinner, be sure you can
Before you go to work for the black-eyed man.

Charles Idaho permitted a slight smile to his stern mouth and then went on:

Once I fired a foreman for hitting a nigger. He hit this nigger one time and then stepped back to see how he'd take it. That was the wrong thing to do, because all it did was make the nigger mad. If you whip a nigger, you want to scare him good. Do a good job when you start. That makes him work better. Well, I called that foreman and give him his time. I knew he wasn't cut out to be a nigger man.

I grew up to it myself. My folks were pioneers on the levee, and when I took my first foreman job, the levees were on the average eight feet high. Today they're better than thirty-five feet. They started raising little walls with wheelbarrows, used mostly white labor for that. Then they came along with slip scrapers and mule teams; and the white labor couldn't handle the mules, so from then on it was niggers on the job. From slip scrapers to high-ball wheelers, then dump wagons and elevator graders, and then tractors came in and the mule teams began to go out. Now it's all these big cow machines rolling on rubber; it's drag lines and cranes and big machinery.

The whole business is a gamble. Your contract calls for so much levee within a certain time limit. And you've got the weather to contend with and your labor conditions. Your levee nigger is a drifter and you know you gonna lose a certain percentage every payday. Anyway, ten to twenty percent. I have lost as high as a hundred percent; didn't have a man to take out a team—they'd gone to town to spend their money. Next day, though, I had a full force.

I've slept down under my own levee when the river was three feet over the top and there was a wall of sacks holding her back. One time had to put my camp on the levee with water all around me for fifteen miles and no way to town except by boat. The whole thing was a gamble and I got out of the business in '35. The prices fell so low you couldn't make money.

Things changed fast. The niggers used to do a lot of singin in the old wheeler days. Nowadays I hardly ever hear it.

Mister Charley, Mister Charley, give me my time.
Go long, nigger, you time behind.

You couldn't get those old levee niggers to work on a farm. They weren't happy unless they were on the levee. Every man had his tent—him and his woman or him and his buddy. Nigger quarters were off to themselves, two hundred yards from the commissary and the headquarters. They could do what they wanted in their own quarters. Rainy days and Sundays they could hang out in the commissary and shoot craps and gamble. I didn't believe in interfering unless there was trouble.

Many foremen allowed their men to carry pistols and they had plenty of killings in those camps, but I never allowed that. One of my gangs I worked for ten years and there wasn't but two shots fired the whole time. I think that's a pretty good record. I told them my tent wasn't bombproof and any shot they fired might hit me, so I wasn't going to have shooting. If anything like that happened, I wasn't going to ask questions, I was just going to tend to the man. Any pistol I found, I'd take it and break it over a wheeler wheel and throw it in the fill, and it's many a one I buried that way.

There was only two of us white foremen to a hundred niggers on the right-of-way and the wheeler gangs. And they needed a whippin at times. I'd go after them with a club or a whip, never with my bare hands—a man would have been a fool to do that—and when I was through with them, they was better workers. Like, if they got fightin, sometimes I'd disarm and strip them and make them fight it out. When they'd get tired, I'd wear um out with a strap and make them fight till they had enough, then whip them till they'd fight till they'd had more than enough, till they could just about wiggle. Naturally, I carried a pistol at all times. I had to. We were the law and everything in those camps.

That's the way all that dirt got moved—in three years I put in seven miles of it, moved seven million cubic yards, handling all nigger labor. We levee contractors created a billion dollars worth of land and property and that big green wall protects that wealth. It's land that produces like no other land in the world. It never needs a nickel worth of fertilizer, where most land costs five or ten dollars an acre a year. All it needs is about two cents an acre spent on the levees. That's what we did down here in the state of Mississippi since my daddy and his folks came over from North Carolina after the Civil War. But it took a type of people that knew how to handle a nigger, because the biggest part of the work was done with mules and there's nobody on earth can handle a mule like a nigger muleskinner. In the old days they'd sing, especially along late in the evenings. But the last ten or twelve years very little singing is done. That began to go out when tractors and cats came in.

THE LEVEE-CAMP HOLLER

In spite of the villainies just described, levee work was attractive to the men of the Delta. Years of plowing had given them the skills required to get work out of a mule team in any weather. On the river, payday came once every week or two, rather than once a year, and in a month a man could pocket more gambling and drinking money than he might earn in a season on the farm. Split away from their little home places and families, these itinerant muleskinners knew the pain of alienation and anomie, yet they enjoyed the freedom of roaming from job to job and woman to woman. If they had to knuckle under to a bullying boss, then they could take out their anger on their weaker fellows. Meantime, they were creating their own culture of racy lingo, humor, tall tale, custom, and song, in which their sociable and ebullient African temperaments could flower. The swampland and the sordid streets of their tent cities became the stage for new acts in the African-American drama, where they could test their manhood, cement their friendships, and enlarge their collective culture. They sang multiple melodies until their mules—all of whom had nicknames— joined in the chorus, sometimes grew so excited that they literally worked themselves to death.

In the thirties, when my father, John A. Lomax, and I were recording across the South, levee camps existed not only along the Mississippi but also on the White River in Arkansas, the Red River in Louisiana, the Brazos and Trinity rivers in Texas, and a score of lesser streams in the vast alluvial plains of the lower South. In these swampy lowlands, indeed wherever land was to be drained, foundations laid, or dirt moved, the black muleskinner appeared with his scoop pulled by a team of lusty mules, and the high, lonesome levee song would soon rise in the air.

> Got up in the mornin, so doggone soon,
> So doggone soon,
> I couldn see nothin, good podner,
> But the stars and moon—
> Oh-oh-oh-oh-oh, but the stars and moon.

The singer is explaining why he's late to work but, like a good worker, he also complains about working conditions in an outfit where all the mules have sore shoulders. The humane law forbade working a mule with a bad shoulder, forcing the animal to grind an open sore against its stiff leather collar. Most outfits disregarded this law, and its constant and flagrant violation became the subject of the muleskinner's perennial complaint.

Well, I looked all over the whole corral,
The whole corral,
And I couldn find a mule, good podner,
With his shoulder well—
Oh-oh-oh-oh-oh, with his shoulder well.

We found this song not only in the Mississippi Valley and the flood plains to the west into Texas, but in every other Southern state as well. Lately, I have looked up all these non-Mississippi levee-holler variants, and every one of them was sung by a Mississippian on his travels or by someone who had learned it from somebody from the Delta.

Charles Peabody, a young archeologist working a site in the Delta, was the first to report on the levee-camp holler. In his journal of 1903 he comments on the difficulty of describing the strange songs his muleskinners were singing:

As to the autochthonous music, unaccompanied, it is hard to give an exact account. Our best model for the study of this was a diligent Negro living near called by our men "Five Dollars" (suggestive of craps), and by us "Haman's Man," from his persistent following from sunrise to sunset of the mule of that name. These fifteen hours he filled with words and music. Hymns alternated with quite fearful oaths addressed to Haman. Other directions intoned to him melted into strains of apparently genuine African music, sometimes with words, sometimes without. Long phrases there were without apparent measured rhythm, singularly hard to copy in notes. When such sung by him and by others could be reduced to form, a few motives were made to appear, and these copied out were usually quite simple, based for the most part on the major or minor triad. The long, lonely sing-song of the fields was quite distinct from anything else, though the singer was skilful in gliding from hymn-motive to those of the native chant.[4]

Peabody also transcribed the free-flowing melody Haman sang, and there is no question that it contains the cadences peculiar to the levee-camp holler that my father and I so frequently recorded all across the Deep South during the 1930s and '40s.

The levee-camp holler therefore seems definitely to be Delta or at least Western in provenance.[5] In fact, repeated recording trips into the area revealed the existence of an extensive genre of songs, called hollers, in the Delta region. For example, every black prisoner in the penitentiary, we discovered, had a holler that was, in effect, his personal musical signature. Heard at a distance, another prisoner could say, "Listen at old so-and-so. Don't he sound lonesome this morning."

All these hollers share a set of distinctive features. They are solos, slow in tempo, free in rhythm (as opposed to the gang work songs), composed of long, gliding, ornamented and melismatic phrases, given a melancholy character by minor intervals as well as by blued or bent tones, sounding like sobs or moans or keening or pain-filled cries, even when they were performed with such bravura that they resounded across the fields. Because they were seldom sung except on the job, even the aficionados of black music have little acquaintance with this wondrous recitativelike vocalizing through which black labor voiced the tragic horror of their condition.

Cap'n, doncha do me like you do po Shine,
Drove him so hard till he went stone blind.

The style of these solo, unaccompanied, idiosyncratic, melancholic hollers runs directly counter to the mainstream of black song in the South and generally round the Caribbean, where song is for the most part on-beat, brisk, merry, sensuous, integrated, choralizing, and accompanied, if not by drums or some other instrument, at least by hand clapping and/or foot stomping. Most black song, both post- and antebellum, even when its mood is somber and serious when the song begins, usually picks up tempo and is transformed into music that can be danced to before it has been sung to a conclusion. Indeed, the bulk of black song, unlike that of Europe, which is usually lyrical, can be danced to—in the case of work songs, making work into a sort of dance.

Major exceptions to this rule are two: the long-meter hymns (the so-called Dr. Watts songs earlier described) and the work hollers of the Delta and the lowland Southwest. Both these forms came into prominence at the time of the decay of the plantation collectivity and the emergence of individualized effort as the main source of survival for Delta blacks. Both mark a sharp stylistic turn away from the on-beat collective song style of most earlier African-American genres and the adoption of a highly individualized solo attack. The favorite long-meter hymn is an ego-oriented appeal for help from God.

Lord, in my trouble I stretch my hand to thee,
Lord, in my trouble no other help I know.

The usual levee-camp holler is a personal appeal to Mister Cholly, the white boss who hires, fires, pays, or doesn't pay him.

Mister Cholly, Mister Cholly, just gimme my time.
Gwan, old bully, you are time behind.

It was in the Delta that blacks entered the levee and land-clearing crews, often forcibly organized, and became for the first time anonymous units of labor instead of being owned by somebody or belonging on some plantation and to an extended family. In this new condition they could see themselves being used up and flung aside, often actually worked to death, alongside the mules they drove. In the earlier plantation situation, under slavery and later on as renters or field hands, they still had some feeling of identification with the bosses they worked for and the place they lived. These relationships were usually attenuated in the levee camps and on the penal farms. There "a nigger wasn't worth as much as a mule." In most societies the individual can look to organized authority as in some sense beneficent or protective, can ask for mercy and help in times of distress and expect to receive it. But increasingly, the laborers of the Deep South, floating from camp to camp, often from prison to prison, came to feel that they had nowhere to turn.

There was, as usual in black tradition, a musical response. It came in the sudden emergence of the lonesome holler, and later the blues, notable among all human works of art for their profound despair. They gave voice to the mood of alienation and anomie that prevailed in the construction camps of the South. In creating these new, critical genres, American blacks called upon ancient African resources, for complaints of this very type existed in the traditions of African kingdoms. Indeed, our Cantometric survey has found very similar songs in Northwest Africa and the Lake States, among the Wolof and the Watusi, for example. A broader look finds that such ornamented, unaccompanied singing is commonplace in the kingdoms and empires of North Africa, of the southern Mediterranean, and of the Middle East. It seems, in fact, that this song type, which we might call the high, lonesome complaint, is one undercurrent of music in the whole of civilized Eurasia—the ancient world of caste, empire, exploited peasantry, harem-bound women, and absolute power—from the Far East to Ireland. A related and ultimately derivative string-accompanied solo style is also present in this same region. It turns up in West Africa, and in the Americas gave rise to the blues.

There are more than hints of this ancient song type in the so-called big songs—the highly ornamented and complex bardic melodies—that entertained the kings of Ireland in ancient times. Throughout this huge domain of empire, which produced early civilization, males generally dominated females, and powerful males had total authority over the less powerful. Only God and his earthly delegates—the emperor, the lord, the high priest—could help. Everywhere in this vast world of classical antiquity, the complaint, the plea for mercy, shaped most cadences to a minor wail. The *muezzin* calls the faithful to worship in this fashion, the farmer drives his animals with such tunes, women rock their babies and keen their dead in this mode, the lover serenades his sequestered sweetheart in this way.

Songs of this type occur in the cattle-raising kingdoms of Northwest Africa, for instance, among the Wolof of Senegal and the Moslemized Hausa of northern Nigeria, and are the stock-in-trade among Saharan pastoralists. A black caravaneer, who loved his camel so much that he kissed her frequently, once sang me a plaintive tune that he said inspired them both on their long, sandy voyages. Thus I am confident that the original of the levee holler will one day be found among the pastoralists of Northwest Africa. Senegalese slaves were prized for their skill with animals, and I suppose that some Wolof, brought to Mississippi, successfully tried out this animal-handling song on his work team, and the melody caught on, for old-time muleskinners agree that these cadences spur on the weary mule.

But what were the emotions of levee-camp men who kept alive the ancient complaints of Africa and of the old world of slavery and tyranny which became the wellspring of the blues? All those wild and melancholy tunes touched my heart, but I had never dug into their background. What held me back? Laziness, fear, timidity, and the same reluctance to enter the sorrow-ridden landscape that perhaps deterred Gorki from a second *Lower Depths*. However, when I returned to the Delta in the more relaxed atmosphere of the 1970s, I found it easy to enter this lost world of the black experience. Committed to a TV program about the origins of the Delta blues, I needed a levee-camp scene and sought out the chief engineer of the levee board for advice. I'll never forget what he told me.

"Used to be, you could smell those camps a mile away, and there was a buzzard on every fence post.[6] Of course, there are none of those camps left today, and not even one mule, because dirt moving is all done by heavy machinery, but there are plenty of old-timers hanging out downtown under the levee who can give you a good story."

Not long afterward, with the help of Worth Long, researcher on the film and veteran of the freedom marches, I was draining a jar with a raffish crowd of levee-camp veterans. This was a great session, but the background sound in the juke drove us to look for a quieter place for the levee-camp interview.

FOUR MULESKINNERS

I chose a huge derelict Mississippi tugboat, a tawny rustbucket three stories high, parked on the river side of the levee, as the backdrop for taping these old-timers in the 1970s. I had them stride down the grassy slope of the levee—four lithe old black men, laughing and relaxed—as if they'd been on camera all their lives. They moved into the shadow of the huge barge and took seats on the big timbers that supported it. I lay on my belly at their feet with the cameraman peering over my shoulder, so that these grizzled muleskinners would loom large on screen as they spoke.[7] Worth Long, my sensitive and sapient guide in these adventures, hovered in the background, giving the scene his blessing. Since we had nipped at a bottle together earlier, these levee veterans felt they were in good hands. In fact, they seemed to relish every moment of their violent adventures. Their mood was serious, but the extravagance of their accounts often had them giggling and chuckling the way survivors of a shipwreck or a natural disaster do a long time after. With the Supreme Court decision on segregation and the freedom marches behind them, they were not afraid to talk, as they might have been in previous decades. The little bunch of survivors included:

Bill Gordon—burly, smiling, but serious, a porkpie hat shading a copper skin and high cheekbones that spoke of Native American ancestry—his role was to tell it straight and unadorned.

Next to him on his left, Walter Brown, the old river runner, pixielike, with a much-broken nose in a nobbled face that life had bashed and slashed, hands gnarled with work and arthritis—he was the legend maker, the poet of facts, often stuttering and popeyed with the excitement of reliving them.

To his right, William S. Hart, sweet and simple-hearted, wearing a sombrero in honor of his movie-star namesake, his little eyes gleaming with happiness as he recalled the exploits of his mule teams.

At their feet and to the right, Joe Savage, by far the youngest and most damaged of them, made musical comments. His front teeth had been kicked out in some jailhouse battle, so that he seemed to be snarling as he sang, twisting his mouth around the empty hole between his fangs, ornamenting the old melodies, shading and shifting his tone color, like a Johnny Dodds, like a South Indian flute player, like a Mississippi muleskinner.

Together these four veteran rivermen raised the curtain on a virtually unknown episode in American history with Joe Savage providing the music cues:

> *Well, I got up in the morning so doggone soon* (he moaned)
> *Till I couldn see nothin but the stars and moon.*

BILL GORDON: You go out there in the morning, plenty mornings you'd have to wait until it get light enough to go to work.

WALTER BROWN: That's right!

B.G.: You'd be standing there in the dark.

W.B.: Standing there in the dark!

B.G.: And when it get light enough, then you go to work. And then you work in the evening, until it get dark and you couldn't see how to come in. They didn't have no electric lights in them times, but those mules just knowed they way in.

W.B.: You couldn't see how to take your mules out. In other words, you would just say it was a free penitentiary. And what I mean about a free penitentiary, you didn't have to ask nobody when you get in, and there wasn't nobody standing out there watching you when you got ready to leave. There were so many men, they didn't stay more than a few weeks . . .

You lived in tents and most times they had dirt bottoms. They would dig ditches around the tent and take shovels and throw dirt up against the tent to keep water from coming in when it rained.

B.G.: See, them tents keep you cool *and* warm. You can put a floor in these, you put baseboard around it, screen it up, just same as a house. You got tables—if you want to cook. You don't wanna cook in your tent, you can have your stove outside.

WILLIAM S. HART: Them tents was on roads just like streets, you know? Sometimes they had two or three hundred tents. Shacks . . .

B.G.: . . . to sleep in—you git in there an go to sleep. The next morning the shack rouster comes around an wake ya up. First time he come around, he'd knock on the tent, he say,

Get up! Sleepin good?
I wish you would.
I hate to call you, but I gotta do.
I don't want ya, but Mr. Charley do.
Say, ya goin?

Say, you sleepin in a good bed an callin it bunk,
You eatin a good sumpin ta eat an you callin it junk.
Say, now ya goin?

So he'd go round the first time. If you wasn up when he back around a second time, he was comin *in* there. You gonna have to come out there, otherwise that shack rouster gonna come in after you.

ALAN LOMAX: What would he come in with?

B.G.: He'd have his stick an pistol.

A.L.: You ever see him shoot or hit anybody?

B.G.: Oh, yeah! I got a lick one morning. He struck at another fella an he hit *me*. Had my head drippin. I was already up. This fellow, when he got after him, he broke and run, so he made a mistake an hit me.

A.L.: But you couldn't fight him back?

B.G.: No, you couldn't fight him back—he got a pistol. Can't fight no pistol. (*laughs*)

W.B.: Let's show the man how that shack-rouster song go. Hand me that piece of steel yonder. . . . See, when they would come round to wake you up, they would have a steel in a diamond shape. And they would rap it, like this, and call for you to git out the bed.

(*Walter Brown produces a frenzy of sound out of a steel triangle, then keeps time to his shack rouster's call.*)

Everybody
Better get up soon.
Got to catch the mules
A-by the stars and moon.

A-git up, boys,
Put on your clothes.
Eat your breakfast—
Git ready to roll.

Ain't you ready?
A-boy, ain't you ready?

JOE SAVAGE *(singing):*

I don't know
But I was told
A-when you git here
You got to solid roll.

Ain't that right?
Ain't you ready?[8]

W.B.: Some of um was like I was. If I didn't feel like goin, I didn't go, you
know. I was just that crazy, you know. I felt I like I was bad and fast as
anybody toted a gun, you know. And I been like that all a my life. I don't
meet nobody no faster than me, and I'm sixty-six years old. I don't tote a
gun now. But when I was in levee camps, I carried my pistol. And if
anything happened, somebody found somebody.

He got his pistol
In his hand.
He'll kill somebody
Or he's gon kill some man.

Ain't you ready?
A-boy, ain't you ready?

W.B.: Monday morning everybody be getting up goin out there three-thirty.
They go catch they mules and harness 'em up and then you go to the
kitchen and eat, and then you go to the pit and you find your wheeler and
you set there till it get light enough for the man breaking out the Johnson
bar for to see how to load it.

J.S.:

Ooo-oo-ooooo . . .

I woke up soon one morning
Bout the break of day.
Lord, I seen my old woman
When she walked away.

The sergeant say, "Hurry."
The captain say, "Run."
I'm gonna take my time,
I'm gonna take my time.

WILLIAM S. HART *(chuckling and chortling with pride over the mules who were comrades on the job):*

I get out there and got my team, man. *I'd* get way back on my a-lines, you know—drivin two great big ol mules, their heads up in the air like that, their harness jinglin, tassles hangin all down the side of um, just takin their time, walkin, just walkin and walkin. Every once in a while, I'd sing. *(His head is in the air, his arms move like the legs of his remembered team as he sings this classic statement of the slowdown.)*

I'm gonna be late in the morning,
I'm gonna be late all day,
I'm gonna be late all day,
I wanna be late all day,
Heyyyy——
I'm gon be late all day
With ol Freddie Mae.

(speaking)

Them big sons a guns—they steppin! *(laughs)* They steppin with me, they *pullin* me up the levee! I'm just raring back on the lines. Them was big sons of guns. Tough. When they'd get on top-a that levee, I'd just raise that line up round they head, say, "Bap!" and we scattered the dirt on down. Then right on down and off that levee I'd go.

I'm gonna be late in the mornin,
I'm gonna be late all day
Wid ol Freddie Mae.

That was my mule!

William S. Hart and Walter Brown are not the first to admire the mule. The mule pulled war chariots in the battles before Troy and was praised by King David in the Bible. The farmers of Italy, Spain, and France contributed to the breed and perfected the animal for agricultural uses, and George Washington himself took a hand in making sure America's mules were of sterling quality. In their peak year, 1930, more than 300,000 mules were plowing Mississippi fields. Certainly, without the mule, farming the Delta would have been impossible. Theodore Savory, the source of this information, sums up the virtues of the mule as follows:

> The mule has more than its share of admirable qualities. It is courageous and intelligent, hard of hide, sure of foot, sound of constitution and able to resist changes in climate and withstand thirst and hunger better than the horse. The mule is markedly sensitive around the head and does not enjoy having its ears fondled; in this respect it differs from the horse and resembles its male parent. It will not accept injustice or irrational treatment but meets them with instant rebuff. The common phrase "a kick like a mule" shows how well known is the animal's major means of protest. . . . They are essentially sensitive spirits in robust bodies, and when their early training has been sympathetically carried out, their behavior is incomparable. . . .
>
> "You can talk to a horse, but you can chat and whisper to a mule."[9]

To this, William Faulkner, who considered the mule the second most intelligent of animals, adds one cautionary note: "He will work for you for ten years, in order to kick you once."

Ray Lum, the great mule and horse trader in Mississippi, preferred mules to horses:

> A mule has got twice as much sense as a horse. You won't jump him in a river. You can pull a horse out of a barn on fire, and the son-of-a-bitch will jerk loose from you, run right back in there and burn up. You get a mule out and he'll thank you for it. . . . Don't ever sell a mule short. If you've been mean to him, he'll remember and kick you when he gets a chance. He'll kick you hard enough to kill your whole soul. I've had my pants kicked off by a little mule. . . .[10]

The old-time black levee men reproached their animals tenderly and punished them like family members, so that men and mules strove mightily together and sometimes even sang in concert.

w.b.: I drove three—Emma near, Ada swing, Martha stick. I did never put a bit in their mouth. When I hitch that bull hook in that wheeler tongue, they'd take off. If they hit a root, I'd say, "Get down," and they'd get down[11] till the harness stand up on they back. And when that loader break out, I tell um, "Hey"—they'd stop, right there. But I didn't never put a bit in they mouth, and you couldn't hook um up in the wrong place. Not to save your life. They knew where they worked, and many a day I hung their bridle lines up on their harness and never took it down.[12] When I rode one I didn't never lead the other ones, they followed. I worked um four years, and didn't nobody do nothin' for um but me. And they knew me just like they knew one another.

I called um "honey." Say, "Look, honey, you ain't doin nothin today." Now they *knew* who I was talkin to, cause I petted um. They'd get out in the pit and they'd get up on a root, Martha would choke down, you know. Cause I had choke strips on um, you know. She'd get out there an she'd stretch out, and her harness come up on her back—she'd whinny, "Whoooo!" I'd say, "Hold it. Uh, get back there." And I walk up there and I turn to Emma, say, "Emma," say, "you ain't doin nothin." And I say, "Ada," said, "and you ain't doin nothin," I say, "and you lettin your sister *down* over there!" And I'd take that line, and I'd come back and hit her, ah . . .

> *Oh, everybody*
> *'Cidin to call me mean.*
> *Cause they see me whippin*
> *On my ol hook team.*

A.L.: And how many people would be singin at one time?

W.B.: Aw, everybody and everybody.[13] You couldn't hear your ears. And some of 'em could sing so good, till the mules would go to hollerin. People don't believe that, but that's true. Buster Williams could start to singin—when his old lady quit him—he could start to singin and the *mules* would go to hollerin. They'd just holler, just holler: "Ahhhh! Ah! Ah!"—like it was twelve o'clock or something.[14] *(laughs)*

> *And tomorrow is payday,*
> *Sunday I'm goin home.*
> *I'm gon hold my baby*
> *In my lovin arms.*

I had whips that I plaited myself, and I had a sea-grass cracker on them, *that* long. But I didn't hardly hit my team. I'd throw that cracker down the side of um an let it pop. That plait was made of the skin off a willow tree, and when I would pop right in his ear, that ol mule would head right up the levee. *(laughter)* Wah-hoo! *(laughs)* I used to love that!

A.L.: You muleskinners could hit a mule with a whip anywhere you wanted to hit, couldn't you?

W.H.: Oh, yeah! Even under the foot!

B.G.: You could hit right up under the front shoulder and knock um down. Take that leather line an hit a mule right up under their front shoulder—he fall just like you shot him in the heart.

W.B.: One time down in the Black River bottoms I had two oxens, and they had as much sense as I did. Ball and Jane—I never will forget um. For instance, they'd come to two trees, about that far apart that both of um couldn't go through there with them yokes on um? Here's what Ball and Jane do. One of um would go through first and turn around and let the other one come through. Then they would back up and they would drag that log through there! I didn't never tell em nothin but, *"Gee, Jane"* and *"Haw, Ball."* That's all I ever had to tell um. That was down there by Chinkapin, Arkansas.

J.S.: Man, they put me behind a plow drivin a white mule—you better not hit a white mule, better not put a spot on it. *(laughs)*

B.G.: And at night you better clean the collars of your mule team. If you didn't clean the collars off, next morning old boss go out there and see a scab on that mule's collar and he'd make you eat it off.

A.L.: Eat it? What was on the collar?

B.G.: A sore off his shoulder. A scab off the mule. He'd make you eat it off.

W.H.: Them big fine mules, what they had, they cost um two-fifty, three hundred, four and five hundred dollars. And they didn't want them misused. The Mercy Man would come around and find out about it. His job was to see that you didn't work a mule with a sore shoulder.

W.B.: That's right, that's the Mercy Man.

B.G.: If a scab was on the mule, and you didn't get his collar off, he go round an check about it, then he come back and find out who it was, he make you eat that scab off of it.

J.S. *(singing):*

Well, I looked all over
That whole corral,

Lord, I couldn find a mule, good podner,
Wid his shoulder well.

An you could tell him, say,

Lord, my wheel mule crippled,
And my lead mule blind.
Lord, I'm gon need some ol body,
I can't shake a line.

That's when you tryin to climb that ramp.
W.B.:

Whoa, tell me, Captain,
What you expect me to do?
Whoa, Ada is crippled
And blinded, too.

Boy, but if he happen to ask you
How come I did leave,
Tell him that I got tired of that rice and salmon
And them black-eyed peas.
Yeah, yeah, yeah,
And them black-eyed peas.

J.S.:

You go down in them quarters,
Tell my buddy Will
That that long, tall girl he's lovin
She gon git im killed.

W.B.:

Well, well, well, well, I got a letter this mornin,
This the way it read:
Hurry home, hurry home,
Your wife and baby is cryin for meat and bread.

J.S.:

> *I bought her a mink coat for Christmas,*
> *I tried to buy a diamond ring.*
> *She said, "I'm sorry to tell you,*
> *Little Joe, but that don't mean a thing."*

W.H.:

> *Went to the commissary,*
> *Tell him myself,*
> *Don't let my woman*
> *Have nothin else.*

I don't let her have nothin else, either.

B.G.:

> *Some call me Slick,*
> *An some call me Shine.*
> *But you can hear my name*
> *Ringin all up an down the line.*

A.L. (TO BILL GORDON): How old were you when you went on the levee camp?

B.G.: About eleven.

W.B.: Me an him went out there bout the same time.

B.G.: I was about eleven. I was too small for to put the harness on my mule—I could put the collar on, but I couldn't put on the harness. The mens would put my harnesses on for me an I'd push the collar, bottom upwards, and then push it up on the small part of the mule's neck.

W.H.: Well, when I come round the levee camp, I's a little kid. Nineteen nineteen—A fella out of Memphis called a "man catcher." Catchin boys, carryin em down to the camps . . .

A.L.: Tell us what a man catcher was.

W.H.: Well, a man catcher is just like a . . . getting up labor for the levee camps, you know.[15]

B.G.: You want some men, right? He'll get um for you.

W.H.: He get so much a man. He git you, and send you down there. Just pay him three dollars a day.

B.G.: Jim Coco caught him here.

W.H.: They send you down there and they'd give you a team, even if you can't drive um.

I didn't know one mule from another. You supposed to know your team, but I didn't know one team from another. I used to catch another man's team and try to harness it for mine. So the corral man help me harness my mules—till I got big enough.

Then, when I got big enough, why I'd just harness my own mules. I used to tie a string on they tails to tell *my* mule from *his* mule! *(laughs)*[16] They come out in the morning tryin to find they mules, and I got um already harnessed. I'd hook um up, and go on out there, haul that man some dirt! Come back in. Oh, I was a cat then!

A.L.: How old were you?

W.H.: I was about eighteen then. I was a man then. I thought I was, anyway. I was working for Charley Silas.

J.S.: Mmm. He's hot—come on now, boy!

W.H.: He was a bad man—they said he was old Jesse James himself. And he'd ride the wildest horse he had. And that horse be just *dancing*. Said he was old Jesse James. And you couldn't slip up on him, you couldn't slip up on him a bit.

W.B.: And he was an *old* man!

W.H.: They said he was ol Jesse James. I used to work for him. He said, "What's your name?" I said, "My name is William S. Hart." "Huh! Shit! You ain't a patch on William S. Hart's ass!" *(laughs)*

I levee-camped from 1919 to '35. I told um all, "Well, man, I go everywhere cause I ain't no one-man's man, and I go everywhere they're payin good money." So, I'd go on a job and get me a load, an come on out. Them others would be slow gettin up the levee, you know? I'd pass them on a run, goin up. Goin on up, goin on up. And when that man throw that clod on up, turn her right back there, and if the dirt be loose, I'd just keep a-going. But if the dirt be stiff, that old buckshot dirt, I'd take my time. You go runnin on with that buckshot and it'll stick on that door and turn you over! *(laughs)*

B.G.: Or jackknife it.

A.L.: How long would it take you to build a hundred yards of levee?

B.G.: Oh, I guess bout couple a months. Cause you didn't have nothin but mules. Have no tractors.

W.B.: In some camps they'd have forty men, some camps wouldn't have but thirty, some camps they'd have twenty-five just depending upon how big the man was. They build their camps according to what size that the man was, how much finance that he had, you know, and how much equipment that he had. Now this man here, George Miller, he got dirt wagons—he don't have slips, he got dirt wagons. A man have to get on the back of it, and trip it when they dump. Then a man got to wind the bottom of it up for to catch the dirt the next time. All right, Charley Silas, he may have slips—

B.G.: —wheelers—

W.B.: —that's a scoop that sets on two wheels, but when you unbuckle it, the bottom of it drop down. It's got a long handle on it, called the Johnson bar. When the pan get full, then the wheeler loader, he pull down on the Johnson bar. It's got a lock system and that buckle. Well, the man with the three mules in the front—what's called the hook team—he knocks loose. When that wheeler loader unbuckle the Johnson bar, the hook team stops, if they're trained. And all you got to do just knock your hitch out. Well, then the two mules carry it on to the dump. Then he'd take that fresno and he'd come back and he would dress it off.

B.G.: The fresno do the work the bulldozer do nowadays.

W.B.: The man that's drivin this slips, he stand up on the handles of it for to keep it from goin in the ground, throwin him over between the mules. Whenever you hit a hard spot, it would throw you over there between the mules. I wasn't but eleven years old, but I was drivin slips.

B.G.: All right, they got a spotter up there. You bring it up there and he never would just say "Dump it" or "Gee" or "Haw," he'd just throw a clod a dirt. He may be lookin cross the river somewhere, just to fool you, and he take a stick or a clod of dirt and chunk it, and you got to dump it where he chunking that thing. You better!

W.B.: That was the *spotter.*

B.G.: If you didn't put it where he said, he had a root layin down there with a big knot on it.

W.B.: That's right.

B.G.: He'd tap you cross the head wit it. You had ta do what he *say to do.* You don't need to try an say what you ain't gonna do, you gonna do what he *say* to do.

W.B.: Whether you saw it or not, but you'd better dump the dirt where that clod fell.

B.G.: Else he'd put that club on you.

W.B.: And then they had a spotter's song.

(begins singing)

I tell my wife an baby,
Whoa, they can look for me.
I got a long holdover,
And I may not never go free.

(speaking)

And they was already free.

(singing)

And I may come limpin,
And I may come lame,
And I may come toppin
Some long freight train.

B.G.: Sometimes it be so cold out there—he wouldn't let you go to the fire—
you'd have to let your lines slip through your hands. Like your wheeler'd
be goin on, you'd have two mules to it, and the mule'd be goin along and
you'd walk along an git up to the fire. See, they had a fire built, for you to
warm goin by. You couldn't stop at it, your wheeler couldn't stop, but you
could let the mules keep a-goin and let the lines slide through your hands
till it get to the end, then you got to catch um. You could never just, say,
stop at the fire and warm.

A.L.: What would they do to you?

B.G.: Would cut your head! Beat it with a pistol or stick or sumpin if you stop.

W.B.: And a lot of times his lines would be covered with frost and them gloves,
when the lines slipped through your hands, your gloves would be full of
frost—just like snow.

B.G.: Yeah, you couldn't stop at the fire and just warm.

W.B.: Now when the bosses came on the levee, they all wore white boots, come
up to here . . .

B.G.: Yeah.

W.B.: . . . and they wore khaki-color pants with button legs—or zip legs. And
they would have on heavy underwear, T-shirts, and heavy wool turtleneck
sweaters. They'd have a pistol on this side [left] and a stick hangin on that

side [right] of their saddle. And you was gonna do what they said, or you was gonna get whipped today.

A.L.: How would they talk to you? What would they say?

W.B.: They didn't never talk to no one man. When they get ready to make a talk, they'd ride right in the middle of the pit. And Ol Man Brown used to take his hat off his head—he wore a big white Stetson, a great big one—and he'd throw it up and he'd shoot six holes in it fore it hit the ground! Then he'd tell somebody down there, "Hand me my hat!"

And they would hand it to him and he'd say, "Now lissen, I'm gon whip you if you stand and I'm gonna kill you if you run. I want you all to do so and so and so. I want you to get me some dirt. I got to finish such and such a station by such and such a time. . . . Is there any questions?" When he asked you that, he'd have his hand on that pistol.

"Is there any questions?" Ain't nobody sayin nothin', an he'd say, "Well, just carry on."

B.G.: Mister Charley, George Miller, Mister Weathers—what them other two bossmen's name?

W.B.: Blair.

W.S.: Mister Tate.

W.B.: Tate. They had camps from Miller's Bend, all the way down here when they was building this levee. Now *they* was *bad mens*. They said Mr. Charley shot Mister Lowrance and Mister Lowrance shot Mister Blair.

A.L.: Can you sing that song?

W.B. *(singing):*

> *Whoa! Mister Charley shot Mister Lowrance*
> *And Mister Lowrance shot Mister Blair.*
> *And then Mister Charley asked him,*
> *"Why were you there?"*
>
> *He said, "You shootin a .38,*
> *And I shoots a .45,*
> *And that .45 is known*
> *To keep me alive."*

(speaking)

And they'd say,

(singing)

> *Yeah, yeah, yeah,*
> *To keep me alive.*

A.L.: What kind of an argument would they get into?

W.B.: You got some mules, all right? You got um in your corral. *I* got some mules, *he* got some mules, and *he* got some mules. The corral boss may get slack and leave the gate open, leave the gap down. Well, all them mules get out on the levee and *you* come and say, "Well, this is *my* mule." *He* goes in, "No, it's *my* mule"—like that, you see.

A.L.: Everybody talks about Mister Charley, sings about Mister Charley. Who was he?

W.B.: Well, ain't nobody actually know who Mister Charley was.

B.G.: They made a song up about him.

W.B.: Yeah. I tell you this, he was a tough man. He used to blow, and you could hear him on the top a that levee. And when he blowed, sumpin was goin to happen.

A.L.: What'd he blow?

W.B. & W.H.: *(in unison):* He'd just blow . . .

W.B.: Whooop!

W. S. HART: Whiiip!

W.B.: And when he did that, sumpin was goin ta happen. There was many men that went there and worked expecting payday and they didn't git nar'un for six or seven weeks! And he'd leave there and hadn't got nothin for his work since he had been there but his food.

(They've shifted into the present tense; the men are reliving their experiences.)

B.G.: Sometimes they give you what you call a drag.

W.B.: Yeah. A drag.

B.G.: Like pay you off five or ten dollars, somethin like that.

W.B.: Yeah!

B.G.: Just for you to gamble with.

W.B.: Yeah!

B.G.: Sometimes they'd miss four and five months.

W.B.: By doin that!

B.G.: Puttin ya off. If someone come along, guy had nerve enough—and make um pay off.

J.S.: Mister Charley T. Silas wouldn pay off!

W.B.: Now, you could go to the commissary. You didn't have to be naked, and you didn't have to be cold, you could go. Every one of um had a commissary.

J.S. *(singing softly)*:

> *Ooo-oo oooo . . .*

W.B.: A—a commissary . . .

J.S. *(singing louder)*:

> *Mr. Charley T. Silas*
> *And old Sandy Moore . . .*

W.B.: . . . an you could go there and get anything you wanted to wear. You could charge something to that doodling book an carry it to the kitchen . . .

J.S.:
> *Two of the richest men*
> *That kept a poor black man poor . . .*

W.B.: . . . and your cook could get anything that she wanted to cook with.

J.S.:
> *Mister Charley gave us payday, boys,*
> *And Sadie gave a drag.*

W.B.: That man, Sadie, is dead!

J.S.:
> *Wunt no difference in that wo— money*
> *That the two men had.*

(speaking) Oh, take it, baby! *(laughs)*

According to another levee veteran, Mister Charley Idaho and Mister Blair split the contract to repair the Coahoma County levee in 1937, Idaho being the "money man" and Blair giving the drag. As he tells it, it was Idaho who shot the Mercy Man, who had walked Charley Idaho's line from end to end without finding one mule with his shoulder well. So, rather than bear the reproach or pay the fine or shut down, "Mister Cholly Idaho shot and killed the Mercy Man. That was way back in the twenties. Nuthin I know. Just something I hear . . ."

W.B.: You know, people that's been here a few years—I guess that's why God didn't kill um all, he left somebody here to tell the story. . . . That Monday morning wunt none of us goin out. He gave us a drag. That was the off day. See, you worked there everyday. See, you had Sunday off—a Saturday evening and a Sunday off. That was payday. But the other days you worked all them days, see.

B.G.: Whole lot of um didn't pay off at all. They give what they call a drag—give you a little sumpin just to gamble with.

W.B.: All it was was a *privileged* penitentiary. When you worked, you wasn't locked up. But other than that, it was just like the penitentiary. They *paid* you what they wanted, they *give* you what they wanted you to have. If you didn't do it like they want it, somebody's gon beat you up.

Stetson Kennedy, in his shattering *Southern Exposure,* tells the story of peonage in the South, with especially grim accounts of forced labor in the turpentine camps. *Rainbow Round My Shoulder,* by Howard Odum, paints similar scenes. But the levee-camp period and its savage inequities are probably the least-known episode in American history. In one of the few written accounts, Roy Wilkins, then an NAACP investigator, reported to *Crisis* magazine:

While there is complaint from workers on all the forms of exploitation, the greatest wail is against the irregular pay day system. The men grumble over the small pay, the long hours, the cursing, the beating, the food, the tents, the commissary fleecing, but they reserve their greatest bitterness for the contractor who "won't pay you even that little you got coming."

I heard of at least two contractors who had paid off in December for the first time since August and September, respectively. This system is a great one for the contractor. The longer the pay days are withheld, the more food and clothes the men buy at the camp Commissary at the high prices in vogue there. There is the money-lending business which all foremen carry on at twenty-five cents interest on the dollar.

Then there are those other deductions: a lump sum, three or four dollars a week for commissary, whether one uses that amount or not; fifty cents for drinking water; fifty cents for the cook (single men pay this); fifty or seventy-five cents tent rent.

If pay days are dragged out two or three months apart, with commissary prices at the pleasure of the contractor, a workman has only a dollar or two of cash money coming to him at the end of three months.[17]

A.L.: Why did you men go into those places? That's what I'd like to know.

B.G.: You didn't *know* no better!

W.B.: You couldn't *do* no better! You was tryin to leave the farm, for fifty and seventy-five cents a day, and go someplace where you could earn a little bit more money. But when you get in those places, well then you would *earn* their money but you didn't get paid.

B.G.: Yeah! You'd get out there, and they would, ah, they say they gonna give you fifteen dollars a week. That's two and a half a day. And payday, he *may* pay you off and then may *not* pay you off.

Sometimes he used to work you out there two and three months and just give you a drag, like ten or fifteen dollars—sumpin to gamble around there in the camp with. Could go down—go to the commissary, and get anything you want, like clothes or stuff like that to wear. But no money. They work you, probably, three or four months, wouldn give you nothin.

So next week, next two weeks, maybe he paid me all my money. But they still wouldn't let me look at him—you couldn't see him. He was back in a little pocket—pay off through a little hole. His eyes look like a dog's eyes.

A.L.: Why didn't you fight back?

W.B.: With what?

J.S.: You couldn't fight all those .44's and .38's.

W.B.: He got a shotgun in his hand and a .44-40 on the side, what you gonna fight him back with?

A.L.: I thought you had your pistol at all times.

W.B.: Well, if you reached for your pocket, if he had not got you with that stick, he was gonna shoot you.

W.H.: They'd have colored bosses, too, round there. They ain't gonna let you hurt that white man.

W.B.: Yeah. They would have colored there. The man, with his wife was runnin the kitchen and the corral boss and the boss. You had three against one any way you turned.

W.H.: "Kill a nigger, hire another one. Kill a mule, buy another one!"

W.B.: That's right. Now I'll tell you. They'd have them rolling wheelbarrows up a runway. It'd be hot, just like this hot now. They got a boss out there tellin you, "Come on with it. Come on with it!" Some of um get hot—they go to dump the wheelbarrow and they would fall out into the pit. The next wheelbarrow of dirt, they'd throw it on the top a you! Leave you right there.

J.S.: Then they had one when I was in Louisiana . . .

(singing)

Oo-oo-oooo . . .

You kill a man in ol Louisiana, boys,
You don't go nowhere.
Boy, you kill a man in ol Louisiana,
You got to hide like a bear.

Hide like a bear, boys,
Hide like a bear.

W.B.: One time I landed in Last Chance, Arkansas. They had a levee camp there, and I had just got in and it was payday, and they was gambling. I was carryin a thumb-cocker. You ain't got to do nothin but just hold that trigger and knock that hammer back, you know. It's gon fire every time it falls.

I was young and crazy then. See, God taken care of me, cause I should've been dead forty years ago, see. But I was a good marksman, you know.

Well, I had been shootin dice and a man try to take fifty dollars from me. He drawed his pistol, and I drawed mine, and we shot, and the bullets hit and fell in the middle of the table. *(laughter)* That's hard to believe, ain't it?

A.L.: Yep! Sure is.

W.B.: But that's true. He shot when I shot and the bullets met, just like that, and fell in the middle of the table. Nobody got hurt. But we got all the money cause the crap house was clear. *(laughs)* Wasn't nobody left.

A.L.: There was no law in those camps, then, huh?

W.B.: No! Wasn't no law. The law wouldn't even come up on top of the levee in Last Chance, Arkansas.

B.G.: They never would come in the camp and rob nobody, but they always lay for ya after you'd get out the camp. They'd always be outside, waitin on ya whenever you come out. They'd put them guns on ya. They don't need you talkin bout you ain't got it—they'd take your money and go ahead on.

J.S.: Back in 1947, when I first came out of the army, I got in trouble right there, Rosedale, and they caught me down here in Greenville. I stayed in Greenville jail down there, that old county jail, and messed in with some *bad* youngsters, and seven of us broke that jail. We sawed our way out of there, took us three nights and days to saw out of that jail. And I was the last one they caught. I was gone, oh, five, ten years before they caught me. They caught me up in Rosedale, and they sent me to Parchman.

> *Got me 'cused of thieving.*
> *I can't see a thing.*
> *They got me accused of forgery*
> *And I can't even write my name.*

> *Bad luck,*
> *Bad luck is killing me.*
> *Boys, I just can't stand*
> *No more of this third degree.*

(sing-speak)

> *Now listen here, boys,*
> *I wanna tell you sumpin.*

(singing)

> *They got me accused of taxes,*
> *And I don't have a lousy dime.*
> *They got me accused of children,*
> *And ain't nar one of them mine.*

> *Bad luck,*
> *Bad luck is killing me.*
> *Boys, I just can't stand*
> *No more of this third degree.*

(sing-speak)

Boy, now looka here,
I wanna tell you one mo thing.

(singing)

They got me 'cused of perjury,
I can't even raise my hand.
They got me 'cused of murder,
An I have never harmed a man.

Bad luck,
Bad luck is killing me.
Boys, I just can't stand,
No more of this third degree.
I'm gone,
So, baby—so long.

Chapter 6

▲▲▲▲▲▲▲▲▲▲

Rise Up, Dead Man

Rise up, dead man, and help me drive my row . . .

PARCHMAN

Only a few strands of barbed wire marked the boundary between the Parchman State Penitentiary and the so-called free world. Like the plantations on the other side of the fence, the state pen was a vast checkerboard of cotton fields cut by wide drainage ditches and graveled roads, sprawling interminably under a hot sky. The land produced the same crop and blacks had the same work to do on both sides of the wire fence. Only the occasional sight of convicts in stripes and of mounted guards carrying shotguns made one realize that this was a prison. But every Delta black knew how easily he could find himself on the wrong side of that fence. As the great Mississippi prison song ironically puts it:

It ain't but the one thing I done wrong,
I stayed in Miss'ippi just a day too long.

The sharecropper loaded with debts he could never pay, or the muleskinner escaping from Mister Cholly, might not at first care too much which side of the barbed wire he found himself on. True, Parchman was a step deeper into hell, but he had lived in one of hell's anterooms all his life and as a boozer, a dancer, a petty gambler—a chief devil in the eyes of the community—was well acquainted with the territory. But the pen soon taught him how wrong he was. It was a Marine boot camp where you never made private; boot camp that ran as long as a man's sentence, and that could mean the rest of his life.

The warden and other officials of this penal system had no interest in or knowledge of penology. As a *New York Post* reporter observed, as late as 1957:

> The state penitentiary system at Parchman is simply a cotton plantation using convicts as labor. The warden is not a penologist, but an experienced plantation manager. His annual report to the legislature is not of salvaged lives; it is a profit and loss statement, with the accent on profit.

These officials and their underlings were filled with a zeal for work that might well be called Southern Protestant Colonial; they had a passion for forcing others to labor hard in the hot fields and woods, and were enraged if there was shirking. Hired on because of their high qualifications as "nigger drivers," the Southern penologists joyously and self-righteously humiliated, bullied, beat, often tortured, and sometimes murdered their charges.

When we first visited Parchman, the state-approved instrument of discipline was a broad strip of leather about four feet long and a quarter inch thick with holes punched in the last foot so it would draw blisters from the bare flesh with each blow and break them with the next. This monstrous contrivance was called "the bat," and Joe Savage remembered it from his time in Parchman.

JOE SAVAGE: They whupped us with big wide strops. They didn't whup no clothes. They whupped your naked butt *(laughs)*. And they had two men to hold you.

WALTER BROWN: Four!

J.S.: As many as they need.

W.B.: I walked through the hall, comin out the kitchen, and looked at it. They had one down an four holdin him.

ALAN LOMAX: Did they ever injure anybody that way?

J.S.: Wooo!

W.B.: Yeah!

J.S.: Kill um! Kill um!

W.B.: They'd kill um like that.

Indeed, the state prisons of the South in many ways resembled Nazi concentration camps, both in the way they treated blacks and in their intimidating effect on the black community. Every black knew, at least by hearsay, what "goin down the river" (going to the state pen) meant. Anything could happen to you; you were at the mercy of lawless men who hated "niggers." The horrid shadow of this remorseless system, in which so many men disappeared, lay over the whole South, carrying a threat that has not entirely vanished. Conditions in these state pens perpetuated the worst aspects of plantation slavery and of the "free penitentiaries"—the levee and forced-labor camps. They transformed many of the society's rebels into hardened criminals, some of whom came to prefer prison life, with its security of three squares and known worries, to life in the free world.

The prisoners rose in the black hours of morning and ran, at gunpoint, all the way to the fields, sometimes a mile or more, their guards galloping behind on horseback. At work they were divided into squads, with the swiftest worker in the lead. The others were required to keep pace with him, and anyone who did not keep up, no matter what the reason, was sure of severe punishment. I met one old-timer, respectfully nicknamed "the River-Ruler" because he'd been the leader of the number-one gang on the number-one farm in the penitentiary for twenty years. The River-Ruler's feet had turned into bags of pulpy bones from the long years of pounding the earth of the penitentiary fields. In the words of the song, he had run and walked "till his feet got to rollin, just like a wheel."

Everywhere we heard of men working till they dropped dead or burnt out with sunstroke. "Knocking a Joe," or self-mutilation, was one way out. The sight of a one-legged or one-armed man who had chopped off his own foot or hand with an ax or a hoe was a common one. Those who "made it," that is, served their sentences and returned to their homes intact in mind and body, had to be "mighty tough peoples."

In the burning hell of the penitentiaries the old comforting, healing, communal spirit of African singing cooled the souls of the toiling, sweating prisoners and made them, as long as the singing lasted, consolingly and powerfully one. This habit of group singing throughout all activities is the very core of African tradition. Africa's great rivers were navigated by chanting paddlers. Gangs of singing axmen, with drummers moving in close to spur them on with hot licks, cleared garden spots in the African jungle. Teams of helpful women slapped clay floors slick and hard or brought in their neighbors' harvests with song. Black Saharans crooned to their groaning dromedaries.

On one West Indian island, where family bust-ups were frequent, I recorded teams of professional singing house movers, who came in when a married couple broke up, sawed their little cabin in two parts, and dragged the lady's half to her mother's place, singing as they pulled. The homemade vessels of the Caribbean were launched and sailed to work chanteys that became the delight of sailors in all the oceans, echoing in distant harbors from Blackpool to Bombay. This musically productive choralizing, that had "brought daylight" into the swamps of the Delta, went out of style as the plantation communities began to break up and the people moved to town. Individualized performance types, like the solo gospel song, the holler, and blues, became fashionable among the maids, farm laborers, and service workers, struggling to climb the lowest rungs of the ladder of American success.

But in the prison camps the group singing that had been an essential African heritage of sociability sustained the black convicts, kept them "normal" and humane. This tradition had given birth to a healthy sense of community in the slave quarters. It had produced a soul-cleansing and sustaining black religious tradition, replete with the noble spirituals that soared round the world. It had transformed the rather stiff amusements of Western Europe's country dance tradition into the peppery southeastern Virginia reel and invigorated the choicest Scots and Irish tunes with black syncopations; in which, as in the popular dances of Latin America, the black slave could hear that his audible presence had become a joyous essential in his social surround. He did not have to wait till evening or when he was at leisure to polish these rhythmic jewels; he amused his friends with them on the job, and so was forever discovering the fit of his music to his environment, to his tasks and to his group. This was the way it was in the old days in the Deep South, the old-timers told us. For every task of river, field, then railroad and construction camp, this habit of singing and working together in rhythm had brought forth a packet of catchy tunes that made the work go merrily in spite of the heat. You sang together on the job, and the responsorial hallies had you shouting at meeting time on Sundays. Thus the basic African group-oriented musical style lived on in the United States.

The hoes, the axes rose and glittered—

I'm calling my diamond,
My diamond bladey . . .

then flashed like a single silver blade as they swung down—

> *They ringing in the bottom,*
> *Drop um down.*

and the earth and the forest thundered under their strokes.

> *Hammer ringin in the live oaks,*
> *Drop um down.*
> *I'm a number-one driver,*
> *Drop um down.*
> *If you drive, I'll ride you,*
> *Drop um down.*

So they overtopped their bosses. Often the axmen stood erect as they worked, their axes swinging high and back over their head, coming almost straight down on the logs at their feet and carving out chips like thick golden slices of cornbread.

You could hear the mighty choruses of the hoe gangs a mile away. Close by, as seventy high-swinging hoes moved grandly ahead like some gigantic mowing machine, sweeping the Johnson grass out in huge swaths, the singing could almost take you off your feet. The sound was like a choir of trumpets and trombones, shot through with tricky harmonies, swinging together on the beat. The term "call and response" is inadequate to describe this black group singing. It was composed of many intertwined parts improvised by the singers joining and leaving the chorus as they pleased, stroking in tones, part phrases, and harmonies just where they were needed to round out the blend. Moreover, the leader and chorus parts overlapped rhythmically as the chorus came in under the leader and replaced him until he was ready with his next line. He, in his turn, overlapped with the chorus, as they held their last note, thus creating moments of polyrhythm. Then the leader swept in with a capping salty phrase, calculated to make everyone smile. Indeed, there was often a sound like gargantuan laughter in the overlapping chorus, as they sent their golden harmonies into the hot blue sky.

> LEAD: *I've got a bulldog weighs five hundred,*
> OVERLAPPING CHORUS: *In my backyard, in my backyard.*
> OVERLAPPING LEAD: *When he barks, he roars like thunder,*
> CHORUS: *All in the clouds, all in the clouds.*

This intertwined, unified, overlapping style is peculiar to black Africa and African America. It is one manifestation of a group-involving approach to communication that allows everyone present to have an input in everything that is happening. Dance, ritual, work, even conversation, are all performed in this overlapping, participatory way. It animates the basketball court as it does the dance floor. Multileveled conversational style, each level understood and reacted to, is the rule in black folk society. Polyphony and polyrhythm are the natural outcome. In African life each task has its own overlapping songs, and these transform the monotonous labor of agriculture into family or neighborhood celebrations such that village life is like a musical.

This habit of making work into sociable play was continued and Creolized in Spanish, French, and English around the Caribbean. My guess is that black work songs became notably more energetic and anguished in the New World, where slave and forced-labor gangs were driven to complete heavy tasks in quick time in all weathers. Gang labor songs sprang into being wherever conditions were particularly hard, as in the malarial rice-growing islands on the East Coast, on the tunnel jobs that pushed the railroads past the Southern Appalachians, among stevedores on the docks and steamboat landings, in the coal mines of Alabama, and in the fertile, but pestilential and heat-drenched river-bottom lands of the Southwest.

In imagery and historic setting these black work songs are as American as the Yankee Doodle or the Ghost Dance, for they were wrested out of the very rock and earth of the Southern land, as black hands broke the soil, moved it, and brought it into production. While rivers of sweat poured down, these trenchant melodies flamed up out of the passionate struggle with nature and resounded in the cruel Southern heavens. In them the African slave, transformed into steel-driving John Henry, put the Bill of Rights into one phrase:

A man ain't nothin but a man.

Although this tradition of communal song began to decline under the individualizing sharecropping farm system, it continued to flourish in the penitentiaries of the South until they were desegregated and reformed in the sixties. My father, John Lomax, and I, recording in the black state prisons of all the Southern states between 1933 and 1947, not only found a great panoply of original songs but discovered that every state pen had developed distinctive work-song styles. Each of these state styles dramatized the struggle of the work group in some original and often thrilling way, at the same time that it helpfully organized and paced the efforts of the participants. No words can describe these effects, but their varied texture can be appreciated on field recordings.[1]

This vein of African-American creativity flourished in the state pens because there it was essential to the spiritual as well as the physical survival of the black prisoners. The establishment of exactly the right tempo is the basis of any successful musical performance, but in the prison chants tempo had a far more crucial role to play. The beat established by the song leader set a practical pace for the work in relation to the kind and size of the task, the weather, the capacities and feelings of the gang. The right tempo increased the flow of well-organized energy, lowered fatigue, and boosted morale by unifying the group and thus vastly increasing its productive output.

These ideas emerged during a conversation at a Parchman prison woodpile where the camp's best singers had been brought together to record. Bull and Bama, Dobie Red and Tangle Eye and 22, who had been singing and chopping like musical tigers, paused, dripping with sweat, while Bama explained:[2]

BAMA: We go out about sunup and we sing practically all the time when we're flat-weeding a ditch.

THE GUARD, CLOSE BY: That's right—some of them sing practically all the time.

ALAN LOMAX: And what if you're working in the woods with axes? If you chop all day long, do you sing all day long?

BAMA: Yessir, there'll be somebody singing the whole day long. Everybody that can chop with an ax, he can sing.

A.L.: Do you think you can slack off a little bit when you sing?

BAMA: No sir. What makes it go so better when you singing, you might nigh forget, and the time just pass away. But if you just got your mind devoted on one thing, it look like the day be longer. You know, a man wouldn't have no business to talking on the job, so best just keep your mind on what you're doing and go to singing, and it go better.

A.L.: What's the most important thing about a good leader? Does he have to have a real good voice or a strong voice or what?

BAMA: Well, now it wouldn't just exactly make any difference about the dependability of his voice or nothin like that, boss; but it take the man with the most understandin to make the best leader in anything. If you bring a brand-new man in here, if he had a voice where he could sing just like Peter could preach, and he didn't know what to sing about, well, he wouldn't do no good.

Then here's a fellow, maybe he ain't got no voice for singin, but he's been cooperating with the peoples so long an been on the job so long, till he know just exactly how it should go, and if he can just mostly talk it and he understand the work so well, it would go good with yuh. No, it don't make any difference about the voice; you can just whistle and, if you know the time and can keep in time with the axes, you can whistle and cut just as good as you can if you were singin. But you have to be done experienced.

A new prisoner, confronting the torture of dawn-to-dark toil in the blazing heat, also faced a musical challenge, which helped him endure his first hellish weeks in the pen; he had to learn how to sing with the prison veterans. These hard boys, who rutted, fought, and killed in overcrowded prison dormitories, could sink their differences, feel the black pride and power of their group, and forget their bitter, bitter cares as their choruses rolled across the field.

I'm choppin in the bottom wid a hundred years,
Tree fall on me, I don bit mo care.

The prisoners all talked about how singing comforted them. One said in a plaintively sweet voice, "When you listenin how the song run, the day just go by mo faster, and befo you know it, the sergeant or the driver is hollerin dinnertime."

I ain't been to Georgia, but I been told
Women in Georgia got the sweet jelly roll.

So the playful eroticism of Africa crept in past the barbed wire and the guards to console the black prisoners. The work-song leaders were always rhyming about the jelly in the biscuit, about women faithless and faithful, women coming with pardons, women forgetting them—women, a worrisome and wonderful thing to a poor prisoner.

Big-Leg Rosie, with her big-leg drawers,
Got me wearin these striped overalls.

When she walks, she reels and rocks behind.
Ain't that enough to worry a po convict's mind?

They sang to little Mattie, counseling her about marriage:

Mattie, when you marry, don't marry a convict man,
Every day be Monday, with a hoe handle in yo hand.

Mattie, when you marry, marry a railroad man,
Ev'y day be Sunday, with a dollar bill in yo hand.

Another leader, nick-named 22 because he was sentenced for twenty-two years, brings in old Dollar Mamie and her expensive tastes, and Bob, who was determined to satisfy them.

Old Dollar Mamie told old Dollar Bob
Dress she want cost a dollar a yahd.

Hush now, Mamie, don't say a word,
You shall have it, if it's in Vicksburg.

It was the quixotically humane practice at Parchman, as in other Southern penitentiaries, to allow well-behaved convicts the opportunity and the privacy to cohabit with their feminine visitors on weekends. The folk theory that you couldn't "hold niggers in the pen without at least a promise of pussy" worked well in practice. The guards and trusties were kept happy with various kinds of payoffs. Wives and sweethearts came visiting; so did prostitutes in plenty, pretending legitimacy. These fancy ladies turned tricks and sold whiskey in sheds and outbuildings. So on weekends and national holidays, some 'victs found solace in the arms of Alberta, Mattie, and old Dollar Mamie. Don't forget Jumpin Judy, immortalized in song for her innovations:

It's Jumpin, Jumpin Judy,
She was a mighty fine girl.
Oh well, she brought that jumpin,
Baby, to the whole round world.

However, it was Rosie who was always on the poor convict's mind. Rosie, little Rosie, *Big Leg* Rosie—the heroine of the Parchman prison farm.

I seen little Rosie in my midnight dreams.
Midnight dreams, Lord, my midnight dreams.

In 1933 forty convicts, assembled by the warden at shotgun point for a Library of Congress recording session, blasted our microphone with their roaring call for Rosie. On return visits to Parchman we tried again and again to capture this powerful sound with hardly adequate equipment. Someday, if ever Mississippi discovers its real cultural roots, all these different versions of *Rosie* we took down over the years will comprise together a magnificent *Rosie* recording. The stereo recording I made in the 1960s will not be the best of these.

By that time the convict chorus had shrunk in size and fervor. Even so, in the 1980s, when work songs were no longer sung at Parchman, I asked a Greenville barroom crowd how many knew *Rosie*. Almost every hand in the room went up: virtually every man there had served time in the pen. So the impossible proved possible. We took some of these crippled-up veterans of the Delta frontier to a site on a bend of their river. They formed up in a ragged line with their heavy hoes, and, staggering a bit, they advanced through the shimmering mirage of heat waves toward the camera, swinging their heavy hoes with the fervor that had cultivated the gardens of Africa and the plantations of the South. And as they reenacted the Parchman field work, they sang to Rosie again—these old derelicts, wobbling under the blast of the sun—with the poignancy and passion of their young, heart-hungry years in the pen.[3]

O Rosie,
O lawd gal.
Stick to the promise that you made me.
Wasn gonna marry till I go free.

Choppin in the bottom with a hundred years,
Tree fall on me, I don bit mo care.
O Rosie,
O lawd gal.

Here is poetry that rings like a hammer on an anvil, that bites the heart, that trills like a bird. Nowhere else in earlier African-American or American folk tradition does one find such disciplined and poignant rhymed couplets. When I transcribe them from field recordings, I am always reminded of the *Greek Anthology*. Indeed, the fire of the Mediterranean *copla* and *stornello* stand in the background of this workman's poesy. And this spare and plangent work-song verse is plainly the main source of the poetry of the blues.

"Good mornin, blues, blues, how do you do?
Good mornin, blues, blues, how do you do?"
"I'm feelin pretty well, good pardner, how are you?"

The skill in devising such telling stanzas had been mastered before the blues began, in the creation of the numberless verses of the work songs. The basis of both types is the rhymed couplet, with a first line variously repeated and a final rhyming line which puts a witty or surprising or powerful cap on the stanza. One man sings of his image of freedom:

I'm going to Memphis when I get parole,
Stand on the levee, hear the big boats blow.

And his buddy ironically rejoins:

You go to Memphis, don't you hang around.
Police catch you, you'll be jailhouse bound.

Movement, going places, transportation were main themes:

Prettiest train that I ever seen
Run from Jackson down to New Orleans.

Here is a tissue of almost nothing, yet it sings superbly. Like most work songs, it caresses the voice, slipping over glottis, palette, tongue, and lips like spring water or good wine. Indeed, prison work chants are the most singable of songs, and I urge everyone who can to try them out for the sheer pleasure of internalizing them. Here's a verse that invokes the magnificence of the Mississippi. The way the group roars *round* and *down* conveys the mighty power of the river and its smoke-plumed packets, beating the water with their huge paddle wheels.

Big boat up the river, turnin round and round,
Struck deep water and she drops on down.

But above all, these prison work songs sound the special despair that burdened the hearts of blacks in the Deep South.

Raise um up higher, let um drop on down,
You won't know the diffrunce when the sun goes down.

I could see the magic wrought by this terse and ardent poetry in its effect on the men who recorded for me that day in the prison woodlot. Their faces blazed with feeling. The songs were theirs—this was their art, re-created as they performed it, following a leader they had chosen and who had to please them or be replaced by another. The leader was weaving a new pattern of verses out of a common stock that was their own, that perfectly stated their feelings, and that differentiated them from their guards and from the free world which was so cruelly punishing them. These songs plumbed the depths of their despair, yet also asserted their determination to endure.

John Henry told his captain,
"A man ain't nothin but a man,
But before I'd let your steam drill beat me down
I'd die with this hammer in my hand."

These men in striped clothes smiled at the good lines. They drove at the work, muscles rippling in the sun, axes biting big chips out of the logs, chips that occasionally rang against the microphone.

Axes walkin, chipses talkin,
    All day long,
    All day long.

Their overlapping African style allowed every man to contribute to the whole effect—a bit of harmony or an improvised comment (like "Let me hear you now" or "Yes, my Lordy, Lord"), even the syncopation of an ax stroke on the log. In fact, that morning in Parchman this little bunch of convicts came up with a new song in the most overlapped, the most syncopated style I had ever heard, something that they had only recently put together out in the Mississippi bottoms. The older men present were unable to join in on this new polyrhythmic "double-cutting" ax song.

Double cutting allows four men to work together in felling a tree, without any interference or danger to the axmen. They stand in a square round the tree, each man on one corner of a square, facing in—the two men on opposite corners chopping together on beat one, the alternate pair on beat two of the song. In this way all four axes can be continuously in motion and all four blades can uninterruptedly chip away at the tree, without colliding. It's a beautiful thing to watch, as well as to hear. The choppers stand with legs wide apart, knees bent, leaning way back and beginning their sidewise swings with a twist of the hips, their axes then flying in, gleaming arcs, and biting deeply and precisely into the tree trunk as they turn in toward it. Two golden chips are started by one pair of blades, then immediately carved out as the next pair strikes—axe one and three together, then two and four together, the pairs alternating—in a Delta pas de quatre.

First comes a down stroke of axes one and three:

WHOP! (At once the lead begins on the offbeat, pair one recovering, pair two swinging in.)

LEAD: *Well, it's early in the morn*
    OVERLAPPING VOICE: *In the mornin*

WHOP! (the stroke of the second pair of ax blades)

LEAD: *Baby, when I rise,*
    OVERLAP: *Lordy, Mama*
LEAD: *Well, it's*
         WHOP!

       early in the morn

    OVERLAP: *In the mornin,*
LEAD: *A-baby,*
         WHOP!

    OVERLAP: *when I rise.*
ALL: *Well, it's early in the morn*
         WHOP!

    OVERLAP: *In the mornin,*
ALL: *Baby, when I rise,*
         WHOP!

    OVERLAP: *Lordy, baby, you have,*
LEAD: *It's I have a misery,*
         WHOP!

    OVERLAP: *Berta,*

LEAD: *Well-ah, in my right side . . .*

WHOP! . . .

This only approximates the intricate pattern of the "new style" that 22 and his bunch were weaving together. It was tricky and highly syncopated, allowing the singers to improvise rhythmic breaks in opposition to the main beat. Where work-song stanzas are generally brief, these ran to a minute or a minute and a half, like an art song or Far Eastern improvisation or a bop solo.

This poetic style seems to be conceived and practiced according to a *vertical* model, which considers the several simultaneous parts of a black choral rendition and allows space for all present to contribute to the entire effect; here the sonorous and verbal aptness of all the interjections is essential to the whole. Such compositional style is difficult for Europeans, especially north Europeans, to perform or even to perceive—at least without the aid of a diagram or a musical score. But it comes naturally to people raised in the black African tradition.

22, a rather slight, wiry, and shy young man, with a troubled look on his face, kept spinning the song, as the four ax blades dovetailed into the live oak. His first stanza speaks for a half-sick prisoner, roused at dawn for a grueling day of forced labor.

*Well, it's early in the morn, in the
   mornin |
Baby | when I rise, Lordy, mama,
Well, it's | early in the morn, in
   the mornin,
A-baby | when I rise,
Well-a | it's early in the morn | in
   the mornin,
Baby, when I rise, Lordy, baby,
You have, it's I have a misery,
   Berta,
Wa- in my right side, well-a
R-in-a my right side, Lordy, baby,
R-in-a my right side, Lordy sugar,
Well, it's I have a misery, Berta,
R-in my right side, well-a.*

Chorus:

Well-a, it's a Lordy Ro-,
*   Lordy-berta,*
Well, it's Lord (you keep
*   a-talkin), babe,*
Well, it's Lord, Ro, Lordy, Rosie,
Well, it's O Lord, gal, well-a.

Well-a whosonever told it, that he   (In the close-knit black
*   told a*   community, both in and out
He told a dirty lie, babe,   of prison, gossip is feared,
Well-a whosonever told it, that he   and the backbiter is hated,
*   told a*   even though his lies may be
He told a dirty lie, well-a,   as improbable as the
Well-a whosonever told it, that he   American Eagle taking wing off
*   told a*   the quarter or the dollar bill.)
He told a dirty lie, babe,
Well the eagle on the dollar, quarter
He gonna rise and fly, well-a
He gonna rise and fly, sugar,
He gonna rise and fly, well-a
Well the eagle on the dollar, quarter
He gonna rise and fly, well-a.

Well, rocks 'n' gravel make-a   (The good song leader
Make a solid road, sugar,   knows he must vary the
Well, it takes a rocks-a, rocks-a   themes of his
*   gravel, make-a*   improvisation from
To make a solid road, well-a,   painful to pleasant, from
It takes-a rocks-a rocks-a gravel,   metaphors of anxiety
*   make-a*   to fantasies of
To make a solid road, well-a,   fulfillment.)
It takes a good-lookin woman to
*   make-a*
To make a good-lookin whore,   (Pronounced "ho.")
*   well-a*
It takes a good-lookin woman,
*   Lord, baby,*

To make a good-lookin whore,
  Lord, sugar,
It takes a good-lookin woman to
  make-a
To make a good-lookin whore,
  well-a.

Boys, the peckerwood a-peckin on
  the,
On the schoolhouse door, sugar,
Well, the peckerwood a-peckin on
  the,
R-on-the schoolhouse door, well-a
Well, the peckerwood a-peckin on
  the,
On the schoolhouse door, sugar,
Well, he pecks so hard, Lordy,
  baby,
Until his pecker got sore, well-a
Until his pecker got sore, Lordy,
  baby,
Until his pecker got sore, Lord,
  sugar,
Well, he pecks so hard, Lordy,
  baby,
Until his pecker got sore, well-a.

(A raunchy play on words,
with the poor white [called
peckerwood because he resembles
the woodpecker] pecking away
at black education so
persistently that his pecker
[penis] gets sore).

Well, hain't been to Georgia, boys
  but
Well, it's I been told, sugar,
Well, hain't been to Georgia,
  Georgia,
But it's I been told, well-a,
Well, hain't been to Georgia,
  Georgia
But it's I been told, Lord, mama,
Well, it's Georgia women, baby,
Got the sweet jelly roll, well-a,
Got the sweet jelly roll, mama,

(Back to the traveling motif,
a visit to Georgia, equally
famous for its race
prejudice and its sweet,
loving women. Shades
of Ray Charles!)

Got the sweet jelly roll, Lord,
  sugar,
Well, it's Georgia women, baby,
Got the sweet jelly roll, well-a.

Chorus:

Well, it's a Lordy Ro-, Lordy
  Rosie,
Well, it's Lord Ro-, Lordy sugar,
Well, it's Lord, Ro-, Lordy Rosie,
Well, it's O Lord, gal, well-a.

On the last chorus, the live oak came tumbling down. 22 and his buddies stepped back, blew on their hands, and grinned. There was back-slapping among the axmen when they heard their recording. They knew they had sung up a storm. Much later, when the record was released, somebody in Harlem found it and, without a word to either 22 or myself, used it to orchestrate Alvin Ailey's *Work Song Ballet*. By now thousands of theater-goers all over the world have applauded this composition from the Parchman woodlot. It is a pity they could not see the dove-tailed pas de quatre for axes performed that day by 22 and his friends Little Red, Tangle Eye, and Hard Hair.

In this anonymous world of the penitentiary, every man is given a distinctive moniker that ticks him off in an apt and sometimes cruel way. This nickname, once slapped on as a joke by a guard or another inmate, can last as long as the convict's sentence, even for life. A fine-looking young mulatto might be teasingly nicknamed "Yaller Gal" and then have to fight off sexual attacks for the rest of his sentence. Our friend Tangle Eye was painfully cross-eyed, but completely accustomed to the guards yelling, "Come up, old Tangle Eye." The Texas singer James Baker was christened Iron Head after a live oak fell on him and he never lost a stroke of his ax or a phrase of his chopping song. The great Leadbelly won his name because of his fabled endurance in the fields as "number-one man in the number-one gang in the Texas pen."

We set down a sheaf of these fanciful black convict nicknames, each one a humorous or witty assertion of the deathless singularity of an individual in the seething anonymity of the prison farms. Each nickname helped to shield a personality from extinction, maintaining the man's privacy by keeping his real name out of prison currency. For these hard-pressed exiles, all dressed alike in striped clothing and herded like animals by guards on horseback, the nicknames asserted and underscored their identities in the darkness of the penitentiary. Moreover, each man also had his own self-composed, identifying musical signature.

You could hear these personal songs—sometimes no more than a few notes long—coming from far away across the fields. These so-called hollers, which belonged to the same family as the levee-camp songs, were pitched high out of a wide-open throat, to be heard from far off. A convict, by raising his holler from time to time during the long day of toil, could announce his existence and fend off the crushing weight of prison anonymity. His signature song voiced his individual sorrows and feelings. By this means, he located himself in the vast fields of the penitentiary, where the rows were often a mile long and a gang of men looked like insects crawling over the green carpet of the crops. Listening to a holler, some con would say, "Lissen at ol Bull bellerin over there—he must be fixin to run," or "That's old Tangle Eye yonder. He's callin on his woman again."

My father and I recorded scores of these "field hollers" or "old corn songs" or "levee-camp hollers," as they were variously called. They were thickest in the river-bottom country, south and west of Memphis all the way into the river lands of Texas. Most of those we found in the Southeast had been imported from the Delta. You can recognize the Delta hollers because they have a shape different from the majority of black folk songs, which tend to be short-phrased, to conform to a steady beat, and to be performed by groups. By contrast, Delta hollers are usually minory solos, sung recitative-style in free rhythms, with long embellished phrases, many long-held notes, lots of slides and blue notes, and an emphasis on shifts of vocal color. They are impossible to notate and very difficult to sing.

As a youngster, I tried to sing whatever we recorded, with varying success, of course, but I never could do a "holler" to my own satisfaction. I tried for years and finally gave up. Then came the moment when a holler spontaneously burst out of *me*. It was the evening of the day I had just been inducted into the army. On this first endless and awful twenty-four hours in a huge army reception center, when I had been yelled at, put down, examined, poked at, handled like a yearling in a chute, I drew KP. It was a sixteen-hour assignment, in which we KP's helped to set the tables for several hundred men three times in one day and then clean up afterward. Along about eight o'clock that evening my feet seemed to be on fire, every muscle in my body was complaining, stinging perspiration was running into my eyes, and my arms were deep in greasy, boiling dishwater. I had never been so miserable in all my life, and there were still two hours to go. At that moment, without thinking, I let loose with a Mississippi holler. Loud and clear, my levee-camp complaint rang through that hellish army kitchen:

Well, I asked my captain what time of day,
What time of day?
And he looked at me, good pardner,
Threw his watch away,
Ohhh——, threw his watch away.

A couple of guys looked up, but thank God most of the others were too unhappy to notice. I went on hollering and the sound got better. I got to feeling *good*. All those years and finally those Delta blue notes were coming out of me. Suddenly, the black KP sergeant appeared. I kept whooping and washing dishes. I felt sure I'd be condemned to another day of KP. But all the black sergeant did before he walked off was to say in a kind of nice way, "Hey, man, you sound like you from down home."

I slid more dirty dishes in the water and hollered triumphantly on. Even my feet sort of stopped burning. I sang all the levee-camp tunes I knew, and got in a lot of the right curlicues.

"How come," I asked myself, "how come I can manage these hollers now, when I never could before."

And then a remark of Leadbelly's came back to me. "It take a man that have the blues to sing the blues."

"You've got to have um to sing um—that's purely it, as the feller says." I could sing them that day on KP because my situation resembled that of the black muleskinners and convicts of the Deep South. I was utterly miserable, physically exhausted, totally humiliated by trained experts in humiliation. I didn't dare complain or talk back, because my fate was in their hands. Submerged in feelings of anguish and despair, at last I sort of had the blues, and so I could sort of holler, at least well enough to pass muster with a Deep South drill sergeant.

That experience on KP brought me nearer to the mystery that surrounds the origins of the Delta blues. Tormented by fatigue, overwhelmed by feelings of helplessness in the face of the implacable power of the military, I at last could feel and sing the blues. Of course, my black friends, doing time in the levee camps and the prison farms, lived their whole lives in far more painful situations than the one that had reduced me to despair on KP. Pushed beyond their physical limits, constantly insulted, unable to talk or fight back, and knowing that no one cared whether they lived or died, their hollers voiced the epitome of despair and, sometimes, rage. In truth, they were like orphans, with both parents dead, left to cruel and indifferent caretakers. Often and again, these case-hardened convicts cried out to their long-dead or faraway mothers, as did Track Horse, a legendary figure in the Texas pen:

Oh it's mama, mama, mama, you don't know,
Oh it's mama, mamaaa——
Mama, you don't know . . .

A great Florida prisoner-composer, Robert McLean, called for his mother to prepare his deathbed:

Mama, mamaaa——(rising into a wild keen)
Come make me a garmeeent——
And make it looong——white and narrooow——

These and other hollers contain original and touching cadences that quite match those of the greatest spirituals. They are as astonishing as if the neighing of horses or the trumpeting of swans had become music. Their wayward strains reveal all sorts of extravagant feelings, and will certainly provide some composer of the future with the language of American dramatic recitative. Some hollers are available on records (see "A Brief Discography"), and I shall do my best to bring the rest before the public.

But thus far they have hardly been noticed—first hidden by jazz, then by Tin Pan Alley, and then submerged in the floodtide of the urban blues, to which they had given birth. The principal blues melodies are, in fact, holler cadences, set to a steady beat and thus turned into dance music and confined to a three-verse rhymed stanza of twelve to sixteen bars. But the unconstrained, improvisatory holler genre remains far richer and more varied, in melodic terms, than the blues.

Into the highly charged pause that followed 22's bopping ax song, there floated Tangle Eye's holler. He had leaned his ax against the live-oak log and, looking wistfully across the Delta plain, he sang in a high sweet voice that at times moaned like an oboe, then leapt into liquid yodeling cries with the fluidity of Sidney Bechet's clarinet. The song told Tangle Eye's story.

Mmmm——hmmmmm——ho, ho, ho, Lawd.
Well, I wonder will I ever get back home?
Hey-hey, oo-hoo, O Lawd,
Well, it must have been the devil that fooled me here,
Hey, hey-hey, for I'm all down and out.

Ay-hey, O Lawd,
Lord, if I ever get back home, I'll never do no wrong.
Well, if I can just make it home,
I won't do no wrong no more.

Mmmm——hmmmmm——
Lord, I left Mae Willie and the baby in the courthouse cryin
"Daddy, please don't go."
Lord, I'll be back home,
Well, Lord, I'll be home one day fore long,
Just wait for me.

Mmmm——hmmmmm——
Lord, I been here rollin for the state so long,
Lord, I'm all down and out.
My friend won't come to see me,
Lord, what's done happen to me?

Mmmmm——hmmmmm——
Lord, if I'd-a listened to what my dear old mother said,
Heyyy——
Boys, she dead an gone,
Lord, Lord, she dead an gone.
Whoo——whoo——what'm I gonna do now?

Years later Roswell Rudd discovered a virtual match for Tangle Eye's holler in a recording from Senegal, an important source for American slaves. When we intercut these two pieces on a tape, it sounded as if Tangle Eye and the Senegalese were answering each other, phrase by phrase.[4] As one listens to this musical union, spanning thousands of miles and hundreds of years, the conviction grows that Tangle Eye's forebears must have come from Senegal bringing this song style with them. This is quite plausible. Ancient British tunes have been found all through America's mountains, as has the French Aquitaine tradition in the Cajun country. But what is special about this and presumably other Delta holler melodies that caused them to survive when most other African tunes were Creolized, or Europeanized?

Most black African music—in Africa and in the New World—is highly rhythmic, group-performed, and sanguine in tone. The solo lamentation is important only in the zones of total tyranny, such as Mississippi, the kingdoms of Africa, and the empires of Eurasia, where the individual—helpless to resist the tax collectors, the recruiting sergeants, the rabid invader, the brutal boss-man—cries out for succor. The regime of slavery, sharecropping, uncertain employment, peonage, imprisonment, and shattered family ties had raised up in the Mississippi male the feelings of the poor man under the bootheel of such ancient tyrannies. Big Daddy had replaced the implacable kings and emperors of the past. Echoes of the age-old Oriental style, somehow handed on by immigrants from African kingdoms to the Delta, provided these hard-pressed folks with the means to voice their despair. And this holler form particularly flowered in the hell pits of prison farms and chain gangs.

Dusk was gathering in the Parchman woodlot. The men were tired and hungry. Jimpson, a wizened little old man who had done no leading all afternoon, began his song, one that voiced the hopes of every man present. Dobie Red, Tangle Eye, 22, Bull, Hard Hair, Little Red, and all the others backed him up, so that his holler rose like a big sad wind into the gathering darkness. It christened Parchman *The Murder's Home*—the murderous home of murder and murderers.

> *Ain't got long, oh mama, ain't got long, I ain't got long.*
> *Lord, I ain't got long in the murder's home.*
>
> *Pray for me—oh mama, pray for me, pray for me.*
> *Lord, I got a long holdover and I can't go free.*

BAMA

After supper the Parchman recording session moved indoors. We passed through the dormitory alleyway, where the guards sat with their guns, safe behind two rows of thick black bars that rose to the ceiling. Back of these gloomy colonnades were two huge prison dormitory rooms of triple-tiered bunks, in each of which a hundred weary and restless convicts were settling down for the night. Past this zone of sweat, tobacco smoke, and the sound of gambling, they brought us into a small bare back room, away from the noise, there to record under the supervision of two good ol boys, one with a pistol on his hip and the other with a sawed-off shotgun across his knees. Presently, the men I had asked for came in—Dobie Red, Bull, 22, and Bama, said to be the star singer of the pen. He had joined the session late, and had been little heard from.

Bama was tall, bright orange-brown, handsome, and supple as a panther. His voice rolled out like a sweet trombone. And his "white folks" laugh—ah-huh, ah-huh, ah-huh—that came between stanzas—tore everybody down. Bama began with his own levee-camp holler.

> *O Lord, I woke up this mornin,*   (Thinking in the cold
> *Man, I' feelin badmmmm——*   emasculated grey of a
> *O babe, I was feelin bad.*   prison morning about
> *Well, I was thinkin bout the good*   the world outside, the
>   *times,*   women outside. Then
> *Lord, I once have hadmmmm——*   remembering the first
> *Well, Lord, ooo——, Boss,*   meeting with a levee-camp
> *She brought me my breakfast this*   woman brought downriver by
>   *mornin,*   boat from Memphis. She'd
> *She didn know my name,*   picked his tent to sleep in
> *She didn know my name,*   and him to cook for.)
> *She said, "Give it to the long line*
>   *skinner*
> *With the brass knob haaamme——."*
> *She said, "Give it to the long line*
>   *skinner*
> *With the brass knob haaamme——."*

Bama broke off with a laugh that rang like a sad copper bell through the grey air of the prison dining hall.

"That's one song that rung up and down the land, boss. This girl was so cockeyed, when she cried the tears ran down her back; she was so knock-kneed till she was crippled and she was blind; she was so black till she spit ink, and when she blew her breath, she blew coal dust; her legs so little, look like she swap legs with a kildee. Now ain't she some good-looking, boss?"

Again the laugh, the guard sitting opposite showing his yellow, gapped teeth and slapping his narrow thigh in cracker glee. Looking at him with a broad grin that veiled his contempt, Bama launched into his version of the yahoo song. This took nerve, because it was the piece that other singers were afraid to sing before whites.

Last year wasn't no good crop year (Thinking of the poverty-
And everybody knowed it. stricken rednecks
Grandpaw raised a bushel of corn scratching in their
And some black rascal stole it. sandy patches in the hills,
 I'm goin home, son, Bama in effect tells the guard,
 I'm goin home, "Sonny boy, I'll leave you
 I'm goin home, son, behind; there's nothing you
 I'm goin home. and yours can do to me.")

Jaybird pullin the turnin plow, (Thinking of the unequal
Sparrow pullin the harrow, division of labor in the South
I'm gonna pull it today, big boy, and how some day the
You gonna pull it tomorrow. tables may be turned.)

Lost my gal the other day, (Now moving on to a fantasy
Where do you reckon I found her? about a promiscuous white
Way down yonder in the old woman, carrying out her
 cornfield forbidden desires for black
Fifteen boys around her. lovers.)

"Gwan, old nigger with the black (The cracker wishing
 boots on, he could drive off the super-
I sure do wish 'twas slav'y, potent black with unchecked
Take this trace chain here violence, but conscious of the
And run you stone crazy." real difference between a slave
and a free man,
"Girl, bring me my shotgun, the cracker then consoles
Rifle ain't got no trigger. himself with the fantasy
We goin down to the party tonight, murder of a Negro casually
Might meet another nigger." encountered.

I'm goin home, son,
I'm goin home,
I'm goin home, big boy,
I'm goin home.

Bama answers again, "Look,
sonny, you can't hold me,
because I'm goin home,
big boy, I'm goin home.")

Bama sounded that big trombone chuckle of his between every stanza of the
yahoo song, and now at the end he looked at me with brimming eyes and said,
"That's enough of that, boss, don't you think so?"

"Where'd you learn it, Bama?"

He had been sitting across the room from me, but in one instant he was on
his knees at my feet, looking up at me in feigned humility—"What was that
you ask me, boss?"

"Get up off your knees, you damn rascal," I said. With the eyes of the white
guard on me, I was trying to respond in harsh, Deep South style.

Bama got up, grinning more broadly than ever, wiped the dust off his knees,
and sat opposite, twisting his cap in his hand. "I learnt that in the country up
in Tennessee, same place I learnt this one about old Stackerlee." Then, calling
upon every mellow nuance of his big baritone, he filled the room with the story
of Stackolee, the badman hero of the Delta.

1.
Now Stackerlee, he was a bad
   man,
He wanted the whole round world
   to know,
He toted a .32-20
And a smokeless .44.

2.
Now Stackerlee told Billy Lyon,
"Billy, I'm sho gon take your
   life,
You have winned my money
And I found a fow-ul dice."

3.
Now Billy Lyon, he told
   Stackerlee,
He said, "Stack, please don take
   my life,
I've got two little chillun
And my po lil weasley wife."

4.
"Now one of them is a boy, Stack,
And the other one is a girl."
"But if you love your children,
   Billy Lyon,
You will have to meet them in
   the other world."

Usually the balladeer tells of the arrest and the demise of Stack, and then of his descent to hell, where he feels so much at home that he takes over from Satan and puts the pitchfork on the shelf, saying, "I'm gonna rule hell by myself"—an appealing fantasy for men considered by their community and themselves to be "devils," proud to be known as "baaad," and accustomed to living under hellish conditions. But Bama, with the flexibility of the black improvisor, shifted these violent feelings to Alberta, summoning her and playfully threatening her, as he might do in a lover's quarrel in the free world.

5.

Alberta, Lord, Alberta,
Baby, don't you hear me callin
  you?
But you's three times seven,
  Alberta,
And you know what you want to
  do.

6.

I'm gonna call up the undertaker,
Lord, I'm gonna ring up Mister
  Morgue,
I'm gonna ask those people
What will Alberta's funeral cost.

Then, in a chuckling voice, he changed directions again to stanzas that were new to me and, judging from their looks of delight, to the others present. The first saluted the pleasures of the world in lines worthy of François Villon:

7.

Now give me water, Lord, when
  I'm thirsty.
Honey, give me whiskey when I'm
  dry,
Give me Alberta when I need her
And heaven when I die.

8.

Now when I gets all up in glory,
Lord, I'm gonna sit down on the
  golden stool,
I'm gonna ask Saint Gab'el
To blow me the Worried Blues.

Bama closed his salute to the "baaad" boy—the blues-singing, dancing sinner and the kind of heaven he hopes awaits him—mocking the converted in such extravagant fashion that everyone in that gloomy room burst out laughing. Even the guard was caught up in the laughter.

"Where in hell were you raised, old Bama?" he asked. "On the farm?"

"Yassuh, boss, on the county farm," Bama replied. He kept up his deep chuckle until the guard stopped laughing.

"How come you get in so much trouble?"

"Well, boss, the way I got in trouble—the first time, the folks was barring me, and I cut and shoot a feller up. So I got in the penitentiary and I worked and worked and worked *so* much, then when I got out of the penitentiary I thought I had worked enough and I decided I could make my living without working and then I commenced putting pistols on folks and that wouldn't do and then I commenced stealing everything that wasn't hot and nailed down and the *po*lice jest commenced to running me every way I turned, so, after I got um started to running me, I just kept on doing wrong—fighting and stealing, you know, and robbing—and sometime I wouldn't be done done nothin, but I been doin so much till, when they'd get me, I'd *due to be got* anyhow. One or two times they arrest me and I told um I hadn't done nothin, they say, "We'll arrest you in egvance—you *gonna* do something." That's the way I just stayed in the penitentiary all the time, boss . . ."

Bama's voice trailed off in a note of mock helplessness as his buddies and the guard giggled together. "Just in and out," the guard said. Bama snapped up the line. "In and out, in and out for the last eighteen years. Yassuh." This last he said in a deep, sad tone as the melancholy of all those lost, bitter years suddenly burst in upon him. With a switch that took my breath, Bama then went back to his clowning. "Done stole everything but a chicken and a hog. I never would bother *them*. Course I *was* figuring on stealing a hog after a boy told me how—see, I never would steal no hog because they holler.

"So this boy told me, 'I stole one last night and he didn't holler a lick.'

"I say, 'How you git him and he don't holler?'

"He says, 'Just get you a loaf of bread and get you some denatured alcohol and pour on the bread and throw in there and let him eat it and then you can walk in there and pick him up and walk all over town and he won't do nothing but just lay there and laugh—heh-heh-heh-heh-heh.' Well, I tried it and they put me here in the penitentiary."

"Bama," I said, "who's the meanest man you ever saw, besides yourself?"

He replied with a rising laugh, "The meanest man I ever seen outside myself, boss, he caught another feller in bed with his old lady, and he got so mad, he killed his old lady, killed the baby, and went out there and killed the cat *and the chickens*. That's the meanest man I ever did see in my life. Now, boss, this is just kidding."

All of this was uttered so ingratiatingly and with so many charming musical inflections that the convict with his problems disappeared behind the whimsicalities of the language and the wit of the telling. By now the white guard was probably satisfied that Bama was the best "white man's nigger" on the farm, an opinion that might save Bama's hide or even his life in the future. When in a hasty remark concealed by lighting a cigarette I begged Bama to talk more seriously, he whispered, "I can't talk out around here," and gave me such a deep and searching look that I immediately gave over asking.

There was nothing more to do. The singers were sung out and they were too nervous to talk. So the recorder was packed up in silence. I could think of nothing to say to these men who were going back to their prison bunks in a moment and in the morning would run to the fields under shotguns. I gave them all the money I had in my pockets, pressing their hands with each gift, and then walked with them through the bullpen. Bama spoke to me under his breath: "When I get out in a year from now, I'm coming to you and get you to recommend me to a job."

"How could I recommend you, Bama, after what you just said about yourself?" I whispered.

"Aw, don't pay that any mind," he said quietly so that no one could hear but me. "I was just uncle-tomming for the white folks."

This whispered remark sent cold chills down my spine at the risk Bama was taking, but he just grinned and turned his back and walked off into the dormitory. The iron door clanged, the great key turned in the lock, and I was alone in the bullpen with the big fat turnkey.

A BURNING HELL

When I get back home, I'm gonna walk and tell
That Brazos River is a burning hell.

I was seventeen when I first heard this song. I stared into the dusty black faces of the convicts who were singing—shame and anger spilled over me. These are my brothers, these are my brothers, I kept repeating to myself. Out of their pain they have made a river of song. How can I repay them for this hard-won beauty?

I glanced at the Stetson-hatted guards in the dormitory. Yonder slack and sun-harsh face by the window, the jaws moving monotonously on a quid, the rotten and yellowed teeth showing occasionally like the fangs of an old wolf, the eyes wolf-yellow; yonder fat one with the catfish mouth, snoring against the black bars, his little bug eyes sealed in sleep; beside him a young black convict stood leaning against the cold bars, hugging them close to his breast as if to smother the hot emptiness that burned in him—a gazelle between two tigers. Even if the gazelle had killed, his deed was done in passion, while the deeds of the tigers, his keepers, were bought-and-paid-for brutality, designed to break men's spirits and make them bow like slaves.

Meanwhile, the powerful voices of the convicts blended and lifted their song like a black marble rooftree raised upon shining columns of onyx harmony. They were singing out of abject misery and utter despair, yet the sound was majestic, as wide as the broad green canefields, as tall as the high blue Texas sky. Just as their African ancestors spoke directly to their ancestral pantheon in song, calling on the gods of thunder, of the sea, and of the graveyard; just as their slave ancestors learned to speak directly to the heroes of the Old Testament, to Old Man Noah, to Little David, to John the Revelator—so these Texas convicts spoke to the sun, addressing her familiarly as Old Hannah.

> *Go down, Ol Hannah, doncha rise no mo,*
> *If you rise in the morning, bring Judgment Day!*

Someday America, someday the whole world, will listen with awe to their singing, engraved imperishably with a diamond needle on an aluminum disc that flashed and spun in the light of that long-ago afternoon. First, the call of the leader, like a lazy glimmer of summer lightning:

> *Go down, Ol Hannah . . .*

And then the grave, deep-toned thundering of his convict chorus:

> *Well, well, welllllllll——*

Then comes the trumpet call of the leader with the golden face and the golden voice:

> *Doncha rise no mo . . .*

The men answer with a roar like a storm about to burst:

> *Doncha rise no mo.*

The high voice of the leader cracks the air like a jagged streak of lightning.

If you rise in the morninnnnn——

and, rising to a wail, splits upon the sky with this agonizing cry:

Set the world on fire . . .

Then in a storm of sound blotting out the landscape, the chorus shouts for the end of the world, and the end of their torment:

SET THE WORLD ON FIRE—SET THE WORLD ON FIRE.

I had been listening in the years before to Bach and Beethoven and Stravinsky, but here on a July afternoon in the Brazos bottoms of Texas these convicts in their shaming stripes outsang those symphonies. I had been soaked from childhood up in Shakespeare, and here was language as noble and perfect as his.

Rise up, dead man,
And help me drive my row . . .

The only American sound that could match theirs was Louis Armstrong's trumpet, but for sheer courage in the face of despair, this Texas convict song was incomparable. These black prisoners had looked death in the face everyday, suffered degradation far more painful than death, and created songs of matchless power to keep their hearts alive.

I was seventeen then, and their courage seemed to me somewhat more than mortal. Now, many years later, as I write this, my opinion has not changed.

These are the rebels against the South, I thought—the "bad niggers," those who refused to endure a black fate mildly and with complacent smiles. They have run blindly and head-on against a system of law administered for the benefit of another group and offering them little protection and much humiliation. The violent actions of these murderers, rapists, and gunmen are individual gestures of protest against the harshness and deprivation of black life in "Niggertown" and in the "quarters." Clearly, their guards treat them as if they were revolutionaries, not criminals. Yes, I thought, if these same hard-featured white guards, who turn their sour smiles upon me because I am white and must share their prejudices, could look into my heart, they would treat me like a black prisoner who dared to question them.

Therefore, I hid my feelings. Nor could I discuss them with my father, who, in spite of his intense sympathy for the prisoners and a genuine concern for black welfare, believed in the overall beneficence of the Southern system. Indeed, at that time, in fact, there were very few white Southerners, and not many Americans, who held different views. What we recorded that afternoon in the Central State Prison Farm in Texas—*The Midnight Special, Pick a Bale of Cotton, Little John Henry, Ain't No Mo Cane on the Brazos*—would help to soften those time-hardened prejudices. Certainly, our own lives were changed. We were encouraged to look for work songs in all the penitentiaries of the South. The faces of the prisoners, so shadowy and fawning in repose, so fiery and powerful in song, their touching and powerful melodies, their graceful, golden voices, all conspired to win our allegiance.

During the next years we made a mournful pilgrimage to the Southern prison farms, a chain of hellholes strung across the land like so many fiery crosses to remind the Southern blacks that chains and armed guards and death awaited them if they rebelled. We became inured to prison food, to prison talk, to prison horror, and to the scorn of the guards who looked upon us as scarcely better than "niggers" because of our interest in the songs of their black charges. We returned again and again, my father in the thirties, myself in the forties and late fifties, to record in the Southern penitentiaries.

We discovered what I believe is America's most moving song tradition, a deathless African-American heritage, created and re-created before our very eyes, as these caged composers bathed their souls with lovely melodies, sweet harmonies, lean and witty poetry, and a shared rhythmic play that psychologically empowered and sheltered them. We shut our ears to everything but their voices. Despite the guards, who sat by during all the recording sessions, despite our own pale faces, which must have seemed like masks of indifference to so many of them, the convicts filled our records with a thousand moving songs, an epic of hot sun and brutality and human courage, mounted upon sincere and profound melodies.

I longed and was unable to talk freely with these newfound brothers of mine whose songs triumphed over their misery. The guards were in the way. I lay awake scheming how I might write down their lives and their thoughts. Burdened with the guilt of my adolescent pecadillos and fantasies, I felt myself as criminal as they, subject to arrest at any moment. Every police whistle, every cruise-car siren blew for me. I fantasied committing some crime so that I, too, could experience what they were experiencing and thus write about them with real understanding. Then one day through the good offices of my Texas friend John Henry Faulk, I met Doc Reese.

Reese, as the result of youthful escapades, had served a sentence in the Texas pen during "red-heifer days," so-called because the lash that drove the prisoners was made of red-heifer hide with the hair still on it. After his prison terms Reese had gone back to school, studied in a Baptist seminary, and become a preacher, a profoundly moving one. But he had not, Faulk discovered, forgotten the work songs he had learned on the river, and I brought him to the Newport Folk Festival. There he and a group of his old buddies, swinging their hoes and axes in front of a forest of microphones, presented their Texas work chants to an astonished youth audience that had come to hear Bob Dylan and the Kingston Trio.

During long talks during rehearsals and after, I found that Doc Reese was not only a beguiling singer but a man of depth and wisdom. Without believing anything would come of it, I nonetheless urged him to write the story of his experiences in prison, especially of the place of singing in the lives of the prisoners. Here is that story, written as freshly as if English had never before been used for literary purposes, the tale of a man who has been to hell and back again. For our purposes it doesn't matter a great deal if that hell is the Texas prison farms along the Brazos or the Parchman State Penitentiary, since they both cast a fearsome shadow over one part of the Deep South. What Doc Reese experienced in Texas certainly held true in the Mississippi prison farm. Only some of the songs are different. Doc speaks for both. He began his account with a blues of his own making.

DOC REESE'S STORY

I was born on the 13th, I'm my mother's only son,
I was born on the 13th, I'm my mother's only son,
Out of all the money in the world, I swear I ain't had none.

I'm the unlucky one, no matter how I try,
I'm the unlucky one, no matter how I try,
I took the plane for California, landed in Shanghai.

I have no schooling, I'm just another fool in town,
I have no schooling, I'm just another fool in town,
The first day I started to school, the sucker, it burnt down.

Often I ponder why I was born black and was forced to undergo so many unjust and unequal things. I feel and I always have felt that, regardless of what I did, mine would be a position of servitude. There was a craving in me, however, that forced me to try to break into a place of comfort, by any means. Stealing was my way.

It was not that I had failed to get proper guidance as to the great evil that this crime actually was, nor was I void of the knowledge of the punishment that would follow, nor did I ever think that I would be able to get around the law. I was imbued with a spirit of vengeance. I felt somewhat elated to have taken something from the white man. I felt I was merely evening up the score. Even if the law did place me in prison I felt justified because, to me, the law was warped to suit the fancies of the white man, whether I was being justly treated by it or no. What I thought was proven wrong to me, but as I thought, many others think, "deep in the heart of the Delta."

I worked at a drugstore in the colored section and, when this store was looted of all the goods on the shelves, I was arrested. Although I had nothing to do with this crime and although I had never before been arrested and had no record at all, I was taken to the investigation cell and blackjacked in an attempt to extort a confession from me. Every ounce of third degree-ism was used against me. Finally, I was released, but with a black mark on my record and my inward feelings enraged. I had not been out of jail a day when an ex-convict made me an offer that was to be my undoing. I was to be turnover man for a gang. This suited me fine, for it would give me the chance to retaliate for the brutal treatment I had suffered.

The gang did a thriving business of looting cafés and I had little trouble in turning over the loot, which was mostly cigarettes. Six months later, when I had just reached the age of seventeen, I was apprehended with a large stock of stolen goods on my hands. They brought the whole gang in for investigation and placed us in separate cells. I managed to get a note to the rest of my boys advising them not to talk. I told them I would take all the blame.

The officers stood me on a brick all night, twisted my arms until they were sore, pressed a pencil under my nose until the pencil broke, but still couldn't get me to clear their books—that is, spill the goods on my buddies. My buddies were released and I was billed and transferred to the county jail to await

Mississippi flood relief camp, 1932 (Courtesy Herbert Hoover Presidential Library)

Hoe team, Parchman State Penitentiary, 1959 (Photo by Alan Lomax)

Convict singing,
Parchman, 1959

Ax-swinging convict,
Lambert camp,
Parchman, 1959 (Photos
by Alan Lomax)

Bama, 1959 (Photo by Alan Lomax)

Lambert camp, Parchman, 1959 (Photo by Alan Lomax)

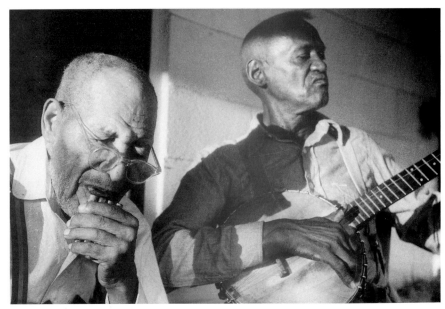

Sid Hemphill and Lucius Smith, 1959

Ed Young, 1960 (Photos by Alan Lomax)

Napoleon Strickland, Como, Mississippi, 1967 (Photo by George Mitchell)

Othar Turner, one of the leading fife and drum musicians, dances to *Shimmy She Wobble*, played by the Gravel Strings Band, 1967 (Photo by William Ferris. Courtesy University of Mississippi Archives)

Fred McDowell with his wife, 1959 (Photo by Alan Lomax)

Sam Chatmon

David "Honeyboy" Edwards, 1974 (Photo by Jim O'Neal. Courtesy Blues Archive, University of Mississippi)

Muddy Waters and Son House (Photo by David Gahr)

Muddy Waters (Photo by David Gahr)

Big Bill Broonzy (Photo by David Gahr)

Memphis Slim (Photo by David Gahr)

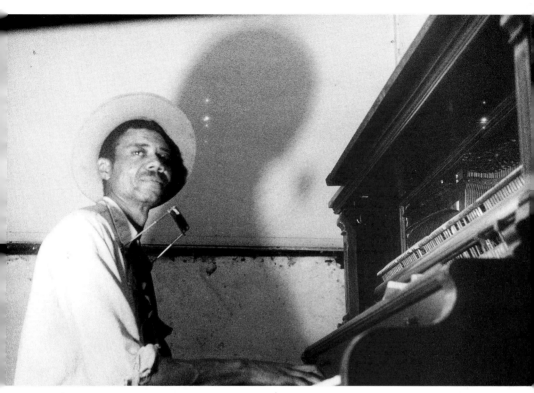

Forrest City Joe Pugh, 1959 (Photo by Alan Lomax)

Forrest City Joe playing harmonica in a cotton field, 1959 (Photo by Alan Lomax)

grand-jury action. As I walked into the bull pen of the county jail, this is what I heard echoing down those cold corridors:

"What the hell do you mean breaking in on us without permission?"

Then one big rough-talking con hollered, "Oyez, oyez, this iron-bound, ass-bursting kangaroo court is now in session!"

I'm not talking to one,
I'm not talking to two,
I'm talking to the judge
And the prosecutor, too.

Jump in your places
Like mules in their traces
And let's get back!

This jim has broke in, so the court is called,
So each one line up against the wall!

I guess this guy must have been kangaroo judge and prosecutor, too, because he walked up to me and began to ask questions:

"What's your name?"

"Doc _____."

"What did *you* steal?"

"I'm accused of four cases of burglary."

"I know you're not guilty," was his jeering remark.

"At least I'm not indicted yet," I answered, somewhat peeved at this line of questioning.

"Guilty or not guilty, we have you charged with breaking into this iron-bound without an invitation and against our wishes. How do you want to plead? Guilty or not guilty?"

"I guess I have no choice in the matter."

"Well, your fine is three dollars or one hundred licks on your natural black ass."

Right there another inmate spoke up, "Please your honor of this most high kangaroo court, we don't need no money. We gets three hots a day and our s—— washed away. Our light bill, water bill, and laundry bill are all paid. We even have mens to watch over us when we are asleep. I make a motion we don't receive this guilty man's money. Let's put those licks on him."

I began to wonder what had become of the money I had left at the desk, and the more I wondered the more frightened I became. The judge interrupted my meditations, "Well, boys, we need his money right now for stamps and some other little articles. So, prisoner, I'm gonna let you send to the desk for the three dollars and we'll let you off easy on this first offense. But let me warn you, don't ever let this happen again."

I was indicted on four separate counts. Each one of them was a burglary committed on the same night at about the same hour in different neighborhoods of town. Just how I managed all those crimes without an accomplice will always be a mystery to me. On the day of my trial I pleaded guilty and asked for the mercy of the court. The mercy was a sentence of twelve years. I left the courtroom pondering what fate held in store for me. What would the prison make of me? Would I ever walk out in the free world again?

My cell mate in the county jail, where we were waiting for transfer to the pen, was a wrinkled-up old fellow named Uncle Frank. Uncle Frank was stooped over from work and mean enough, I believe, to steal the pennies off a dead man's eyes. Some of the boys called him One-Wing Frank on account of him missing one hand, and he told me how he lost his hand:

"When I first went down on the river, I tried to work hard and make it in the way they told me, but, shuh, man, they'd beat you anyhow. Look like to me they took delight in it. They beat on me till one day I run off. In my young days I could run, man! And I outrun all the dogs and the hosses they sont after me.

"But I was foolish, too. I got clean away into the next county, then I stole me some clothes and went to town and got drunk wid one of the pretty big-hipped gals. What did she do but turn me in. They took me on back to the farm and whipped me till I was raw as beef. Right then I made up my mind that I wouldn't work no mo. So the next day out in the bottom, I knocked this joe, a permanent one." One-Wing held up his stub arm. "Yeah, I never did no more heavy work after I chopped off this hand."

After hearing Uncle Frank's story, dark thoughts used to come rolling through my mind as I lay in my cell at night. Then one morning I heard chains rattling down the corridor of the jail and somebody hollered that Uncle Bud had come and Black Betty was waiting.

Now you must know that in red-heifer times a man by the name of Bud Russell operated the transfer wagon that collected the prisoners from all over the state and brought them to the pen. They called him Uncle Bud and they sang many songs about him.

Yonder comes Bud Russell.
How do you know?
I know him by his big hat
And his forty-four.

He walks into the jailhouse
With his chains in his hand.
I heard him tell the captain,
"I'm the transfer man."

They used to sing that song to Uncle Bud's face. They sang a different song behind his back:

Uncle Bud, Uncle Bud was a man like this,
Couldn't get a woman, he'd use his fist.

Uncle Bud had corn that never been shucked,
Uncle Bud had gals that never been _____.

So ever after on, they call any man that operates the wagon "Uncle Bud," no matter what his name is. In place of Black Maria, we call Uncle Bud's old wagon Black Betty.

Uncle Bud had come and Black Betty was waiting! It seemed to me as if my whole body had turned cold as ice. I got up off my bunk and couldn't seem to get my feet down on the floor. Could hear my joints crack whenever I took a step. We were called out in the corridor and they gave us a necktie—a long chain with a Regent lock for the knot in every necktie. Thus I marched out of that jail and into the black, wire-enclosed truck, where Uncle Bud stood watching with his submachine gun under his elbow. When we started, I peeped through a heavy black wire grating to tell my old hometown goodbye. We were a full chain—eighteen men, two white women, and one colored woman.

At two o'clock the same afternoon we rolled up to the walls. This was the main unit of the prison system with the hospital, the shoe shop, the place where they made automobile license tags, the school, the trusty shack, the auditorium, the dining room, the big steel dormitory, and also the death house. The building had old-fashioned towers and funny-shaped windows all over it. Maybe it looked good at one time, but now it seemed to me all black and smoky and greasy like an old kerosene stove. When I walked in, I felt I had walked into a big pair of black jaws and they had closed down behind me.

They stripped us, fingerprinted us, and gave us a bath and a medical examination. We were allowed to keep only our belts and our money was placed to our account for us to draw on whenever we wanted. Most of us were issued white duck clothes. To the escapees and parole violators they gave stripes. Then they marched us to our sleeping quarters. The reception committee was waiting.

"Hey, there, old Big Head!" I didn't turn around, because I didn't know they were talking to me.

"Yes, I mean you." This time the jim tapped me on the shoulder. "We gonna call you Big Head because you got a head as big as a punkin and empty as a gourd."

Like every man who enters the prison, I now had my convict alias. The boys christen you as soon as they see you or as soon as they latch on to you. And that name is likely to stick to you until you leave the prison. I tried to grin at the man.

"Well, Big Head—if you know how to talk—where did you fall from?"

"Houston."

"How much time you doin?"

"Twelve years."

"That's just schoolboy time. I could do that in my shirttail and never show my black behind."

"How much time do you have?" I asked him. His name, I found out later, was Iron Jaw. He was a man that liked to talk.

"I have a hundred and twenty-five years for a number of crimes . . . Well, Big Head, you ain't gonna be lonesome. They's enough boys here from Houston to work all the farms in the river bottoms."

The bell in the tower rang and we got in line and marched into the dining room. To my surprise the scaugh was all right. I asked Iron Jaw, "Do they feed this way all the time?"

"Here in the walls they do. The members of the prison board come here a lot. But when you get down on those farms in the Brazos bottoms, you may never see a decent meal for months. The farms are rotten—rotten sleeping and eating, rotten hard work, and rotten bosses. Bout all you can do is gamble."

"Well, that's gonna be hard on me because I don't gamble. Don't have any luck."

"That's good, cause you can't win in the pen. These guys can outcheat the devil. After the lights go off at ten, come on over to my bunk and we'll talk."

At the time I thought Iron Jaw looked at me in a funny way, but I told myself that I was feeling jumpy. So after lights I went to his bunk and we began to chat. Right off he asked me, "Did you have a wife in the streets, old Big Head?"

"Yes, I've got a wife and one kid about two months old."

"Well, what do you think she's doing tonight?"

"I don't know. Hope she's thinking about me."

"More likely she's out with Joe the Grinder, if she's like the other gals."

"She wouldn't do that, I don't believe."

"Man, you think she's gonna wait for you twelve flat years?"

"Maybe I'll get parole," I muttered. I was feeling low in my mind by now and I wished I never had come to talk to this man who seemed to want to torture me with thoughts of home. As he went on talking, I began to think he had been well named, for his voice rang like iron.

"We all have that hope when we first come down here, but we soon find out we are the forgotten men. I had some broads promise they would be true to me when I first fell, but, since the months turned into years, those promises is forgot and the letters have stopped coming."

I started to get up and walk away from Iron Jaw's bunk, but he grabbed my arm. His voice became more friendly, "Did you see that slick cat sitting across from us in the dining room with all those starched clothes on?"

"Yeah."

"He is really making it easy here. He's a gal-boy we call Rosetta."

"What's a gal-boy do?"

"What does a woman do in the streets?" Iron Jaw asked me.

"You mean wash and cook?"

"Women do more than that, you know as well as I do. Haven't you ever heard of a punk?"

I said I had.

"Well, Rosetta is a punk, and you have him just like you would your wife."

"You mean he has what my wife has?"

"Something just as good and when you have him, you won't ever have any use for a woman again. Now listen, Big Head, I can help you a lot while you're here. I have some good connections and I can keep you from going to the farm. Besides, I can let you have all the dough you need, if you will be my gal-boy. Would you like that?"

It was my first day in prison and I didn't want trouble with any man. I spoke just as easy and quiet as I could: "I'll tell you, Iron Jaw, I never hold any hard feelings for what a man thinks or does, but, when I was born, I was a man-child. When I get low enough to take my mother's place, I will jump in my own ass and break my damn neck."

The day I left the walls on transfer to the farm I was worried, but I was glad to get away from Iron Jaw's looks. I had been afraid all the time he would try to do some dirty deed and get me in trouble. As we neared the farms, we looked through the dust flying up from the wheels of the big truck and could hear the men singing:

> *Black Betty's in the bottom,*
> *Let your hammer ring,*
> *Black Betty's in the bottom,*
> *Let your hammer ring.*[5]

Squads of men were scattered out across one of the biggest cotton fields you ever saw. The rows ran straight away from the road until they came together in the distance and wiggled in the heat from that old hot broiling sun. "It is a burning hell," I thought.

"Christ, man, that don't look like no farm. Mo like a garden," the boy next to me remarked.

It looked like the people had crumbled up the clods by hand. The song of the hoe squads got louder. The convicts were chopping all together, and when they'd raise those hoes, the blades would catch the sun and twinkle like a rainbow. The rainbow came falling down as the men struck in time to the song:

> *Black Betty's in the bottom,*
> *I can hear her roar,*
> *She's bringing some po sucker*
> *With an achin soul.*
>
> *She'll bring you here and leave you,*
> *Let your hammer ring,*
> *For a hundred summers,*
> *Let your hammer ring.*
>
> *Black Betty's got a baby,*
> *Let your hammer ring,*
> *Damn thing's gone crazy,*
> *Let your hammer ring,*

Dipped its head in gravy,
Let your hammer ring.

They carried us to the building, where we were unchained. The guard on the truck gave our papers to the building steward and we were assigned to tank number three. The tanks were big and high dormitory rooms with four rows of bunks in three tiers. One end of each of the tanks faces on the picket and these ends are closed off by big black steel pipes that run from floor to ceiling. Steel doors open into the picket and there the guards and the building tenders stand watch with their clubs and guns.

A large, black, smooth-skinned, gross-talking Negro met us at the door. This was the building tender for tank three and he had an expression on his face just exactly like an old coon your dog has got cornered up in a wire fence. He turned out to be as mean as he looked. He ordered us to sit down. One of the boys took his time about it and the building tender slapped him to the floor.

"When I tell you to do anything, I mean do it, understand?" He looked at us with a wolfish smile. "Where'd you come from, boy?" he asked a slim guy standing next to me.

"I'm from the capital."

"I guess since you fell out the governor's mansion you come down here to run everything, but get this straight. The cap'n run the farm and I run this tank. There ain't but three ways that you can make it here. They are hard ass, suck ass, or haul ass. If you gonna hard ass, you gotta have an iron ass, a brass belly, and a heart of steel, because we been practicing on hard guys for years and we know how to crack you. To suck ass, you got to be an ace sucker; you gotta look like you enjoy it. If you gonna haul ass, you better be ready to outrun the shit eaters and swim the big muddy river."

This man was a convict like me, and probably had more time than I did. He turned to Joe, one of my fall buddies, and said, "Where'd you come from, old yellow gal. I bet you're fine and I'm gonna have you for my boy." He laughed like a wolf while he ran his hand over Joe's legs. And what he said came true. The first night we were in the tank he came to Joe's bunk and Joe pushed him off. The next day the building tender, Old Love they called him, claimed Joe had broken a rule and he beat Joe down to the floor with his club. He kept on beating him and putting him up for punishment with the captain till Joe gave in. From then on, until he got tired of him, Old Love made things easy for Joe. That boy turned punk for true. He *made* him into a gal-boy. To me, this is the worst thing about prison life. Everyone knows it goes on—warden, captain, guards and all—yet nobody does anything about it.

Old Love went on talking to Joe: "How much time do you have?"

"Two years."

"Two years? You won't even find out where the captain s——! What did you steal?"

"I was sent up for assault and attempt."

"I know assault and attempt. Assault on some white man's window and attempt to steal what he had on the inside. You can assault and attempt here on the weeds and Johnson grass in this good captain's cotton . . . Now, Shorty, what's your story?"

"I'm from Dallas with a double fan [ten years—two hands]. I tried to do away with all the weed out there."

"So you're a sniffler! Well, you can't sniff here unless you want to use alfalfa . . . Now listen, you bulls, my rules are simple. No loud talking, no spitting on the floor, bathe often, git offa your bunk when the bell rings in the morning, and don't forgit to make it up when you git off it. Holler 'Alley boss' when you want to get up at night and don't leave your bunk until the night man give you the word to go ahead on. In the morning, the captain will tell you which squad to catch, and then you'll go to the fields."

We were assigned to our bunks and the rest of the day was passed in talk about the streets with the sick boys who were staying in the building. About six-thirty the turnkey drug his keys across the bars to notify the picket boss that the squads were coming in from the fields. This picket boss was a big brute with a look like Dillinger in his bloodshot eyes and a potbelly that hung almost down to his knees. We called him Dough Belly behind his back.

"Number one plow, boss!" yelled the turnkey.

"That's right," Dough Belly hollered back.

"Number two plow, boss."

"Let um come."

"Twenty of um, boss. Captain say put this un in the hospital."

"I got um."

And so the squads were checked into the tanks. The men were wet with sweat down to their socks. Their faces were dusty and their eyelashes hung with dirt. They were cursing a steady curse till the building sounded like a big nest of mad bumblebees. As many of the 'victs as could ripped off their dirty clothes and rushed to the showers in the rear of the tanks. One young bull sat down on the bunk opposite me and began to look at me the way a cow looks at a new gate.

"My name's Fast Black," he told me. "What do they call you?"

I told him my name. "Well, how're things on the streets?" he inquired. "Is the jims and janes still knockin theirself out?"

"The streets are on the beam and the janes on the ball. The jims are on the cut as sharp as tacks each and every day."

"That sounds fine, man." Fast Black smiled. "I'm down here wrestling with a long stretch and it's knockin me, but I'll be out there some sweet day afterwhile . . . Now look here, after supper we'll have a talk and I'll wise you up to what goes on around this place."

I thought about Iron Jaw and I mumbled something. This Fast Black looked like an all-right jim, but then how could I be sure?

We fell in line with our hands on the right shoulders of the men just ahead of us and marched in to supper. There I got my first taste of prison-farm scaugh. The best you could say about it was that there was a plenty—slices of coarse bread, slabs of hog meat, piles of vegetables cooked tasteless—stuff like that. The rest I will tell you in a prison song I learned:

You wake up in the morning
When the ding-dong ring,
Go marchin to the table,
See the same damn things.
It's on the table,
Knife, fork, and pan.
If you say anything about it
You're in trouble with the man.

After supper, they had mail call and opened the commissary. Some of the boys marched off for school. Then in an hour Old Love hollered, "Let's ride um," meaning we should get in our bunks. We mounted and I heard Fast Black whisper, "Hey, want to know why they call me Fast Black?"

"Uh-huh."

"It's because I'm so dark, old Big Head."

"Lissen, if you're a friend, call me Doc, will ya?"

"Okay, Doc."

"Tell me about the squads, Fast Black. Which one is the best to get on?"

"Them squads is all hard if the boss don't like you. Talk humble and don't grumble; act like your head's been bored for the simples; then maybe your boss won't ride you. Now here's the way the squads is laid out.

"There's number one hoe squad, where they put all the hard asses and haul asses. They make that squad *roll*. They have to set the pace for the rest of the squads in the field. Try to work um so hard they'll make a break, then they can lay the punishment on um. Number two hoe squad moves a little slower but must stay on the tail of number one. They push number one if it ever drag ass in the field. Number three is gen'ally the easy squad and do easy jobs, like shucking corn. Number four is boys who ain't well and can't keep up, but they make um work anyhow because they so tough to handle in the building. Number five is called the 'pull-do's' because they got to be pulled to make um do *any* work. Some are cripple. Some just contrary. They the last to get to the field, riding while the rest of us trots ahead of the boss's horse."

You shoulda been on the river, nineteen and nine,
Number one was runnin, number two was flyin,
Number three was hollerin, number four was cryin,
Number five was draggin, and the pull-do's dyin.
Why don't you wake up, dead man, help me drive my row?
My row is so grassy, I can't hardly go.
They have murdered my partner, plan on killin me.
If I get my chance, buddy, I'm gonna try to run free.

The next morning I was assigned to number four hoe squad, same as my new buddy, Fast Black. I felt good till I saw our boss. The men called him old Easter Rabbit because he didn't have but one big long tooth in the front of his face and when he chewed his tobacco his ears wiggled just like a rabbit eating. But that was the only thing about him that resembled a rabbit. The rest of him was part snake and part bear. He had a high whiny voice and more words of profanity than the Japs have rice.

"Just don't never talk nothin where he can see your lips movin," Fast Black told me while we were trotting to the woods ahead of old Easter Rabbit's horse. "That old devil's about half deaf and he'll think you're cussing at *him*."

After we got out in the bottoms, Easter Rabbit called me over to his horse. "Well, high-pockets, I guess you've come down from Huntsville to tell us how to run this farm."

"No sir."

"What's that you say, god damn your black soul?" he said. "Don't mumble at me."

"No, boss, I just wants to get along," I said very loud.

"Well, you can get along, if you watch yourself," he said. "But, goddammit, if you get tough, I can get a whole lot tougher. What'd *you* do in the streets, old nigger?"

"Worked in cafés, shine parlors—whatever I could find," I said.

"Well, you gonna get some blisters on those soft hands of yours now, you soft-bellied bastard," he whined. "And the only shoes you'll get to shine are mine. You can start right now."

Easter Rabbit gave me a kick with the toe of his boot. "Now I want you to walk down there and take a look at that river. Anytime things get too hot for you here, you can always try to swim across," he grinned.

I stood and looked at the old Red Brazos. It was swift and wide and full of drift logs, tangles, and mudholes. A million ideas swept through my mind while the men sang this song:

I was standing on the river when the ship passed by,
I looked and saw my mother, turned my head and cried.

If I ever do get wounded and pass away,
You can tell my people these are the things I say—

Give my clothes to my sister, give Papa my diamond ring,
Give my shoes to my sister, don't give my wife a doggone thing.
If my mother don't want my body, cast it in the deep blue sea
Where the catfish and the alligators can fight over me.

We kept on down into the bottom, deep down in there where the sun don't never shine because the woods are so thick and heavy. The boys say the trees down there look like old ghosts standing in some lonesome graveyard. We grouped up, four men to a tree.

"Old Big Head, you watch us strike a few times," said Bad Eye, a bulky guy who had been on the river for sixteen years and had natural life for murder, "and then you come on in. You strike with Gizzard Lips and I'll strike with Butter Bowl."

Those guys could make an ax do tricks. Alternate men around the tree struck together, in a steady rhythm: "Blam-lam, blam-lam, blam-lam." On the upstroke they'd twirl their ax helves round in their palms so those double-bitted heads would flash like diamonds in the sunshine. I fell in with Gizzard Lips and Bad Eye began to sing:

> *Why don't you ring, old hammer?*
> > *Hammer ring,*
> *Ring-ho, ring-ho,*
> > *Hammer ring.*

We all sung the "hammer ring" and Gizzard Lips began to "preach" to his diamond, which is what he called his ax.

> *I'm gonna preach to my diamond,*
> > *Hammer ring,*
> *If you walk, I'll ride yuh,*
> > *Hammer ring,*
> *And if you ride, I'll drive yuh,*
> > *Hammer ring,*
> *Cause I'm a number one driver,*
> > *Hammer ring,*
> *The axes is a-walkin,*
> > *Hammer ring,*
> *The chipses is a-talkin,*
> > *Hammer ring,*
> *Looky, looky yonder,*
> > *Hammer ring,*
> *I think I see sperrits,*
> > *Hammer ring,*
> *A-walkin in the timber,*
> > *Hammer ring.*

Every man in our squad was striking to the rhythm of Bad Eye's song. Every man was swinging on that hot beat of his. The blood was running warm in my veins and I felt lifted up like I have in church sometime. There wasn't any more Easter Rabbit, no more bullying building tender, no more prisoners—just that old live oak and the axes biting them big chips and the song rising right through those dark woods up to the blue sky. About the time old Bad Eye began to talk about the "sperrits in the timber," I heard somebody holler, "Timbohhhhh——"

That long, lonesome holler nearly scared me to death. I looked up in time to see one of those big live oak trees come crashing down—whoomp! The ground shook when it hit. Then old Bad Eye began to sing again:

My diamond's caught afire,
  Hammer ring!
It's burnin up the timber,
  Hammer ring!
And I need a little water,
  Hammer ring!
To cool my diamond,
  Hammer ring!

By eleven o'clock there was a big patch of sunshine in those dark bottoms where we had been working. Also, breakfast had begun to seem about a day ago. My little guts felt as if they were about to be eaten up by my big guts. Fast Black was the first one to see the wagon coming with our dinner, or "johnny," and he began to holler:

Believe I spied the johnny, believe I spied the johnny,
Believe I spied the johnny, God Almighty God knows.

Coming over yonder, coming over yonder,
Coming over yonder, oh my Lordy.

She's rockin dead easy, she's rockin dead easy.
She's rockin dead easy, God Almighty God knows.

When the wagon got to the johnny grounds, plates were laid out on the ground in rows. Each convict got down by his own plate. The pots were passed along the lines and we ate, with the guards eating and sitting in a big circle around the edge of the johnny ground. Johnny lasts an hour in winter and two in the summer. Dice games usually take place as soon as dinner is over, and those who do not participate get with their friends and venture into the streets of the past.

"Getting over here by old Big Head, boss!" Bad Eye hollered to the johnny boss.

"Go ahead, old Bad Eye, but I don't want to hear too damn much noise out of you," replied the boss. Bad Eye slid along the ground until he was in our crowd. "You from Houston?" he asked as soon as I was near.

"Yeah."

"How much time they give you?"

"I got twelve years for my silly little game. It was all right at first, but looks like it'll be hell at the close."

"You can make it, if you try," he encouraged me.

"That's right, Doc," said Fast Black. "Just keep your mouth shut and your asshole open and you can roll right on."

"It don't make no diffunce whether you got a long time or a short one," said a voice behind us. "You a dead man anyhow soon's you come down on these farms." It was Butter Bowl talking. He was a short chubby fellow, and this was the first time I heard him say a word all morning. "Naw, hell, it don't make no diffunce. After all this mess, you won't care whether you live or die." He looked at me and his eyes looked like a dead man's eyes. They caused a cold chill to run down my spine. "We in a dead man's hole," he muttered like he was talking to himself.

About that time the field boss called for his horse and then hollered, "Raise um up, raise um up." The 'victs slowly got up off the ground, where some had been lying asleep and dreaming of the streets. The squads were counted out and we went back to the woods. The diamonds began to shine again and a song broke in the air. It was an encouraging song. It told about how you might get lucky and win.

1.

Way out in Californy
Where old Stewball⁶ was born,
All the jockeys in the country
Said he blew there in a storm.
> *Well, bet on Stewball*
> *And you might win, win, win,*
> *Bet on Stewball*
> *And you might win.*

2.

His bridle was made of silver,
His saddle was made of gold,
And the price on his blanket
Hasn't never been told.

3.

That little bell was tapped on,
That big bell, it fairly tone.
Old Stewball came to the startin
Like a criminal to be hung.

4.

Old Molly ran like lightning,
Like an express passenger train,
But old Stewball swept around
  that racetrack
Like a midnight shower of rain.

5.

The cuckoo, it done hollered,
And the turkle dove, it just moan.
I'm a poor boy in trouble
And a long way, way from home.

6.

Now ain't these hard times?
Buddy, don't I know?
Now ain't these hard times?
Buddy, don't I know?

The axes were walking. The old live oaks were tumbling all around us, but old Butter Bowl was hardly striking. It looked like his mind was away off somewhere. Easter Rabbit finally noticed it and began to really chew the rag.

"Butter Bowl, you sorry son-of-a-bitch, if you don't go to work, nigger, you won't cost the captain a cent for supper. I'll have you put in that hole and kept there on bread and water till you're thin enough to see through, you fat-assed, no-account bastard. I'll give you the hot-house blues."

Butter Bowl ducked his head down and mumbled, "Go to hell, old squabblin man. Hell, I'm workin." Easter Rabbit couldn't hear what he said, but he saw his lips working.

"That's all right, I know you want me to kiss your ass. Maybe I'll have the captain kiss it when he gets here, you sorry blue-black ape. You so sorry, come to think of it, you must have been an accident. Your mama went to the outhouse and out you dropped."

That made Butter Bowl hot and he said in a loud voice, "If your mama had you, I know you must be an orphan, because no woman could live after seeing she had brought a thing like you into the world."

"Cap'n, Cap'n," Easter Rabbit went to squawlin, "come get this impudent son-of-a-bitch. He's not been doin a goddamn thing but talkin all day."

The captain came riding over and called Butter Bowl up to his saddle, caught his nostrils with a pair of pliers, and mashed them together. "Old Butter Bowl, you sorry, nappy-headed, hard-ass bastard," he yelled, "when are you gonna do some work? Every boss I put you under says you won't work. Well, either start rolling or try to beat these dogs to the Brazos. I'm gonna send to Huntsville and get some leather for your ass and every time one of these bosses ask me to, I'm gonna let you have it. I don't think you have as much ass as I have leather."[7]

Butter Bowl fell back into the dust as the captain gave him a kick. That night, when he went to the building, he was put in the cuffs. His hands cuffed behind him, he was left to sit flat on the concrete until after midnight. We had a four-thirty rising bell in the summer.

The next morning Old Love, the building tender, woke up on the wrong side of the bed and began to roar just like a lion. He had lost a lot of money in a crap game the night before and he was raging.

"Come off those damn bunks, tighten them damn sheets, and fold them blankets right. I don't want to hear a goddam sound out of any of you. Whose damn bunk is this?" he yelled as he stood by my bunk.

"It's mine," I said, half afraid.

"You're a new nigger, ain't you?"

"Uh-huh."

"Well, if I have to tell you about this bunk again, I'll put so many knots on your damn head you won't be able to put that damn head of yours through that damn door."

I went to makin the bed over again, and he walked down the aisle and stopped at Butter Bowl's bunk. "Get your sorry ass over here, old Butter Bowl. You may do what you want to out there in the fields and cuss the bosses, but in here you gonna make your damn bunk up."

Butter Bowl came, walking slowly, and, as he approached his bunk, Old Love let him have it. He hit him on the right side of the head and the blow rang through the entire building. Now, Butter Bowl never had building trouble before. He had been respected as a man and avoided by the tenders. When Old Love hit him, he put his hands up to his head, half dazed, with the blood running in his eyes. He saw Love reaching for his dirk and he turned and ran up the alley with Love right on his heels, cutting him at every step. He ran to the back of the building, snatched the top off a commode, and whirled just in time to let Love have it against his head. The top shattered and a sharp piece stuck into Love's head. Love lost his dirk and club and Butter Bowl began to beat him down to the floor, growling, "You low-down, belly-crawling bastard, you been fooling with us too long. This time you grabbed the wrong man."

By this time the assistant building tender had grabbed his club and was rushing to help Old Love. As he moved in, Gizzard Lips rose to Butter Bowl's defense. Gizzard Lips was a small Negro, about five feet four inches tall, weighing about one hundred and forty pounds, but he was tough as a boot and didn't take any fooling with. He came up with a curse on his lips, "You ratty trusties ain't gonna beat that boy up for nothin without first havin hell outa me."

He went in with his six-inch chin gleaming. The building tenders were in a panic and Dough Belly, the picket boss, was shouting, "Old Love, Old Love! Bring him up front and I'll shoot him." The fight was raging. Gizzard Lips stabbed Old Love. The assistant building tender clubbed Gizzard Lips. Butter

Bowl was hitting like a V-8 Ford and was as bloody as a butcher. Old Love was growing weak from the loss of so much blood.

The turnkey let the building tenders off tank number two and this put the odds against the two 'victs. They were beaten down to the floor and dragged to the front, where they were kicked insensible. All were taken to the emergency room and given first aid and then to the hospital, where they were sewn up. On the fourth day Love and Butter Bowl died, and Gizzard Lips was charged with murder and ninety-nine years were added to his life sentence.

I was filled with fear and hatred of this place and all I had seen. My friends, Fast Black and Bad Eye, seemed to have deserted me. They didn't want to talk. We just kept our heads down and walked like dead men.

We were chopping cotton. I was afraid I could not chop as much as was required of me, but I was trying. Down the rows behind me I heard the noise of another fight starting. I looked back and this is what I saw.

Cold Blood, the picket boss, had been blamed for the killing I have just told of. For punishment he had been transferred to the pull-do squad and he was hot about this. He was taking his bad temper out on an old cripple fellow named Lew, who had a hard time keeping up. One of the other bosses, in kidding Cold Blood about his squad and how sorry it was, told him that if *he* was carrying that nigger Lew, he would use a grass rope on his ass and make him keep up. So this day in the cotton field Cold Blood ordered several of the boys in his squad to grab old Lew and spread-eagle him. "I'm going to give you something to make you keep that damn row up," he remarked.

Old Lew raised his hoe and said, "If any of you sorry sucker-asses come up to me, I'll cut your neck off down to your asshole."

The boys, quite naturally, would not go up to him. Finally old Cold Blood got off his horse, loaded his shotgun with buck shots instead of with bird shots, and began to chase old Lew around. Cold Blood was so fat and so soft that he could not even catch that cripple old man at first, but he finally got in reach of him and struck Lew on the shoulder with the barrel of his gun. The gun went off and blew away half of Lew's shoulder.

"Don't shoot me no mo, boss," Lew pleaded as he fell to earth. Cold Blood walked back a few steps to where he had dropped his extra shells and loaded his gun again. Then he approached Lew with a curse on his lips. "I'll put you out of your misery, you right sorry old hard-ass nigger," and he laid his gun on the side of Lew's head and blew the top of his head off. He then mounted his horse and ordered the men to go to work. All the gangs in the field had stopped and were watching what happened. When Cold Blood had done his dirty deed, Easter Rabbit and all the bosses began squabbling and pushing on down the line. We rolled on while a couple of the trusties dragged Lew to the wagon. An investigation was held, but nothing was ever done about this incident. Cold Blood is still a guard on the Big Brazos.

We rolled on under that sun. Old Bad Eye began to sing. It was the first time he'd sung since Butter Bowl had been murdered.

> *My mama called me, Lawd, Lawd, Lawd,*
> *And I answered, "Ma'am."*
> *"Ain't you tired of rollin, O Lawd, Lawd,*
> *For that big-hat man?"*
>
> *My pappy called me, Lawd, Lawd, Lawd,*
> *And I answered, "Suh."*
> *"If you tired of rollin, O Lawd, Lawd,*
> *What you stay there fuh?"*
>
> *My sister called me, Lawd, Lawd, Lawd,*
> *But I ain't got long,*
> *"Just a few more summers, O Lawd, Lawd,*
> *And I'll be gone."*
>
> *Well, they's some in the buildin, Lawd, Lawd, Lawd,*
> *Some on the farm,*
> *Some in the graveyard, O Lawd, Lawd,*
> *And some goin home.*

Somehow that mournful old song crept into my ears, and I began to sing, too. I knew Bad Eye was talking to me. Talking to the rest of us. I knew he'd made a lifetime sentence and was subject to parole this year. He was telling us that if he could make it, we could, too. You could hear us for a mile. We made a big sound that rolled over that old green cotton field like a big wind, rising. All the guards rode with their guns out that day.

On the johnny grounds Fast Black got to talking about hauling ass. He was trying to get me to go with him. "We can outrun anything they got on this river. Ain't no use in staying here and getting killed. Might as well die trying to get away."

Bad Eye listened and didn't say much at first. Then he began to talk to us and we listened because he was an old 'vict and knew the ropes. "They ain't no use in tryin to beat the system," he said. "I tried it every way I know. Only thing to do is to throw your time the way they tell you to and then leave out of this Southern country. Lissen what I tell you now. I know. I been through all of it."

We had a two-hour johnny that day and Bad Eye told us his whole story. This was what he said:

"The first hitch I threw was five years for stealin a hog. I really stole him, too, because I had a large family and they were hungry. I eased up to old Moster's pen and with my long knife in my hand grabbed that hog and rammed that goddamned knife clean through his heart. Man, that hog fell over without a squeal. I put that hog in my sack and toted him to my shack and, you talking about happy! Them little nigger babies of mine was really happy. The next morning when the table was set, we had spare ribs for breakfast.

"But you know I was a plum fool! I had left a plain trail of blood right to my door. Old Moster come to my house and he axed me, 'Old Bad Eye, what did you steal my hog fer?' "

"I said, 'What you mean—steal your hog?'

" 'But, boy, I saw the blood all the way to your door.'

"This made me mad as hell. I reached up on the wall and got my shotgun and told him to get away from my door or I would make a sifter of him. He went on away, all right, but the sheriff come with a posse and took me to jail and in a few days I was in prison.

"This pen was a hell of a place then, son. Put me in number-one hoe squad and we had to roll in that hot sun all day long. If a man fall out wid de sun, they just drag him out the way and let the work go on. They *drove* you down here in them times—niggers and whites, mens and wimmens. It was in red-heifer days when we used to sing:

You oughta been here in 1904,
You could find a dead man on ev'y turn row.

You oughta been here in 1910,
They was drivin the wimmen like they do the men.

"Well, in about three months old Mos' come and got me out. I worked for him till I paid him for the hog. Then I made enough money to buy me a little plot of ground and moved my family into my little shack and I was really on easy street. Even bought me a rubber-tired buggy. Man, I was the proper guy and all the janes wanted to ride with old Bad Eye, but I had me a special big-hipted mama and she toted a razor for anyone she caught flirting with me. I be damn if I don't believe she'd have used it on me!

"One day me and my old lady and three pretty kids just like me were coming from town. The dark clouds began to show in the west and I tapped Old Blue, my fast-stepping mare, to hurry her on home. There was a low bridge on Onion Creek and I wanted to get over it before the water covered it. The rain begin fallin—a regular flood. When I got to the creek, the water was over the bridge, but I thought I could make it over. The old mare stepped in and we started across. It looked to me like we was gonna make it when a big bust of water swept the buggy off the bridge. My wife and chillun were drowned.

"Ever since then, seems like I been half crazy. I kept my place, but I didn't do much farming. Had Sattidy-night suppers when all the niggers would round up in there to have they times. They pretty gals used to get me to sing this little old song:

I got a letter Miss Annie was dead, my boy!
I got a letter Miss Annie was dead, God dog!
I got a letter Miss Annie was dead,
She got choked on a crawfish head, God damn!

Ain't but the one thing worry my mind, my boy!
Ain't but the one thing worry my mind, God dog!
Ain't but the one thing worry my mind,
A house full of women, not one of them mine, God damn!

Bad Eye continued telling us young jims his story:

"One night we were having a big supper. A young white boy and a young upstart nigger came riding up on some fine horses. They had been drinking chock and were acting rowdy, trying to get some of those big-legged, pretty gals to go down on the creek with them. These were some beautiful dames about eighteen years old. Their tits looked like a couple of electric light bulbs and just to look at them made an old man like me feel sixteen.

"Well, those gals didn't want to go, but they grabbed them anyway and started toward the creek. The gals began to call on their dads, but do you know they own pappies was afraid to do anything because this young white boy had money! I sat there until I began to think about how my own little gals would have been just about the age of these gals, if they had lived. In no time at all I reached up and got my old .45 and started for the creek.

"I got there just as the white boy was tearing the clothes from the gal. I said, 'You rotten son-of-a-bitch, leave that gal alone,' and about that time the young nigger further down the creek upped an ran. But the young white man was a bully and he invited me to his ass. Told me I didn't have a damn thing to do with white folks' business. This made me damn mad and I told him, 'Listen, you damn clay-colored son-of-a-bitch, if you don't turn that gal loose, I'm gonna turn this .45 loose!'

"He thought I was bulling him and kept on tearing the gal's dress. I raised my gun and fired. He fell. The crowd came running when they heard the shots, but I slipped away and gave myself up to the sheriff. A mob tried to get me, but they moved me to another jail. When I was tried, they gave me life.

"I went down on the river and the bosses all tried to make my road look hard because I had killed a white man. They tried in every way to kill me, but they couldn't. Finally, I decided to run away. I got me some pepper and the next day, when we went in the bottoms to cut wood, the lead nigger begin to sing a song that give me the running-away blues:

Captain, if I beat you to the river, what would you do?
Would you do me this favor? Lemme make it through,
Lemme make it through.

Captain, if I beat you to the river, you can count me gone.
I'll be in Lou'siana, tryin to cool my bone,
Tryin to cool my bone.

"I listened to this song and I got worried. I eased behind a brush pile like a bat out of a burning barn. From there I hit the bushes and headed for the big river. That old song was still ringing as I stood on the banks of that old red-colored river. It was boilin, wid big logs and old brush. Look like the whole river was full of suckholes and whirlpools.

"I leaped in and swum to the other side. About a mile through the thickets I came to a farmer's house where some clotheses were hanging on the line and quickly changed. Didn't have no hat or shoes, but I figgered by staying off the road I might not be noticed. Hadn't went but a mile till I heard a truck over in the next lane. Then I heard the shit eaters barking. Didn't take me long to climb a tree and from there I peppered the air, but in less than ten minutes the whole pack was around that tree. I knew I had failed.

" 'Here I is, boss,' I hollered, 'glad to go back and go to work.' When I come down, he beat me with his whip and trotted me all the way back to the building. Next morning I caught the number one squad and went back to cutting wood."

"And where you got to now?" Fast Black asked him. "You're still on the river, aincha? You're still taking all this stuff from these sorry bastards we gotta call 'boss' and 'cap'n.' Ev'y day you walk out in these fields you liable to be kilt."

"But looky here, Fast Black, I made it, throwed my nineteen years on my lifetime sentence. I'm liable for clemency right now."

"You may get a pardon and you may drop dead," said Fast Black.

"And look at you," Bad Eye went on, "you only got six years and you'll be out in no time."

"I won't live that long. I'll tell one of these bosses just what I think of him. Naw, me an Doc here are gonna try to make it to the Brazos line—"

"Raise um up, you sorry bastards," hollered Easter Rabbit. We grabbed our hoes and went back to the field. Now, as everybody knows, conversation is not permitted the convicts while they're working. But in our songs we had a way to talk right on. Today it was old Bad Eye giving good advice to me and my friend Fast Black. He was singin the song about old Rattler, the fastest dog they ever had on the Brazos.

Early one Sunday mornin,
    Here, Rattler, here,
Captain called the dog sergeant,
    Here, Rattler, here.[8]

He ran so fast till he looked like a streak,
You should have seen that dog a-workin his feet.

The Texas Special was a-runnin downhill,
But Rattler pass it like it was standin still.

Soon as he heard old Rattler's cry,
Old Beatum wished for wings to fly.

Here, Rattler,
Here, Rattler, here,
Here, Rattler,
Here, Rattler, here.

"Just the same," Fast Black told me when we were washing up for supper, "I'm gonna make it for the river just as soon as I can. You might as well come with me."

Right then I wasn't studying about trying to outrun those dogs, but something happened to change my mind. The new tender, named Creepin Jesus, who was put in Old Love's place on tank three, asked me did I want to be schoolteacher for the camp. That would mean I wouldn't have to go in the field no more. No more Easter Rabbit. No more hard rolling under the barrels of a shotgun. But the way Creepin Jesus looked at me when he made the proposition, I knew what *he* wanted. So I told him I didn't have enough education to teach.

Creepin Jesus was no bully like Old Love. He was worse. He *kept* after me. He pestered me to death. I made like I didn't know what he meant, but every day I felt more like telling Fast Black I'd go along with him when he made his break.

One night I woke up and felt a hand under my mattress. It was Creepin Jesus. He jerked his hand out and held up a homemade dirk, the kind the prisoners sometimes manage to make and hide around theirself for protection. If they find one of those daggers on you, you're *bound* to be in trouble.

"All right, old Doc," Creepin Jesus said right low, so he wouldn't wake nobody, "I got the goods on you this time. What do you say? Want to be my boy and have me forget this? Or want me to turn you in?"

Just about that time a great big pair of hands slipped around that building tender's throat and cut his wind off short. Fast Black had grabbed him. Before I knew what was going on, Bad Eye snatched the dirk out of Creepin Jesus' hand and placed the point right over his heart. "Don't move, you rotten son-of-a-bitch, or I'll cut your heart out," Bad Eye told him. "I oughta kill you now, but I give you a chance. Leave Doc alone and forget about this dirk or get ready to die. You gonna do like I tell you?"

Creepin Jesus couldn't say nothing, so he sort of waggled his head up and down. "And get this, you slimy bastard," Bad Eye say. "If you spill to the white man, I'll get to you somehow and kill you deader than hell. I might go, but I'll carry you with me. Understand?"

Creepin Jesus nodded his head again, so Fast Black and Bad Eye let him go. He didn't even look around. Went down that aisle like a lizard looking for his hole. My two buddies mounted their bunks and nobody even turned over. It was like a nightmare that hadn't even been dreamt. Creepin Jesus never did so much as speak to me again. Fact was, he got himself transferred to tank number one the next week.

He didn't forget Bad Eye, though. He paid him back, at least I will always think it was him did the dirty deed. Bad Eye had a life sentence. He'd served sixteen years of it and had earned ten years good time. That meant he could be paroled, because nineteen years on any sentence, if a man have a good record, make him eligible for clemency. The Prison Board had sent the investigator to interview him and this man had sent in a favorable report on Bad Eye. Bad Eye was looking every day for his pardon to come from the governor. He was always humming the old song about

I'm gwine away to leave, my time ain't long,
The man gonna call and I'm goin home.
Then I'll be done all my grievin, whoopin, holl'in, an cryin,
Then I'll be done all my studyin about my great long time.

Then one day in cane-cutting time they called him out of our squad and placed him in number one hoe, the squad that led the rest. When Bad Eye ask him, the captain mumbled something about needing all his best men in number one squad. So that morning Bad Eye left us. Later he told us what had happened.

The boss on number one squad was the man Bad Eye had slipped away from that time he'd made it to the river. He still held a grudge against Bad Eye. When they got to the field, this boss said to Bad Eye, "Well, old nigger, I notice the board's been out to see you."

"Yassuh, boss, after sixteen years on this old river, I think it's about time."

"What you gonna do when you git out?"

"I dunno, boss. I think I move to Kansas City and git me a job. I hear times is good up there in the war."

"Don't build your dreams too high," said the boss, "you might be disappointed."

That night, when the squads were checked in the building, Bad Eye was ordered to get on the barrel, and for what no one knew. When he later secured his record, he found he had been "impolite." A letter from the board told him that, since his record was not clear, his case would be reconsidered later on.

Bad Eye won't talk to anybody, no more'n to ask for his victuals. He just stares ahead of him all day like he was seeing ghosts. Fast Black is making ready for the day when he's going to try and run out from under those shotguns. He wants me to be his buddy and go with him, and I can't see much reason why I shouldn't. Every day we slop through the cold mud down between the cane rows. The cane leaves cut our hands to the bone. The northers blow right through our cotton convicts' stripes. Not far away the big muddy river flows through the bottoms, the barrier between us and everything we want and love. None of us knows whether we shall cross it in this life or in the next . . . Some days when the winter rain whips across the field, I can hear my friend Bad Eye talk to the river. And all us prisoners heist the song behind him. Maybe our folks will hear it when the wind goes moaning by.

Little boy, little boy, how did you git so long?
Must of killed your rider in the high sheriff's arms.

Little boy, little boy, you should have stayed home,
Picked up chips for your mammy, blowed your daddy's horn.

Let it be noted that Doc Reese, the man who told this tale of the Sugarland penal farm, was rescued from prison rape by comrades who loved him enough to risk their lives and their chance for parole for their friend. This was certainly because Doc was a lovable man. Among his many endearing qualities, one that weighed heavily on the scale of prison loyalties, was his singing voice, which was spicy keen and strong enough to chase a lake of bourbon. Thus one might say it was the old African pattern of the singing brotherhood that brought Doc through the burning hell of the Texas pen.

Chapter 7

▲▲▲▲▲▲▲▲▲▲

The Hills

SID HEMPHILL

Senatobia is in "the Hills," a different world from the Delta. Thin, clayey soil. Everything turned grey and scorched by midsummer. Empty houses in erosion-gutted, weed-grown fields. Few cars on the road. You're liable to be the only customer in a grocery store, where the sweet-sour of pickles-jawbreakers-flypaper is a half-century heritage. Softer, slower speech than in the Delta. A milder eye. Real backwoods astonishment over strangers. Antebellum atmosphere. Here, where the bones and gristle of the land showed in the erosion washes, lived Sid Hemphill, the "boar-hog musician of the hills."

Off the gravel a couple of miles through sparse scrub oaks and starved broomweed pastures, we found Sid Hemphill's shack at what appeared to be the fountainhead of all erosion. It teetered on a small lip of land which the running sores of the rain gullies had almost eaten away and from which they had sprangled out, ten and twenty feet deep, to carve, gut, and destroy the surrounding field. One slender bridge of land linked Sid's dwelling and the pasture gate. Across this final crumbling bridge I gingerly drove. There were no dogs or chickens in the yard. The sagging, unpainted door in the weathered-grey, warping house was closed. My heart sank. Here, in this graveyard of a place, I would miss my man. He was dead, ill, away. I walked across the crazy porch and was about to knock when the door flew open. Sid Hemphill, whom the blind harp blower called "the best musician in the world," stood in the doorway.

No one had told me that Sid Hemphill was blind, but it was the last thing you'd recall about him. His face blazed with inner light. He ran rather than walked everywhere. He could never wait for his wife to bring something, but always darted up to find it himself. His speech, which could not keep pace with his thoughts and designs, had become telegraphic and brusque.

"I learnt to play from my daddy. He was a good un. Told me he got all his tunes from his colored cousin. Down in South Mississippi. An awful fiddle player." ("Awful" here means very skillful and brilliant.)

"I'm sixty-five. Be sixty-six in next month, if I live . . . I can play—I don't know, sir, hardly—lemme see—play guitar, fiddle, mandolin, snare drums, fife, bass drum, quills, banjo, pretty good organ player. Come on out here. I'll show you."

Sid sprang up, knocked out his pipe on the chimney, and dashed out the front door. He stepped across his precarious butte, as lively as a youngster, dragging me to the door of his smokehouse. "There," he flung it open. Twoscore bulging tow sacks hung from the rafters, but instead of smoked hams and sides of country bacon and skins of sausage, they were stuffed with musical instruments—drums, fiddles, mandolins, guitars, fifes, and cane pan-pipes, well protected by the gunnysacking against the damp. Sid proudly opened the bags and poured out before me a rural instrumentarium, most of which he had crafted with his own hands.

"Course I makes my own fiddles. Several good fiddle makers round here—but it ain't often you find a man kin make a good drum." He thumped and riffled to prove his point. "My bands play for all picnics hereabout. The folk like fife-and-drum music to dance by. I has several diffunt bands and I send um all about."

So here in the Hills was the music of three or four past Delta generations; here was a hoedown fiddler such as Phineas Maclean and George Adams danced to, but still making a good living by tootling and scratching out his breakdowns for the Hill folk. And Sid knew them all. I reeled off the list of fiddle tunes that had stumped my Delta folks. Old Blind Sid said "Sho!" to every title, a trifle impatiently. Then he cross-questioned me and called off a flock of local tunes that were new to me. "Here's one way we play," he snatched up his fiddle, tuned it with a sweep or two, and began sawing away—a simple tune of two phrases, bowed so heavily the fiddle sounded almost like a drum—then in a voice that was bold and sure, in the harsh, shouting tones of a truly African singer, he sang the refrain.

> *You cain't read,*
> *You cain't write,*
> *You cain't get no supper tonight.*
> > *You cain't eat,*
> > *You cain't stay,*
> > *On the eighth of Januway* (Old Christmas).
>
> *You cain't read,*
> *You cain't write,*
> *You cain't eat no supper tonight.*
> > *You cain't eat,*
> > *You cain't shine* (dance),
> > *You cain't talk to the gal of mine.*

"I been playin that ever since I was a little boy. See, one time I ask my daddy to play me the fiddle"—Sid drove on rapidly, exhilarated by his music. "So he say, 'Son, if you want to play the fiddle, whyn't you play it yourself?' Then he bust me over the head."[1] Sid rocked with laughter. "Well, I went off, stayed six months, and I came back. I could outplay him.[2] Old man tell me, 'Go down and watch them hogs. They down in the lot.'

" 'They ain't down in the lot.'

" 'They must be in the cornfield.'

" 'Go call your dogs, then.' " Without further ado Sid pulled his bow across his big, crude country fiddle, producing the wild whoop a man uses to call his hounds. "Aieee, go on, old dogs, catch them hogs," he hollered. "Sooey, sooey." We were off to a musical hog hunt, Sid fiddling a drone figure with a driving rhythm that sounded at various times like a locomotive, a pack of hounds on a hot trail in the brush, a herd of razorback hogs hitting hell-for-leather through a canebrake, and a cotton gin gone to Memphis on a spree. The cords and veins stood out in his strong neck as he shouted to his dogs and his companions— "Look out there, boys. Catch um. Sooey, sooey." The sweat rolled down his forehead. His blind eyes fairly popped with excitement. Hog-killing blood lust sounded in the pig squeals that punctuated his country fiddle tune. Years later I heard the match of this music in the lion-hunting music of the Niger. Hemphill was playing the European fiddle the way his African granddaddy must have made it sound when he first tried it out in the slave quarters.

You need to rest after music like this *Panola County Razorback Hog Killing*. I picked up the panpipes—a set of hollow canes of varying lengths, bound together with the tops even. Pan, the goat god, is to be seen playing sets of pipes like these in Greek friezes, and they're the principal folk instrument of Rumania even today. The Indians of the highlands of South America play the *rondador*, a set of more than a score of pipes. Sid's pipes were of two sizes—one with a set of four tubes, the other of ten. I had never before seen this instrument in all my journeys in the South.

"Them's the quills," said Sid. "That's old folks' music. Music of olden time. Back yonder almost everybody used to play on quills.[3] Now, ain't hardly common no more. I makes my own. Sho, I'll make you all you want, a quarter a set . . . Nawsuh, if you please, I'd druther you wait till tomorrow. My band playin a picnic at the Fives, and fellow in the band is a really good quill player. I'm just half-hand at it . . . ."

Night had almost caught me on Blind Sid's island in the bitterweed. After we agreed to meet at the picnic the next afternoon, I shook his pale, freckled hand. That wild, sad, braying fiddle of his rolled around in my head until late that night. Next morning I was feeling quite ill. I had had enough of the field—too much dust, too much sun, too much irony. I was washed up and longing to get the hell away.

PO WHORE'S KINGDOM

It was a bad-luck Saturday in a county that seemed almost deserted. The few people that we met all had various notions about the location of the Fives, where the dance was scheduled. We tried every corner of the county, drove many hard miles in the blinding sun, and smothered in dust before somebody said, with a chuckle, "Oh, you must mean the Funky Fives, Po Whore's Kingdom. That just up the road a little piece. I'm goin to that picnic myself."

A mile up the road I heard the band. At first I didn't recognize the tune, puffed somewhat plaintively on the fife with a ruffling snare-drum background. When I could see the band, old Sid with his fiddle and the others under a tree at the edge of the dusty lane, I realized that they were playing *The Sidewalks of New York* as it might have sounded deep in the Congo.

At that moment my little Ford scraped bottom and refused to go farther. I backed up off the road, got out, and, snuffling back my hay fever, walked up the grassy road and into the dusty field where the band sawed and thumped away. I wish I could say that the next hours were a joyous and replenishing experience. I wish I could say that on August 15 at Sledge, Mississippi, the black farmers of Mississippi repossessed the earth with their laughter and their dancing. Actually, hardly anyone had come to the picnic, and I was too inexperienced to appreciate the treasure Lewis Jones and I had discovered. Sid's music represented an early phase of African-American music—not only that, but a clear revival of African tradition, kept alive in the Mississippi backwoods. As we have looked more deeply into the tradition of northeast Mississippi Hill country, we have found instruments, musical styles, and dancing that link the black South to the black Caribbean and, no question of it, to the dance of Africa as well.

That afternoon in the Funky Fives I had only an inkling of all this. I was half sick and there was nothing to eat and nothing to drink except for the local brand of firewater, not so potent but more savage than Haitian *clairin*. Nonetheless, when Will Head (bass drum), Sid Hemphill (violin and snare drums), Lucius Smith (five-string banjo), and Alec Askew (guitar), and a fife player let loose, I was riding gain, and the big Presto recording gear did a fine job as old Blind Sid topped himself by shouting out the work-song version of *John Henry:*

1.
This is the hammer
Killed John Henry,
Laid him low,
Laid him low.

2.
Take this hammer
To the captain,
Tell him he's gone,
Tell him he's gone.

3.
When you hear that
Bulldog a-barkin,
Somebody roun,
Somebody roun.

4.
When you hear that
Peafowl a-hollerin,
G'ina rain,
G'ina rain.

5.
I don't like no
Right black woman,
Black myself,
Black myself.

"It would take me a good while to count up the songs I know—somewhere like a hundred," said Blind Sid. "I can play any kind of church song a man want to hear *and* reels."

It turned out Blind Sid was a composer, a rural rhymester who had celebrated many of the dramas of Panola County in the longest ballads I had ever heard a black man perform. One ran to twenty-six stanzas, and he just had a "sketch" of the local railroad wreck called *The Carrier Railroad*—a twenty-one-verse sketch. It is the story of a reckless engineer named Dave Carr, who wrecked a train on the local lumber baron's railroad. "It was popular back in 1903 and '04. Everyone except Mr. Carrier heard it," said Sid. The short phrases, delivered pell-mell and with high energy, conveyed the excitement the puffing locomotive stirred up in the Delta backwoods.

1.
Last, one Monday mornin
It come a shower of rain.
9 come to Ballantine
Goin like a fast train.

2.
It was Dave Carr on Mister
*   Carrier's engine,*
Mr. Carrier, he looked and
*   laughed,*
"Tell you, Dave Carr,
Don't run my train too fast."

3.
Mister Dave told Mister Carrier,
*   man,*
"Don't you know I know your
*   rules,*
Tell you, Mister Carrier,
A train ain't no mule."

4.
Mister Dave told Mister Carrier,
"Man, fire me at your will.
Every time it come a shower of
*   rain,*
It can't run up Johnson's hill."

Sid's next ballad ran to almost the same tune, at a slightly slower tempo. It relates the high spots in the history of Jack Castle, a local "bad nigger." As Sid remarked, winding his story up at stanza 26, "I could have put that record plumb out to the other side, but I hardly ever play that anymore. He done more than I told you and every bit of it's in the song.

"Jack, they call him Jack Castle, because that the name of the white family he live with so long. Jack was a very, very roguish man. Raised right up here in these hills, but all he think about was stealing and playing the bully. He wanted to be known as a bad nigger and he told me, 'Sid, by God, make one about me—what I done.' That's how I come to make this song. Now listen. This is Sid Hemphill singing *The Roguish Man*, made in 1903":[4]

1.
I went down to Pritchett,
West come a-runnin back.
I'm gonna tell you, Bill
    Armstrong
Done put the ball to Jack.
        My honey babe,
        Why don't you come home?

2.
Old Jack walked in the house,
    boys,
With his pistol in his hand,
He's cussing Bill Armstrong
Like he wasn't any man.

3.
Bill Armstrong shot Jack in the
    head,
Shot once on the floor.
"Tell you now, Jack,
You aren't bull'in me no more."

4.
Old Jack got well that time
And Jack, he wasn't sore.
Next trouble Jack got in
He broke in Mister Lawrence'
    store.

5.
Laid old Jack in jail that time,
He didn't have nary friend,
Sentenced that poor boy
To five years in the pen.

6.
He stayed in the pentenshuh,
Five years long,
Come back and say to Mister
    Castle,
"Can I stay here at home?"

7.
Mister Castle went to Miss Sue,
"Miss Sue, I'll tell you it's a sin.
I'm gonna let old Jack stay here
With us again."

8.
Last one day Mister Castle
Goes out in the field.
Jack goes down to his meal
    house
And steals all his meal.

9.
Old Jack walk around the
    backyard,
Say, "I got to have some
    fun—"
Went in Mister Castle's back
    room
And stole his clock and run.

10.
Mister Springfield told Jack,
    "Jack,
You have fixed it so
They don't want you
In the jailhouse no mo."

11.
Jailer told old Jack,
"Jack, we done left it alone.
We don't want you in this
    jailhouse—
Have to go back home."
        My honey babe,
        Why don't you come home?

Sid added, "A fellow finally killed Jack about his stealing—up here around Pritchett."

I would be the last to say there is much nobility in this tale. It describes with accuracy the status of "the bad Negro" in back-country Mississippi in the early 1900s and the liberties allowed him by his white protectors (and admirers?). Being a "bad Negro," ready to carry out violence against his own color on the order of his white boss, yet so often in trouble that "they don't want you in the jailhouse no mo," was one way to build a reputation in the palmy days of Panola County.

I listened to Blind Sid with gathering excitement, realizing that he was a ballad maker as protean as Woody Guthrie, who had come into his prime as a composer in the epoch of classic black ballad-making at the turn of the century. All of his compositions were in the vein of *Frankie* and *The Boll Weevil*. He was of the company that had created this genre, and in him one could observe its processes. The distinctive features of his ballads and presumably of these black narrative songs in general was that people could dance to their music. They all were set to syncopated dance tunes, unlike the reserved and text-oriented traditional ballads such as *Barbara Allen* or *Jesse James*. Indeed, Sid performed his local ballads with string-band accompaniment as part of his repertory for local dances, so that these local narratives of bad men and railroads were, in effect, dance music. This was their secret power.

To be sure, Sid sang ballads on other occasions, but always with the dash and the driving rhythm that made local dancers hop and shake. Mounted on sexy rhythms, even the bloodiest and most gloomy yarns evoked the pleasure-filled atmosphere of the country hoedown and the barrelhouse. This was what made *Frankie and Johnny* and *Casey Jones* irresistible. Moreover, this rhythmic transformation returned the ballads to their ancient ambience, when the whole community danced while the story unfolded, something one can see today only in Africa and remote parts of Europe, such as the Orkneys and

Asturias. The very root of the word "ballad" is dance—*ballare* and *bailar* mean to dance in Italian and Spanish respectively—an impression that came vividly alive in the pell-mell rush of Sid's ballad performances.

Sid, like Woody Guthrie, always composed a basketful of stanzas for his songs. It would scarcely seem possible for another singer to remember the whole song. Indeed, Sid remarked that he seldom sang them all on any one occasion. Perhaps this is one fashion in which ballads grow—starting with more than enough material, which is then cut and edited as the song travels to other singers. The length of Sid's ballads, on the other hand, may simply identify him as a composer and singer of more antique stamp than one ordinarily encounters; in the old days there was plenty of time to listen.

"Here's one I made up a little later than the others," Sid said. "I just kep a-hearin um talkin about boll weevils. Boll Weevils eatin up all the cotton those days. I was making up songs them days and I went out on it."

"You never heard any other boll-weevil song?" I asked, for I felt sure that the ballad had originated in Texas, where the boll weevil first appeared.

"Nawsuh," said Sid, "I hadn't never heered nary un at all. It may have been out, but I never heered it. Here's the original boll weevil."

As he sang his boll-weevil ballad with a passage of fiddling between stanzas, I mentally compared it to the Texas version I had grown up with.

SID'S VERSION
I'm gonna sing you something,
The latest of my own.
Sing you about the boll weevil
Is trying to take our home,
 Ain't got no home,
 Ain't got no home.

That farmer went out in the field
 one mornin,
That boll weevil's flyin in the air,
Went out there this evenin,
Done moved his family there,
 Havin a time,
 Havin a time . . .

AN EARLY TEXAS VERSION
Have you heard the latest,
The latest of the songs?
It's about the little boll weevil
Picked up both feet and gone,
 Jus lookin for a home,
 Jus lookin for a home.

The first time I saw the boll
 weevil,
He was sittin on a square,
Next time I saw the boll weevil,
He had his whole damn family
 there.
 Just lookin for a home . . .[5]

I felt as I listened that Sid's verses were plainly half-heard and hasty reworkings of the more cogent original. In this case Sid had followed a practice normal to many black folksingers—because they improvise and remake songs as they perform, they usually say, when asked, that they have "composed," that is, arranged them. I had my doubts about Sid's claim to *The Boll Weevil,* but there could be little question of the originality of the next ballad he sang, *The Strayhorn Mob,* an account of a local lynching that pridefully named the lynchers. Sid appeared to find nothing grim about the subject or the song itself. He was a ballad maker in a country where lynching was so much accepted that "one of the men in the mob, Mister Sam House, writ it all down and told me to make up a song. I played it for him many a time and he liked it too good. Then Mister Norman Clayton—you must know him—he was in the thing, too. He used to get me to play it, pitch me fifty cents, and by the time I play four or five verses, he laugh and go on. His daughter do the same way."

"Who was it they lynched, Sid?" I asked.

"Lemme see, now," Sid scratched his head, "Lemme see . . . You know, I just fergit who it was!"

Just whom it was they lynched apparently didn't matter in Panola County, at least not so much as who attended the lynching party—even to the blind black singer commissioned to celebrate the event. Not until I had listened to Sid's song many times did I appreciate his artistry. In the refrain, repeated low and murmurously—"laid him low, they laid him low"—Sid expresses his sympathy for the mob's victim. The mob he describes as afraid to face the lone jailer—sneaking in the backdoor of the jail to make their kill, then running, like a pack of cowardly boys, all the way home to their own community. Of course, like all Southern mobs, Sid points out, they were all cleared in court. That was the way things were done back in those bad old days.

1.

Them boys around Strayhorn
They didn't have a job,
Went to Senatoby
And had a big mob,
    Laid him low,
    Laid him low.

2.

They went round to the jailhouse—
"Jailer, we want the key."
Say, "Oh, boys, if you get the key,
Well, you will have to murder me."
    We'll lay you low,
    We'll lay you low.

3.

Some walked round the jailhouse,
Stepped in at the gate,
Some of um made a shot
With a thirty-eight.
    They laid him low,
    They laid him low.

4.

Well, you talk about some runnin
    then,
All of um run jest like wheels,
(Wish) I'd-a been there to see um
    run,
Seen Mister Will Springfield.
    Seen him run,
    Seen him run.

5.

Well, talkin about the mob,
Hasn't been one since
Talkin bout Mister Hunter
When he jumped the courthouse
    fence,
        When they laid him low,
        They laid him low.

6.

Mister Norman Clayton told the
    boys,
"Boys, now all of y'all wait.
We'll git back to Strayhorn,
If we can follow a trottin gait."
        Laid him low,
        Laid him low.

7.

Senatoby boys was really mad,
But they didn't play so bad,
Scared to fool with the Strayhorn
    boys,
Mr. Sam House was s' bad.
        He'll lay you low,
        He'll lay you low.

8.

Mister Strayhorn told the boys,
"Tell y'all a certain fact,
The hounds get on the track,
They brought the boys back—"
        But they laid him low,
        They laid him low.

9.

When they tried the Strayhorn
    boys,
They did not try them here,
Tried the boys most anywhere,
But they all sho came clear.
        They laid him low,
        They laid him low.

10.

When they tried the Strayhorn
    boys,
Did not try um alone,
Tried the boys most anywhere,
But they sho came home.
        They laid him low,
        Laid him low.

Whereupon the fife player, with the drums and guitars beating out a somber rhythm behind him, wailed and squeaked through a tune they called *The*

Death March. The country folk listened with stony faces, their wild, kinky hair covered with dust, while the terrible afternoon sun beat into the yard with a rhythm more violent than the drums. It was music harsh and crude and vital and rank as milkweed. I realized something was pouring into the mike that had never been recorded before—a sound that Davy Crockett might have heard as he rode through these hills on the way to Texas.

The fife player put his instrument aside and Sid handed him the panpipes, a set of the quills. Sid picked up the drumsticks and began a riffling march rhythm. "This here is *Come On, Boys, Let's Go to the Ball*," Sid hollered. Alec slid the four-hole panpipe back and forth across his lips, blowing little primitive flutelike sounds out of the canes, and between every tone, producing a strange, choked sound with a violent intake of breath on the offbeats—a style for naked stomping into the fat and wrinkled warm earth, not for these eroded lanes, a tune such as the African Pygmies have played from time immemorial, moving in a circle, each dancer blowing one note on his little cane flute and whooping on each intake of breath. Alec played *The Devil's Dream* on his pipes in this Pygmy style, and in one passage sang between piping breaths a strange little melody, breathed out in puffy aahing sounds, following this with a passage of "Eeeh-y, oophy" murmured somewhere in the deeps of his nose. Then there was *Emmaline Take Your Time*, rippling on a strange scale in savage triplets out of the ten-hole panpipe. Now at last I was recording a music that suited the early days of this wild country when blacks and whites and Indians fished and hunted and swilled whiskey and ran from the great Mississippi in the shadowy edges of the American jungle. I know now it was older still.

"Tell me, Alec," I said, "where did you learn to play like that?"

"I learnt from a cousin down in Como forty, fifty years ago, when I was a little boy. His name was Jeems Lomax."

"My grandfather was named James Lomax," I said in astonishment. "Where was your cousin from?"

"Oh, he come from down round Quitman County."

"That's where my grandfather lived before he went to Texas," I said.

"Maybe you-all's related," said Blind Sid, beginning a laugh in which we all joined and which has lasted me until today.

I didn't get back to Mississippi for almost twenty years. Much of that time I was recording in Europe, yet there I kept remembering Blind Sid Hemphill and my putative cousin, James Lomax. As I roamed the hills of Italy and

Spain, the raw, wild sound of Sid's band often ran through my dreams. In those years I was compiling the first global recorded anthology of folk and primitive music. As my perspective broadened and I came to have a view of Africa and Europe, it dawned on me that on that dust-laden summer afternoon in Po Whore's Kingdom in Mississippi, I had stumbled onto an outcropping of African music in North America.

Drums were paramount in Sid's band, as they had been in Africa. Drums had been forbidden the American slave as too dangerous a rallying sound and had survived only in tolerant New Orleans in the dances on Congo Square. But Blind Sid had a smokehouse full of drums and was the commander of drum orchestras that called the people of backwoods Mississippi to march and to celebrate, as such orchestras had done in Africa, and the sound of their cadences, whether hooted on panpipes, sawed on rusty fiddle strings, or shouted hoarsely over the orchestra by Blind Sid himself were clearly like those I had on the black African discs in my world anthology. Sid's fiddling conjured up the bowed lute playing of the bards of Sudan. His panpipe, with its whooped and implosive notes, pointed to Pygmy roots. These similarities could not be represented in music notation—here my European musicologist friends threw up their hands—but they were nonetheless there. I was brooding over a systematic way of representing such stylistic differences. Meantime, when I played tapes of Blind Sid and Son House and the other geniuses I had recorded in the Deep South, European friends demanded to know more about the music than I could tell them.

BACK DOWN SOUTH

I was afraid to write or to inquire by phone about Blind Sid because I was afraid to learn that something dreadful had happened to him. It had become an article of my private religion never "to go back." So often when I had returned to a good recording site, I found that the best people had passed away or withered and their communities had gone to pieces. At last, however, at the end of a long recording trip through the South, I made a circuitous and cautious approach to Sid's country in northeastern Mississippi. On the way, I stopped in Oxford, William Faulkner's hometown. I had always wondered what Faulkner's home folks thought about him. Not much, I discovered. They gossiped with me about his drinking habits, his sexual peccadillos. Few properly appreciated his writing, it seemed, and one local authority assured me that

Faulkner was not even the best writer in his family—that John Falkner,[6] his brother, could write rings around him and that it was a darn shame that Bill's undeserved fame and good luck had eclipsed a much more promising talent.

I'll admit that I heard this rather absurd local gossip with some malicious pleasure. Although I admired Faulkner as a stylist and had been shaken by his doom-filled tales of a declining gentry, I resented his bitter caricatures of the upward-striving poor whites—the Snopeses, as he superciliously called them. We Lomaxes had been Mississippi poor white trash. Moreover, my years of song collecting among the backwoods folk of the South had convinced me that they were among the gentlest, most charming and amusing people on this earth. I wondered what embattled Bill Faulkner felt when he read *Let Us Now Praise Famous Men*.

I had another bone to pick with the ghost of the great writer as I invaded his fictional Yoknapatawpha County with my recording machine. How could he have so neglected the other side of the story—the black side? In his novels most blacks appear as servants, brooding over their white folks as they slide slackly downhill, caught up in pitiful addictions or petty vanity, wantonly throwing away their lives and treasures, obtusely failing to face the true source of their own feelings of despair and guilt: that they and their folks had cruelly exploited and mistreated their black neighbors and out of sheer greed had kept the blacks of Mississippi in a state of poverty and humiliating dependence.

The conviction grew, during years of Southern fieldwork, that Faulkner's dark Southern canvas hid more than it portrayed. His chronicles of white decadence and tragedy served to conceal the real identity of Mississippi from the world, from his fellow Southerners, not to say from himself. The longer I listened to the life stories and songs of the black folk of the Delta, the more his work puzzled me. One-half of Mississippi, perhaps the more interesting half, had been left out of the his account. Faulkner scarcely gives the reader a hint at what black life or feelings are like. His blacks are exotic background, lay figures who hardly do more than voice despairing and perhaps ironic comments on the self-destructive behavior of their "beloved" masters. The hero of *Intruder in the Dust* is the one black who does stand out, who sticks up for himself, yet he does so out of a sense of his personal dignity, not as a member of the black majority. Meantime, the blacks had cleared most of the land and made most of the crops in Mississippi, while their white bosses sipped mint juleps in the shade and "wondered what those niggers would be up to next."

As I talked to the black levee-camp workers, farmers, prisoners, mothers, and children of the Delta, as I comprehended that the music they had made out of their tribulation was becoming the music of the whole world, I wondered how Faulkner could have remained so provincial. Did he ever hear such music, such songs as are described in these pages? He must have, yet it wasn't clear. Maybe the blacks simply kept up their masks when they talked to him. Perhaps he was too preoccupied with the hurt of his own folks to have time to try to find out what was going on in the shanties of "Niggertown" where his servants lived, and in the shacks where his tenants tangled together in sleep.

The bartender in my favorite hangout in Oxford slid another bourbon along the bar and droned on: "I suppose Bill could write well; they paid him enough for his books—and God knows how much he made in Hollywood—but I never could get into them myself. We always did think his brother was the talented one in the family . . ."

Weary of this nonsense, I decided to risk finding all dead and no survivors, to go back and look up Blind Sid and his people. Faulkner's indifference to his black neighbors was simply not to be endured.

"Hey, you reckon there's anybody in town that could introduce me up in Panola County?" I asked the bartender. As the local authority on everything, he knew just the man, the administrator of home relief. "Just about all the darkies up in that way draw some kind of government money—better than working, don't you know?" he called after me.

The relief administrator turned out to be a low-key and friendly black, whom I have never until this moment thanked, because I lost the notebook with his name in it. This kind gentleman insisted that he had never stopped to listen to the picnic music of Panola and Tunica counties, but had heard it was quite unusual. He could, however, guide me to it, because some of the musicians were his clients.

Soon I was eating his dust on the gravel roads that led me into a folk-song collector's paradise, where in a few days I recorded Fred McDowell, a blues-man quite the equal of Son House and Muddy Waters but, musically speaking, their granddaddy; the Young brothers, with fife-and-drum music out of the springtime of the black frontier; and then finally Blind Sid Hemphill, still alive and fiddling. As we crossed over the border into unconventional America, the road, as it usually does, became a muddy lane with axle-threatening ruts and crevasses. At its end we came to Ed Young's country shack, with a mule barn and a peach orchard out back. Lean hound dogs swarmed out from under the front porch. A yardful of shy children looked on as their daddy came to the front gate to see who these white folks were.

The best adjective for Ed Young was winsome. He was a little guy, slim, graceful, and gentle. He danced with the grace of a Pygmy—in fact, I believe that he, like a few other fantastic black musicians I have met in America, was of Pygmy descent. He spoke with a Mississippi drawl that put chocolate icing on his words and made his speech sweet to hear, giving it an African lilt that may explain why white Southerners adopted this drawling style. And when Ed played what he affectionately called his "fice"—a fice, or feist, is Southern for a really talented bitch hound, who always trees her coon—when he cocked his fice into the air and blew, he looked like Pan, and, from the effect he had, may have sounded like Pan as well. Everyone started dancing.

Pan, the Greek embodiment of pleasure—you remember the pictures and the bas-reliefs—played his pipes in a dancing semicrouch. This is the black-African, Pygmy playing posture, and it was Ed Young's music-making stance. He always danced as he played, his feet sliding along flat to the ground to support his weaving pelvis, enticing someone in the crowd to cut it with him, turning this way and that, always with dragging feet and bent knees, and always leaning toward the earth.

His brothers Lonnie and G. D. Young played with him, Lonnie at the tail of the orchestra beating the bass drum, and G. D., a tiny sprite of a man—like a little dried-up ginger root and just as peppy—on the snare drum. Once you looked closely, you saw that the mainspring of the action was Lonnie and his bass drum. Lonnie was tall, lean as a country hound, with a flat, shiny roach of hair on top, always laughing quietly and, when his drumsticks were breaking out, always dancing. Movements flowed from Lonnie's midsection throughout his body. He played the lead in the band's polyrhythm, his padded sticks making a low, murmurous, but heated comment on the squeals of Ed Young's fife, as G. D. Young, the little brother of the bunch, riffled the snare drum. They went in for subtle stuff, quiet stuff. They capered without lifting their feet; their shoulders, belly, and buttocks separately twitched to the beat.

The dance, as you might suppose, began at once, the Young brothers supplying the music, and as participants there were wives, flirting half-grown daughters, cousins, kids, neighbors drifting in—all experts at the Delta slow drag. The chocolate tape was sliding off the reels and across the silver recording heads, while the needles on two meters jumped to the beat in the face of the big Ampex. This was 1959 and I finally had German mikes and a Cadillac of a recorder and was doing stereo—the first stereo field recordings made in the South. You should hear the recordings⁷—for me, a life's dream realized.

Oree came first. It had no words, just an occasional low-pitched howl from

Lonnie, answering the high call of the fife. The women pulled their skirts tight, tight around buttocks and thighs, and an old lady "balled the jack," rotating her hips and squatting lower and lower till her dress tail stirred the dust and everyone shouted for joy. As she wound smoothly back to her upright stance, her shadow looked like a big bird, rising up in the orange light of the kerosene lanterns.

The Young brothers were players, not talkers. Shirley Collins, the lovely English folksinger who was along for the trip, asked them questions.

SHIRLEY COLLINS: Where did you learn *Oree*?
LONNIE YOUNG: It's just a made-up song. That's all I know.
S.C.: Who made it up?
L.Y.: Oh, I just got to sittin down thinkin and I just decided to play it. I had heard other folks, you know. But I decided to play it and I jus made it on up.

In this improvisatory black oral tradition, every performance is original, a fresh and intentionally varied re-creation or rearrangement of a piece. So when asked, most blacks will properly say that they had made up the tune or song. Shirley tried again after the next song, which had brief but cryptic lyrics:

Jim and John had a race
Pahnnnn_____
Jim beat John to the same old place
Pahnnnn_____

Shirley, whose songs generally run to several stanzas, asked, "Are there only two verses?"

L.Y.: That's right, didn't have but two.
S.C.: Who made it up?
L.Y.: My cousin.
S.C.: Where is he from?
L.Y.: He did stay in White Station, but he may be dead now. Me an him used to play together all the time.
S.C.: Who's Jim and John?
L.Y.: Jim and John are just some folks' names.
ED YOUNG: We just wrote us a song and named it.
S.C.: What were they racing about?

Then, guessing the answer to her question, Shirley and the whole group burst out laughing.

The sweet African sounds washed across the sandy yard and Ed, too, began to ball the jack, turning while he sank slowly toward the earth, until he was close enough to reach out and caress the ground with a wide sweeping gesture. Then, while he slowly spun erect again, he drew the fingers of his right hand across his brow, leaving there a powdery trace, as if, by this token, he declared himself to be a child of Mother Earth, and, as he rose like a bird from the dust, out of his cocked flute poured raptures of goat cries, bird songs, and lovers. We looked on with brimming eyes as this black sprite of a man magically recalled his ancestry in this bit of African choreography. Each time I saw him perform, he repeated this dramatic movement, whether he danced on the ground or on a stage, where there was no dust to mark his forehead. One night onstage at Newport when he knelt and performed this earth-covering gesture, he drew a roar of applause from the vast audience. I always hesitated to ask him what it meant, and, in fact, never did find out what he intended, but I am sure this sign will turn up in a film of African ritual. This remarkable gesture bears witness to the black African reverence for the earth, manifested in rolling on the ground in religious ecstasy (Holy Rolling), "getting down" (becoming serious), and much more. Ed, when he stroked the earth, appeared to renew his energy and then played with more fire.

But an even more general and important African pattern was unfolding before us—the trait that gives black dance music its flexibility and warmth. The Young brothers were surrounded by their audience and were dancing with them, dancing as they played. An electrifying rhythmic exchange was going on between the musicians and the others—a dancer breaking out and a musician responding, and then the reverse. True democracy—if you could hack it. See that little shavetail kid make his move toward that bass drum and watch Lonnie beat the break for him. This is so, so different from the non-African practice where the orchestra sits apart and plays for the others to dance, controlling their movements with music. In the white European case the orchestra (maybe with a director) calls the tune; in the black case there is constant interplay within the whole group, with the musicians picking up hot rhythmic licks from the dancers nearby them so that everyone is dancing.

Watching the Young brothers' line of fife and drums sashay across the yard, enclosed by their dancing family, I saw in my mind's eye the jazz parades of New Orleans, where the band is a pulsing artery in the belly of a huge dancing throng. I remembered the Mardi Gras parades in Trinidad and Rio and the wild *rara* parades of Haiti and the films I'd seen of African processionals, and I could see that this family party in northern Mississippi belonged to that African tradition. A dancing orchestra of winds (sometimes voices) and percussion play in polyrhythm, in close, hot interaction with their dancing audience. This, I feel, is the social, the behavioral source of the multiple rhythms and of the rhythmic freedom of hot, of black music, which is constantly enriching itself from its social surround.

Such constant turn taking—earlier I've called this overlapping—promotes group or collective improvisation. Band or dance-group members are constantly breaking out into improvisations, stimulated and supported by the ensemble. Same for the chorus, and the solo singer if there is one. But don't forget the rhythmic level—the body involvement—the rock-steady beat and the dancing. Here interchange and breaking go on constantly between the dancers and between the dancers and the dancing or improvising orchestra. All this is out in the open in Mardi Gras, in a black street parade, at a drum dance in Haiti, in Ed Young's backyard, but it continues, just below the level of vision, in jukes, barrelhouses, and dance halls where black orchestras play for dancing. If you look closely, you can see the physical interplay between members of the band and between them and the folks on the floor. This is a multirhythmic situation, where everybody is playing round the beat, where everybody feels free to pick up from everybody else—and it is the rich resource that the orchestra draws upon and nourishes with its hot licks and polyrhythms.

This black approach to orchestration has changed and is continuing to change music everywhere. In a very real sense, everybody in the world— especially the young people of Eurasia—is trying to learn it. But it isn't easy to adopt its social strategies and become part of the rhythmic collective of dancers and players. You have to change your sense of togetherness as well as your movement style. You can't manage that just by counting beats and playing the counted patterns through the ends of your fingers or dancing them with your legs and feet. The beats have to originate in the middle of the body, as with Ed and Lonnie, then flow through the limbs. The results of taking the non-African road and trying to play hot rhythms with the extremities are manifold, ingenuous sometimes, and often offensive. They are called everything from hard rock to funk, from minimalism to *Einstein on the Beach*. However, our business is not with these Eurasian rhythmic struggles but with how the Delta blacks used their African heritage to transform the European music they encountered.

Look at what folks like the Young brothers did to the fife-and-drum orchestra, the mainstay of the European military. Consider first *The Spirit of '76*,
three musicians marching into battle, proud, erect. Playing in unison for
unison marching, such fife-and-drum corps played a key role in the wars of the
eighteenth century, their paradiddles marshaling and directing the troops in
battle. Right on past the Civil War, American kids thrilled to this sound, as
the local home-guard drill teams turned out on the 4th of July and other
patriotic occasions, and there are still lots of active fife-and-drum teams in the
Northeastern states.[8] All this is another thing entirely from the Young brothers, slouching along with their hip twisting, their hot licks, and an occasional
Watusi leap.

Thomas Jefferson's slaves formed a fife-and-drum team as their contribution to the War of Independence. The idea was not outlandish, since fife-and-
drum bands had been popular among blacks all through the British colonies.
Indeed, blacks had often been assigned to play military music in early America; one document tells of a black fife-and-drum corps playing for a Confeder-
ate regiment. When I recorded in the Windward Islands in the late fifties, I
found that red-hot fife-and-drum combos dominated the celebrations of An-
guilla, St. Kitts, and Nevis, playing jigs, reels, and quadrilles, later called
square dancing on the American frontier. That matched what Sid Hemphill
had to say, for I did find him again, alive, if not quite kicking.

SID AND LUCIUS

Sid at ninety-one was literally bent double with age, twisted into an inverted
L. His band had been superseded by smaller combos, without fiddles or
panpipes. But Sid could still play fiddle and quills, and I was a more ripened
listener. He and his very agreeable compadre, Lucius Smith, still barked in the
sergeant-major style that all members of the eldest black generation affected.
Conversation was like an exchange of rifle volleys.

ALAN LOMAX: Were your people musicians?
SID HEMPHILL: My daddy.
A.L.: What did he do?
S.H.: He played fiddle and farmed.
A.L.: How many in the family?
S.H.: It was six of us boys played music. Six of us. And one didn't. Seven.

A.L.: You had a family band.

S.H.: Yes, we had a whole family band, before the boys all married and their wives stopped them. You know a colored man's wife is contrary.

A.L.: How do you mean?

S.H.: Want the husband to do what they say do.

A.L.: Was your wife contrary, too?

S.H.: Yes, but I didn't pay her no 'tention. Went right on and played. She hid my guitar, and I looked everywhere till my mind tell me to look in the tater cellar. And time I opened the cellar door up, first thing I struck it. Went to hollerin then.

A.L.: What did they call your band?

S.H.: Hemphill. Had two snare drums, bass drum, fifes, these quills, and a fiddle. We played all over Coahoma County, parts of Quitman, Senatoby, parts of Tunica, and on up in Tennessee. Our job was to play picnics. August and July we played bout every day of the week, outside of Monday. Danced to a fare-you-well—promenade—swing your partner—all that stuff.

> *I went up on the mountain,*
> *And give my horn a blow,*
> *Think I heard my true love say,*
> *"Yonder comes my beau."*
> > *Wo beaver dam, wo beaver dam,*
> > *Beaver dam, honey, can't you understand?*

He bore down heavily with his fiddle bow in the noisy, heavily syncopated style that the slaves introduced into Southern fiddling. The song goes back a hundred and fifty years to the days of the beaver trappers. Sid then picked up his quills and blew and puffed out a tune with a gapped African scale. It had only one phrase, much varied, and its text was cryptic frontier double entendre, like the songs I had heard at the drum dances in the Bahamas and elsewhere in the West Indies.

> *Emmaline, take your time,*
> *Got nowhere to go . . .*

The verses were shouted hoarsely like rough trumpet breaks; they merged into the hooted and squealed notes that came after every puff on the pipes. Meanwhile, old Lucius frailed away on his banjo, loosely strung so that the strings, which were raised high above the fingerboard, slapped and buzzed with every stroke. The musical menu was early African-American—an African instrument (the panpipe, tootling away like a Pygmy circle of one-note pipes) and the banjo, played like a strung drum, presumably much as American slaves handled it after they introduced it into the United States. Highly energized syncopations gave rise to cross rhythms in this prehistoric jazz ensemble. Indeed, this orchestral type—a wind section (the panpipes and the voice) in polyrhythm with percussion (the buzzing, thumping banjo)—had the same shape as the New Orleans jazz-parade band—winds in polyrhythm with percussion—an orchestral type that our world survey shows is peculiar to black Africa. The black fife-and-drum bands and the New Orleans jazz orchestras, already discussed, belong to this African orchestral family.

The next time I saw Lucius Smith, Sid Hemphill was dead and Lucius had turned ninety. Surrounded by admiring female relatives, Lucius sat, as it were enthroned, in the family parlor, ready to be filmed, his hair arranged in a sort of poodle cut around his gleaming brown face—two white puffs over each ear and another one on top of his head—as bright and fractious as an old gentleman could possibly be. Lucius was prepared to challenge my every question, barking his replies like a commanding officer. I was trying to find out whether his generation shared the common view that dance music is sinful and can condemn you to hell. He burst out:

LUCIUS SMITH: All of us goin to hell. *(laughs)* We're all goin.

ALAN LOMAX: You think everybody's goin to hell? Everybody in the world?

L.S.: Well, show me one gon be saved, then we'll talk.

A.L.: Me!

L.S.: Well, can you prove it?

A.L.: No, I can't.

L.S.: You ain't . . . you won't prove it . . . you ain't never died, either.

A.L.: Well, nearly, one time! *(laughs)*

L.S.: Well, if you ain't died, you don't know where you goin. *(laughs)* You may go rotten, so. How do we know? That's it! Ain't been nobody could tangle me yet.

A.L.: Well, I want to try to tangle you. Tell me, what was your profession all your life?

L.S.: Oh, plowin a mule. We didn't make no music much till summer, you know. Didn't have time while we were farmin. Made music in the summer when the folks call for us.

A.L.: You wish you'd done somethin else?

L.S.: Well, I had to do somethin to make a livin. Wunt doin nothin but plowin a mule at that time. That's all. The mule'd make his livin an mine, too. When they put the tractor in, they made away with the mule, but they done killed um out before that come—worked um to death. A mule couldn't tell you nothin. He couldn't tell you to stop. You'd get on an ride from here to Memphis. All he had to do was to go. He didn't know where he was goin. And you settin up there kickin im in the side, "Come up there! Come up there!" Didn't know whether his head hurt or whether it didn't.

A.L.: They treated some folks like that, too.

L.S.: I ain't got to that.

A.L.: Get to that.

L.S.: Well, here we come—way back yonder, all you worked for is your clothes, way back yonder. They paid fifty cents or forty cents a day. I picked cotton thirty-five cents a hundred. Chopped cotton from sun to sun—two bits and forty cents. My Daddy chopped cotton on a Saturday, and started at one, and chopped till sundown, for twenty cents. That's it.

A.L.: Those folks must have been mighty mean.

L.S.: Well, you see, everything was cheap at that time. Get a whole hog's middle for a dollar. Sugar four cents and three cents a pound. Everything was cheap. Cotton five and six cents a pound. Cotton seeds around eight cents to seven cents a bushel. Things was cheap at that time. But somebody was gettin the money, though.

I keep a-tellin you, things in bad shape, things in bad shape, bad shape. It gets worse and worse. Young folks got it now.

(Lucius's old eyes began to twinkle and I knew something was in the air.)

L.S.: And they think old folks ain't got no sense, and they the ones that ain't got it. I done been over the road—I know.

(At that moment a drumbeat sounded in the house. An inner door flew open and out stepped a young woman beating a huge red bass drum that completely hid Lucius from view as it passed him. When it came to rest, he cackled in triumph.)

L.S.: Never saw anything like that, did you? I knew it!

A.L.: Where did you get that drum?

L.S.: Got it from Loudon and Loudon [Ludwig & Ludwig Drum Company], up in Indiana. Come out of Indiana. We put in the order and they made this drum.

A.L.: How far could you hear it beat?

L.S. *(judiciously)*: Well, now, a drum supposed to be heard a mile to the inch. This drum's thirty-six inches big, so it's supposed to be heard thirty-six miles. But since there's so much electric in the air, you can't hear um far as you used to.

A.L.: Tell me that again, I don't quite understand.

L.S. *(more emphatically)*: *I said drums supposed to be heard a mile to the inch. This drum's supposed to be heard thirty-six miles.* But since there's so much electric in the air, it catch the sound, can't hear it like you used to. Fifty, sixty years ago—can't hear it like you used to. The electric all everywhere knock the drum sound down.

(As I pondered this observation in Panola County acoustics, the young lady drummer chimed in.)

JESSIE MAE HEMPHILL: Would you think that I used to tote that drum on my shoulder?

A.L.: You can't carry that drum. *(I could barely see Lucius over the top of it.)*

L.S. *(gently)*: Oh, she used to play it a whole lot.

J.M.H.: Big as it is, I used to carry it.

L.S.: See, she's Jessie Mae Hemphill. Hemphill's grandaughter.

J.M.H.: I don't look like I could, but I used to carry that big drum all around the picnics and play it.

A.L.: Did you play with your grandfather? Tell us about it.

J.M.H.: Ever since I was nine years old, I played drums with my grandfather.

L.S.: And her daddy, too!

J.M.H.: And with my daddy. We played music with him, too.

A.L.: Wasn't it unusual for women to play the drum?

J.M.H.: Yeah, didn't see no women hardly beat no drum, no women.

L.S.: Sometimes the mens between the plow handles and we couldn't get nobody. We could get her when we couldn't get the men.

J.M.H.: I'd take their place, see. And I'd tote that drum with him *(points to Lucius)* when they couldn't get a man to come. And I'd be right there with Uncle Lucius.

L.S.: Sometimes we'd be short of men, and then her aunties could play—her mama—all them could play.

J.M.H.: Yeah, my mama, Rosie, Sidney . . .

L.S.: When we couldn't get the men, we used them.

J.M.H.: So we'd just have a woman group. There was four of us with my mother and Virg and Rose and Sidney and then I was the baby. I could beat um, when I was nine.

L.S.: We played string music and this drum with it, but the fiddle would go louder than this drum.

A.L.: The fiddle music would ride on the bass drum?

L.S.: *(shaking his finger)* A fiddle is the leading music of the whole world, outa all the music. The fiddle leads all the music and the banjo's the next.

A.L.: Why does the fiddle lead all the music? I don't understand?

L.S.: Well, I don't know, I couldn't tell you. But it's the leader. If anybody can play um. But that's the question now, can't nobody play um.[9] All the fiddle and banjo pickers about gone. And you young folks ain't studied 'bout um. Ain't studied nothin but automobiles and how much a dollar buy of gas. *(laughs)*

J.M.H.: But when my grandaddy was alive, he could make anything. He made me a drum, he made me a fiddle. And he could play all a this music that we had. Every music that we had, he could play.

L.S.: He'd play down to an organ, down to a piano, down to a jew's harp, which you could put in your mouth. He was a music man. Then he learnt all of us. He learned us. Good as ever been through here, Panola County, he was. Given to him. Sid Hemphill.

In Sid Hemphill's young days, when the Mississippi land and cotton boom was on, every community had its own jump-up band for celebrations and picnics. For the whites, the story was different. Their largely British heritage equipped them to sing ballads and lyric songs and hymns, usually without any accompaniment, and to dance to the music of the fiddle or small string combos. All other music was imported from the city or learned from sheet music. The brass marching band was generally manned by semiprofessionals, playing from notes or by rote. Orchestral music was not a part of their British folk heritage, as it was for black America. In black Africa, every village could field a number of native orchestras and everyone could participate, at least with complex patterns of clapping. Soon the blacks were to change all that.

Everywhere in the New World, slaves and lower-caste black freedmen absorbed the instrumental traditions of their local European overlords and created their own dance orchestras, and improvised head arrangements of the tangos, sambas, rumbas, merengues, fox-trots, cakewalks, and numerous other regional dance styles that dance-mad American Creoles invented as they courted across race and language lines. With Sid Hemphill and the Young brothers we meet two surviving examples of this widespread Southern-black frontier dance-orchestra tradition.

In the United States, becoming a professional musician was a permitted way for a black man to achieve and move up the caste-class ladder. The few extra pennies or dollars that the black musician earned put him a notch up economically; he became a catch for all the girls. From the days of slavery until the present, talented blacks, using their inherited cultural skills, took on and developed this role creatively. Handy in Memphis and the black jazzmen in New Orleans were able to afford conventional instruments to create local urban music, and then mightily advance themselves and their families in the world.

In less prosperous or backwoods neighborhoods, talented blacks like Sid Hemphill developed orchestras of homemade and hand-me-down instruments, yet still impressive for their size, the range of their repertory, and the catchiness of their orchestrations. We know some of these—the old-timey hoedown combos of the Southeast, the black Cajun music of the Southwest, the jug bands of Memphis, not to mention the innumerable black orchestral types in Latin America, such as the *rara* bands of Haiti. The African-American tradition, then, always seems to evolve specialized and rather complex orchestras to provide music for its community dances. All these orchestras provided extra income for their participants, money that might move their families up the class line. The biographies of Jelly Roll Morton, of Danny Barker, of Handy, all testify to that story.

The blind musical maestro of Panola County, Sid Hemphill, could field several kinds of orchestras—various sizes of string bands for entertainment and square dancing, fife-and-drum teams for the syncopated "marching" at picnics. (Stack Mangham told the same story about Friars Point.) The picnic season came in July and August, when small farmers, renters, and sharecroppers laid by their crops and the religious attended revivals, the worldly went dancing, and, because the Hill country wasn't so "strict," many did both. The picnics, often sponsored by a political candidate or some moneyed town dweller who wanted to show his country relatives a good time, were open to the public and largely financed by sales of homemade barbecue and drinks, with red-eye whiskey out in the dark back of the wagons.

The three biggest picnics took place on the 4th of July, Masonic Day in August, and Labor Day, but smaller affairs might occur on any weekend in the lay-by season. A local ball game took up the afternoon, and the music began toward dark with maybe three or four hundred people kicking up dust—there was no dance floor, they danced on the ground—right through till Sunday.

The grass on the dance ground might be knee-high when the dancing began, Ed Young remembered, but at the end it was gone and the dancers were slow-dragging in the dust. The fife players sometimes blew for ten straight hours, "blew till their eyes bugged out" as one drum corp after another dropped out and were replaced. Slathers of time for the musicians to improve, for the boys to show off their hot moves to the girls, and for lovemaking away from the lantern light.

I asked her if she loved me,
She said she loved me some,
She threw her arms around me
Like a circle round the sun.

THE PICNIC

The picnics I attended in 1978 were fairly small affairs, but one became so raunchy that at last the local black sound man demanded that we shut off our cameras. What follows is a description of what is on that videotape:

After dark at the picnic ground, a hundred or so people, dressed in their best, are gossiping, strolling about, eating barbecue, making out in cars, or listening to the music. In the cleared space in front of the barbecue stand, Jessie Mae Hemphill, Blind Sid's granddaughter, a red plastic flower in her hair and dressed to kill in a white silk dress and white, high-heeled pumps, has hold of the bass drum and is pouring out a hard-driving beat. Napoleon Strickland, widely reputed fife player, is blowing a high sweet obbligato. The young crowd watches with excitement as he goes to his knees, then falls on his back and rolls in the dust of the picnic ground, like a mule rolling in the grass after his harness is off, his big, thick legs waving in the air but never losing the beat. He comes back to his knees, covered with litter and looking very awkward in his green pants and purple shirt as he sways before the drum. Jessie Mae's face is stiff with concentration as she heats up the beat.

Women drummers are rare, even here in Mississippi, but she and all her sisters learned how to make music from their grandfather, Blind Sid. "We had an all-girl band, just as hot as anybody else's," she told me. Now she's really lighting up this picnic. A powerful man in a brown silk shirt and a white sombrero takes a very wide stance before the drum and begins to salute it with stiff torso movements. I haven't seen this before in the United States—the pelvic salute to the drum which is an everyday dance gesture in the West Indies. There, when a woman has danced her move out, she approaches the drum with knees wide and squats briefly on the face of the lead drum or swishes her skirt across it. That decisively stops the music. At other times, in *vaudou* ceremonies, dancers make pelvic gestures toward the drum to honor the holy music that is inspiring them. I never expected to see this African behavior in the hills of Mississippi, just a few miles south of Memphis.

Napoleon begins to blow high tremulous phrases, like a child calling its mother in the night. The young man wearing a green shirt and lavender shoes spreads his legs before the bass drum like a woman about to receive a man. He balls the jack, arms wide as a bird in flight, waves of movement rising from his taut pelvis up through his trunk to his head. He takes the rim of the bass drum between his legs, touching his crotch to it, and his pelvis rotates in little movements of intercourse. A tall, skinny man in a brown shirt is peeping over his shoulder as if to see whether sex is taking place. This man next assumes the push-up position, parallel but close to the ground, and pretends to screw it. Green Shirt and Lavender Shoes falls to his knees and makes like a dog in heat. Oh-oh . . . The young snare drummer cocks his leg. Jessie Mae Hemphill drums on with steady concentration. Boys, girls, children, adults crowd close. "Ayaaaa-aya-aye," calls Nap as he gasps for breath between his endless phrases on the fice.

There are now four young men saluting the drum with their hips. Nap is kneeling on the ground, facing them. Brown Shirt horizontally screws the earth. Nap raises his hand palm up and out and shouts wordlessly, then recommences his tremulous phrases. The breaks boil out of the drum. Nap cries out senseless, wordless speech and puts his straw hat on the young drummer. Then things really heat up. Nap and his two young drummers dance entwined, face to face, their thighs interlocked, their hips rocking and bucking. Nap is behind one of the lads, symbolically screwing him from the rear, touching him. This lad, for his part, receives the slim youngster in a green shirt who is wearing Nap's hat. These are his drummers—their thighs are dovetailed and they are simulating sex, balling the jack as partners, holding on to each other so as not to fall. All this masculine exhibitionism challenges the women, who thus far have been onlookers, to join the dance.

Nap has grabbed a big woman and is dancing with her. The lads start dragging girls into the dance. A woman begins, arms raised high. She's leaning back and grinding away, her hips bucking, showing that she really knows what to do when a man is inside her. The bucking rolls through her whole body as she leans back with wide-open thighs. Lime-Green balls the jack with scotch bottle in hand. Green Shirt mounts the bass drum, which is slung between his legs. He bends clean over so that he can beat one side with both drumsticks on the top.

The girls are being drawn in. The first takes on man after man, and her sisters begin to buck and jerk in sympathy. They explode into giggles and melt into the dark. The musicians are in a row on their knees facing the crowd, Nap still blowing away. One drummer covers his snare with his body. Green Shirt is copulating with his drum rim as he beats. He reaches under his crotch and plays on the side facing the earth with the padded stick, beating the upper side with the bare stick; it is a very anal performance. He continues to make love to the bass drum, his thighs wide, his pelvis changing pace as he carries on with this symbolic sex act. Napoleon advances toward him. He leans back and takes the bass drum onto his belly, feeling the vibes in his crotch.

At this point the black Mississippi sound man demanded that we stop shooting, and since I had enough for my film, I agreed. I understood his concern. The normal American audience might mistake this sexually hyperactive, virtually all-male dance for a homosexual orgy, which it most certainly was not. All-male erotic dancing has always been a part of African tradition. Our world survey of dance styles shows that pelvic, shoulder, and belly articulation are frequent in the dances of Polynesia, Indonesia, South India, and the Near East (belly dancing), and well-nigh universal in Africa. It is an old trait, more hallowed by time than the northern habit of holding the body stiff and upright in the dance. John Marshall filmed Bushmen in dances that imitated the mating of various animals they hunt, the aim being to insure rewarding hunting. In Africa, both boys and girls, during their periods of initiation, are taught dances that mime copulation in order to prepare them for the duties of marriage.

Mixed-couple dancing is rare except in Europe. In most agricultural regions, as in Africa, the sexes dance in separate choirs, dramatizing each gender's particular concerns. That was what these young Panola County drum dancers were doing—competitively showing off the steely muscles of their backs, loins, and buttocks, as well as their skills at winding their hips, just as they had that afternoon exhibited their mastery of baseball on the local diamond. The young women watched with appreciation, as well as anticipation,

I presume, and later on, when a bluesman hooked up his amplifier and began to play, they cut the mustard just as the boys had done, dancing in little clumps, in rows, in couples, sometimes with male partners, using body movements just as openly sensuous as those of the young men earlier on. It was like a coming-out party, where the community sponsored every stage of the courtship process and where everyone had the opportunity to show off their feelings and their talent.

One message was writ large. This Panola County fife-and-drum music was not an antique, it was Africa come to life in America. The heat and beat of the music were a co-creation of the dancers and the musicians, who danced as brilliantly as they played. Dance was music and music was dance, and both were powerfully and positively genital. These country people were having fun with their bodies—shaking it on down out there in the dark—fun that might shock Calvinist sensibilities, but which harmed no one, hurt no one, not even themselves. They were giggling, smiling, grinning, and laughing as they played their rhythmic sexual games, carrying on in ancestral ways. Undoubtedly, the celebrations of black pioneers of the Delta had been just as joyfully erotic.

NAPOLEON

Not many days later we went calling on Napoleon Strickland, the fife-playing generalissimo of the all-night picnic. He and his mother work as tenant farmers on a sizable plantation and live in one of its standard houses, painted red, with a green sea of cotton lapping right up to their back porch. We found Napoleon in the kitchen, fashioning a new cane fife. He was stripping down a piece of cane with his sheath knife, while a poker was being heated in the elegant little wood range balanced on bowed legs near the center of the bare room. Napoleon has Russian teeth, small, even—upper and lower—and orangy white from smoking. You see almost all of them when he grins. He is very often pleased and so a strange orange-white light constantly flickers in his round and otherwise expressionless chocolate countenance, like the candled smile of a jack-o-lantern.

Majesterially, he draws the red-hot poker out of the coals and, holding up a section of cane, says, "Now this is something you go fishing with, but I'm gonna fix it so it will make music." He puts the cane down on the floor and, holding it steady with his foot, burns the first finger hole into the barrel, then puts the poker into the coals again. "Now I'm gonna show you how I make it sing."

He holds the flute up to his lips and licks the place where he will blow it. Then he burns in that hole. Next he licks his other fingers and spreads them along the barrel, locating the other finger holes in accordance with his normal way of spreading his hand along the barrel when he plays. These tuning points are marked with spit. He nicks the chosen wetted points with his big clasp knife—"See, I takes my knife and I swings each one of them out."

"How far apart do you put the holes?"

"About a half an inch, I think."

Here we witness black magic. No micrometer, not even a ruler or a pattern, has controlled the tuning of this fife. The finger holes are simply set a comfortable and familiar distance apart, where his fingers naturally fall when he's playing. He carefully burns out and enlarges these holes, one after another. He delicately touches the end of the cane. "When the sound come out this end, you got it made," Napoleon opines. "Now I'm gonna burn the jintes out of the cane." So saying, he pushes the red-hot poker up the barrel of the new fife, and as he burns through each joint of the cane, delicate notes of smoke rise in the kitchen air. Withdrawing the poker, he blows the barrel of the fife clear of smoke, shavings, and cinders. He rubs the cane to cool it off, "Now," he says proudly and with his widest grin, "here's the fice, and I'll do it like this."

He puts it to his lips and begins to blow mellow notes. Jim and John are soon running their eternal race up and down their African scale. Again black magic! If you know it, you can call up the spirits of your ancestors four thousand miles and three hundred years away. Your fingers fall in the right places along the cane, and out comes music even the Pygmies would applaud. I try him with an idea I heard about from my trombone-playing friend Roswell Rudd, that the wind player gets his notes by singing the song inside his head.

Napoleon nods enthusiastically. "Yeah, before I can blow it on this fice, I gotta make the song come out of my mouth." He silently mouths the tune. It's an extraordinary sight, as if he were eating something he liked. The sound is a mumble.

"What are you doing inside your mouth there?"

"I'm singing the song inside my mouth, exactly." He starts to mouth silently, and I ask him to sing out loud.

"*Jim and John, they had a race . . .*" He mumbles the refrain, the fife part. Then mumbling—singing—

"*Jim beat John to the same old place . . .*" Then the whole refrain mumbled, with chewing motions, all the while nodding and smiling, as if the tune tasted good. I thought of what a black trumpeter out of a New Orleans marching band once said to me:

"I can read notes, all right, and I do that when I have to. But when I'm really playing, the notes get in the way of what I'm hearing in my head."

Yeah, talk to me, horn man. You've defined the difference between the folk tradition—the improvisatory, head tradition—and the scored, written-down tradition. In the latter, the performer is tied down by the score; in the former he can add his own feeling to every note, to every phrase. This is crucial to the story of the Americanization of black music, since both the African and the African-American traditions have been, until very lately, entirely "head" traditions, no less rich for that. This meant that as the songs were orchestrated, the sound and color of the notes and phrases continuously shaped the course of the melodies. This is obvious when you hear blacks sing. They shift tonal color at times with almost every phrase—moaning, keening, chuckling, braying, growling, whining, pleading, giggling. Napoleon Strickland has just shown us how that rainbow of tonal eloquence is unleashed in black wind playing. His story of how he makes his fice sing explains the enormous emotional power, the endless charm of Louis Armstrong, Johnny Dodds, and the great early virtuosi of the horn. They were singing to us, confiding in us, through their horns.

A dime-store harmonica was all the horn Napoleon Strickland needed. The harmonica was probably the instrument that replaced the panpipe and the fife right across the South. You can entice this cheap German toy to sing blue notes, to play gapped scales and glissandi, to howl like a foxhound on the trail, to wail like a locomotive on a downgrade. I once took a slow-motion film of that greatest of harp blowers, Son Terry, and watched him lifting quarter tones off the back of his harmonica with his fingertips. He would beat his cupped hands and make blatting trumpet notes. Most of all, by muting the harp, as Napoleon was doing, he could make it sing the blues, the harp taking up the phrase just as the singer leaves off and moaning right on for him.

On this wild, blue, rainy Mississippi day Napoleon is building a lovely sound out of the Delta favorite:

Now she's gone and I don't worry,
I'm sitting on top of the world . . .

His cupped hands form the sound bridge between the end of the harp and his ear. Moisture dampens the corners of his eyes. He truly mourns. A slow freight chugs powerfully in the bass register of the harp. He moves into a dance tune, a simple figure played over and over that makes your feet itch. He says:

"I'd be walkin down the roadway over in the night, you know, blowin—

Black Mattie, will you be something to me?

"I didn't yet know much about harp, but when I heard it say something about *Black Mattie*, I turned that thing around and looked at it and say, 'Why, I believe this thing will call *Black Mattie*. I believe I can blow that tune.' So I kept on. Couldn do much at first, but when I commenced truly blowin, I said, 'My life's done changed.' " Napoleon laughingly goes on, "Why, I can just walk along and do this thing. It keeps me happy when I'm off by myself."

The harmonica became a companion because it could answer back—it could sing the melody with almost human nuance; Napoleon and others could make it "talk" the words or moan them. In Southern folk tradition the admired player is the one who can make his instrument speak, and this tendency is ultimately African. There, where many languages employ tone to define meaning, the talking drums can transmit complex messages. Any spoken phrase has its own melody, which may be handily translated directly into song. These conventional tonal systems did not survive in the new Creole languages invented by the slaves. However, these Creole idioms were all more melodious than their European source languages; all used pitch and tone color in a generous degree in everyday speech.

One important function of melody (in English, at least) is to enhance the emotional impact of a given stretch of speech, to allow this heightened communication to be uttered without disrupting the communication. You can sing things that you cannot say. The melody gives the words an emotional intensity that is inappropriate in everyday speech.

However, since black country English is more highly charged, more loaded with nuance, more varied tonally than everyday English, so, too, is black melody. To get the feel of this, try speaking a black song like *Go Down, Moses* or *Swing Low* to the pitches of its melody. You'll discover in each of these songs a hidden charge of great emotion. Thus, when a black musician like Napoleon has his instrument talk the tune, he unleashes strong and subtle feelings. When the guitar or harmonica begins to answer the player back, the emotional content of the phrase can well make you laugh or cry.

I believe that very few white singers or musicians have understood this. Most simply imitate and improvise upon the charming tonal material they hear on records, without realizing that what they are playing with is not just "music," not just notes, but heightened speech as well. The melodic color of each phrase captures the significance of some particular passage of speech and it must be delivered with great nicety, so as not to lose the nuance of the original phrase. If it is varied, the changes must fit the expressive color of the original language or else the song will be vulgarized. In other words, non-Creole speakers are liable to butcher black improvisatory style, because they do not know the language they are singing, just as a Christmas carol might be missung and spoilt by a black bluesman. The results might be amusing, but would not touch the heart in either case. The former, the non-Creole case, has recently filled the whole environment with a freewheeling, misbegotten mis-use, by young white rockers, of the severe and subtle musical language of the blues. It has been misspoken and misplayed for so long with such huge success that a false and gauche musical idiom seems now about to drown out all the other melodic systems of the world, including that of the Mississippi Delta, its parent.

THE DIDDLEY BOW

This playful-voiced, multitonal approach to making music—which is a normal property of African style—has been transferred to stringed instruments, a crucial step in the birth of the blues. On this wild, blue, rainy day in the red sharecropper's shack, where the dull green of the cotton field laps up to the back door, Napoleon Strickland, a dedicated dance musician, sits next to the cast-iron kitchen stove fashioning a *diddley bow*, the one-stringed African-American descendant of the oldest of all instruments. Its earliest ancestor is the mouth bow, a hunter's bow held in front of the open mouth as resonator—the image of an Ice Age hunter playing one appears on the cave wall at Lascaux; it has been found among the Bushmen and very widely in black Africa;[10] I've recorded mouth bows in Arkansas and in the mountains of Georgia.

The other and perhaps more direct ancestor of this primordial chordophone is a one-stringed zither from the Congo. Its vibrating string is a sliver of fiber cut out of the central stalk of a large palm leaf[11] and raised up at each end by two bridges. This toylike zither rests on the ground or on top of a gourd resonator, and often two children play it, one beating out a spiky rhythm with two little sticks, the other sliding a metal cup or gourd along the palm fiber to play a very "glissy" tune.[12]

Napoleon is busy now creating an American equivalent of this African zither. He strips a worn-out kitchen broom of the steel wire that binds the broomstraws to the handle.

"Musn get in a hurry now or I'll mess up," he says as his chocolate fingers deftly unwind the coiling wire. "Now I'll just show you how to make what some folks call a one-string guitar, and I call a jitterbug. I been makin me jitterbugs ever since I was a little boy."

Most of us know "jitterbug" as a term for a forties dance style, but the root of the word seems to be African. It seems to refer to a little bug or a small child, crawling on the floor.[13] Napoleon is clearly a jitterbug, diddley-bow expert. It takes him only minutes to manufacture one. His actions swiftly follow his words. "I nails a brad on each end of my board [about three feet of a one by three]. Then I winds my string [holding up his four-foot length of broom wire] round each of them brads. Then I puts in my bottles at each end."

He shoves two square brown snuff bottles under each end of the wire, and they lift it a couple of inches off the board. He pushes left and right to tighten the wire, trying and changing the pitch. His smile lights up. "You hear that thing? We got it going. Now I just need to put it where I can pick it." He gets up then and nails the finished diddley bow (jitterbug to him) across an open doorway at about shoulder level. The tuned string faces him.

In some cases the one string is nailed to the side of a house, and the whole house serves as a resonator. I've seen a diddley bow strung vertically along the supporting post of a front gallery. The player sat on the gallery railing with his arms around the post and fretted his diddley bow vertically. The tune he chose to play was the oldest children's song in the English language:

Frog went a-courting, he did ride,
Sword and a pistol by his side.

The slider made the steel wire go "hunh-hunh," just like the frog in the ballad, and the player said, "That's one I used to sing when I was just a kid."

In America, too, the one-stringed zither was the particular delight of black children, who took out their longing for a banjo or a guitar with a jitterbug.

One man remembered nailing his baling wire to the cabin floor, lying beside it and strumming it, stroking it. What better consolation could there be for the little black kid, smarting from the severe discipline of a hard-pressed mother, who perhaps has told him to "dry up and quit your crying," than to have his jitterbug softly whine and moan his troubles. Certainly, this child's zither from the Congo became more versatile in America, where a stout piece of baling wire took the place of the palm fiber.

Napoleon now shows us another American innovation—the replacement of the African gourd-cup slide by a bottle—in this case another brown snuff bottle, a symbol of forbidden adult pleasures. He holds this slide between the thumb and forefinger of his right hand. The right hand actually encircles the string, the bottle poised above the string, the other fingers curled under it and used to damp and pick notes, as the bottle strokes out the tune along the stretched wire. The forefinger of the left hand, meantime, is sweeping vertically up and down across the string, producing a steady, syncopated beat that runs all through the piece. This counters the changeful buzzing, whining, ringing, more melodic sound of the bottle as it glides along the string. These notes are sometimes damped with the side of the finger that holds the slide, leaving the third left-hand finger free to add another beat when desired.

I ask your patience for this elaborate description of what I saw in our video of Napoleon. The observation of how Napoleon produces tricky multipart rhythms out of his diddley bow offers a close-up view of the complexity of Mississippi guitar style. In effect, Napoleon has made a small orchestra out of his one-stringed instrument, with plucked drum parts and a slider melody part. He plays a different beat pattern with each hand—two against three, or six against eight—and lays in the melody on top of these. It's a good deal more complicated than patting your stomach, rubbing the top of your head, and scratching your ear all at the same time. Napoleon manages this with ease, since from childhood he has practiced patting games like *juba* to make himself perfectly bilateral, as well as multileveled, so that he can do different things with his right and left sides, meanwhile moving his feet and middle body and shoulders to other beat patterns. This polyrhythmic skill he now transfers to picking, stroking, and damping his one-stringed instrument.

The root of this multilaterality is the black dance. Often the dancer adopts a wide stance with slightly bent knees and arms evenly presented. Movement comes from the middle body and moves outward along the limbs, each of which can then respond to different aspects of the beat. To facilitate coacceleration, the African gaze is not eye-to-eye or eye-to-foot, as in Europe, but eye-to-torso so that the initiation of the rhythmic pulses in other dancers or in the orchestra can be picked up and reacted to at their inception.

This central impulse system facilitates intersynch and makes shifting in and out of synch easier. It also obviates the need for unison, since at any moment the movers can pick up cues of rhythms coming from the bodies of other dancers and fall into perfect synch with them or, in the usual African case, improvise on the other's beat plan. Thus an African dance group can move in perfect synchrony, conforming to the basic beat, while each dancer can vary level, direction, posture, and limb movement rather freely without reducing the powerful impact of rhythmic togetherness. This intertwining of flexibility and precision allows black groups to achieve a level of synchrony with ease that a Euro-American dance group can only attain after long rehearsal.

We watch Napoleon at his diddley bow, playing this black multileveled game of perfect synch with himself. His straight-ahead, bilateral approach to his instrument links him to an ancient African heritage: the favorite instruments of Africa's heartlands are played evenhandedly—drums, xylophones, harps, lyres, mbiras, whistles, flutes, clapping hands. In all of these the rhythmic and melodic functions are handled symmetrically with both sides of the body. In North Africa and, of course, in Eurasia a unilateral playing-position approach is more usual, with the rhythmic function on one side, the melodic on the other. Jelly Roll Morton, the king of New Orleans jazz pianists, spoke for his African heritage when he insisted that a good jazz pianist must have a left hand as active as the right. Eurasians tend to be more active in the treble clef and on the right side.

Now Napoleon, standing in front of his jitterbug, is playing melody and rhythm with both hands. The one-stringer is giving out wild little cries and squeals. Occasionally, Napoleon sings long, slow, wordless phrases in a muffled sweet voice that the sliding snuff bottle repeats and comments upon. If there are words in his song, they are too slurred to be understood. Napoleon prolongs some notes, sliding from tone to tone, the one-stringer trailing him, filling in the pauses. In fact, this is really a holler, like the prison, levee-camp, and cornfield hollers—a slow, rhythmically free, lonesome tune—now set to an appropriate string accompaniment. The slide trails the melody, moans like a harmonica, or whoops like a fife between phrases, while a swift, hot, dancing ostinato lick—*duh-duh daah, duhduhdaahdud*—rolls out of the left hand. We're hearing the holler made into a dance on the one-stringed zither. This is undoubtedly an instance of an ancient African process that gave rise to new dance songs, as plaintive as they were sensuous. These free-flowing melodies, expressive of the sorrows of the epoch of black history, are made to resound, as if sung on a stringed instrument, which at the same time produces the hot rhythms of a complex and highly erotic new dance style. Like Evans, I believe that this event was unique to the Delta region, since apparently both the diddley bow and the holler had a local flowering in this part of the South.

Napoleon Strickland also captains the next part of this journey toward the blues. He's sitting on the gallery looking out over the long cotton rows. His mother, a woman with a life of hard work showing in every line of her face, is rocking quietly close by, looking at her son with sadness and pride. Napoleon loves, lives, eats, thrives on music. He is playing a blues on a battered green dobro, a kind of steel guitar. Instead of a snuff bottle as a slide, he wears the broken-off neck of a coke bottle on the second finger of his left hand. His round brown face under his porkpie straw hat registers sincerity, joy, intensity, puzzlement. A speech impediment makes it hard to understand the lyrics of his song.

"I don't like to play this tune but once in a while, you know, but sometimes I gets the blues." He plays on, his feet moving continuously, changing beat patterns. Sometimes the right heel is tapping three beats against two in the left. Then the right foot holds the beat, while the left divides it. He picks the melody with the index finger of his right hand over against a continuous thumb beat.

Worked all the summer, part of the fall,
Took my Christmas in my overhalls.

As he sings, he whops out broken chords on the bass strings with the slide. Then between verses, the bottle neck becomes more active. First it plays a run on Big E, next on Big B, then he slides it all the way up, playing the melody on little E. Meantime, he adds to the rhythmic complexity by hammering on, pulling off, and pushing the melody strings with the first finger of his right hand. Again, as in his performance on the diddley bow, Napoleon is playing melody and rhythm with both hands. He has transferred the diddley-bow style to the guitar and has enriched it by adding chords and the wide tonal possibilities of a six-stringed instrument to the slide style.

Most important, however, the *guitar is now singing the blues*, moaning the blues, crying the blues, with a nearly human voice. Moreover, it's singing in English, black English, with none of the nuance left out. Such precise intonation was difficult to achieve on less precisely tuned African instruments. But each of the exactly milled and tuned strings of the guitar offers a range of notes that, with the subtle manipulations of fingerwork and slide, can be made to emit the nuance of speech and really talk the blues in every register, as well as define other wordless feelings with the utmost delicacy. Meantime, the slider ignores the European scale, marked by the frets on the guitar neck, by simply sliding over them and stopping where the voice part breaks. Most heartbreaking of all are the sounds that come out of the treble strings, choked high up on the neck, which are made to cry out in ineffable agony, as well as ecstasy, as the mood turns from sorrow to orgasm. Here the private woes of the little orphaned boy, lying on the floor and stroking his diddley bow, can at last be heard. The nuance-laden poetry of the blues now sounds through an instrument.

So black country guitar pickers taught their instruments to sing the blues and, at the same time, to serve as one-piece dance orchestras, evoking the multiple patterns of the old-time string band by beating, picking, plucking, hammering, pushing, and sliding. This new six-string virtuosity so fascinated the black working class that a lone bluesman with a guitar was enough for a dance or a party. His music kept everybody happily on the dance floor and his lyrics, sung and picked, told everybody's story. Napoleon Strickland had learned his licks from one of the finest of these single-handed country entertainers, a man whom the Rolling Stones also came to admire and imitate—Fred McDowell. The Young brothers had suggested that I look Fred up. At that time he was farming in the same worn-out country that starved the Youngs down to the bone. He and his wife, sitting on their gallery for some cool at the end of an August day, looked like a couple of hungry blackbirds.

FRED McDOWELL

Fred was a quiet, silky-voiced, stoop-shouldered fellow, eager to record. That very evening he invited in a couple of neighbors to help out—one man to play second guitar, and his aunt, Fannie Davis, to provide the wind section by blowing on a fine-toothed comb wrapped in toilet paper. We recorded outdoors after dark, by flashlight. No wind was blowing, and the katydids were out of season, so we could take advantage of the living quiet of open air and the natural resonance of the earth and the trees. The mixer and the stereo had room for this multidimensional sound, with one mike for Fred's voice, one for his picking and its backup, and one for his aunt's humming and wheezing through the comb. The sound we captured made us all deliriously happy. The blues, speaking through Fred, sounded like a deep-voiced black herald of the *loi*, with a silver-voiced heavenly choir answering him from the treble strings. When we played his recording back to him, he stomped up and down on the porch, whooping and laughing and hugging his wife. He knew he had been heard and felt his fortune had been made. His old auntie, sitting on the ground near me where I was riding gain, kept patting me and saying, "Lawd have mercy, Lawd have mercy!"

The road Fred opened up that night took us back to the days before the blues was frozen in its modern conventional form of a three-line stanza, made up of a questioning or troubling first line, repeated twice, and an answering rhyming or punch line, thus:

The blues jumped a rabbit, run him a solid mile,
The old blues jumped a rabbit, run him a solid mile.
When the blues overtaken him, he cried like a baby chile.

Some of Fred's blues had the four-line form, like *Careless Love* and *See, See, Rider*, with the first line repeated three times before the rhyming line. Others simply consisted of one line repeated over and over, until Fred wanted to have a guitar or a comb break and introduce a new idea. These songs have the informality of the holler and the pieces that Napoleon moaned to his diddley bow. Maybe Fred's best number was a sexy dance tune called *Shake Um On Down*, that now the whole world jumps to.

But Fred never left the blues; you could tell because of the blue notes—flatted thirds, sevenths, fifths, that he and his aunt were producing. These flattened or narrowed intervals—a flat third is smaller or narrower than a normal third—are the signature of the blues; the sound that makes them different. European and American musical theory is centrally concerned with the subject of scales; and much has been made of the way that exotic music deviates from the familiar European scale. Thus the phenomenon of these "strange intervals" has been endlessly discussed. Indeed, they do have a powerful effect, coming as they do on points in the scale that are turning points for melodic movement.

There has been much critical writing about this matter,[14] many of the best technicians pointing out that these flatted or "blued" intervals are frequent in African music, and some suggesting that the American blues scales result from the adaptation of African scale patterns to the European diatonic scale. These theories offer insight into the musical background of blue notes, but they leave me unsatisfied, because they fail to explain the special appeal of this music and to connect it to its cultural background.

I hold that music and culture are interconnected, in fact that music is a communication about, a mirror of culture. In the Cantometric world survey of musical style, we learned that interval size is correlated cross-culturally to those factors that restrict the social independence of the individual. For example, the class- and caste-bound societies of the Orient, where strict rules of etiquette enveloped each person in a network of rules, are notorious for their use of quarter tones and other intervals of less than a second. At the other end of the scale, the songs of egalitarian hunters and gatherers, like the African Pygmies and Native Americans, abound in big leaps, like octaves and fifths. The sub-Saharan black-African tradition, where only a modest level of social layering stiffened social intercourse, is characterized by a frequent use of sizable intervals, especially thirds and fifths. Flatted—that is, narrowed—intervals sometimes occurred in black-African as well as African-American music, but at nowhere near the frequency that they came to have in the blues of the Delta. Here, as all agree, they signal a melancholy, a depressed mood, one which blacks say and know is the product of the caste system that hems them in. Therefore, I attribute this shift to blue (or narrowed) intervals in the music of the Delta after 1900 to the painful encounter of the black community with the caste-and-class system of the post-Reconstruction period. The two main studies of Delta life[15] describe the social malaise of this era when the black plantation community and the black family system were shattered and blacks ended up on the very bottom of the social heap as day laborers and sharecroppers and had to begin to fight their way upward in order to survive. Homelessness and orphaning were the order of the day for Delta working-class blacks, creating the wellspring of melancholy whose theme song was the blues.

The notable feature of the music of this period is that thirds, fifths, and even larger intervals are just as prevalent as they had been in black Africa and in African-American shouts and spirituals, but that these intervals are now very frequently flattened, or narrowed. The many big leaps give a sense of freedom (a permissive sex code, a feeling of social equality within the community—*I'm just as good a black man as you are!*), but the narrowing or blueing of the intervals tinge them with irony and sadness, as the impact of an emerging caste-class sytem negates these positive feelings—*(They don't see me as nothin but a black face!)*. This idea may explain the extraordinary effect that blues melodies seem to have cross-culturally: they rouse pleasant, erotic feelings, but simultaneously evoke a sense of world-weariness and melancholy. Narrowed large intervals—you could try this notion out on your favorite instrument. The music of Russia, where communal villages came to be ruled by Oriental conquerors, has a similar sociomusical texture.

Fred McDowell's recordings for me, as they appeared on the Atlantic label,[16] won him instant and extraordinary fame. After their release in 1960, he cut fourteen LPs, and the Rolling Stones invited him to Europe. They made much of him, wined and dined him, and bought him a silver-lamé suit, which he wore home to Como and was buried in, for he died soon after, much reduced by the life that fame and fortune had too late introduced him to. Certainly it is a blessing that he was so thoroughly taped, for no one on records, perhaps, performed the sweet old country blues so well as he. His mellow, multitonal vocal style lends subtle pathos to every phrase of his songs and evokes eloquent responses from his gnarled and work-wise plowman's fingers. His journeys up the treble strings take us into the region of heart cries or, at times, of tender ecstasy. You feel that the underlying mood of his music is as grave as the tragic destiny of his people. Yet the dancing beat that rocked the barrelhouse all night long rolls and jangles joyously.

The young English intellectuals and artists, moving into rock, fell in love with this music, and through them, and in the hands of the likes of Eric Clapton, the slide guitar style became a main orchestral ornament of the international rock movement. Unfortunately, in spite of displays of mass hysteria at their every appearance on stage, these urban translations of Mississippi slide guitar have gone aesthetically and emotionally flat. Today's rock guitarist slides out the notes of his music with unmatched virtuosity, but succeeds only moderately in having his guitar intone or cry out the poetry, or, if it does, these passages are inexpressive and the effect is mechanical and dull, even though delivered passionately and triple forte.

One problem is that, after you have respoken a blues line in Liverpoolese or New Jerseyese, the flavor of some tonal patterns of the language has been changed and diminished and the songs end up saying "Come on, baby, let's truck" or words to that effect. To my jaundiced old Southern ears, moreover, many rock guitarists are more concerned with showing off how many notes they can get off and how many chords they know than what the song has to say or how the guitar can speak it to them. Their fooling around in the upper register adds to the frenzy of public concerts, but these devices are so frequent and so calculated that they have become abstractions of the feminine sexual climax they represent, as mechanical and gelid as a crate of condoms. This is not what Fred McDowell and Napoleon Strickland and their friends intended.

What they and other bluesmen accomplished was the completion of an aesthetic revolution that profoundly changed both African-American and then Euro-American music. As we have seen, solo singing and then solo-accompanied blues tended to displace the older group black styles to which everyone present could contribute. The same thing held true for the folk traditions of Great Britain—the new, more virtuosic accompanied style steadily replaced earlier unaccompanied styles, such as the solo ballad. In the British traditions, carried over to the American frontier, the unaccompanied ballad singer and the unison choral performance of game songs, chanteys, and hymns were the usual song-performance modes, while instruments were reserved for dance tunes or reflective airs, but only infrequently for accompaniment.

Aside from the moribund Gaelic harper tradition, there were no solo-string-accompanied song styles in Great Britain in the last several centuries, until they began to pour in thick and fast from the United States—the Virginia reel, minstrel songs, jazz, blue-grass, rock. The first to become widely popular were minstrel pieces, the second were the black ballads, like *Frankie and Albert*, and the third wave was the blues. Early minstrel hits, like *Old Dan Tucker* and *Old Zip Coon*, are plainly black in origin or inspiration. They, in turn, stem from earlier fiddle, and wind banjo-accompanied ditties such as Sid Hemphill and the Young brothers played. This plantation music making gave rise to both the blackface minstrelsy, which held the American stage for a century, and to songs in the mountain hoedown style, which are clearly black in style, such as *Lynchburg Town* and *Sourwood Mountain*. Old-timey, blue-grass, and country thus are rooted in the African-American accompanied tradition, which is but one of the American offshoots of the many solo-string-accompanied styles of West Africa.

It is fascinating to recall that West Africa—the seat of the slave trade—has long had solo-string-accompanied bardic tradition, with evident connections to the Moslem, the Mediterranean, and ultimately the Asian world. This essentially Eurasian kind of music making, close kin to the solo-lament type discussed earlier, dominates the entire landscape of ancient imperial civilization in Asia and the Mediteranean. Homer smote 'is bloomin' lyre, David played on his harp and sang in the courts of kings. Their art, practiced by adept and trained specialists, was intended to hold audiences spellbound, and thus to eliminate group participation. This bardic focus on the single performer symbolized the extreme centralization of the power of kingdoms and empires, and was thus well-known in Mediterranean Europe and North Africa. It was also important in the African kingdoms of the Lake States, in Sudan, and in the West African kingdoms. Indeed the griots, such as the virtuosic bards of Senegal, accompanying themselves on complex stringed instruments backed up by rhythm orchestras, still play a leading role in the life of many West African communities. They are social satirists, whose verses once on a time dethroned chieftans.

The bluesmen of the Delta continued this satiric tradition, depicting, as far as they dared, the ills and ironies of life in their caste-ridden society. Musicologists generally agree that America's black bluesmen have, in essence, reconstituted the high art of the African griot. Indeed, we can assert that through the work of performers like Sid Hemphill, Blind Lemon Jefferson, Charley Patton, and their like, the griot tradition has survived full-blown in America with hardly an interruption. Indeed, the performance patterns of the African and the American performances are virtually identical, even though different kinds of lutes, different scales, and different languages are employed in the two zones.

In both cases, too, the griot and the bluesman perform in the midst of an active and noisy crowd that constantly comments on and dances to their music. This very African habit continued in the black ghettos of the United States. Subsequently, in the Delta and generally in America, at least, the solo-virtuosic style, backed by the recording industry, tended to swiftly displace the old group-produced work songs and spirituals. With every step in "modernization" the specialist tended to replace and silence the collective. In the next chapters we can observe the rise of the virtuoso among Delta country bluesmen.

Chapter 8

▲▲▲▲▲▲▲▲▲▲

Bluesmen

DELTA BLUESMEN

The blues ain't nothin but a woman on a po boy's mind,
The blues ain't nothin but the po man's heart disease . . .

I got the blues and I'm too damn mean to cry,
I got the blues and I just can't be satisfied . . .

The blues ain't nothin but a low-down achin chill,
Ain't never had um and I hope I never will . . .

It take a man that had the blues to sing the blues . . .

The blues have been mostly masculine territory. Of course, women have and do sing the blues. But down in the land where the blues began, the majority of real, sure-enough, professional, and aspiring-to-be-professional blues singers—who, as they put it, "followed the blues"—wore pants. Indeed, no truly respectable Delta woman was supposed to sing the blues even in private. Women sang the church songs, which were regarded as spiritual and sacred. To join the black folks' church and remain a member in good standing, you had to forswear all wordly things—first and foremost dancing and the music of the dance, the blues, which were the devil's own. All women of repute belonged to the church, where their good sisters were ready with help in times of trouble. Woe betide the sister who slipped and was caught dancing to the blues; she might be put out of the church and lose the support of the feminine community.

On the other hand, women were attracted to these devilish blues musicians because these gents with guitars and harmonicas usually had a little money in their pockets. They could give a woman a good time, buy her a drink or a present, pay for the fun she gave them. The money from playing in jukes, barrooms, and plantation hops on weekends might not look like much, but it put the bluesman ahead of most other folks in the Delta plantation world. Bluesmen could afford to dress better, drink more, gamble more, have more good-looking women, maybe even give up farming. In the Delta the blues and other secular songs were left to the men who didn't care what was said about them and claimed not to be afraid of hellfire, where the blues would surely put them. However, sooner or later most men joined the church and gave up the sinful ways of the world, including the blues. There they found a welcoming committee of their womenfolks, good church workers who stood back of the preacher and solid community values.

Music and the ministry were the principal professions available to men of wit in the Delta. Many of the most ambitious tried them both—Son House, Big Bill, Muddy Waters, to name a few. Many blind men combined the two and became strolling religious street singers, groping through the hostile blackness of Jim Crowed streets, terrified they might bump into a white woman. Nonetheless, through the continuous rehearsals of street-music performance, they became the finest of the black musicianers—men like Blind Lemon Jefferson, Blind Willie Johnson, Blind Willie McTell, Blind Gary Davis, to name some of the stars of this melancholy occupation (see the discography for their incredible recordings).

The bluesmen's skill with the guitar gave them great power among their music-and-dance-mad brothers. The six-string, to one who understands its resources, is a portable orchestra, capable of sounding several parts at once. It backs up and responds to the mordant wit of the singer, and at the same time provides dance music for a roomful of people. The lone bluesman could pocket the fee for a whole orchestra. One astute observer remarked that as dance halls grew bigger to accommodate the crowds of prosperous times, pianos and small combos began to replace the lone guitarist. *Boogie-woogie* or *The Fives* on an upright with the front out and buzzers on the strings could reach to the back tables in a big noisy barroom. A generation of piano wizards appeared who devised an African, orchestral way of playing this parlor instrument. A bit later, all sorts of amplified guitars appeared in the hands of Southern honky-tonk musicians.

The tonality of the music began to change with these influences; the African-like scales, which had sounded the cool melancholy of the blues, were muted. Later, with the electronically amplified instruments Muddy Waters and other urban bluesmen introduced, electronic tone replaced that of steel and wood, and the guitar began to lose its human voice. Through all these changes, now so important to a world that vibrates to the blues from very far off, through all this urbanization, the power of the Mississippi bard endured. One man with one guitar in a lonely room or a studio or Detroit or Chicago could cook up a new way of messing around on his guitar that would turn on all the little women between both the oceans. That was a job for a man rather than a woman.

With few exceptions, only women in show business, women of questionable reputation, women who flaunted their loose living, publicly performed the blues—women like Mamie Smith, Bessie Smith, and Memphis Minnie. The list isn't very long. These female blues singers toured the black vaudeville circuits or performed in city nightclubs; that is, they all performed in comparatively protected venues—on stage, up and out of reach of their admirers—and, between appearances, relaxed in backstage areas out of bounds to the public, in the company of peers. They did not sing in the street or play in jukes and barrooms, where they would inevitably be subjected to sexual advances of every sort, mild to life-threatening.

Not many women would risk playing a guitar before an audience. Even Rosalie Hill, daughter of maestro Blind Sid Hemphill, taught by him to play guitar as her mother and sisters could, confessed to feeling "funny" about getting up in front of folks and picking the blues. There was more to this than the black religious folk belief that all lutelike instruments, the guitar in particular, were the devil's own riding horses. None of the Hemphills took that idea seriously. The Cantometric world survey shows that men play stringed instruments far, far more frequently in public than women. In many cultures such music making is restricted to dancing girls, prostitutes, and other professionals.

There is another consideration. I believe, along with the great Curt Sachs, that instruments like the guitar and violin are shaped like the feminine body and have phallic necks. Holding and manipulating such a sex symbol in public seems to be an act appropriate only for men. In Italian, for example, an evening of lovemaking is termed *a la chitarra.*

The way in which blues musicians have come to handle guitars makes this symbolism far more overt. The guitar is butted against the hips, with the neck pointing straight ahead, and handled in a masturbatory way. Meanwhile, the strings are choked down close to the sound hole, and plucked, stroked, frailed, as if female erotic parts were being played with, while the instrument itself emits orgiastic-like sounds. In other words, the modern rock guitarist, following Jimi Hendrix, is only making explicit the eroctic symbolism previously implicit in blues performances. The necked lute, which probably originated among the sex-starved shepherds of Central Asia, has always uttered small, high-pitched sounds like a woman weeping for her lost love or squealing with pleasure in the arms of her lover.

Gender differences favored the male singer. He was unlikely to be raped or violated by his admirers, and if he exercised some caution, he could reap a rich and enjoyable sexual harvest, companioning lonely or displaced women, as he moved from place to place. Nonetheless, the blues musician, working his magic in the corner of a bar or on the front porch of a cabin in a cotton patch, lived at an emotional storm center—of pent-up passion or rage heated up by plenty of booze. As a privileged and sexually attractive stranger, he frequently aroused envy or jealousy in the hearts of locals. Often he had to flee for his life or, like Leadbelly, stand and fight for it.

Many, many bluesmen beside Robert Johnson were murdered or wounded on the job. Most carried weapons for self-protection, and a large percentage served time for their almost inevitable involvement in crimes of violence. This was no life for a woman; it was too risky; it took you far away from your steady man and your children, as Madonna and other women in rock must have discovered. These are distractions that most women are simply not interested in for very long.

But other factors entered in. Few Delta women sang or composed the blues precisely because they did not live the blues in the sense that their men did. Feminine lives were rock-hard and filled with sorrow, but they did not face alone the humiliation, the danger, the deprivation, and the orphaning of Delta life in as direct a fashion every live-long day as did their men. Both boys and girls were orphaned, as Delta family life broke down and marriages dissolved under the pressure of an iniquitous economic system, but these events overtook boys far more than girls.

A boy often had to leave his home and community when a new husband appeared. Often he had to fend for himself on the roads when he was only eight or ten, thence perhaps to be drawn into permanent peonage by a labor recruiter. The lives of women as mama's helpers, wives, mistresses, mothers, domestic workers, and churchgoers sheltered and protected them from much of the brutalizing interracial experience their men knew. (They certainly experienced other humiliations, about which little has yet been told.) Feminine moves were from kitchen to kitchen, generally within the circle of the extended family, rather than from camp to camp and boss to boss. Girls chopped cotton and sometimes plowed, but dealing with a mule all day, every day, and with the white man every payday was not their destiny. It was the men, not the women, who created a song style meant to keep a team of mules surging in the collar from dawn till dark. The women were not expected, when times got really hard, to seek their fortunes, walking the roads, riding the blinds, hoboing from one construction camp to another, and so they were not, all their lives, faced with the police, the walking boss, the chain-gang guard, the nigger-drivers, whose common aim was to keep the black man down.

Housed somehow, if only in pitiful shanties, the women were not always looking for a home, finding it, quarreling, being kicked out, moving on again—you gotta keep moving, you gotta keep moving, following the work—this was not the heart of feminine experience, nor was it the experience of the small percentage of the Southern blacks who somehow managed to rise in the world. It was the unique and constant experience of very many working-class black males, and it was among them, among their artists, that the blues arose. Again, this is not to say that women did not suffer as keenly as men under the cancerous social system of the post-Reconstruction South, but the suffering had a different source and they could bring it to the church and wail, sing, and shout it out in company with their sisters, as the men usually did not.

Orphaned by their society, the itinerant Delta bluesmen created songs that appealed to women for sympathy and a place to hang their hats. As we shall see in what follows, it was the degree to which each bluesman experienced the sense of pain and loss that accompanies the disappearance of parents, which determined the way they sang the blues. Those bluesmen who grew up in solid families or were left to the care of beneficent grandparents or other caring relatives seem less agonized, at least to my ear—men like Big Bill Broonzy, Sam Chatmon, Leadbelly. Those who had been traumatically orphaned and heartbroken early in life became, it seems to me, the most heartfelt wailers later on. In this group I would put, for instance, Son House, Blind Lemon, Charley Patton, and, above all, Robert Johnson. All were damaged by poverty, by homelessness, by Jim Crow justice, by mistreating women, but the pain was sharper for the orphaned ones.

Lord, I'm a poor boy and a long ways from home,
And I ain't gonna be treated thisaway.

I'm broke and I ain't got a dime.
Ev'ry good man gets in hard luck sometime.

I'm a good old boy, just ain't treated right,
Freezin ground was my foldin bed last night.

Make me a pallet on your floor
So your good man will never know.

These verses incorporate three of the songs that old-time Delta bluesmen see as the oldest of the blues, "the first blues, the ones we heard when we came along"—*Poor Boy a Long Ways from Home, One Dime Blues*, and *Make Me a Pallet on Your Floor*. All have the older four-phrase stanza form, three lines repeated and then a rhyming punch line, one of the lyric forms frequent in Southern white lyric tradition and in the black spiritual. All the songs sound the main themes of the blues—orphaning, homelessness, injustice, sexual conflict—and I imagine were successfully employed by hoboing bluesmen, whose dulcet tones had charmed the weary mules on the levee, to win some Southern cooking and some down-home loving in the country lanes of the Yazoo bottoms. Where they worked their true magic—these melancholy and sensual rhymes and a whole river of others in this vein—was at the weekend dances and little country suppers and barrelhouse hops that supplied the principal diversions for Delta blacks.

THE SLOW DRAG

I remember one of these occasions of the blues. I believe, but I cannot be certain now, that Muddy Waters invited me or took me there, but it may have been some other time or place, because in those years I dropped in on many of these affairs.

The Delta countryside was drenched in moonlight, edged in black by woods. From where we turned off on the rutted road, we could see the little shack far off, its windows shining orange from kerosene lamps, and from it came a deep, powerful rhythm, as if someone were beating a huge drum yonder in the moonlit cotton patch. No melody yet, only this heavy beat, growing stronger and stronger as we picked our way past barbed-wire gates, tires spinning in the sandy loam, and finally drove into the yard, into a shower of nervous chickens coming down from the chinaberry trees, and could hear the bluesman's voice and the crying of guitar strings over the continuing beat.

Cars and buggies and a couple of mules ringed the yard. A knot of men clustered round a lamp-lit cooncan table. We edged through the crowd on the little front gallery and peered in and discovered the source of the mysterious drumbeat. The wooden floor of the shack was, so to speak, a drumhead, responding, first of all, to the double rhythm of the bluesman's feet as he stomped out an accompaniment to his playing. Then at his side a youngster was pulling the broom, dragging the head of a broom over the rough boards in a diagram of the beat, causing the floor to vibrate like a rub-board and and the massed straws of the broom to rattle and swish like the swats in a rhythm section. This rhythmic source was reinforced by the feet of the couples who packed the steamy room and were performing the *blues*, also called the *slow drag*, a name that well describes it.

The couples, glued together in a belly-to-belly, loin-to-loin embrace, approximated sexual intercourse as closely as their vertical posture, their clothing, and the crowd around them would allow. Slowly, with bent knees and with the whole shoe soles flat to the floor, they dragged their feet along its surface, emphasizing the off beat, so that the whole house vibrated like a drum. It was that sound we had heard a mile away in the moonlit night.

Nowadays, of course, the slow drag is known everywhere American music has penetrated, and it is as casually entered into as the waltz or the fox-trot, not seeming especially sexy, since everyone today is doing some form of balling the jack. But in 1902, when my father was recording on the Brazos River, a white planter, swearing him to secrecy, took him far out in the bottoms to a tightly shuttered sharecropper cabin, where they were allowed to peep in and see the black tenants doing "the blues" or the slow drag, a dance considered to be so obscene that my father never told my mother about it until years afterward.

The slow drag was, I believe, an innovation at that time, and it may well have been then the most erotic dance on earth. The Choreometric survey of dance style offers these facts. First, foot sliding with a wide stance is African. In the slow drag it combines with the mixed couple, which is largely European. We Westerners, culturally myopic about the rest of the species, tend to think the face-to-face mixed-couple dance is a human universal. In fact, this pattern is rare in the world. In most cultures the sexes dance in segregated groups, or in mixed groups, but rarely as mixed couples. Only in West Africa and especially in Western Europe do the partners face each other, ready for action, so to speak. Moreover, it is only in the waist-swinging courtship dances of Western Europe, our survey shows, that partners continuously hold on to or embrace each other. This expression of the singular importance of the nuclear family in Europe seems to have made a powerful impression on the black slaves when they encountered it. Two things occurred.

In the first place, black ministers, perhaps reacting to the shock that their followers must have felt at the untoward eroticism of the waist swings their masters were performing, ruled against the dance even more strongly than their Calvinist preceptors. They condemned everything to do with dancing as totally out-of-bounds for the godly. Dancing was defined, not only by the facing waist swing, but by another Eurasian feature—*foot crossing*. Your African heritage was to shuffle or slide your feet, but if you crossed your feet, you were hell-bound. Thus arose an anomalous and confusing sacred/sinful dichotomy that has painfully split the black community ever since—into those who gave up dancing (the European foot-crossing type) and all secular music and those who would not. The emotional conflict over this prohibition was particularly hurtful for people of African cultural background, since the dance is the very heart of African creativity. Black dancers and dance musicians in America have ever since felt themselves to be Satan's own children. After leading a life of inward fear and conflict over the matter, they often have felt they must give up their dearest pleasures, as they grew old, out of a lively fear of hellfire. Their wives, meanwhile, felt duty-bound to nag them about the matter until they caved in, joined the church, and cut dancing out of their lives.

All this lies in the background of bluesman Robert Johnson, who has lately become something of a national celebrity, because it is said he sold his soul to the devil in return for his musical skills. In fact, however, every blues fiddler, banjo picker, harp blower, piano strummer, and guitar frammer was, in the opinion of both himself and his peers, a child of the devil, a consequence of the black view of the European dance embrace as sinful in the extreme.

The black-couple dance, of course, was far more erotic than the white, because of the pelvic and belly movements normal to the black dance tradition. Thus in every black colonial area, the held-at-a-distance European quadrille or waltz position was transformed by various degrees of middle-body movement and partner contact into the sexy colonial American dances that have since captured the world—the rumba, the tango, the merengue, the fox-trot, and many more—all stamped as the most erotic dances of the modern era. In them the partners of mixed couples embrace face-to-face, their middle bodies in contact, as they rotate, flip, shake, and touch moving middle bodies. The blues—the slow drag—is probably the most licentious of all, for here the partners stay pressed as close together as possible, just as if they were in bed, belly-to-belly, thigh-to-thigh, crotch-to-crotch, both arms round the other's neck and, holding this position, grind their hips together slowly so that their mounting sexual excitement may be coexperienced. By skipping most of the preliminaries of courtship, the slow drag helps the dancers to decide quickly whether they want to have sex together or not.

This dance dominated the room on that long-ago moonlit night in Mississippi. Most of the men wore overalls and brogans, the women skimpy cotton dresses. They were poor people—sharecroppers and renters—having their Saturday-night bust. Their white whiskey ran down our gullets like fire and brought on a sweat. There was local barbecue for sale, spicy and delicious. People were having fun. Laughter greeted some of the most ironic sallies of the blues singer, who, without any thought or need of a microphone or amplifier, was filling that little Delta dance room with his voice and his guitar.

A dollar is round and rolls from hand to hand,
Just the way these Clarksdale women move from man to man.

I'm gonna buy me a pistol, long as I am tall,
I'm gonna shoot my woman just to see her jump and fall.

As one verse followed another, dwelling on domestic quarrels, the fickleness and the venality of women, and the endless disappointments of love, Delta style, I noticed that a ring of women encircled the bluesman, praising him and egging him on. Sometimes only the top of his hat could be seen over the feminine hairdos. The more caustic his antifeminine comments, the more they called out praise and reached out to fondle him.

This was not the respectable church crowd. These gals were out for a good time. Some of them had probably quarreled and fought with their men; Delta cotton-patch women often won these domestic battles. Some were looking for a new man or were planning to switch dates, somewhat in the way that the anthropologist Norman Whitten describes in the dances of black coastal Colombia.[1] Perhaps they enjoyed hearing the bluesmen denounce their rivals, their treacherous sisters. Perhaps these masculine complaints made them feel powerful, reminding them of what they could do to some man who wounded them. At the same time, they might sympathize with the male victim, yearning to be the one he chose for consolation, to replace the false one, to give him sex and mothering.

Like a feminine crowd at a rock concert, these mean, mistreatin mamas shoved in close round the singer. In this public place they felt free to open their arms to him (something they could never do if he weren't singing), to show off what sexpots they were, what mothers they were, in front of everybody. They yearned to console the lonely, heartbroken bluesman. They encouraged him to go on to another tale of sexual conflict, another story that would also end with a man longing for a woman he has mistreated or who has mistreated him. Above all, they were on display, in the market for a new lover, a new man. The sensuality of the blues, the erotic intimacy of its dance style, accelerated their decisions about new partners.

It was with such an audience in such theaters on ten thousand such nights that the bluesmen ripened their skills and rhymed their river of ironic verse. As we shall see in the accounts that follow, the personalities of these modern troubadours were extremely varied, yet all sang one part of the same story and all could boast, touching their guitar strings, *"I've got a home everywhere I go."*

Bluesmen often risked trouble by taking advantage of this situation. Eugene Powell remembered: "If I'd see a woman I wanted, her husband couldn carry her home. I'd pick that guitar hard. I'd sing hard. I've had women come up and kiss me—didn't ask could they kiss me—just kiss me right then—just grab and kiss me. Just to be safe, I'd always ask a woman if she was married. Right away she'd tell me, 'No.' Her husband might be right nearby, but long as he was out of earshot, that woman would deny him. That tickled me sometime and I'd sing right on.

I said, Tell me, sweet mama, how you want your rollin done?
Tell me, sweet mama, gal, how you want your rollin done?
She say, "Slow and easy, like my old-time rider done."

Roll my belly, mama, roll it like you roll my dough,
Want you to roll my belly, like you roll my dough,
I want you to roll me, sweet mama, till I tell you I don't want no mo.

EUGENE POWELL

Eugene Powell, one of the veterans of the thirties, who cut some lovely sides for Bluebird, still plays exquisite music. His fingers are a bit stiff, but they can ask every string to match the color of the notes he's singing. He virtually smacked his singer's lips over every wicked nuance in the lines above; his eyes twinkled and he smiled a wicked snaggletoothed smile as he sang.

"I wasn't but three days learnin how to pick a guitar. See, what I wanted to do was to sing and pick the guitar like a man. I learnt how when I was a seven-and-a-half-year-old boy, but I wanted to sing like a full-grown man. Grown men always sing bout some woman, you know. I was just a boy, but I wanted a woman. You know how children is," he said with a laugh. "I didn't know what to do with a woman, but I wanted one anyhow. I tried to sing in a real low voice:

(Taking a low, rumbling tone)
Whoa—oh, get up in the mornin, I'm 'onna do like Buddy Brown,
I'm 'onna eat my breakfast, boys, I'm gonna lay back down.

But it come out like so.

(Taking a comical falsetto)
Gonna get up in the morning, I'm 'onna do like Buddy Brown,
Gon eat my breakfas, I'm gon lay back down.

(We all laugh.)

In Powell's stories about his untrammeled, mischief-filled boyhood, we encounter another side of the blues: the gift of making merriment out of deprivation—the madcap play of a bunch of little orphans, with no adult to look after them or hold them down, a source of the ungovernable impudence and fun that runs through so much of the blues:

I went on something scandalous. When Mama leave home, I'll tell you what I'd do. I'd give a ball. Ain't nobody round. Mama and them gone. Just us children—I'd go an look though, first. Then I'd say, "Goddam! Git on down here, you goddam niggers, and let's have a time. Let's ball some! Call ourselves ballin."

I'd get the dishpan and wash it out good and clean, and then I'd pour in a little piece of molasses. They was bears on the can—called it Bear Brand Molasses—and mix in peaches—had Bear Brand Peaches, too. I'd pour it so deep with molasses, and I'd cook flapjacks.

Now them other kids was makin money. They'd break old dishes and glasses and use the pieces for money. Then here they come, buyin stuff from me fast as I could cook it. And I had some meat fryin in the grease with them flapjacks, and they'd buy that and they'd holler, "Give me another dollar and a half of them goddam good pork chops and molasses." I'd send um some mo, send em some mo, and they'd pay and eat up so fast I had to say, "They ain't no mo." Then that mean old boy, he come at me.

"Goddam, don't I see molasses in that pan?"

"Yeah, but I sold all I want to sell. It's my time to eat now."

"Hell, the joint belongs to you and you can eat when you get ready, but right now we gon get what's in that pan!"

Us get into it, and round and round the house we'd go.

Mama and them, they sold whiskey at that time, some whiskey, called it "Peach an Honey," and one they called it "Banana Brandy"—that was some sweet whiskey. Mama sat that jug over behind the trunk. She had marked it, and I didn't know she had marked it outside the jug on the paper. Anyhow, when she come back, I'd had that knocked down bout so far, so Mama knowed somebody had been in it. Everybody was sayin, "No, it wasn't me." And she said, "Well, I'm gon whip all of ya!" Them others was sayin, "Well, he done it!"—they all tell the truth on me after they found out that they gon get a whuppin. Well, she kinda thrashed me around there a lil bit an tol me I better not go in it no mo, and then she left an went visiting again.

I just tell y'all the truth—that was the best-tastin whiskey. I said, "Well, I reckon this whiskey gon get me killed, but I'm gon ahead on drink me some of it." The jug was bout that far from the bottom. I drunk it down till it got bout that far, and it was so good I drank it down further; then I went cryin bout I was gonna get a whuppin for doin it. So I went and got that jug. I said, "Well, I'm jus gon go on an let Mama kill me and I's goin to hell—be done with it." So, I got the jug and I drinked it all up. When Mama come, all of it was gone. You know children think they can fool old folks. I tole Mama, "That whiskey waste outa there or else that jug had a hole in it and done leaked out on the bottom somewhere."

Mama said, "You a liar, you fool, you! You know that jug ain't got no hole in it!" She wouldn't whup me right then cause I was drunk, you know. Like if I was goin to the door thataway, I had to start way over here, you know, way over there cause I'm gonna sure curve, you know. I go over there to the door to go outdoors to calm myself, gonna step down the steps and there wasn't no steps there. Boy, I done some steppin. I hit the ground, and boy, you talkin bout some hurt! It was too bad to cry. I couldn't open my mouth, just went "Annhhh"—that way.

All this Eugene told us with many delighted chuckles. For him these memories of a turbulent childhood were neither tragic nor disturbing. Everyone he knew grew up that way—trained to fight or flee for their lives from childhood up. The world of the blues was no child's garden of verses. It was frontier, it was ghetto; it was also shaped by old African traditions, that had trained boys in Africa to be the armed defenders of their village and their nation and now prepared American black youngsters to fight for their neighborhoods and to survive in the harsh worlds of slavery, peonage, and, often, prison. Although Eugene was raised poor and was left to his own devices by a busy mother, neither his blues singing nor his reminiscences express any feeling of deprivation:

Every time Mama leave there, my nephew, me an him would get into it. He's an old bad boy. He wanna be a man, you know. I wanted to be a man. And I knew he didn't like for nobody to bother 'im. I'd always reach down there and get three little rocks. I'd say, "First, second, and the third one is the law. I'm gon have to do somethin with this one." And I'd do um this way. [He makes a flipping motion with his hand]. I say, "Well, I reckon I'm gon have to get the corner of the house on im." That's what I had to do. Get the corner of the house where I could run an git away from him cause he'd try to kill you! He'd be standing up there with a half a brick in his hand, gritting his teeth.

I would just barely drop the rock on im. If he just look any way, I'd tap him with that rock. And then that nigger'd git after me, and be runnin me round the side a the house, knockin off half the house, look like. "A-wham!" with them half bricks. I thought I'd git away from im, but I couldn't hardly walk, cause I had some ol things in my heels, they call um sandspurs. They just stick my foot so bad, so I run up in a tree by the church, went way up in the tree and waited awhile. He looked up an he seen me. "Yonder he is! Goddamn, we gon git im down." They went in the house and got my rifle—I tell you, tain't no story—a .22 rifle. I'm lucky to be livin! Them ol boys shootin at me with that rifle. Them bullets say, "Pow! Zzzzumm!"—right by my head. Looked like they said, "Hmmm-mm-mmm!" hummin right by my ear.

Boy, I fell out that tree and start to runnin. And he was right behind me with a great big brick, you know. I run on to Ol Man Cook's house and an old lady—she's sittin up in there sewin, old lady in white. I didn't have time to tell her, "Let me come in," I just runned in anyhow. He was right behind with that brick.

That old lady was sewin an quiltin, and she said, "Hup, hup, hup! Where you goin?!"

I said, "I comin in here."

"What you comin in here for?!"

I said, "That boy trying to kill me. You see him with that rock?"

You know, children be scared a ol folks—they ain't no mo, but they used to be.

"Boy, git outa here with that rock fore I git somethin and tear you up! What are you doin around my house with that brick?"

He said, "That ol boy hit me an run, I'm gon git im." Well now, she runnin me out there, gettin me outa there now.

"Git on back out there, both of ya! Git on out there!" Well, I hated to go out there cause he's gon try an rap me with that brick. But, boy, I made up my mind good. I went out there and I was on that top step an I made a spring, hit that ground, and I dug off like a car. Them first tracks, I scored them out. Boy, he run me on back home. I said, "Well, I got to try to make it the best way I can." So, I snatched that rifle from um an took that rifle to pieces, and that's why I'm livin today and able to sing the blues.

Now little girl, gal, where you get your sugar from?
Little girl, little girl, where you get your sugar from?
You must have been down in Louisiana
And got it right off the sugar farm.

Ain't it lonesome, sleeping in a big bed by yo'self?
I said, ain't it lonesome, sleeping in a big bed by yo'self?
When you can't be with the one you love, honey,
Keep lovin someone else.

A study of child-rearing practices in the Deep South finds that black working-class mothers raise their boys to be aggressive, roughly teasing and challenging them, yet at the same time they enforce obedience with blows and beatings, so that boys become accustomed to a threatening environment and to bearing pain.² All this prepared the black bluesmen for the difficulties and dangers that faced them at every turn when they set out with their guitars to live the life of the blues. Between songs Eugene recalled the risks and the raunchiness of that life:

I had a woman down there, name Annie Mae. She could play guitar pretty good, too, and I'd carry her with me to help me out on them suppers, you know. She could sing good. So, I went down there one Saturday evening, and she kept on gappin around and gwine on—had done quit actin like she had been actin.

Well, I said to her, I said, "Annie Mae," I said, "come here."

She said, "Well, I'll come cause I wanna tell you sumpin," said, "Me an you done quit."

Well, I sat there awhile, then I got up to leave and that woman followed me way down the road with her brother's pistol. Gon kill me. Yeah. She'd come on awhile and catch up with me and then walk along the side of me, I thought she had the gun cause she would be scared to walk the road at night. So she stopped me an' I stopped to see what did she want. And she said, "I oughta kill you."

I said, "Kill me bout what? I oughta be killin you, you done quit me for that other boy," and I said, "And I ain't tryin to kill you," I said, "cause if you live, I can get you back again, but if I kill you, I can't. But I don't want you back no mo," I said, "so I ain't gon kill you." So, well, while she went on down the road a piece goin back home, and she stopped me again. I wait and see what she wanted. She said she tryin to make her mind up to shoot an kill me. Then she got way up the road, then she said, "Well, I'm gon go back now." And she went back.

The next time she called me, I wouldn't stop. I kept goin, I went on. I got way up that road out on 61. An' I was playin that ol piece about *Highway 61 Is the Longest Highway I Know.*

And then, when I head in round down Hollandale, they heard my guitar, way down the road about a mile, way in the night about twelve or one o'clock. And when I got there, they was already up—settin out there in they pajama suit and nightshirts an things, hopin I would keep playin my guitar.

Oh, Highway 61, baby, is the longest highway I know.
Oh, Highway 61 is the longest road I know.
It run from New York City down to the Gulf of Mexico

I used to play with the man they call the Devil's Son-in-Law. Richard Harney was his name, but he named himself "Hacksaw, Devil's Son-in-Law." He'd say, "You better come on and get acquainted with the Hacksaw. I'm the Devil's Son-in-Law."

He had long fingers, bout that long, okay? Picked much guitar. Me an Hacksaw, we'd go in them jukes where the Seabird was rollin. We'd stand around there a little while an some of um would see me.

"How bout you playin us a piece? Come on!" Them big-shot gamblers, they'd throw us two or three dollars, an' we'd fall on them guitars. So, the house-man come in there, and he ain't gettin no money goin in the Seabird now, and say, "Y'all gon have to leave, cause this is the way I make money, on my Seabird."

When we attempt to leave, everybody say they gonna leave, too. "If you don't let them play, we ain't gonna stay here. We don't want to hear that Seabird, we wanna hear them men play them guitars."

Well then, he'd have to let us play, you understand. He didn't offer us nothin for playin, but we would make more than I probably woulda charged him, because everybody was throwin money, just throwin money. Everytime we'd play, we'd get two or three dollars. Us started to make money then, and we'd stay there and play all night. If I seed some woman I liked, I'd come whoppin the blues down hard, an' Hacksaw would tell me,

"Go on an' play it like you want it," he say, "I'm gon put some gravy around this stuff here. I feel like seein the people *wade in the blues!*" Then he'd go on further, say, "Go ahead an play, I'm gon put some omelette aroun this music."

I'd be playin blues, you know, doin somethin with my guitar, and he near about killin his, playin it so hard an doin so much to his guitar that folks would get all distracted watchin him.

So, well, we leaved from there—goin back along the road just about first dusk.

Hacksaw say, "Do you know where a singer out here could drop round and see somethin?"

I said, "Yeah. There's some stayin in that house yonder."

See, I knowed one round through there. "Let's lay um down a little blues when we go rollin by."

We got on the gravel road, walkin. I come up playin the guitar an he come up gettin behind me on it, and them folks come to the door.

"Hey y'all!" they said. "Come by here an play us a piece!"

Oh man, that sound good to us. [*laughs*] We wouldn't git no better than that. We were where we could play and our food come free of charge, and our monkey was free, too. We'd get free monkey. [*laughs*] They used to like us to play that ol piece bout *Tight Like That*. You remember it, doncha?

Wearin my pants above my knees,
Just might get it with who I please.
It's tight like that, yes, tight like that.
Do you hear me talkin to you,
Baby, it's tight like that.

Old Uncle Jack with his wooden leg,
I'll hold his head while you set the peg.
Cause it feel so good, tight like that.
Baby, don't you hear me,
Talkin bout tight like that.

Mama killed a chicken, thought it was a duck.
She put him on the table with his feet stickin up.
Oh tight like that, yes, tight like that.
Don't you hear me keep a-tellin you,
Baby, it's tight like that.

Had a little dog, his name was Ball,
Gave him a little taste and he want it all.
Tight like that, yeah, it's tight like that.
Don't you hear me talkin to you,
Baby, it's tight like that.

A note of unconflicted and happy eroticism rings out here. Songs like this—all the little double- and triple-entendre rhymes of the ring games, of black minstrelsy, of ragtime, jazz, the blues, and rock—have gradually chiseled away at the starchy standards of nineteenth-century propriety, until American pop today has burst past all bounds. Earlier it was "tarararaboom-deray" and "jadah-jadah jing-jing-jing;" earlier it was code words like "jelly roll," "salty dog," "trucking," and "rocking." Nowadays the language of song employs the explicit argot of the streets. In all this the driving force has been the sexually more permissive African cultural tradition, in which fertility rather than continence is a central value. An African myth, recorded by Harold

Courlander, captures a view of sexuality miles away from European mythology and literally oceans away from the Calvinist morality it encountered in the Southern United States. To paraphrase briefly:

When the great Olorun distributed powers to the orishas, he gave Babalouaye inordinate sexual strength. Babalouaye was constantly lying with women. Even on the one day when Olorun had asked him to restrain himself, Babalouaye said, "Olorun gave me this power and I will use it whenever I wish." Then he had intercourse with Oshun. On the next day he woke with a body full of sores and soon died of syphilis. Oshun appealed to Olorun to bring Babalouaye back to life, but no avail. She tried many wiles and failed, but at last she found some wonderful magical honey and sprinkled his house with it. Olorun was overcome with a desire for the honey and asked Oshun for it, but Oshun steadfastly refused to give him any, until he brought Babalouaye back to life. So at last Olorun brought Babalouaye back to life, and Oshun gave Olorun the honey he wanted. As for Babalouaye, he returned to the pursuits and enjoyments he had had before.[3]

The Devil's Son-in-Law, Hacksaw, and his friends, rollicking in the shanties of the Delta, remained happily devoted to this worldview. Not even the old mothers of the church had been won over to the discomforting idea that sex was sinful and wrong and to be shunned if possible. Witness to this were the black folktales of the Delta, which we heard during the breaks between the dance sets, as we washed down hot tamales and spicy pork barbecue with lashings of corn whiskey:

You might not believe this, but there was a woman once who never had had no man. This woman lived away out in the woods, you know, by herself. And she never did 'low no mens in her house. Couldn't nobody, see, nobody be there. So there was a man in town one evening about three o'clock, you know, he was a cow buyer and he was talking to the people at the market and they told him about this here woman, name Annie. Man say:
"Don't nobody go around and see Annie?"
"No, I never did hear nobody goin over and seeing her."
"I wonder who go with her?"
"I don't know. Nobody there at all."
"Tain't?"
"No."

"Well, I'm goin over there tonight and I'm gonna get on her."

He went and bought up a lot of cows and he drove um past this woman's house. He says, "Hello."

She says, "Hello."

He says, "Now, lady, could I stay here all night tonight?"

She says, "Why, mister, I don't 'low no man to stay here."

Says, "Well, I ain't no man. I'm a woman hater."

"Woman hater?"

"Yeah."

"All right. Bein you is a woman hater, you can stay here all night."

So when he got down, he went on in the house. She says, "Ain't got but one bed."

He says, "Why, I can sleep with you then. I'm a woman hater." It's hot, in summer, so him and her laying in the bed, you know, laying there with his shirt up and prick near as hard as a brick.

Directly she looked over there and seen that thing, she said, "What is that?"

"Them my cows."

She felt down a little lower and she said, "What is that?"

"Them my oxen."

So he lays on across her and he feels her and says, "What is that?"

She said, "That's my hole of water."

He lay there awhile. He say, "Well, lady, can I water my cows in your pond?"

She say, "Yeah."

So he gets on her, commence gettin it from her. And it got kinda good to her, she thought he could go in deeper, she said,

"Listen, drive your cows on in." So he left it right there. It get so good to her, she said, "Listen, drive the cows and oxen all into the clear water. Damn hole ain't boggy."

When the laughter had died down, we heard about the old lady washing at the spring:

There was this lady used to do her wash at a certain spring and a fellow went over there to get him some water, you know, and he went to the spring and got him a drink of water, and he noticed her washing. She just washing and she didn't pay him no 'tention. He looked there and slipped up behind her, he did what he wanted, and thought he'd slip on off, you know. But she hollered and told him, say, "Mister, I washes here every Friday."

One of the younger men in the circle raised up his glass and proposed a toast to the preachers:

Once there were three preachers
Was going to the installation.
They was riding along in this coupe car—
Baptist, Methodist, and the Sanctified preacher.

The Baptist preacher said,
"Let's stop and take a drink."
The Methodist said, "Let's do so."

And they all got out and walked in the jinte.
The Baptist preacher, he called for a pint,
The bartender, he threw it to him.
The Baptist preacher passed him the buck.
He knocked the top off and began to drink.

The Baptist preacher say,
"God made man, He made him big and stout,
And left a place for his rail to hang out."
He drank and passed it to the Methodist preacher.

The Methodist preacher say,
"God made woman, he made her big and stout.
Jesus Christ sewed her up until the thread give out."
He taken his drink and passed it to the Sanctified preacher.

The Sanctified preacher say,
"Glory, Halleluyah, it makes me shout
Just to think of the place where the thread give out."

Then M. C. Orr capped the session with his epic of the nymphomaniac queen of Africa, another tale from the endless *Decameron* of the Delta:

Once there was a queen offering a thousand dollars to the man that fuck her a hour. The queen sent her guards out to look for a man that could. They go and they walk and they walk and they walk until eventually they found one. They said, "The queen is offering a thousand dollars for the man that fuck her a hour." He say, "I'm the man; take me on up there." They say, "Now listen, if you can't, they're gonna chop your neck off." He say, "That's all right; take me on up there." Carried this guy on up there and he begin to fuck. He begin at one o'clock and went until fifteen minutes after one, and the queen throwed off. She called the guards and say, "Cut his neck off." He say, "Wait, lady, wait," he say, "give me a chance." He say, "If you don't cut my neck off, I'll guarantee you I'll go get a man who will fuck you an hour." She say, "If you don't, then I'm gon chop your neck off and his'n, too."

And so she give him a chance, and they went out, the guard following him. And they walked, and they walked and they walked, they looked and eventually they saw a great big man sitting under a tree. He was cracking hickory nuts with his dick and busting them on his nuts. They walk up to the man and say, "Mister," say, "the queen's offered a thousand dollars for the man that fuck her a hour." He say, "I'm the man; take me on up there." He say, "Now, if you don't fuck the queen a hour, they're gonna chop your neck off and mine too." "All right," he say, "take me up there."

They carried the guy up there and he started in at two o'clock. The guy began at two and he fucked her until two-thirty and nobody said a word—until three and nobody said nothing. He fucked her till three-thirty, and the queen was unconscious. He fucked her until four, and the guards began to get uneasy, and they decided to bust the door down and see what was the trouble. And the man was sitting up on the side of the bed with a teaspoon, pouring it in her.

This is the first time a Lomax has ever reported on the erotic lore we discovered. The Library of Congress gave such material the Greek symbol Δ (delta) and made it inaccessible save to specialist scholars and congressmen— it was by law their library and, of course, they had special privileges. In these days of "letting it all hang out" it's hard to recall the prudishness of that earlier period, when, for instance, *Ulysses* by James Joyce could not be legally published or sold in the United States. The Supreme Court decision ruled against this censorship in 1933. It was only in 1960 that the first scholarly paper on erotic folklore was read before the American Folklore Society. Since its author, the famed sexologist Gershon Legman, could not afford to come from France to present his work, it was read to the group by a psychoanalyst, specially invited for the occasion. The chairman of that session ordered the doors closed and locked and suggested to the women present that they might want to leave before their delicate feelings were violated. None left, by the way, and in the rush of scatology that for a few years filled the American folklore quarterly, female scholars figured prominently as authors.

However, if my father and I had included the so-called dirty songs in our 1930s anthologies of American folk songs, the books would have remained unpublished. We had the opportunity to present and celebrate the huge panorama of American folk song and establish its value with the general public for the first time. It never occurred to us to endanger this goal by including erotic material. Even now I feel some reluctance to take this step. By so doing one fosters the tormenting ambivalence of our social code which, on the one hand, rewards sexually stimulating entertainment of every sort and, on the other, idealizes fidelity in romantic and marital relationships as a support to the keystone of society, the nuclear family. Moreover, like much pornography, many tales display a harshness about sexual matters that I find both unpleasant and unreal. Usually, they treat women as objects in a way that many if not all women find repugnant.

It is for this very reason that I have included pornographic lore at this point in this essay on bluesmen. The blues portray a pain-filled landscape inhabited by women "who study evil all the time." I believe that the hearts of these women may have been hardened by the careless macho attitudes expressed in such tales as these, and that the feminine betrayals, of which the bluesmen constantly complain, are in some degree acts of revenge upon the men for their selfish insensitivity. This is an undercurrent in the portraits of the bluesmen that follow.

SAM CHATMON

By the time I met Sam Chatmon in the 1970s, he had a white beard that stretched below his belt buckle. He was well into his eighties, had played the blues all his life, first as a member of a family blues band that made commercial recordings in the twenties, and later as a popular figure on the college lecture circuit. His family story shows how the blues emerged from country square-dance bands like the one Blind Sid commanded. After a lifetime they still filled his heart and mind.

"I always keeps the blues. That's my daily occupation—the blues. I go to bed with them. I git up with them!" he chuckled. He began to tell me about a current affair.

"My love is just like a faucet. She can turn it off, then she can turn it on. You know I come home the other night, I come in there, I looked in my livin room, it was all nasty. Went on in the middle room, the bedroom—it was nasty. Went on down in the kitchen, it was all dirty. I turnt round to my ol lady, I say, 'Hey! Listen! What you gon aim to do here?' She says, 'Not no more than I done done.' I said, 'Well, listen, this is your last time you stayin here with me.' Said, 'You get your clothes and leave, I mean right now! And I mean it.' " Sam picked up his guitar and added to the story:

I told you you could go
And don't come back to Sam no mo.
Woman, it's your last time
Shaking it in the bed with me.

Says, I told you to your face
I had another good girl to shake it in your place.
Babe, it's your last time
Shaking it in the bed with me.

Oh, you shake it, you can break it, hang it on the wall.
Throw it out the window and run round and grab it just before it falls.
Shake it, you can break it, hang it up on the line.
I don't want your love cause it shore ain't none of mine.

I told you in the spring,
When the birds all began to sing,
Woman, it's your last time
Shaking it in the bed with me.

Well, you kicked all my cover off the bed and on the floor.
You better be glad, sandfoot, you ain't gonna get to kick it no more.
Now you wear your miniskirt way above your knees,
Now you can shake your jelly with every other man you please.

I told you you could go
And don't come back to Sam no mo.
Woman, it's your last time—
Shaking it, I mean twisting it,

Doing that monkey dog,
And that slop in the bed with me.
Oh go, baby!

The chilly brutality of these verses reflects what was said and shouted and screamed in the domestic quarrels that took place in the shacks and shotgun houses of the rural black ghetto. The keenest pain of poverty and homelessness is losing love and family, and the constant refrain of the blues is the faithlessness of lovers. Those hard decades, when the people were uprooted, were the years of careless love when the women, like dollars, rolled from hand to hand. In his next blues, Sam remembers how it felt to go home from his night watchman's job in Hollandale and find "another mule kicking in your stall."

It's love, oh love, oh careless love,
Says you broke my heart and you didn't care.
Says your love's run cold, I tell you, woman, it hurts my soul,
With your love, oh love, oh careless love.

Someday, I may get lucky again.
I said, someday, I may be lucky again.
Well, someday I mean I may get lucky again
Just to find me another loving friend.

Throughout West Africa and the West Indies song composers maintain the social order. When people feel they have been treated unjustly by their lover, they run to the song maker or launch a song themselves to punish the faithless one. To avoid direct and sometimes fatal confrontations, these public reproaches often employ veiled language and usually name no names. Even so, the whole community understands the who, what, and why of the complaint. The villain of the piece (a wayward girl, an erring spouse) may reform or, if too humiliated, leave town. I remember one Haitian Mardi Gras song that drove an incestuous father out of the village. Many blues, and many blues verses, began that way.

Corinna, Corinna, where'd you stay last night?
Your shoes ain't buckled and your clothes don't fit you right.

Sam went on to tell his family history, quite bitter enough to explain his life-long addiction to the blues.

SAM CHATMON: About my blues—man, I has the blues everyday. I can make up a song anytime I wanna make it up, cause I keeps the blues. I was raised about sixteen miles this side of Jackson, comin towards Vicksburg. My daddy, he was a slavery-time man, married and had children in slavery times. He went by Chatmon cause his master was Old Man Chatmon. He first was a Madden, he said, then him an his mother were sold to Mister Chatmon. And then he had to wear the name of Chatmon. He said the old ladies, old colored ladies, they would always be the ones to take care of the young kids. And they had a trough to mix bread and stuff up in so the children could eat.

ALAN LOMAX: The kids ate out of a trough?

S.C.: Yeah, a trough! Just like pigs! My daddy tol me all these things and I don't forget um. The next thing he tol me, he said, he was in the Civil War.

A.L.: Was he in the war on the Southern or the Northern side?

S.C.: Well now, he was on the side he didn't get no pension! He didn't get no money at all. Now Old Man Isley, he was on the side where him and his wife both drawed pensions. But my daddy didn't draw no pension. He told me they killed so many men in the Battle of Vicksburg, they didn't have no bridge to cross, so they'd take men and throw um in the branch, in the creek, till they could drive the wagons on 'cross.

A.L.: What did your father say about how he felt when he was freed?

S.C.: Well, he felt the same way. It was like it had never come. The colored folks have come a long way, but still, I say a lot of us has a fear yet of what was back there in them days. Used to be, when we'd go to a white man's house, we'd have to go around to the back. Now, it's done got to the place where you go to the front and knock, but I go to the back yet! Cause I was raised up like that. Your teachin's what your mother and father gives you, you just can't hardly get out of it, it grows with ya. What your mother or father taught you, you believe it's right yet.

A.L.: Did your father work as a house servant or did he work in the field?

S.C.: He worked in the field awhile, but he played music in slavery times. They had him and Old Man Miller for their fiddle players. Yeah, he was a fiddler in slavery times. He was born in 1825. That's near as I can come there, and he died in '34, made 'im a hundred an' nine years old. And my grandma, she was a hundred and twenty-six. And I'm tryin to make it to eighty. I got about two more months. *(laughs)*

A.L.: Do you remember any of the tunes that he played to you?

s.c.: Yeah, I remember practically all of um. All of um is just ol things bout *Can't Get the Saddle on the Old Grey Mule* and *Little Liza Jane*.

> *Hey, Liza,*
> *Little Liza Jane,*
> *Oooh Liza,*
> *Little Liza Jane.*
>> *Steal that gal with the red dress on,*
>> *Little Liza Jane,*
>> *Who's been there since I was gone,*
>> *Little Liza Jane.*
> *O Liza,*
> *Little Liza Jane,*
> *O Liza,*
> *Little Liza Jane.*
>> *You get there before I do,*
>> *Little Liza Jane,*
>> *Tell Lil Liza I'm coming too,*
>> *Little Liza Jane.*

When they'd finish that one, they'd say, "Everybody promenade to the bar!" All the men would carry their ladies to the bar and give um drinks. After a while they'd get ready to start back again on sumpin else. Old Man Miller and my daddy didn't have no guitars, nothin but fiddles.

> *Chicken in the bread pan pickin up dough.*
> *"Granny, will you dog bite?" "No, chile, no."*
> *Can't get the saddle on the ol grey mule,*
> *Can't get the saddle on the ol grey mule,*
>> *Whoa mule, whoa mule,*
>> *Can't get the saddle on the ol grey mule,*
>> *Whoa mule,*
>> *Can't get the saddle on the ol grey mule.*

a.l.: You had a whole musical family, didn't you?

s.c.: Yeah. Sisters, brothers, and Mama—all of us played, the whole family. All my nephews, they can play. Peter Chatmon, up here in Memphis, they called him Memphis Slim, that's one of my sister's boys.

Sam's voice betrayed a proper avuncular pride. Memphis Slim, whose star rose late in the blues firmament, was one of the greatest blues pianists and singers of all time. The reader will encounter him full-scale in chapter 10 of this volume—a star performer who can also be heard on CDs.[4] Slim's career peaked overseas in the 1970s, when this cotton-patch pianist ran his own nightclubs in Paris and Tel Aviv.

s.c.: Well, I'm his uncle. All us could play. Have you ever heard Charley Patton? Well, Charley Patton's my brother. Charley Patton picked the blues. He was a good bluesman, but he could clown better than he could pick.[5] He'd take his guitar and put it all behind his head and all tween his legs and keep a-pickin. Nothin but the blues.

There was nine of us. We played for parties everywhere. For colored and white, too. All we wanted was the money. If we would play two hours and a half, we'd get five dollars a man. When we'd get through with us crops, late on by in June or July, we'd all get together and take a tour all up through Memphis, Chicago, and different places like that. We played *Donna, Somebody Stole My Gal, Sit Right Down and Write Myself a Letter.* See, we was playin jus jazz music. One of our special numbers was the one about "I love my coffee and I love my tea, but the doggone Sugar Blues soured on me."

Memphis Minnie—she was a little, slim, dark woman with short hair. Her big hit was about the bumblebee and she talked about how the bumblebee had the best old stinger she ever see and bout it stingin her till she got sore. And how it oughta come back and sting her some mo. The people all went crazy about that stuff. She was raised up there in Jackson, Mississippi. She married a boy named Charlie McCoy. We all stayed there in Jackson. Bout fourteen or fifteen of us played together. Every Saturday night we would divide up—let four or five go play at this place, and four or five go to the other, and four or five go to the other. That's the way we got around.

We played for white folks more than we did colored. White folks had somethin to hire you with and colored folks didn't. A. J. Lewis, he was a double millionaire. And John Gaddis—he was a millionaire. I played for all them people. They wouldn't want the *T.B. Blues* and such as that. They wanted nothin but the *Sugar Blues* and the *St. Louis Blues* and then, fox-trots.

To Sam, the blues were first of all another kind of dance music. He sang about the bitterness of Delta love in a rather matter-of-fact voice, without either the keening of a Robert Johnson, the ironic merriment of Eugene Powell or Papa Charlie Jackson, or the rage of Son House. Perhaps he was too old to care, but I suspect that because he came from this stable family background, the anguish of the blues did not touch him as deeply as it did others.

As Sam and his folks careened around the Midwest in their jalopy, chasing success from gig to gig, they dedicated a song to America's fathomless optimism:

> *Lost all my money, ain't got a dime.*
> *Bad luck and women, I'm leavin them behind.*
> *But after all this hard travelin*
> *Things about comin my way.*

And they created, or at least first recorded, the song that has brought hope to countless broke-and-hungry, hung-over jailbirds, and the rest of us when we're in that mood:

> *Troubled in mind, I'm blue,*
> *But I won't be blue always.*
> *The wind gonna rise*
> *And blow my blues away.*

A.L.: What do you think the blues are all about, Sam?

S.C.: The blues is about a woman. If your wife or anybody misuses you, you make up a song to sing. Instead of tellin her in words, you'll sing that song. So, when you be singin that song, you have your mind direct on how she done treated you. That's what the way it was in slavery times. My daddy said when the folks in slavery times wanted to sing sumpin to his old massa, they would hum an old corn song [another term for a holler like those of the levee camp and prison].

A.L.: Remember the words?

S.C.: No sir. He never would tell me that. But they said they would hum them old songs late in the evening, so the white man could hear um and know something's troublin um. That's the way that you'd sing to a woman . . .

> *When I come to your house and knock upon your door,*
> *I hear a strange voice say: "Get away from there, you can't git in here*
> *no mo!"*

Well, that's bound to give you the blues! When they ask me, "What is the blues?" I tell them, "The blues ain't nothing but a cow wanna see her calf. *(laughs)* That's all the blues is."

Well, I know that woman sure gonna jump and shout,
Hey, I know my woman sure gonna jump and shout,
When that Greyhound bus roll up to Hollandale, Mississippi, and Sam
comes steppin out.

I said, "Baby, don't sell it, please, don't give it away."
I said, "Baby, don't sell it, please, don't give it away.
You just put it on ice and freeze it, woman, oooh, I'll wake it up
someday (Oh yes I will, boy)."
You know, I got them blues.

(guitar sings)

I got the blues to see my baby, I said, "Don't turn your love on me so
strong."
I got the blues to see that woman, but I don't want her to turn her love
on Sam so strong.
Cause your love is just like a faucet, baby, oh, you can turn it off, can
turn it on.

At eighty, Sam's voice sometimes cracked a little, but when he turned to the straight blues, his lips curled masterfully around the syllables, his lean, wrinkled fingers and broad, curved-back thumb stepped out a powerful, grave accompaniment, and no nuance of this cruel tale of parting escaped him.

I went down to that river, oh, thought I'd jump and drown.
I thought about the woman I was loving, boys, I turned around.

I went down to that depot, asked the man how long the train been gone.
He said, "It's been gone long enough for your woman to be at home."

I'm going down to that railroad, lay my head on that railroad track.
I'm gon think about the woman I'm loving, and man, I'm gonna snatch it
back.

Scarcely noted commonplaces of Delta song, these lines are unmatched anywhere in world literature for sheer despair. They voice the feelings of the deprived and humiliated individual, which we will find over and over again as we move further into the land where the blues began.

JACK OWENS

Past woods and cornfields sprouting out of the sandy upland soil and at the end of a narrow dirt lane lined with milkweed and sunflowers, we came to the desolate shack of bluesman Jack Owens. Several windows were boarded shut. No one was about; there were no chairs on the front gallery; the ill-kept front yard, behind the barbed-wire fence, was empty. Two big white shoats, rooting and snorting in the hogpen, were the only evidence that the place was inhabited. Conforming to country good manners, we stopped at the front gate and made our presence known by "hollering" the house—"Jack, Jack." Nothing stirred. We waited a few minutes before we knocked on the back door. Nobody came. But since we had been assured that Jack Owens was at home that day, we persisted. A good five minutes had passed before his grizzled face appeared at the doorway,

I left it to Worth Long, my black coproducer, to tell our story, that we were filming old-time bluesmen in Mississippi. To him Owens denied that he played the blues or that he ever had played them. No promise of money or fame could move him. He stuck to his story—he didn't understand why we had come to him, because he knew nothing about no blues nohow, and never had owned a guitar in his life.

David Evans, the leading musicologist of the blues, had told us that Jack Owens was the finest old-time guitar picker he had found in Mississippi. But Jack didn't know no Mister Evans. We knew that Jack had run a country juke in this very house for many years, making dance music and selling homemade whiskey to his neighbors. When we referred to this, Jack hinted that we had somehow lost our way and had come to the wrong address. Apparently, he thought we were "the law." Just as we were about to give up, he said, "Tell you what you might do. You might go talk to Bud Spires. I hear folks say he's a mighty blues man."

With that he backed into the house, shut the door, and left us to the white shoats. A miserable moment. Usually, when the collector persists against such reluctance, things end badly—"You can lead a horse . . ."—but we were determined to tape the man Evans had praised, and we set out to find Bud Spires, without having a clue about who he was or where he lived. The search through the maze of country lanes round Canton took most of the day. The last lap, the approach to Bud Spires's house, was gloom-filled, because we knew by then that Bud Spires was blind, "blind as a bat," the man said.

We found him, however, crouched over a television set. He sprang up and moved to meet us like a basketball forward—a tall, powerful, shambling fellow with a big mustache over a wide grin. He was delighted with our mission.

"Jack is my buddy, man. We been partners the longest time. See, I plays with him. Wait till you hear us. You wait. We the best, the best in the West. Can I get him to play? Can a duck fly? Can a hound dog bark?

"Listen, don't pay no attention to what old Jack say. He's kinda scarified, you know. He come from the old time—back, way back. He's scared of white folks. He's still got that old stuff in him. You know—'Yaasir—yas, yas—' " Bud whined, then exploded into chuckles.

"Come on, man, let's get started. We gonna cut us some records today." This husky blind man hustled us out the house and gamboled across the yard to our vehicle, calling out to his family, "See you all in the after while, after we make our broadcast." As we rolled along toward Jack's, he pulled out his harmonica and entertained us with a blues in which good sex is compared to driving a high-powered automobile.

> *Don't get mad with me, boys, if your buggy don't ride like mine.*
> *Don't get mad with me, boys, if your buggy don't ride like mine.*
> *Cause it's an easy-ridin buggy, rarin to go all the time.*
>
> *Springs in the front, springs behind,*
> *Springs in the middle, boy, you can't find.*
> *It's an easy-ridin buggy, rarin to go all the time.*
>
> *I rode the buggy last night, night befo.*
> *I'm goin back tonight, I'm tryin to ride it some mo.*

Bud was a one-man, red-hot singing orchestra, accompanying himself on the harmonica, putting rough, bluesy chords after some lines and squealed comments to underscore the sexiest images. Sometimes his instrument almost disappeared in his mouth as he both blew and sucked notes out of its metal reeds.

When we reached Jack's house, Bud took over. "You-all got a guitar Jack can pick on? Okay. Now let me handle him."

He was right. With Bud present, Jack became a different person. In a rather courtly way, he simply canceled out our earlier visit, and appeared on camera with a twinkle in his eyes and a charming country grin. With Bud's harmonica adding a soulful second voice over his right shoulder, Jack Owens launched straightway into the main theme of the blues, the main consequence of lower-caste poverty—the heartbreaking fickleness of women.

Lord, it's nothin but the devil,
Oh, change that woman's mind.

It must be the devil,
Lord, it must be the devil, baby,
Lord, change that woman's mind.

(Bud Spires: *"Hello, devil!"*)

Well, it's nothin but the devil, baby,
Will change that woman's mind.

Jack Owens opens every song with guitar and begins with variations on the main theme of his blues, set in a rhythmic figure that establishes the rock-steady beat of the whole piece. Then his voice rings out like a glass of moonshine struck with a silver knife, every note touched with pain. He dwells on the blue notes, emphasizing them with glides and bits of tremolo. Like all great actors and speakers, he proceeds slowly, polishing each phrase, then, in the African manner, pauses for a response from his chorus—Bud's delicate harmonica breaks and the plangent comments of the guitar. The celluloid thumb pick and the two metal finger picks on the first two fingers of his right hand put a sharp, sometimes snarling edge on the notes. His tempo and his mood are grave, even though he often smiles over some of the lines.

Devil got religion, baby,
Well, the devil got religion, baby,
Joined the Baptist church.

I wondered where he'd learned his songs. Jack replied in his accustomed grave manner. Bud Spires filled in the pauses in African style— in which one may lead but never completely dominate the conversational space. His comments supported and never interrupted Jack, but provided a second musical voice, right on the beat.

JACK OWENS: Learned my pieces right out in the cotton field, plowing.
> BUD SPIRES: Cotton field.

JACK: I ain't learned nothing in no town . . . ain't been to town hardly. *(He chuckles and wipes the sweat off his arms with a big bandana.)*
> BUD: Didn't know what town was, did you? Shuh!

JACK: Naw! Naw, I learned all my blues in the country. Right here out in the country.
> BUD: In the fields.

JACK: Fields, picking the cotton, plowing, hoeing, picking peas, all that kind of mess.
> BUD: Picking cotton or either hoeing, don't make no difference.

JACK: That's where we learned this mess at. That's the reason we don't know no other pieces.
> BUD: We learned something.

ALAN LOMAX: Have you been a farmer all your life?

JACK: All my life . . . been farming out here all my days. Ain never had no . . .
> BUD: Plow a mule in the daytime, pick guitar at night.

JACK: That's right, that's all I do. Nothing but a farmer.
> BUD: Sho!

JACK: *(turns his hat around on his head)* Daddy's and things was a farmer. That's all I knowed. Raised chickens and a few hogs, something to eat around here. Farm out there in the field.
> BUD: Whew! *(wiping sweat away)*

JACK: That's all I ever knowed. *(He pulls his hat brim down and peers out into the gathering dusk.)* That's all I ever knowed.

> *Lord, hard times here everywhere I go,*
> *Lord, hard times, baby gal, driving you door to door,*
> *Hard times, baby gal, driving you to my door.*

As Jack Owens sings, he chords an unobtrusive but highly charged background to the song. It is as if an inspired black gospel quartet were improvising, using fragments of the main melody as backup. The runs on the bass strings elicit broken chords in the baritone and tenor registers, while the harmonica drops in a wailing tag of melody a half mile higher—all performed so fluidly that the strings seem to be singing with Jack rather than accompanying him. The refrains—the repeated lines—like "door to door," "drag me down," are repeated in the guitar part, in haunting harmonies. The whole thing is bare-bones simple, but profoundly romantic. Jack's voice sounds like a shawm that can speak Southern. The guitar sings along with him in a wistful barbershop-quartet style. Its notes, drawn out of brass by steel and edged with acid, melt into strange but elegant background harmonies and pungent countermelodies. This, one feels, is deep blues, as profound as *cante jondo.*

I ain't gwine no higher, baby, Lord,
Lord, stay right here, old baby gal, till you drag me down,
Drag me down, till you drag me,
Stay right here till you drag me . . .

Lord, hard times here everywhere I go,
Hard times, baby gal, driving you door to door,
Hard times, baby gal, driving you to the door,
Hard times driving you door,
Hard times, baby gal, driving you door to door.

Jack stared off over the dull green of the cotton fields and struggled to remember how his life began. His account was halting and dreamlike, but you saw the orphaned black boy, holding on to the guitar his absent father had left him.

"I don't know how old I is, but I'm just goin on what they say. My uncle say I was sixty-seven years old, but they told me up yonder in that old folks' home I was seventy-five. I been foolin round playin an old guitar a long time.

"My daddy left me here in Mississippi when I was about eleven years old. He played church music on the guitar. Church songs. I run on and drug that old guitar of my daddy's round, all round the floor—I remember, just as good. That guitar had twine strings on, what you fish with. Kep a-foolin with that old guitar till I went out in the field and I picked around there till I learnt me some kind of little old song. My daddy didn't know when he come down here to see me, he didn't know I knowed how to play them blues—he didn't know that. I start to playin them, you know, playin them round, by being just left for my own out there, playin them little old songs. I got so I could pick some. My uncle tol me, 'Why, you can really *play*. Why don't you git out and play for some of them dances.' And that's how I got started."

Lord, I want a woman, baby . . .

ALAN LOMAX: How long have you been plowin?
JACK OWENS: All my days, since I got up.
A.L.: How many times you been married?
J.O.: Three times.
A.L.: Any children?
J.O.: None, none, none.

Singing and making music are a kind of dreaming out loud, pulling the listener into the dream and thus taking care of his deep needs and feelings. Jack's blues concern the time when the family system of the South was breaking up under economic pressure. Jack's own father left him when he was a shirttail kid, so that in his tenderest years he couldn't answer those perennial Southern questions: Just whose boy is you? What is yo name, boy? And the cry of the orphan rings out in all his blues, as it does in Robert Johnson's.

Those who refused to endure the humiliation of being black in the Jim Crow South were abruptly leaving. Giant machines were taking over the jobs on plantation and levee; unemployment was endemic for those who stayed behind. The men were on the prowl. In one of Jack's best blues, the "kid man" is on the front steps, singing through the screen, asking to be taken on as a temporary replacement for the man of the house.

Lord, I went to, to her house
And I sat down on her steps.
Lord, come right in, pretty boy,
My good man just now left.
Good man just now, good man just,
Good man just, good man just, good man just,
Good man just now left.
Good man just . . .

Well, if I can't come in
Let me sit down fore your door.

Lord, I'll leave so easy,
Baby gal, your good man never know.
Good man never, good man never,
Good man never, good man never,
Good man never know . . .

The song reminded me of a newly minted and highly syncopated ax song I had recorded earlier at Parchman (see page 268). In the stanzas of the *Catfish Blues* the lines are fragmented into a sort of chanted e. e. cummings verse, so that single images are highlighted and the verse ends in a series of brief phrases, like dance moves, with the guitar answering phrase by phrase.

JACK OWENS (singing):
    Lord, if I
    Was a fish
    Swimmin in the
    Deep blue sea,
    Have all you pretty baby gals
    Fishin after me
    Fishin after
    Fishin after
    Fishin after me.
BUD: *Well, I've got,*
    I got a little woman, you-all,
    She got a color, right fair brown,
    But she's got a new way of lovin me
    An it just go down.
JACK: *Lord, take me,*
    Take me, baby gal,
    Won't you try me
    One more time?
    Oh take me, baby gal,
    An-uh try me one more time,
    Try me one time
    Try me one
    Try me one
    One

> *One*
> *Give me one more time,*
> *Baby gal, one . . .*

With Jack, the truly orphaned one, not sure just what his real name was, forever seeking his father, the pain touches every phrase with heartbreak.

DAVID EDWARDS

Friars Point sleeps in a crook of the levee. The oldest town in the county and, in the years of the steamboat, the county seat, it now lies quietly in the shadow of the man-made green hill that runs all the way from Memphis to New Orleans, cut off from the Mississippi by miles of swamp and willow thicket. The fine old houses in the white district have retreated deep into their green lawns and behind their shade trees and flowering bushes. The sound of train whistle and bus claxon on the main lines of travel through Clarksdale never disturb them. Buried in greenery, Friars Point snoozes quietly, waiting for the whistle of the steamboat that will never make a landing or, perhaps, for the rumble of the Mississippi that may one day slide through the levee and wash this little town quietly off the map.

Only on Saturday afternoon will you find anything doing along Main Street. Saturday afternoon in Friars Point, when folks stroll up and down and drink Cokes, waiting for the evening and its adventures in other, livelier parts of the country, we found our friend from the Dipsie Doodle, that wild young rooster David Edwards. He was at the center of a crowd of blacks in front of the drugstore, his harmonica protesting that it was not a golden trumpet and yet doing pretty well at it; his guitar pouring out cascades of blues breaks, hotter than the July afternoon. We edged in closer and heard:

> *Lord, lemme tell you, lemme tell you*
> *What Uncle Sam will do,*
> > *He will take you out of jitterbuggin*
> > *Put you right in a khaki suit.*
> *Lemme tell you, lemme tell you*
> *What Uncle Sam will do,*
> > *Stop you from all that jitterbug,*
> > *Man, put you in that khaki suit.*

Everybody laughed. Dave flashed a smile and flung another shower of glittering notes over us as his fingers danced down the fingerboard, and then, with a hot, choked-down beat stated his thesis:

Oh yeah! I would rather be an army man,
Oh yeah! I would rather be an army man,
I'm gettin tired of ridin these buses, baby,
Lord, I believe I'll ride some trains.

David could make the guitar "speak the blues like a natural man." He proceeded to make a flowery speech while the harmonica, in the frame around his neck, moaned and shouted like the reed section in a hot band. It was very tricky stuff, but Dave was very cool about it, standing there with a sharp Stetson cocked far back and his drape-shape double-breasted coat buttoned up, "whipping his instruments down to a fine gravy" like he wasn't even trying.

The crowd gave Dave a spatter of country applause, dropped a few nickels in his hat, and began to drift away. A Holy Roller "singing band" had opened up in a vacant lot across the street. The women with their shrill voices and their stomp-time tambourines were too tough for Dave, so he sauntered off down the dusty little street, tossing arpeggios and swift bass attacks over his shoulder, because he really couldn't stop playing.

Fresh from the offices of two Mississippi high sheriffs, I didn't shake his hand right there in the street. Way back there in 1942 the air remained empty between us as I said hello and we chatted pleasantly about the blues. Dave played a little bit more for me, proving, as I had thought, to know mostly "commercial" blues, and soon was in the car, showing me the way to his house. There, in privacy, we shook hands and exchanged surnames, a small courtesy that, because it lay outside the mores of the South, worked warm magic.

"I'm a boy that likes to *go*," said Dave, "been so far away from Miss'ippi, I didn't think I'd ever get home. Missouri, Tennessee, Alabama, Georgia, Florida, Chicago—all those states—I just loves to ramble. If it wasn't for this army draft business holding me down, I'd be gone now. They ain't nothing doing around here.

"Oh, you'll find a lots of good musicianers around this country. Look Quick from over in Burrville, he plays that Charley Patton style. Tom McClennan, he's on records, down in Yazoo City, a guitar picker, a real one. Buddy Boy in Jamestown. Old boy they calls Pop Corn right here in Gunterson plays a pretty good box. Little Willie, guitar, in Crenshaw. I reckon Black Albert down at Leland is the best five-string banjo picker. Bo Chatmon, he compose *Sittin on Top of the World Blues,* old-time blues fiddler. He recorded with the Mississippi Sheiks, way back yonder when I was a kid. I've played with all of them, but I reckon I learnt the most from Andrew Moore in Indianola. That's just a step from Shaw, Mississippi, where I was born . . ."

These names in the yellowed pages of my field notes of fifty years ago point guilty fingers at me. All these little-known masters of the blues are dead. I feel now that I should have followed up those leads. But I couldn't have recorded them all—there was only one recording machine—and besides, we were doing a balanced picture of the Delta. Our plan limited us to a visit to each artist's favorite musician.

Dave said, "Well now, if you want my favorite, I believe the best we got around here, besides me, is a fellow name McKinley Morganfield. We calls him Muddy Waters for short."

The now world-renowned Muddy Waters was only locally known at the time. Even so, it is striking that Dave Edwards had not mentioned the now legendary Robert Johnson, who had already recorded, and whom he has lately claimed as a close acquaintance. At that time, of course, Johnson was less important in local opinion than Charley Patton, the Mississippi Sheiks, and many other local bluesmen. And of course Johnson was already dead, after a very brief career, much of it lived out far from the Delta.

Dave had us turn into a gate off the gravel road to his uncle's house, where he was staying. My notes on that visit are meager. Dave was in a hurry to get to "town." "A crazy and dilapidated two-room shotgun house on Paul Grey's place," I wrote. "Cracks in the floor so wide you can see the ground. Kitchen booming with flies. Own a home? No. Own a farm? No. Own an automobile? No. Own a radio? No. Own a Victrola? Yes, in bad repair. Own stock? No. Some chickens. Some vegetables. No milk cows. Grandma, never attended school. Augustus, head of family, 2nd grade. Estella, wife, 5th grade. Minnie, 3rd grade. Dave, 27 yrs. old, wife's cousin, 4th grade . . ."

Meantime, Dave had put on his other suit, sharp-toed shoes, slicked his hair back, and was warming up his guitar for Saturday night in Clarksdale. The mosquitoes were at work on us. His family, surveying Dave with some pride, waved us on. They did not relish a ten-mile walk back from town at midnight. On the way in I asked Dave if he'd ever been married.

"I settled up with a women the first time when I was twenty-three. Mary, I stayed with her a year. Then along came a man she'd been with before. He come in one evening and asked me to play him a piece and said he'd give me a drink. I told him, "No, I thank you." I was scared he'd try to pizen me. Well, that man took Mary off with him one day when I wasn't home, and he made her stay with him for a week at the point of a pistol. And after that we didn't have no more peace no more. He had put something on her . . .

"Well, I left outa there. It didn't make me no diffunce. The women are all right in they way, but they all on fast time. If you ain't got no scratch, they won't bother with you. Like the old boy say:

Some peoples loves whiskey,
Some peoples like a toddy,
Take me home, sweet mama,
Cause I ain't got nobody.

"Two things a musician likes, that's whiskey and women. And the womens likes us better than they do the average working man. I have my girlfriends scattered out good, plenty in Clarksdale, plenty more in Leland, some in Shaw, more in Memphis. Whenever I stop, I find me a friend. The biggest portion of women likes their friend-boy to play music. They takes it as a compliment. And they likes these sharp-toed shoes and different things. So I gets for nothing what costs these hardworking men two dollars . . . Oh, I reckon I must have four or five children scattered here and about other country places. Here's my toast I tell um all:

My back is made of whalebone,
My belly is made of brass,
I save my good stuff for the working women
And the rest can kiss my ass.

We were both laughing when I dropped David Edwards on the main drag in Clarksdale. "If you want to find me, the peoples in Solomon's saloon can always tell you where," he told me, and moved off through the crowd. That night I made a round of the little country balls in Coahoma. In every juke I met another Seabird, eating up the nickels and giving out with music that Tin Pan Alley had decided Southern blacks should like. On my way home to bed around eleven, I spotted Dave on a street corner in Clarksdale, proudly ripping off another blues—the only live music in the county that night, except for the mournful exhalations of the two blind bards.

Sometime later Dave and I spent an afternoon with my recording machine. It turned into a rather exhausting question-and-answer session, for Dave had made commercial recordings and felt hesitant about spilling the beans before a microphone. Every time he could escape my probing, his hands would again begin to flash over the guitar strings, bringing out those coldly brilliant figures of which he was so proud. Here, omitting most of my queries, is what he told me.

"My daddy played violeen and guitar, what he had picked up in South Miss'ippi—different old-time pieces like *Joe Turner* and *Stagolee*. He did what you call just frail a guitar. Nowadays that frailing don't go; what peoples like now is for a man to pick a guitar—make it speak the words. But my daddy just naturally frailed—I fergit all the words:

Stagolee, Stagolee,
Stagolee, he was a man,
And they kilt poor Stagolee.

Dave, using just his thumb pick, played a savage, simple rhythm, the guitar strings snapping and clashing until the instrument sounded just like a set of drums. "That's the old-time way," he said. "Well, I wanted to be a musician like my daddy. When he was singin, I'd try to pick up the songs. Then I got him to show me the song. He sat with me and put my fingers on the fingerboard till I learnt D, A, then G, C, F, B flat, back to C. A long, short, G seventh . . . The first guitar I owned, my daddy paid eighteen dollars for it. And he used to beat me all the time about it. You know, I'd be supposed to be working in the fields and I'd slip home to play, and then they'd be angry and beat me.

"See, my daddy was a farmer. I guess he cleared around five hundred dollars a year at that time, and when the war was on he made fifteen hundred, bought him a hack and some good instruments. Those days Mama would go to the dances right with him, but after a while she got converted and joined the church and got him to quit playing the blues."

"He just gave up the world," I said.

"Just gave it up," Dave replied.

"Do you think there's any harm in this music?"

"I don't believe so."

"Well, what if you get shot? Do you think you'd go to hell?"

"Oh, *now*, naturally I would."

"You just hope you lucky and not get shot?"

"I hope I be lucky."

"If you were playing a guitar at a dance and drinking and someone was to shoot you dead, you'd just go to hell?"

"I *believe* I would."

"You think Robert Johnson went the wrong way?"

"Yes."

"So you think all these blues are the devil's business?"

"Well, I believe the *blues* is. And I'm the devil's child right now. I guess it's been seven or eight years since I been to church. If I'm not a church man, I just won't be a hypocrite."

The "devil's child" grinned at me as he began his version of the famous early jazz tune that runs "Hesitation stockings, hesitation shoes . . ."

Hellitakin stockins, hellitakin shoes,
The hellitakin woman give you the hellitakin blues.
> *Tell me how long do I have to wait?*
> *If you'll be my brown,*
> *I'll pay you forty dollars down.*

"I can remember the folks singin that when I was just about four or five years old. Another one I liked real well at that time was the *Jelly Roll Blues*:

Jelly roll, jelly roll,
Hangin on my mind.
It hypnotized my daddy
And run my mama blind.
> *I love my jelly,*
> *I love my jelly roll.*

Look here, Mama,
Why don't you stop Sis?
She's standin on the corner
Doin the double belly twis.
> *I love my jelly,*
> *I love my jelly roll.*

"Did you understand what that song meant at that time?" I asked.

"It wasn't long till I did," Dave told me. "You take from this part of the country—they start out at ten and eleven years old—they do everything everybody else can do. If they don't be doing it, they trying to do it. They think they be doing it, if they wouldn't be doing nothin. I remember a game we kids used to play when I was real small. All the little gals be dancing, you know, and when it get good to um, they'd raise their dress up about to their ankles and say—

'*Do you want a little bit of this I'm got?*'
'*Mm—no'm, ah-no, ma'am!*'

"She get her dress about halfway up her leg—

'*Do you want a little bit of this I'm got?*'
'*Mm—no'm, ah-no, ma'am!*'

"She get her dress up above her knees, she'd holler—

'*Do you want a little bit of this I'm got?*'
'*Yes, ma'am! Mm—yes, ma'am!*'

"That's what we called a play game when I was a child, but we'd be hidin when we played *that*. In '26, there was a gal maybe two years older, wanted to show me about everything. She just told me to come on. I wanted fun. I wanted to know what we were going to do. She showed me and we made everything all *right*. Anyhow, I thought I was doin good. I done what I was doin it my *way*."

Dave leaned back and laughed right on down to the soles of his shoes.

"What happened when the old folks caught up with you?" I asked.

"Well," said Dave offhandedly, "some of um did try to beat us, but when you get too far gone, you just too far gone. You take a kid around and they start doing that and the old folks try to beat um to stop um, they ain't getting nowhere. If the young folks want it, they'll leave home, see.

I love my jelly,
I love my jelly roll . . .

"I followed country dances for years, playing four or five hours on a Sat'dy night, watching all them peoples get drunk and do the chicken scratch, the black bottom, the scrawnch—where they go right down to the floor shimmying—sometimes they call that the sweet tail—but after while I got tired of all that and I left out.

"How I left home the first time, a boy came through, name Old Willie, and he carried me away to Memphis—I hadn't never been no further than Greenville before. It was a year before I saw home again and by then I really knew something about music.

"Old Willie was a slim brownskin fellow, played guitar and piano. He had me around, playing different places with him and taking little odd jobs when we wouldn't be playing. We had a mighty good time, drinking, getting to know different friends, boys *and* girls—I couldn't just generally tell you how many girls I had since I been rambling around. I got to know every musician in Memphis, nearly about—Dewey, the jug blower. Ukelele Pete, played a ukelele-tip violin. Tango Allen, Osa Brown. Buddy Doll, he's a midget about two feet high, and the peoples gives him right smart just to see him play. They all hustlers—what I mean by hustling, playing beer taverns and things like that.

"Course the biggest they done was drinkin—could drink up the Mississippi river if it was whiskey—and some of um do worse than that. Cokey John, he snuff cocaine, and when he can't get that, he drink anything—shoe polish, strained through light bread—can heat, take it out the can, burn it, and drink it. He say it make him 'jiggified'—make him feel good. He'd get limber and he could play that guitar then.

"It's pretty hard to guess at it, but in a year we'd make two or three hundred dollars, hustlin. Like last week I was playin at a tavern in Memphis and we got eighteen dollars for just three of us. *One* night I got twenty-six dollars for a strang band. You can do pretty good at hustlin, if you can play all the late numbers—not them *old* songs like my daddy plays, we don't know nothing about them *old* numbers. What we play is what they records, the peoples like Mister Melrose up in Chicago.

"See, Mister Melrose in Chicago, he have boys that writes up talents for him—one in St. Louis, Mister Ralph Limbo, and Mister Spier in Jackson. That way he gets in tetch with the good blues players, he books them out and haves them on the road and they make *good*. Then they plays they new blues for him and he records. He used to pay twenty-five dollars a side for a record, that fifty dollars a record, real good money. He don't give no royalty, not unless you're blind or afflicted, but he put your name on the record. Whomsoever sing the song, that's your record. Who owns the song? Well, all I know, your name on the record, if you sing it.

"Here, lately, they cut that money down. They cut from twenty-five a side to seven fifty a side. I don't know why. They say records got cheap, but yet and still they want you to record. There must be something in it or they wouldn't want you to record all the time.

"The last time I went to Chicago for him I made eight records for ninety dollars outside of expenses and all I want to drink. And I met Lonnie Johnson, Tampa Red, Walter Davis, Pinetop, Roosevelt Sykes, and Memphis Minnie.[6] She was a tall brownskin woman with a mouth full of gold and she could nachully pick a guitar. But she'd throw that guitar down and turn a trick with somebody for three, four dollars. I met all the good musicians and I watch um all and picked up different chords and things. Sometimes they'd show me chords for friendship, sometimes I'd pay um for a lesson, but now I can go with the best of um, I don't care who it is. He can just tune up his instrument, go to playing, and I'll catch him.

"Other times I be's on the road, hustlin and hoboin. I ask some guy what train I catch out of here to such and such a place. Maybe he say the M and O or the Cotton Belt or the Katy. I'll ride that to the crossroad and I'll see my way to another train—the Missouri Pacific, the Illinois Central. I get that connection and then along comes the Southern or maybe I catch the Frisco. Just continually changing like that, catching different trains, I get one or two thousand miles away from home and I get the blues and it put me on a wonder.

Late hours of midnight
That old freight begin to reel and rock.
Next station it come to
This old freight train is bound to stop.

Sometimes I begin to wonder
Will I ever git back home.
I been hoboin so long
Till I take the jungle to be my home.

"That's the jungle song what the hoboes sing in the jungle. Guys have much fun in the jungle sometime," Dave went on quietly and wistfully. "We goes up town, git us some pig foot and a bucket, go to cookin and eatin. Have us a jug. Somebody sing and pick a guitar. And you meet some white guys on the road that will treat you better than your own color *ever* will treat you. I've known white guys to meet me, say, 'You wait, I'm going off awhile and knock up a little money,' come right back and say, 'What do you-all want to eat and drink?'—give *me* better treatment than I ever had *any*where in my life.

"See, some days, this guy liable to have a quarter in his pocket. That night, when they git to a city where they goin, they have fifteen or twenty dollars. Where they git it? Well, they got different ways to git *that*. Every man don't do the same thing to git that money. That's the reason they're on the road, see. People staying at home, they ain't thinkin of nothin but workin and tryin to pull their shift somewhere. But the guys on the road, they got an attitude[7] and they know a way to git that money—if you's a good prize fighter or something like that, you gonna run into *some*place where you'll get a break, if you have an attitude to git hold of something. Not everybody's a musician, they ain't lookin for that. Now me, I got that talent and anywhere I land I can sit right down and make me up a song about whatsonever people want to hear. Like one time hoboin in through this country, me and Old Willie got caught and put on the county farm. So I made up a song to sing to the boys . . .

Oh, you got to ro-o-o-oll, just like the hunter's hound,
Lord, if you can't roll, get your britches down.

I ain't got so many mornins to git up soon.[8]
They git you up, baby, by the light of the moon.

Oh, you got to roll, just like a wagon wheel,
Way they treat you, baby, they heart made outa sheet-iron steel.

"Another time, too, up in Illinois, they caught me and my buddy on a freight and about to put us on the pea farm, but I sung um a new song and the special agent let us off."

"Dave," I said, "how about making up a song right now to prove what you told me."

"You just name the subject," Dave said. "Just give me a title and I make you the blues."

I thought a minute. I wanted to give him a notion that would adapt itself to the blues, and I tried to think of something that was not already recorded in another place. At last I said, "How about the *Wind Howling Blues*?"

Without a moment's hesitation, Dave reached way down the neck of his guitar and began to make wind howl and cry out of the treble strings. Then, after an ornate flourish of bass runs, he sang the following blues, sucking more wind sounds out of his harmonica at the tail of every phrase:

Baby, don't you hear the wind howlin, howlin all around the door?
It howls so lonesome, Lord, Lord, it ain't gonna howl no more.

It's thunderin and it's lightnin, baby, and the wind begin to blow,
Lord, my baby told me this mornin, now-now, that she don't love me
*   no mo.*

Lord, it's snowin outdoors, rainin on my old windowpane,
I'm gonna quit you, Black Mattie, you know, it's a low-down cryin shame.

Black Mattie's face go to shinin, baby, just like the risin sun,
Lord, the high-brown powder, that lipstick, baby, Lord, ain't gonna help
*   old Black Mattie none.*

Well, now look here, little Mattie, do you think that's kind,
Take my love this mornin and then leave poor old Dave behind?

It was really a very fine blues, not "made up" on the spur of the moment, of course, but, like all folk improvising, *woven* from appropriate fragments of earlier blues. The new tag "wind howling" simply opened the way to the main subject matter of the blues, the fragile and troubled sexual relationships of the outcaste poor, as they moved into urban life. Both hillbilly songsters and bluesmen sang endless variations on the theme of lost love. Among blacks, however, women had more stable resources of income, while men were more often homeless and hungry. And so in this very masculine genre, the male was constantly throwing himself on the mercy of a woman. No wonder women were crazy about the blues. *Wind Howling Blues* was thus simply a variation on an old theme. Still, it had a sufficiently new atmosphere to *seem* brand-new. I was properly astonished and Dave was pleased.

"I could record that," he said, "if I get back up North."

"Where do you like to live best?" I asked him.

"I like *some* parts of the North."

"Why?"

"Well, everybody is the same there—treated just alike. We all go the same beer tavern. Sit down to lunch at the same table together. You do's what you want to do up there. Down South you can't do that. This is a country for white *mens* and colored *womens*. They can have the ones they wants. That leaves me out."

I confess I was surprised that this young rapscallion would talk so soberly and frankly to a white man like myself. "Why don't you go North?" I asked. Dave answered me with his "favorite blues, made up about three weeks ago."

When I first started out to bummin, babe,
Lord, I bummed from town to town.
Now, now they gonna get me in the army
And them Japs will turn me around.

"Have you volunteered, Dave?"

"I ain't *axed* for it, but I will go, if I *have* to go."

"How do you think it's gonna turn out?"

"Can't hardly tell. It's just like going to court—you can't tell how you're coming out." And with that smiling comment Dave Edwards walked off through the Mississippi sunshine, his Stetson cocked back on his head, tossing runs and arpeggios over his shoulders, because he couldn't stop playing the blues . . .

MUDDY WATERS

People had told us we must hear McKinley Morganfield—better known by his nickname, Muddy Waters. So one extra hot July afternoon we went out to the Sherrod Plantation, a place friendly to our project, and set up the recording machine in a room off the commissary. It was by far the best equipment I had ever had in the field. It cut high-fidelity sound onto sixteen-inch acetate discs, which meant that singing and talking could go on for almost fifteen minutes before disc space ran out. John Work, the director of music at Fisk, Elizabeth, my then wife, and I hadn't long to wait.

Presently, Muddy Waters came in, a husky, curly-headed, dark-brown–skin fellow. His round, rather flat face and his Chinese-like eyes made him look like a friendly dark Eskimo. It was barefoot time in the South, and he was barefooted, so I had an excuse to follow my Southern raising and shed my own shoes. Muddy was a bit nervous because he'd lent his guitar to a friend, but when he began to fool around with the Martin I'd brought along, we all began to smile. Soon the emerald needle of the recorder was cutting a blues track that literally made pop music history. Muddy called it *Country Blues*.

Minutes seem like hours and hours, now,
Oh, it seems like days,
Seems like my little woman oughta stop,
Stop her low-down evil ways.

Muddy Waters kept singing this tune even after he became a star of the urban blues and the idol of young rockers. At the Beatles' first press conference in New York, a reporter asked them what they most wanted to see. They immediately replied, "Muddy Waters and Bo Diddley."

"Where's that?" asked the culturally ignorant reporter.

The Beatles snickered. "You Americans don't seem to know your most famous citizens."

Mick Jagger named his Rolling Stones after a line from one of the blues Muddy recorded at Sherrod's on that long-ago day. In fact, the session has become a sort of holy occasion in the minds of blues lovers, so much written-about and discussed that young blues scholars seem to know more about what went on than I do. I remember thinking how low-key Morganfield was, grave even to the point of shyness. But I was bowled over by his artistry. There was nothing uncertain about his performances. He sang and played with such finesse, with such a mercurial and sensitive bond between voice and guitar, and he expressed so much tenderness in the way he handled his lyrics, that he went right beyond all his predecessors—Blind Lemon, Charley Patton, Robert Johnson, Son House, and Willie Brown. His own pieces were more than blues; they were love songs of the Deep South, gently erotic and sentimental. When they were commercially recorded later on and then widely imitated by the young stars of rock, they brought about a revolution in Tin Pan Alley.

Muddy's style so impressed me that I recorded his two finest blues twice, and later included both of these blues in the first set of records published by the Library of Congress. This compilation aimed to present the finest things we had found in our survey of the whole country, and Muddy's work definitely belonged in this prime category. His first song, given without any prompting from me, began with a murmurous tenderness, the slide guitar echoing the melancholy and sensuous syllables.

Was gettin late over in the evenin, child,
I feel like blowin my horn (making love).
I woke up this mornin,
Find my my little baby gone.

Late on in the evenin, man, man,
I feel like blowin my horn.
Well, I woke up this mornin, baby,
Find my baby gone.

Well, now, some folks say
The old worried blues ain't bad.
That's the miserabliest feeling,
Child, I most ever had.
Some folks tells me
That the worried blues ain't bad.
Well, that's the miserabliest feeling, honey now,
Ooooh, girl, I most ever had.

Muddy's song departed from the rigid AAB, three-line blues formula most of his contemporaries used. Instead, Muddy was rhyming variations on the four-phrase song form—ABAB in outline—using syncopations to make eight lines out of four. In two stanzas of hyperbole, he measured his hurt, the moments that turn his thoughts to death, the empty hours and desolate days of longing for his faithless jenny.

Well, brooks running into the ocean,
The ocean, the ocean runnin into the sea,
If I don't find my baby,
Somebody goin, gon bury me.
Brooks run into the ocean, child,
Ocean run into the sea,
Well, if I don't find my baby, now,
Oh well, girl, you gon to have to bury me.

Yes, minutes seem like hours
And hours seem like days,
Seem like my baby
Will stop her low-down ways.
Minutes seem like hours, child,
And hours seem like days,
Yes, seem like my woman, now,
Oh well, girl, she might stop her low-down ways.

Well, I'm leaving this morning
If I have to ride the blinds
I feel mistreated, girl,
You know now, I don't mind dyin.
Leaving this morniiin (he yodels a little here),
If I have to, now, ride the blinds.
Yes, I been mistreated now, babe,
And I don't mind dyin.

Here was a poem as artful, as carefully structured as an eighteenth-century love lyric, yet marvelously shaped for singing. In the first two stanzas the poet announces the sorrows caused by his inconstant mistress. The next two state his boundless romantic melancholy. In the envoi he threatens a departure that may result in his death, a formula as old as the troubadours. The whole song has far greater coherence than most blues, not just because it is tied to a single theme, but because it so crisply depicts an age-old strategy men use to get their way with women. The girl is teased and cajoled into compliance with accusations of hardheartedness and fickleness.

In a second variant, a cover recording taken at a later date, Muddy retained the same structure. However, comparison shows how textual improvisation shapes the folk blues. Like every blues singer, Muddy had a stock of floating stanzas used in building any song he sang. In this case he cut back on romantic hyperbole and used two openly phallic verses that warn his neglectful lover that he might seek consolation on up the road. Here Muddy clearly establishes, at the very beginning of his career, the main source of his own blue feelings—sexual frustration. Virtually all of his compositions deal with this theme and little else. For him, even the magical mojo hand was a mode of dominance over women. *Country Blues* begins with a variation of the familiar opening stanza:

Well, it's gettin late on the evenin,
I feel like, feel like blowin my horn.
I woke up this mornin, find my,
My little easy, my little easy gone (easy rider lover).

Minutes seem like hours and
Hours now, oh it seems like days.
Seems like my little woman
Better stop her lowdown ways.

I b'lieve I'll go back to Memphis, boys,
Gonna have some of this here hambone boiled (a phallic pun).
I done laid round Clarksdale and
I'm bout to let my old, my little old hambone spoil.

Yes, I'm goin back to St. Louis,
I'm gonna have my little churnin done (another sexual image).
I can't find no country woman can make my low-down,
My little old butter come.

Well now, bye-bye, babe, I ain't got me
No more to say.
Just like I been tellin you, gal,
You gonna have to need my help some day.

A last chord sounded on the Martin. Muddy looked up with a shy smile. The dark acetate chip was curling quietly at the center of the black disc. There was space for talk in the magic moment just at the end of a performance. I realized I had recorded a masterpiece. I tried to be careful—not to ask leading questions, but simply to get this very shy artist to talk about his songs.

ALAN LOMAX: Tell me, if you can remember, when it was that you made that blues.

MUDDY WATERS (*softly*): I made it about the eight of October in 'thirty-eight.

A.L.: Do you remember where you were, what you were thinking about?

M.W.: Arkansas—I was changing a tire on my car. I had been mistreated by a girl, and it got running in my mind to sing this song. (*Several agonies at once—the Arkansas bottoms, miles from everything, mosquitoes and gnats stinging, hot as hell, squatting in a muddy road, trying to get the car jack to work, and thinking about that special new girl going out with everybody else.*) So I just felt blue and the song fell into my mind and come to me just like that and I started singing. (*So that's how one of the great blues was born, or so Muddy said. I tried again.*)

A.L.: Tell me the story of it, if you don't mind, if it's not too personal. I want to know the facts of how you felt and why you felt that way. (*I wasn't to learn them.*)

M.W.: I just felt blue, and the song fell into my mind and came to me and I started singing.

A.L. (*trying another tack*): What other blues do you remember running to that same tune? *(In fact, there are only a few blues tunes, and many texts sung to each one.)*

M.W.: This song came from the cotton field. My boy put the record out—Robert Johnson. He put out *Walking Blues.*

This was the first time Johnson's name had been mentioned in our interview. I had waited to see whether Muddy would bring him up and the name of Son House as well—whether this younger man would acknowledge his debt to them. But Morganfield had no trouble doing that, for he was confident of his own powers. He brought them up himself. Johnson's song began:

I woke up this mornin,
Feelin round for my shoes.
Told everybody
I've got these old walkin blues (in some versions, *leavin blues*).
Woke up this mornin,
Feeling round, oh, for my shoes.
You know by that
I've got those old walkin blues.

It may be that Muddy took his inspiration from that record—this sort of borrowing is common in the fluid field of blues song making. The Johnson *Walking Blues* has a different first verse than *Country Blues,* shares with it verses 2, 3, and 4, and ends with a couplet about a gal who had Elgin⁹ movements from "her head down to her toes." Johnson's records were then in circulation, so Muddy could have used his *Walking Blues* as a model for his *Country Blues.* In fact, both songs seem to be derived from *Gypsy Blues,* earlier recorded by Son House. Since both men were protégés of House, it is likely that Son House was the source for both. There can be no final answers to such questions, since all good bluesmen are constantly revising even their favorite numbers, adding things from the common stock of the blues, so that no two performances by a country bluesman are ever exactly the same. Conformity and constant performing began to alter this habit when bluesmen came to town and turned professionals, and the needs of bandsmen and recording directors curtailed this freedom.

All three variants of the present song are set to the ABAB, four-line verse form that breaks into eight with interpolations—a Son House signature. There is no question, however, that Muddy's variant is far more cogent, much less a melange of wandering stanzas, and this cogency empowered the new type of sentimental pop-blues form that was to make Muddy Waters' career.

A.L.: Did you know the tune before you heard it on record?

M.W.: Yessir, I learned it from Son House; that's a boy that picks a guitar. I been knowing Son since 'twenty-nine. He was the best. Whenever I heard he was gonna play somewhere, I followed after him and stayed watching him. I learnt how to play with the bottle neck by watching him for about a year. He holp me a lot. Showed me how to tune my guitar in three ways—nachul, Spanish, and cross note.

A.L.: Did you know Robert Johnson?

M.W.: No, I didn't know him personally. I just see him at a distance when he was through here playing.

A.L.: Was House a better player than Johnson is, you think?

M.W. *(chuckling):* I think they both about equal.

A.L.: Did you play every day when you were learning how? How much did you practice?

M.W.: An hour and a half to two hours.

A.L.: Every day?

M.W.: Every day.

Most black folk musicians practice whenever they can—many hours every day. This was true for Leadbelly, who was happiest with a guitar in his hands, true for New Orleans jazzmen. Much of this practice consists of playing a few tunes over and over again, with variations, until they acquire high polish, until the players know them so well they can perform them even while juggling their instruments. Such intensive rehearsal lies back of the effortless improvisations in jazz and the blues. Ambitious Muddy worked hard on his guitar; he hoped it would be his ticket out of the Delta someday.

A.L.: What was the first piece you ever tried to learn?

M.W.: *How Long Blues* by Leroy Carr.

> *How long, how long,*
> *Has that evening train been gone?*

How long, how long,
Baby, how long?

This song, one of the early blues hits by the amazing creator of many early blues hits, had the urbanized quality that Muddy was trying to put into his blues. It was also the theme song of his life—he couldn't wait to get away from the farm to seek his fortune up North. But Muddy was no rambler.

M.W.: When you travelin round, you don't know where you gonna sleep at night. That's a poor show. I was born in Sharkey County in Rolling Fork. My father was a farmer and musician, and we didn't see too much of him. Then my mother died, and my grandmother took me over and brought me hundred miles north to Coahoma County. We settled down way out in the country, where there wasn't another house in sight. My grandmother raised me, along with my uncle. So I've been pretty much brought up on this plantation, lived here for the last nineteen years.

Muddy's black extended family took him in after he lost his immediate parents, so he didn't feel as homeless and orphaned as many of his contemporaries. He grew up in a hardworking, stable home. I believe that shows in his relaxed, rich vocal style, which is so much less tense and agonized than that of Son House or Robert Johnson, and in his later blues, when his vocalizing became mannish and assertive. Still, his Mississippi experience was no bed of roses.

"I started working in the field when I was about ten, for fifty cents a day, maybe seventy-five. Didn have much time for school. Later on I went to St. Louis, but I came back to take care of my grandmother, trying to make something out of farming."

That this hadn't amounted to much became obvious when we filled out the family questionnaire used in our survey of Coahoma music makers. This document paints a stark picture of a sharecropper family in a brown four-room shack in the middle of a cotton field.

Residents in the month of July, 1942, were—
1) McKinley Morganfield, head of family, 29, completed 3rd grade.
2) Sally Anne, his wife, 27, 6th grade.
3) Joe Grant, uncle, 32, no schooling.

4) Ola, grandmother, 64, no schooling.

Non-resident, Adeline Morganfield, 8 years old, outside child.

The family farms 8 acres on shares, owns no work stock, no cattle, 4 hogs, 7 chickens, no fruit trees, a small vegetable garden, and jointly clears between $100 and $300 dollars per year after paying commissary debts. This family tried their fortunes near Blairsville, Arkansas, for one year, then returned to Sherrod's.

All family members belong to the Century Burial Association. The grandmother and wife attend church regularly, M.M. frequently enough to try preaching for a time. His wife and other family members go to dances every Saturday night all over the county. About dancing, M.M. has this to say:

"I don't dance—quit trying. Just wasn't no hand to dance. You be dancin with a girl, and people snatch her and go. So I never did try to learn."

M. M. owns a 1934 V-8 Ford, drives to Clarksdale 3 or 4 times a week "to look around," to nearby Drew and Lula, Mississippi, for the ride, and to Memphis once or twice a year.

M. M. seldom plays the table model, spring wound Victrola (phonograph) he owns. He has the following records: *Black Pony Blues; Kind Lover Blues*, Arthur Crudup. Bluebird B 8896. *Death Valley Blues; If I Get Lucky*, By Arthur Crudup. B 8858. *Sweet Lover Blues*, by Peetie Wheatstraw, Vocalion 3396. *Crawling Kingsnake* by Tony Hollins, Okeh 06351, along with a Bluebird of Sonny Boy Williamson, a Decca Record of Jay McShann; and sermon by Eldert Oscar Saunders on Conqueror.

His favorite instruments are: 1) Guitar, 2) Piano, 3) Harmonica. His first instrument was harmonica. His favorite radio star is Fats Waller. His favorite recording artist is bluesman Walter Davis on the Bluebird label. He likes Negro better than white music, because it has more harmony, especially in the blues line.

His repertory includes

Pop songs: Dinah, I Ain't Got Nobody, The House, St. Louis Blues.

Country and Western pieces: Home on the Range, Deep in the Heart of Texas, Boots and Saddles, Missouri Waltz, Be Honest with Me.

Country blues: County Jail Blues, Thirteen Highway and Angel Blues by Walter Davis, Down South and Sugar Mama and Bluebird Blues by Sonny Boy Williamson; and his own blues Rosalie, Ramblin Kid, Number One Highway, Canary Bird Blues, Country Blues and I Be's Troubled.

The most popular pieces at local dances: Blues, plus some of the following numbers—Corinna, Down by the Riverside, Chattanooga Choo-Choo, Blues in the Night, Darktown Strutters Ball, Red Sails in the Sunset, Bye Bye Blues.

Clearly, Coahoma blues musicians like Muddy Waters were exposed to the pop music of the day and composed with such models in mind. He began early, beating rhythm on buckets, singing all the time. His first childish composition was *I Don't Want No Black Woman Charley-hamming My Bones*. Just what "a black woman charley-hamming his bones" meant to little Mackinley Morganfield, grown-up Muddy Waters was never able to remember or explain. It was a buried childhood memory, which I suspect expressed the incoherent fury of a little boy who had been painfully chastised. After all, he was raised by his grandmother, who almost certainly believed that sparing the rod spoiled the child, and who probably used a hickory switch to "learn" him his notably quiet good manners. Those Deep South grandmothers not only were devoted but were severe disciplinarians. Once, a black friend of mine told me that she took revenge on her grandmother by going way out in the woods and beating on a tree stump, yelling "Take that, you old black bitch, take that!" Both this woman and Muddy Waters grew up to be highly ambitious and successful people, who had been given a sense of self-respect and a drive to achieve by their strong and caring grandmothers.

Nonetheless, Muddy's songs were loaded with his mistrust of women, his dependancy on them, his need to control them. His muleskinning holler was a truly violent fantasy about his faithless lover:

Ummm (he moaned)—*what you want me to do?*
I done give you my money, died for you.
   I was sittin here talkin with this little old woman,
   Beggin for "kitty-tom," Lordy, beggin for "kitty-tom."
I'll take my .32-20 (a pistol) *and lay you in your grave,*
And the day of resurrection you gonna rise again.
   When I was a little lad, at home and be bad,
   My father, he grab me and shuck the bad away.
Everybody keeps on hollerin about old Dangerous Doom.
When I, oohhh, get my .32-20, I'm gonna be dangerous, too.
   I were waiting for my summer change.
   As soon as the wind rise, I'm goin away.

This submerged hostility toward women was to remain the main theme of his blues. The Delta system appears to have disillusioned Muddy more than angered him. In fact, he composed the *Burr Clover Blues* to help his boss (with whom he was on good terms) succeed in a soil-improvement experiment. When we recorded this blues in 1942, Muddy was a devoted member of the Son Simms Four, a string band of the kind Handy had heard in the area earlier. Veteran Son Simms (who had accompanied Charley Patton on some of his early Paramount recordings) played a jazzy fiddle in the lead; Louis Ford seconded on mandolin, with Percy Thomas on second guitar; while Muddy played lead guitar and did most of the singing. Old-timer Son Simms recalled that the earliest blues were *Joe Turner*, about the long-chain man who took prisoners off to the work camps, and *Make Me a Pallet on the Floor*. "That's how these women will do you, when you're off from home," said Simms. "They don't want to get the bed nasty with them and their kid man, so they put some old quilt down on the floor so they can do their business."

Make me down a pallet on yo flo', (3 times)
Now make it so yo man won't never know.

Make me down one bunk up side yo wall,
Make it just as long as I am tall.

I love you, baby, cause you's so nice and brown,
Cause you tailor-made, ain't no hand-me-down.

"And their good man will never know," Louis chimed in. "It's just like that old toast we boys used to say." He raised his glass:

Old Aunt Milly from Salt Lake City,
The way she'd do it was really a pity.
She starts with tectish and ends with gas,
She's got a Cadillac pussy and a Packard ass.

Son rejoined:

Johnson grass and a monkey's ass
Are very sad to see,
But a whiskey flask and a whore's ass
Will be the death of me.

"Enough to give the governor the blues," said Simms, as everybody chuckled. "Now here's you a blues out of the olden times." And with the band trailing along, he sang these traditional stanzas:

Your hair ain't curly and your doggone eyes ain't blue,
If you don't want me, what in the world I want with you?

The fiddle moaned and the mandolin spun silver-blue runs.

Don't a man feel bad, when the good Lord's sun go down,
He ain't got a soul to throw his arms around.

Now looky here, babe, what you want me to do?
I've done all I could, honey, just to get along with you.

We're so familiar with the blues today that we take them for granted. We often forget that the blues is the only song form in English that allows the singer (anyone) to pose problems, raise issues, make complaints, and then provide a cynical or satirical response. Musically speaking, the first phrase of the blues raises a question—it often ends on a high note, leaving the problem unresolved, the question unanswered. The clinching phrase usually descends to a low note, roundly concluding the matter. There are such improvisatory forms in Latin languages—the Spanish *copla*, the Italian *stornello*, the Portuguese *fado*—but there was none in English till the muleskinners and blues singers of the Delta filled this poetic gap, which none of the great poets of the English tradition had done. The blues has the magical property of allowing you to improvise a comment on life. At the same time, its music keeps you "shaking that thing"—a pattern that is patently African.

At our second session Muddy Waters took the opportunity to record more of his own compositions, all deviations from the standard three-phrase couplet in the direction of pop song form—*Rosalie, I'm Bound to Write to You* and *You Gonna Miss Me*, another reproachful blues. He told us, "Men get the blues when their woman quit them. I don't hardly ever have the blues myself. Mostly, I don't have the blues when I play them; I just plays um."

If the river was whiskey
And I was a diving duck,

I would dive to the bottom
And never would come up.
    Ah-hah, you gonna miss me,
    When I'm dead and gone,
    Ah-hah, you gonna miss me,
    When I'm dead and gone.

Within a year I had sent Muddy discs of two of his songs released by the Library of Congress that he could play on his home phonograph and even put on the jukeboxes in Clarksdale. What moments those must have been for him! For the first time he could be certain that he was as good as anybody else on the singing Seabird. Thoughts of becoming a preacher evaporated. He'd never been very religious anyway. He consulted his grandmother and she gave him her blessing. So one rainy day when the fields were knee-deep in mud, he sent word to his boss he was sick and caught the Illinois Central north to Chicago. The words of his favorite blues were coming true:

Well, if I feel tomorrow
Like I feel today,
I'm gonna pack my suitcase
And make my getaway.
I be troubled, I'm all worried in mind,
And I never be satisfied,
And I just can't keep from cryin.

Yeah, I know my little ol baby
She gonna jump and shout.
That ol train be late, girl,
And I come walkin out.
Lord, I'm troubled, I'm all worried in mind,
Yeah, and I never'll be satisfied,
And I just can't keep from cryin.

Yeah, now goodbye, baby,
Got no more to say,
Just like I been tellin you,
You're gonna have to leave my way.
Lord, I'm troubled, I'm all worried now,

Yeah, I never'll be satisfied,
And I just can't keep from cryin.[10]

I didn't see Muddy again for about ten years. By then he was driving a big Cadillac; I was still in a Ford. "Hi, Lo," he grinned, noting our shift of status. Robert Palmer, James Rooney, and other blues historians have told the tale of his extraordinary success in Chicago, how he came to dominate the capital of the blues. I shall leave most of that in their hands and dwell on only one phase of the story. Muddy Waters, like Ellington, became a great band leader. He recruited an all-star combo that played his sound and backed his singing, but, while most black blues bands soon broke up, Muddy, like Ellington, held his band together for years on end, leaving time for his orchestral ideas to ripen. In the maelstrom of the Chicago blues world, such stability is unusual, an achievement due to Muddy's deep-rooted sociability. In African musical tradition leader and chorus constantly alternate, and leadership changes, so that everyone present takes a break. As Muddy himself explained:

When one of my band members goes over big, I really like it. A lot of people ain't like that. They don't want to give their band members a break. Some of them want to sing sometimes. Some of em can't. I let them all try. They feel good behind that, you know. Everybody wants to be a star. So I give em a chance. Just let them please their own mind and they feel more freer working. . . .[11]

They played almost every night in one of the thousands of little bars and clubs where the black working class had its fun. The hours were very long indeed. Muddy remembered: "Mostly we had a late hour license—three and four and five o'clock in the morning. On Saturday night go to about five. Summertime it was daybreak. Go in there in the day and leave in the day—next day."[12] And they had to play hard and loud to get a hearing, because, true to black tradition, everybody present felt free to talk, shout, whoop, holler, laugh, quarrel, dance, fight, maybe all at the same time, but never remain passive and silent. Muddy had to change his style to cope with this problem.

When I went into the clubs, the first thing I wanted was an amplifier. Couldn't nobody hear you with an acoustic. Wherever you've got booze, you're going to get a little fight. You get more of a pure thing out of an acoustic, but you get more noise out of an amplifier.[13]

Thus Muddy began to build the big sound into the blues. He learned to stay tight on mike and make the loudspeakers shout and groan over his crying guitar, with the rhythm guitar pumping the bass in the background.

Soon an amplified harmonica joined him center stage, not moaning softly in the background but pressed against the microphone; it shrilled, howled, and baahed like a musical windstorm. Muddy felt good, because the harmonica had been his first instrument, and he felt better when Little Walter from northern Louisiana joined him—"he knew *what* to put in there—and *when* to put it in there." More important, the addition of the harmonica transformed the blues combo from a country string band into a wind-plus-string orchestra—the main Eurasian orchestral type. This black remake of Western orchestration style gave his music a broader audience appeal.

The records were doing well; the band was working all year round, but Muddy wanted to go after a bigger African-Eurasian sound and a bigger audience. He told James Rooney:

> Another change was the piano. If you get the piano in there you get a whole full bed of background music. . . . I kept that backbeat on the drums plus full action on the guitar and harmonica and the piano in the back, then you've got a big sound. It was in my head. Nobody ever told me about it.[14]

Muddy not only altered his singing style to match this big sound, but the image his blues presented as well. Muddy Waters, the Delta wallflower, the muleskinner complaining that his woman had done him wrong, now took the role of the sharply dressed, supervirile dude, with money in his pocket, with all the women in town on his trail. He shouted and growled out his mannishness in songs like *I've Got My Mojo Working, I'm Ready,* and *I'm Your Hoochie Coochie Man.*[15] These songs made it clear that the black working class had moved up several notches, from "boy" in the Deep South to "I'm a man" in the Middle West. That message rocked the black clubs in the forties, and it was just what British youth, breaking away from parental control, wanted for their rock revolution in the fifties and sixties.

In spite of his newfound prosperity and his world fame, Muddy remained a serious Delta bluesman, deeply attached to the blues aesthetic and steadfast in his loyalty to the blues masters from whom he had learned his art.

> I had it in my mind I wanted to play close round Son House—between Son and Robert. I did Chicago a lot of good. A lot of people here didn't hear Son

or Robert Johnson because they didn't get a chance to. . . . You see, the blues is tone, deep tone with a beat. . . . By itself that sound would never have made it in Chicago. I guess I'm one of the first people who was thinking of that sound, learning on that sound and when I got here I found people could get close to that sound.[16]

Muddy here brings us close to the process out of which jazz and much American music has come—the black adaptation of European instruments to an African-European orchestral style. Of course, there was loss as well as gain here—in this case, the loss of the subtle eloquence of the country blues as the amplifiers roared and the piano shaped the harmonica.

The last time I saw Muddy Waters was during the Poor People's March on Washington in 1968. Thousands of the black poor, many coming in mule-drawn wagons, converged on the Capitol to lobby for a better deal, meanwhile living in a village of tents in the parks adjoining the Washington Memorial. I had been asked to organize culturally relevant entertainment for the encampment, and there ensued a mighty singing of black folk music along the Potomac, where the black delegates rested after their marches on the Capitol and the White House. Muddy Waters, then cresting in popularity, seemed an obvious choice for a program. When I got him on the phone in Chicago, he immediately agreed to come. "Sure we'll help out. We'll just drive on down overnight and get to town the morning of the concert," he told me in his deep grave voice.

When I called the march headquarters on the day of his concert, they had nothing to report about Muddy. On the off chance, I went looking for him at the concert site, at the foot of the Lincoln Memorial, overlooking the Reflecting Pool. There, in the shade, was a big Cadillac, with feet sticking out of some of the windows. Muddy was snoozing at the wheel. He looked up with that sleepy, crooked grin of his. "Hi, Lo," he said and we laughed.

"Yeah, we had a nice ride down. Left old Chi at nine last night and got here in time for breakfast. Went by the headquarters this morning, but those preachers didn't seem to know who we were. So we came on out here to wait for you." The carful of sleepy bluesmen, including Little Walter and Otis Spann, chimed in, "Don't you worry. We'll sleep when we get back to Chicago. Show us where we set up at."

Later that day a host of Muddy's folks gathered to hear him. At the far end of the Reflecting Pool, the icy finger of Washington's monument lifted skyward. Nearby, Lincoln brooded in the shadows of his marble temple. At his feet sat the folks whose ancestors had been bereft by his murder. They had come to present their case to the country—some driving from the Deep South in wagons pulled by mules, some bused in from the slums of Midwestern cities. Underemployed, badly housed, pushed toward despair and crime by poverty, sharing only crumbs from the rich table of America's boom economy, this was the black lobby—the welfare mothers, the street gangs, the jobless. They had been knocking on doors, visiting their congressmen, marching, the young, angry ones wanting to break out, then always falling back on peaceful protest, all pretty much in vain. The Nixon White House had ignored them and their distinguished black leaders. Ahead lay the final mass meetings that their leaders hoped would reach the country's heart and win something for their people back home. Meantime, they were relaxing in the cool of the evening. Muddy, their main man, was standing where Marian Anderson and Reverend King had stood, telling their story the way they felt it.

Well, if I feel tomorrow
Like I feel today,
I'm gonna pack my suitcase
And make my getaway.
I be's troubled, I'm all worried in mind,
And I never be satisfied,
And I just can't keep from cryin.

Back of the poetry that expressed their discontent rose the big sound that Muddy and his friends had been cooking up, the sound of their new wind, strings, and percussion combo. It had many voices: a closer-miked harmonica, wailing and howling in anguish and anger like the wind off Lake Michigan; Muddy's lead guitar, with the bottle neck crying out the blues all up and down the six strings, a rhythm guitar behind, both amplified by big speakers so every crying note, every beat, could be heard a quarter mile away; a drum set, heavy on the back beat, traps, blocks, and cymbals sizzling and cracking in counterrhythms; a big bass fiddle, transformed by Willie Dixon into a tuned zither, slapped and plucked to emit a bass countermelody like a bull about to charge; and swanking it on a grand piano, Otis Spann, filling in all the cracks with surging boogie.

This was America's newest orchestra, rich with unconventional harmonies and polyrhythms, far more African than any jazz band—an orchestra built around singing, highly rhythmic yet subtly supporting and amplifying the vocal part, going back through Son House to the one-stringed diddley bow, to the very roots of African-American music in Mississippi.

The audience, folks from the ghettos of the Midwest and the Deep South, knew this sound. It was theirs. They had danced it into being on a thousand thousand nights in barrooms and at house parties. Now the old Delta music, rechristened rhythm and blues, was on stage in the nation's capital. A roar of applause swept across the Reflecting Pool into Lincoln's marble house. The politicians might not be listening, but soon the whole world would be dancing to this beat and singing these blues.

Chapter 9

▲▲▲▲▲▲▲▲▲▲

Big Bill of the Blues

The story of how and why the blues moved North and established its new capital in Chicago is part of the life history of Big Bill Broonzy, the John Henry of blues singers. As he wrote me:

> My mother and father told me this story   they said in 1892 it came a big flood and they lost every thing they had an had to move to the hilles an in 1893 the started another croop an the had just brout a nuff money on his crop to last untell the 24 of June.
>
>   the had 12 children all ready an he left to go get some moar food he left on the 23 of June an did not get back untell the 28 of June he brought back food a nuff for him an my mother an 12 childern but when he got back my mother hade twins an that wase me an my sister lanie he was looking for one but it wase too
>
>   it wase a old lady by the name lizer thompson she was the midwife for all the women down ther the did not ust a doctor at that time when my father come home ant lizer met him at the door an told him say Frank you done a good job that time he said what do you mean she said i mean yo shot both barel that time yo have got twins a boy an a girl. . . .

So in a letter Big Bill Broonzy, blues singer for a generation of black people begins his life story. So he spelled it out—this folk poet whose melancholy and whose laughter has shouted out of the jukeboxes of saloons and rib joints from Chicago to Miami.

My daddy stood still for a while and then he said, "I just got food for twelve and now I've got fourteen." Then he caught his breath and said to Aunt Lizer, "Okay. Lead me to them."

So she did. And my mother kissed my dad and said, "Ain't you lucky?" And my dad said, "Like hell I'm lucky. I brought enough food for twelve and now it's fourteen," he said, "What can I do now? This is all the food they would let me have on this year's crop."

My mother told my dad, "Don't worry. It will be a long time before they'll want meat and bread. Until then they can live on milk and corn meal gruel."

And my dad still said, "Like hell I'm lucky." . . . And that's the true story of how Big Bill was born. Which is me. The reason I know it's true is because I've heard my daddy tell it so many times. The reason he kept the whole thing on his mind was that this was the first time he had ever cussed in his life, and it was the last. I never heard my daddy cuss in my whole life except when he was telling this story of how me and my twin sister, Laney, was born.

Frank Broonzy—a big Baptist, a deacon in the church—was strict with his children, like most of the other country blacks who sharecropped forty acres of cotton in the Mississippi bottom counties in the 1890s. He didn't permit them to fish or hunt or shoot marbles on Sunday, or sing the devil's songs.

If Big Frank had known that June day in 1883 that his son would grow up to be a "guitar-picking child of the devil," he might have done some sure-enough cussing. To Frank and his fellow Baptists any song not a hymn was the devil's music. Big Bill heard the old folks tell about a boy who sat whistling the blues on the steps of the church house and about an old man who came up to the young blasphemer, shook his finger in his face, and told him, "Boy, you'll be sitting here tomorrow but you won't be whistling." Next day, they found the boy dead there on the church house steps. "Cose I didn't see that," said Big Bill sagely. "That's what papa and them told me."

The Broonzys were black sharecroppers. They ran to size. Frank Broonzy stood six feet two and a half inches tall, carrying two hundred and forty pounds of solid bone and muscle under a light skin. His mother was half white, sired by a white slave owner upon one of his slave girls. Frank's mother raised him in the house to "flunky work," chopping wood and milking the cows and doing around for the white folks, hoping he would escape the harsh labor of a field hand. But Frank married a dark-skinned girl, slim and beautiful. His mother called her "black Nettie," until the couple moved away out of reach of her bitter tongue. They went up the river from Louisiana into Bolivar County, Mississippi—Delta land, where the cotton grew higher than a man's head— Delta land, with the levees still too low to protect the farms from the yearly rises of the river.

"In a rise, we used to move up to the hills until after the water went down," Big Bill recalls. "Most folks lost their household stuff and their hogs, goats, cows and, chickens. And a lot of people lost their lives. . . . You could hear um on top of houses and up in trees—just out there in the dark somewhere— crying and hollering all night long. Sometimes people would start after um and you wouldn't never hear of them again. . . . I remember how we'd wade out for miles and miles. We'd most in ginerally throw chunks of wood in front of us and when they'd whirl round and round, we'd know it was one of them dangerous currents and we'd try another road."

Maybe Frank Broonzy brought his Nettie to Bolivar County because he had heard of Mound Bayou, the only independent black community in the state of Mississippi. In Mound Bayou black men owned big plantations and worked black sharecroppers. Mound Bayou planters built fine houses, put up a railroad station, bricked in some storefronts, sent representatives to the Reconstruction Congress, educated their children abroad in Paris and London. A Mound Bayou black man belonged for decades to the Republican National Committee. Then something—was it hate or pride or prejudice or racial sabotage?—something choked the hope out of this little town. Its boarded-up stores, the big mansions haunted by the quarrels and the murders that have shattered the leading families, the dusty station with its peeling signboard, all wore a bereaved and desolate look, so that you breathed easier after its empty windows were left behind.

But in 1870, when Frank Broonzy came there to try his luck, Mound Bayou was a hopeful place, and he was looking for something better than Louisiana. What he found was the sharecropping system, where you'd go to the commissary and tell how many kids you got—the age and the size—and they'd give you food accordingly. He left twelve kids at home when he went to the commissary for meat and meal. When he got back he found fourteen in the house. He had put himself in debt to bring pork, flour, and salt for twelve Broonzys. Aunt Lizer, the old midwife, cackled at him, "You shot both barrels off that time." His wife, Nettie, patted his hand and smiled tremulously: "Ain't you lucky?" He looked at them both like enemies and, for the first and only time in his life, Big Frank cussed.

There will be little more in this story about Big Frank Broonzy. He worked hard and died easy, resting in Abraham's bosom. This is the story of his twin son, birthed on that painful June day in 1893, a son named Big Bill, who topped his father by three and a half inches; Big Bill, who dropped the plow handles and the Bible, picked up the fiddle and took the devil for his patron; Big Bill, who became a poet for working-class blacks from coast to coast, striding through the jungles of the entertainment rackets as surely as Big Frank had walked the dark woods of Bolivar County.

Unlike most of the bluesmen discussed thus far, Bill was no orphan; he never had to worry about who his daddy was or where his mama was; he graduated from a solid family into a solid country marriage. And he was a working man most of his life. The first tunes he played were for the rowdy jollifications of the Southern backwoods; and notes of country joy sound all the way through Bill's many recordings, even his blues. Nowhere in his recordings does he wail and keen like Son House, Blind Lemon, and Robert Johnson. Yet in his vein he is as fine a blues artist as any of them.

Big Bill encountered all the humiliation and injustice both the South and the North imposed on blacks in that preintegration period. But his spirit was unbroken and his vision of life remained undistorted. Indeed, he struck back against Jim Crow as no other bluesman of that time did, in verse as good as anything Langston Hughes or Sterling Brown ever wrote. His hard-hitting *If You're Black, Get Back* and his ironic *It Was a Dream* are classic American songs of protest. Everyone who knew Big Bill respected him and looked up to him as a wise and dignified man. Indeed, he was wise and he was dignified, even though his songs echo the ironic and the reckless laughter of his burdened people.

Here, then, is Big Bill's story, word for word, as he gave it to me in the 1940s.[1] He spoke in a slow and almost mournful tone, at times stammering and halting as some painful memory was concealed or only partly expressed, or again in the measured style of a truly reflective man, chuckling often over the absurdities of life:

Well, I was born in Mississippi, in the year 18 and 93. I was born on a plantation and I stayed there until I was eight years old. Then my daddy and mother, they brought us—me and my twin sister and about eight more of us—to Arkansas—that was Langdale—Langdale, Arkansas. My daddy had got in touch with a white man there who would give us more food and better supplies. So we moved to Langdale and I was raised there. My daddy started a crop and I holp chop cotton and pick cotton and my daddy said, "You can plow when you're fifteen."

Every night I would bring me some cornstalks home and I'd go out in back of the barn and rub them cornstalks together and make music and the children would dance. That was my cornstalk fiddle. I rubbed it hard when I wanted a loud tone and I rubbed it easy when I wanted to play soft. I used to play *Turkey in the Straw, Joe Turner, Take Me Back Blues*, and *Uncle Bud*.

Uncle Bud, Uncle Bud, he's a man in full,
He walks all around like a Jersey bull.

Uncle Bud's got corn that never been shucked,
Uncle Bud's got gals that never been touched.

And all the children would do jig dances, like *Cuttin the Tobacco, Ballin the Jack*, and *Falling off the Log*.

One time at a country picnic I heard a musician the folks called See-See Rider playing a cigar-box fiddle. That was the only name I ever knew him to have—See-See Rider. All I know, he was old when I knew him and the best musician in that part of the country. He's been dead now thirty-five years.

See-See Rider used to play at the barrelhouses down home. He lived at Reydell, Arkansas, right on the Arkansas River, and he used to play fiddle all through that country for both white and colored. He had him a homemade band—fiddle, guitar, and bass—all made by himself, but he was so well liked, he never had to pay no fare on the train. He got his name from an old blues he was always singing:

See, see, rider, see what you done done,
Made me love you, now your man done come.
    Hey, hey, hey, hey.

I'm sitting down laughin, when I stand up I'm cryin,
I done lose my baby and I believe I will lose my mind.

I hate the day I ever left my home,
Ever since my baby left me, everything is going on wrong.

I was born in Mississippi, my daddy brought me to Arkansas.
What can you do with a woman, when she won't gee or haw?

If your woman want to leave you, you better let her go.
She will get another man and make a pallet on your floor.

Don't never say what a woman can't make you do,
She will say she is taking in clothes, make you hold the
light till she get through.

When you see me comin, heist your windows high,
When you see me leavin, hang your head and cry.
Hey, hey, hey, hey.

I hung around Old Man See-See Rider till I figured out how his guitar and fiddle were made. Then I went to the commissary and they give me a cigar box and a big wooden box, and me and my buddy name Louis made a guitar out of the big box and I made a fiddle out of the cigar box. Then I went to the woods and cut a hickory limb and I stole thread from my mama to make a bow. Way we got strings, me an Louis would go to the picnics and barrelhouses and wait for See-See Rider to break a string. We would tie them broken strings together and put them on our homemade instruments. And when See-See Rider seed I knew how to play, he holp me fix the strings and showed me some few tunes, so Louis and me could play *Shortnin Bread* and *Old Hen Cackle* and *Uncle Bud.*

We had to keep our instruments hid under the house, because our mothers wanted us to be preachers. We would go to church and when we would come back, we would sneak under the house and get our fiddle and guitar and then out into the woods. The other children would follow and we'd have a dance way out where their folks couldn't find us.

One day the old folks had gone to town and all of us kids got in the chicken house. We had killed three of my mother's chickens and the girls were cooking them. The kids were dancing while Louis and me played *The Chicken Reel.* We had things going good, but a white man heard us and walked in on us. We both had got beatings from our mothers about playing, but he just wanted to know what we were playing and we told him See-See Rider said it was a homemade fiddle. He laughed and said, "Well, what's that on the fire?"

I didn't want to tell him, but he said not to be scared because no one gonna bother us and he told us to play some more. We played all three pieces that we knew and he told us, "Bill, you and Louis come with me," and we did. He taken us to his house and carried us out on the sun porch and called his wife and kids and some friends who was visiting his wife from town. Me and Louis was scared to death almost, and he said, "Boys, start playing just like you did in the hen house."

We started playing and I sang and all the white people and the cook and the handy man came in and started dancing and patting their hands. By that time it were dinnertime and he asked the cook what she had for dinner and she told him "baked ham." He said, "These boys like chicken," so she cooked us chicken and plenty of it. When we'd picked them chicken bones bare, he carried us home and lied for us—told our mother and father we had been cleaning up the commissary and paid us two dollars apiece. My mother told him, "You can work um any time." That white man laughed and said, "I will come by and get um again."

It was three or four weeks before we seen him again, but we would practice every time we got a chance. One day he came and got us and told us he had something for us. He sent to Sear and Rowback in Chicago and got us a brand-new fiddle and a guitar. We opened the box and got them out, but we couldn't play them. My homemade fiddle had only one string and the new one had four. He just laughed and told us to come every day and practice. I practiced for a long time till my brother-in-law showed me how to tune the fiddle. He could tune it, but he couldn't play it, and I could play it but not tune it. So they used to pay him to tune and me to play. So I played for those white peoples a long time and I also holp my daddy raise cotton.

That's the way I was raised there at Langdale until I was twelve. Then we left Langdale and went to a place called Scotts Crossing, Arkansas. Now I must tell you about me and my sister Laney, my twin. It used to be we wouldn't eat or go nowhere without each other. We slept together until I was thirteen years old. Fact of the business, we didn't know no difference between girls and boys yonder in the country. Girls in my days would ride calves and hogs and climb trees just like boys, and we would throw a ball as hard at one of them as at a boy. So I didn't know no difference between me and Laney till one day I'll tell you about.

Me and Laney we went down to the pond, crawfishing. We waded around there awhile up to our waists nearly and I noticed some blood on the water. I ask Laney if she was hurt and she told me no, but I thought she might have cut herself on one of those sharp canes down there, so I carried her out on the bank. We couldn't find no place that was cut, but Laney kept on bleeding and

I like to was scared to death. I carried her most of the way home, and when Mama come out and saw, she snatched Laney up and took her in the house and shut the door. Left me standing out there on the porch. And I still didn't know what was the matter.

When I'd start to ask her, Mama'd shush me up. So then they separated us. They knew Laney wouldn't let me go off without raising sand, so my daddy told her he was taking me to the store to get some dewberry pie—we were both crazy about dewberry pie—and he taken me off in his wagon and didn't stop till he got me to my older sister's. That's where Laney's crying come off—when he didn't show back up with me that evening. I stayed gone for eight months and, when I come home, Laney seemed just like one of my other sisters. Today she's five feet eleven inches tall and weighs two hundred and sixty pounds—all solid—to my two hundred and two. She's the mother of fourteen children.

Now I'm going to tell you a tale on my family, to show you what sort of family I come from. It seems like my father, like most men down South and up here, too, had him an outside woman. Maybe he had more than one, but this one in particular my mama heard about. When she did, she took action. She sent me out to harness our two best mules to the buggy, and by the time I got to the front door, there she was, with her old hat jammed over her eyes, and my daddy's shotgun in one hand and a box of shells in the other. She got in the buggy with me driving, and we didn't stop for three hours, till we come to a little crossroads with one country store.

There was an old feller on the front gallery and my mama hollered and ast him where Miss Nettie lived. He tole her it was an old yaller house down the road about three miles. Mama snatched up the reins and the buggy whip, and it looked like that buggy hardly hit the ground before we come to that yaller house, settin up away from the road up on a hill. "You stay here, now Bill," my mama told me, and she walked up the hill toward the house. When she got to within hollerin distance, she called out, "You, Frank Broonzy, come out of there."

I swear it wasn't no more than a couple of minutes till the back door opened and a women with her clothes about half on went runnin away through the garden. My mother leveled down her and shot both barrels, but she must have missed her. Before she could load up again, that women had disappeared in the woods. I reckon that must have been Nettie.

My mama sort of laughed, then she hollered, "You can come on out now, Frank." And pretty soon, my father came out the front door, down the steps, and walked past us and got in the buggy. My ma sat in the front with him and

I sat in the back. Just about the only thing I heard my father say was, "Well, that's the last time." My mama just nodded. Then she put her arms around his neck, so I got to hold the shotgun all the way back home. That's the only trouble my folks ever had that I know of, and that's doin all right when you consider how long it takes to raise fourteen children.

Well, around about then I joined the church, was baptized, and came to be a good member. I was a pretty good songster—people liked it—and so I put away my fiddle and after a while, I started to be a preacher. In fact, I was a preacher for almost four years, after I got to be nineteen years old, but I kept right on working on levee camps and road gangs and I learnt lots of them old hollers.

The hame string's poppin and the collar's cryin,
This time tomorrow I'll be down the line.

Men in the bottom hollerin, "Whoa! Haw! Gee!"
Women in the quarters, hollerin, "Don't you murder me."

I married in 1914. She was seventeen years old and I was twenty-one. Her name was Gertrude. We was church members together and we was always around different places together. I liked her and she liked me, so she said. Fact of business, she proved it because she started a family. We had chicken and cake and ice cream at our wedding. Up to her I hadn't ever known a woman in my life.

Well, I started out on my own place. I was a good Christian, and I didn't run around and I had stopped playing the fiddle. But Christian's one thing and money's another; I had to quit church because they wouldn't pay me no money to preach. One day I was in the field dirting some cotton, a white fellow come along and asked me, said, "I heard you could play the fiddle." I told him, "Yessir, I can play, but," I said, "I have to have some guy play the guitar with me." So he says, "All right, you take this note and get whatsoever instruments you need. And we'll pay you fifty dollars to play for this picnic we're having."

I told him "Yassuh" and I went on to the house and I told Gertrude I would refuse. But Gertrude, she got in after me, and them days, whatsoever she said went with me, so, in spite of my mother and my dad being good Christians and Baptists and not thinking it was right for me to play blues and barn dances, I went through with it anyway. Christian's one thing and money's another. Me and Louis and Jerry Saunders played for that three-day picnic and made the fifty dollars and fourteen dollars in tips to boot.

Me and them boys played around dances for white people all over the country—at fish fries, picnics, and all kinds of big gatherings all down through Arkansas and Mississippi and some parts of Texas. Generally, they'd dance Thursday night, Friday night, and Saturday night. We had different tunes we'd play—for waltzes, *Over the Waves* and *Missouri Waltz*—old ragtime numbers such as *Sally Goodin, On the Road to Texas*, and *Uncle Bud* for fast dances like one-steps and two-steps and the square dances with figgers . . . I lived a pretty good life after I started playing the fiddle. See, they'd pay us fifty dollars apiece for a three-day picnic and then they'd always throw us a little change. Sometimes we'd make fifteen, twenty dollars a night apiece. Up North here they call it tips, but down home we called it—just give, freely give. The money I'd make while I was off playing, my dad taken it and he saved it and bought a plantation for us and a nice home. So from then on we lived pretty good.

Why didn't I play for Negro dances? Well, you see the way the white man is in the South is this. Anything's good, they think it's too good for the Negro, see. Now my uncle had a barber shop, had six chairs in it, but no Negroes could go in there and get no haircut, see. It wasn't the matter my uncle didn't *want* to cut Negroes' hair, because he *like* to cut hair on Negroes. And he had cut Negroes' hair all the time until one white man happened to go in there and find out he was a durn good barber and knowed how to handle clippers and scissors and combs. So therefore they didn't want him to work on Negroes, says, "Well," says, "that Negro's a good barber; he's too good to work on Negroes."

Same thing about me. When I started playing music, white man told me, he says, "You too good to be playing for Negroes." See? "You should be playing for white people." And therefore they wouldn't allow me to play for my own people. Wanted me to play for white people all the time. So that's the way I started playing for whites. They would say, "Now you can play for so-and-so, then for such and such a person—you don't have to play for Negroes." So I never did play for no Negroes until after I got away from around my home and come to Chicago . . . Because, you see, if you play for colored people, why they just pronounce—just consider you as a bum musician down there. The white folks want all the good things for themselves.

The same thing they figure about a real nice-looking colored woman. They think she's too good for a Negro man, make no difference if she *do* want one. The white man'll get salty because she's too good for a Negro, so therefore, that starts a big rumor rolling around amongst them there and they'll hire her as a cook or maid and they'll keep her for themselves. What I would say about it—what they enjoy, they just don't want the Negro to enjoy. That why they kept me playing for *their* dances until I got so that I could get about the world and then I left from down there.

Well, I played music, but I still plowed and raised cotton and corn. One day I was plowing and I looked up and see the white boss coming. When he got up to me he said, "Well, Bill, I'm sorry, but I got to have five men go to be examined today." He called my name and the names of four more and we all taken our teams out from the plows and went up to the store and hitched up the wagon and went to town. This white man said, "Now when you fellows get up there to be examined, let me know what happened and what they do to you and all that." So when we got back and told him, he says, "I'm gonna try to keep you from going because you're good workers. I don't want you to go the army."

So at last one day he came out and told us, "You five fellows, I did all I could to hold you, but you have to go to town today." So we got in town and went around to the courthouse and they walked us down to the railroad station. Train standing there. They lined us up and a friend of mine, name Seburn—he was five from the end of the line, and I was on the tag end—so we were playing around and you know the old saying—"If you're on the tail end of the line, you're a dead dog's tail"—and I didn't want to be a dead dog's tail, so we were kidding around and I pushed Seburn out of his place. And just about that time the man came along, tagging folks, and when he got down to the end of that line, he didn't have no tag for Seburn. Seburn went on back home, see, and I had to go to the army.

They carried us to Camp Robinson in Little Rock and they give us what they call Camp Robinson lemonade [a very strong purgative]—they had a barrel of it there. We drink it and jump the fence. Then they give us shots in the arm and shoulders and asked us what part of the service we want. So I said, "Engineer"—I had learned how to handle engines in the gin or the rice pump, so I was interested—but the only engines I seen in my outfit was some big mules we had.

In about a month they shipped us to Newport News and from there to Brest, France. I didn't know where I was going a bit more than a goat. When I knowed anything, this thing was out in the middle of the ocean—I really didn't know whether it was an ocean or a sea and I didn't know what to think because I never had seen so much water before in my life—the biggest water I had seed was the Mississippi River—and when I looked around we was too devilish far out to see any land anywhere. Some were seasick and some were scared, but there wasn't nothing for me to be scared of. I hadn't never rode a ship that big before and so I just got satisfied at whatsoever was going on.

We got in Brest, France, and then they shipped us out to different places. I don't know the names of all the places where we went, but it was in France. I didn't get to the front. I was in one of those supply companies—those labor battalions—digging up stumps, building barracks, cutting down trees, putting in *good* roads where there never was a road before—we did all the dirty work, as I say.

How did I feel about that? Well, what was there for you to feel? Practically all of us there, that's the same kind of work we was used to doing—the dirty work. And some of the officers say—I've heard um say it in presence of me, when some guy had the nerve to ask um for different jobs—they say, "You have that to do because you don't know anything else." Some of the boys did get good jobs—cooks and what we called flunkies—and the rest of us had the same old hard work we had at home.

See, lots of the officers were Southern. I'm sure of that because you could tell the way they treated the Negro—anyone who would speak up for his rights generally got punished. And what made us salty was the white boys on the other side of the highway could come over to *our* camp and shoot craps with us, but we couldn't go over on *their* side because they had us quarantined. They say they were trying to break up the germs—they didn't want the germs to get over amongst the white soldiers, said the germs was over amongst the colored—that's what they *say*. All I know is one time the white and colored boys got together and the colored found out they was getting different rations and well, those boys raised sand at the mess hall and so they shipped um to the front right away. There were some tough Negroes in that bunch and I heard the lieutenant tell one of them, "We'll see how tough you'll be up there at the front." Well, I saw those boys come back later on and they was all kinds of shapes. So I didn't get about much. I saw plenty of Franch girls and they looked good to me, but I never did get with um like some of the boys did. It was hard to get out.

One thing I did get out of the army—I couldn't read or write and I had to keep worrying the fellows to help me write home. So every day I tried to write something or read something. I practiced reading in the stockroom, looking at the labels on the different cans and boxes. I learnt to spell out c-a-n-d-y and t-o-m-a-t-o—on like that until finally I got so I could write home to my mother. I was twenty-seven years old then.

About singing, well, we sang to our mule sometime, but most it was church songs, because most of the boys were scared to death. Most of us accepted prayer and didn't do much singing. Had more crap games over there than songs. Had to wear gas masks a lot, too, and some places we couldn't even light cigarettes, so I don't remember no special songs outside of the old muleskinning blues.

Git up in the mornin so doggone soon,
Can't see nothin but the stars and moon.

Look all over the whole corral,
Couldn't find a mule with his shoulder well.

Told my captain my feet was cold.
"Goddam your feet, let the wheelers roll."

I didn't know when the war was over, they kept us so busy cleaning up—filling up holes in the highways, sawing up trees that had blowed across the road. Lot of times a little man would get up on a box and call us to listen, but I was salty and I didn't pay no attention. I thought we was just moving again and, man, I hated that moving—walking twenty-five to thirty miles without stopping in mud up to your knees. So I didn't know the war was really over until we were on our way back home, and I guess I didn't believe it till we got back to New York and were on our way to Camp Pike in Little Rock to get discharged.

My people was living way down in Arkansas and so I had to go down there to my family. I had a wife and a kid, you know. So I got off the train at this place—had a nice uniform an everything and I met a white fellow that was knowing me before I went in the army and so he told me, "Listen, boy," he says, "now you been in the army?"

I told him, "Yeah."

He says, "How did you like it?"

I said, "It's okay."

He says, "Well, you ain't in the army now." Says, "And those clothes you got there," says, "you can take um off and get you some overhalls," says, "because there's no nigger gonna walk around here with no Uncle Sam's uniform on, see, up and down *these* streets." Says, "Because you've got to go back to work."

"All right," I told him. I said, "Well, what about-uh-uh if I haven't got any clothes? This is all the clothes I have. I been gone two years," I says, "and I haven't got any clothes and I haven't any money to buy any."

So he said, "We haven't got anything to do with that." Said, "But we'll let you have some overhalls—to work in." Says, "Fur as you a *suit* of clothes, you don't need that noway until you make up for the time you been gone. What you've got to do is to go to work and pay for some of them things that you wore before you left here."

So I told him, I said, "Well, the things that I wore before I left here." I said, "they're all worn out now and gone. My brother wore um out for me," I said. "Fact of business, I *paid* for those things once."

"Well," he says, "you still got a bill up there."

So he give me overhalls to wear to go to work and that's all. They wouldn't let us—wouldn't let me have anything—no clothes, no suit of clothes and shirts and things—nothing but work shirts and work clothes. So that's how it was when I got back to my hometown in Arkansas. I found something else, too. Things were different between me and Gertrude. It look like she didn't sympathize with me no more.

The army takes the life out of a man, in a way. It make a man get to the place where he don't want to take nothing off nobody. That's the way I felt when I come back. I didn't want nobody telling me nothing—*nobody*—you know what I mean. Don't tell me what I've *got* to do! And my wife, before I went in the army, whatsonever she said, went. After I came out, she tried the same thing, telling me I shouldn't do this and I shouldn't do that. Well, I wouldn't stand for that from her and the same thing about the white men I had to work for. They'd try to tell me this and tell me that and I didn't care no more about a white man than I did a black man, see, and whatsoever he try to tell me that I *had* to do, that's where we fell out. So I just left outa there and I haven't lived in the South since, and I don't expect to live there no more if I can help it.

Maybe you don't understand. The main reason I left home was because I couldn't stand eating out of the back trough all the time. In the army I had been used to being considered as a man irregardless. I had got used to being clean all the time—having plenty clean, good clothes and a place to bathe and fix myself up. At home I had been just dumb to the fact. I thought that was the right way to be treated, and when I found out it was the wrong way, I just wouldn't take it no more. That's from being in the army, see. Fact of business, after I found out that there was more of the world than just Arkansas and other people was living in other parts of the world and doing a durn sight better than what I was, which I had thought I had been doing good down there, I said, "What the heck," I says, "down here a man ain't nothing nohow. He never gits to be a man down here. It's always 'Boy' until you git too old, then they call you 'Uncle.' You never be called a man in the South, you know that! Not a Negro. I made up a blues along those lines.

Plowhand have been my name,
Lawd, for forty years or more.
Lawd, I've did all I could
Tryin to take care of my so-and-so.

I ain gon raise no mo cotton,
I declare I ain gon try to raise no mo corn.
Gal, if a mule started to runnin away with the world,
Oh, Lawd, I'm gon let him go ahead on.

I wouldn't tell a mule to get up,
Lawd, if he set down in my lap.
Lawd, I'm through with plowin,
That's what killed my old grandpap.

I done hung up my harness, baby,
Lawd, I done throwed my overalls away.
Lawd, now goodbye, old plow,
Big Bill is goin away to stay.

Every night I'm hollerin
"Whoa, gee, get up" in my sleep.
Lawd, I'm always settin my back,
Ho, Lawd, to keep my little plow from goin too deep.

So I left home one night—it was in January 1920. I went home that evening and my wife was telling me what I should do about money matters, that I should go to the railroad instead of trying to hang around there and farm—I should go to the railroad and get a job like several more of the boys who had been lucky enough to get jobs there when they came back, making good cash money—and here I was working on a plantation, working by the day, farming and cutting logs and doing around—so I should go and work on the railroad, too—and I had tried and I couldn't get the job because I didn't know nothing about a railroad at that time, so I just told her, says, "Okay," I says, "now I'm gonna show you what I'm *gonna* do."

Feel like holl'in, I feel like cryin,
I feel so bad, baby, I just feel like dyin.
  But if I can feel tomorrow,
  Ooooh, like I feel today,
  Lawd, I'm gonna pack my suitcase,
  Babe, I'm gon make my getaway.

Cryin in the mornin, cryin at night,
I cry all the time, baby, cause you just don't treat me right.
  But if I can feel tomorrow . . .

Sittin down and laughin, tears came rollin down.
I'm crazy about a woman, and she done left this town.
  But if I can feel tomorrow . . .

Goodbye, Arkansas, hello, Missouri,
Gal, I'm goin up North, I declare I ain't foolin.
  But if I can feel tomorrow . . .

That night about eleven a freight come through there. I caught that freight and I rode on North just singing the blues.

SWEET HOME, CHICAGO

. . . an I went to Chicago on the 8 day of febeary 1920 and I got acrint with Charlie Jackson Jim Jackson Blind Balke Blind Lemon lonney Johnson Bumblebe slim mo raney idder cox Bessie smith mamie smith tricks smith Ethel Wather leror car Barbcue Bob shorty george georgia tom tamper red clarance williams   i made my first recording in 1926 on the Paramount recording co under mayo williams they gave me the name Big Bill then becos ther was a litl Bill already on record   since that time i have made over 260 songs of my own ritting . . .

In coming to Chicago, Big Bill was not traveling alone. In the years between 1914 and 1920 a half million Southern black rural farm workers decided they "couldn't stand eating out of the back of the trough all the time" and moved North into the big centers of industry where, they had heard, their folks "was doing a durn sight better." In four years, fifty thousand blacks poured into Chicago's South Side. Thus began the flood of emigration from the farms of the South into the ghettos of the cities that continues to this day, transforming millions of rural blacks into city dwellers. They early learned in the slums, and at the incredible tempo of boom-time America, the facts of blizzards, tenement living, restrictive covenants, political corruption, heavy work in industry, and the sharp loneliness of city streets. However, they still were doing better; constant fear and humiliation had disappeared from their lives and decent jobs at reasonable pay were available. In the evening, when the folks went out on the town, such a hilarious, wild, moody, and eccentric sound arose in the gin mills and dance halls on the South Side—such a wailing of clarinets, such a braying of trombones, such a singing of trumpets, such a river of rhythm from pianos, guitars, and drums, such a torrent of passionate songs burst out, that the last barriers of musical propriety were swept away. This floodtide of bittersweet, sexy sound swept the big cities of the Midwest, and soon all America became a land of jazz and the blues, paying tribute to its capital city, Chicago.

King Oliver, King Louis Armstrong, King Jelly Roll Morton, Queen Ma Rainey, Queen Bessie Smith, Queen Ethel Waters—all the royalty of hot jazz were crowned in Chicago. During the twenties and thirties, jazz bands booked out of Chicago to New York, Hollywood, Pittsburgh, Paris, London. The tunes were arranged in Chicago, taking their names and much of their color from its streets and amusement halls. The great record dates were set up there. White disciples (Bix, Benny, Hoagy, Wild Bill, Mezz, and a host of others) were instructed there. It was, in the words of a blues, "sweet home, Chicago," this windy city, and out of it a big wind of hot dance music blew right around the world.

Jazz was entertainment music that expressed the brash confidence of the industrial boom between the wars. The multicultural roots of this essentially Creole music gave it the international savor needed to capture a world audience. Its blue notes reflected the anomie of an increasingly uprooted population. Jazz, which had begun as commercial music in the tenderloin district in New Orleans, became then more commercial, more falsely exuberant, more full of self-conscious showmanship as it was taken up by the smart boys of the music industry. Almost before it had begun to grow, jazz was made respectable, brought under control, and made to serve the purposes of the amusement industry rather than to express the anger, the anxiety, and the aspirations of the blacks who had created it. Nonetheless, the blues still pervaded jazz, albeit in subtle and hidden fashions—in hot tone color, in the hundreds of breaks and riffs that are at the basis of jazz improvisation. When a band gets hot, the trumpets are bound to sing, "I got the blues, but I'm too damn mean to cry." Indeed, the blue feeling attracted a very blue and lonely twentieth century to jazz.

However, the blues of the professional jazzman are never quite the real thing. To many New Orleans musicians the blues were "the music of the inferior longshoremen along the river," perhaps acceptable as a rich theme for improvisation. As they turned professional entertainers, the jazzmen lost contact with the mass of blacks who worked in stockyards, steel mills, and cotton fields and lived in slums; the successful men found a stable family life, at the time when most Southern blacks were experiencing the dissolution of the old rural family life. A glance at the lyrics of the so-called blues composed by jazzmen shows one immediately that these musicians never had the blues in the sense that Big Bill and his friends knew them.

I love my coffee,
I love my tea,
But the doggone sugar blues
Soured on me.

But the sharecroppers turned steelworkers and the washerwomen turned mill hands in Chicago still wanted the real blues. They also needed new lyrics to illuminate their new experiences in clear and ironic language, set to the simple melodies that reminded them of home and might be sung or played by almost anyone. So the blues came to town on their own, unobtrusively and unannounced, riding the Illinois Central freight from Memphis. Singers like Big Bill hustled into Chicago from all over the Deep South and played the crowded ghettos of the South Side. The industrial centers of the whole Midwest received a tide of black Southern laborers and their home-grown entertainers. They played at house-rent parties. Their "skiffle" music ran on into the morning or until the cops raided the flat. Their big country voices, accustomed to reaching out across a mile of cotton field or levee, rang out over the drunken confusion of the barrelhouses and jukes and nickel-a-drink dance halls. Hundreds of these singers, of every degree of professionalism, in every town with a Negro population, rhymed out thousands of blues couplets every year, and several sensitive editors have woven this popular verse into big books that portray the story of a people on a painful, blood-spattered march toward a new life.

The most professional and productive of these blues composers moved in and out of Chicago or else lived in the town. Tampa Red came from Florida. Blind Lemon came from Dallas. Jim Jackson came from Memphis. Lonnie Johnson came from New Orleans. Blind Blake came from Pittsburgh. Memphis Minnie came from Mississippi. Leroy Carr came from Mississippi. Furry Lewis came from Arkansas. In fact, the vast majority originated in the Mississippi Delta. They gathered in Chicago because there were paying jobs for them in taverns and dance halls, and also, for the first time, they could put their songs on record.

At first Columbia, Victor, and Brunswick, devoted to improving the public taste with Italian opera and the tunes of Broadway, turned up their noses at this alley music. Then Paramount Recording Company, a branch of the Wisconsin Furniture Corporation, began to record black jazz and blues and spirituals. Every black, North and South, who had the money bought a phonograph. Every young buck, courting his girl on Saturday night, brought along the latest Paramount hit instead of a box of candy. Paramount at first had no distribution system; it didn't need one. Pullman porters, running out of Chicago, bought stacks of records for a dollar a copy and sold them at bootleg prices on runs from Texas to Florida. For the first time, the rural black could hear his own voice singing in accent, language, and melody that were native to him about his own special concerns and problems.

When sales of these early records skyrocketed, the big companies hastened to engage the best singers and put smaller diskeries like Paramount out of the running. The shamefully titled "race" record business sprang up, whose managers swindled and cheated the musicians. They made vulgar demands on the naive and wonderful black artists who wandered into their studios, demands that cheapened the music. In August Wilson's play *Ma Rainey's Black Bottom*, one such recording session is portrayed in memorably bitter and tragic terms.

Recording directors with one hand pocketed royalties that belonged to the singers; with the other they held out a pen, which the illiterate and often blind musicians touched with a trembling hand, thereby assigning copyrights of their songs to these musical gangsters. In spite of the poor taste and the cultural depravity of these entrepreneurs, the masters of the blues managed to set down on records the most powerful songs of this or perhaps any other generation in America. While snobbish boards of directors kept the microphones of European record companies closed to the musical hoipolloi, American recording companies, out to make a buck, waxed music and musicians who broke every rule in the book of musical respectability. Thus the birth of the blues was recorded as it was happening, and so memorably that perhaps the genre can never be killed.

This was the world Big Bill Broonzy stumbled into in February 1920, hoboing out of Arkansas to Chicago on the Illinois Central Line. It is in this world that Big Bill, still a slum dweller, still singing every night for stockyard and steel-mill laborers, became a giant figure:

I landed in Chicago February 2, 1920, hoboing on a freight train. I had a brother up there and he knowed a friend and he called him up that night. He asked me, "You wanta go to work?" I told him, "Yeah." So in about four days I got a job at the America Car Foundry and I worked there for about two years. Then I worked at the Phoenix Foundry and at the American Brake Shoe, first as a molder's helper, then as a molder—steam all around me, hot iron falling, but I liked it because I got more money than I ever had before—thirty-five to forty a week as a helper, then fifty to fifty-five as a molder.

I'm a steel-driving man from that steel-driving land,
I have a mind to carry out John Henry's plans.

I got a ten-pound hammer, they all like to hear it ring,
It rings just like them barrelhouse women sing.

I ain't John Henry, I am just John Henry's friend,
Where he left off at, that's where I just began.

When I start driving, women come from miles around,
They love to see me drive that steel on down.

Of course, there was no union. The whites, doing the same work, got more than the Negroes. At first I didn't pay that any attention. I still was just a Southern man in my ways. But after I had my second job and got to be molder and to know what I was doing around there, I heard the boys say, "Man, if you're white, you're *all right*!" From hearing that, I made my blues about

Me an a white man working side by side,
This is what it meant,

He was getting a dollar an hour,
I was getting fifty cents.
  If you white, you all right,
  If you brown, stick around,
  But if you black, oh buddy!
  Get back, get back, get back.

Then I got me a job with the Pullman Company, cleaning cars and cleaning up the yards, stuff like that around, and I got to be good enough to be a Pullman porter. I made about five or six runs and then I had started playing music around and making money out of that, so I quit. See, I was acquainted with Frank Braswell on the job. I told him about my fiddle and he got to telling me about what you could do with a guitar and he introduced me to John Thomas, Charlie Jackson, Ed Strickland, Kid Music, and a lot more. I bought me a guitar for a dollar and a half, and me and John Thomas played around with it for about a year. Charlie Jackson—he had the first big blues hit with *I'm Gonna Move to Kansas City.*

It takes a rockin chair to rock, rubber ball to roll,
A brownskin woman to satisfy my soul.
  I'm gonna move to Kansas City,
  Baby, where they don't low you.

Charlie taught me how to make my music correspond to my singing. At last me and John Thomas was talking one day and he say, "Let's go down and make some records." I said, "Who you gonna see?" He say, "We going down to see Ink Williams."

There was a gang of guys sitting around the office there and I played a couple of pieces. Mister Williams, he told me to go back home and rehearse some more, because I wasn't good enough. I turn around to go and a guy ask me my name. I told him and say, "I don't know *you.*" Then everybody laughed and told me it was Blind Blake. I like to fell out. Blake was the best guitar picker on records. Well, he took my guitar—my little dollar and a half guitar that I had at the time—and he set down and began to show me what a guitar could do. He made it sound like every instrument in the band— saxophone, trombone, clarinets, bass fiddles, pianos—everything. I never had seed then and I haven't to this day yet seed no one that could take his natural fingers and pick as much guitar as Blind Blake. He could make a guitar just speak the blues! Of course, Lonnie Johnson is good, but I don't give him so much credick because he plays with a pick. Blind Blake played with his natural fingers.

Blind Blake could shake hands with a woman and tell her what color she was, whether she was light-skin or dark-skin or real dark. He could hear you talk and, he may never see you no more in maybe six months, but the minute you say "Hello, Blake," he'd know. He could get about all over the world by himself, and he was a jolly fellow, the jolliest fellow you ever seed in your life to be a blind man—always out on some party, pitching a booger-rooger, drinking a barrel of whiskey, and having a ball. In fact, I reckon that's what kilt him in the end. They say he was coming home real late one night in one of these sure-enough Chicago blizzards and he must have slipped down or something and, by him being so fat, he couldn't get up and he froze to death before anybody found him. That's how they say he died.

Anyhow, Blake played so much guitar that I started to put the whole mess down and forget it. Yet unstill I went on back and John Thomas showed me some more chords and we rehearsed and rehearsed around there about a year. So Mister Williams told us to come on down again—that was in '26—and he said, "Okay, you play all right now. I'll let you make a record." So we did—me and John Thomas stuck our head in the big horn they used then and sung *The Big Bill Blues*.

> *Some folks say the Big Bill Blues ain't bad,*
> *Must not have been the Big Bill Blues I had.*

And we made the *House Rent Stomp* about these little parties people give to take up money for their rent, selling white lightning, chittlin's, pig's feet, and stuff like that. We made two more—*Tadpole Blues* and *Tear It on Down*—but Williams said I didn't play *Tear It on Down* good enough, so he gave that number to Barbecue Bob to record.

I never got a penny out of any of them records, as I know anything about. I heard the record sold good, too. We was supposed to get a hundred and fifty dollars, but Williams told me that John Thomas got the money in front by telling some kind of tale that he had to go off and bury his father or something. Then they told me I broke the microphone patting my foot and singing and they had to take out of our money for that. So I told um it was all right, but I didn't record no more until '28 when I met Lester Melrose and I started recording under him. Then I went to Champion, back over to Piermont, and then to a gang of different companies—Banner, Perfect, Gennett, Black Pattie, Vocalion, Victor, and all them different things. Then around '31 I come to New York and made a whole lot of records in '31 and '32—*Milk Cow, Truckin Little Woman, Louise, Just a Dream*—so many I can't remember them all, blues to fit every subject.

I haven't seen my milk cow three long weeks today,
I haven't had no sweet milk since my milk cow strolled away.

If you see my milk cow, tell her to hurry home,
I ain't had no sweet milk since she's been gone . . .

See that woman comin down the road,
Jumpin and jerkin, like a Model T Ford,
        She's a truckin little woman, don't you know! (3 times)
        She's a truckin little woman, here from Tennessee.

That little gal that I'm singing about
Is strictly tailor-made and it ain't no doubt,
Built up round right from the ground,
She can look up as long as you can look down.
        She's a truckin little woman, don't you know! . . .

I didn't get no royalties, because I didn't know nothing about trying to demand for no money, see. Sometimes they would tell me that a number of mine didn't sell so good. I'd say that, well, I was hearing folks play my records around where I lived, but they'd just tell me that they just put them records out around where I was so I could enjoy listening to them, but that my records didn't go other places. And just whatsonever they said went, see? I'm principled up like this. I really don't want to have no connections with a man that I got to fight him and raise sand to try to get anything out of him for what I've done. Until I started running in this music business, I had never lived around no people that would kill they own brother, like, for a lousy dollar, or would rob they own family for a few nickels. I'd always been around people that they making a little something, they'll give you something, too. So, well, these guys would give me just enough to sort of live on and, by me being the way I am, I just let it go.

I made more playing in taverns and nightclubs than I ever did out of records. Little I made out of um, I couldn't have bought a car, let alone a house for my mama, like I did in 1939. But you ain't gonna make enough out of playing in no club to buy stuff like that; you eat and live it all up. The jobs don't run thick enough. What I'd do was get me a job in some foundry or something and work. Sometimes I worked on levee camps and then I helped lay steel from Texarkana into St. Louis on the Missouri Pacific. That way I could always send my mother five dollars or two dollars a week and my wife and I could scratch along with about ten dollars every week. But I never made no whole lot from my records.

Sometimes I think I never will record no more. See, I never got a royalty till 1939 and '40, the year I made *Just a Dream* and *Done Got Wise*. And when I add it up, maybe altogether I drew $2,000 from all my two hundred sixty numbers. Those guys ain't never told me *just* how many records they sold, and if they do, how do I know they giving me the straight of it? I just can't figger that out. I can't understand it. If a man want me to sing and play and he like what I do, he should be glad to pay me something for it—not that I have to jump on him or cause trouble between us for me to collect a lousy dime—he getting his and I just go to hell! If I'm the cause of his getting something, why don't he give me some? But a lousy guy that lets you work your head off and then gets on easy street and leaves you still where you were. I don't understand people like that. It's just outrageous to me.

In fact, these recording directors were just as villainous as Big Bill says they were. I interviewed a number of them at the time, and they bragged about how they had cheated the black country bumpkins who recorded for them. Moreover, they were men of vulgar tastes, interested only in the bottom line—in sales. They had a crude sense of which songs and which types of music had sold well, and they insisted on having more of the same. Thus scores of recordings were made in slavish and uncreative imitation of others. Called "covering," this practice is now general in the record industry, and results in the public being battered from every side with the same songs, week after week and month after tedious month, while creativity waits in the wings.

The "race" record "producers" had also perceived that the blues were improvised and often consisted of extravagant fantasy and language. They encouraged their singers to produce cheap "novelty" blues, the sillier the better. *The Dentist Chair Blues, The Fire Detective Blues, The Broadway Street Woman Blues, The Oil Well Blues, The Western Union Blues, The Gold Tooth Papa Blues, The Tootie Blues, The Bakershop Blues,* and literally thousands of other titles flooded, then jammed, the narrow marketplace, drowning the poignant and often profound poesy of the earlier country blues in oceans of superficial swill. This remarkable folk style was also trivialized musically, simply to get product onto the market. Recording sessions were got through as quickly as possible, essentially because the recording directors had no respect for the music and the artists they were recording. The musicians, who in the evenings set private parties afire with their inventions, were simply "going through the motions" in the commercial recording studios. It is to the credit of the players and their tradition that some of the beauty still shines through. But the main result was that commercial catalogues filled up with miles of trash, routinely performed, and the public gradually lost interest.

In 1939 I systematically played my way through the Columbia, Victor, and Paramount catalogues, and found the material could not compare to the music we were then recording in the rural South, both without funds to pay singers and with a dinky little disc recorder. There were many gems among the dross, of course, because the companies were documenting, though in a halfhearted and half-baked way, a period of intense creativity by highly original musicians. Yet most of the material, which blues fans now so revere, struck me at the time as the product of a wasted opportunity. What might have been done by record producers and companies who cared about these artists, understood their traditions, and wanted to help them! In the end, there is something wrong-headed about selling dreams—and songs are, after all, dreaming out loud. In the case of the blues, the balance sheet and the Hit Parade had been substituted for the age-old human process of the community voting on songs as they were being sung and created. This was the process that gave rise to the epic beauty of the early blues, but could only distantly support the bluesman, getting his "numbers" ready for a record session, such as we saw depicted in *Ma Rainey's Black Bottom.*

Big Bill went on: "See, all these numbers I recorded, practically, were mine. Maybe ten or twelve were other guys' numbers, but the rest I wrote. Now back in those days some of these guys were better musicians than I was—fact of the business I'm not so good now—so these record people took lots of my numbers and give um to other guys to make, instead of me. The Yas Yas Girl made *Want to Woogy*, Lil Green made *Country Boy Blues*. Arthur Crudup recorded a number of mine called *Rock Me, Baby* under the name of *Rocking Chair Baby*. And I could tell you a gang more things like that. Those musicians never paid me and I never asked um to. What's the use of my sueing? For what? What I would get is a lawyer that would turn right around and do me in all over again—get him four or five hundred dollars from the other side and leave *me* in the hole. And, I don't know, I don't want to lose my friendship with a man over a dollar. If one of those boys makes one of my numbers and can get something out of it, I hope him good luck. That's just the way I was raised. I like a friend better than a lousy dollar any day of the week. I never made no big sum in my life, but I always lived pretty good and had something stowed away, and lot's of these guys haven't had that same luck."

It may seem strange to many that Big Bill should have expressed no more active resentment against the inequities of a world that brought him such puny rewards for his songs. Truly, he was of a naturally calm and philosophical turn of mind. Undoubtedly, he thought often how much better off he was than those he left behind him in the South. He always had a job—from 1920 to 1925 for the Pullman Company; from 1925 to 1927 as a grocery boy; from 1927 to 1934 as a molder in a foundry; from 1934 to 1936 on WPA; from 1938 to 1943 in the Merchandise Mart. With a regular salary, supplemented by income from his club dates and his records, he lived better than most blacks on the South Side, especially those newcomers from the South who came to Chicago without education or skills to help them.

Yet Bill had more in mind than this. He knew he was lucky to be alive. He was thinking of how many of his good buddies—blues blowers, boogie pianists, and guitar pickers—had lived by violence and died by violence. Singing in the dance halls and gin mills where the desperate and the reckless children of the devil come to have their fling, the makers of the blues rub shoulders with violence every night they work. With raw whiskey going down, raw passions rise to the surface. Women are making a play for new men. Men are out looking for a new girl or a fight to work off steam and liven up a Saturday night. And, although some of the masters of the blues like Tampa Red stay on one side next the piano and smile blandly while life roars by on the dance floor, many of the great blues blowers have been such men as to outdrink, outfight, and outlove their audiences. Instead of sitting quietly at the center of the whirling dance of reckless, angry folk, such men spun at the vortex. So like the good, the princes of the blues often died young.

Bill's size kept him out of trouble. He lived up to his name. Bill was big—way over six feet, with a six-foot wing spread and great hands, feet, and head. When there was trouble in a bar where he was playing, he had only to rise from his chair on the bandstand and look around, and things would quiet down. I've seen that. He was clearly not a man to be toyed with. But even so, Big Bill knew he was lucky to be alive. He thought of his half brother,

Washboard Sam—"easy to get insulted, just crabby that way, who stays in jail more than he does out." He remembered Peetie Wheatstraw, another Devil's Son-in-Law, making his last record about "an old hearse coming rolling," then dying that same night in a collision on the highway between Chicago and Detroit. He remembered Blind Boy Fuller, who slowed down the fast pace of his life a little too late and died of heart failure at thirty-four. He thought of Leadbelly and of the scar that circled his neck from ear to ear and of the times Huddie had to kill to keep from being killed. He recalled how some woman slipped poison into Blind Lemon Jefferson's coffee when this great old pioneer of the blues at last had begun to live well and grow fat from prosperity. He remembers how Robert Johnson, the best poet of the blues after Blind Lemon, died, like his Texas master, of poison from the hand of a dark girl down in Bogalusa, Louisiana. And then he thinks of how it went for Sonny Boy Williamson—the ruff of wild hair sticking up under his black ten-gallon hat, the wild, addled laughter bursting out through the reeds of his harmonica, and then dead, an ice pick in his temple, lying in his own blood on the pavement with his sweet grin twisted into pain. Big Bill, whose size and cool judgment have kept him out of trouble, knew that he was lucky to be alive. Moreover, they had taken some of the Delta out of Bill:

I'll tell you how I wanted to be. After I got out the army. I wanted to be presentable and be around in public places and get along with people, not be out there trying to kill one another and things like that. Being in the army opened my eyes and let me know that people could be human beings, not be beasts and kill one another and fight just because you's out there and one guy has got one woman and every man wants that same one woman and everybody want to kill one another about her. The woman wants the man, let her have him, that's all there is about it.

You take down at my home—if a Negro woman is nice-looking and she wants a Negro man for her husband, but the white man want her, for her and her family to get along all right and be satisfied down there and keep whatsonever they got, this Negro that has got this woman got to give her up. Then you take the Negro man—he wants a Negro woman and the other Negro's got her, so he says, "I'm gonna take this woman away from this man," and so they get together and somebody gets killed . . . Well, all of that's unnecessary stuff. If the Negro woman wants the white man, to my idea, whatsonever man she wants, if it's a Japanese, German, Greek, or Polish, or whatsonever he is—let it go.

I've been like this. I'm very slow about women. Course, I've gone out on parties with women and played and laughed with them, but I never just been out with and got to bed with this woman and that woman. I never did live that way, because I always had my own woman and carried her around with me. I did that when I was a young man and now that I'm an old man I still do that. Well, I did monkey around with a couple of girls before I went to the army because I thought that was something you had to do, but after I was in the army and never had a chance to get at no women and I got along so well and weighed two twelve when I come out, I figured it was just nonsense to run around.

I ain't got no clothes,
I'm here all alone.
All the clothes I've got, boys,
I've got them on.
    Just old ramblin Bill,
    Just old ramblin Bill,
    Someday I might get married
    And I might settle down.

I'm just like a piano player,
Carry nothin but my hat.
I plays women where I find um,
And I leaves um where I plays um at.
    Just old ramblin Bill . . .

Course, I've seed a lot of women I'd like to get ahold of as far as that's concerned, but as for me running up to a nice-looking woman and go to meddling, I never did that in my life. I'm fifty-three years old now, and I never did whistle at a strange woman in my life, and you won't never see me standing on a corner hollering at a woman I don't know—I never did that in my life. And, fact of the business, I never had to bother another man's woman in my life, because when I get rid of one woman, I got another one in sight. That's the way to stay out of trouble. I been in this life, playing around nightclubs and barrelhouses and honky-tonks since 1935. Even before that I played all through the South amongst the white folks and at these, what they call, double picnics with the Negroes dancing on this side and the white people on that side; but I never had no trouble because I always had my own woman, see, and, fact of the business, maybe she was sneaking out. So long as I didn't see it too plain, it wasn't nothing for me to squawk about. So long as I got service, what the heck, I didn't give a darn where she went.

I got a letter,
It come to me by mail.
My baby said she was coming home,
And I hope that she don't fail.
　　I feel so good,
　　And I hope I always will.
　　I feel like a jack with a jenny
　　Over behind a hill.
　　I feel so good,
　　I feel like balling the jack.

I'm going down to the station
Just to meet the train.
You know, I can't miss seeing my baby
When I got dead aim.
　　I feel so good . . .

I love my tea,
I love my Gordon gin.
When I get high, boys,
I feel like floatin round in the wind.
　　I feel so good . . .

That way I never did run into no trouble in my life, never had but one fight in my life and that was when I was young and foolish. I'll tell you how that come about. See, I was the kind of a boy that I was crazy about my mother. I always figgered my old man could take care of himself, but anything anybody did to my mother, why they got on me when they did that. Well, my mother always had a gang of chickens and ducks and guineas and different stuff like that around the place, and so one morning she called me and she says, "Bill, get up," she says, "I'm missing two chickens."

I says, "Well, Mama, how do you know you missed two chickens? Did you count um?"

She says, "Now, son, you know I know my own chickens. I know when one is out—when I call um and they don't show up." Now, see, I was always the kind of a fellow I want to get the right point of a thing before I get in an argument or anything like that so I say, "Well, now," I says, "which one is gone?"

She say, "It's two of my Domineckers that's gone."

"Well, Mama," I says, "where do you think they've gone? You think Frank or Dave or Lije stole um and cooked um?"

"Naw," she says, "because I *give* David and Lije two and Frank one." See, they was my married brothers and they would steal chickens from my mother just as quick as anybody else.

"Well," I told her, "you go to *they* house and you gonna find your chickens." So she lit out and, in going by this guy's house, we call him Lucky, she found chicken feathers and she knowed them feathers and they started arguing about it and he told my mother she was a damn liar. When she come back and told me that, I went down there intentionally to kill him. I was seventeen years old then. I stole my daddy's Winchester and went on down there and waited for him. When Lucky come up and I asked him did he steal my mother's chickens and why he didn't make some kind of excuse and tell her he'd pay her or something, he says, "I didn't take your mother's chickens."

I said, "Did you call my mother a damn liar?"

He said, "I don't know whether I did or not." So I up with my Winchester and made four shots at him and missed him each time. While I was shooting, he was running, and he got away, and that was all right. I never did see him no more until after I come up to Chicago and he said, yes, he had stole her chickens, and I told him then that all I wanted him to do was to go apologize, and when he didn't, that started the hell. Then me and Lucky laughed over it. Well, that was the only time I ever had a fight with a man. I never had no ups and downs no more. There's no need of that nohow. People can live without that, at least I can.

Now let me tell you about how I make my blues. Soon as something jump up in my mind, I put it right down. You got to put down that verse that comes to you just when it comes to you and let that take effeck on you first, then the others will come with the feeling. Me, I got to get my feeling to sing a blues. I've heard so much blues sung with words that didn't seem to mean so much, yet unstill they would bring the folks right up out they chairs. It's the feeling in um. You got to have that feeling and you got to let it control your singing. Blues can't be wrote down to do much good, because I don't care how much you write one down, they ain't no blues singer in the world that can sing one three times the same way. He bound to change his blues around if he feeling it. And I tell you another thing—a good blues man don't play so much when he singing, because when you're moving them fingers too devilish fast, it takes away from your voice. The feeling all goes into your fingers.

Big Bill fell silent, his eyes veiled in brooding. He was far away from the furnished room, which was his home after all these years of rambling. The light of the unshaded ceiling light showed harsh poverty—a sagging double bed, two straight chairs, a cardboard wardrobe, and a trunk in the corner. Bill was lonely, and he felt old. His wife, he had said, quietly, "she *been* gone."

All his life Big Bill had been learning to live without his heart's desires. His severe Baptist family had cooled his heart to love. The army had taken the joy for him out of the feckless and carefree existence of an Arkansas black entertainer. His Southern white boss had stripped him of his uniform and his pleasure in rural life. His recording managers had substituted bitterness for satisfaction in his role as a leading racial singer. His life in the ghetto jungles of Chicago and Harlem, where poverty breeds noisy confusion, vice, and crime and threatens every human relationship, had undermined his faith in people.

Yet in spite of this crippling experience, Big Bill was basically untouched, still merry-hearted, strong, and dignified. Everyone felt that. I saw this country-raised, Southern-bred barrelhouse singer walk out of a party where a drunken black salesman had used the term "nigger." Stung by Bill's quiet contempt, the man had furiously cursed Bill for minutes. When he had run out of epithets and wind, one of the younger men turned upon him—"Fellow, Big Bill was right and you were in the wrong. See, Bill, he studies about things."

As if in reply to a question, Big Bill said to me, "You can't put no feelings down on paper." The remark seemed to be aimed at me. I put up my notebook and pencil. "Naw, naw, that's not what I'm referring to," Bill reassured me. "I'm talking about the blues. What I mean is you can't put down the music in the blues on no paper!"

Big Bill was talking about the problems of a country musician, who plays by ear, when he encounters city music, with its rigid rules and its dependence on written notes. Much of the charm and the excitement of the early blues records depended upon the free way in which the instruments improvised on the blues as they were unfolded by the singer—the piano indulging in a ripple of treble chuckles at some ironic phrase, the guitar repeating the crying tones of the singer, "talking" the words on pulled treble strings, the bass stomping its big feet in frenzied approval of an apt "punch line." But now, Bill was telling me, this happy day of ad lib recordings was gone.

"You know what they tells me now?" said Bill. "These young boys playing this here bebop? They tells me the blues is old-fogeyism. They done give it all up. It don't rate no more in these modernest times. And they mean it! Don't you try comin in one of these joints on the South Side and singin one of these down-home Arkansas blues. Man, they'll beat you to death."

Giving up "old-fogeyism" meant singing and playing in tune with the piano, that is, shifting over from the traditional scales of the Delta, which fitted black communication style, into the neutral and unfamiliar diatonic scale developed over the centuries in European fine-art music. The Delta scale and its intervals, which were at times flatter or sharper than those of the piano, underlay the accustomed Delta modes of expressing anguish, desire, bitterness, amusement, and a host of other emotions, habitually employed by African-American folksingers. Big Bill makes clear what a violent and sudden loss this was for native Delta bluesmen. They also had to accompany their songs in a new way.

Formerly, they had sought for instrumental devices that enhanced the unconventional tonalities of their new-fangled sung poetry. Under the "educated" dispensation they had to change that approach and follow the rules of conventional harmony, playing the chord sequences that grew out of the harmonies rather than out of their unconventional vocalization. Thus, like other pop singers, they became subject to the orchestra, and so more like one another. When amplified and electronic instruments took the stage, a further depersonalization ensued. The resonances and overtones of these louder instruments came to dominate all performances, and singers began to give up both their individual and their regional styles. The incredible variety of the twenties and thirties gradually gave way to a virtuosic, electronic sameness that came to afflict the blues of the city.

Big Bill worked out a compromise tonal approach and used it in recording commercial songs he devised. But he felt this style was far less satisfisfying than what he had grown up with. He recalled that earlier, rural style in the hollers and work songs he recorded for me.[2] It was rich with emotional nuance, one aspect of the contribution that American blacks have made to the expressive potential of American sung English. But they have been damned for their pains, and wherever the half-educated arrangers and adapters of black music assumed control, this same impoverishment has taken place. It has gone so far now that listening to a very talented black soul or rock singer is more like hearing a concert artist who feels free to swing rather than a carrier of the genuine and much richer African-American tradition that Big Bill grew up with. *Molto peccato!*

Bill couldn't help laughing as he told about the absurd difficulties he encountered in arranging a recording session. "Take the blues now—how'm I gonna know in advance what I'm gonna play? I won't know till I done done it. But nowadays you walk in a studio without no music for the different instruments and they tell you they don't know what to play—they will say that and yet those same guys wouldn't have been eating around here a few years ago if they couldn't play the blues by ear. I been knowing them all for years. Pete Johnson, Albert Ammons, Count Basie—all of um—they wasn't nothin but barrelhouse blues players a few years ago, playin all night with nothin in the world in front of um but a big drink of whiskey. Now *they* tell *me* they can't play blues if it ain't wrote down.

"It's all just a racket. First I got to pay a guy to take down what I'm playin on guitar. He fool around three or four hours on a piano and make himself maybe ten or twenty dollars. See, *he* say I don't play correctly chords, and he has to change um. Then I got to call in another racketeer to make parts for the different instruments in the combo. Then comes rehearsal. I got to pay for that, too.

"All them musicians come in the studio. Got they dark glasses on. Some of um wearin their little bebop goatees. The piano player set up the music. Maybe he can really read, maybe. But them other guys can't read notes no more than I can. They just see the chord changes in the letters. So over come the trumpet man. He poke his head way out his coat collar and take a long look at the music. A good long look. Probably so hung over he can't even read the title. Then he go back and sit down and play whatever come easiest to him like he been doin all his life.

"And I got to change my stuff to suit *them*. If I get really in the blues, they can't play with me and it ain't no band in the world *can*. They holler and say, 'Cut out all that old-fogeyism, Bill, for Christ's sake. Play the note, fellow, play the note.' You got to be so perfect now, the blues ain't no pleasure no more. You're always in a strain, worrying if you gonna make a bad chord.

"What make me so hot is that these same guys telling me can't play nothin.

They don't know but one move in the blues and when they through with that, they done. That's why all these records sound so much alike. You can't tell when one leave off and the next one start, if it wasn't for the nickels dropping in the Rockolas. All these guys have gone money-crazy, that's all in the world it is. They don't believe in fellowship. Whom they're dealing with—they don't give a durn about that. Not just one of um.

"I misses my old piano player, good old down-home boy they call Joseph. Now he's dead, they ain't no piano player can follow me when I get the blues and start really playin. He the only man that ever could. His mama tried to get him to take lessons. He told her, 'Damn the lessons. I know enough to play what I want to play.' "

Twenty to thirty years ago the blues came to town. Hoboing into Chicago, Detroit, and Indianapolis on slow freights from the Deep South. High-pitched hollers from the cotton fields and riverboats. Angry growls and jackass brays made on trumpets and trombones by players who didn't know the proper way to play but knew what they wanted to say.

For three generations the hot, blue, and boogie records of Big Bill and his comrades had been the daily song fare of the entire black working class and, reaching beyond this group, has now colored all American music. Now, at last, the city had caught up with these country musicians. A new generation of half-trained jazz musicians demanded that Bill give up his country ways—his "bad chords," his "whooping," his "ad-libbing"—the qualities that underlay the originality of Bill and his music—the blueness of the blues. To these youngsters, with their smattering of city sophistication, all this was "old-fogeyism."

Like a true folk composer, Big Bill would be surprised if anyone criticized his songs as unfinished, rough, or hastily contrived. He worked on order for years, the recording managers calling upon him for eight or a dozen new blues to be ready for the next day. Many of his songs he improvised in the studio. But there is another, more important point. Like most blues singers I have known, Bill did not keep a copy of any of his own records. For him, these were songs in their first stages, which he would not expect a singer to reproduce without his own changes, just as he himself never repeated them exactly. These are the seeds of finished blues—most will die, some will grow and flower, but all will contribute to the power of the great dark river of the music which, better than any other art form, provides an expressive outlet for the American tragedy, which is the loss of love.

EVIL-HEARTED BLUES

Sometimes I'm so evil,
Don't even love myself,
Don't even love my woman
Or nobody else.

Now I'm so evil,
Don't care if the sun don't shine.
I feel like killin you, baby,
And goin on down the line.

Sometimes I love to gamble
And stay out all night long,
But when I get busted, gal,
I swear you done me wrong.

I can't be satisfied,
I can't sleep at night,
The devil's got the best of me
Cause I ain't been livin right.

JUST A DREAM

I dreamed I was in the White House,
Settin on the president's chair.
I dreamed he shake my hand,
Said, "Old Bill, I'm glad you're here."
    But it was a dream, man,
    Just a dream I had on my mind.
    When I woke up next morning,
    Jim Crow did I find.

I dreamed that I got married,
Raised up a familee.
I dreamed I had ten children
And they all looked just like me.
    But it was a dream, man,
    Just a dream I had on my mind.
    When I woke up next morning,
    Not a child could I find.

I dreamed I had a million dollars,
Had a mermaid for my wife.
I dreamed I won the Brooklyn Bridge
On my knees shootin dice.
I dreamed I played policy,
Played the horses, too.
I dreamed I winned so much money
I didn know what to do.
    But it was a dream, man,
    Just a dream I had on my mind.
    When I woke up next morning,
    Not a penny could I find.

I dreamed I was up in heaven,
Settin down around the throne.
I dreamed I had an angel
Layin back in my arms.
I dreamed I went out with an angel,
And I had a good time.
I dreamed I was satisfied
And nothin to worry my mind.
    But it was a dream, man,
    Just a dream I had on my mind.
    When I woke up next morning,
    Not a pinfeather could I find.

Chapter 10

▲▲▲▲▲▲▲▲▲▲▲

Blues in the
Mississippi Night

I spent a lot of time with Big Bill Broonzy when he lived in Chicago in a rented single room lit by a single light bulb hanging at the end of a fly-specked wire. I watched as he wrote lyrics for his next blues session with a stub pencil on a school tablet. Bill seemed to me as wise as he was big, and warm and talented. He introduced me to Memphis Slim and Sonny Boy Williamson. Over a midnight bottle of bourbon, I learned that Memphis and Bill had grown up in the Arkansas River bottoms, and I surprised them by singing some snatches of Arkansas prison work songs that I knew. Memphis looked at me quizzically and then began to chuckle. Big Bill winked, and although I never asked, I believe they thought that perhaps I had served time in the Arkansas pen, as apparently they had. There was no other way I could have heard these prison tunes. At any rate, the atmosphere warmed, and we talked of many things as the bottle went round, and time passed pleasantly and we all decided they should do a Chicago blues concert in the "Midnight Special" series I was then producing at Town Hall in New York.

When they came to New York, they slept over at my place in the Village in order to save hotel money. They entertained my daughter Anna and sampled our Southern cooking. That night in 1946 the trio tore down the house at Town Hall, discovering that their Delta music was appreciated by an audience they had never known about. The moment seemed right for a productive recording session. They were eager for it. I took them to Decca, where we could have a whole studio to ourselves that Sunday. We had a couple of drinks.

I put my little one-celled Presto disc recorders on the floor, and I sat at their feet, flipping the discs, as they reminisced.[1] There was only one microphone. Memphis began with a song of his own:

You got to cry a little, die a little . . .

and when the last golden chords died away, I said, "Listen, you all have lived with the blues all your life, but nobody up North here understands where they come from. Tell me what the blues are all about."

That was about the last thing that I said for two hours. My Chicago friends began a conversation with each other that grew more intense as the afternoon wore on. I think that they really forgot that I was there as they talked, played, and sang to each other. It was almost as if the Mississippi night had closed in around them while they reminisced, creating a sort of one-act play about the strange and tragic events of Delta life. In doing so, they recapitulated the whole substance of this book.

Big Bill, who was older than the others, took a Socratic role, gently drawing his young friends into deeper and deeper levels of the drama. Memphis Slim, then one of the finest blues pianists in the world, who bore a mood of erotic and comradely pleasure everywhere he went, offered humorous counterpoint to Bill's graver observations. Sonny Boy, with all his madcap gifts, was a little simple, and his two friends would gently kid him, so that he, in great delight, could take the comic role in the play.

"The thing about the blues is," Big Bill said, his voice ringing out with authority, "it didn't start in the North—in Chicago, New York, Philadelphia, Pennsylvania, wha'soever it is—it didn't start in the East, neither in the North—it started in the South, from what I'm thinking."

"Blues started from slavery," Memphis muttered, half to himself.

"And the thing that has come to a showdown, that we really want to know why, and how come, a man in the South *have* the blues," Bill went on. "I worked on levee camps, extra gangs, road camps and rock camps and rock quarries and every place, and I hear guys singin *uh-hmmmm* this and *mmmmm* that, and I want to get the thing plainly that the blues is something that's from the heart—I know that, and whensoever you hear fellows singing the blues—I always believed it was a really heart thing, from his heart, you know, and it was expressing his feeling about *how* he felt to the people.

"I've known guys that wanted to cuss out the boss and was afraid to go up to his face and tell him what he wanted to tell him, and I've heard them sing those things—sing words, you know, back to the boss—say things to the mule, make like the mule stepped on his foot—say, 'Get off my foot, goddam it!' and he meant he was talking to the boss. 'You son-of-a-bitch,' he say, 'stay off my foot!' and such things as that."

"Yeah, blues is kind of a revenge," Memphis broke in. "You know you wanta say something, you wanta signifyin like—that's the blues. We all have had a hard time in life, and things we couldn't say or do, so we sing it."

"How do you sing a thing like that?" Bill asked.

"Well, like a friend of mines was down working on the railroad, and he sang some songs for me, a little number called

Oh, ratty, ratty section,
Oh, ratty, ratty crew.
Well, the cap'n gettin ratty, ratty boys,
You know I'm gonna rat some too.

He couldn't speak up to the cap'n and the boss, but he still had to work, so it give him the blues, so he sang it—he was signifying and getting his revenge through songs."

"And he didn't quit because he didn't know where he gonna find his next job," Bill added.

"Probably had one of those jobs you *couldn't* quit," Memphis chuckled.

"Man, how they gonna hold you?" from Sonny Boy, querulously.

"They hold you like this, Sonny Boy. They didn't have no payday on them jobs. They give you an allowance in the commissary store for you and your woman. You draw on that allowance, so much a week, and after it was up, that's all you got, see? Maybe sometimes you didn't get no pay at all."

"Yeah," Memphis joined in. "Most of us didn't know how to read and write and figure and so they charged us what they wants. They charged us twenty-five dollars for a side of side meat. And you gonna stay there till you paid for that meat, maybe gettin twenty-five cents a day wages. When you take a notion to leave, they tell you, 'Well, you owe us four hundred dollars.' "

Big Bill took up the story. "Suppose you be working a team of mules, and one of them gets his leg broke and you have to kill him—that's your mule! Yessir, that dead mule is one you bought and you gonna work right on that job till you pay for him or slip off some way."

"And if you say anything about it," Memphis said seriously, "you might go just like the mule. All odds are against you, even your own people."

"That's right," agreed Bill. "The white man don't all the time do those things. It's some of your own people at times will do those dirty deeds because they're told to do them, and they do what they're told."

Treat a group of people as if they had no right to dignity, allow these people no security, make them bend their knees and bow their heads, and some of them will conform to slavery in their own souls. Perhaps these so-called Uncle Toms are the most grievous result of the slavery system.

Bill interrupted my reflections: "Looky here, Memphis. Did you ever work for the Loran brothers?"

"You mean those guys that built all these levees up and down the river from Memphis? Sho, man, I've worked for the bigges part of the Loran family—Mister Isum Loran, Mister Bill Loran, Mister Charley Loran—all them. I think them Lorans are something like the Rockefeller family. When a kid is born, *he* Loran junior. They got Loran the second, Loran the third, Loran the fourth. They always been and they is still—Loran brothers—some of them big businessmens in towns, some of them running extry gangs and levee camps and road camps. And *they* were peoples wouldn't allow a man to quit unless they got tired of him and drove him away."[2]

"That's right," Memphis chuckled. "And remember how the boys used to sing:

I axed Mister Charley
What time of day.
He looked at me,
Threw his watch away.

All the way from the Brazos bottoms of Texas to the tidewater country of Virginia I had heard black muleskinners chant their complaint against Mister Charley, but the score of singers all disagreed about his identity. I grinned with excitement. Maybe I had at last discovered the identity of my elusive Mister Charley.

I asked my second question of the evening. "Who is this 'Mister Charley'?"

"Mister Charley Loran," Bill immediately responded.

"What sort of man is he?" I asked.

"Well," Memphis drawled, "now I couldn't hardly describe him to you. You know, it's hard for a colored man to talk like a white man anyhow."

(Memphis was talking for my benefit now. He had been reminded there was a white man listening there. He began to rib me gently.) "Mister Charley was one of them *real* Southerners; had a voice that would scare you to death whenever he'd come out with all that crap of his. Always in his shirtsleeves, I don't care how early in the mornin and how cold it was."

"Night or day." Big Bill began to chuckle with him. "Didn't make no difference to Mister Charley what time it was."

"Don't care how early he'd get up, you gonna get up, too. He'd holler:

Big bell call you, little bell warn you,
If you don't come now, I'm gonna break in on you.

And he *meant* it."

"Sho he did," laughed Big Bill. "He the man originated the old-time eight-hour shift down here. Know what I mean? Eight hours in the morning and eight more in the afternoon."

Sonny Boy kept adding eight to eight and getting sixteen and going off into peal after peal of high, whinnying laughter. In this shared laughter I felt the three had again accepted me. I asked another question.

"I'd always heard of this Mister Charley in the song as 'the Mercy Man.' Is *he* the same as Charley Loran?"

"Naw, man, that's Mister Charley *Houlin*, the best friend we ever had down in this part of the country, really a friend to our people. He was the man we all run to when somebody mistreated us," Big Bill told me.

"Otherwise known as the Mercy Man," Memphis added. "I remember an incident happened in Hughes, Arkansas. They had a fellow there named Charley Holan that were running a honky-tonk."

"That's right," Bill put in. "A barrelhouse, they call it."

"He had a lot of property there, this colored feller name Holan. So they hired a sheriff there, and-a, so this sheriff were living in one of Charley Holan's houses. And he wouldn't pay Charley no rent, he were just staying there; and so every time that Charley would ask him for some rent, he'd whip Charley Holan. So *he* happened to be, as they say, one of Charley Houlin's Negroes. So, Charley Holan finally got up enough nerve to go tell Charley Houlin; so that Charley told the police, say, 'Saturday evening at one o'clock, meet, I'm killing you or you kill me.' And I mean, that's no joke, that's what happened. So he met him that evening and he told him, say, 'Well, I came to kill you—you been messing with one of my Negroes.' So the police went to get his pistol, and Charley shot him through the heart. So they pulled him over out the street, and let the honky-tonk roll on . . .'' Softly, seeing it, wondering about it, he repeated, "Yeah, man, let the old honky-tonk roll *right* on."

"Toughest place I ever seen," said Big Bill, "were some of them honky-tonks in Charley Loran's camps. Negroes all be in there gamblin, you know, and some of them short guys couldn't quite reach up to the crap table—and I've seed them pull a *dead* man up there and stand on him."

"Yeah, stand right on him," said Memphis.

Big Bill had more to tell. "Pull that dead man up there, and stand on him and still keep shooting dice, see. And I've heard them come around and say, 'If you boys keep yourselves out of the grave, I'll keep you outa jail.' "

"That's right," said Memphis. "And I've heard them say, 'If you kill a nigger, I'll hire another one. If you kill a mule, I'll buy another one.' On the levee camps they used to say, when fellers would be so tired from carrying logs or something like that, or clearing new ground, he say, 'Burn out, burn up. Fall out, fall dead.' Yeah, just keep rolling, that was the best you could do. Work yourself to death or either you was a good man."

"Main thing about it is that some of those people down there didn't think a Negro ever get tired!" Big Bill's ordinarily quiet voice broke with a sound that was half sob, half growl. "They'd work him—work him till he couldn't work, see! You couldn't *tell* um you was tired."

"Why couldn't you?" I asked.

"They'd crack you cross the head with a stick or maybe kill you. One of those things. You just had to keep on workin whether you was tired or not. From what they call 'can to can't.' That mean you start to work when you just can see, early in the mornin, and work right on till you can't see no more at night."

"Only man ever helped us about our work was Charley Houlin, the Mercy Man," said Memphis. "He used to come out and say, 'Those fellows are tired; give um some rest.' Ain't he the man, Bill, cut them sixteen hours a day down to eight?"

"Right in this section he was," Bill replied.

"How did he do it?" I asked.

"Why, he and his son, Little Charley, just didn't like the way things was going on, so they just come in and taken over, that's all. Otherwise they was the baddest men down through this part of the country. Both of them was ex-cowboys from Texas and sharpshooters. Could shoot like nobody's business. So after they taken over, that made it a lot better. And it's still better today."

"You mean the people were just scared of Old Man Houlin and his boy?"
I asked.

"That's right," Memphis said. "I'll tell you how bad they was scared. You
know, they passed a law in Arkansas—no hitchhiking. I was trying to get a ride
to Little Rock, and so a feller by the name of Mister Cut, he was the baddest
feller down from the latter part of Arkansas."

"Yeah, he is, too," added Bill.

"So he says," Memphis went on, " 'What are you doing hitchhiking here,
feller, er, boy?' I say, 'I am trying to get home to work.' He say, 'Where you
work at? Who you work for?' I say"—Memphis imitated the mild and insinuating way he made his reply—" 'I work in Hughes for Mister Charley Houlin.'
You know what he told me? He say, 'Come on, I'll take you there.' "

Sonny Boy, Big Bill, and Memphis threw back their heads and laughed,
laughed quietly and long, as if they shared some old joke, burdened with irony,
but bearable out of long acquaintance.

"Any other time, or if you had been with any other man, or if you don't be
working, you'd have got a whipping, or went to jail or to the levee, went to the
farm . . ."

"Went on the farm and work for no pay," said Bill.

"That's right," Memphis went on, "but since I was working for Mister
Charley, he taken me to Mister Charley."

"Yeah, he was even scared to bother you because you was one of his men."

"Mister Cut take me in his car," said Memphis. "Even gave me a drink!"

Bill, shaking his head in wonder, chuckled, "They'll do that, too."

"You know, Memphis," Big Bill continued, "you and I worked in all kinds
of camps—levee camps, road camps, rock quarries, and all—but what I want
to get at is, how we lived in those places? You know, the way we lived in those
tents and things like that, and the food we had to eat was scrap food from what
other people had refused—old bags of beans and stuff they couldn't sell."

Memphis, beginning to howl with laughter over the old and painful joke he
recalled, interrupted, "They take all that stuff and they put it in a pot, and they
had a name for it in the camp I was in—'La-la-lu. If I don't like it, he do.' But
you like it, you like it."

"Yeah, that right," Bill agreed. "I know what you mean."

Big Bill continued, forcing us to savor the dirt, see the hoggish way the men
had to live. "They have those big truck patches they call um down there, truck
gardens, and they just pull up greens by the sackful, you know, and take um
to the lake or creek, sort of shake um off in the water and throw um in the pot.

In one of them fifty-two-gallon pots, you know, and cook all the stalks and the roots—"

Memphis, beginning to laugh his big laugh again, broke in. "And if you found a worm in your greens and say, 'Captain, I found a worm here,' he'd say, 'What the hell do you expect for nothin?'"

Big Bill and Sonny Boy burst out in great yells of laughter, as Memphis hurried on to top his own story: "And then some feller over 'long table says, 'Gimme that piece of meat!' "

"Yeah, I've heard that," Big Bill gasped out between the gusts of laughter that were shaking his whole body. Sonny Boy couldn't sit still any longer; his laughter was riding him too hard. He went staggering around the studio room, beating his arms in the air.

When we had recovered from this healing laughter, Memphis added thoughtfully, "Those guys seemed to get a kick out of the whole thing."

"Did you ever see those guys they called 'table walkers'?" Bill asked.

"Yeah, many times," said Memphis.

"He get up from way down the other end of the table and walk right down through the table and pick up what you got."

"Those guys," Memphis said respectfully, "those guys, they were what you call tough people; they know they get a whippin."

"Pull that .45 and walk the table," Bill remembered.

"Yeah, he knew he gonna get a whippin," Memphis said. "He pull that .45 on us, an when the white man comes, the white man whip him with his .45 right there on him. The white man wouldn't have no gun or anything. He just come and say, 'Lay down there, feller, I'm gonna whip you.' " Memphis spoke quietly, with bitter, weary irony. "So this tough man would kick the gun out of his scabbard and give him a whippin." There was a pause. We could all see the big black figure cowering on the earth and the white man standing over him with a stick, beating him as he might a chicken-killing hound. After a moment, almost in a whisper, Memphis continued, "After this table walker get his whippin, he'd pick up that big pistol he toted and go on back to work."

Well, you kicked and stomped and beat me,
And you called that fun, and you called that fun.

If I catch you in my hometown,
Gonna make you run, gonna make you run.

"Yeah," Bill said. "Then maybe this guy that took the beating would come out there on the job and kill one of his buddies, kill one of us. That happens. I've seen that many times."

"In the meantime," Memphis added, "if you were a good worker, you could kill anybody down there, so long as he's colored. You could kill anybody, go anywhere."

"You mean"—Big Bill rapped this out—"you could kill anybody down there as long as you kill a *Negro!*"

"Any Negro." Memphis's voice was flat and painstakingly logical, as if he were reading the rules out of a book. "If you could work better than him. Don't kill a good worker—then you were sorry. If you did, you go to the penitentiary."

Stagolee, he went a-walkin in that red-hot broiling sun.
He said, "Bring me my big pistol, I wants my forty-one."

They were both entertainers. They had made their way safely and even pleasantly through their violent world, their guitars slung around their necks like talismans. Wearing these talismans, they had entered into all the secret places of this land, had moved safely through its most dangerous jungles, past all its killers, who, seeing their talismans, had smiled upon them. They lived the magic life of fools. (Remember the hard, drawling voice: "I got a nigger on my place that can keep you laughin all day. I don't know where he gets all the stories he tells and them songs of his. Reckon he makes them up, nigger-like. And sing! Sing like a mockinbird. You ought to hear him. You'd split your sides.") Now these buffoons with their clear artist's vision were making a picture of their world, a terrifying picture of a place in which they were perfectly at home.

"You know, Bill," said Memphis, "we had a few Negroes down there that wasn't afraid of white peoples and talk back to them. They called those people crazy."

"Crazy people, yeah," said Bill. "I wonder why did they call them crazy, because they speeak up for their rights? I had an uncle like that and they hung him. They hung him down there because they say he was crazy and might *ruin* the other Negroes. See, that is why they hung him, because he was a man that if he worked, he wanted pay; and he could figure as good as the white man, and he had a good education better than some of the white people down there. Lot of them would come to him for advice."

"The white people there were about as dumb as we were," Memphis broke in.

Big Bill went on. "I remember one time my auntie had a baby boy; he was about two or three years old. The white man came up there one day and he told him, he says, 'Say, Gerry,' he says, 'I want you to get that woman out there and put her to work.' Says, 'There's no woman here sits up and don't work, set up and in the shade, but Miz Anne.' And my uncle say, 'Well, who is Miz Anne?' He says, 'Er, Miz Anne is my wife.' My uncle say, 'Well, I'm sorry, mister, but my wife is named Anne, too, and she sit up in the shade.' Say, 'She don't come out.' The man say, 'No nigger sits up there without working.' My uncle look at him. 'Well, that's one Miz Anne is a *Negro* and she ain't going to work in the field.' And he jumps off his horse. Well, my uncle whipped him, and run his horse on away, and then beat him up and run him away from there." Bill went on in a flat and weary voice to finish his story. "So, the white man went to town and got a gang and come out there after him that night, and he shot all four, five of them until they finally caught him."

"And hung him," muttered Memphis.

"Fifty or sixty of them come out there and got him and killed him." Bill began to speak with mounting rage. "That was on account of he was protecting his own wife, because he didn't want his wife to work out on the plantation when she had a baby there at the house to take care of and she was expecting another one pretty soon."

"I've seed this happen," Bill went on, "in the South, that one white boy down there was liking the same girl that this colored boy was liking, and he told this colored boy not to marry this colored girl because he wanted her for hisself, and the boy told him that he loved her and he was going to marry her. He say, 'Well, you can't get no license here.' So the boy run off, him and the girl, and went off to another town and they got married and they come back there and the man asked them was he really married to her. And he said, 'Yes.' So the girl figured that if she show him the license he would leave her go, and so she showed him the license; then they went and killed his daddy and they killed her. Then they killed his mother and then one of his brothers, he went out to try to protect them, and they killed him so they killed twelve in that one family. That was in 1913. The boy was named Belcher, that's the family got killed. That was at a place called Langdale, Arkansas, way out in the woods from Goulds, Arkansas."

Without any more feeling than one would recall a storm or a flood or any other past disaster, Memphis commented, "Yeah, I heard of that, heard all about it."

"It was no protection at all that the poor people got in place like that back in those days," Bill went on with calm anger. "You try to fight back, then it's not just you they're gonna get. It's anybody in your family. Just like if I got three brothers; I do something and they can't catch me, they catch the other brothers."

"Anybody in the family," added Memphis.

"*You* might do something and get away and run off, but why do somethin or other and get your whole family killed? You know what I mean?"

"I know it!"

"That's what they got on you. And if they got a girl in the family that they like, you just want to let him have her, because if you don't, he'll be liable to do something, you know, so outrageous, because when they see a Negro woman they like, they gonna have her if they want her."

If I feel tomorrow like I feel today,
If I feel tomorrow like I feel today,
Stand right here and look a thousand miles away.

"What they call a bad Negro in the South is a Negro that will really fight his own people," Bill went on. "The Negro that will fight the white man, they call him crazy, they don't call him bad, fact of the business, because they say he's gone nuts. The white man will call a Negro a bad seed . . ."

"He'd *ruin* the rest of the Negroes," Memphis interjected. "He would open the eyes of a lot of Negroes, tell um things that they didn't know. Otherwise," he chuckled, "he was a *smart* Negro."

"And he'd go around and get the *Chicago Defender* and bring it down here," said Bill. "You know what I mean, git it down here and read it to the Negroes."

"Speaking of the *Chicago Defender*," Memphis interrupted, "I were in a place called Marigold, Mississippi. And you know, they had a restaurant in there and in back they had a peephole. And I thought they were gambling back there or something, and I went back there to see was they gambling. In fact, I was kinda stranded—I wanted to go back there and shoot a little crap and make me a little stake. And you can imagine what they were doing back there. They were reading the *Chicago Defender*, and they had a lookout man on the door with a peephole. If a white man come into the restaurant, they'd stick the *Defender* into the stove, burn it up, and start playing checkers." Memphis laughed. "That's the way they had to smuggle the *Defender* down there. That's what they really call a bad Negro, a Negro that had nerve enough to smuggle the *Chicago Defender* down in the state of Mississippi where they didn't allow them to put um off there."

"That's what makes the Negro so *tetchious* till today," Bill said. "He has been denied in so many places until if a gang is in a place and they say 'You fellers get back' or 'Get over there' or 'Don't stand there' or something like that, they figger right straight that they're pointing at *them*—a lot of times they don't mean that. They really mean they don't want *nobody* standing there, but the Negro thinks, straight off, they referrin to him because he's black."

Sonny Boy had been listening to his two older friends for a long time. He had had no experience of the deeps of the South—the work camps, the prison farms, the wild life of the river that they had known. He was a boy right off the farm, whose half-mad genius on his Woolworth harmonica was gradually leading him out into the world.

But Sonny Boy knew how it was to feel "black and *tetchious*."

"Well, boys, I'll tell you what happened to me. My mother she bought a mule from, er-uh, Captain Mack. You know he's the boss of the county road—"

"Where's that?" asked Bill.

"Jackson, Tennessee. He's the boss on the county road, you know. They take you out on trucks and you build bridges, and you dig ditches and things like that. He sold my mother a mule, so by me bein young and everything, mother gave me the mule, and nachully, young boys, I'd run the mule. Course, the mule, he was a nice-looking mule. Well, finally, the mule got mired up in the bottom, and the mule dies—"

"Wait—wait a minute," Bill cut in.

"Is that the mule you married?" asked Memphis.

Sonny Boy began to stutter.

"That must be the mule you bought the hat for," Memphis cracked, and they burst into guffaws of country laughter, while Sonny Boy kept stuttering his story.

"Naw it ain't! Now listen! Just this old mule got *mired* up and died down there in the bottom."

"I understand."

"Yeah. So Captain Mack, he told my mother, say, 'I'm just crazy to get that damn boy out there on the country road, I'm gon do him like he did that mule.' And so my mother had to scuffle to keep me offa there. Every little move I'd make, he was watching me. And after all, he'd done sold the mule, and she paid him. But he say I kill the mule—"

Big Bill interrupted sharply, "That word, that word. We'll go back to that word they have down there: 'Kill a nigger, we'll hire another'n. Kill a mule . . .'" And here Sonny Boy joined in, "buy another'n."

Bill went on, "See, all those things go into the same word. The fact of the business, back in those days a Negro didn't mean no more to a white man than a mule."

"Didn't mean as much!" said Memphis.

"Didn't mean as much as a mule," said Sonny Boy.

"You'll agree to that?" asked Bill.

"Now I agree to that," answered Sonny.

"Well, that's the point we gittin to now." Bill went on, "You see, now you take a mule, they sell the mule. All right, then, there was times when they sold a Negro, too. What they looked at was just a face of a black man."

"I know a man at my home, they called him Mister White, that had a plantation about fifty or sixty miles square and he didn't even want a Negro to come through his place. The government highway ran through his land, you know? What they call a pike, a main highway where everybody had to go, but he built a special road, ran all around his place, and when you got there it was a sign said NEGRO TURN. You had to turn off the highway and go all around his plantation."

"I knew him, I knew him well," Memphis muttered.

"And this Mister White had all white fences around his place. The trees, he painted them high as he could reach. All his cattle, his sheeps, goats, hogs, cows, mules, hosses, and everything on his place was white. Anytime one of his animals have a black calf or a black goat—whatsonever it was—Mister White give it to the niggers. Even down to the chickens. He had all white chickens, too. And when a chicken would hatch off some black chickens, he'd say, 'Take those chickens out and find a nigger and give um to him. Get rid of um. I won't have no nigger chickens on this plantation!'"

"And I've known," Bill continued, "it was a Negro and a white man standin at a railroad crossing, you know, just as you get into town? Negro and white man, just standing there talking. The white man was telling that Negro what he wanted him to do, and another Negro come drivin a wagon with a grey mule and a black mule to the wagon. So this Negro drive up to the crossing, and the rails was kind of high there, see, and the wheel hit the rail, and the mule was tryin to pull over and he kept sayin, 'Git up, Git up!'

"So the white man holler up there, ask him, 'Hey,' says, 'do you know that's a white mule you talkin to?'

"And this Negro say right quick, 'Oh, *yes sir*! Git up, *Mister* Mule.' "

Bill and Memphis began to guffaw, and after a moment, when he got the point of the joke, Sonny Boy's laughter burst over him in torrents. Again he staggered off, howling with glee and beating his arms helplessly in the air. So we all laughed together, blowing the blues out of our lungs with laughter.

"Well, how about that Prince Albert tobacco, you know," gasped Memphis, when he could speak again.

"I've heard of that," said Bill.

"You know, if you go in a store, you didn't say 'Gimme a can of Prince Albert.' Not with that white man on the can."

"What would you say then?"

"Gimme a can of *Mister* Prince Albert."

We were caught up in gales of squalling laughter that racked Sonny Boy. We were howling down the absurdity, the perversity, and the madness that gripped the land of the levee, a beautiful and fecund land, rich in food and genius and good living, and song, yet turned into a sort of purgatory by fear.

Now for an instant we understood each other. Now in this moment of laughter, the thongs and the chains, the harsh customs of dominance, the stupid and brutalizing lies of race, had lost their fallacious dignity, but only for an instant. The blues would begin again their eternal rhythm, their eternal ironic comment:

The blues jumped a rabbit, run him a solid mile.
When the blues overtaken him, he hollered like a baby chile.

"Yeah," said Bill, his face becoming somber, "that's the way things go down around these little Southern places—enough to give anybody the blues."

They had begun with the blues as a record of problems of love and women in the Delta world. They had located the roots of these miseries in the stringent poverty and racial terror of black rural life. They recalled the pleasures and dangers of the Mississippi work camps, where the penitentiary stood at the end of the road, waiting to receive the rebellious. Finally, they came to the enormities of the lynch system that threatened anyone who defied the rules. Then, overwhelmed by the absurdities of the Southern system, they laughed their way to the final curtain in true African style.

For me, the session was a triumph. Here at last, black working-class men had talked frankly, sagaciously, and with open resentment about the inequities of the Southern system of racial segregation and exploitation. An exposé of that system was on record. Also, a new order of eloquence in documentation had emerged out of a situation where members of a tradition could present their own case to each other. They had themselves stated why and how the blues had arisen in their homeland in the Mississippi Delta.

But Big Bill and his friends had another reaction to the recordings. I had agreed, perhaps mistakenly, to play back what they had recorded. The bluesmen listened with mounting apprehension and, in a powerful rush of words, attacked me for making the records, demanded that they be destroyed, then finally asked me to promise that I would never reveal their identities.

"Why, why?" I demanded. "What could you be afraid of, way up here in the North?"

"You don't know those peoples down there," they said.

It didn't matter that the three of them lived in Chicago. When those Deep Delta peckerwoods heard the records, they'd come looking for them. If they couldn't find them, they'd go after their *families*, burn down their houses, maybe kill them all out, Bill and Memphis assured me. This was America in 1948, but these three great artists of the blues, whose records right at that moment were spinning on jukeboxes all over the South, were terribly afraid.

So I promised to conceal their identities if the recording were ever released—an unlikely event so far as I could see—and I kept my promise until 1990. When this trialogue was published in the magazine *Common Ground* in 1948, I invented a fictitious setting and changed all the names. This fiction was maintained even in the 1959 United Artists release of the session, and the whole story was never told until the summer of 1990 when Ryko released the interview on a CD. There the three men finally played their own parts. There were warm reviews, four stars in *Entertainment Weekly*, and a national prize. At last America seemed ready to hear the tragic story that lies back of the blues. By then Sonny, Big Bill, and Memphis, all three, were dead.

Even after we had talked the matter out on that long-ago Sunday in New York, our mood remained subdued rather than triumphant. We knew we had made a real breakthrough and had opened up a dark period of history that had previously been hidden—they felt that as much as I did—yet a pall had fallen over our friendship. I invited them to stay on in New York, but though they were still glowing from the great success of their concert, they pled urgent business in Chicago. They were polite, but they wanted to go home at once. They caught the next train west and I heard no more from them for years, even though, after the reviews of the Town Hall bash, Bill and Memphis began to get bookings in white clubs and eventually ended up working and living in Europe.

When I brought my recording gear back to the Delta twenty years later, in 1959, I decided to try to find out more about their hero, Charley Houlin, the Texan who shot down the sheriff to protect his renters. It was a dreamlike experience to drive through the Arkansas River bottoms, seeking the hero of my friends' legend of the good white man, and even more like a dream to drive into Hughes, Arkansas, the scene of the gunfight, and to discover, from the first person I met there, that Charley Houlin was still alive.

"You'll find Charley on _____ Street over cross the tracks. You can't miss his place; it's got big wide steps." Through the elm-lined streets of the old Delta town, across the tracks to the colored section, there was the sign HOU-LIN'S PLACE at the head of a broad wooden staircase. I left Shirley in the car, climbed the stairs, and pushed open the swinging saloon doors. The big barroom was empty except for a good-looking Creole lady who was polishing the long mahogany bar. Behind her rose a huge mirror bordered below by a triple row of bottles and decorated with an impressive array of revolvers, rifles, and shotguns in easy reach. When I asked for Mister Houlin, she turned and called in a soft voice, "Charley," and to me, "He'll be right out."

While I waited, I looked at all those guns and thought over what a black down the street had told me: "Charley Houlin is the fastest shot in Arkansas. Everybody knows that. Them state troopers don't even slow down in front of Charley Houlin's door, they just drive on by."

The Delta, especially the Arkansas side of the river, was still frontier in 1959, and Charley Houlin looked as if he'd stepped out of *Gunsmoke*. Compact, blond-haired with touches of grey, poker-faced, well groomed in West Texas style, he had the cold blue-eyed gaze of a gunman. We howdied and had a drink. He told me he'd left Texas because "things were gettin slow down there," had done well in Arkansas and decided to settle. I wanted to ask him more about his adventures, but I never got up my nerve. There was a reserve in Charley Houlin that kept one at a distance. When I told him I was recording black music, he turned to his Creole lady: "He ought to get together with old Forrest City Joe, oughtn't he, hon?"

That August afternoon I found Forrest City Joe Pugh sitting on the front gallery of a tavern identified in shaky lettering as THE OLD WHISKEY STORE, playing guitar for a group of loungers. I listened awhile, bought him a drink, and as we drove out into the country to find his musical buddies, he pulled out his harmonica and began to blow in the screaming, far-out style of Sonny Boy Williamson. Joe could play as well when the harmonica was inside his mouth or when he blew through his nostrils, as in the normal fashion. He also sang around and over the mouth harp so that the voice and instrument became one stream of continuous sound. When he finished, he knocked the spit out of the instrument and chuckled. "Someday this thing gonna buy me a car like yours!"

We found his favorite guitar player, Sonny Boy Rogers, weighing his last sack of cotton at the wagon down a muddy lane. It was cotton-picking time, everybody had money in their pockets, and Sonny Boy was in high good humor. Soon we were back in town with a carload of young blues musicians.

By nine o'clock the stereo recorder was sitting on the bar of a honky-tonk. Forrest City Joe and his two-piece band, Boy Blue with His Two, along with their girlfriends and other connoisseurs of the blues, were lapping up the liquor and pouring out the honky-tonk blues. No New York technician would have approved of the acoustics. Between takes the place was a bedlam, but the emotional atmosphere was mellow and marvelous. This was the first stereo field recording trip. When the musicians and their friends heard the "thwack" of the rhythm section coming from speaker A, and the squeal and moan of the singer–harp blower from speaker B, delight and approval were universal. The crowd danced during all the playbacks. The tall talk and the cussing led to some loud and inconclusive fights.

Forrest City Joe was at the top of his form. He convinced us both that I had discovered a new blues star. He played piano and guitar. He raved on through his harmonica, playing old pieces and improvising new ones. He moaned the story of a recent unhappy affair:

She used to be beautiful, but she lived her life too fast.
Now she runnin round,
Tryin to drink out of everybody's whiskey glass.

I had a good racket of sellin whiskey,
I told my baby so.
She wasn satisfied till she went to town
And let the chief of police know.

She used to be beautiful, but she lived her life too fast . . .

One thing, one thing, old buddy,
Forrest City Joe can't understand—
She cooked cornbread for me,
She cooked biscuits for her man.

She used to be beautiful, but she lived her life too fast.
Now she runnin round town,
Tryin to drink out of everybody's glass.

As I watched these wild young Arkansas blacks playing their "rocking" blues (with two guitars, drums, harmonica, and a heavy backbeat—very different from the country blues I normally recorded), I began to see how African their music making was. In sum, they were incredibly sociable—constantly interacting, clowning, and dancing with each other and the lively crowd around them; endlessly playful, laughing, making musical jokes, handling their instruments and their voices in all sorts of ways, always improvising with tone, text, tune, rhythm, and harmony; and supremely energetic—singing loud, playing hard, accenting powerfully, pushing the tempo, performing as if their very lives depended on every phrase. Think of James Brown at his peak, Louis Armstrong at his hottest, a Brazilian or Trinidadian carnival ramping down the avenue, a strolling street bard in West Africa with his mates tossing calabash rattles like Magic did a basketball—and you're looking at Forrest City Joe, Boy Blue, and their mates all that night in Hughes, Arkansas.

Two generations of white rockers have tried to emulate this style and have thus far failed, because the whites have not yet grasped the body-based African rhythmic scheme, which allows great intensity without being overemphatic, which fosters playfulness without being silly or losing the beat. Forrest City Joe and his friend had it all. That they were as clearly African as the Benin bronzes you can hear for yourself if you compare their recordings with matching cuts from Senegal and other parts of West Africa.

About 1 A.M., Charley Houlin came by to listen awhile. Then, as he told me good night, he suggested I make a visit to nearby West Memphis. "But you better check in with the sheriff when you get there. They keep West Memphis pretty tied down, if you know what I mean." I didn't, but I told him I would check in with that sheriff. By 3 A.M., I could scarcely see the typewriter to tap out the contracts with these eager young beavers of the Arkansas blues. At 4 A.M., I loaded the machine into the car. The youngsters went off to get a nap before their cotton-picking day began. Joe wanted another drink and he deserved one.

As dawn came to Honky-tonk Row in Hughes, we had the machine packed into the car. We were both very happy. Joe was on records, bound, he thought, for stardom. Things had changed for the better. The 1954 Supreme Court decision was behind us; black and white kids were attending the same schools in the Delta. Here in Hughes he and I, black and white, had been able to fraternize in public without getting into trouble. Joe couldn't stop sounding off. He was so happy about the future he began to make up another world, better than the present one.

"What was the fastest man you ever heard of?" he asked the air, and then supplied the answer: "It was a man run so fast that God struck at him with lightning and missed. Missed three times. At last God gave up and said, 'Go, cat, go! . . .'

"That man so cross-eyed he had to lay flat on his back to look down the well. When he dug a well, the water tasted bent. And he was ugly! He was so ugly that he stood off God and scared the devil to death. That way he died when he got ready!"

We were weak with laughing. Two drunks, who had been listening, were staggering helplessly on the sidewalk, begging Joe to stop before he killed them. As for Joe, he seemed possessed of all the magic of black wit and music. The only way to say goodbye was to buy him another fifth and beat it. When I looked back, Joe had become a dusty, ragged figure between the railroad tracks and the honky-tonks.[3]

I followed Charley Houlin's instructions to the letter. When I reached West Memphis, my first act was to drive straight to the sheriff's house so as to establish my identity and clear myself. The sheriff was away, but I chatted for a few minutes with his wife, explaining to her, as she rocked and crocheted, what I wanted to do in her town. "I reckon it's all right. You just go on," she told me. "I'll tell the boss when he comes home."

Most of West Memphis seemed to consist of saloons and eating places. I walked into the biggest, loudest bar, got hold of a stein of beer, and wandered over to the crap table to watch the game. Gutbucket blues were growling on the jukebox. There was a low platform in one corner, clearly intended for live music. Things looked good. I was hanging out by the crap table, soaking in the icy beer and looking for somebody to ask about the blues, when I felt something hard poking me in the ribs. Then there were two somethings, one on each side.

I did the conventional thing. In spite of the beer mug, I put up both hands and looked over my shoulder. Two very unpleasant-looking deputies with badges had me at pistol point. In good round American they asked me who the hell I was and what I was doing there. I was looking to find blues singers; I had heard there were lots of blues singers playing in the bars. It seemed I was a goddam liar and "no such of a thing" and "we don't want your kind muscling in here," they insisted as they shoved me toward the door, and "we know what to do with your kind," as they pushed me out the front door and into their squad car.

One sat in front and drove, the other in back with his pistol stuck in me. I was getting scared and I managed to tell them that I had done what I was supposed to do, I had tried to check in, I had gone by the sheriff's house, like Mr. Houlin told me, and had checked in. But that was another goddam lie, I was told, you just don't want what's coming to you. I didn't, and I rather begged them "let's drive by and check with Mrs. Sheriff."

Well, why not, it won't take but a minute, and then we'll show you up for the lyin mmmp you are and then—but anyway we headed out for the sheriff's house. Thank God Mrs. Sheriff was still rocking and crocheting on the front porch. Very, very politely they helloed and then they told her who they had in the car and she said she'd see. She got up from her rocker and came out to the car and looked in and said, "That's him. That's the one. He was by here this afternoon."

They thank-you-ma'amed her and so did I. As they drove off, however, they explained to me again that, check or no check, Houlin or no Houlin, they didn't want my kind snooping or muscling in or whatever it was I was doing in West Memphis and I should get in my car and my tires should burn the pavement until I had left there. They dropped me at my car and again let me know that they didn't want to see me around town that evening.

I followed instructions. I went to the motel, where I'd stashed Shirley for safety's sake, and we did burn rubber and got out of West Memphis, Arkansas. As we drove along through the darkling river bottoms, I realized we were close to Hamp's Place, the country honky-tonk where this tale began. I tried to tell Shirley how it was when Willie B. and William Brown and I had crossed over that river bridge twenty years earlier, about that long-ago mellow evening, when we were young and reckless and full of whiskey. Down deep we had felt helpless in the face of giant and implacable injustice. But since then, things had taken a better turn.

My encounter with the West Memphis cops was *old* stuff; the *new* was the session I'd had with Forrest City Joe and his friends. And that had taken place right in the heart of the Delta. The free and easy feeling of those happy hours symbolized profound shifts in Southern mores. Doors were opening that had been closed to blacks for centuries. Perhaps Gunnar Myrdal had been right when he said that Constitution was the very marrow of American folklore, and that once the Jim Crow rules had been declared unconstitutional by the Court, most of the white South would go along with that decision. Of course, some places were changing more slowly than others. But the main social barriers had been breached. Moreoever, it was clear that the blues, with its tide of African irony and rhythm, would surge on, uncheckable, like the big river down there under the bridge, laughing and singing to itself about the new times coming.

The sun gonna shine in my back door some day,
The wind gonna rise and blow my blues away . . .

Acknowledgments

▲▲▲▲▲▲▲▲▲▲▲▲▲▲▲▲▲▲▲▲▲▲

I have many people to thank for contributions on fieldwork data—Samuel Adams, John Work, and mainly Lewis Jones, who collaborated on the whole Coahoma County survey. The Library of Congress Folk Song Archive, of which I was then in charge, furnished recording instruments and other equipment, and the records of the songs are now in the Archive. John Faulk and, especially, Elizabeth Harold contributed important interview material. In all my Southern work I am indebted to my father, John A. Lomax, who generously included me in his field trips and shared his joy in and reverence for black folk music with me. I thank Shirley Collins, the talented English folksinger, who assisted me on the 1959 field trip, as well as Worth Long and John Bishop, who worked with me when I returned to the Delta in 1978 to shoot footage for the *American Patchwork* series. For providing their wonderful photographic work to this endeavor, I wish to thank William Ferris, Jeff Todd Titon, George Mitchell, Jim O'Neal, Frank Driggs, and David Gahr. For background research on the levee camps, I am indebted to James Cobb of the University of Tennessee at Knoxville; for other background research, to David Evans and his seminal studies of Delta music, John Cowley, and Barry Dornfeld. I wish to thank Gerry Parsons of the Library of Congress and Cavett Taff of the Mississippi Department of Archives and History. Carol Kulig made valuable suggestions in the last stages of editing. Gideon D'Arcangelo, my editorial and research assistant, has helped in many ways to bring this book to fruition, especially in editing the photographic sections.

Song Appendix

OLD RATTLER
As Sung by Doc Reese

1.
Early one Sunday mornin,
    Here, Rattler, here,
Captain called the dog sergeant,
    Here, Rattler, here.

2.
"Old Eatum, old Beatum, old
    Cheatum's done gone,
    Here, Rattler, here,
And I'll give you a marrow bone,
    Here, Rattler, here."

3.
"I don't want your marrow bone,
    Here, Rattler, here,
I want those trusties that are long
    gone,
    Here, Rattler, here."

4.
"Catch um, old Rattler, bite um, old
    dog,
    Here, Rattler, here,
And I'll give you a marrow bone,
    Here, Rattler, here."

5.
Just as soon as the chain set Rattler
    free,
He had his nose to the ground and
    his tail like a tree.

6.
He found the trail of the trusties
    three,
Just where they passed the live oak
    tree.

Another version of this song appears in *American Ballads and Folk Songs*, collected and compiled by John A. Lomax and Alan Lomax (New York: Macmillan, 1934), p. 66.

7.
When he came to the river he leaped
   right in,
He was on the trail of the missing
   men.

8.
To the other side old Rattler went,
There he picked up the same old
   scent.

9.
He ran so fast till he looked like a
   streak,
You should have seen that dog
   a-workin his feet.

10.
Soon he begin to growl and moan,
A sign he was bringin the bacon
   home.

11.
Old Cheatum had climbed up very
   high,
Thinkin old Rattler would pass him
   by.

12.
Rattler circled the tree just twice,
Then he perched there like a
   well-trained fice.

13.
Old Cheatum was another of
   Rattler's finds,
He had gotten tired and was left
   behind.

14.
Then Rattler ran on with determined
   mind,
Left all of the others far behind.

15.
The Texas Special was a-runnin
   downhill,
But Rattler pass it like it was standin
   still.

16.
He was on the trail of the men who
   had gone,
And he rode old Eatum right to his
   home.

17.
He ran to the window and barked at
   the door,
Then he heard old Eatum cross the
   floor.

18.
Rattler begun to yell and scream,
He wanted old Eatum, what I mean.

19.
At last old Eatum heard the sergeant
   say,
"Come out, old Eatum, go back and
   stay."

20.
Old Eatum come out with his hands
   in the air,
He knew his run had got him
   nowhere.

21.
Now old Beatum thought he was
   travelin alone,
But Rattler soon showed him he was
   wrong.

22.
Soon as he heard old Rattler's cry,
Old Beatum wished for wings to fly.

23.

He kept on runnin with all his
  might,
When he looked back, Rattler was in
  sight.

24.

Old Beatum wondered what he
  would do,
"If Rattler get to me, I know I'm
  through."

25.

"Come here, sergeant, and call off
  your dog,
I'll go to the farm and cut your
  logs."

  Here, Rattler,
  Here, Rattler, here,
  Here, Rattler,
  Here, Rattler, here.

OLD STEWBALL
Will Stark's Version

1.

Old Stewball, Old Stewball,
I know him of old,
You run in London
Twelve long years ago.

2.

When the word was given
For the hosses to go,
Stewball, he started
Like an arrow from a bow.

3.

On the day that was 'pinted
For the hosses to run,
The ladies and gentlemen
From Baltimore come.

4.

The ladies did holler
And the gentlemen did squawl.
The children cried, "Look, look,
At noble Stewball."

5.

Old Bonnie's a fine hoss,
Had a long tail and mane,
Stewball can pass her
Like showers of rain.

6.

"Old Master, old Master,
I'm risking my life
To win all this money
For you and your wife."

7.

"Stick fast to your saddle,
Say, rider, don't fall.
You won't be jostled
By noble Stewball."

8.

Master bet hundreds,
And Missus bet pounds,
Master was winner
But Missus took down . . .

FRANKIE AND ALBERT
Will Stark's Version

1.
Frankie was a good woman,
Everybody knowed,
Paid eighty-one dollars
For Albert's suit of clothes.
    He's her man,
    But he done her wrong.

2.
Frankie went to the barroom,
Asked for a glass of wine.
She asked the loving bartender,
"Have you seen that man of mine?
    He's my man,
    But he done me wrong."

3.
The bartender said, "Yes, Frankie,
I ain't gonna tell you no lie.
He left here about an hour ago
With the girl they call Alice Fly.
    He's your man,
    But he done you wrong."

4.
Frankie went out on down the
    street,
She heard a bulldog bark.
"Sholy that must be Albert,
Hidin in the dark.
    He's my man,
    But he done me wrong."

5.
Frankie went to the hop joint
And she didn't have no fear.
She see Albert smoking a hop seegar
And the women all buying him beer.
    He's her man,
    But he done her wrong.

6.
She shot him once and she shot him
    twice,
And he fell down on the floor,
Say, "Turn me over, baby,
The bullets hurt me so."
    He's her man,
    But he done her wrong.

7.
Frankie went to Albert's mother
And fell down on her knees,
Says, "I have killed your son, Albert,
Forgive me, if you please.
    He's my man,
    But he done me wrong."

8.
Albert's mother told Frankie,
Says, "Please take my advice,
Don't never love a poor man so
That you have to take his life.
    He's your man,
    But you done him wrong."

OLLIE JACKSON
Will Stark's Version

1.
Hush, girls and boys,
Don't you all say a word.
I'm gonna sing you a new song now
That you haven't ever heard.
　　When you lose your money, learn
　　　　to lose.

2.
On Saturday night
'Tween eight and nine o'clock,
Ollie Jackson, the gambler,
Made two fatal shots.
　　When you lose your money, learn
　　　　to lose.

3.
Ollie Jackson was a gambler,
Dick Carr was the same—
"Let's go down to Bill Curtis's place
Where they havin a big crap game."
　　When you lose your money, learn
　　　　to lose.

4.
Dick Carr had the dice,
Bet six bits he passed.
Ollie Jackson faded him
And that was po Dick's last.
　　When you lose your money, learn
　　　　to lose.

5.
When the bet was on,
Dick Carr's pint was nine.
He grabbed um up and rolled um in
And out comes seven flyin.
　　When you lose your money, learn
　　　　to lose.

6.
Ollie Jackson win the bet.
Dick wouldn't turn it loose.
Dick started for his pistol
And Ollie said, "It ain't no use.
　　When you lose your money, learn
　　　　to lose."

7.
Ollie Jackson shot Dick Carr,
He dropped down to his knees,
And Dave Carr throwed up his hands,
"Don't kill my brother, please."
　　When you lose your money, learn
　　　　to lose.

8.
Babe Carr, he jumped up,
Started around the table.
Ollie leveled that Colt of his,
Shot Babe below his navel.
　　When you lose your money, learn
　　　　to lose.

9.
George Fountain says, "Boys,
This will never do."
Curtis said, "You done spoke too
　　late,
He shot Babe through and through."
　　When you lose your money, learn
　　　　to lose.

10.
Dick Carr and Babe,
They both fell near in line.
Five minutes afterwards,
Carr brothers, they were dyin.
　　When you lose your money, learn
　　　　to lose.

11.
When the shootin was over,
Ollie looked big and stout.
He put his pistol in his pocket
And done the slow drag out.
 When you lose your money, learn
 to lose.

12.
When the inquest was over,
Folks listened and they looked.
They all spoke very well of him
Except Joey Fountain and Big Foot.
 When you lose your money, learn
 to lose.

13.
Mrs. Carr said to the sergeant,
"I wish you had come soon,
And 'rested Ollie Jackson,
A little Kansas City coon."
 When you lose your money, learn
 to lose.

14.
On 19th and Chestnut
Was heard a distressin noise,
How two bully gamblers met their
 death,

Two Kansas City boys.
 When you lose your money, learn
 to lose.

15.
The day was set for the trial,
All the rounders stood in line
To see would Ollie Jackson
Have to do some time.
 When you lose your money, learn
 to lose.

16.
George Fountain and Big Foot,
They both done all they could,
But if Ollie had got one hundred
 years,
It would have done them boys no
 good.
 When you lose your money, learn
 to lose.

17.
Now, boys and girls,
Please take my advice,
Never try to gamble
With a pair of loaded dice.
 And when you lose your money,
 learn to lose.

THE ROGUISH MAN
Composed by Sid Hemphill

1.
I went down to Pritchett,
West come a-runnin back,
I'm gonna tell you, Bill Armstrong
Done put the ball to Jack.
 My honey babe,
 Why don't you come home?

2.
Old Jack walked in the house, boys,
With his pistol in his hand.
He's cussing Bill Armstrong
Like he wasn't any man.
 My honey babe,
 Why don't you come home?

3.
Bill Armstrong shot Jack in the
head,
Shot once on the floor.
"Tell you now, Jack,
You aren't bull'in me no more."

4.
Sent for Doctor Parnell,
He didn't even try—
Said, "It wasn't no use to work over
Jack
For he will sholy die."

5.
Brought Jack to his sister's,
Told all his friends,
"He's been bull'in round
Ballantine's,
Better not bully there again."

6.
Sent for Doctor Daniel,
Doctor Blair come mighty quick.
"I'm gon tell you
Jack's in a mighty bad fix."

7.
Doctor worked on Jack
As much as we could tell.
Help of Doctor Daniel,
Jack, he got well.

8.
Old Jack got well that time,
And Jack, he wasn't sore.
Next trouble Jack got in,
He broke in Mister Lawrence' store.

9.
They laid old Jack in jail that time,
He was layin on his bunk,
Studyin about that money
In Mister Castle's trunk.

10.
He went in Mister Castle's house,
Mister Castle hadn't come back.
Jack pushed his hand in Mister
Castle's trunk,
Got his money sack.

11.
Mister Jim Mabie and Mister Price
told Jack,
"Jack, we are vexed.
You come and got the money,
Now we got to break your neck."

12.
He says, "Yes, Mister Mabie, you
and Mister Price,
You is on the track.
Run my hand in Mister Castle's
trunk,
Got his money sack."

13.
Mister Jim Mabie told Jack, "Jack,
You don't tell us no tale.
Put you in this buggy
For Senatoby jail."

14.
Mister Jim Mabie had Jack in the
buggy,
Got near bout Strayhorn.
"Stop here, Mister Mabie,
Lemme steal you a feed a corn."

15.
Laid old Jack in jail that time,
He didn't have nary friend.
Sentenced that poor boy
To five years in the pen.

16.
He stayed in the pentenshuh,
Five years long.
Come back and say to Mister Castle,
"Can I stay here at home?"

17.
Mister Castle went to Miss Sue,
"Miss Sue, I'll tell you it's a sin,
I'm gonna let old Jack stay here
With us again."

18.
Last one day Mister Castle
Goes out in the field.
Jack goes down to his meal house
And steals all his meal.

19.
Old Jack walk around the backyard
Say, "I got to have some fun."
Went in Mister Castle's back room
And stole his clock and run.

20.
Mister Castle told Mister Springfield,
"You 'port him, t'won't be no use.
Send old Jack to the Senatoby jail
And they'll turn old Jack a-loose."

21.
Jailer told Mister Springfield,
"We have fixed it so
Jack done stole so much,
Don't want him in the jailhouse no
    mo.''

22.
Mister Springfield told Jack, "Jack,
You have fixed it so
They don't want you
In the jailhouse no mo."

23.
Jailer told old Jack,
"Jack, we done left it alone.
We don't want you in this jailhouse,
Have to go back home."
        My honey babe,
        Why don't you come home?

BOLL WEEVIL
As Sung by Sid Hemphill
(Compared with an early Texas version)

SID'S VERSION
1.
I'm gonna sing you something,
The latest of my own.
Sing you about the boll weevil
Is trying to take our home.
    Ain't got no home,
    Ain't got no home.

AN EARLY TEXAS VERSION
1.
Have you heard the latest,
The latest of the songs?
It's about the little boll weevil
Picked up both feet and gone.
    Jus lookin for a home,
    Jus lookin for a home.

2.

That farmer went out in the field
   one mornin,
That boll weevil's flyin in the air,
Went out there this evenin,
Done moved his family there.
      Havin a time,
      Havin a time.

3.

The farmer went to the boll weevil,
Says, "Boll Weevil, where in the
   world your home?"
"I stays over in Texas,
Won't be here very long.
      Got to have a time,
      Got to have a time."

4.

Farmer says, "Boll Weevil,
I thought I buried you in the sand."
"I'll be back next spring
When you spadin up your land."

5.

That farmer said to the boll weevil,
"How come you head so red?"
"Eatin all the farmer's cotton,
But he tryin to kill me dead."

6.

The farmer went to the merchant
For to get his wife a dress.
Boll weevil says, "Now, farmer,
I sho got you best."

2.

The first time I saw the boll
   weevil,
He was sittin on a square.
Nex time I saw the boll weevil,
He had his whole damn family there.
      Jus lookin for a home . . .

3.

The boll weevil is a little black bug,
From Mexico, they say,
He come to try this Texas soil
And thought he better stay.
      He was lookin for a home . . .

4.

The farmer taken the boll weevil
And buried him in the sand.
The boll weevil said to the farmer,
"I'll stand it like a man."
      It'll be my home . . ."

5.

The farmer ax the boll weevil,
"What makes your head so red?"
"I've been wandering this wide
   world over,
It's a wonder I ain't dead.
      Ain't got no home . . ."

6.

The banker got half the cotton,
The merchant got the rest.
Didn't leave the po farmer's wife
But one old cotton dress,
      And it's full of holes,
      And it's full of holes.

7.

The farmer went to the merchant then
For some dippin and chewin.
Boll weevil say, "Now, farmer,
Ain' nothin doin.
        You cain't have a dime,
        You cain't have a dime."

8.

The farmer went to the merchant then,
Gonna get him a bucket of lard.
"Cain't get nothin, farmer,
The boll weevil got yo job."

9.

The farmer ax the boll weevil,
"What in the worl you tryin to do?"
"I'm tryin to carry six rows
And my chillun all carryin two."

I BE'S TROUBLED
Composed by Muddy Waters

Well, I know somebody
Sho been talkin to you.
I don't need no tellin, girl,
I can watch the way you do.
I be's troubled, I be all worried in mind.
Yeah, an I never'll be satisfied
And I just can't keep from cryin.

Yeah, my baby she quit me,
Seem like Mama was dead.
I got real worried, gal,
And she drove it to my head.
I be troubled, I be all worried in mind.
Yeah, an I never'll be satisfied
And I just can't keep from cryin.

Notes

▲▲▲▲▲▲

▲ Preface

1. The reader interested in further exploring these findings is referred to the following works by Alan Lomax: "The Homogeneity of African–American Musical Style"; *Folk Song Style and Culture*; *Cantometrics*, a handbook with training tapes available from the University of California Extension Media Center in Berkeley; *Blues in the Mississippi Night*, a recording available from Rykodisc; and *Jazz Parades: Feet Don't Fail Me Now* and *The Land Where the Blues Began*, available from Pacific Arts/PBS Home Video. All of these selections are listed in the bibliography, discography, and filmography. The reader is also referred to the works by David Evans, Robert Farris Thompson, and Melville Herskovits listed in the bibliography.

Chapter One ▲ My Heart Struck Sorrow

1. Howard Odum's magnificent *Rainbow Round My Shoulder*, a multivolume verbatim account of the songs and wanderings of a black bluesman, first published in the 1930s, in addition to Wulf Sachs's *Black Hamlet*, the biography of a South African witch doctor, inspired me to begin to use the recording machine to create "oral histories" of Southern black and other folk musicians. In the recorded biographies of Leadbelly, Jelly Roll Morton, Aunt Molly Jackson, and numerous others, I sought to portray the factors governing the growth of musical traditions. Two of these studies appeared in print—*Mister Jelly Roll* (1949) and *The Rainbow Sign* (1959)—but most remained unpublished. I worked over the large corpus

of Mississippi material accumulated in the Coahoma surveys of 1941–42, but produced no results satisfactory to me. Other recording trips to the Delta (1947, 1959, and 1979) added wonderful new things to my collection. However, it wasn't until I returned to the study of these data, equipped with the results of the Cantometric world survey of performance style, that I began to make sense of them.

From 1963 to 1982, I directed the Cross-Cultural Study of Expressive Style at Columbia University where, along with my research team, I developed Cantometrics, a system for measuring song style on a global scale, and Choreometrics, for measuring dance style. See my *Folk Song Style and Culture* (1968) in the bibliography. With these ethnographic tools I was able to see how various aspects of African and European traditions were favored by social circumstances and utilized by Mississippi artists in the development of a series of styles that answered their changing needs. This book is a narrative account of these findings—which might, in technical terms, be called operations on the data. Some, perhaps, will find my history unsatisfactory or distasteful, but I feel that I have found a way of explaining these data, over which I have been brooding for nearly fifty years, and of providing a viable explanation for the emergence of the blues, the most popular song form that we know anything about.

2. I believe this was the same William Brown who recorded later in the narrative with Son House and earlier with Charley Patton.

3. See discography.

4. See discography.

5. In fact, according to well-documented accounts, Johnson died in 1938.

6. Fiddling Joe Martin played mandolin, Leroy Jones played harmonica, and, to my surprise, William Brown turned up to play second guitar. My recordings of this session have been published in England and elsewhere (see discography).

7. Many Delta old-timers called this the first blues they ever heard. Others spoke of *Joe Turner.*

8. Hortense Powdermaker, in her ethnography of a nearby Delta community, compared this Deep South handshaking rule to the taboos she had encountered in her studies of primitive Melanesia:

> To violate this strong taboo is to arouse the resentment, suspicion, fear, which attend the breaking of taboos or customs in any culture. If a Melanesian is asked what difference it would make if he failed to provide a feast for his dead maternal uncle, his attitude is one of complete bewilderment

and strong fear at the mere suggestion, he would resent it as an invitation to general disaster. The title taboo is sensed as equally essential to the *status quo* in Mississippi. To question either is to question the whole system. . . . (*After Freedom*, p. 45)

9. At the time we met in Clarksdale, neither David Edwards nor I realized that he would become one of the best-known Delta bluesmen. He had already done some commercial recording and asked me to use one of his stage names, so in all my field notes I called him Joe Williams. A fuller portrait of him is to be found in chapter 8, pp. 394–405.

10. See chapter 7.

11. See pp. 314–25 for the story of Sid Hemphill.

12. See discography.

13. Charles Haffer continued discussing his repertoire: "I used to sing *Stagolee, Casey Jones, Frankie and Albert, Shortnin Bread, Bill Bailey.* And there was a song about

Skinner, skinner, you know the rules,
Eat your supper, curry your mules.
You don't curry him, curry him right,
You'll see it on payroll Saturday night.

"That originated on the levee camps back in the nineties. See, I used to live close to a levee camp once and would pick up those things. You hear um going down the road—didn't have no streets where I come from—whistling and singing those things, and people would learn um just like they learn songs on the radio today—us people that didn't belong to the church:

All you people oughta be like me,
Drink your gin and let your cocaine be.
Hey, honey, take a whiff on me.

"We had songs for cutting wood, making the ax sound with your song:

Ever since I left my captain,
I been goin down,
Been goin down.

"And they'd be a whole crowd of um singing this song on the railroad:

This is the hammer
Killed John Henry.

Won't kill me,
Won't kill me.

"But back in my day people didn't think there was no good could come out of a levee camp. Levee-camp people were dangerous people, they thought. They were gamblers, you know. They kill one another, push the dead man under the crap table, and gamble right on. In those days they'd go right out on the farm and gamble. Back then the law couldn't go on a white man's place and get nobody. White folks could get their people out of anything they done. You're a good worker—ain't nobody could bother you. That made the people who were not good Christians very rude. So the Christians didn't think much of the gamblers. They have certain things they abhor. If a girl was making love to a man, they thought that was a terrible thing. It ain't no harm in these things now, it's practically all right."

Old Man Haffer chuckled long and richly, as I added, "I guess a lot of folks did it anyhow."

"Of course they did. But the attitude was different. You take music. I came along at a time when the church people thought it was a terrible thing to have a piano in the church. They was afraid of a piano. They thought it was the devil.

"When people started going North, they came back with this piano idea and the old heads thought they was getting away from the old landmark, trying to turn the church into a barrelhouse. Sometimes when the piano was brought in, there would be a big fight and a lot of people would quit the church because they thought the church was going into sin."

Chapter Two ▲ There Is a Hell

1. Much of the sociological material in this chapter was gathered by Lewis Jones and his Fisk University associates and summed up by him in two unpublished monographs, "The Mississippi Delta" and "An Ecology of Counties," edited by Lewis Jones in the 1940s. These sources, as well as conversations with Jones, are cited and paraphrased here.

2. An example: In the disastrous Mississippi flood of 1927, the waters did not recede for months, and thousands of homeless black laborers were held at gunpoint in concentration camps on the levee so that Delta landowners would not lose their labor supply. Even though these acts of willful peonage were brought to the attention of then President Hoover, he claimed he had no jurisdiction over the matter, and the blacks were forced to remain for months without tents or beds and with the most miserable food, repairing the levee at gunpoint. Red Cross supplies,

sent for relief purposes, were seized by the planters and sold to blacks in order to put them further into debt.

3. An old spiritual warns against foot crossing:

> *Sister, better mind how you walk on the cross,*
> *Yo foot might slip and yo soul be lost.*

Whereas a wide stance was usual in black African dance, a narrow stance with foot crossing is typical of clogging or stepping or other forms of West European dancing. The newly converted slaves came to view foot crossing as a lure of Satan.

4. B. A. Botkin, *Lay My Burden Down*, p. 107.

5. They were Joycie Stith, Caroline and Henry Joiner, Hester Jones, Annie Anderson, Fannie Jackson, Louise Smith, James Clark, Tom Jones, and Charley Drake.

6. Botkin, *Lay My Burden Down*, p. 55.

7. John Hebron Moore, *The Emergence of the Cotton Kingdom in the Old Southwest*, p. 84.

8. Allison Davis et al., *Deep South*, p. 244.

9. George Mitchell, *Blow My Blues Away*, p. 160.

10. Ibid., pp. 184–85.

11. Powdermaker, *After Freedom*, p. 208.

12. Abram Kardiner and Lionel Ovesey, *The Mark of Oppression*, p. 114.

13. This story is excerpted from interviews with Walter Brown conducted by Alan Lomax in 1979 in the Delta. Much of this footage is included in *The Land Where the Blues Began* (Pacific Arts Home Video, PBS 260).

14. Theodore Rosengarten, *All God's Dangers*, p. 15.

15. This was in the early 1940s.

16. Powdermaker, in *After Freedom*, observes: "It can be roughly estimated that no more than twenty-five or thirty percent of the sharecroppers get an honest settlement" (p. 86). "A couple who sharecropped and rented for fourteen years, say they cleared money only three times: $50, $60, $100" (p. 94). "In a study of eighty families in the Yazoo Mississippi Delta, it was found that the diets of over 50% were ten percent or more below standard in protein, calcium, phosphorus, and iron. The consequences have been the wide prevalence of pellagra" (p. 79).

17. Davis et al., *Deep South*, pp. 230–31.

18. Ibid., pp. 238–41.

19. When there was cotton to be picked or chopped, many planters simply took black children out of school and sent them to the field, if their parents hadn't already done so. In 1941 the Fisk survey of 100 families on King and Anderson, where conditions were comparatively good, showed that the median for grades completed was five.

20. See Paul Oliver, *Dwellings: The House Across the World* (Austin: University of Texas Press, 1987).

21. Mitchell, *Blow My Blues Away*, pp. 79–81.

22. Ibid., pp. 91–92.

23. Ibid., pp. 90–91.

Chapter Three ▲ The Ugliest and the Fastest Man

1. William Ferris, *You Live and Learn*, p. 192.

2. Charles Joyner, *Down by the Riverside*, p. 194.

3. See Roger D. Abrahams, *Positively Black* and *Deep Down in the Jungle*, and Alan Dundes, ed., *Mother Wit from the Laughing Barrel*.

Chapter Four ▲ Lonesome Whistles

1. William Ferris, *You Live and Learn*, p. 61.

2. *Roustabout Holler* from the book *Our Singing Country*, collected and compiled by John A. Lomax and Alan Lomax, pp. 350–51.

3. "Yazoo Delta railroad cars, with the initials Y. D. written in gold letters on their sides, inspired the railroad's nickname 'Yellow Dog.' Moorehead is the community where the Southern crosses the Dog and the place where Handy heard the man playing and singing the old blues—'I'm going where the Southern cross the Dog' and making the guitar talk it with his slider" (Ferris, *You Live and Learn*, p. 98).

4. They're handling more than a ton of steel.

5. See John Dollard, *Class and Caste in a Southern Community*.

6. See pp. 129–30.

7. Harold Courlander, *A Treasury of Afro-American Folklore*, p. 286 (material excerpted from *Drums and Shadows: Survival Stories Among the Georgia Coastal Negroes*, Savannah Writers Project, WPA, University of Georgia Press, 1940).

8. Classic Southern fiddle tunes, both with clear black influence.

9. See song appendix.

10. In chapter 6, pp. 302–3, find the Mississippi Penitentiary variant, where prisoner fancy, so focused on escape, has endowed Stewball with epic properties.

11. See song appendix for full text.

12. See song appendix for full text.

13. This was 1939. Fifty years later Clarksdale was to experience a far worse period of cocaine addiction. The song, which was sung as a lighthearted ditty in the relatively drug-free thirties and forties, now has tragic implications.

14. From Ferris, *You Live and Learn*, p. 81.

Chapter Five ▲ The Levee

1. Excerpts from letters home to New York State by William Hemphill, who worked as a junior engineer in the Yazoo–Mississippi Delta District under Major T. G. Dabney in 1904. This manuscript was graciously contributed by Dr. James Cobb of the University of Tennessee at Knoxville, who has written a definitive history of the Delta (see bibliography).

2. Ibid.

3. The black section of Clarksdale.

4. Charles Peabody, "Notes on Negro Music."

5. Stack Mangham, Handy's sponsor in Clarksdale, said the levee hollers had been there as long as the levees themselves.

6. H. N. Olds, an engineer, inspected sixty-five camps in 1929 and found that few provided any form of toilets and that "conditions were putrid" (Olds, *Report*, p. 8).

7. The interested reader can see part of this dramatic scene in *The Land Where the Blues Began* (Pacific Arts Home Video, PBS 260).

8. For another version of this holler, see "Shack Bully Holler," in John A. Lomax and Alan Lomax, *American Ballads and Folk Songs*, p. 45.

9. Theodore Savory, "The Mule," pp. 103–4.

10. From Ferris, *You Live and Learn*, pp. 188–89.

11. The mules would squat down near to the ground to make a hard pull.

12. He drove without reins.

13. Up to this moment I had thought that the levee songs were unaccompanied solos. Apparently, many different muleskinners hollered simultaneously, creating a "heterophony" to which the mules contributed their share. We should try to re-create this scene and discover its African sources.

14. Nate Shaw, Alabama farmer, recalled the meal schedule his mules were accustomed to:

> My mules was used to eatin at dinner times, used to be eatin at every feedin time—mornin, noon and night. 'Bout twelve o'clock them mules would ask for feed. They'd look around, anywhere they was; they knowed me—any animal knows his master; he may not know the name of him, but he knows the man that feeds him. They know; they got sense just like people; they got their kind of sense and people got theirs. Them mules looked to see me, out twelve o'clock and I hadn't fed em—"agh-agh-agh-agh-agh-agh." I'd look around and they standin lookin right at me with their heads up—"aagh-agh-agh-agh-agh." The animals knowed me and they was askin for their dinner or breakfast or supper. Anywhere, at home, in the lot, or if you'd have em out on duties, they know when their feedin time come. . . . (Rosengarten, *All God's Dangers*, pp. 449–50).

15. Archie Green, in his *Only a Miner: Studies in Recorded Coal-Mining Songs* (Urbana: University of Illinois Press, 1972), shows that "levee camp" became a general term for all sorts of construction camps, dirt-moving jobs, and land-clearing operations, where peonage and forced labor were frequent practices.

16. A report on the ways of the cattle-raising Nuer in East Africa tells how the ten- and eleven-year-old herd boys tied strings on the tails of the family cows in order to locate them at night in the village corral of thorns.

17. Roy Wilkins, "Mississippi Slavery in 1933," pp. 81–82.

Chapter Six ▲ Rise Up, Dead Man

1. See discography.

2. For recordings of this session, see *Negro Prison Songs from the Mississippi Penitentiary*, Tradition Records TLP 1020.

3. This scene occurs in *The Land Where the Blues Began* (Pacific Arts Home Video, PBS 260).

4. See *Roots of the Blues*, Atlantic 1348.

5. This Texas work song and others in this story can be heard on records from the Library of Congress. See discography.

6. See the song appendix for the more sober ballad variant—the broadside ballad about a magical Irish racehorse, *The Noble Skubald.* Convict singers give the piece epic touches and end it with lyric verses about the woes of prison life

7. Official whippings were administered in Texas with a broad black leather strap that blistered rather than cut. Due to past abuses, there is a state law forbidding the use of the leather without the permission of the head of the penitentiary system.

8. The full twenty-five stanzas of this improvised Texas work-song epic can be found in the song appendix. The text illustrates how balladlike songs were "sung together" by the black work songs.

Chapter Seven ▲ The Hills

1. This story of the quixotic father challenging his son to make music on his own is a common one.

2. Robert Johnson had a similar learning curve; see pp. 14–15.

3. Uncle Remus talks about "the quills." And they were well known in the Southeast in antebellum times.

4. For the whole ballad, see the song appendix.

5. See the song appendix for the remainder of the song.

6. This may explain why William added a "u" to the spelling of his last name, thus changing Falkner to Faulkner!

7. See *Roots of the Blues*, Atlantic 1348.

8. David Evans, in "Black Fife and Drum Music in Mississippi," pp. 95–96, summarizes the research on this matter by Eileen Southern in her book *The Music of Black America*, as follows:

> . . . as early as the seventeenth century blacks may have "picked up" the
> skills of fife or drum playing from the militia units in New England and the

Middle Colonies. . . . During the eighteenth century there are numerous reports of black fifers and drummers. In fact, during this time Negroes and Indians were allowed to enroll in the colonial militia only as drummers, fifers, trumpeters, and pioneers. For the election of slave "governors" in Hartford and Wallingford, Connecticut, in the 1750's parades were held with marching to the music of fife and drum bands. Later in these celebrations songs were sung in African languages to a different combination of instruments: the fiddle, tambourine, banjo, and drum. In 1765 two black drummers were used to call the citizens to a meeting. Advertisements for slaves or notices of runaways during this century attest to their skills on a variety of instruments including drum and fife as well as the German flute. Numerous black fifers and drummers served during the Revolutionary War, and the names of several are known. Between 1818 and 1844 Frank Johnson's Colored Band working out of Philadelphia was one of the most popular groups in the country. They were primarily a marching band of woodwind, brass, and percussion instruments; but on occasion a fifer and drummer would play to give the regular bandsmen a rest during parades. They could also constitute themselves as a band for dances. In 1832 Dan Emmett, a white man who later became a famous minstrel showman, received instruction in fife and drum at Newport Barracks, Kentucky, from John J. "Juba" Clark, almost certainly, from his nickname, a black man.

9. That is, play in the heavily bowed, syncopated African-American style of Blind Sid and his predecessors.

10. Among the Kissi of Liberia, the musical bow, an instrument that can be made to "talk," is much favored by children. See David Evans, "Afro-American One-Stringed Instruments," p. 241.

11. Ibid., p. 235.

12. Ibid., p. 237.

13. Ibid., p. 210.

14. See David Evans, "African Elements in Twentieth-Century United States Black Folk Music." See also Gunther Schuller, *Early Jazz: Its Roots and Musical Development* (New York: Oxford University Press, 1968).

15. See Dollard, *Caste and Class in a Southern Town,* and Davis et al., *Deep South.*

16. See discography.

Chapter Eight ▲ Bluesmen

1. See Norman Whitten and John Szwed, eds., *Afro-American Anthropology.*

2. Carol B. Stack, *All Our Kin: Strategies for Survival in a Black Community* (New York; Harper & Row, 1975).

3. Harold Courlander, *Tales of Yoruba Gods and Heroes* (New York: Crown Publishers, 1972), pp. 11–12.

4. See *Blues in the Mississippi Night* in the discography.

5. Sam was wrong in putting Charley Patton down because he juggled his guitar. Many of the great Southern virtuosi, black and white, play games with their instruments, holding them between their legs, behind their backs, over their heads, swinging them to and fro, throwing them up and catching them right on the beat—in a word, dancing playfully with their instruments, which they often endow with human names. The practice is rootedly African, I believe, for there musicians are constantly shifting the position of their rattles and stringed instruments, tossing drums in the air between strokes, and the like, playing with them, as did their slave, then black-minstrel, descendants. Here is the source of Uncle Dave Macon's medicine-show routines with his five-string banjo.

Many critics consider Charley Patton the seminal figure in the blues, though clearly his relative, Sam, hardly agrees. Patton, whose voice and guitar style had the raw power of a middle-buster plow, recorded early, and some of his blues, such as *Shetland Pony Blues,* were copied by a wide range of other bluesmen.

A hard-drinking, serious, and highly original artist, his work strongly influenced Son House, Willie Brown, and other musicians who, in their turn, taught their art to Muddy Waters and Robert Johnson. Thus some critics portray him as the key figure in the history of the blues. This view is too simplistic, to my mind, because it is based on the study of the handful of musicians who were recorded, and an intimate knowledge of the even smaller number whose records were distributed commercially. In fact, there were hundreds, if not thousands, of singers working in the blues idiom during its peak period between 1900 and 1950, in the fertile cotton country south and west of Memphis. The blues heartland was the Yazoo Delta, but there were little Deltas all the way to the Trinity River bottoms near Dallas. In them flourished a throng of blues singers, whose names we shall never know. It is the European focus on the great-man theory of history and the American mania for crowning champions that cause us to attribute the rise of a folk tradition to one singer who happened to be well recorded. Perhaps, if I was forced to choose one man, I would choose Blind Lemon Jefferson, the master guitar stylist, whose records outsold Patton's many times over during the same epoch.

6. The musicians he names were all well-known blues recording artists on RCA Victor, musicians whom the Melroses often used in their recording sessions.

7. Maybe Joe meant "aptitude" or something similar.

8. "Soon" means early, very early.

9. Elgin was the brand name of the watch most commonly known in the Deep South.

10. For more verses to this song, see the song appendix.

11. James Rooney, *Bossmen*, p. 129.

12. Ibid., p. 126.

13. Ibid., p. 126, p. 112.

14. Ibid., p. 122.

15. Arnold Shaw, *Honkers and Shouters*, p. 296.

16. Rooney, *Bossmen*, p. 114.

Chapter Nine ▲ Big Bill of the Blues

1. By the fifties, Big Bill was interviewed again by the Belgian writer Yannick Bruyoghe, and this version of his life story, a charming but different view of the man, appeared in *Big Bill Blues: William Broonzy's Story* (New York: Macmillan, 1955).

2. See *Blues in the Mississippi Night* in the discography.

Chapter Ten ▲ Blues in the Mississippi Night

1. This innovative dramatic interview was first presented in a lecture to the New York Folklore Society in 1947. It was first published as "I Got the Blues" in *Common Ground* (1948) and later included in Alan Dundes's anthology of African-American folklore, *Mother Wit from the Laughing Barrel* (1973). The recording of the interview, *Blues in the Mississippi Night*, was first released by United Artists (UAL 4027) in 1959. In all these cases the identity of the participants was disguised as they had requested. It was not until the interview was reissued by Rykodisc (RCD 90155) in 1990 that the true identity of the bluesmen was made public.

2. The Lowrance brothers, whose base camp was located in Mississippi County, Arkansas, have become legendary. Their camps were singled out by the govern-

ment sanitary inspector in 1929 as being dangerously unhealthy. Apparently, Lowrance family members (I suspect this name is a Southernization of some appellation such as Lorentz) lived in Memphis in the thirties, for there are directory listings for Blair Lowrance and William Tate Lowrance as levee contractors and for Lucy Lowrance, widow, perhaps of the notorious Isum. Henry Truvillion, Texas veteran of the levee camps, remembers how Isum roused the men on his camp:

"Long about three, four o'clock you can hear Isum Lowrance (*killed mo men up and down the Mississippi than the influenzy*) knockin on the ding-dong with his nigger-punchin .44.

Who dat knockin on de fo'-day dong?
Mus be Isum Lowrance, cause he don knock long.

"Den Mr. Isum Lowrance spoke up his own sef, says,

Raise up, boys, raise up, raise up—
Breakfas on de table, coffee's gettin col',
Ef you don come now, goin throw it outdo's.
Aincha gwine, aincha gwine, boys, aincha gwine?

Sampson Pittman, whom I interviewed in Detroit in 1938, had worked for the Lowrances in Arkansas and told me that "the Lowrance brothers is seven companies of um, each seven brothers: one Charley Lowrance, Lawrence Lowrance, Eddie Lowrance, Clarence Lowrance, and Blair Lowrance, Ike Lowrance, levee contractors."

"Where do they live?" I asked.

"All throughout the states of Arkansas, Louisiana, Mississippi, and Georgia. They were pretty tough. Charley Lowrance is the best of all, he owns a farm in Garders, Arkansas."

Pittman, an excellent guitar player, had the habit of telling wild tales of his Southern adventures to the beat of his instrument. Safe in his Detroit apartment, a long way from retribution and with the whiskey flowing, he improvised a fantastic tale of how Lawrence Lowrance bamboozled one of his roughest muleskinners. I quote a fragment of this dramatic reminiscence:

Mister Charley, Mister Charley, what's the matter with you,
Although I have done everything, partner, you asked me to do.

"Now look here, Slim, they tell me that you is known to be the baddest shine that lives on the line. Is it true about you carrying two .45's around, and is it a fact that every time you kill a man that you puts a notch on your gun? Let me look at your gun, Slim. Mmm, mm-mm, pretty tough guy.

"Now Slim, I'll tell you, I'm an official in the camp. I'm going to buy everything to try to please you. I don't want no trouble out of you and I guess you is the same by me. Now do you know this is Mr. Lawrence Lowrance talking to you, Slim?"

"Yeah, I don't care nothing about Mr. Lawrence, no more than I do no one else."

Lowrance then proposes that Slim prove how good a marksman he is by shooting at a barrel floating down the river. When Slim has emptied both his pistols by shooting at this floating mark, Lowrance draws his own pistols.

"Do you know this is Mister Lawrence, Mister Lawrence Lowrance? Slim, I didn't like your look when you first walked in the camp and I told Bullwhippin Shorty to tell you that I want to see you this morning and this is what I want you to tell Slim. Out of all the flour that I could buy, you call it Java, you call the best mules costing me 250 dollars each, you call them shaving tails. Slim, I don't like that. Now listen, Slim, you get on the Government Ridge and let your feet run away with your body."

Sometimes the tables were turned on the wily Lawrence Lowrance, as Big Bill Broonzy makes clear. Bill calls him "Lost Lorand," as indeed he was when he got too far from his home country.

"I do remember I was working on levee camp for the Lorand brothers, the baddest men in the White River bottom. So the one we called Mister Lost Lorand, he went to a town not far across the Mason-Dixon line. They had Negro police there and they didn't allow nobody to carry a pistol. But Mister Lost Lorand had two .45's, one on each side.

"This Negro police walked up to Mister Lorand and said to him, 'It's against the law to carry a gun in this town. Did you know that?'

"So Lorand said to the Negro police, 'Say, Negro, do you know who I am?'

" 'No, I don't,' said the Negro police. 'So tell me, who is you?'

" 'I'm Lost Lorand.'

"Pulling out his big .38-40 pistol and cocking it in Lorand's face, the Negro police said, 'Mister Lorand, you once was lost, but now you're found.' He hand-cuffed Lorand, took his two .45 guns, and took him to jail.

"The news traveled all over the South and North because that Negro was the first to arrest a bad white man and there was Negro police in all Southern towns and in the North, too, but they just arrested other Negroes, because white people don't break the law, they make it. You had to be black to break the law.

"So when Mister Lorand came back to White River bottom he was better to Negroes, and at the meeting one day he got up and told all of us this story just like it happened. He said he had never thought a Negro could or would ever have nerve enough to attempt to arrest one of the Lorand brothers."

It was thirty years later in Belgium, a mighty ways from the Delta, that Big Bill laughed over the tables being turned on one of the old-time levee bosses. (See William Broonzy, *Big Bill Blues*.) Mostly, these "old tush-hogs" had it their own way. There was Tom Paine, "a forky-tailed devil," who transferred prisoners to the pen. There was Forrest Jones, operator of one of the filthiest camps on the river in De Soto County, Mississippi, who is said to have shot the Mercy Man. Pittman remembered them all.

> *I worked on the levee, long time ago,*
> *And ain't nothing about the levee camps that I don't know.*
> > *Partner, partner, partner, don't you think I know,*
> > *Say now, I ain't no stranger, I been down in the circle before.*
>
> *No, there ain't but the one contractor on the levee that I fear,*
> *Your Bullyin George Hulan, they don't 'low him back here.*
>
> *Now there's Mister Forrest Jones, ain't so long and tall,*
> *He killed a mercy man and he's liable to kill us all.*
>
> *Now Mister Charley Lowrance is the Mercy Man,*
> *The best contractor, partner, that's up and down the line.*
>
> *Now when you leave out West Helena, on Highway 44,*
> *The first camp that you get to it is called "Rainymo."*
> > *Partner, partner, partner, don't you think I know,*
> > *Say now, I ain't no stranger, I been down in the circle before.*

Much of the above comes from "Shack Bullies and Levee Contractors" by John Cowley, who, in this valuable article, quoted at length from my field recordings for the Library of Congress. Most of the excerpts quoted are drawn from these recordings of mine.

3. This footnote is a tombstone. A few weeks after I left Arkansas, I received a letter with the horrifying news that Joe Pugh was dead. It was a matter of a big car, driven too fast. The end of his hopes was there—smashed against the windshield. The whole thing still brings tears back of my eyes, even as I write these words.

A Brief Book List

Abrahams, Roger D. *Deep Down in the Jungle: Negro Narrative Folklore from the Streets of Philadelphia*. Chicago: Aldine, 1970.

———. *Positively Black*. Englewood Cliffs, N.J.: Prentice-Hall, 1970.

———. "Playing the Dozens." *Journal of American Folklore* 75 (1962): 209–20.

Albee, Edward. *The Death of Bessie Smith*. New York: Coward-McCann, 1960.

Botkin, B.A. *Lay My Burden Down: A Folk History of Slavery*. Chicago: University of Chicago Press, 1945.

Broonzy, William (as told to Yannick Bruyoghe). *Big Bill Blues: William Broonzy's Story*. New York: Macmillan, 1955. London: Cassell, 1955.

Calt, Stephen, and Gayle Wardlow. *King of the Delta Blues: The Life and Music of Charlie Patton*. Newton, N.J.: Rock Chapel Press, 1988.

Charters, Samuel. *The Country Blues*. New York: Holt, Rinehart & Co., 1959.

———. *The Bluesmen: The Story and Music of the Men Who Made the Blues*. New York: Oak Publications, 1967.

———. *The Legacy of the Blues: Art and Lives of Twelve Great Bluesmen*. New York: Da Capo Press, 1977.

Cobb, James. *The Most Southern Place on Earth: The Mississippi Delta and the Roots of Regional Identity*. New York: Oxford University Press, 1992.

Cohn, David L. *Where I Was Born and Raised.* Boston: Houghton Mifflin, 1948.

Courlander, Harold. *Negro Folk Music U.S.A.* New York: Columbia University Press, 1963.

———. *A Treasury of Afro-American Folklore.* New York: Crown Publishers, 1972.

Cowley, John. "Really the 'Walking Blues': Son House, Muddy Waters, Robert Johnson and the Development of a Traditional Blues." *Popular Music,* 1:57–72 (Cambridge: Cambridge University Press, 1981).

———. "Shack Bullies and Levee Contractors," Parts One and Two. *Juke Blues,* nos. 3 and 4, Winter 1985–Spring 1986.

Daniel, Pete. *Deep'n As It Come: The 1927 Mississippi River Flood.* New York: Oxford University Press, 1977.

———. *The Shadow of Slavery: Peonage in the South, 1901–1969.* Urbana: University of Illinois Press, 1990.

David, John R. "Frankie and Johnnie: The Trial of Frankie Baker." *Missouri Folklore Society Journal* 6 (1984): 1–30.

Davis, Allison, Burleigh B. Gardner, and Mary R. Gardner. *Deep South: A Social Anthropological Study of Caste and Class.* Chicago: University of Chicago Press, 1941.

Dollard, John. *Caste and Class in a Southern Town.* New Haven, Conn.: Yale University Press, 1937.

Dorson, Richard M. *American Negro Folktales.* Greenwich, Conn.: Fawcett, 1956.

Dundes, Alan, ed. *Mother Wit from the Laughing Barrel: Readings in the Interpretation of Afro-American Folklore.* Englewood Cliffs, N.J.: Prentice-Hall, 1973.

Evans, David. "Afro-American One-Stringed Instruments." *Western Folklore* 29, no. 4 (1970): 229–45.

———. "Black Fife and Drum Music in Mississippi." *Mississippi Folklore Register* 6, no. 3 (Fall 1972): 94–107.

———. "African Elements in Twentieth-Century United States Black Folk Music." *Jazzforschung* 10 (1978): 85–110.

———. "The Origins of Blues and Its Relationship to African Music." In *Images de L'africaine de l'antiquité au XXe siècle,* edited by Daniel Droixhe and Klaus H. Kiefer, pp. 129–41. Frankfurt: Peter Lang, 1987.

Ferris, William. *Blues from the Delta*. Series edited by Paul Oliver. London: Studio Vista Limited, 1970.

————. *Afro-American Folk Arts and Crafts*, special edition of *Southern Folklore Quarterly* 42, nos. 2 and 3 (1978). Revised edition, Boston: G. K. Hall & Co., 1982; Jackson: University Press of Mississippi, 1986.

————. *Local Color*. New York: McGraw-Hill, 1982. New York: Anchor Books/ Doubleday, 1992.

————. *Encyclopedia of Southern Culture*. Charles Wilson, co-editor. Chapel Hill: University of North Carolina Press, 1989. New York: Anchor Books/ Doubleday, 1992.

————. *"You Live and Learn. Then You Die and Forget It All": Ray Lum's Tales of Horses, Mules, and Men*. New York: Anchor Books, 1992.

Handy, W. C. *Father of the Blues: An Autobiography by W. C. Handy*. Edited by Arna Bontemp. 1955. Reprint. New York: Da Capo Press, 1985.

Hawes, Bess Lomax, and Bessie Jones. *Step It Down: Games, Plays, Songs, and Stories from the Afro-American Heritage*. New York: Harper & Row, 1972.

Herskovits, Melville J. *The Myth of the Negro Past*. Boston: Beacon Press, 1941; rev. ed., 1958.

Hurston, Zora Neale. *Mules and Men*. 1935. Reprint. New York: HarperCollins, 1990.

Jackson, Bruce, coll. and ed. *Wake Up Dead Man: Afro-American Worksongs from Texas Prisons*. Cambridge, Mass.: Harvard University Press, 1972.

Jones, Lewis W. "The Mississippi Delta." Unpublished monograph, Fisk University Social Science Institute, Nashville, Tenn., 1941.

Jones, Lewis W., et al. "The Ecology of Counties." Unpublished monograph, Fisk University Social Science Institute, Nashville, Tenn., 1941.

Joyner, Charles. *Down by the Riverside: A South Carolina Slave Community*. Urbana: University of Illinois Press, 1989.

Kardiner, Abram, and Lionel Ovesey. *The Mark of Oppression: Explorations in the Personality of the American Negro*. New York: World Publishing Co., 1962 (first edition, 1951).

Keil, Charles. *Urban Blues*. Chicago: University of Chicago Press, 1966.

Kennedy, Stetson. *Southern Exposure*. Garden City, N.Y.: Doubleday, 1946.

Leadbitter, Mike. *Delta Country Blues*. Sussex, England: Blues Unlimited Publications, 1968.

Lee, Peter, ed. *Living Blues: A Journal of the African American Blues Tradition*. University, Miss.: Center for the Study of Southern Culture, University of Mississippi, 1991.

Lomax, Alan. *Mister Jelly Roll*. New York: Duell, Sloan & Pearce, 1949. Reprint. New York: Pantheon Books, 1993.

———. *The Rainbow Sign*. New York: Duell, Sloan & Pearce, 1959.

———. *The Folk Songs of North America*. Garden City, N.Y.: Doubleday, 1960.

———. *Folk Song Style and Culture*. New Brunswick, N.J.: Trans-Action Books, 1968.

———. *Cantometrics: An Approach to the Anthropology of Music*. Berkeley: University of California Extension Media Center, 1977.

———. "I Got the Blues." *Common Ground* 8 (Summer 1948): 38–52.

———. "The Homogeneity of African–Afro-American Musical Style." In *Afro-American Anthropology*, edited by N. Whitten and J. Szwed, pp. 181–201. New York: Free Press, 1970.

Lomax, John A., and Alan Lomax. *American Ballads and Folk Songs*. New York: Macmillan, 1934.

———. *Negro Folk Songs as Sung by Leadbelly*. New York: Macmillan, 1935.

———. *Our Singing Country*. New York: Macmillan, 1937.

Mitchell, George. *Blow My Blues Away*. Baton Rouge: Louisiana State University Press, 1971.

Moore, John Hebron. *The Emergence of the Cotton Kingdom in the Old Southwest*. Baton Rouge: Louisiana State University Press, 1988.

Odum, Howard W. *Rainbow Round My Shoulder: The Blue Trail of Black Ulysses*. 1928. Reprint. New York: Krause 1972.

———. "Folk-Song and Folk-Poetry as Found in the Secular Songs of the Southern Negroes." *Journal of American Folklore* 24 (July–September 1911 and October–December 1911).

Olds, H.N. *Report of Preliminary Sanitary Surveys of Labor Camps Maintained by Contractors Engaged in Mississippi Flood Control Operations, 1929–30*.

U.S. National Archives, Record Group 90, United States Public Health Service Files for 1924–1935, Box 43.

Oliver, Paul. *Blues Fell This Morning: The Meaning of the Blues.* New York: Horizon, 1960.

———. *The Story of the Blues.* London: Barrie and Rockliff, The Cresset Press, 1969; Philadelphia: Chilton Books, 1969.

———. *Savannah Syncopators: African Retentions in the Blues.* London: Studio Vista Limited, 1970.

———. *Shelter in Africa.* New York: Praeger, 1971.

———. *Songster and Saints: Vocal Traditions on Race Records.* Cambridge: Cambridge University Press, 1984.

Oster, Harry. *Living Country Blues.* Detroit: Folklore Associates, 1969.

Palmer, Robert. *Deep Blues.* New York: Penguin Books, 1981.

Peabody, Charles. "Notes on Negro Music." *Journal of American Folklore* 16 (1903): 148–52.

Powdermaker, Hortense. *After Freedom: A Cultural Study in the Deep South.* New York: Atheneum, 1969.

Ramsey, Frederic. *Been Here and Gone.* New Brunswick, N.J.: Rutgers University Press, 1960.

Rooney, James. *Bossmen: Bill Monroe and Muddy Waters.* New York: Dial Press, 1971.

Rosengarten, Theodore. *All God's Dangers: The Life of Nate Shaw.* New York, Knopf, 1974.

Sackheim, Eric, and Johnathon Shahn. *The Blues Line: A Collection of Blues Lyrics.* New York: Grossman Publishers, 1969.

Sacre, Robert, ed. *The Voice of the Delta: Charley Patton and the Mississippi Blues; Traditions, Influences, and Comparisons.* Liège, Belgium: Presses Universitaires Liège, 1987.

Savory, Theodore H. "The Mule." *Scientific American* 223, no. 10 (December 10, 1970): 102–9.

Shaw, Arnold. *Honkers and Shouters: The Golden Years of Rhythm and Blues.* New York: Collier Books, 1978.

Southern, Eileen. *The Music of Black America: A History.* New York: W. W. Norton, 1971.

Stearns, Marshall and Jean. *Jazz Dance: The Story of American Vernacular Dance.* New York: Schirmer, 1964.

Thompson, Robert Farris. "Aesthetic of the Cool," *African Arts* 7, no. 1 (Autumn 1973).

———. *African Art in Motion.* Berkeley and Los Angeles: University of California Press, 1974.

———. *Flash of the Spirit: African and Afro-American Art and Philosophy.* New York: Vintage Books, 1984.

Titon, Jeff Todd. *Early Downhome Blues: A Musical and Cultural Analysis.* Urbana: University of Illinois Press, 1977.

Whitten, Norman, and Szwed, John, eds.. *Afro-American Anthropology.* New York: Free Press, 1970.

Wilkins, Roy. "Mississippi Slavery in 1933." *Crisis: A Record of the Darker Races* 40, no. 4 (April 1933): 81–82.

Wilson, Al. *Son House.* Collectors Classics, Blues Unlimited, Bexhill-on-Sea, 1966.

For further bibliographical references concerning the blues, see the following:

Hart, Mary L., et al. *The Blues: A Bibliographical Guide.* New York: Garland, 1989.

Herzhaft, Gérard. *Encyclopedia of the Blues* (Fayetteville: University of Arkansas Press, 1992).

A Brief Discography

▲▲▲▲▲▲▲▲▲▲▲▲▲▲▲▲▲▲▲▲▲▲▲▲▲▲▲

Afro-American Blues and Game Songs. Library of Congress AAFS L4.

Afro-American Folk Music from Tate and Panola Counties, Mississippi. Library of Congress, AAFS L67.

Afro-American Spirituals, Work Songs and Ballads. Library of Congress AAFS L3.

Big Bill Broonzy: Good Time Tonight. Columbia CK 462192 [CD].

Blind Lemon Jefferson—King of the Country Blues. Yazoo 1069.

Blind Lemon Jefferson/Son House. Biograph BLP-12040.

Blind Willie Johnson: Praise God, I'm Satisfied. Yazoo 1058.

Blues Classics by Sonny Boy Williamson. Blues Classic 3.

Blues in the Mississippi Night. Features Memphis Slim, Big Bill Broonzy, and Sonny Boy Williamson, as told to and recorded by Alan Lomax. Notes by Alan Lomax. Salem, Mass.: Rykodisc, 1990 (RCD 90155). The recording on which Chapter 10 is based.

The Blues Roll On. Recorded in the field and edited by Alan Lomax, assisted by Shirley Collins. New York: Atlantic, ca. 1960 (Atlantic SD-1352) [LP]. Forrest City Joe and others.

Bo Carter: Greatest Hits 1930–1940. Yazoo L-1014.

Bo Diddley/Muddy Waters/Little Walter: Super Blues. Checker LPS-3008.

Chicago Blues Anthology. Chess 2CH 60012.

David "Honeyboy" Edwards: I've Been Around. Trix 3319.

The Griots: Ministers of the Spoken Word. Ethnic Folkways FE 4178.

Gus Cannon and Noah Lewis: Volume Two. Document DOCD-5033 (Austrian).

Jim Jackson: Kansas City Blues. Agram AB 2004.

King of the Delta Blues: The Music of Charlie Patton. Notes by Stephen Calt and Don Kent. Newton, N.J.: Yazoo (Shanachie), 1991 (Yazoo 2001) [CD].

Let's Get Loose: Folk and Popular Blues Styles from the Beginnings to the Early 1940's. New World Records NW 290.

Living Chicago Blues, Volumes 1–4. Alligator Records, ALCD 7701–7704.

Masques Dan, Côte d'Ivoire. Ocora OCR 52.

Masters of the Delta Blues: The Friends of Charlie Patton, Featuring Son House, Tommy Johnson, Willie Brown, Kid Bailey, Bertha Lee, Ishmon Bracey, Louise Johnson, and Bukka White. Notes by Don Kent. Newton, N.J.: Yazoo (Shanachie), 1991 (Yazoo 2002) [CD].

McKinley Morganfield a.k.a. Muddy Waters. Chess 2CH-60006.

Memphis Jug Band. Yazoo 1067.

Memphis Slim and His House Rockers, featuring Matt "Guitar" Murphy: Memphis Slim—U.S.A. Pearl PL-10.

The Mississippi Blues 1927–1940. Origin Jazz Library OJL-5.

The Mississippi Blues No. 2: The Delta, 1929–1932. Origin Jazz Library OJL-11.

Mississippi Blues: Library of Congress Recordings 1940–1942. Notes by Ray Templeton. Crawley, West Sussex, England: Interstate Music Ltd., 1991 [1973, 1979] (Travelin' Man TM CD 07). Contains material from Chapter 1.

Mississippi Folk Voices. Southern Culture.

Mississippi Fred McDowell: Delta Blues. Arhoolie F 1021.

Mississippi John Hurt—Avalon Blues. Rounder 1081.

Mississippi John Hurt—1928 Sessions. Yazoo 1065.

Mississippi John Hurt—Worried Blues. Rounder 1082.

Muddy Waters: Down on Stovall's Plantation. Testament T-2219.

Musique Kongo. Ocora OCT 35.

Musique Toma Guinée. Vogue LDM 30107.

Negro Blues and Hollers. Library of Congress AFS L59.

Negro Prison Songs from the Mississippi Penitentiary. Tradition Records TLP 1020. Contains material from chapter 6.

Negro Work Songs and Calls. Library of Congress AAFS L8.

Really! The Country Blues. Origin Jazz Library OJL-2.

Robert Johnson: The Complete Recordings. Columbia C2K 46222.

Roots of the Blues. Recorded in the field and edited by Alan Lomax, assisted by Shirley Collins. New York: Atlantic, ca. 1960 (Atlantic SD-1348) [LP].

Roots of the Blues. Edited by Alan Lomax. New York: New World Records, 1977 (80252-2) [CD].

Sam Chatmon: The Mississippi Sheik. Blue Goose 2006.

Sleepy John Estes, 1929–1940. Folkways/RBF 8.

Son House: The Complete Library of Congress Sessions 1941–1942. Original recordings by Alan Lomax for the Library of Congress. Crawley, West Sussex, England: Interstate Music Ltd., 1990 (Travelin' Man TM CD 02).

Son House: The Legendary 1941–1942 Recordings in Chronological Sequence. Arhoolie/Folklyric 9002. Contains material from chapter 1.

Son House, Willie Brown, and Others: Walking Blues. Flyright LP 541.

Sounds of the South. Recorded in the field and edited by Alan Lomax, assisted by Shirley Collins. New York: Atlantic, ca. 1960 (Atlantic SD-1346) [LP]. Contains material from chapters 1, 2, and 7.

South Mississippi Blues. Notes by David Evans. Somerville, Mass.: Rounder Records, 1988 (Rounder Records 2009) [LP].

Tampa Red: Guitar Wizard. RCA/Bluebird AXM2-5501.

Traveling Through the Jungle: Negro Fife and Drum Band Music from the Deep South. Testament T-2223.

Wolof Music of Senegal and the Gambia. Ethnic Folkways FE 4462.

For more complete listings of blues recordings, consult the following discographies:

Dixon, Robert M. W., and John Godrich. *Blues and Gospel Records: 1902–1943.* 1977. Reprint. Saint Clair Shores, Mich.: Scholarly Press, 1982.

Oliver, Paul, ed. *The Blackwell Guide to Blues Records.* Oxford and New York: Blackwell Reference, 1989.

Scott, Frank, et al. *The Down Home Guide to the Blues.* Pennington, N.J.: A Cappella Books, 1991.

Atlantic Records is reissuing the recordings of Alan Lomax's Southern fieldwork of 1959–60 as a four-CD boxed set entitled *Sounds of the South.* Here the reader can listen to Ed and Lonnie Young, the best fife-and-drum combo discovered in America, reviving African tradition intact in the Delta hills; Blind Sid Hemphill sparking hot rhythms with his quills, an instrument as old as music itself, at an afternoon hog roast in Senatobia; Fred McDowell's slide guitar *singing* the blues, accompanied by his aunt on a comb wrapped in toilet paper; the lining hymns and anguished sermons of the Southern black church; Holy Rollers "getting happy"; polyphonic shouts from the Georgia Sea Islands; children's game songs recorded in the backyard; the rowdy honky-tonk piano in the backroom of Charley Houlin's place. Then, this rich vein of African-American music-making is set beside the countervailing background of white song from the Southern backwoods, showing how, in the high-speed string combos of bluegrass, for example, these very diverse traditions interpenetrated and influenced each other. Originally entitled *The Southern Heritage Folk Series*, it includes the following titles: *Roots of the Blues* (Atlantic LP 1348), *The Blues Roll On* (1352), *Negro Church Music* (1351), *American Folk Songs for Children* (1350), *Blue Ridge Mountain Music* (1347), *White Spirituals* (1349), and *Sounds of the South* (1346).

A Brief Filmography

▲▲▲▲▲▲▲▲▲▲▲▲▲▲▲▲▲▲▲▲▲▲▲▲▲▲▲

Beale Street. Produced by Alexis Krasilovsky, Ann Rickey, and Walter Baldwin, distributed by the Center for the Study of Southern Culture (hereafter referred to as CSSC), 1981 (29 min., 16mm and ½″ video, B&W).

Bessie Smith. Produced by Charles Levine, distributed by Film-Makers' Cooperative, Canyon Cinema Co-op, 1968 (13.5 min., 16mm, B&W).

Black Delta Religion. Produced by Judy Peiser and William Ferris, distributed by CSSC, 1974 (15 min., ½″ video, B&W).

The Blues Accordin' to Lightnin' Hopkins. Produced by Les Blank, distributed by Flower Films, 1969 (31 min., 16mm, color). Available on ½″ video from CSSC.

Blues Houseparty. Produced by Eleanor Ellis, directed by Jackson Frost, distributed by CSSC, 1989 (57 min., ½″ video, color).

Blues Like Showers of Rain: Lightnin' Hopkins. Directed by John Jeremy, distributed by CSSC (30 min., ½″ video, B&W)

Most of these listings were drawn, with permission of the editors, from *American Folklore Films and Videotapes: An Index*, edited by William Ferris and Judy Peiser (Memphis, Tenn.: Center for Southern Folklore, 1976), and the *Southern Culture Catalog*, distributed by the Center for the Study of Southern Culture (CSSC) at the University of Mississippi.

Blues Maker. Produced by the University of Mississippi Center for Public Service and Continuing Studies, distributed by CSSC, 1969 (14 min., ½″ video, B&W).

Born for Hard Luck: Peg Leg Sam Jackson. Produced by Davenport Films and the Curriculum in Folklore at the University of North Carolina at Chapel Hill, distributed by CSSC, 1976 (29 min., ½″ video, B&W).

Bottle Up and Go., Produced by Judy Peiser and William Ferris, distributed by CSSC, 1980 (18 min., ½″ video, color).

Chicago Blues: Muddy Waters. Produced by Harley Cokliss, distributed by CSSC (50 min., ½″ video, color).

The Delta Blues Festival. Produced by the University of Mississippi Telecommunications Resource Center, distributed by CSSC, 1985 (30 min., ½″ video, color).

Delta Blues Singer: James "Sonny Ford" Thomas. Produced by William Ferris and Josette Rossi, distributed by CSSC, 1970 (44 min., ½″ video, B&W).

Faulkner's Mississippi: Land Into Legend. Produced by University of Mississippi Division of Continuing Education, distributed by CSSC, 1965 (32 min., ½″ video, color).

Festival. Produced by Murray Lerner/Patchke Productions, 1967 (95 min., 16mm, B&W). Scenes of the Newport Folk Festival, 1963–66.

Give My Poor Heart Ease. Produced by William Ferris/Yale University Media Design Studio, distributed by CSSC, 1975 (20 min., ½″ video, color).

Gravel Springs Fife and Drum. Produced by William Ferris, Judy Peiser, and David Evans/Center for Southern Folklore, distributed by CSSC, 1971 (10 min., ½″ video, color).

The Land Where the Blues Began. Produced by Alan Lomax, distributed by Jane Balfour Films, Ltd. (overseas), Pacific Arts Video (home video #PBS 260), and the Association for Cultural Equity, 1981 (60 min., ¾″ video, color).

Mississippi Delta Blues. Produced by Judy Peiser and William Ferris/Center for Southern Folklore, distributed by CSSC, 1974 (18 min., ½″ video, B&W).

Mississippi Delta Blues. Produced by Anthony Herrera, distributed by CSSC (29 min., ½″ video, color).

Mississippi Steamboatin'. Produced by Walter Lewisohn, distributed by CSSC (16 min., ½″ video, color).

The Parchman Trials. Produced by Mississippi Educational Television, distributed by CSSC (60 min., ½″ video, color).

Ray Lum: Mule Trader. Produced by Judy Peiser and William Ferris/Center for Southern Folklore, distributed by CSSC, 1973 (18 min., ½″ video, color).

Return to the River. Produced by Mississippi Educational Television, distributed by CSSC, (60 min., ½″ video, color).

Reverend Gary Davis/Sonny Terry: Masters of the Country Blues Series. Produced and distributed by Yazoo Video (#501), a division of Shanachie Records, 1991 (60 min., ½″ video, color).

Roots of American Music: Country and Urban Music, Parts 1, 2, & 3. Produced by University of Washington School of Music, distributed by University of Washington Press, 1971 (40 min., 33 min., and 23 min., 16mm, color). Performances by Son House, Fred McDowell, Mance Lipscomb, the Georgia Sea Island Singers, and others.

Shoutin' the Blues. Produced by Agrinsky Films, distributed by CSSC (16 min., ½″ video, color).

Son House/Bukka White: Masters of the Country Blues Series. Produced and distributed by Yazoo Video (#500), a division of Shanachie Records, 1991 (60 min., ½″ video, color).

Sun's Gonna Shine. Produced by Les Blank, distributed by Flower Films, 1968 (10 min., 16mm, color). Available on ½″ video from CSSC.

Three Songs by Leadbelly. Produced by Blanding Sloan and Wah Mong Chong/Folklore Research Films, distributed by Film Images, 1945 (8 min., 16mm, color).

To Hear Your Banjo Play. Produced by Alan Lomax and Creative Age Films, distributed by Audio Brandon Films, 1947 (16 min., 16mm, B&W).

Two Black Churches. Produced by William Ferris/Yale University Media Design Studio, distributed by CSSC, 1977 (20 min., ½″ video, color).

A Well Spent Life. Produced by Les Blank, distributed by Flower Films, 1971 (44 min., 16mm, color). Available on ½" video from CSSC. Portrait of the Texas bluesman Mance Lipscomb.

Yank Rachell: Tennessee Tornado. Produced by Michael Atwood, distributed by CSSC, 1989 (30 min., ½" video, color).

Index

▲ ▲ ▲ ▲ ▲ ▲

Song Titles and First Lines

▲▲▲▲▲▲▲▲▲▲▲▲▲▲▲▲▲▲▲▲▲▲▲▲▲▲▲▲▲▲▲▲▲▲▲▲▲